Studies in Celtic Histor

GAELIC INFLUENCE IN THE NORTH

CW91432719

STUDIES IN CELTIC HISTORY

ISSN 0261-9865

General editors
Dauvit Broun
Máire Ní Mhaonaigh
Huw Pryce

Studies in Celtic History aims to provide a forum for new research into all aspects of the history of Celtic-speaking peoples throughout the whole of the medieval period. The term 'history' is understood broadly: any study, regardless of discipline, which advances our knowledge and understanding of the history of Celtic-speaking peoples will be considered. Studies of primary sources, and of new methods of exploiting such sources, are encouraged.

Founded by Professor David Dumville, the series was relaunched under new editorship in 1997. Proposals or queries may be sent directly to the editors at the addresses given below; all submissions will receive prompt and informed consideration before being sent to expert readers.

Professor Dauvit Broun, Department of History (Scottish), University of Glasgow, 9 University Gardens, Glasgow G12 8QH

Professor Máire Ní Mhaonaigh, St John's College, Cambridge CB2 1TP

Professor Huw Pryce, School of History, Philosophy and Social Sciences, Bangor University, Gwynedd LL57 2DG

For titles already published in this series
see the end of this volume

GAELIC INFLUENCE IN THE NORTHUMBRIAN KINGDOM

THE GOLDEN AGE AND THE VIKING AGE

FIONA EDMONDS

THE BOYDELL PRESS

First published 2019
The Boydell Press, Woodbridge
Paperback edition 2023

ISBN 978-1-78327-336-2 hardback
ISBN 978-1-83765-027-9 paperback

The Boydell Press is an imprint of Boydell & Brewer Ltd
PO Box 9, Woodbridge, Suffolk IP12 3DF, UK
and of Boydell & Brewer Inc.
668 Mt Hope Avenue, Rochester, NY 14620-2731, USA
website: www.boydellandbrewer.com

A catalogue record of this publication is available
from the British Library

CONTENTS

ILLUSTRATIONS

Figures

Maps

Basemap data © 2014 Esri

Illustrations

Tables

ACKNOWLEDGEMENTS

This book has been gestating for a long time, and it has become something of a historical artefact in its own right, encompassing various layers of my life. I started my research as a doctoral student in the History Faculty at Oxford University, where I was immensely fortunate to be guided by two highly committed doctoral supervisors (and now good friends), Professor Thomas Charles-Edwards and Professor John Blair. I am also grateful to my examiners, Professor Thomas Clancy and Dr David Griffiths, for their judicious assessment of the thesis and their continued support throughout my career. I benefited from interactions with many other staff and students at Oxford. I cannot name them all, but I would like to thank my New College friend Noël Sugimura, with whom I shared the 'matter of glorious trial' that is doctoral work.

I subsequently moved to the Department of Anglo-Saxon, Norse, and Celtic at Cambridge University. The ASNC ethos proved formative as this work started to evolve into a book, and I am grateful to my ASNC colleagues for sharing their wonderful multi-disciplinary world with me: Professor Paul Russell, Professor Máire Ní Mhaonaigh, Professor Rosalind Love, Professor Simon Keynes, Dr Richard Dance, Dr Judy Quinn and Dr Elizabeth Rowe. I also thank the Fellowship of Clare College, in particular the rowing squad, for their congenial environment. This book benefited from the process of teaching, notably the 'History of the Gaelic-speaking peoples, 400–1200', and I learnt much from the students who took that course.

I eventually returned home and became the Director of the Regional Heritage Centre, based in the History department at Lancaster University. I would like to thank Dr Sam Riches and Ann-Marie Michel, my colleagues in the RHC, for their commitment and good humour. I would also like to pay tribute to my predecessor, Professor Angus Winchester, for his vision for the Centre, as well as his inspiring scholarship.

Across the field more generally, I have benefited from many conversations with colleagues over the years. Again, I cannot name them all, but I mention in particular Dr Alex Woolf and Dr Clare Downham. I would also like to thank Professor Jón Víðar Sigurðsson for hosting me at Oslo University during an ERASMUS exchange, which enabled me to immerse myself in Scandinavian history and languages. I am deeply grateful to Caroline Palmer at Boydell & Brewer, and to the editors of Studies in Celtic History, for the immense patience that they have shown during the production of this book.

I have been fortunate to receive funding from various sources over the years. While I was still at school, the Scott Trust enabled me to pursue two courses at Sabhal Mòr Ostaig. This started my life-long interest in Scottish Gaelic, which culminated in a CertHE by distance learning. The AHRB (now the AHRC) supported my Masters and doctoral research, and since then I have received two Newton Trust grants and a CRASSH Fellowship, which enabled me to carry out some additional research. I have also received funding towards publication costs from the Hunter Archaeological and Historical Trust, the Cumberland and Westmorland Antiquarian and Archaeological Society, and the Historic Society of Lancashire and Cheshire.

Acknowledgements

Some of the knowledge contained in this book was formed during my childhood. In particular, I have benefited from many journeys on the M6 and the M74, and on CalMac and Manx Steam Packet ferries. I thank my parents for inspiring me on these trips, and I hope that this book is an appropriate tribute to their own interests. It reflects my mother's belief in the importance of learning languages, and my father's understanding of landscape through the eyes of the mountaineer. Sadly, during the gestation of this book a number of close relatives have died, and I remember in particular Genevieve Edmonds, Doris Crossley (née Heaney), Harry Crossley and Roger Fowles. I have benefited from the support of a wide network of family and friends, including my cousin Mark and my mother-in-law Oriel.

Finally, I would like to dedicate this work to my young sons, Aidan and Chad, in the hope that they are inspired by their saintly namesakes. I also dedicate it to their father, my husband Jonathan, who more than lives up to the meaning of his own name.

The maps in this volume were made by Fiona Edmonds using ArcGIS® software by Esri. ArcGIS® and ArcMap™ are the intellectual property of Esri and are used herein under license. Copyright © Esri. All rights reserved. For more information about Esri software, please visit www.esri.com. The Roman road dataset is Blackwood, Carol. (2017). GB Roman Roads, [Dataset]. EDINA. https://doi.org/10.7488/ds/1777.

ABBREVIATIONS

AC   *Annales Cambriae*, cited from:
          John Williams (ab Ithel) (ed.), *Annales Cambriae*, Rolls ser. 20 (London, 1860).
          David N. Dumville (ed. and transl.), *Annales Cambriae, A.D. 682–954: Texts A–C in Parallel* (Cambridge, 2002).
          Henry Gough-Cooper (ed.), *Annales Cambriae*, http://croniclau.bangor.ac.uk

AClon   Denis Murphy (ed.), *The Annals of Clonmacnoise being Annals of Ireland from the Earliest Period to A.D. 1408* (Dublin, 1896; repr. Felinfach, 1993).

AFM   John O'Donovan (ed.), *Annála Ríoghachta Éireann: Annals of the Kingdom of Ireland by the Four Masters from the Earliest Period to the Year 1171* (Dublin, 1849).

AI   Seán Mac Airt (ed. and transl.), *The Annals of Inisfallen* (Dublin, 1951).

ALC   William M. Hennessy (ed. and transl.), *The Annals of Loch Cé* (London, 1871).

AR   Dermot Gleeson and Seán Mac Airt (eds), 'The Annals of Roscrea', *PRIA* 59 C (1957–9), 137–80.

ASC A   Janet Bately (ed.), *The Anglo-Saxon Chronicle: A Collaborative Edition, 3:MS A* (Cambridge, 1986).

ASC B   Simon Taylor (ed.), *The Anglo-Saxon Chronicle: A Collaborative Edition, 4:MS B* (Cambridge, 1983).

ASC C   Katherine O'Brien O'Keeffe, *The Anglo-Saxon Chronicle: A Collaborative Edition, 5:MS C* (Cambridge, 2001).

ASC D   G. P. Cubbin (ed.), *The Anglo-Saxon Chronicle: A Collaborative Edition, 6:MS D* (Cambridge, 1996).

ASC E   Susan Irvine (ed.), *The Anglo-Saxon Chronicle: A Collaborative Edition, 7:MS E* (Cambridge, 2004).

AT   Whitley Stokes (ed. and transl.), 'Annals of Tigernach', *Revue Celtique* 16 (1895), 374–419; 17 (1896), 6–33, 119–263, 337–420; 18 (1897), 9–59, 150–97, 267–303; repr. 2 vols (Felinfach, 1993). AT cited from the 1993 reprint.

AU   Seán Mac Airt and Gearóid Mac Niocaill (ed. and transl.), *The Annals of Ulster (to A.D. 1131)* (Dublin, 1983).

AU2   William M. Hennessy and B. Mac Carthy (ed. and transl.), *Annala Uladh: Annals of Ulster*, 4 vols (Dublin, 1887–1901).

BAR   British Archaeological Reports

BLITON Alan James, 'The Brittonic language in the Old North: a guide to the place-name evidence', 3 vols: http://www.spns.org.uk/bliton/blurb.html

C & G   W. G. Collingwood and T. H. B. Graham, 'Patron saints of the diocese of Carlisle', *TCWAAS*, 2nd ser. 25 (1925), 1–27.

Canmore	Historic Environment Scotland, 'The Canmore database', https://www.historicenvironment.scot/archives-and-research/ archives-and-collections/canmore-database/
CGH	M. A. O'Brien (ed.), *Corpus genealogiarum Hiberniae* I (Dublin, 1962).
CI	Thomas Charles-Edwards (ed. and transl.) *The Chronicle of Ireland,* 2 vols (Liverpool, 2006)
CIIC	R. A. S. Macalister, *Corpus Inscriptionum Insularum Celticarum*, 2 vols (Dublin, 1945–9).
CKA	Benjamin T. Hudson (ed. and transl.), 'The Scottish chronicle', *The Scottish Historical Review* 77 (1998), 126–61.
Corpus I	Rosemary Cramp, *Corpus of Anglo-Saxon Stone Sculpture Volume I: County Durham and Northumberland*, 2 vols (Oxford, 1984).
Corpus II	Richard N. Bailey and Rosemary Cramp, *Corpus of Anglo-Saxon Stone Sculpture Volume II: Cumberland, Westmorland and Lancashire North-of-the-Sands* (Oxford, 1988).
Corpus III	James Lang, *Corpus Anglo-Saxon Stone Sculpture Volume III: York and East Yorkshire* (Oxford, 1991).
Corpus VI	James Lang, *Corpus of Anglo-Saxon Stone Sculpture Volume VI: North Yorkshire* (Oxford, 2002).
Corpus VIII	Elizabeth Coatsworth, *Corpus of Anglo-Saxon Stone Sculpture Volume VIII: Western Yorkshire* (Oxford, 2008).
Corpus IX	Richard N. Bailey, *Corpus of Anglo-Saxon Stone Sculpture Volume IX: Cheshire and Lancashire* (Oxford, 2010).
CPNS	William J. Watson, *The History of the Celtic Place-Names of Scotland* (Edinburgh, 1926).
CS	William M. Hennessy (ed. and transl.), *Chronicon Scottorum*, Rolls Ser. 46 (London, 1866).
DB Chesh	Philip Morgan and Alexander R. Rumble (eds), *Domesday Book: Cheshire*, Domesday Book 26 (Chichester, 1978): cited by code number. Christopher Lewis (ed.), *The Cheshire Domesday*, Alecto County Edition of Domesday (London, 1991): cited by folio number.
DB Derbys	Philip Morgan (ed.), *Domesday Book: Derbyshire*, Domesday Book 27 (Chichester, 1978): cited by code number. David Roffe (ed.), *The Derbyshire Domesday*, Alecto County Edition of Domesday (London, 1991): cited by folio number.
DB Yorks	Margaret L. Faull and Marie Stinson (eds), *Domesday Book: Yorkshire*, Domesday Book 30, 2 vols (Chichester, 1986): cited by code number. A. Williams and G. H. Martin (eds), *The Yorkshire Domesday*, Alecto County Edition of Domesday (London, 1992): cited by folio number.
eDIL	'Electronic Dictionary of the Irish Language', http://www.dil.ie/#
EMC	Fitzwilliam Museum, Cambridge, 'Early medieval corpus of coin finds', https://emc.fitzmuseum.cam.ac.uk/
HB	*Historia Brittonum*, cited from: Theodor Mommsen (ed.), 'Historia Brittonum cum additamentis Nennii', in *idem* (ed.), *Chronica Minora saec. IV. V. VI. VII*. 3, MGH Auctores Antiquissimi 13 (Berlin, 1898), 111–222. John Morris (ed. and transl.), *Nennius: British History, and the Welsh Annals* (London, 1980).

HE	Bede, *Historia ecclesiastica gentis Anglorum*, cited from: Bertram Colgrave and R. A. B. Mynors (ed. and transl.), *Bede's Ecclesiastical History of the English People* (Oxford, 1969). Michael Lapidge (ed.), in *idem* and André Crépin (ed. and transl.), *Histoire Ecclésiastique du Peuple Anglais*, 3 vols (Paris, 2005).
HR	*Historia regum*, in Thomas Arnold (ed.), *Symeonis monachi opera omnia*, Rolls ser. 75, 2 vols (London, 1882–5).
HSC	Ted Johnson South, *Historia de Sancto Cuthberto* (Cambridge, 2002).
J-F	Edward Johnson-Ferguson, *The Place-Names of Dumfriesshire* (Dumfries, 1935).
MGH	Monumenta Germaniae Historica
MM	The Manx Museum Catalogue
MT	R. I. Best and Hugh Jackson Lawlor (eds), *The Martyrology of Tallaght* (London, 1931).
OE	Old English
OIr	Old Irish
ON	Old Norse
PAS	Portable Antiquities Scheme, 'Database', https://finds.org.uk
PNCu	A. M. Armstrong *et al.*, *The Place-Names of Cumberland*, 3 vols, English Place-Name Society 20–2 (Cambridge, 1950–2).
PNDerbys	Kenneth Cameron, *The Place-Names of Derbyshire*, 3 vols, English Place-Name Society 27–9 (Cambridge, 1959).
PNEY	A. H. Smith, *The Place-Names of the East Riding of Yorkshire and York*, English Place-Name Society 14 (Cambridge, 1937).
PNIOM	George Broderick, *Placenames of the Isle of Man*, 7 vols (Tübingen, 1994–2005).
PNLa	Eilert Ekwall, *The Place-Names of Lancashire* (Manchester, 1922).
PNNY	A. H. Smith, *The Place-Names of the North Riding of Yorkshire*, English Place-Name Society 5 (Cambridge, 1928).
PNWe	A. H. Smith, *The Place-Names of Westmorland*, 2 vols, English Place-Name Society 42–3 (Cambridge, 1967).
PNWY	A. H. Smith, *The Place-Names of the West Riding of Yorkshire*, 8 vols, English Place-Name Survey 30–7 (Cambridge, 1961–3).
PRIA	*Proceedings of the Royal Irish Academy*
PSAS	*Proceedings of the Society of Antiquaries of Scotland*
RCAHMS	Royal Commission on the Ancient and Historical Monuments of Scotland
SCBI	Sylloge of Coins of the British Isles
SSNNW	Gillian Fellows-Jensen, *Scandinavian Settlement Names in the North-West* (Copenhagen, 1985).
TCWAAS	*Transactions of the Cumberland and Westmorland Antiquarian and Archaeological Society*
TDGNHAS	*Transactions of the Dumfriesshire and Galloway Natural History and Antiquarian Society*

PREFACE:
AN EVENTFUL VOYAGE

A fierce sea lashes a boat that is transporting a very precious cargo. A group of people huddle by the shore; they watch the scene with dismay and pray for a safe outcome. The helmsman vainly tries to steer, but this is not an ordinary storm. Three waves miraculously turn into blood as they break over the side of the vessel, and the voyage is abandoned.

This dramatic scene is a depiction of the attempt to send the relics of St Cuthbert to Ireland. It belongs to a series of miniature pictures that accompanied accounts of the saint's life and miracles in a manuscript from Anglo-Norman Durham.[1] The incident took place in the 870s, a decade that straddled the eras covered in this book: the Golden Age of the seventh and eighth centuries, and the Viking Age.[2] The episode encapsulates the enduring nature of Gaelic influence in the Northumbrian kingdom, for Cuthbert was a renowned Northumbrian saint, and the attempted voyage took him towards Ireland, a key part of the Gaelic cultural world.

The Northumbrian kingdom was the most northerly of the Anglo-Saxon polities. In its heyday the kingdom stretched across much of modern-day northern England and southern Scotland, from the River Mersey to Ayrshire and from the Humber Estuary to the Firth of Forth. This extensive area includes landscapes that are prized in the modern day for their untamed appearance: swathes of heather moorland on the Pennines and the Border Hills, and sharp peaks formed from volcanic rock in the Lake District. Yet the kingdom also encompassed areas rich in agricultural potential, especially for cattle-rearing. These areas sustained a wealthy nobility, important churches and incipient urban centres. The Northumbrian elites travelled widely, forged links with other kingdoms, and developed an appetite for exotic goods. At the northern and southern ends of the kingdom, the great coastal indentations of the Humber and the Forth could be traversed to reach Anglo-Saxon Mercia and the Picts, respectively. Two long coastlines opened the kingdom up further to external influences. The western coast is lapped by the Irish Sea and the North Channel, over which sailors voyaged to the Gaelic world: Ireland, western Scotland and the Isle of Man. The eastern coast opens on to the North Sea, and travellers could set sail from here to south-eastern England, Francia and Rome. The cultural contacts established along the eastern coast have been researched in considerable detail, and I would

---

[1]   See front cover image: Oxford, University College, MS 165, p. 143, fol. 73r, dated by Kauffmann, *Romanesque Manuscripts*, 66–7; Lawrence-Mathers, *Manuscripts in Northumbria*, 84–108, esp. 104. Farmer, 'A note', suggests that the manuscript was created in Durham for a private patron. For further discussion of the incident, see below, 114.

[2]   The term 'Viking', with its long-standing capital letter, has come under much scrutiny in recent scholarship; see Jesch, *The Viking Diaspora*, 4–10 for a helpful guide. I use the term to refer to raiding (while acknowledging the relationship of this activity to trade and settlement) and to define the period from the end of the eighth century to the eleventh.

not claim that Gaelic influence outweighed those links, or indeed that the two were mutually exclusive.[3]

These diverse cultural influences came together in the Northumbrian kingdom during the seventh and eighth centuries. The ensuing phase of intellectual and artistic creativity has become known as the 'Northumbrian renaissance' or the 'Golden Age'; the latter term is also used in an Irish context.[4] This was a political high point, a time when Northumbrian kings wielded influence well beyond the borders of the kingdom. During the ninth century, the Northumbrian elites were subsumed by internal difficulties, which formed the background to the capture and conquest of York in 866–7 by a 'Great Army' of Scandinavian origin. The kingdom fell apart, and some areas became vulnerable to the expansion of other dynasties. The notion of a Northumbrian kingdom lived on, however, in the political unit centred on York until at least the mid-tenth century. Northumbrian culture endured for even longer, and mingled with Brittonic, Scandinavian and Gaelic influences on the northern and western edges of the former kingdom. Thus the history of the Northumbrian kingdom, from its rise until its fragmentation, provides a fruitful opportunity to investigate cultural interaction in an early medieval setting.

This book focuses on Gaelic and Gaelic–Scandinavian influence in the Northumbrian kingdom, from its emergence in the early seventh century until its division between the English and Scottish realms during the eleventh century. It is the first work to investigate Gaelic influence in the area over such an extended period. The quality of the evidence varies from locality to locality and over time, and so it is impossible to build up a comprehensive picture of every part of the kingdom across all four of the centuries under investigation. Nevertheless, the evidence is sufficient to argue that links with the Gaelic world were more pervasive, long-lived and multi-faceted than has been recognised hitherto. A nuanced picture can be drawn, one that takes into account different phases of cultural contact and influences emanating from several directions. I devote particular attention to the western and northern parts of the Northumbrian kingdom, which were closest to Ireland, Gaelic-speaking parts of Scotland and the Isle of Man.

The study also differs from earlier treatments of Gaelic influence in the Northumbrian kingdom by adopting an interdisciplinary approach. The term 'Gaelic' refers in the first instance to language, as I discuss below,[5] but those who came to Northumbria had an impact beyond the purely linguistic. This book also covers political links, routes of communication, ecclesiastical contacts and material culture. An interdisciplinary approach inevitably has pitfalls, and it is necessary to examine the limitations of each type of source material, but it can be helpful to compare and contrast different categories of evidence. The approach has the added benefit of shedding light on the west and north of the Northumbrian kingdom, regions that are poorly recorded and have bequeathed no early medieval manuscripts. Here I argue that their inhabitants enjoyed close links with the Gaelic and Gaelic–Scandinavian worlds.

[3] Frankish links with the Anglo-Saxon world are considered by Levison, *England and the Continent*; Story, *Carolingian Connections*; Palmer, *Anglo-Saxons*. For Rome, see Matthews, *The Road to Rome*; Tinti (ed.), *England and Rome*.

[4] For the Northumbrian usage see, for example, Kendrick, *Anglo-Saxon Art*, 119; Cramp, 'The Northumbrian identity', 1, 10–11; Neuman de Vegvar, *The Northumbrian Renaissance*. For 'Golden Age' in an Irish context, see Ó Cróinín, *Early Medieval Ireland*, 196.

[5] See below, 5.

I do not provide an exhaustive treatment of all of the relevant categories of evidence. I have devoted particular attention to texts, personal name studies and church dedications, whereas my study of material culture and landscape history draws to a greater extent on work conducted by other scholars. This approach is determined partly by my training as an historian with a strong interest in languages and names, and also by the emphases of existing scholarship. Manuscripts, palaeography and intellectual links have previously gained, or are currently enjoying, attention in works on contact between the Gaelic and Anglo-Saxon worlds.[6] In contrast, personal names and church dedications have been relatively neglected, and there remains much to discover in Ireland's very rich textual corpus. A century ago, the celebrated scholar and artist W. G. Collingwood wrote 'the pictures of these times can only be given as an historical novel, because any other form would claim too much for the authenticity of details'.[7] I aim to show that the evidence adds up to a picture of enduring and varied Gaelic influence, and I hope that the material presented in the current book will encourage further specialised work to refine that picture.

[6] See below, 99–100.
[7] *The Likeness*, preface.

CONCEPTS AND HISTORIOGRAPHY OF THE NORTHUMBRIAN AND GAELIC WORLDS: MEDIEVAL TO MODERN

This book explores the evolution of contact between Gaelic and Northumbrian spheres over the course of four centuries. One event encapsulates the complexity of the theme, namely, the Northumbrian king Ecgfrith's raid on the plain of Brega in Ireland (684). The expedition occurred in defiance of the revered churchman Ecgberht, who saw it as an unwarranted attack on a people who had never harmed the king. In a similar vein, the Northumbrian historian Bede characterised the raid as an attack on *gens innoxia, et nationi Anglorum semper amicissima* 'an inoffensive people who had always been friendly to the English'. Bede saw Ecgfrith's subsequent defeat and death in battle against the Picts as just punishment for this *impietas* 'wickedness'.[1] The event continued to haunt depictions of relations across the Irish Sea for many centuries, as seen in Conchubranus's mid-eleventh-century *Vita Sanctae Monennae*, where the incident is recast in light of contemporary themes in Irish–English relations.[2] This later retelling echoes Bede's picture of complex connections, involving not only enmity but also ecclesiastical bonds and friendships forged in exile.[3]

Bede framed his account as a momentous incident in the interactions between *gentes* 'peoples'. The protagonist, Ecgfrith, was *rex Northanhymbrorum* 'king of the Northumbrians', and a representative of *natio Anglorum* 'the nation of the English'. Those attacked, the *gens innoxia*, were the inhabitants of Ireland, for which Bede used the terms 'Hibernia' and 'Scottia'. When describing the aftermath of the battle in Pictland, he wrote of *Scotti, qui erant in Brittania*, indicating that 'Scotti' was a term for the inhabitants of the pan-Gaelic world. Thus in this account we see complex groupings of people: Scotti targeted in Ireland, but also resident in Britain; Northumbrians who were also English. For Bede, 'the medieval world was undoubtedly a world of peoples, *gentes*', as Rees Davies wrote.[4] Yet how far did this consciousness seep through society, and how is it manifested in our sources?

---

[1] *HE* IV, 24 (26), 1 (ed. Lapidge, II, 350–3; ed. and transl. Colgrave and Mynors, 426–9). When citing Bede's *Historia ecclesiastica gentis Anglorum*, I use Michael Lapidge's 2005 edition (which is accompanied by a French translation) and that of Colgrave and Mynors (1969), which is still widely referenced.

[2] 'Conchubrani Vita Sanctae Monennae', I.14 and I.15 (ed. Esposito, 215–17; ed. and transl. Ulster Society for Medieval Latin Studies, 268–73).

[3] I discuss the relationship between this episode and the raid on Brega in my forthcoming article 'Irish hagiographical representations'. On Bede's nuanced, though favourable, portrayal of the Irish, see McCann, *'Plures de Scottorum regione'*, 24–8.

[4] Davies, 'The peoples', 4. In this chapter, I follow Davies's translation of *gens* as 'people' to allow for the varied, and sometimes ephemeral, groupings encompassed by that term in the Insular world. In other contexts, scholars have sometimes translated the term 'race'; for an example, see Geraldine Heng's seminal new work *The Invention of Race*, 7, 124.

I begin by exploring how early medieval writers conceptualised peoples, before examining contemporary terminology for the Gaelic and Northumbrian worlds. I then review the historiography of the topic, arguing for an appreciation of the complexity and enduring significance of Northumbrian-Gaelic relations.

Concepts of early medieval peoples

When early medieval scholars wrote of groups such as the Northumbrians, they were not merely reporting on the world around them; rather, their works were deeply rooted in biblical and classical learning. The presentation of Old Testament peoples influenced portrayals of contemporary groups, for the *populus Israhel* was unified by a shared consciousness and law, as well as the covenant with God. The term *populus* could be rather specific, for example differentiating the *populus Romanus* from the barbarian *gentes*, but this distinction was breaking down during the early medieval period.[5] The Vetus Latina and Vulgate Bibles tended to use the term *gens* for a people (sometimes in contexts where 'nation' appears in modern English translations) and this usage influenced the vocabulary of early medieval writers.[6] Another touchstone for the understanding of peoples was Isidore of Seville's widely influential *Etymologiae*. He famously stated: *Gens est multitudo ab uno principio orta, sive ab alia natione secundum propriam collectionem distincta.* Isidore was attempting to redefine the *gens*, moving away from the Roman image of the barbarians to one that was relevant to the Visigothic kingdom.[7] He went on to enumerate the nations descended from Japheth, Ham and Shem (drawing on Genesis 10) and to discuss the location and characteristics of peoples in his day. The Old Testament also provided a model for rulership, for the Israelites petitioned their judge, Samuel, to appoint a king to lead them *sicut universae habent nationes* 'such as all the nations have'.[8] In a similar way, kingship often underpinned nationhood in the medieval period, notwithstanding modernist scepticism about the existence of nations prior to the eighteenth century.[9] Medieval *gentes* had diverse political manifestations, ranging from communities unified by law to loose military confederations; furthermore a

---

[5]   Scheil, *The Footsteps*, 101–91 discusses the concept of the *populus Israhel* in late antique works and early medieval England. For the *gens/populus* distinction, see Geary, *The Myth of Nations*, 50, 61–2; Tugène, *L'idée de nation*, 73–8; Schustereder, *Strategies*, 20.

[6]   For example, I Samuel 8:20, *et erimus nos quoque sicut omnes gentes*: *Biblia Sacra Vulgata* (ed. Weber and Gryson, 376); and similar in the various Vetus Latina versions (I Reges 8, 20): Vetus Latina Institut, *Vetus Latina Database*: https://brepolis.net/apps/vld/index.html. Translated in the King James Version: 'that we also may be like all the nations', and in the New International Version: 'then we shall be like all the other nations'. Cf. Hastings, *The Construction*, 16–17.

[7]   Isidore, *Etymologiae* II.1 (ed. Lindsay, no pp. given; transl. Barney *et al.*, 196). 'A *gens* is a number of people sharing a single origin, or distinguished from another *natio* in accordance with its own grouping' (translation adapted). For the context, see Wood, *The Politics of Identity*, 7–8, 13, 60–1, 76–7, 147–79; Reimitz, *History, Frankish Identity*, 10.

[8]   I Samuel 8:5; *Biblia Sacra Vulgata* (ed. Weber and Gryson, 376). The term *natio* is discussed in Hastings, *The Construction*, 3; Reynolds, *Kingdoms and Communities*, 256; Dumville, 'Did Ireland exist in the twelfth century?', 116.

[9]   Medieval nationhood is discussed by Stringer, 'Social and political communities', 10–11, 21–34; Hastings, *The Construction*, esp. 1–13. They challenge historians who have portrayed nationhood as a phenomenon of modern history, such as Hobsbawm, *Nations and Nationalism*, 9–10, 14–45; Anderson, *Imagined Communities*, 41–9.

large *gens* could include smaller *gentes*.[10] This flexibility in defining a people should be borne in mind when examining the interaction of Northumbrians and Gaels.

The mental universe of early medieval writers was divided into peoples, but it is less clear how the groups termed 'Gaelic' or 'Northumbrian' were manifested in reality. No longer is it possible to follow the discredited views of the nineteenth-century scholars who conceived of ethnicity as an innate biological feature.[11] Since the late twentieth century, historians have widely followed anthropologists in arguing that ethnic identities were flexible and prone to manipulation.[12] The historian Reinhard Wenskus independently came to the view that the Germanic peoples were the product of a process known as *Stammesbildung* (the word used in ensuing scholarship is *Ethnogenese* 'ethnogenesis'). Disparate warbands would join in confederations, coalesce around a leading kindred (*stirps regia*) and adopt their origin myth. In this way a *gens* emerged, ruled by an elite who transmitted cultural customs (the *Traditionskern* 'kernel of tradition') to their followers.[13] The 'Vienna School' of Herwig Wolfram, Walter Pohl and others have further developed and refined the ethnogenesis model. There is now a sophisticated understanding of 'strategies of distinction', that is, ways that participants and observers constructed late-antique ethnic groups.[14] In its current form, the concept of ethnogenesis allows for considerable variety and nuance, and is far from a 'rigid model, a straitjacket'.[15] That said, aspects of the concept are still being debated, such as the extent of Roman influence in the societies that emerged in the wake of the empire.[16]

Much of the scholarship relating to ethnogenesis concerns the barbarian peoples who moved across the Roman frontiers of continental Europe, often as disparate and linguistically diverse armies. Language was rarely a prerequisite for unity, for military confederations often included speakers of several tongues. Even in the case of the Strasbourg Oaths (842), where the armies of Charles the Bald and Louis II were presented as monolingual speakers of Romance and Germanic tongues respectively, the distinction was partly symbolic.[17] In contrast, language seems to have been a much more prominent factor in forging group identities in northern Britain

---

[10] Wenskus, *Stammesbildung und Verfassung*, 46–7, 50; Wolfram, *The History of the Goths*, 5, 12; Kahl, 'Einige Beobachtungen', 67, 81; Reimitz, *History, Frankish Identity*, 69. Hiberno-Latin writers of the seventh century might use the term in a specific way, for a ruling kindred with deep lineage: Charles-Edwards, *Early Irish and Welsh Kinship*, 141–65; idem, *Early Christian Ireland*, 96–100.

[11] See below, 19–20.

[12] Barth, 'Introduction'. It is worth noting Helmut Reimitz's more recent distinction between ethnic identity and ethnicity: *History, Frankish Identity*, 7–8.

[13] Wenskus, *Stammesbildung und Verfassung*, esp. 32–8, 46–82. Some of his views were anticipated in 1907 by Chadwick, *The Origin*, 153–91, as noted by Murray ('Reinhard Wenskus', 67); Wood, *The Modern Origins*, 300.

[14] Pohl, 'Introduction', 5; idem, 'Telling the difference', 21–2.

[15] The quotation is from Bowlus, 'Ethnogenesis', 242.

[16] Goffart, *Barbarian Tides*, balanced by Pohl, 'Introduction', 2–3, 6–7; idem, 'Telling the difference', 39, 63–9. For other areas of criticism, see Gillett, 'Was ethnicity politicized?'

[17] Nithard, *Historiae*, III.5 (ed. Müller, *Nithardi historiarum libri IIII*, 35; transl. Scholz, *Carolingian Chronicles*, 161), discussed by Ayres-Bennett, *A History*, 16–21. For instances where there is no correlation between linguistic and political identity, see Wenskus, *Stammesbildung und Verfassung*, 96–100; Wolfram, *The History of the Goths*, 210, 231; Wickham, *The Inheritance*, 5, 100, 481.

and Ireland; indeed, Bede wrote of *quinque gentium linguae*.[18] The Britons were unified by their vernacular language, while remaining militarily and politically fragmented. They called themselves *Cymry* (**com-brogi* 'inhabitants of the same *bro* 'locality'), a designation that dated back to Roman times, when speakers of the vernacular (*Cymraeg*) distinguished themselves from speakers of Latin.[19] Gaelic identity was similarly rooted in a common language, and underpinned by a prolific vernacular literature, which was partly shaped by clerics who were literate in Latin. The Northumbrians did not have their own language, being part of the wider English-speaking sphere, but distinctive dialect features developed within the kingdom.[20]

The use of medieval peoples as a framework for understanding cultural interaction has its limitations.[21] The consciousness of belonging to one people was often relevant to those in the higher social strata, including the literati and court circles, who could in turn disseminate such ideas to other sectors of society.[22] Yet as Eric Hobsbawm noted of more recent times, the 'view from below' is hard to recover, and peasants were often the last to be captured by 'national consciousness'.[23] Local allegiances persisted underneath broader identities: the residents of Annandale, for example, were identified with their river valley in the Roman period (*Brittones Anavionenses*) and again in the twelfth century.[24] At the start of the period Ireland comprised many *túatha* – entities that defy easy definition – but that were essentially groups of people with their own king. It would have been vital to know whether one belonged to an *aithechthúath* ('unfree client people') or a free people.[25] An individual might have held allegiances to locality, region, and nation, each layer of identity being empha-sised in different contexts. In some Bavarian cemeteries of the post-Roman period, for example, female costume alluded to local links and to far-flung origins, whereas male dress reflected membership of regional armies.[26] Gender influenced the ways in which an individual experienced membership of local groups and *gentes*.

In my study, then, the topic of Northumbrian–Gaelic interaction includes links at a regional and local level, such as the strong and enduring connection between the Furness peninsula and the Isle of Man, alongside the high-political dimension.

[18] HE I, 1, 3 (ed. Lapidge, I, 114; ed. and transl. Colgrave and Mynors, 16–17) 'five languages of peoples'.

[19] Charles-Edwards, 'Language and society', 711–15; Woolf, 'The Britons', 373–9; Charles-Edwards, 'The making of nations', 22–9.

[20] Johnston, *Literacy and Identity*, esp. 27–31. Johnston focuses here on Irish identity, and indeed the vast majority of surviving texts are from Ireland. Iona-based scholars such as Adomnán were involved in this milieu, as Johnston notes at *ibid.*, 33, 37. For Northumbrian dialect, see Hogg, 'Old English dialectology', 396–9; Toon, 'Old English dialects', 417, 435, who notes that Northumbrian dialect is sometimes characterised as 'a loose conglomerate of individual varieties'.

[21] My understanding of 'cultural' in this context follows Barth, 'Introduction', 9 as a term relating to facets of group behaviour.

[22] Geary, 'Ethnic identity'; McKitterick, 'Conclusion', 333: 'literacy had repercussions right down the social scale'; *eadem, History and Memory*, 5–7.

[23] Hobsbawm, *Nations and Nationalism*, 12; cf. Schustereder, *Strategies*, 26.

[24] Edmonds, 'The expansion', 63, citing Rivet, 'The Brittones Anavionenses'. In general, see Reynolds, *Kingdoms and Communities*, 266; Pohl, 'Ethnic names', 12–13; Halsall, *Barbarian Migrations*, 38–9.

[25] Byrne, 'Tribes and tribalism', 130–7, 158–61; Charles-Edwards, *Early Irish and Welsh* Kinship, 143–5; *idem, Early Christian Ireland*, 102–6; MacCotter, *Medieval Ireland*, 22–3, 88–91, 108. Ó Corráin, 'On the "Aithechthúatha" tracts'.

[26] Hakenbeck, *Local, Regional and Ethnic Identities*, 102–5, 143.

This approach supports my overarching argument that Gaelic influence took diverse forms, and varied in intensity, across the Northumbrian kingdom.

The Gaelic-speaking world

I now turn to the specific terms used in the study, starting with 'Gaelic', for the Gaelic-speaking world gave rise to the cultural influenceṣ that I trace in this book. In taking a pan-Gaelic view, I do not wish to downplay links between Northumbria and Ireland, which have long been perceived as a significant aspect of the 'Golden Age'. Rather, I wish to highlight a whole range of possible connections involving Ireland, the Isle of Man and the nascent Scottish kingdom.[27] Nor do I wish to claim that the Gaelic-speaking world was intimately interconnected and coherent at all times in the early medieval period. Recent studies of late-medieval Gaelic high culture, a time of flourishing patronage in the Isles as well as in Ireland, have veered away from the idea of an integrated 'culture province' in the thought-world of bardic poetry.[28] It is worth asking what the notion of Gaeldom meant to early medieval writers.

The tightest bond between the Gaels was their language. Kenneth Jackson coined the term 'Common Gaelic', and viewed the language as tightly unified during the linguistic phase known as Old Irish.[29] The evidence for dialects in Old Irish is slight, which may suggest that it was a high-register scholarly language. It was perhaps promoted by the politically dominant group called Féni, and certainly by scholars whose interests spanned the lay and ecclesiastical worlds.[30] Jackson saw Gaelic as relatively unified throughout the Middle Irish period (*ca* 900–1200), with no distinction between the literary and spoken registers.[31] More recently scholars have noted the emergence of some distinctively Scottish-Gaelic features, which must have been marked in speech, and also permeated the written medium. One example is the system of eclipsis, an initial mutation of consonants that developed distinctively in Scottish Gaelic.[32] Galloway was a significant exception to this rule: here eclipsis followed the same pattern as Irish and Manx.[33] Thus Gaelic had dialectal differences, as well as common features that were most pronounced in the literary sphere. The commonalities can make it difficult to discern the precise sources of Gaelic linguistic influence in the Northumbrian kingdom.

A broader sense of Gaelic identity emerged, which was rooted to some extent in these linguistic ties. The vernacular term *Goídel* was borrowed from Welsh *gwyddel*

---

[27] On the historiography of the Gaelic world, see Ellis, 'The collapse', 449–51.

[28] McLeod, *Divided Gaels*, 4–7, 114, *contra* Jackson, 'Common Gaelic', 77. Cf. Ó Mainnín, '"The same in origin and blood"', 6.

[29] Jackson, 'Common Gaelic', 80–6. 'Old Irish' is a long-established term, but 'Old Gaelic' is also used; see Ó Baoill, 'A history of Gaelic to 1800', 5.

[30] For dialects: Thurneysen, *A Grammar*, 12; Ahlqvist, 'Remarks'; Russell, '"What was best"', 439–43; Murray, 'Dialect in medieval Irish?' For Féni: Charles-Edwards, 'Language and society', 727–9; *idem*, *Early Christian Ireland*, 512, 583–4; *idem*, 'The making of nations', 32. The scholarly register is discussed by McCone, 'Zur Frage der Register', 89–97.

[31] Jackson, 'Common Gaelic', 79. Here he was drawing on O'Rahilly, *Irish Dialects*, 248.

[32] Ó Maolalaigh, 'Place-names as a resource', 14, 24; *idem*, 'The Scotticisation of Gaelic', 241–58. More generally, see Ó Buachalla, 'Common Gaelic revisited'.

[33] Ó Maolalaigh, 'Place-names as a resource', 29–30; cf. in general, O'Rahilly, *Irish Dialects*, 117; Thomson, 'The continuity', 172; for links between Galloway, Man and Ireland, see below 120–6, 145–6, 161.

'wild man' no earlier than the seventh century.[34] A tale quickly arose to explain the creation of the language (*Goídelc*), as related in the early core of *Auraicept na nÉces* ('The Scholars' Primer'). *Goídelc* reportedly emerged during the confusion of tongues following the building of the Tower of Babel; a group that included the eponymous protagonist Gáedel formed it from the finest parts of all languages. The tale emphasises the importance of language in forging a community, for when groups left the Tower they consisted of *cach combérlaid* ('everyone speaking the same language') not *cach comcheniúil* ('everyone of the same kindred').[35] The idea of common descent soon augmented the linguistic foundations of Gaelic identity, as intimated by genealogical poetry as early as the seventh century. These ideas were fleshed out in the historical poem of the renowned Irish scholar Máel Muru Othna (*ob.* 887), and detailed at length in *Lebor Gabála*, a weighty work of the eleventh century.[36] Meanwhile Scottish writers drew on the origin legend of the Gaels (albeit without reference to *Lebor Gabála*) to demonstrate the antiquity of Scottish kingship.[37] The linguistic concept of Goídil did not disappear entirely, as witnessed by Gall-Goídil 'Foreigner Gaels', who first appeared in Ireland in the 850s and later re-emerged in what is now south-western Scotland. These people seem to have been Gaelic speakers, even if their behaviour or background marked them out as being in some way 'foreign'.[38]

A shared Gaelic identity was perceptible to outside observers, notably the Latin writers who described the Gaels collectively as Scotti.[39] It is important to establish the connotations of this term at the time when Northumbrian scholars started to use it, for its scope evolved. The fourth-century writer Ammianus Marcellinus recounted the disruption caused by three Insular peoples, the Picti, Scotti and the elusive Attacotti in the turbulent 360s.[40] The expansion of the Scotti (or at least the broadening of the term's remit) must have occurred by the fifth century, for Orosius placed Scotti on the Isle of Man as well as in Ireland.[41] By the later seventh century, it was possible

---

[34] The borrowing postdates the change of Brittonic *w*- to *gw*-, completed by the end of the eighth century: Jackson, *Language and History*, 389–91, refined by Sims-Williams, *The Celtic Inscriptions*, 211–14, 288; cf. Charles-Edwards, 'Language and society', 723. The date is supported by the date of syncope in accusative and dative plural: *Goídelu, Goídelaib* (Ó Murchadha, 'Nationality names', 56).

[35] *Auraicept na nÉces* §1 (ed. Ahlqvist, *Early Irish Linguist*, 46); Charles-Edwards, 'The context', 76–8; Russell, '"What was best"', 405–6.

[36] 'Nuadu Necht ní dámair anflaith' (ed. O'Brien, *CGH* 115a, 1–4; ed. Meyer, *Über die älteste irische Dichtung*, 39–42). For the dating, see Ó Corráin, 'Irish origin legends', 57–64; *idem*, 'Creating the past', 192–3; 'Can a mbunadas na nGáedel?' (ed. Todd, *Leabhar Breathnach*, 220–71; ed. Best *et al.*, *The Book of Leinster*, III, 579); Carey, 'In search', 437–9. *Lebor Gabála Érenn* I, 16, 102 (ed. Macalister, I, 36–7, 166–7); Carey, *The Irish National Origin-Legend*, 19–22.

[37] A thirteenth-century synthesis of these traditions underpins the account of Scottish origins in Fordun, *Chronica gentis Scottorum*, I, 8–19 (ed. Skene, I, 9–21). See the new edition by Broun, *The Irish Identity*, 36–8 and for discussion, *ibid*. 11–81, 130–1.

[38] Herbert, 'Sea-divided Gaels?', 96–7; Clancy, 'The Gall-Ghàidheil', 21; see below 69–70.

[39] The term emerged in the fourth century. Mac Neill, 'Ancient Irish law', 267 suggested it was a nickname meaning 'raiders'; cf. Ó Murchadha, 'Nationality names', 55; Márkus, *Conceiving a Nation*, 77–80.

[40] Ammianus Marcellinus, *Res Gestae*, xxvi.4.5, xxvii.8.1 (ed. and transl. Rolfe, II, 586–9; III, 52–3). On the Attacotti and the Roman army, see Freeman, *Ireland and the Classical World*, 9–10; Raftery, *Pagan Celtic Ireland*, 216.

[41] Orosius, *Libri historiarum adversum paganos* 1.2.80–2 (ed. Zangemeister, I.12).

for Adomnán of Iona (*ob.* 704) to write of *Scotti Brittaniae* 'Gaels in Britain'.[42] This is not to say that the term 'Scotti' always referred to the broad community of sea-divided Gaels; in some cases the title *rex Scottorum* might be better translated 'king of the Irish'.[43] By the tenth century, 'Scottish' terminology was increasingly associated with the incipient kingdom of the Scots in what had been Pictish territory. 'Scotia' was used as the Latin translation for the Gaelic 'Alba', a term that originally applied to all of Britain and then became restricted to the area between the Forth and the Spey.[44] The shifting nature of the term 'Scotti' should be borne in mind when translating the works of early medieval writers.

So far I have established that Gaelic consciousness was tangible during the early medieval period. This form of affinity was, however, often an undercurrent in the identities that took root more prominently in the different parts of the Gaelic world, and became more politically potent. Turning first to Ireland, there was a concept of a long-standing traditional law, *Fénechas*. Its name was related to the term Féni, which designated the confederation led by Uí Néill, as well as the Irish as a whole. A common legal tradition – underpinned by vernacular literacy – offered a powerful sense of unity in an era when peoples were often perceived as communities of law, custom and descent.[45] Ecclesiastical scholars conceived of Ireland's inhabitants as a people on the biblical model and as a constituency for conversion; St Patrick, indeed, saw a letter headed *vox Hiberionacum* 'the voice of the Irish' in a vision.[46] The Ireland-wide scope of Patrick's mission came to be emphasised in later hagiography, and it underpinned the claims of his chief church, Armagh, to primacy in Ireland.[47]

Seventh-century scholars developed a theory of Irish over-kingship, in which the prehistoric site of Tara became a talisman of Ireland-wide power: *caput Scotorum* 'the capital of the Scotti' (in this context, the Irish).[48] Even if the greatest kings of Tara – drawn mostly from Uí Néill – left parts of Ireland untouched, the concept of Irish rulership had emerged. It went on to influence the political ambitions of the most powerful Irish rulers in the ninth and tenth centuries, who were often designated *rí Érenn* 'king of Ireland'.[49] Brían Bóroma (*ob.* 1014) was the first to extend his power across the entire island, and even beyond, using personal authority to

---

[42] Adomnán, *Vita S. Columbae*, I.10, I.36, II.46 (ed. and transl. Anderson and Anderson, 34–5, 64–5, 178–9).

[43] As in the reference to Domnall mac Áedo in a poem edited in Strecker, *Rhythmi Computistici*, 695–7, dated in Ó Cróinín, 'Early Irish annals', 80. Domnall is elsewhere called *rex Hiberniae*; see Ó Cróinín, *Early Medieval Ireland*, 74. This is not to deny that Domnall's victory at Mag Roth (637) had severe ramifications for the Dál Riata *cenéla* in Britain; see below, 38–9.

[44] For the terminological shift, see Broun, 'The origin'; Dumville, 'Ireland and Britain'. For the dual meaning of *Alba* as a Pictish legacy, see Broun, *Scottish Independence*, 71–98, 164. Ross, *The Kings*, 41–2, 143 outlines the importance of the Spey.

[45] Charles-Edwards, *Early Christian Ireland*, 580; and in general, Reynolds, *Kingdoms and Communities*, 256–8. Johnston, *Literacy and Identity* offers a powerful argument for the importance of literacy. Compare Sarah Foot's interpretation of English identity ('The making of *Angelcynn*'), and in general, Hastings, *The Construction*, 19–25, 30–1, 39.

[46] Patrick, *Confessio* (ed. and transl. Hood, 27, 46); Ó Corráin, 'The Church', 266–84.

[47] For example, the seventh-century text *Liber Angeli* §8, 13, 18, 28 (ed. and transl. Bieler, 184–91).

[48] Muirchú, *Vita Sancti Patricii* I.10 (ed. and transl. Bieler, 74–5), preserving Bieler's translation of *Scotorum*, which is appropriate in context. Cf. Bhreathnach, 'Temoria: caput Scotorum?', 68–73; Charles-Edwards, *Early Christian Ireland*, 481–521.

[49] Herbert, '*Rí Éirenn, Rí Alban*', 64–6; Herbert 'Sea-divided Gaels?', 94–6.

mobilise armies across provinces.[50] By the end of the period covered in this book, then, a robust and politically influential sense of Irish identity had come to the fore. This development would have been perceptible to those based in the Northumbrian kingdom, many of whom were themselves being absorbed into the larger political unit of *Engla lond* 'England'.

Moving across the North Channel, the evolution of Gaelic culture in Argyll and the Isles would have been perceptible to those on the northern and western flanks of the Northumbrian kingdom. The timescale for the settlement of Gaelic speakers is controversial, and the evidence is meagre and complex. The key figure in the traditional account is the Dál Riatan leader Fergus mac Erca, who reportedly spearheaded the settlement of Argyll from Antrim *ca* 500 AD; the associated annal entries are, however, far from contemporary.[51] Bede, drawing on a Pictish source, reported a similar migration that was led by *dux Reuda*.[52] In a much-debated article, Ewan Campbell has highlighted the lack of archaeological support for these migration accounts, and proposed that the Gaelic language developed on both sides of the North Channel in prehistoric times.[53] Against this, the second-century writer Ptolemy offered the Brittonic (not Gaelic) name *Epidii* for the inhabitants of Kintyre (Ἐπίδιον ἄκρον). This evidence is not conclusive, however, since Ptolemy was dependent on Brittonic-speaking informants.[54] The trans-marine political link between Dál Riata in Britain and Ireland had certainly emerged by the late seventh century, when the core elements of *Míniugud Senchasa Fer nAlban* 'Explanation of the history of the men of Britain' were composed. They portray Erc (Fergus's father) as having sired six sons who went to Britain and six who remained in Ireland.[55] The text identifies three principal kindreds (*cenéla*) in Britain, but in reality power ebbed and flowed between a number of groups, and the wider Dál Riatan kingdom was slow to emerge.[56] This decentralised view of the Dál Riatan polity may offer a key to unlocking the gaelicisation of Argyll and the Isles, indicating that rule by Gaelic-speaking dynasties progressed in a piecemeal fashion. From a Northumbrian perspective, then, Dál Riata was at once part of the wider Gaelic world and an entity riven with internal rivalries.

The next major phase of Gaelic expansion occurred in the late ninth/early tenth century, and it is equally mysterious. The traditional view, dating back to the tenth

---

[50] Ní Mhaonaigh, *Brian Boru*, 33–7, and for the influence of scholarship on kings, Ó Corráin, 'Nationality and kingship'; with literary examples, Ní Mhaonaigh, 'Perception and reality', 135–9.

[51] AT [500] (ed. and transl. Stokes, I, 84); CS [499] (ed. and transl. Hennessy, 34–5); AClon 501 (ed. Murphy, 74); AFM 499 (ed. and transl. O'Donovan, 160–1). Dumville, 'Ireland and North Britain', 191, argues that this entry was a tenth-century insertion into the Clonmacnoise branch. Charles-Edwards (*The Chronicle of Ireland*, I, 83–4) leaves open the possibility that it belonged to the Iona chronicle.

[52] *HE* I, 1, 4 (ed. Lapidge, I, 118; ed. and transl. Colgrave and Mynors, 18–19); Duncan, 'Bede, Iona', 3–4, 16–17, 33–4; Fraser, *From Caledonia to Pictland*, 145.

[53] Campbell, 'Were the Scots Irish?'

[54] Ptolemy, *Geographia*, II, 3.1 (ed. Nobbe, I, 67); Freeman, *Ireland and the Classical World*, 70. For critiques of Campbell's article, see Armit, 'Irish–Scottish connections', 2–3; Halsall, *Worlds of Arthur*, 133.

[55] *Míniugud Senchasa Fer nAlban* (ed. and transl. Bannerman, 41, 47). Here I follow Bannerman, *Studies*, 104–7, 154–6 for the date of the political connection, and Dumville, 'Ireland and North Britain', 208–9 for the notion that several core elements of the text were brought together in the tenth century.

[56] Fraser, '*Dux Reuda*'; idem, *From Caledonia to Pictland*, 121–2, 145–7, 249–50; Dumville, 'Political organisation'.

century, is that the Dál Riatan king Cináed mac Ailpín conquered Pictland, laying the foundations of the kingdom of Alba and the medieval Scottish realm.[57] Historians now see the gaelicisation of Pictland as a long-running process, dating back to the 'polyethnic' society of the eighth century, and stretching forward to the renaming of Pictland as the kingdom of *Alba* by the year 900, if not beyond.[58] What is clear is that a powerful kingdom was evolving north of the Forth during the tenth century, and that its kings derived their legitimacy from the Gaelic world. Anglo-Saxon chroniclers increasingly restricted 'Scottish' terminology to this territory, a usage that may have been pioneered in the English-speaking world by the Northumbrians, thanks to their links north of the Forth.[59] Meanwhile Scandinavians settled in the former Dál Riatan heartlands in the west, leading to the emergence of a Gaelic–Scandinavian culture. The results varied from area to area, as exemplified by the names *Innse Gall* 'islands of the Foreigners' for the Hebrides and *Earra-Ghàidheal* 'coastline of the Gael' for Argyll.[60] Both of these cultural zones influenced the Northumbrian kingdom as it fragmented during the Viking Age.

The Isle of Man sits in a pivotal location in the Irish Sea, yet the fragmentary state of the textual evidence obscures its significance in the early Gaelic world. Ogam stones – written in an alphabet developed in Ireland – attest the presence of Gaelic speakers during the fifth and sixth centuries, and possibly later.[61] They fall into two distinct groups: four in the south of the Island are written purely in ogam, and at least one in the north (at Knock y Dooney) features bilingual ogam/Latin inscriptions of a type known in Wales.[62] By the eighth century, the balance of power had shifted to the Britons, and the person commemorated as 'Guriat' (Gwriad) on a Manx cross may be identifiable with the Gwriad, father of Merfyn, progenitor of Gwynedd kings.[63] Gwriad may have ruled over a mixed population of Britons and Gaels, as was appropriate to an island located in the middle of the Irish Sea.

The continuity of Manx Gaelic (*Gaelg*) during the Viking Age has been a controversial subject. Some scholars have proposed that Norse temporarily superseded Gaelic, as the dominant language at least, and others have forcefully defended the permanence of Gaelic.[64] The idea of Norse ascendancy rested on an apparent lack

---

[57] As in the text known as 'Chronicle of the Kings of Alba', which contained tenth-century elements: CKA (ed. and transl. Hudson, 148, 152); see below 50.

[58] Fraser, *From Caledonia to Pictland*, xii, 293–305, 325–6; Woolf, *From Pictland to Alba*, 59–67, 87–126, 320–2, 341; Broun, *Scottish Independence*, 73; Márkus, *Conceiving a Nation*, 247–78.

[59] Woolf, 'Reporting Scotland', 233–4; Milfull and Thier, 'Anglo-Saxon perceptions', 218.

[60] I give the names here in Modern Scottish Gaelic forms. See also the different fates of the island and mainland *cenéla*: Woolf, *From Pictland to Alba*, 100.

[61] For the dating of the early inscriptions, see Sims-Williams, *The Celtic Inscriptions*, 346, 363. There may have been a faint ogam inscription on the eighth-/ninth-century slab from Ballavarkish keeill (MM 52; *CIIC* no. 1068, II, 191; Wilson, *Manx Crosses*, no. 52). See Kermode *et al.*, *The Manx Archaeological Survey*, I (report 3), 33–4; *idem*, *Manx Crosses*, Appendix B 15–18. However, Wilson ('Stylistic influences', 318–19) notes that the ogam is no longer detectable.

[62] MM 5; *CIIC* no. 520, I, 479–80; Wilson, *Manx Crosses*, no. 5; Kermode, *Manx Crosses*, appendix A. For the names, see Jackson, *Language and History*, 173; Charles-Edwards, *Wales and the Britons*, 148–52.

[63] MM 69; *CIIC* no. 1066, II, 190; Wilson, *Manx Crosses*, no. 69; Kermode, *Manx Crosses*, 121–3. The identification cannot be proven, as noted by Wilson, 'Stylistic influences', 313, but the name is Brittonic (Sims-Williams, *The Celtic Inscriptions*, 148–9, 366).

[64] Norse dominance: Marstrander, 'Det norske landnám', esp. 46–7, 336; *idem*, 'Remarks', 290. Discontinuity of Gaelic: Gelling, 'The place-names'. Continuity: Thomson, 'The continuity'; *idem*, 'Language in Man'.

of Gaelic place-names in the earliest ecclesiastical documents, a key source of such names (Rushen Abbey's 'abbeyland bounds') having once been assigned to the fourteenth century. Yet Basil Megaw's redating of the 'abbeyland bounds' to the mid to late thirteenth century exposed a fatal flaw in this argument.[65] Megaw proposed that the Viking-Age elite spoke Norse and the lower echelons Gaelic, but this scenario underrates the number and variety of Norse place-names on Man.[66] I would argue that there was considerable bilingualism at various levels in Manx society, as was advantageous in a world that looked out to the Irish Sea and the Isles. Indeed several of the Island's impressive runic inscriptions show traces of Gaelic syntax.[67] Certainly Rǫgnvaldr Guðrøðsson (*ob.* 1229), an illustrious Manx ruler, was the subject of an Irish bardic poem, which flattered the Manx king in terms reminiscent of Ireland's legendary past.[68] The Island was a vital entrepôt in the transmission of Gaelic influence to the Northumbrian kingdom.

Finally, it is worth noting that Gaelic influence can be detected throughout the North Atlantic. The Faroe Islands are of particular interest because they lie on the sea-roads between Iceland, Norway and the Hebrides. Irish and Scottish hermits left a tangible legacy in the form of cross-slabs,[69] and they may have been the pioneers who gathered peat and cultivated barley and oats.[70] Scandinavians established much larger colonies in Iceland and the Faroes during the Viking Age. Some sagas – written down much later – emphasise the importance of organised movements from Norway, often in the face of political strife.[71] The Viking world can be seen, however, as an interconnected diaspora in which new opportunities were also open to Scandinavians based in Ireland and the Hebrides. Men and especially women (wives, slaves or colonists in their own right) moved to the North Atlantic, leaving a legacy in the DNA of the modern Icelandic and Faroese populations.[72] Gaelic influence can also be detected in personal names, epithets and place-names, all of which have striking parallels in north-west England.[73] This point is significant because it suggests that the diaspora encompassed areas stretching from the former Northumbrian kingdom to the North Atlantic.

---

[65] Megaw, 'Norseman and Native', 265, 270–2. Gelling accepted the redating in her 1978 article 'Norse and Gaelic', 258, while retaining her broader argument.

[66] Fellows-Jensen, 'Scandinavian settlement'.

[67] Language contact: Thomson, 'The interpretation'. Syntax: Olsen, 'Runic inscriptions', 225–6; Marstrander doubted Gaelic influence ('Om sproget', 243–8, 256), noting parallels in Scandinavia, but for a broader argument about Gaelic influence on idiosyncratic features of Norse in Man, see Page, 'Celtic and Norse', esp. 140.

[68] 'A poem in praise of Raghnall' (ed. and transl. Ó Cuív); Ó Mainnín, '"The same in origin and blood"', 6–8.

[69] Dicuil, *Liber de mensura orbis terrae*, VII.6–15 (ed. and transl. Tierney, 72–7). Skúvoy cross-slabs: Stummann Hansen and Sheehan, 'The Leirvík Bønhústoftin', 46–7. Others are harder to date: see Arge, 'The Landnám', 104–5; Fisher, 'Cross-currents', 162–4.

[70] Edwards and Borthwick, 'Peaceful wars'; Church *et al.*, 'The Vikings', 231. Pre-Viking settlement in Iceland remains controversial; a recent discussion is Kristján Ahronson, *Into the Ocean*, 75–130, which argues that an artificial cave was constructed in the early ninth century.

[71] For example, *Færeyinga saga*, ch. 1 (ed. Ólafur Halldórsson, 3; transl. Faulkes, 5). For its complex and layered history, see Mundal, 'Færeyinga saga', 44–6.

[72] The concept of diaspora is analysed by Abrams, 'Diaspora and identity'; Jesch, *The Viking Diaspora*, esp. 68–81. For the DNA evidence, see below 56 n. 83.

[73] Bugge, *Vesterlandenes indflydelse*, 359–65; Craigie, 'Gaelic words' (although compare his more sceptical 'Gaels in Iceland'); Lockwood, 'Some traces'.

Northumbrian terminology

I will now move on to the term 'Northumbrian', which is my preferred way of refer-ring to the kingdom at the heart of this study. It offers a clear description of the area in which I trace Gaelic influence, that is, the kingdom at its height. The term was contextual in its usage, and I do not claim that all of the inhabitants thought of them-selves as Northumbrian first and foremost. Some will have remained loyal to smaller regions; others were inspired by the notion of a greater 'English' unit. Writers based in the Gaelic world referred to English speakers collectively as *Saxain*, although this term might be qualified by *tuaiscirt* 'of the North'.[74]

The roots of the Northumbrian kingdom lie in the shadowy post-Roman period. From the darkness emerges a complex mixture of *Romanitas* ('Romanness'), Brittonic culture and the 'Anglian' communities from whom the Northumbrian kings traced descent. The emergence of Anglian communities in northern England is ill-docu-mented, but one possible model appears in Gildas's *De excidio Britanniae*, which I take to be a work of the mid-sixth century. Gildas related that a leader of the Britons concluded a *foedus* 'treaty' with a band of Saxons, a word that designated various peoples who originated across the North Sea.[75] Whether or not this particular episode is relevant to Northumbria, it highlights one way in which Anglian warriors might have arrived. A related possibility, as Bede famously recounted several centuries later, is a migration from Angeln in northern Germany to Britain.[76] Such migrations were traditionally credited with cultural change in parts of northern England; aspects of material culture, such as cremation and female dress, were indeed imported from the German/Danish border or Norway.[77] These markers of Anglian culture are, however, very unevenly distributed within the territory that became Northumbrian, being most prevalent on the fertile edge of the Yorkshire Wolds.[78] A variety of factors, such as competition for power or social structure, prompted communities to adopt new customs and costumes.[79] Isotope analysis is now shedding light on the varied backgrounds of those buried in cemeteries that have yielded Anglian artefacts. For example, a sample of the deceased from West Heslerton cemetery (Yorkshire East Riding) grew up locally and to the west of the Pennines, as well as in Scandinavia.[80]

---

[74] For example, AU 913.1 (ed. and transl. Mac Airt and Mac Niocaill, 360–1).

[75] Gildas, *De excidio Britanniae*, 19–23 (ed. and transl. Winterbottom, 23–7, 94–7). I am not persuaded that Gildas considered the northern and Saxon invasions contemporary, based on the interpretation of *interea* ('meanwhile') at the start of ch. 22 (Halsall, *Barbarian Invasions*, 519–26 and *Worlds of Arthur*, 187–91). It does, however, appear that Gildas misplaced this episode, as argued by Sims-Williams, 'The settlement', 6–15. For the date of writing, see below 28.

[76] *HE* I, 15, 2 (ed. Lapidge, I, 164; ed. and transl. Colgrave and Mynors, 50–1); Rix, *The Barbarian North*, 89.

[77] For a culture-historical view, see Leeds, *The Archaeology*, 68–82, although he stressed the heterogeneity of the incomers in 'The distribution', 3, 78–80. For artefactual parallels across the North Sea, see Hines, *The Scandinavian Character*, 13–14, 35–109, 270–85; Martin, *The Cruciform Brooch*, 19–28, 87, 175–6, 191–232.

[78] Cramp, 'Anglo-Saxon settlement', 266–9; O'Brien, *Post-Roman Britain*, 62–77; Lucy, 'Changing burial rites', 16–18; *eadem, The Early Anglo-Saxon Cemeteries*, 27–8, 85–6, 89, 98–9, 104–5.

[79] Halsall, *Barbarian Migrations*, 27–9, 128–9, 156, 350–3, 361, 377, 386–92 (competition); Lucy, *The Early Anglo-Saxon Cemeteries*, esp. 21, 50 (social factors).

[80] Budd *et al.*, 'Investigating population movements', 134–6 (oxygen data); Montgomery *et al.*, 'Continuity or colonization' (strontium data).

Thus I would characterise the emergence of the Anglian community as a process in which common culture helped diverse groups to solidify, including some men and women who had moved across the North Sea.[81]

There are further hints of these diverse origins in the names of the Deirans and Bernicians, the forerunners of the Northumbrian kingdom. The former may have been based on Brittonic *derw* 'oak' (sometimes understood as *deor* 'brave man'); the latter on *berna* 'hill pass'.[82] Notwithstanding this complexity, by the eighth century Northumbrian genealogists were presenting the Bernician and Deiran kings as descendants of the Germanic god Woden. A fragmentary migration story also implies distant origins for the Bernician figure Oessa.[83] The emergence of these dynasties is a key element of the story of the future Northumbrian kingdom. Oessa's grandson Ida is the first securely attested Bernician king, whose reign started in 547 according to a regnal list available to Bede.[84] Ida's people may originally have dominated the area around Hadrian's Wall although he came to be associated with the coastal site of Bamburgh.[85] The Northumbrian genealogies also contain a pedigree for Edwin, whose father Ælle was the first attested king of the Deirans.[86] The Deiran and Bernician kings emerged as rulers of peoples rather than firmly defined territories: Edwin ruled *regnum Deirorum* 'the kingdom of the Deirans' *de qua prouincia ille generis prosapiam et primordia regni habuerat*, according to Bede.[87] The high-ranking Deiran and Bernician leaders were increasingly drawn into a wider Anglo-Saxon network, as is strikingly shown by the grave of a young woman discovered at Loftus (Redcar and Cleveland, North Yorkshire) in 2007.[88] She was buried lavishly on a bed – a rite otherwise unknown in Northumbria – and her followers wore southern English fashions.[89] Conversion to Christianity further enhanced this broader 'English' consciousness, for Gregory the Great conceived of a mission to

---

[81] This is how John Hines explains the emergence of Anglian dialect: 'Philology, archaeology', 29–33; *idem*, 'The becoming', 54–9.

[82] Oak: Hind, '*Elmet* and *Deira*', 547–52; Hamp, 'On notable trees', 44. 'Brave man': Breeze, 'The origin'. Cf. James, *BLITON*, svv. Forms such as *Deivyr* only appear in the Gododdin A-text and are probably late. Hill pass: Jackson, *Language and History*, 701–5, but note that this element does not survive in Modern Welsh. For the political significance of the names, see Orton and Wood, *Fragments of History*, 110–11; cf. Koch, *The Gododdin*, xl.

[83] Dumville, 'A new chronicle fragment'.

[84] *HE* V, 24, 1 (ed. and transl. Colgrave and Mynors, 562–3; ed. Lapidge, III, 182); Kirby, 'Bede and Northumbrian chronology', 515.

[85] Orton and Wood, *Fragments of History*, 113–14; compare Halsall, *Worlds of Arthur*, 249–52, 305–6 for emergence of Anglo-Saxon kingdoms in strategic interior zones.

[86] Dumville, 'The Anglian collection', 30, 32, 35 (texts), 45–50 (textual history), *contra* Sisam, 'Anglo-Saxon royal genealogies', 289, 292–4, 329, who saw the genealogies as a Mercian production. Dumville, 'Kingship, genealogies', 77–80 for contemporary relevance. Ælle's rule is placed at the time of the Gregorian mission, i.e. 597: Bede, *Chronica Maiora* in *De temporum ratione* (ed. Mommsen, 309; transl. Wallis, 226); Miller, 'The dates', 41–2.

[87] *HE* III, 1, 1 (ed. Lapidge, II, 14; ed. and transl. Colgrave and Mynors, 212–13 (my modified translation)) 'from which *provincia* he (Edwin) had derived the origin of his people and the foundations of his royal power'. For the Deirans and Bernicians as peoples, see Blair, 'The boundary', 49; Wood, 'Monasteries', 11–12. However, the division of the Northumbrian dioceses would have formalised the Bernician/Deiran boundary: *HE*, IV, 12, 3 (ed. Lapidge, 256, 258; ed. and transl. Colgrave and Mynors, 370–1).

[88] Hines, 'The becoming', 54; Geake, *The Use of Grave-Goods*, 129–36.

[89] Sherlock, *A Royal Anglo-Saxon Cemetery*, esp. 118, 121, 129–31.

the *Angli*, a term that the archbishops of Canterbury and Bede applied to all of the Anglian and Saxon Christians.[90]

I would identify the seventh century as a pivotal time when Northumbrian identity began to supplant Anglian, Bernician and Deiran affinities. The Bernician king Æthelfrith exercised power over the Deirans, and his Deiran successor Edwin managed the same in reverse. Æthelfrith married Edwin's sister, Acha, and their son Oswald is said by Bede to have welded the two polities together.[91] Bede's writings demonstrate the move towards Northumbrian consciousness: he consistently placed his people north of the Humber and adopted the term *Northanhymbri*, even if he did not invent it.[92] Bede promoted the pan-Northumbrian view of history by using a king-list that presented a single line of Northumbrian kings. The list was included with an early copy of *Historia ecclesiastica*, and an extended version circulated with the genealogical compilation known as the 'Anglian collection'.[93]

By the early eighth century, the concept of 'Northumbrian–Gaelic' interaction would have been meaningful to elite and educated members of society. That is not to say that local loyalties disappeared; indeed, Bernician/Deiran rivalries dissipated only gradually.[94] Similarly, former Brittonic kingdoms retained some distinctiveness within the Northumbrian kingdom. Half a century after Edwin expelled the king of Elfed/Elmet, the *Elmedsætan* appeared in the tribute list known as the 'Tribal Hidage'.[95] A key factor in the assimilation of such newly conquered areas was how closely they would be tied to royal interests. The Northumbrian kings operated a circuit around *villae regis* (royal centres) where they consumed food renders, fostering local relationships through feasting and the distribution of largesse.[96] The Deiran and Bernician rulers may have gravitated towards their ancestral circuits, which took in areas of cultivable, cleared land.[97] On the other hand, the west and north offered productive areas of mixed farming such as the Eden Valley, which

---

90 For example, Bede wrote of *de mensibus Anglorum* and *Anglorum populus* in *De temporum ratione* §15 (ed. Jones, 329; transl. Wallis, 53–4). Cf. Richter, 'Bede's *Angli*'; Wormald, 'Bede, the Bretwaldas', 118–121. Brooks, *Bede and the English*, 15–19 argued that Bede was countering an emerging Saxon identity.

91 *HE* III, 6, 3 (ed. Lapidge, II, 44; ed. and transl. Colgrave and Mynors, 230–1).

92 For example, Bede, *De temporum ratione* §4557 (ed. Jones, 516; transl. Wallis, 226). The phrase *Nordanhymbrorum gentis episcopus* may have already featured in the text of the Council of Hertford: *HE* IV, 5, 2 (ed. Lapidge, II, 226; ed. and transl. Colgrave and Mynors, 350–1); cf. Wallace-Hadrill, *Bede's Ecclesiastical History*, 226–8. Nick Higham has argued that the concept of the Northumbrians was of southern English origin: 'Northumbria's southern frontier', 396–8. The term was sufficiently new to require explanation in *HE* I, 15, 2; II, 5, 1; II, 9, 1 (ed. Lapidge, I, 164, 310, 330; ed. and transl. Colgrave and Mynors, 50–1,148–9, 162–3); cf. Tugène, *L'image*, 63. Peter Hunter Blair's argument that the vernacular *Norðanhymbre* originated first is no longer accepted (Blair, 'The Northumbrians', 98–104).

93 Cambridge University Library Kk. 5. 16, fol. 128v (the Moore manuscript); Blair, 'The *Moore Memoranda*', 245–50; Dumville, 'The Anglian collection', 32, 35–6.

94 *Vita Gregorii Magni* (ed. and transl. Colgrave, 98–101) presented Æthelfrith as a tyrant who expelled Ælla's rightful heir, Edwin. Cf. Wood, 'Monasteries', 11–12.

95 The earliest text is printed in Dumville, 'The Tribal Hidage', 226–7. Such names often appear in the genitive plural: Baker, 'Old English *sǣta*', 45. Dating: Davies and Vierck, 'The contexts', 225–7, 288–92 *contra* Higham, *The Kingdom*, 115–16. There is debate about whether the text is Mercian (Davies and Vierck, 'The contexts', 225–6) or Northumbrian (Brooks, 'The formation', 62).

96 Charles-Edwards, 'Early medieval kingships', 28–33.

97 Designated 'cultural cores' by Roberts, 'Northumbrian origins', 121, 123.

became associated with Northumbrian queens.[98] Yet the area may have eventually become a haven for a discarded and disgruntled branch of the Northumbrian royal line.[99] The territories closest to the Gaelic world were prone to fall out of the Northumbrian royal orbit, a point graphically illustrated by Northumbria's fragmentation during the Viking Age.

Northumbrian identity changed in significant ways from the 860s onwards. The various versions of the 'Anglo-Saxon Chronicle' provide an insight into the use of Northumbrian terminology by those within the kingdom as well as by outside observers in the south of England. The common stock of the Chronicle was compiled at the Wessex court of King Alfred (*ob.* 899), and it describes the Northumbrians as a people, *Norþan hymbre*, using the directional form *norþan* ('to/from the North').[100] One strand of the chronicle's common stock traced the movements of the heathen Great Army, a branch of which settled in the land of the Northumbrians.[101] The Great Army was initially presented as an occupying force, but from the 920s Scandinavian potentates were acknowledged as *Norþhymbra cyning* 'king of the Northumbrians' in a northern continuation of the original chronicle.[102] The *de facto* scope of the kingdom, York and its hinterland, co-existed with a lingering concept of a larger Northumbria. The leaders who submitted to Edward the Elder at Bakewell included Rǫgnvaldr (based in York), the sons of Eadwulf (based in Bamburgh) *7 ealle þa þe on Norþhymbrum bugeaþ ægþer ge Englisce ge Denisce ge Norþmen ge oþre* 'and all who live among the Northumbrians, both English and Danish, Northmen and others'.[103] The rulers of York sought the support of the Northumbrian *witan* 'council', which included the archbishop of York, while the rulers of Bamburgh were descended from a Northumbrian royal or noble lineage.[104] Yet other allegiances pulled the two areas apart, notably the Danish identity that linked the military elites of York with more southerly areas of Scandinavian settlement. Danish identity had legal, regional and political dimensions, and it encompassed those of both Scandinavian and English descent in the Danelaw.[105]

The final challenge to Northumbrian consciousness was the politically driven extension of English identity in the tenth century. The concept of *Angelcynn* was cultivated in King Alfred's court circle as a way of unifying the West Saxons and the Mercians, and staving off the Viking threat. Alfred drew inspiration from Bede's *gens*

---

[98] Phythian-Adams, *Land of the Cumbrians*, 58, 97–9, 111–12; Rollason, *Northumbria*, 52 describes the area as a possible Northumbrian heartland. On queens, Charles-Edwards, 'Early medieval kingships', 31–2.

[99] See below, 48.

[100] Bede's *Nordanhymbri* preserves the directional form. The ASC common stock sometimes used *Norþ hymbre* in relation to Alfred's reign.

[101] *Þy geare Healfdene Norþanhymbra lond gedælde 7 ergende wæron 7 hiera tilgende* 'And that year Hálfdan shared out the land of the Northumbrians and they proceeded to plough and support themselves'. ASC A [876] (ed. Bately, 50); ASC B [877] (ed. Taylor, 36); ASC C [877] (ed. O'Keeffe, 61); ASC D [876] (ed. Cubbin, 26); ASC E [876] (ed. Irvine, 50; transl. Whitelock, 48); cf. McLeod, *The Beginning*, 214–15.

[102] For example, Sigtryggr in ASC D [925] (ed. Cubbin, 41; transl. Whitelock, 68).

[103] ASC A [920] (ed. Bately, 69; transl. Whitelock, 67–8). Downham, '"Hiberno-Norwegians"', 144, argues that the extended list of Scandinavian peoples was meant to impress.

[104] ASC D [947] (ed. Cubbin, 44; transl. Whitelock, 72); Rollason, *Northumbria*, 249.

[105] Reynolds, 'What do we mean', 406–13; Innes, 'Danelaw identities'; Hadley, *The Northern Danelaw*, 300–6, 309; Abrams, 'King Edgar', 172–9. For the shifting nature of the term 'Danelaw', see Abrams, 'Edward the Elder's Danelaw', 128–33.

Anglorum, despite the Saxon origins of his own dynasty.[106] The expansion of Alfred's grandson Athelstan into the Northumbrian kingdom led to the adoption of the title *rex Anglorum*, and Northumbria finally lost its independence in 954. The Wessex kings recognised the distinctiveness of the northern elites, as witnessed by charters of Eadred and Eadwig that refer to their rule of the *Angli* (south of the Humber), *Norþanhimbre* (Bamburgh), *pagani* (in York?) and *Brittones* (the Cumbrian kingdom, which incorporated parts of western Northumbria).[107] The English kings tended to appoint different earls for York and Bamburgh until the mid-eleventh century, when the tenure of the two earldoms was combined. At this time a pan-Northumbrian consciousness can be glimpsed in the legal tract *Norðleoda laga* 'the law of the north people', which is associated with Archbishop Wulfstan II of York (*ob.* 1023).[108] Thus I would argue that a concept of the Northumbrian people continued to co-exist with the regional identities that re-emerged during the Viking Age. I therefore investigate Gaelic influence over the long sweep of Northumbrian history from the seventh century to the eleventh.

Interdisciplinary approaches to cultural interaction

So far I have considered how early medieval writers portrayed Northumbrian and Gaelic peoples, and I have examined other forms of identity that intersected with those concepts. Yet the thought-world of texts may not have translated smoothly to the realities of life in the Insular world. There is no reason to assume that 'Northumbrian' and 'Gaelic' consciousness generally left concrete and coherent traces in contemporary material culture. It is worth discussing the interrelationship of different types of source material, and the academic disciplines that interpret them, in relation to the theme of cultural interaction.

Movements of people and ideas preoccupied scholars of the 'culture-historical' school during the late nineteenth and early twentieth century. They plotted distributions of structures, artefacts and languages in order to trace migrations and contacts. Some of this work led to advances in the understanding of sites and artefact typologies.[109] However, the 'radiocarbon revolution' of the mid-twentieth century, and the consequent redating of significant sites, undermined the diffusionist approach.[110] Meanwhile, the horrors of the Second World War spelled the end of studies that sought the origins of modern peoples and polities in the prehistoric and early medieval periods.[111] There was still a place for interdisciplinary work in other areas of 'medieval studies' (*Mediävistik*), which continued to accommodate a number of

---

[106] Bede's influence: Wormald, '*Engla lond*', 10–14; Foot, 'The making' (also noting Alfred's promotion of learning). For Saxon usage elsewhere, see Reynolds, 'What do we mean', 402, 405.

[107] For example, *Charters of Burton Abbey* no. 9 (ed. Sawyer, 14–15); Sawyer, *Anglo-Saxon Charters*, 200 (S548). I follow Keynes, 'Welsh kings', 98–9 on *pagani*. For other views, see Brooks, 'English identity', 51; Downham, 'Religious and cultural boundaries', 18.

[108] *Norðleoda laga* (ed. Liebermann, I, 458–61; transl. Whitelock, *English Historical Documents* I, 469–70); Wormald, *The Making* I, 391–4. References to the Britons reflect (re)-conquest of Cumbrian lands by the Northumbrian earls: Edmonds, 'The emergence', 209.

[109] See, for example, Childe, *The Dawn*, esp. 322–40 for prehistoric Britain and Ireland.

[110] See below 185–7.

[111] Trigger, *A History*, 163–74, 185, 244.

disciplines. Some polymathic scholars practised several of them; F. T. Wainwright is a notable example.[112]

The New Archaeology, or Processualism, of the 1960s occasioned a radical rethink. A focus on cultural evolution, internal changes and adaptation to the environment replaced the external stimuli that had dominated 'culture-historical' work. Philip Rahtz's New Medieval Archaeology aimed to release his discipline from the status of 'handmaid of history' by treating sources for the most part autonomously.[113] Some archaeologists took this approach to the extreme by separating archaeology from any textually informed historical context in order to avoid the cross-contamination of results.[114] Ian Hodder challenged the systems- and rules-based approach of the New Archaeology during the 1980s. He refocused attention on the thought-world lying behind the creation of material culture, and on the importance of placing artefacts in their historical context.[115] Hodder suggested that scholars could 'consider the archaeological record as a "text" to be read', thus highlighting fruitful links between history and archaeology, while acknowledging the unique remits of the two disciplines.[116] In medieval archaeology, some scholars had already become uncomfortable with the complete separation of different types of evidence, given that texts and material culture emanated from the same society.[117]

In these circumstances, it became possible for historians and archaeologists to ask complementary questions about cultural interaction once again.[118] One example is the reception of Immanuel Wallerstein's 'world-systems theory', which emphasises the supply of raw materials from peripheral areas to those at the core. Some archaeologists have explored the application of the approach to pre-modern periods, highlighting the precariousness of large-scale networks and the role of political force.[119] Meanwhile, historians have weighed up this theoretical perspective in relation to the methods and remit of Global History.[120] Recent thinking about the Middle Ages on a global scale has underlined disparities in the survival (or indeed existence) of both written and material evidence across different areas of the world. This situation has encouraged historians to embrace a variety of methodologies; as Mark Whittow wrote: 'there is an almost universal commitment among those exploring the medieval centuries to an approach that unites texts and material culture, together increasingly with evidence from the biological and physical sciences'.[121]

---

[112] Wainwright, 'Problems and policies'; *idem, Archaeology and Place-Names*; cf. Jaritz, 'Interdisciplinarity', 713.

[113] Rahtz, *New Medieval Archaeology*, 12–13, 18–19; quotation at 3; compare more generally Clarke, 'Archaeology', 18.

[114] Reece, 'Sequence is all', 114.

[115] Hodder, *Reading the Past*, 77–102. Hodder frequently cites Collingwood's *The Idea of History* as a source of inspiration in this chapter.

[116] Hodder, *Reading the Past*, 118–46, 153–5, quotation at 122.

[117] Driscoll, 'The New Medieval Archaeology', 105–9; cf. the response by Rahtz, 'The Nuer Medieval Archaeology', 110–11.

[118] It could be argued that the search for interdisciplinary methods has never ceased. For example, Horn and Ritter ('Interdisciplinary history', 429) note the foundation of the *Journal of Interdisciplinary History* in 1970.

[119] Wallerstein, *The Modern World-System I* focused on the period from the sixteenth century onwards. For consideration in relation to the early medieval period, see for example, Barrett *et al.*, 'What was the Viking Age?'. Cf. Trigger, *A History*, 332–3.

[120] An example focusing on the period 600–900 is Dudridge, 'Reworking the World System paradigm'.

[121] Whittow, 'Sources of knowledge', 46.

The term 'interdisciplinary' is not as transparent as it seems, however, and there is scope for debate about the ways in which disciplines can be combined. In practical terms there are differences between separating the source material before attempting a grand synthesis – the approach advocated by Philip Rahtz – and interweaving different types of evidence. A scrupulous example of the latter is John Hines's examination of material culture and literature from early medieval times to the present day.[122] In more theoretical terms, there has been debate about the remit of the term 'interdisciplinary', and even whether there are clear disciplinary boundaries.[123] The challenge of interdisciplinary work continues to increase, as new fields begin to shed light on the early medieval period. DNA studies are an increasingly rich seam of evidence, but they reveal a different aspect of an individual's background from the aspects of cultural identity that texts and archaeology may highlight.[124] Even so, there is an increasing trend for DNA specialists to relate their evidence to language, culture and historical developments, thus broaching questions that require interdisciplinary investigation.[125]

An essential prerequisite for interdisciplinary work is a question that only two or more disciplines can answer.[126] My question is: what was the nature of Gaelic influence in the Northumbrian kingdom? As noted already, cultural contact operates at various levels, it affects different social strata, and it varies in geographical reach. No single type of source material illuminates this phenomenon fully, and in some cases I am pursuing the kinds of unrecorded social experiences for which, in Robin Fleming's words, 'we have to put aside our copies of the Anglo-Saxon Chronicle and look instead to the mountains of contemporary material excavated by archaeologists'.[127] Indeed, surviving evidence of all types is fragmentary, even exiguous, in some parts of the Northumbrian kingdom, and so it is only sensible to gather all of the material. How, then, is it possible to present a rounded view of cultural interaction from these rapidly proliferating, and sometimes apparently contradictory, sources of information? My approach is to explore the nuances of selected types of evidence, notably textual and onomastic, as well as selected types of material culture. I will examine each type of material before drawing general conclusions, for some of the material is little studied in its own right. I provide a synthesis and an analysis of cross-cutting themes at the end of the book.[128] This is not to deny the challenges of interdisciplinary work, including the difficulty of conducting specialist research into every type of source material. I have sought to achieve 'disciplinary adequacy' in all of the approaches deployed here, that is, an understanding of the scholarly

---

[122] Hines, *Voices in the Past*.

[123] For example, Moran, *Interdisciplinarity*, 13–15 (flexible use of the term) *contra* Newell, 'Decision making', 257–260 (integrationist perspective).

[124] Evison, 'All in the genes?', 288. For further critiques, see Hills, *Origins of the English*, 67; Halsall, *Barbarian Migrations*, 451.

[125] For example, Cavalli-Sforza, *Genes*, 134 ff. The University of Leicester's project 'The impact of diasporas on the making of Britain' is an example of an interdisciplinary project working on these questions: https://www2.le.ac.uk/projects/impact-of-diasporas. Cf. Nelson, 'Why re-inventing medieval history is a good idea', 28–31.

[126] Repko, *Interdisciplinary Research*, 35–7, 74, 84–9.

[127] Fleming, *Britain after Rome*, xxi.

[128] For the challenges of synthesising different types of evidence, see Wainwright, *Archaeology and Place-Names*, 89–97; Hills, *Origins of the English*, 13.

frameworks in which research has been conducted.[129] I seek to highlight the limitations, as well as the potential, of each type of source material for understanding Gaelic influence in the Northumbrian kingdom.

Historical interpretations of Northumbrian–Gaelic contact

Having established my usage of the terms 'Northumbrian' and 'Gaelic', and discussed their limitations in relation to non-textual evidence, I will end by discussing broader aspects of the historiography. As R. G. Collingwood observed, 'no historical problem should be studied without studying … the history of historical thought about it'.[130] I will assess the reasons why previous scholarship has rarely highlighted the variety and longevity of Gaelic influence in the Northumbrian kingdom. While the Lindisfarne–Iona link has loomed large in historical writing, other dimensions of the theme remain relatively obscure. Even if I depart from that trend, it is enlightening to consider why previous historians took a different view.

The first explanation is that the kingdom straddled the future Anglo-Scottish border. Once the border emerged, Northumbrian history increasingly became attached to the English story.[131] In the late-medieval period, the term *Northumbria* became associated with an English royal county, *comitatus Northumbriae*, which encompassed Durham and Northumberland.[132] Late-medieval writers occasionally applied the term *Northumbria* to the whole of late-medieval northern England, including the areas west of the Pennines, but normally it was restricted to Durham and Northumberland.[133] This usage foreshadows its modern sense as a synonym for north-east England, particularly in heritage-related contexts. It is not surprising, therefore, that the western and northern edges of the kingdom have been relatively neglected in the historiography of the kingdom. The vestiges of Northumbrian religious heritage were recast as aspects of royal, national or local devotion in southern Scotland.[134] Meanwhile, the emergence of a perceived Highland–Lowland divide in late-medieval Scotland created a symbolic division between Gaelic culture and the border area.[135] The Gaelic heritage of the Scottish kingdom remained important to the legitimacy of Scottish kingship, yet the *Inglis* tongue of the Lowlands was gradually redefined as Scots, the language of the Scottish nation, while the Gaelic of the Highlands was termed 'Erse' (Irish).[136] The consciousness of linguistic and cultural

---

[129] Repko, *Interdisciplinary Research*, 60, 193–224; cf. Horn and Ritter, 'Interdisciplinary history', 446.

[130] Collingwood, *Autobiography*, 132.

[131] Also noted by Higham, *Ecgfrith*, 2–3, 14.

[132] King and Pollard, '"Northumbria" in the later middle ages', 73–4.

[133] *Ibid.*, 84–5.

[134] Turpie, *Kind Neighbours*, 95, 115–16, 139.

[135] Broun, 'Attitudes of *Gall* to *Gaedhel*'; MacGregor, 'Gaelic barbarity', 7–15. A twelfth-century example is Guillaume le Clerc's portrayal of Fergus of Galloway as the son of a coarse peasant in *Roman de Fergus* (ed. Frescoln 40–2; transl. Owen, 6–7). The classic description of the Highland–Lowland divide (though of debatable date) is in Fordun, *Chronica gentis Scottorum*, II, 9 (ed. Skene, I, 42).

[136] Mason, 'Civil society', 112–14; Murison, 'Linguistic relationships', 81; MacGregor, 'Gaelic barbarity', 19–20, 36–40; Newton, *Warriors of the Word*, 52–3.

separation accelerated in the early modern period, one marker being the Statutes of Iona (1609).[137]

A second explanation for the relative neglect of my subject is that the history of northern England has never been a central part of the wider English story. The study of the English nation has tended to focus on the centre of government in the south-east of England.[138] The Northumbrian kingdom did not conform to the broader pattern of 'Anglo-Saxon' history and was incorporated into *Engla lond* at a relatively late stage. Northern English antiquaries devoted attention to the bishopric of Durham throughout the early modern period and beyond, thus helping to preserve the memory of Northumbria's 'Golden Age'. Their work focused on regional concerns rather than a broader Insular context, however.[139] Similarly, the 'New Northumbrians' of the Victorian period revived consciousness of the early medieval kingdom against the backdrop of northern England's industrial powerhouse.[140]

The third, and most significant, explanation is the stereotype that Saxon and Celt (whether Gaelic or Brittonic) inhabited distinct and antagonistic spheres. The idea of a disjunction between England on the one hand, and Ireland, Scotland and Wales on the other, goes back to medieval times. The twelfth century saw the emergence of a new notion of Englishness that sought to unify the Anglo-Saxons and the Normans against Scottish, Irish and Welsh 'Others'.[141] The English kings and literati adopted a myth of British rulership focused – somewhat ironically – on King Arthur, and used it to promote English imperial ambitions.[142] Furthermore, Anglo-Norman writers held Gaelic ecclesiastical influence in far less high esteem than Bede and his counterparts.[143] The reputation of the Golden Age of Northumbrian Christianity, and its debt to Gaelic missionaries, would be restored to some extent during the Reformation period.[144]

The eighteenth century witnessed important steps forward in the study of the Celtic languages, following Edward Lhuyd's discovery of kinship between Gaelic and Brittonic languages. Antiquaries also took to using the term 'Celtic', although often not in the same ways as modern scholars.[145] The polarised views of Celts and Saxons reached their zenith in the nineteenth century, just as History was emerging as an academic discipline.[146] This was the period in which medieval origin myths were

---

[137] Withers, *Gaelic Scotland*, 7, 73–4, 113; Newton, *Warriors of the Word*, 29–32, highlighting the ensuing measures of 1616.

[138] Jewell, *The North–South Divide*, 2–3, 22, 31.

[139] Sweet, '"Truly historical ground"', 112–22.

[140] Colls, 'The new Northumbrians'; *idem*, 'Gaelic and Northumbrian'.

[141] Gillingham, *English in the Twelfth* Century, chs 1, 3, 6, 8.

[142] MacDougall, *Racial Myth*, 12–15.

[143] One example is Ailred of Rievaulx's attitude to Galloway; see below, 112–13.

[144] For the reception of Bede among Catholic writers during the Reformation era, see Highley, *Catholics Writing the Nation*, 118–123. For the scholarly advances in Anglo-Saxon studies associated with the early Church of England, see Niles, *The Idea*, 51–73.

[145] Lhuyd, *Archaeologia Britannica*. For antiquarian usages, see Stukeley, *Abury*, 11, 15, 24, 45; Kidd, *British Identities*, 185, 187–8; Farley and Hunter, *Celts*, 24–5. I adopt the linguistic usage in this book. Sims-Williams, 'Celtomania and Celtoscepticism' is a superb overview of the topic. As he notes on p. 4, disciplinary differences are evident in the usages of the term. For an archaeological take, see for example James, 'Celts, politics'.

[146] Reuter, *Medieval Polities*, 4; Wood, *The Modern Origins*, 16, 328.

revived and adapted to suit modern nation-states.[147] At this time the term 'Anglo-Saxon' developed international currency as an ethnic/racial, as well as an historical, term, leaving some very problematic legacies in the modern day.[148] Writing at the height of the British Empire, the historian E. A. Freeman stressed the Anglo-Saxon aptitude for governance while giving the Britons and the Irish dismissive treatment.[149] Meanwhile, Celtic stereotypes were turned on their head and used to challenge English cultural and political dominance, especially in Ireland against the backdrop of moves towards independence.[150] Scholars who examined Celtic/Anglo-Saxon interaction were unusual; they included the poet and critic Matthew Arnold, who sought the origins of English Literature in a dynamic blend of styles, while reiterating some well-worn stereotypes.[151]

In more recent times, research has more frequently crossed cultures and borders, as exemplified by the concept of the 'Irish Sea province', which became popular among archaeologists in the 1960s.[152] Meanwhile Nora Chadwick encouraged historians and literary scholars to range across the English and Celtic worlds in publications such as *Celt and Saxon* (1964).[153] Around the same time, D. P. Kirby produced a doctorate on relations between Northumbria and Celtic Scotland, a work that has some themes in common with my current book.[154] There has also been critical assessment of the concept of the 'Celtic Church', a method of Church organisation that was ostensibly common to Wales and Ireland and fundamentally different from the system in England. Scholars are now more inclined to trace diverse modes of ecclesiastical organisation across Britain and Ireland, and to place the Insular churches in their broader Late Antique context.[155]

The development of the 'New British History' (or preferably 'Archipelagic History') in the late twentieth century also lends itself to the study of the Northumbrian

---

[147] Curtis, *Anglo-Saxons and Celts*, 66–9; Young, *The Idea*, 71–8, 96–103. More generally, see Geary, *The Myth of Nations*, 15–40; Wickham, *The Inheritance*, 3; Wood, *The Modern Origins*, 109, 199–211.

[148] On the emergence and usages of the term 'Anglo-Saxon', see Reynolds, 'What do we mean'; Frantzen and Niles, 'Anglo-Saxonism and medievalism', 2–3; and in a linguistic context Momma, *From Philology to English Studies*, 128–9. For the international nineteenth-century context, see Young, *The Idea*, 172–230; Niles, *The Idea*, 265–77. The present book was already in draft by 2017, when some important new works on modern connotations and appropriations of the term emerged; one example is Dockray-Miller, 'Old English'. I have therefore been unable fully to assimilate this recent discussion in the current book, but it will have profound ramifications for the future study of early medieval history.

[149] Freeman, *The History*, I, 3–4, 14–22, 33–5. In later works he allowed for the presence of Britons, but focused on the English: 'The latest theories'. For his attitude to the Irish, see Curtis, *Anglo-Saxons and Celts*, 79–81. The historiographical context is discussed in German, 'Britons, Anglo-Saxons', 347–59; Wood, *The Modern Origins*, 202–11.

[150] Curtis, *Anglo-Saxons and Celts*, 108–16. More generally, see Edwards *et al.*, *Celtic Nationalism*; Leerssen, 'Celticism', 12–13.

[151] Arnold, *On the Study*. For stereotypes, see Sims-Williams, 'The visionary Celt'; Young, *The Idea*, 140–64. Arnold drew on the work of the Breton writer Ernest Renan ('La poésie').

[152] For example, Alcock, 'Was there an Irish Sea culture-province?'; see below, 73.

[153] Chadwick (ed.), *Studies in Early British History*; *eadem* (ed.), *Studies in the Early British Church*; *eadem* (ed.), *Celt and Saxon*. Nora Chadwick brought to completion the final publication of her husband, Hector Munro Chadwick, the pioneering *Early Scotland*; cf. Edmonds, 'H. M. Chadwick'.

[154] Kirby, 'A new survey'.

[155] Davies, 'The myth'; cf. Hughes, 'The Celtic Church'. For the modern reception of the concept of 'Celtic Christianity', see Meek, *The Quest*.

kingdom. The approach promotes the comparison, and tracing of contacts, between England, Wales, Scotland and Ireland.[156] It has been criticised for a focus on 'anglicisation', that is, the extension of English power across the archipelago.[157] Such an approach would indeed be problematic in relation to the tenth century, when English dominance was more of an aspiration than a reality, and even more so for the heyday of the autonomous Northumbrian kingdom. In contrast, my book investigates influences travelling in the other direction, those emanating from the Gaelic world. I therefore favour a version of the Archipelagic approach in which influences travel in numerous directions, and the various communities 'interact so as to modify the conditions of each other's existence'.[158] I avoid the term 'anglicisation' on other grounds too, namely, that it underplays the level of regional variation within England. In my view, Northumbrian history sits most comfortably in the context of Middle Britain – what is now northern England and southern Scotland – rather than as an adjunct to English history alone.[159]

Another criticism of 'New British/Archipelagic History' is that it distracts from the importance of broader European developments.[160] This would indeed be dangerous for, as David Rollason has shown, a European perspective is valuable for study of the Northumbrian kingdom. Moreover, some major recent explorations of early medieval society, economy and culture have been painted on a broad-ranging European and Mediterranean canvas.[161] Yet to my mind the Archipelagic perspective and European perspectives are not mutually exclusive: 'the triangular connection between England, Ireland and Gaul was very important', as James Campbell observed.[162] The point is illustrated by the career of the Northumbrian churchman Willibrord, whose missions to the Continent emanated from Ireland.[163] In this book I devote attention to the Irish Sea, the North Channel and the Forth–Clyde isthmus; but that is because they are relatively neglected conduits, not because they are more important than, or removed from, the Carolingian world.

Medieval historians have recently pursued cultural interaction on an even larger scale by opening up the study of the Global Middle Ages. A major theme in explorations of wide-ranging, transnational contact is trade in luxury and exotic goods. At first glance, the areas that I am studying seem to lie at the very edge of such mercantile concerns; the closest trading nexus to the west of the Northumbrian kingdom was Chester and the Wirral, while the northern borders of the kingdom lay at the

---

[156] Pocock, 'British history'; Grant and Stringer, 'Introduction: the enigma'; Cohen, 'Introduction', 4–6.

[157] Brown, 'British history', 117; a point acknowledged by Pocock in 'The limits', 312–13. For nuanced treatments of 'anglicisation' in the late-medieval period, see Frame, *The Political Development*, esp. 1–4; Davies, *The First English Empire*, esp. 2; Hammond, 'Domination and conquest?', 70–1, 77, 79.

[158] Pocock, 'The limits', 317.

[159] This perspective was pioneered by Barrow, 'The pattern', and has been seen more recently in Woolf, *From Pictland to Alba*; Fraser, *From Caledonia to Pictland*; Higham, *Ecgfrith*. For the term 'Middle Britain', see Jotischky and Stringer, 'Introduction', 1, 4.

[160] For example, Canny, 'The attempted anglicization', 147; see Morrill, 'The British problem', 14–15, for a defence.

[161] Rollason, *Northumbria*, esp. 4–5. For broad-ranging works that incorporate the Insular world, see Wickham, *Framing the Middle Ages*; Smith, *Europe after Rome*.

[162] 'The debt', 343.

[163] Ó Cróinín, 'Rath Melsigi'; Richter, *Ireland and her Neighbours*, 149–56. Palmer, *Anglo-Saxons*, 64–5 provides an overview of the various influences on Willibrord's career.

end of the North Sea coastal trade network.[164] There are hints that the edges of the Northumbrian kingdom yielded raw materials that were traded over long distances; for example, isotope analysis indicates that lead extracted from Cumbrian and Pennine ores flowed into the Viking-Age trading centre of Kaupang in Vestfold (Norway).[165] Perhaps the prime attraction of the Cumbrian foothills was cattle farming, which intensified from the tenth century onwards, offering new opportunities to those who could exploit the lack of high-level control.[166] Such smaller-scale movements add up to a bigger picture that falls within the purview of the Global Middle Ages.[167]

This discussion of historical writing has revealed the intellectual trends that have hindered or helped discussion of Northumbrian–Gaelic relations over the last millennium. Significant scholarly shifts have taken place in recent times: the hard-and-fast distinction between 'Celt and Saxon' is breaking down in historiography, and scholars have transcended national boundaries in history writing. It would be inappropriate to take these lines of thought to the extreme and claim that there were no significant differences between the Northumbrians and their Gaelic-speaking neighbours. My appraisal of contemporary terminology has underlined the separation between the two *gentes* in the thought-world of medieval scholars. Furthermore, the Northumbrians were part of a broader *gens Anglorum*, and this relationship would have a decisive impact on the attitude of tenth-century Wessex kings. For the most part, Northumbria was to be absorbed into *Engla lond*, rather than incorporated into a looser *orbis Britanniae*. The seeds of English separation from Gaeldom were being sown, but in other ways the tenth and eleventh centuries saw the culmination of Gaelic influence in the Northumbrian kingdom.

---

[164] See below, 95, 221.

[165] Skre, 'From Kaupang and Avaldsnes', 239; *idem, Things from the Town*, 428. Mineral richness may partly explain the expansion of the kingdoms of Northumbria and Strathclyde, as suggested by John Maddicott ('Two frontier states', 31) and Daniel Elsworth ('The extent', 97), respectively.

[166] James, 'A Cumbric diaspora?', 193–4, 203; Edmonds, 'The expansion', 58–9.

[167] Holmes and Standen ('Introduction', 34) write of 'connections across very different registers: local, mid-range and global'. For further insight into the global perspective, see http://globalmiddleages.org.

2

EXILES AND EMPERORS:
GAELIC–NORTHUMBRIAN POLITICAL
RELATIONS IN THE GOLDEN AGE

Movements of people along ancient pathways and seaways often take on a timeless air, yet cultural influence occurred against a backdrop of rapid political change. Marriage alliances, court intrigues and great battles played their parts in determining the strength of ties between different parts of the Insular world. In this chapter I examine the political dimension of Gaelic influence in the Northumbrian kingdom, and provide a chronological framework for the thematic studies that I tackle elsewhere in this book.

The main sources of information about political vicissitudes are texts, especially chronicles, but there are limitations to what they reveal about Northumbrian–Gaelic contact. The ecclesiastical context of chronicling affected the type of information recorded; battles tended to be interpreted through the lens of biblical parallels or as signs of the coming apocalypse.[1] By the late seventh century, churchmen were cultivating skills for interpreting scripture and dating Easter, including *computus*.[2] Easter tables might be annotated with references to events and reigns, and such records arguably underpinned annals, along with other material such as late-Roman chronicles.[3] Bede is a striking example of a scholar whose expertise in *computus* influenced his chronicling activity, and he incorporated chronicles into his computistical treatises *De temporibus* (703) *and De temporum ratione* (725).[4] Bede also appended a series of annals to *Historia ecclesiastica*, and his example was followed by a later copyist (most likely based in York), whose continuations to 766 appear in a select group of continental manuscripts.[5] These 'northern annals' were continued further, to at least 802, and they have been attributed to the circle of the great scholar Alcuin of York on the basis of Latin style and points of detail. The annals were incorporated into a late-tenth-century historical miscellany, twelfth-century northern texts and the northern recension of the Anglo-Saxon Chronicle, which most probably emerged in

---

[1] Coleman, *Ancient and Medieval Memories*, 115–27; Flechner, 'The Chronicle of Ireland', 428, 432, 441–9.

[2] Coleman, *Ancient and Medieval Memories*, 139–46; Wallis, *Bede: The Reckoning*, lxviii–lxxi, notes the influence of *computus* on Bede's historical method, especially *De temporum ratione*.

[3] For example, Poole, *Chronicles and Annals*; Miller, 'The disputed historical horizon'; Ó Cróinín, 'Early Irish annals'; Story, 'The Frankish annals'; more guardedly Evans, *The Present and the Past*, 145, 171–3; for a sceptical view, see McKitterick, *History and Memory*, 97–100.

[4] *De temporibus* (ed. Jones, 601–11; transl. Kendall and Wallis, 126–31); *De temporum ratione* (ed. Jones; transl. Wallis). On the link between Bede's *computus* and historiography, see Wallis (transl.), *Bede: The Reckoning*, lxviii–lxxi.

[5] *Continuatio* (to 766) (ed. and transl. Colgrave and Mynors, 572–7); for the manuscripts containing the *Continatio*, see *ibid.*, lxvii–lxix. For the text's background, see Story, 'After Bede', 180.

York in the early eleventh century.[6] There is something of a lacuna in Northumbria's history in the early ninth century, until a later set of northern annals (888–957) becomes available. This text was incorporated in the compendious twelfth-century work *Historia regum*, which was most likely written by Symeon of Durham. These annals also informed the 'northern recension' of the Anglo-Saxon Chronicle.[7]

One limitation of the chronicle evidence is its uneven survival across the Northumbrian kingdom. Durham's monastic library has remained partly intact, and some texts were preserved on the Continent, but northern and western areas of the kingdom are poorly represented.[8] Literate men and women dwelt in those regions too, as witnessed by the painted lettering unearthed on fragments of plaster at St Patrick's Chapel, Heysham (Lancashire).[9] A chronicler based at this church, perched on a rocky headland above the Irish Sea, could have told remarkable stories, but sadly they are lost. A northern British chronicle was ultimately transmitted to Wales and preserved in the core of *Annales Cambriae* and *Historia Brittonum*, the latter being a compilation of various texts put together in North Wales *ca* 829–30.[10] Texts written in the Gaelic world also shed light on the Northumbrian kingdom, notably the reconstructed 'Chronicle of Ireland', whose genesis has provoked much debate. I am persuaded that the chronicle began life on Iona in the late sixth century, shortly after its foundation by St Columba. Northumbrian information was incorporated because of Iona's close connection with the kingdom.[11] A copy of the Iona Chronicle moved to the Irish Midlands *ca* 740, and this text formed the core of various daughter chronicles that diverged after 911. They form two main branches, the 'Annals of Ulster' and the Clonmacnoise group; entries that appear in both branches will have been in the 'Chronicle of Ireland'.[12]

The textual evidence is limited by its unremitting focus on the elites. This perspective may not be entirely misleading for a study of political connections, for the nobility were among the most mobile sectors of society. Those who ventured outside their own kingdoms lacked the legal protection afforded by their kin group, or the social network offered by lord–client relations.[13] Travelling was a precarious

[6] *Chronicle* (to 802): see for example *HR* (ed. Arnold, II, 30–68); Rollason, *Sources*, 17–18; *idem*, *Northumbria*, 15–16; Story, *Carolingian Connections*, 126–33. It is unclear whether the twelfth-century witnesses all drew on the tenth-century miscellany or independent texts. Cf. Blair, 'Some observations', 86–7; Lapidge, 'Byrhtferth'.

[7] *HR* (ed. Arnold, *Symeonis monachi opera omnia*, II, 91–5); Blair, 'Some observations', 104–11; Rollason *et al.*, *Sources*, 27; Rollason, *Northumbria*, 17; Downham, 'The chronology', 36–8. See Keynes, 'The manuscripts', esp. 542, 545, 547–8 for the northern recension of the ASC.

[8] Mynors, *Durham Cathedral Manuscripts*, 1–2. For the Continent, see Levison, *England and the Continent*, 143–7; McKitterick, 'The diffusion', 402–4.

[9] Potter and Andrews, 'Excavation and survey', 117–22; Higgitt, 'Anglo-Saxon painted lettering'.

[10] Hughes, *Celtic Britain*, 70–2, 85, 94–5; Dumville, 'On the North British section', 211–14. Evans has shown that this text was independent of the 'Chronicle of Ireland', although a British and then Northumbrian chronicle might have fed into Iona's chronicle in the seventh century: 'The Irish chronicles', 16–24, 38–9.

[11] Bannerman, *Studies*, 9–26; Evans, 'The Irish chronicles', 27–35; *idem*, 'Irish chronicles', 44–5; Ó Corráin, *Clavis*, II, 932.

[12] The chronicle has been reconstructed by Thomas Charles-Edwards, *CI*; Hughes performed groundwork in *Early Christian Ireland*, 100–7. The Clonmacnoise branch is discussed in Grabowski and Dumville, *Chronicles and Annals*, 53–6, 209–26. Mc Carthy, *The Irish Annals* esp. 103–6, has postulated transmission of the common source through several churches down to *ca* 1019, but the received view is defended by Evans, *The Present and the Past*, 3–6, 17, 67–72, 115, 225.

[13] Charles-Edwards, 'The social background'.

business, and those who had access to ships, supplies and personal introductions could reduce some of the dangers. The hazards may have increased for women; some travelled on pilgrimage, to meet their betrothed and to settle in new lands but we know less about their journeys than those of their male counterparts.[14] That said, isotope analysis of tooth enamel increasingly indicates significant mobility around the Irish Sea throughout the early medieval period.[15] Women and children were among those who moved, and they played vital roles in cultural interaction.[16] While it is only possible to gain a partial insight into political interactions, there is sufficient evidence to support my argument that the Northumbrian kingdom was connected with several different parts of the Gaelic-speaking world during the Golden Age.

The Britons and the Irish Sea

The Northumbrian kingdom was underpinned by the shadowy post-Roman polities of the northern Britons. The great bulwark of Hadrian's Wall ran across the territory from the Solway Firth to Tyneside, and it played a role in the evolution of the Northumbrian kingdom. The northern frontier troops had become embedded in their local environment, and these garrisons evolved into warbands.[17] By the sixth century, the elites north and south of the Wall combined *Romanitas* with Brittonic culture, and their kings were remembered in medieval Welsh poetry.[18] The Britons had a history of both contact with, and hostility to, groups to their north and west: a striking example is the group of Brigantian refugees who huddled on Lambay, an island near Dublin, as their territory in northern England fell under the sway of the Romans.[19] I argue that Northumbrian kings assumed some of these pre-existing links and enmities.

A line of military installations demarcated Roman territory along Hadrian's Wall and the coast as far as Maryport (Cumbria, formerly Cumberland).[20] Forts and harbours were established further south at Ravenglass, Lancaster and (for a time) Kirkham, which lay at or near the port named Σεταντιων Λιμην (*Setantion limen*) in Ptolemy's second-century Geography.[21] The name of the Setantii is related to Ptolemy's river name *Seteia* and also has an intriguing resemblance to Setanta, the boyhood name of the Ulster hero Cú Chulainn in *Táin Bó Cúailnge*.[22] The epic tale comes down to us in manuscripts of the twelfth century and later, although the first recension may

---

[14] Bitel, *Women*, 228–32; Jesch, *The Viking Diaspora*, 89–90.
[15] Hemer *et al.*, 'Evidence of early medieval trade'; Hemer *et al.*, 'No Man'; Symonds *et al.*, 'Medieval migrations'.
[16] Hadley and Hemer, 'Microcosms of migration'; Shepard, 'Networks', 117–18.
[17] See below, 26–7.
[18] Fraser, 'St Patrick' for *Romanitas* north of the Wall; Koch, *The Gododdin*, xiii–xxxiv for the mix of peoples at Catraeth.
[19] Rynne, 'The La Tène and Roman finds'; Raftery, *Pagan Celtic Ireland*, 200–3. Ptolemy's *Geographia*, II, 2.7 (ed. Nobbe, 65) places some Brigantes in south-eastern Ireland.
[20] Birley, 'The Roman fort'; Breeze and Dobson, *Hadrian's Wall*, 7–39, 44–5, 51, 75–6, 81; Collins, *Hadrian's Wall*, 12–13. There is debate about the length of the line: compare Potter, *Romans*, 359 (maximalist) with Bellhouse, *Roman Sites*, 3, 61–4 (minimalist).
[21] Ptolemy, *Geographia*, II, 3.2 (ed. Nobbe, I, 68); Rivet and Smith, *The Place-Names*, 456–7; Shotter and White, *Roman Fort*, 2, 16–23; Howard-Davis and Buxton, *Roman Forts*, 21–37, 76.
[22] *Táin Bó Cúailnge: Recension I*, lines 444–5 (ed. O'Rahilly, 14; *Táin Bó Cúalnge: from the Book of Leinster*, lines 796, 908–12 (ed. O'Rahilly, 22, 25).

have gestated for centuries before that.[23] If Setanta derived from Setantii (which is only a tentative possibility) the loan would fit best in the fifth century AD, indicating Irish-Sea contact around that time.[24] The Roman defences did not, indeed, cut off contact across the Irish Sea and the Wall: these borders are no longer seen simply as mechanisms to keep barbarians out, but rather as permeable zones.[25] Roman goods arrived in Ireland, clustering around the Boyne Valley and the north-east, while client leaders distributed Roman items to the north of Hadrian's Wall.[26]

The exclusion of certain groups from these Roman patronage networks prompted a new wave of raids by Picts, Scotti and Attacotti.[27] The threat was sufficient to warrant construction of new 'Saxon shore'-style forts in Lancaster and on the Welsh coast, and the stationing of marines on the Lune Estuary.[28] The attacks peaked in 367 with the eruption of violence that Ammianus Marcellinus called *barbarica conspiratio* ('barbarian conspiracy'); it took the highly regarded Count Theodosius two years to deal with the aftermath.[29] The trouble was facilitated by the so-called *areani/arcani* (frontier scouts), who betrayed the positions of the Roman troops to the barbarians.[30] This fleeting piece of information is significant because it implies close contact between Scotti, Picts and the Britons in the inter-wall zone. The 'barbarian conspiracy' was taken very seriously, notwithstanding Ammianus's exaggeration of Count Theodosius's achievements, and Roman leaders continued to wage campaigns against Picts and Scotti later in the fourth century.[31]

The redeployment of some Roman troops to the Continent did not end this pattern of warfare. Numismatic and structural evidence is accumulating for fifth-century

[23] Andrew Breeze has amended *Seteia* to *Meteia*, making a link with the Celtic root **met* 'reap' ('Three Celtic toponyms', 161–3). *Seteia* could, however, be pre-Celtic (cf. Ekwall, *English River-Names*, liv–lv; Parsons, 'Clarifying Ptolemy's English place-names', 172, 175). The -*nt* of Setantii is Brittonic. A recent suggestion is that the Setantii dwelt in the Wirral and South Lancashire, which would fit with the Irish links at Meols: Shannon, 'From Morikambe to Morecambe', 47–9.

[24] Mac Neill, 'Varia I' raised concerns about sound changes, which were answered by Bergin, 'Varia I', 233–4; cf. Guyonvarc'h, 'L'anthroponyme irlandais'. The conditions for the loan are that *t* > *d* voicing had occurred in Brittonic, but *chw* had not yet developed at the start of the word, cf. OIr *sant*, Welsh *chwant* (Vendryes, *Lexique étymologique … RS*, s.v. *sant*; eDIL, s.v. *sant*). The presence of a long *e* in some instances of *Sétanta* may reflect a perceived link with *sét* 'path' (Bergin, 'Varia I', 235). I am grateful to Paul Russell for advice on these points.

[25] Whittaker, *Frontiers*; Goetz, 'Concepts'; Collins, *Hadrian's Wall*, 2–4. Cf. Clark, 'The Northumbrian frontiers', 15–47 for the early medieval period.

[26] Freeman, *Ireland*, 2–13; Raftery, *Pagan Celtic Ireland*, 206–19; Ó Floinn, 'Early Christianity', 13–17; Hunter, *Beyond the Edge*, 32–6, 51; *idem*, 'Hillfort and Hacksilber', 6–7.

[27] Hunter, *Beyond the Edge*, 52–4; Fraser, *From Caledonia to Pictland*, 59–60.

[28] Casey, 'The end of the Roman army'; Shotter and White, *Roman Fort*, 3, 16–17, 23–7, 29–30; Shotter, 'Numeri barcariorum'; Potter, *Romans*, 365–6. For debate about the relationship of Lancaster's fourth-century fort-plan to earlier forts, see Wood, 'Roman Lancaster', 41.

[29] Ammianus Marcellinus, *Res Gestae* XXVII.8, XXVIII.3 (ed. and transl. Rolfe, III, 50–7, 130–7); den Boeft *et al.*, *Philological and Historical Commentary*, 184.

[30] Ammianus Marcellinus, *Res Gestae* XXVIII.3.8 (ed. and transl. Rolfe, III, 134–7); cf. Mann, 'The northern frontier', 40; Breeze and Dobson, *Hadrian's Wall*, 142–5, 148, 241–2 for their identity as local militia.

[31] For the impact, see Breeze and Dobson, *Hadrian's Wall*, 236; Laycock, *Britannia*, 111–13, *contra* Gerrard, *The Ruin*, 22–5. The Gallic Chronicle of 452 placed Magnus Maximus's victory against Picts and Scotti in the third year of Gratian (383–4) (ed. Burgess, 67). Stilicho's activities appear in a panegyric written in 400: Claudian, *De consulatu Stilichonis*, II, lines 247–55 (ed. Birt, 211–12); cf. Miller, 'Stilicho's Pictish war'.

inhabitation of Wall forts, although there is uncertainty about the official involvement in this twilight phase.[32] The *Notitia Dignitatum*, which survives only in fifteenth- or sixteenth-century copies, purports to record administrative and military organisation in the 390s, with revisions down to 425.[33] The section pertaining to Hadrian's Wall has recently been rehabilitated, and it depicts northern frontier forts under the command of the *dux Britanniarum*.[34] Several scenarios have been proposed for the fate of the soldiers after this point; to my mind, the most persuasive is the model developed for the reuse of two granaries at Birdoswald fort. The southern granary was redeployed as a hall until its roof collapsed, sealing a worn coin of Emperor Theodosius (388–95), and the then-derelict northern granary was reconstructed twice in timber. The halls may be associated with the transformation of the fort's garrison into a warband, who would protect local inhabitants in return for supplies.[35]

It is worth considering the implications of this 'warband model' for the coastal forts, some of which appear in *Notitia Dignitatum*.[36] Taking Maryport as an example, modern excavations around the eastern defences have revealed late-Roman structures and coins.[37] There is also a plaque bearing a Chi-Rho symbol and two probable post-Roman stone monuments.[38] Recent excavations have yielded intriguing evidence to the north of the fort: a ditch filled in the late fourth century, postholes for a very substantial timber building, and seven long-cist burials, one of which was filled with soil containing a late-Roman coin.[39] This post-Roman community surely evolved from Maryport's garrison and its dependants, who would have been skilled in countering seaborne attack. I suggest that the survival of such fort communities deterred Irish settlers from the coast of what is now north-west England. There was a different situation in Wales, where numismatic evidence and a gap in *Notitia Dignitatum* suggest troops were indeed withdrawn from coastal forts. Irish veterans of the Roman army may then have been entrusted with coastal defence, as suggested by the ogam-derived inscription on the coffin from Rhuddgaer, opposite Segontium fort (Caernarfon) across the Menai Straits.[40]

The continuing imperative to defend the western coast is revealed by Gildas's *De excidio Britanniae*, which places several phases of raids by Picts and Scotti after the

---

[32] Collins, *Hadrian's Wall*, 33, 88–96. The apparent scarcity of late military metalwork is debated by Böhme, 'Das Ende', 492, 521–2; Coulston, 'Military equipment', 59. Halsall suggests the occupants were paramilitaries: *Barbarian Migrations*, 195–7; idem, *Worlds of Arthur*, 216–19, 285–6.

[33] *Notitia Dignitatum*, Oc. XL (ed. Seeck, 209–13).

[34] Hodgson, 'The Notitia Dignitatum'; Collins, *Hadrian's Wall*, 38–48, *contra* Collingwood and Myres, *Roman Britain*, 289, 296.

[35] Casey, 'The end of garrisons'; Wilmott, 'The Late Roman transition'. Stratigraphic evidence contradicts the abandonment and reoccupation theory of Dark, 'A sub-Roman re-defence'; Dark and Dark, 'New archaeological and palynological evidence'.

[36] The case for and against Maryport as Alione in *Notitia Dignitatum*, Oc. XL, 53 (ed. Seeck, 212) is discussed in Jarrett, *Maryport*, 15–16; Breeze and Dobson, *Hadrian's Wall*, 293–6; cf. Rivet and Smith, *The Place-Names*, 243–5.

[37] Jarrett, *Maryport*, 39–40, 48, 56.

[38] Collingwood and Wright, *Roman Inscriptions of Britain* I, nos 856, 862–3 (285, 287); Dark, 'New archaeological and palynological evidence', 60–3.

[39] Symonds, 'Maryport's mystery monuments', 17–21.

[40] Casey, 'The end of the Roman army'. The *Seguntienses* had moved to Illyricum by the time of *Notitia Dignitatum*, Oc. V, 65; VII, 49 (ed. Seeck, 118, 134). The use of Irish foederati was suggested by Collingwood and Myres, *Roman Britain*, 282–3; cf. Rance, 'Attacotti, Déisi'. I am grateful to Professor Nancy Edwards for alerting me to the Rhuddgaer coffin (Williams, 'Leaden coffin').

usurpation of Magnus Maximus (*ob.* 388).[41] I am persuaded that Gildas was writing in the mid-sixth century because his obituary appears *ca* 570 in the 'Chronicle of Ireland', which drew on contemporary or near-contemporary material.[42] Gildas's account is chronologically problematic, and he presents the invasions through a biblical lens; nonetheless, he had obtained some information from descendants of those who endured the raids.[43] Gildas refers to depredations *duabus ... gentibus transmarinis vehementer saevis, Scotorum a circione, Pictorum ab aquilone.*[44] I see the adjective *transmarinus* as a reference to the seaborne nature of the raids, whether they came from Atlantic Scotland, eastern Scotland or Ireland.[45] Elsewhere, Gildas refers explicitly to seaborne raids from Ireland, which tallies with St Patrick's abduction from Britain in his youth *cum tot milia hominum.*[46]

From the sixth century onwards, Irish groups settled in south-western Britain, western Wales and the Isle of Man. Their presence is seen in Irish personal names in Latin inscriptions and Irish inscriptions written in the ogam alphabet.[47] The raids were staved off by diplomatic links and intermarriage between Irish and Brittonic dynasties, contacts that also promoted the spread of Christianity in Ireland.[48] Isotopic analysis of skeletons from several Manx cemeteries indicates considerable mobility between the Island and coastal regions around the Irish Sea during this period.[49] The north side of the Island was closely linked with the lands of the North Britons, whereas the south side came more strongly under Irish influence, a distinction indicated by the distribution of ogam, bilingual and Latin inscriptions.[50] Some scholars identify what is now south-west Scotland (especially the Rhinns of Galloway) as another area of Irish settlement on the basis of place-name evidence, but these names may well have been coined at a later stage. The authenticity of a possible ogam stone from Lochnaw on the Rhinns peninsula (Dumfries and Galloway) is still under discussion.[51] Even if there was no full-scale Irish migration to the Solway region, there were cultural and religious links across this stretch of sea.[52] The long-cist graves found in the recent excavations at Maryport have yielded white quartz

---

[41] Gildas, *De excidio Britanniae*, 14, 17–18, 20 (ed. and transl. Winterbottom, 21–4, 93–5).

[42] AU 569.3 [570], and a doublet added in one manuscript at 576.6 [577] (ed. and transl. Mac Airt and Mac Niocaill, 84–5, 88–9); AT [570] (ed. and transl. Stokes I, 109); AI [567] (ed. and transl. Mac Airt, 74–5); *CI* 570.3 (transl. Charles-Edwards I, 108); Stancliffe, 'The thirteen sermons', 109, 177–80. See also Woods, 'Gildas'.

[43] For the schematic and biblically influenced treatment of the raids, see O'Loughlin, *Gildas*, 116; Halsall, *Worlds of Arthur*, 190. For *transmarina relation*, see Thompson, 'Gildas and the history', 209–12; Sims-Williams, 'Gildas and the Anglo-Saxons', 7.

[44] Gildas, *De excidio Britanniae* 14.1 (ed. and transl. Winterbottom, 21, 93): 'by two exceedingly savage overseas nations, the Scotti from the north-west and the Picts from the north'.

[45] Cf. the plunder taken *trans maria* (overseas), and raiders in coracles: Gildas, *De excidio Britanniae* 17.3, 19.1 (ed. and transl. Winterbottom, 22–3, 94). *Contra* Wright ('Gildas's geographical perspective', 87) and Fraser (*From Caledonia to Pictland*, 43), who link these references to origin myths.

[46] Gildas, *De excidio Britanniae* 21 (ed. and transl. Winterbottom, 24, 95); Patrick, *Confessio* § 1 (ed. and transl. Hood, 23, 41): 'with so many thousands of people'.

[47] Thomas, 'The Irish settlements' (the pottery evidence is now discounted); Sims-Williams, 'The five languages', 22, 32; Charles-Edwards, *Wales and the Britons*, 174–91.

[48] Swift, *Ogam Stones*, 23, 49, 127–8; Ó Floinn, 'Early Christianity'.

[49] Hemer *et al.*, 'No Man'.

[50] Charles-Edwards, *Wales and the Britons*, 150.

[51] Canmore, ID 60396; Katherine Forsyth (pers. comm.). For place-names, see below, 160–1.

[52] Thomas, *The Early Christian Archaeology*, 16–17; *idem*, *Christianity in Roman Britain*, 285; Symonds, 'Maryport's mystery monuments', 21.

pebbles, a biblically inspired practice that is attested around the Irish Sea.[53] Cross-Solway connections also provide a context for Whithorn's famous fifth-century Latinus stone, which features a Latin inscription in Roman capitals.[54] Roman capitals also feature alongside ogam on the bilingual pillar stone at Knock-y-Dooney, Isle of Man, where an Irish name is represented both in Irish and British Latin.[55]

The elite patrons of Roman-inspired monuments eventually founded kingdoms, of which Rheged was the greatest and yet most elusive. Urien of Rheged reputedly dispensed his largesse at *Llwyfenydd* (probably the River Lyvennet in the Eden Valley) and he was lord of Catraeth (Catterick, North Yorkshire?).[56] These place-names appear in the so-called 'historical poems' of Taliesin, which come down to us in a thirteenth-century manuscript. The other main body of 'Old North' poetry, the Gododdin *awdlau*, exists in two versions in the late-thirteenth-century manuscript *Llyfr Aneirin*. There has been much discussion about the date of composition of the poetry in relation to both linguistic features and content.[57] My stance is that some of the stanzas had emerged in northern Britain by the seventh century, whereas others could have been composed in Wales on the model of the earlier verses as late as the twelfth century.[58] If it is correct to locate Rheged in north-west England on the basis of this information, its rulers must have taken up the duty of protecting the Cumbrian coast. Indeed the phrase *tra merin Reget* ('across the sea of Rheged') appears in *Llyfr Taliesin*, although not in one of the 'historical poems' but rather a prophetic poem that seems to date from the tenth century or later in its current form.[59]

Archaeological evidence opens up the possibility that Rheged stretched across the Solway. The fort and town of Carlisle, capital of the *civitas* of the Carvetii, has long been characterised as the heart of Rheged. The evidence from Carlisle is not as prolific as might be expected for a key centre, although significant areas remain to be investigated, such as the castle's interior.[60] The fort's barracks blocks eventually collapsed, while the *principia* (headquarters) continued into the fifth century with modifications.[61] Strip houses and an impressive townhouse continued to be used,

---

[53] Revelation 2:17; Crowe, 'A note'; Hill, *Whithorn*, 73–4, 469, 472–3.

[54] *CIIC* no. 520, I, 499–501; dated in Tedeschi, *Congeries lapidum*, 295–7; Forsyth, 'The Latinus stone', 23–4, 28, 30–6.

[55] MM5; *CIIC* no. 520, I, 479–80; Kermode, *Manx Crosses*, appendix A; Wilson, *Manx Crosses*, no. 151. For the epigraphy, see Tedeschi, *Congeries lapidum*, 301–2; Forsyth, 'The Latinus stone', 35. For the name, see *Language and History*, 173; Charles-Edwards, *Wales and the Britons*, 148–52.

[56] *Poems of Taliesin* VIII; IX.10 (ed. Williams, 9, 11); cf. IV.21, VII.19, VIII.27 (ed. Williams, 4, 8, 10); Hogg, 'Llwyfenydd'. The river name may derive from **leman/liman* 'elm' (Modern Welsh *llwyfen*). Andrew Breeze places *Argoed Llwyfain* in the vicinity of Lyvennet ('The names', 60–1). For debate about Catraeth, see Clarkson, *The Men of the North*, 100–9; Dunshea, 'The meaning'.

[57] Compare Koch, *The Gododdin* (a reconstruction of the Ur-text) with Isaac, 'Gweith Gwen Ystrat', noting the late development of the prosthetic vowel (*ystrat* for *strat*).

[58] Cf. Thomas Clancy's description of the early northern material as *disjecta membra* ('The kingdoms', 165). An example of a twelfth-century Gododdin-inspired poem is *Hirlas Owain* (ed. Williams in Bramley *et al.*, *Gwaith Llywelyn Fardd* I, 193–206).

[59] 'Yn wir dymbi Romani kar' (ed. and transl. Haycock, *Prophecies* 8, line 80, 158), note the reference to the tenth-century kingdom of Deheubarth. Cf. Dunshea, 'The Brittonic kingdoms', 164–6. The syntax does not support Clarkson's interpretation 'Rheged beyond the sea': *The Men of the North*, 71.

[60] McCarthy, 'The kingdom', 12–13; *idem*, *Roman Carlisle*, 147.

[61] Zant and Howard-Davis, *The Carlisle Millennium Project*, I, 334–7, 351–2, 357–8; McCarthy, *Roman Carlisle*, 134–6.

along with a post-built structure at Stanwix, across the River Eden.[62] Some archaeologists have suggested that the core of Rheged lay further west, in the Rhinns and
Machars peninsulas, where there was an important citadel at Trusty's Hill. Trenches
on the summit of the hillfort have recently revealed a timber-laced rampart that was
constructed in the sixth century. There is also a sherd of E ware, an imported pottery
that is found in quantity at nearby Whithorn and the Mote of Mark.[63] The regional
rulers would have benefited from controlling the exotic goods that accompanied the
pottery, redistributing them in order to forge networks of clients.[64] Whether they
were the rulers of Rheged is another matter; the nearby place-name 'Dunragit' is
suggestive, although its interpretation is not straightforward.[65] One possibility is that
the rulers of Rheged emanated from a core territory in the Eden Valley, and then built
up temporary trans-Solway overlordships.[66]

Control of the seaways was a high-stakes endeavour for kings around the Irish
Sea in the sixth and seventh centuries. A select group of rulers benefited from control
of Continental imports; for example, Dál Fiatach redistributed the exotic goods to
other kingdoms in north-eastern Ireland.[67] Dál Fiatach were the leading dynasty of
the Ulaid, and they often supplied over-kings of the *cóiced* (the 'fifth' of Ulster) in
the face of rivalry from a group of peoples known as the Cruithni. These struggles
can be reconstructed from eleventh- and twelfth-century genealogies and regnal lists,
which drew on earlier material.[68] The Ulaid were understood to have ruled over a
large area of the north of Ireland prior to the rise of Uí Néill, but were now confined
to the east of the River Bann.[69] They were also active on the sea, as shown by their
expedition to the Isle of Man in 577, from which they returned in 578 according to
entries in the Chronicle of Ireland. The information probably derives from contemporary records kept on Iona or at Bangor (Co. Down); either way, the chronicler was
not far from the action.[70] This maritime activity was magnified in the minds of later

---

[62] McCarthy, *A Roman, Anglian and Medieval Site*, 45–69, 136, 359, 368–71; McCarthy, *Roman Carlisle*, 89–90, 138–9; Keevill *et al.*, 'A solidus'; Oxford Archaeology North, 'Stanwix primary school', 8, 14.

[63] McCarthy, 'Rheged', 370–4; Toolis and Bowles, *The Lost Dark Age Kingdom*, 38–40.

[64] Laing and Longley, *The Mote of Mark*, 104–13; Hill, *Whithorn*, 297–326. Control: Campbell, *Continental and Mediterranean Imports*, 117, 124, 134; compare Wooding's more varied model: *Communication*, 5, 68.

[65] The earliest form is *Dunregate* 1535, featuring Gaelic *dún*, which would most likely have been coined or adapted after the eleventh century. For a Brittonic etymology, see *CPNS*, 156. Cf. Williams, *The Poems of Taliesin*, xl–xli; MacQueen, *Place-Names in the Rhinns*, 92; Clarkson, *The Men of the North*, 71.

[66] McCarthy, 'The kingdom', 21; Clancy, 'The kingdoms', 162.

[67] Campbell, *Continental and Mediterranean Imports*, 112–14.

[68] *Clann Ollaman Uaisle Emna* (ed. and transl. Byrne); *Senchas Síl hÍr* (ed. Dobbs); cf. the incom-
plete version in *CGH* 156 a 25–158 42 (ed. O'Brien, 269–86); Ó Corráin, *Clavis*, III, 1588–9. King-lists: *Ríg Ulad* in *The Book of Leinster* (ed. Best *et al.*, I, 192–4); *CGH* 161 b 32–161 bc 46 (ed. O'Brien, 322–3); Meyer, 'The Laud synchronisms', 484–5. Our understanding of this *cóiced* rests heavily on the work of Byrne, *Irish Kings*, 106–29, now augmented by Charles-Edwards, 'The province of Ulster'.

[69] Byrne, *Irish Kings*, 107–8; Bannerman, *Studies*, 2; Charles-Edwards, 'The province of Ulster', 40, 49.

[70] AU 577.5, 578.2 (ed. and transl. Mac Airt and Mac Niocaill, 88–9); AT [577] (ed. and transl. Stokes, I, 112); CS [577–8] (ed. and transl. Hennessy, 38–40); *CI* 577, 578 (transl. Charles-Edwards, 111). An alternative to the notion of the Bangor chronicle is the idea that Iona's annal-
ists included detailed information about the Ulaid and Cruithni, as suggested by Smyth, 'The earliest Irish annals', 33–41. O'Rahilly, *Early Irish History*, 253 and Hughes, *Early Christian Ireland*, 119–23 supported the Bangor chronicle.

writers, to the point where the Dál Fiatach king Báetán mac Cairill was accorded the title *rí Érenn ocus Alban* 'king of Ireland and Britain' in an eleventh-century text.[71] Another group with an interest in the Isle of Man were Conailli Muirtheimne, one of whose members is commemorated on a fifth- or early sixth-century ogam inscription at Ballaqueeney on the Island.[72] The Conailli were located on the southern margins of the territory dominated by Ulaid and they became politically visible in the seventh century, perhaps under the aegis of Uí Néill. Thus Irish kings seem to have been jostling for control of the Isle of Man.[73]

This was to change in the seventh century when the Isle of Man shifted to Brittonic control, in turn creating an opening for Northumbrian expansion. Bede described King Edwin (*ob.* 633) as subjecting *Meuanias Brettonum insulas, quae inter Hiberniam et Britanniam sitae sunt* to his control. Bede adopted Orosius's term for the Isle of Man but he changed its affiliation from the *Scotti* to the *Brettones*.[74] These Britons may have been a Manx or Manx–Galwegian dynasty, which some scholars link with a pedigree in the major Welsh genealogical collection known as the 'Harleian genealogies'. The Tudwal and Merfyn named in this pedigree have been identified with a king in the *Miracula* of St Nynia of Whithorn (*Tudvael*), and a man who was killed on the Isle of Man, respectively.[75] In short, the Northumbrians became part of a struggle for the seaways that was already playing out between Brittonic and Gaelic kings.

Insular politics in the early seventh century

I will now examine the ways in which Northumbrian kings developed political links and enmities. I argue that their contacts radiated across the Gaelic world. Bede's *Historia ecclesiastica gentis Anglorum* gives the impression that the seventh century was the highpoint of Gaelic influence in the Northumbrian kingdom. So vital is Bede's portrayal of these interactions that it is worth considering factors that influenced his work. Secular affairs were more to the fore in Bede's work than in one of his model texts, Eusebius's *Historia ecclesiastica*.[76] Bede situated Northumbrian history in the broader context of the *gens Anglorum*, as was appropriate for a text commissioned by Abbot Albinus of Canterbury, whereas his information about the Gaelic

---

71 *Senchas Síl hÍr* (ed. and transl. Dobbs, 'The history', 322–5, 328–9); cf. *CGH* 156 b 40–1 (ed. O'Brien, 275). Báetán's reputation for maritime prowess was transferred to his father in the twelfth-century *Clann Ollaman Uaisle Emna* (ed. and transl. Byrne, 63, 77).

72 MM2; Kermode, *Manx Crosses*, 98–9; *CIIC* no. 504, I, 482; Wilson, *Manx Crosses*, no. 2. The name could be Old Irish *Conual* or Brittonic *Cynwal* (Sims-Williams, *The Celtic Inscriptions*, 90, 125, 309, 320). The presence of MUCOI, the Irish designation for a people, favours identification with the Conailli (McManus, *A Guide*, 102, 104, 111, 113).

73 Thornton, *Kings*, 185–95. Dáibhí Ó Cróinín has persuasively suggested that Báetán expelled the Conailli from Man: *Early Medieval Ireland*, 72.

74 *HE* II, 5, 1; II, 9, 1 (ed. Lapidge, I, 310, 332; ed. and transl. Colgrave and Mynors, 148–9, 162–3): 'the Mevanian islands of the Britons, which are located between Ireland and Britain' (Man and Anglesey)'. Cf. Charles-Edwards, *Wales and the Britons*, 149, 174, 190.

75 *Miracula Nynie episcopi* (ed. Strecker, 948–50; transl. MacQueen, *St Nynia*, 90–1) AU 682.2 (ed. and transl. Mac Airt and Mac Niocaill) *inmano* (translated by Mac Airt and Mac Niocaill as 'while captive (?)'; *CI* 682.2 (transl. Charles-Edwards, I, 164).

76 Eusebius's work was known to Bede through Rufinus's translation: Markus, *Bede*, 8–9.

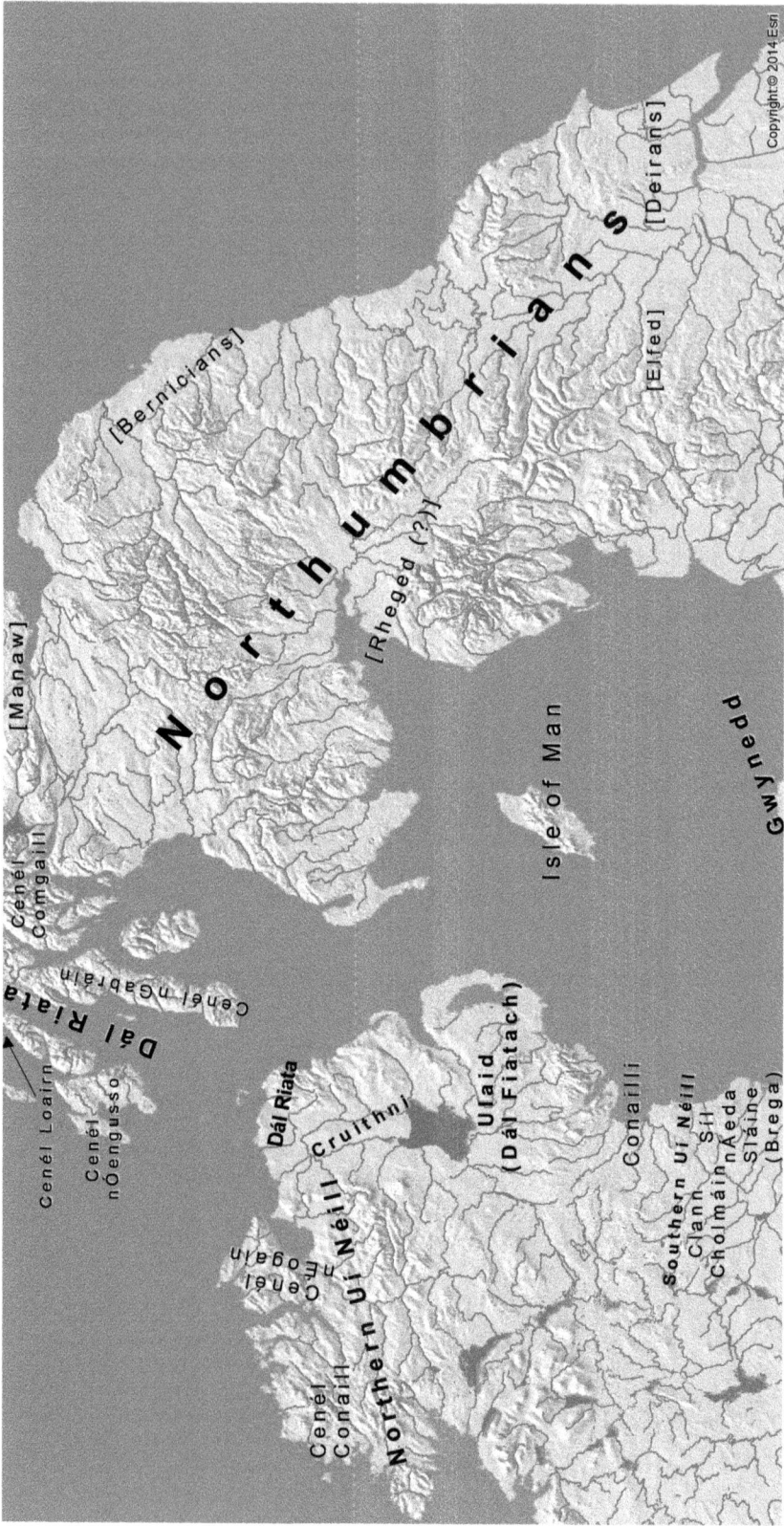

Map 1: *Northumbrian relations with the Insular world in the mid-seventh century*

world came partly through a Pictish intermediary.[77] Bede's expertise in biblical exegesis, notably his commentary on I Samuel, conditioned his understanding of Insular interactions.[78] Bede associated the Britons with *perfidia* 'treachery', a word that recurs in his discussion of Saul's history in the commentary on 1 Samuel, whereas the *gens Scottorum* were *nationi Anglorum semper amicissima*.[79]

Even so, the first recorded encounter between the Northumbrians and the Scotti was a battle, which took place at Degsastan in 603.[80] Degsastan lay in the territory of the North Britons, and I suggest that they are key to understanding the episode. Two formidable kings were involved: Æthelfrith of Bernicia and Áedán mac Gabráin of the Dál Riatan kindred Cenél nGabráin, which was based on Kintyre. Áedán was reaching the end of a career in which he had dominated the Dál Riatan *cenéla* and campaigned further afield, encroaching on Brittonic territory. The Iona chronicle records Áedán's 582 victory in *Manu*, which is more likely to be the Brittonic/Pictish region of Manaw on the Forth than the Isle of Man (*Eumania*).[81] Meanwhile, Æthelfrith *plus omnibus Anglorum primatibus gentem uastauit Brettonum* 'ravaged the Britons more extensively than any other English ruler'. Bede modelled his account of Æthelfrith, *rex fortissimus et gloriae cupidissimus* 'a very brave king and most eager for glory', on Saul, the first king of Israel.[82] It is nonetheless credible that Æthelfrith sought power over the Britons, for the Tweed Basin was being opened up as an area for Bernician settlement during his reign.[83]

The exceptional site at Yeavering lay on the upland edge of this area, and its earliest medieval buildings may date to the mid/late sixth century. The balance of British and Anglian influence in this phase is debatable; the structures belong to the early medieval building tradition seen elsewhere in England, which itself drew on Roman and Continental 'Germanic' styles.[84] There was already an enormous enclosure in local palisade style, which has been interpreted as a cattle corral.[85] This provides a clue to the process of expansion in the uplands: Áedán and Æthelfrith

[77] *HE* preface, 2–3 (ed. Lapidge, I, 96, 98, 100, 102; ed. and transl. Colgrave and Mynors, 2–7). For Bede's Pictish sources, see Evans, 'The calculation', 188–90; Fraser, *From Caledonia to Pictland*, 99–100, 237–8, 240–1, 275. Evans, 'Irish chronicles', 44–5 discounts Ecgberht of Iona as the intermediary, *contra* Duncan, 'Bede, Iona', 39–41.
[78] For example *In primam partem Samuhelis* 2, 15, 27–8 (ed. Hurst, 134). *Sed et hodie ...* highlights the relevance to contemporary kingship; cf. McClure, 'Bede's Old Testament kings', 87, 94–5; Thacker, 'Bede and the ordering', 54–6; Brown, 'Bede's neglected commentary', 128–9.
[79] *HE* IV, 24, 1; V, 23, 5 (ed. Lapidge, II, 350; III, 176; ed. and transl. Colgrave and Mynors, 426–7, 560–1) 'always very friendly towards the English nation'; Thacker, 'Bede, the Britons', 138–9.
[80] The date is given by Bede and ASC E (ed. Irvine, 22). The Chronicle of Ireland's misplacement of the battle in 600 reflects the process of merging sources: *CI*, I, 38–9.
[81] AU 582.1 (ed. and transl. Mac Airt and Mac Niocaill, 90–1); AT [579.1, 580.1 – doublet] (ed. and transl. Stokes, I, 113–14); *CI* 582 (transl. Charles-Edwards, 112–13). *Bellum/Cath Manann* features a *–nn* stem genitive, nominative *Manu*. The A- and B-texts of *Annales Cambriae* use the name of the Isle of Man (*Eubonia/Eumonia*), but this entry was probably inserted in the tenth century (Grabowski and Dumville, *Chronicles*, 209–26, esp. 216). For the scope of Manaw, see Clancy, 'The kingdoms', 160–1; Charles-Edwards, *Wales and the Britons*, 4–6.
[82] Wallace-Hadrill, *Early Germanic Kingship*, 76–8; McClure, 'Bede's Old Testament kings', 82–3.
[83] Smith, 'Brito-Roman', 9–11; O'Brien and Miket, 'The early medieval settlement'.
[84] Scull, 'Post-Roman phase I', challenging Hope-Taylor, *Yeavering*, 154–7, 209–13; cf. James *et al.*, 'An early medieval building tradition', 199–205; Gardiner, 'An early medieval tradition', 235–9.
[85] Hope-Taylor, *Yeavering*, 78–83, 205–9, 280; O'Brien, 'The Great Enclosure' (noting the difficulty of dating it).

were competing for cattle tribute from the Britons.[86] In a broader European context, Chris Wickham has stressed the importance of resources in determining styles of rule, and in this respect northern Anglo-Saxon kingship looks similar to rulership in other parts of the Insular world.[87] The rich body of legal material from Ireland shows that cattle were fundamental to socio-economic relations during the seventh and early eighth centuries. Increasingly it looks like the same was true in parts of Anglo-Saxon England, although the textual evidence is poorer.[88] Áedán and Æthelfrith were among the most successful of the overlords, and they were in a select group of kings who extended their control across a range of territories and peoples.[89]

Æthelfrith's successes prompted Áedán to muster a great army and march to Degsastan. The location was *celeberrimus* 'very famous' in Bede's day but sadly it is no longer famous enough to be identified. The most popular candidate, Dawston in Liddesdale, is not a linguistically good match for *Degsastan*, and in my view it lies too far south.[90] The Upper Tweed Valley would be a more suitable location: it was disputed territory in the sixth century and the *stan* might have been one of the inscribed monuments that had been constructed there.[91] Both sides endured significant losses, but Áedán's army was annihilated and he was forced to flee.[92] *Degsastan* was far from a straightforward conflict; indeed, Hering son of Hussa (Æthelfrith's Bernician predecessor) guided Áedán's army, according to the northern recension of the Anglo-Saxon Chronicle.[93] Æthelfrith's rise to power must have driven Hussa's family into exile with Cenél nGabráin. A marriage alliance between the two houses would explain why one of Áedán's sons bore the name Conaing (OE *cyning* 'king').[94]

Another participant in the battle was Máel Umai mac Báetáin (*ob.* 610), who killed Æthelfrith's brother. This information is found only in the Clonmacnoise branch of the Chronicle of Ireland, which raises the suspicion that it was added in the tenth century.[95] The mention of Máel Umai can, however, be placed in the context of interaction between his kindred, Cenél nÉogain of the northern Uí Néill, and Cenél

---

[86] Charles-Edwards, 'Early medieval kingships', 30–1; Campbell, 'Comparing early medieval polities'; Fraser, *From Caledonia to Pictland*, 173.

[87] Wickham, *Framing the Middle Ages*, 56–7. There has been debate about whether, and how, the next stage of tribute-taking (from client kingdoms) differed between Anglo-Saxon England and Ireland. See Binchy, *Celtic and Anglo-Saxon Kingship*, 20–31; Wormald, 'Celtic and Anglo-Saxon kingship', esp. 164; Charles-Edwards, 'Celtic kings', 73–7.

[88] McCormick, 'Cows, ringforts'; Kelly, *Early Irish Farming*, 27–8; Banham, *Anglo-Saxon Farms*, 75–106; *eadem*, 'Insular agricultures', 32–4. For the north-west European context, see Loveluck, *Northwest Europe*, 69.

[89] Fleming, *Britain after Rome*, 206.

[90] Suggested by Skene, *Celtic Scotland*, I, 162, challenged by Jackson, *Language and History*, 612; Stenton, *Anglo-Saxon England*, 77 n. 2. Smith, 'Brito-Roman', 9, suggested that Addinston (Lauderdale) contains Áedán's name, but early forms do not support this idea (Williamson, 'The non-Celtic place-names', 11).

[91] For example the Yarrow Stone, Whitekirk: *CIIC*, no. 515, I, 491–3; Elliot, 'Prehistoric', 14. For arguments in favour of Tweeddale, see *British Battles* (forthcoming) by Andrew Breeze.

[92] *HE* I, 34, 2 (ed. Lapidge, I, 262, 264; ed. and transl. Colgrave and Mynors, 116–17).

[93] ASC E [603] (ed. Irvine, 22). For Hussa, see the Bernician king-list: Dumville, 'The Anglian collection', 32, 36; *HB* 63 (ed. Mommsen, 206; ed. and transl. Morris, 37, 79).

[94] Conaing appears in AU 622.2 (ed. and transl. Mac Airt and Mac Niocaill, 110–11); AT [620] (ed. and transl. Stokes, I, 135); CS [622] (ed. and transl. Hennessy, 55–6); *CI* 622.2 (transl. Charles-Edwards, I, 132). *Míniugud Senchasa Fher nAlban* (ed. and transl. Bannerman, *Studies*, 41, 48, cf. 87, 94–5).

[95] AT [599] (ed. and transl. Stokes, I, 123); *CI* 600.2 (transl. Charles-Edwards, I, 121); Evans, 'The Irish chronicles', 21.

nGabráin. Just over a decade earlier, an alliance had been forged by Áedán mac Gabráin and the leading Uí Néill king, Áed mac Ainmere of Cenél Conaill, at Druim Cett (*ca* 590).[96] After Áed died in 598, Colmán Rímid of Cenél nÉogain, brother of Máel Umai, emerged as the most prominent Uí Néill leader.[97] Brian Lacey has argued that Cenél nEógain were not viewed as an Uí Néill dynasty at this time, and while this is debatable, it does seem that Cenél Conaill and Cenél nÉogain were pursuing distinct agendas.[98] Thus Áedán mac Gabráin may have sought to replace his Cenél Conaill alliance with links to Cenél nÉogain, procuring their support at Degsastan. Already at this early stage it is possible to identify a range of friends and foes of the Bernicians among the Gaelic-speaking rulers.

After Degsastan Æthelfrith went from strength to strength, dominating the Deirans (and marrying a Deiran princess), and campaigning as far west as Chester. Æthelfrith was killed *ca* 616 by Rædwald of East Anglia, who had harboured the Deiran exile Edwin. The battle ensured Edwin's rise to Deiran kingship, and he quickly extended his power over Bernicia.[99] Æthelfrith's children went into exile among the Picts and his erstwhile Dál Riatan foes, who lay beyond Edwin's reach.[100] Edwin was orientated more towards the south, as seen in his marriages to the Mercian princess Cwenburg and the Kentish Æthelburg, and he was the first Northumbrian to extend *imperium* over the Southumbrian realms.[101] He also had links to Gwynedd, having been an exile there according to later, but apparently independent, Welsh and Anglo-Norman texts.[102] At an early stage he took over the Brittonic kingdom of Elmet in the Pennines, killing its king, and founding a royal vill.[103] His trans-Pennine contacts also encompassed Rheged, if a record of his baptism at the hands of Rhun, descendant of Urien, is to be believed. This contradicts Bede's account of Edwin's baptism by Paulinus, but most likely reflects a North British tradition that was incorporated into the early ninth-century *Historia Brittonum*.[104] Having made the Brittonic kingdoms tributary, Edwin may have called on them to provide naval service, which would explain how he was able to take control of the Isle of Man.[105]

The conquest of Man brought Edwin into the Irish Sea zone and into conflict with Fiachnae mac Báetáin (also known as Fiachnae Lurgan). Fiachnae's maritime interests continued the pattern set by Báetán mac Cairill (*ob.* 581), a predecessor

---

[96] Anderson and Anderson, *Adomnán's Life of Columba*, xvii–xviii; Bannerman, *Studies*, 82, 157–70; Ó Cróinín, *Early Medieval Ireland*, 73. For the date, see Sharpe, *Adomnán*, 312–14; Meckler, 'The *Annals of Ulster*'; Fraser, *From Caledonia to Pictland*, 138–9.

[97] Some later texts call him king of Tara: 'The Laud genealogies' (ed. Meyer, 293); *CGH* 137 a 8 (ed. O'Brien, 124); cf. Charles-Edwards, *Early Christian Ireland*, 484.

[98] Lacey, *Cenél Conaill*, 289–319.

[99] *HE* II, 12, 2–5 (ed. Lapidge, I, 354–62; ed. and transl. Colgrave and Mynors, 176–9); ASC E [617] (ed. Irvine, 23).

[100] *HE* III, 1, 1 (ed. Lapidge, II, 16; ed. and transl. Colgrave and Mynors, 212–13).

[101] *HE* II, 5, 1; II, 14, 1–2 (ed. Lapidge, I, 310, 370; ed. and transl. Colgrave and Mynors, 148–9, 186–7).

[102] *Trioedd Ynys Prydein* (ed. and transl. Bromwich, 58); Geoffrey of Monmouth, *Historia regum Britanniae* XI.190 (ed. Reeve and transl. Wright, 262–3).

[103] *HB* 63 (ed. Mommsen, 206; ed. and transl. Morris, 38, 79); AC A & B [616] (ed. Williams (ab Ithel), 6); ed. Gough-Cooper [a173.1], [b642.1]); *HE* II, 14, 3 (ed. Lapidge, I, 372; ed. and transl. Colgrave and Mynors, 188–9).

[104] *HB* 63 (ed. Mommsen, 206; ed. and transl. Morris, 38, 79); *De temporum ratione* (ed. Jones, 525; transl. Wallis, 228); *HE* II, 14, 1 (ed. Lapidge, 368–9; ed. and transl. Colgrave and Mynors, 186–7).

[105] Higham, *Ecgfrith*, 62.

in the over-kingship of north-eastern Ireland (and quite possibly the kingship of Tara).[106] Whereas Báetán had belonged to Dál Fiatach, the leading dynasty of the Ulaid, Fiachnae was from the Cruithni. Fiachnae had defeated his Dál Fiatach rival, Fiachnae mac Demmáin, though the tables would eventually be turned.[107] Fiachnae mac Báetáin would have seen Edwin's conquest of Man as a threat, and this would explain his raid on Ráith Guaili in 623. Several scholars have identified this *ráith* as a fort in Ireland, either in the south-west or close to Fiachnae's own region in the north-east.[108] Yet it is worth considering the possibility that 'Ráith Guaili' is the Iona chronicler's adaptation of the Brittonic name for Bamburgh (*Din Guaire*).[109] The substitution of *ráith* for *dún* is not difficult to explain since both meant 'fort', and *Guaili* could be a miscopying of *Guairi*. Bede wrote that kings of *Scotti in Britannia* desisted from battle with the Northumbrians after Degsastan, but this would not apply to Fiachnae, who was king of the Cruithni in Ireland.[110] The case for identifying Ráith Guaili with Bamburgh is strengthened by the eighth-century Irish tale *Compert Mongáin*, which opens with Fiachnae *i n-imnisiu fri Saxanu* 'in warfare against the Saxons'. This tradition was no doubt elaborated in the tale *Sluagad Fiachnae maic Báetáin co Dún nGuaire i Saxanaib 7 primsluagid hErend archena* 'Hosting of Fiachnae mac Báetáin to Dún nGuairi among the Saxons, and the first hosting of Ireland besides'. The tale is now lost, but its title features in two lists of tales that derive from a tenth-century text.[111] Edwin had set his stamp on Bamburgh's region by this time, as seen in the impressive timber hall and Roman-inspired theatre at Yeavering.[112]

Edwin's maritime activities also impinged on his former hosts in Gwynedd, whose heartland was Anglesey. Edwin used Man as a stepping stone to Ynys Môn (Anglesey), perhaps taking advantage of a power vacuum upon the retirement or death of Cadfan, who is commemorated as *rex sapientissimus opinatissimus omnium regum* on an inscription at Llangadwaladr (Anglesey).[113] By 629 Edwin was challenging Cadfan's son Cadwallon for control of Anglesey and Cadwallon went into

---

[106] *Clann Ollaman Uaisle* (ed. and transl. Byrne, 64, 77); *Ríg Ulad: The Book of Leinster* (ed. Best *et al.*, I, 193); Meyer, 'The Laud synchronisms', 484. For Báetán and Fiachna as possible kings of Tara, see *Senchas Síl hÍr* (ed. and transl. Dobbs, 64–5); *CGH* 137 a 5, 11 (ed. O'Brien, 124); Charles-Edwards, *Early Christian Ireland*, 482–3, 499–50. Byrne (*Irish Kings*, 112) suggested that the mysterious *Féchno* of the earliest Tara regnal list was Fiachnae. For the list, see *Baile Chuinn* (ed. Bhreathnach and Murray, 84–5).

[107] AU 602.3, 626.1 (ed. and transl. Mac Airt and Mac Niocaill, 100–1, 114–15); AT [601, 625] (ed. and transl. Stokes, I, 124, 139); CS [502, 626] (ed. and transl. Hennessy, 45–6, 57–8); CI 602.3, 626.1 (transl. Charles-Edwards, I, 122, 134). For the descent of the two Fiachnaes, see *Senchas Síl hÍr* (ed. and transl. Dobbs, 338–9, 68–9); *CGH* 143 b 1, 161 bc 34, 162 b 53, LL 330 c 43 (ed. O'Brien, 155, 323, 327, 409).

[108] For Ráith Guaili in Munster, see Jackson, 'On the northern British section', 27–8; Breeze, '*Scéla Cano meic Gartnáin*', 93–4. For Ráith Guala in Co. Down, see Hogan, *Onomasticon*, 572; 'Onomasticon' updated by Ó Corráin, 2400. I am grateful to Russell Ó Ríagáin for drawing this *ráith* to my attention.

[109] AU 623.3 (ed. and transl. Mac Airt and Mac Niocaill, 112–13); AT [624.3] (ed. and transl. Stokes, I, 136); CS [623] (ed. and transl. Hennessy, 55–6); CI 623.3 (transl. Charles-Edwards, I, 132); cf. HB 61, 63 (ed. Mommsen, 205–6; ed. and transl. Morris, 37–8, 78–9).

[110] HE I, 34, 2 (ed. Lapidge, I, 264; ed. and transl. Colgrave and Mynors, 116–17).

[111] *Compert Mongáin* §2 (ed. and transl. White, 71, 78); *ibid.*, 25–7 for dating. For the tale-list, see Mac Cana, *The Learned Tales*, 48, 59; Toner, 'Reconstructing', 118.

[112] Hope-Taylor, *Yeavering*, 51–3, 58–63, 125–41 (hall A4); 119–22, 124, 241–4 (theatre: building E).

[113] CIIC no. 970 (II, 129); Edwards, *A Corpus III*, 180–3: 'the wisest and most renowned of all kings'.

exile in Ireland; I suggest that he travelled to Edwin's foes among the Cruithni.[114] Edwin's bitter struggle with Cadwallon was well remembered in Welsh poetic tradition, including the potentially seventh-century poem *Moliant Cadwallon*. Cadwallon dramatically reversed his fortunes by allying with the Mercian king Penda, killing Edwin, and dominating the Northumbrian kingdom for the best part of a year.[115] Thus Edwin's interest in the Isle of Man drew him into the wider politics of the Irish Sea region and eventually to his death.

The Northumbrian powerhouse

The return of Æthelfrith's sons ushered in a new phase of political contact, which underpinned the peak of Northumbrian power in the mid-seventh century. The sons drew on friendships forged in exile: Eanfrith had been living in Pictland and fathered a future Pictish king;[116] other sons developed a close relationship with Iona and Cenél nGabráin.[117] At the battle of Fid Euin in 629, Osric son of Albruit, a *rígdamnae* (potential king), fought alongside the grandsons of Áedán mac Gabráin against the Cruithni. Osric appears only in the Clonmacnoise branch of the 'Chronicle of Ireland', and it has been suggested that his name was a tenth-century addition deriving from Bede's reference to the Deiran king Osric son of Ælfric.[118] However, there is some detailed material about the Cruithni in this strand of the Clonmacnoise branch, and Osric is a plausible Bernician name. He may have been the son of an Ælfred who belonged to a collateral branch of the Bernicians, perhaps a grandson of Hussa. The syntax of the entry leaves open the possibility that Osric was also a grandson of Áedán.[119]

The first attempt of a son of Æthelfrith to return from exile was unsuccessful. Eanfrith assumed power over the Bernicians while Edwin's nephew Osric took control of the Deirans. The two kings forsook their baptism and were eventually slain by Cadwallon during an *annus horribilis* that was erased from the Northumbrian

---

[114] *Trioedd Ynys Prydein* (ed. and transl. Bromwich), triad 29; AC A & B [629] (ed. Williams (ab Ithel), 6; ed. Gough-Cooper [a186.1], [b657.1]).

[115] AC A & B [631] (ed. Williams (ab Ithel), 7; ed. Gough-Cooper [a187.2], [b658.1]); *HE* II, 20, 1; III, 1, 2 (ed. Lapidge, I, 394, 396; II, 17, 19; ed. and transl. Colgrave and Mynors, 202–3, 212–15); *Canu Cadwallon ap Cadfan* (ed. Gruffydd, 25–43); for arguments in favour of its authenticity, see Breeze, 'Seventh-century Northumbria'; Koch, *Cunedda*, 186–7. I do not follow Woolf ('Caedualla *rex Brettonum*') in seeing Cadwallon as a North British ruler because I place more weight on the Anglesey–Man axis.

[116] Talorgan son of Anfrith, who features in the eighth-century core of the Pictish king-lists (ed. Anderson, *Kings and Kingship*, 248, 262, 266, 280).

[117] Fraser, *From Caledonia to Pictland*, 155–8. Iona's lay founder, Conall, was a member of Cenél Comgaill, but thereafter the kindred supported the church at Kingarth, whereas Cenél nGabráin favoured Iona.

[118] For the nature of the annalistic testimony, see Dumville, '*Cath Fedo Euin*'; for the influence of Bede, see Evans, 'The Irish chronicles', 22. Stokes, 'On the linguistic value', 426–7, discussed the name-forms.

[119] David Dumville ('*Cath Fedo Euin*', 125) raised the question whether 'Ulster (or Scottish) information about the earlier seventh century was able to reach tenth-century Clonmacnoise in quite good shape'. In his view this is not 'an easy option', though there is other material of this nature in the Clonmacnoise branch. For discussion of *Albruit* and *Ælfred*, see *ibid.*, 123; Moisl, 'The Bernician royal dynasty', 105–6, 109.

king-list.[120] Their reigns threw into relief the achievements of Oswald, another of Æthelfrith's sons, who was presented as an outstanding example of Christian kingship. This image of Oswald is heavily indebted to Bede's *Historia ecclesiastica*: Bede saw Oswald as the personification of an Old Testament warrior king under the guidance of a holy man, Áedán. Their co-operation fulfilled an ideal of pastoral work based on Gregory the Great's writings.[121] Gaelic links were but one element of Oswald's multi-faceted political interests. He brought the Deirans and Bernicians together once again, aided by his mother's Deiran lineage.[122] He was the overlord of the Southumbrian realms, and he demonstrated his power there in association with his godson, King Cynegils of Wessex.[123]

Nevertheless, Oswald's connection with the Gaelic world took several forms. The Britons continued to act as conduits: Oswald is likely to have ordered the *obsessio Etin* (siege of Edinburgh) in 638, and western citadels came under Northumbrian influence.[124] The metalworkers at the Mote of Mark adapted their styles to reflect Northumbrian taste, and a Northumbrian brooch has also been found at Trusty's Hill.[125] The latter was burnt down shortly afterwards, while the Mote of Mark continued to thrive, probably remaining in the hands of a local leader who paid tribute. One attraction of the hillforts was their political and economic links across the Irish Sea, which may explain why they were allowed to continue as going concerns. Nicholas Higham has made the attractive suggestion that Oswald appointed his brother Oswiu as his deputy in the region and brokered Oswiu's marriage to Rhiainfellt, who was most probably a princess of Rheged. While Bede did not acknowledge this marriage, it is attested by *Historia Brittonum* (drawing on a northern British source) and a list of queens in the ninth-century core of the Durham *Liber Vitae*.[126]

Oswald's strongest links with the Gaelic world were those forged in exile in Dál Riata. Adomnán of Iona recounted that Oswald had been baptised on Iona with twelve retainers, and that he experienced a vision of St Columba on the eve of his battle against Cadwallon. Adomnán also described Oswald as *totius Brittanniae imperator a Deo ordinatus* 'emperor of all Britain ordained by God', drawing inspiration from depictions of ordination in the Books of Samuel and the Irish idea of over-kingship.[127] The Iona community apparently accepted Oswald's over-lordship, and they may have welcomed Oswald as their protector at a time when Cenél nGabráin's political fortunes had suffered a major blow. Domnall Brecc, a grandson of Áedán mac Gabráin, dramatically broke his alliance with the northern Uí Néill kindred Cenél Conaill at the battle of Mag Roth (Moira, Co. Down), 637. He switched his allegiance to the king of the Cruithni, Congal Cáech (king of Tara),

---

[120] *HE* III, 1, 2 (ed. Lapidge, II, 17, 19; Colgrave and Mynors, 212–15); Dumville, 'The Anglian collection', 32, 36.

[121] McClure, 'Bede's Old Testament kings', 94; Thacker, 'Bede's ideal', 146, 152.

[122] *HE* III, 6, 3 (ed. Lapidge, II, 44; ed. and transl. Colgrave and Mynors, 230–1).

[123] *HE* III, 7, 1 (ed. Lapidge, II, 44, 46; ed. and transl. Colgrave and Mynors, 232–3); Rollason, *Northumbria*, 38.

[124] AU 638.1 (ed. Mac Airt and Mac Niocaill, 120–1); AT [640.1] (ed. and transl. Stokes, I, 144), CS (ed. and transl. Hennessy, 64–5); *CI* 638.1 (transl. Charles-Edwards, I, 141).

[125] Graham-Campbell, 'The Mote of Mark', 49–50; Laing and Longley, *Mote of Mark*, 148–56, 168; Toolis and Bowles, *The Lost Dark Age Kingdom*, 27, 44–7, 132–4.

[126] *HB* 57 (ed. Mommsen, 203; ed. and transl. Morris, 36, 77); *The Durham Liber Vitae* (ed. Rollason and Rollason, I, 93); Higham, *Ecgfrith*, 80.

[127] Adomnán, *Vita Sancti Columbae*, I.1 (ed. and transl. Anderson and Anderson, 14–17); Enright, *Iona*, 60–1 (Old Testament influence); Dumville, 'The English', 49 (political theory).

but the pair were heavily defeated.[128] The disaster upset the Iona community, for Cenél Conaill were Columba's own kindred.[129] Bede claimed that Oswald *denique omnes nationes et prouincias Brittaniae, quae in quattuor linguas, id est Brettonum Pictorum Scottorum et Anglorum diuisae sunt, in dicione accepit.*[130] While Oswald's rule was widespread, it appears that he favoured Cenél nGabráin above other kindreds, which highlights the complexity of Northumbrian–Gaelic relations. This diplomatic pattern was disrupted by Oswald's death at the hands of the Mercian king Penda in 642. Shortly afterwards, the leader of Cenél nGabráin, Domnall Brecc, was killed by Owain of Dumbarton. Owain was an ally of Cenél Comgaill, another Dál Riatan kindred, who had not thrived under Oswald's overlordship.[131]

Oswald's brother, Oswiu, ultimately continued the Northumbrian hegemony. It took time for him to dominate the Deirans, and he waged a long struggle against Penda, which culminated in his recognition as the holder of *imperium* in the south.[132] A Mercian rebellion ended this status, and thereafter Oswiu focused his attention on northern Britain.[133] Oswiu had a detailed grasp of the politics of Gaeldom, having been in exile with Oswald. The brothers' close relationship with Iona would have endeared them to Columba's kindred, Cenél Conaill, but Irish genealogists linked Oswiu with a different northern Uí Néill group, Cenél nEógain. They identified Fín, daughter of Colmán Rímid, as the mother of one of Oswiu's sons, the future King Aldfrith. It is hard to see why an Irish scholar would have fabricated this genealogy any later than Northumbria's political Golden Age.[134] Indeed, a context for the union can be found in the long-standing pattern of co-operation between his Dál Riatan hosts and Cenél nEógain.[135] Fín was at least seven years older than Oswiu, but it is just possible that they met while Oswiu was in exile; alternatively Oswiu may have spent time with Cenél nEógain while acting as Oswald's deputy in the west of Northumbria. Oswiu's marriage to Rhiainfellt of Rheged took place around this time, and had ended by the time of his accession, when he married Edwin's daughter,

---

[128] Clonmacnoise-branch chronicles identify the key participants as Domnall mac Áeda (king of Tara, of Cenél Conaill) and Congal Cáech: AT [636] (ed. and transl. Stokes, I, 143–4); CS [636] (ed. and transl. Hennessy, 84–5); CI 637.1 (transl. Charles-Edwards, I, 140). AU 637.1 (ed. and transl. Mac Airt and Mac Niocaill, 118–19) notes the battle but not the participants, probably because of eye-skip. For Congal Cáech as king of Ulster, see *Book of Leinster* (ed. Best *et al.*, I, 193); as king of Tara see the early legal tract *Bechbretha* §32 (ed. Charles-Edwards and Kelly, 69).

[129] Adomnán, *Vita Sancti Columbae*, III.5 (ed. and transl. Anderson and Anderson, 190–1).

[130] *HE* III, 6, 1 (ed. Lapidge, II, 42; ed. and transl. Colgrave and Mynors, 230–1) 'at length held under his sway all the peoples and kingdoms of Britain, divided among the speakers of four different languages, i.e. of the Britons, Picts, Gaels and English' (I have modified the translation).

[131] AU 642.1 (ed. and transl. Mac Airt and Mac Niocaill, 122–3); AT [641] (ed. and transl. Stokes, I, 146); CS [640] (ed. and transl. Hennessy, 86–7); CI 642 (transl. Charles-Edwards, I, 142–3). Some of the details only appear in the Clonmacnoise branch, but they are confirmed by the Strathcarron stanza in both versions of the *Gododdin*: *Canu Aneirin* (ed. Williams, lines 966–71, 972–7 (39); transl. J. P. Clancy, *The Triumph Tree*, 114). For the Cenél Comgaill–Dumbarton alliance, see Fraser, 'Strangers', 109–12; Higham, *Ecgfrith*, 85–6.

[132] *HE* II, 5, 1 (ed. Lapidge, I, 312–13; ed. and transl. Colgrave and Mynors, 150–1).

[133] *HE* III, 24, 1–5 (ed. Lapidge, II, 134–43; ed. and transl. Colgrave and Mynors, 288–95).

[134] CGH 140 a 39–40 (ed. O'Brien, 135); 'The Laud genealogies' (ed. Meyer, 294); Ó Riain, *Corpus genealogiarum sanctorum Hiberniae* (ed. Ó Riain, 175). The latter lists both Colmán Rímid and Cenn Fáelad of Brega as possibilities for Fín's father, but the weight of evidence points to the former. Fraser (*From Caledonia to Pictland*, 217) suggests genealogical manipulation.

[135] Cenél nEógain fought Cenél Conaill in a naval battle off Kintyre on the same day as Mag Roth; note also the alliance at Degsastan (603). See above, nn. 95, 128.

Eanflæd.[136] Oswiu and Oswald's personal contacts in Gaeldom may have attracted retainers and their families to Bamburgh. The isotope analysis of skeletons buried in the Bowl Hole cemetery – while not allowing for precise localisation – indicates that some individuals had grown up in western Scotland or Ireland. Others came from further south in England, pointing to similar contacts there.[137]

There are hints that Oswiu enforced a more intrusive form of rule on his tributary territories than Oswald. The Bernicians took over native political centres in the far north-east and the west, including Dunbar and perhaps also the fortress of *Iudeu* on the Forth.[138] Northumbrian noblemen started to settle in these areas; at Lockerbie, for example, a Yeavering-style hall replaced an earlier post-built structure.[139] Oswiu continued to act as the protector of Cenél nGabráin, and it may be no coincidence that they appear pre-eminent among the wider Dál Riatan entity in the late-seventh-century sections of *Míniugud Senchasa Fer nAlban*. By this time, Cenél nGabráin had subordinated their neighbours Cenél Comgaill, and together these *cenéla* were identified as the descendants of Domangart, son of Fergus Mór. Domangart was known as Domangart Réti, which links him with the *dux Reuda* whom Bede noted as the founder of Dál Riata in Britain.[140] Nevertheless, Oswiu's overlordship was not uniformly welcomed. An early manuscript of Adomnán's Life includes an extract from an earlier Life of Columba by Abbot Cumméne of Iona (657–69), which lamented the outcome of the battle at Mag Roth. Cumméne wrote of the ensuing subjection to *extranei* 'foreigners' (most likely the Northumbrians) *quod suspiria doloris pectori incutit*.[141] Oswiu's long reign provided time for his policy towards subject kingdoms to harden, and he eventually died in 670.

Northumbrian–Gaelic relations became even more fractious in the reign of Oswiu's son, Ecgfrith. His contacts were oriented more towards the south than towards the Gaelic world. His mother was the half-Kentish Eanflæd, he spent part his childhood in Mercia, and his wives were the East Anglian Æthelthryth and the Kentish Iurminburg.[142] Nevertheless, the politics of his northern and western neighbours were key to his reign. Ecgfrith countered an uprising in the tributary southern Pictish area; meanwhile, the leading Pictish kingdom of Fortriu (now understood to be in northern Pictland) passed to his cousin, Bridei.[143] Ecgfrith then turned his attention southwards, fighting the Mercians on the Trent in 679. The Iona chronicler noted the death of Ælfwine son of Oswiu in the battle, which indicates that Iona remained

[136] Ireland, 'Aldfrith', 75; Higham, *Ecgfrith*, 82–3.
[137] Groves *et al.*, 'Mobility histories', 469–70. The Bowl Hole cemetery included men, women and children: Groves *et al.*, 'The Bowl Hole early medieval cemetery'; Groves *et al.*, 'The Bowl Hole burial ground'.
[138] *HB* 65 (ed. Mommsen, 208; ed. and transl. Morris, 38, 79); Perry, *Castle Park, Dunbar*, 66–77.
[139] Kirby, *Lockerbie Academy*, 4, 43–54.
[140] *It e téora trena dáil riatai .i. cenél ngabráin cenél n-óengusa cenél loairnd móir*: *Míniugud Senchasa Fer nAlban* (ed. and transl. Bannerman, *Studies*, 42, 49); Fraser, 'Dux Reuda', 1–4; idem, *From Caledonia to Pictland*, 145.
[141] Adomnán, *Vita Sancti Columbae* (ed. and transl. Anderson and Anderson, 190–1) 'which fills the breast with sighs of grief'. See *ibid.*, xxiii–xxviii for the identification of the *extranei* as the Northumbrians. Fraser, *From Caledonia to Pictland*, 165, suggests Cenél Comgaill.
[142] *Vita Sancti Cuthberti auctore anonymo*, IV.8 (ed. and transl. Colgrave, 122–3); *HE* III, 24, 2; IV, 17 (19), 1 (ed. Lapidge, II, 136–7, 292–3; ed. and transl. Colgrave and Mynors, 290–1, 390–1).
[143] *Vita Sancti Wilfridi* 19 (ed. and transl. Colgrave, *The Life*, 40–3). Bridei was Ecgfrith's *fratruelis*: *HB* 57 (ed. Mommsen, 202; ed. and transl. Morris, 36, 77); Fraser, *From Caledonia to Pictland*, 200–1. For the relocation of Fortriu to the north of the Mouth, see Alex Woolf's seminal article 'Dún Nechtain'.

interested in the Bernicians.[144] Ecgfrith also tightened his grip on Brittonic territory in the west, as revealed by Stephanus's *Vita Sancti Wilfridi*, which admittedly had an unforgiving attitude to Britons. The *Vita* describes the consecration ceremony at Ripon and the granting of various Pennine estates, which had been vacated by Britons fleeing the sword.[145] Carlisle had become a royal centre by this time, and Queen Iurminburg was resident there when Ecgfrith rode into Pictland to wage an ill-fated battle at *Nechtansmere* (which is most plausibly located at Dunnichen in Angus) in 685.[146]

Bede attributed Ecgfrith's defeat and death in battle to his decision to invade Ireland in 684.[147] The reasons for the attack merit consideration, for it cast a long shadow over Gaelic–Northumbrian relations. The Chronicle of Ireland, probably drawing on the Iona Chronicle, reveals that Ecgfrith targeted the plain of Brega, where the currently dominant Uí Néill kindred, Síl nÁeda Sláine, resided. Their king, Fínsnechta Fledach, was king of Tara, as proclaimed in the poetic regnal list *Baile Chuinn*, which was initially produced during his reign.[148] Some commentators have explained the raid as a strike against Ecgfrith's half-Uí Néill brother, Aldfrith; against this, Aldfrith was arguably Ecgfrith's favoured successor rather than a threat.[149] Thomas Charles-Edwards has identified an ecclesiastical dimension, suggesting that St Wilfrid claimed authority over the northern half of Ireland, where churches still preserved old methods of calculating Easter.[150] Another scenario is a pre-emptive attack against a grand alliance of Picts, Britons and Uí Néill. Indeed, the leader of the campaign, Berht, belonged to a dynasty of Northumbrian sub-kings in southern Pictland.[151] The case for Brittonic involvement is weakened by reliance on the seventeenth-century 'Annals of Clonmacnoise', which refer to an 'alliance of the Irish with the Brittaines'.[152] The idea that Berht had an interest in Ireland may, however, be supported by the idea that he was related to the Berrihert and Berechtuine who were commemorated in the Glen of Aherlow and Tulach Léis na Saxan (Tullylease, Co. Cork) in the south of Ireland.[153]

---

[144] *HE* IV, 19 (21); V, 24 (ed. Lapidge, II, 308–9; III, 184–5; ed. and transl. Colgrave and Mynors, 400–1). AU 680.4 (ed. and transl. Mac Airt and Mac Niocaill, 146–7); AT [680.4] (ed. and transl. Stokes, I, 165); CS [676] (ed. and transl. Hennessy, 104–5); *CI* 680 (transl. Charles-Edwards, I, 163).

[145] *Vita Sancti Wilfridi* 17 (ed. and transl. Colgrave, *The Life*, 36–7).

[146] *Vita Sancti Cuthberti auctore anonymo*, IV.8 (ed. and transl. Colgrave, *Two Lives*, 122–3). The traditional location makes sense if kings from further north and south were fighting over the overlordship of southern Pictland. For an alternative, see Woolf, 'Dún Nechtain', 184–7.

[147] *HE* IV, 24 (26), 1 (ed. Lapidge, 350–3; ed. and transl. Colgrave and Mynors, 426–9).

[148] AU 685.2 (ed. and transl. Mac Airt and Mac Niocaill, 148–9); AT [685.2] (ed. and transl. Stokes, I, 168); CS [681] (ed. and transl. Hennessy, 106–7); *CI* 685.2 (transl. Charles-Edwards, I, 165). For composition of *Baile Chuinn*, see Byrne, *Irish Kings*, 91, 104; Bhreathnach, '*Níell cáich úa Néill nasctar géill*', 61–2.

[149] Yorke, *Rex Doctissimus*, 8; *eadem*, 'Adomnán', 36–40; *contra* Moisl, 'The Bernician royal dynasty', 120–4; Smyth, *Celtic Leinster*, 120–1.

[150] Stephen, *Vita Wilfridi* 21, 53 (ed. and transl. Colgrave, 42–5, 108–9); Charles-Edwards, *Early Christian Ireland*, 432–5; *idem*, 'Wilfrid', 256–8.

[151] Fraser, *From Caledonia to Pictland*, 201, 244; Higham, *Ecgfrith*, 203–4.

[152] AClon 680 (ed. Murphy, 109).

[153] All of these names contain the element *be(o)rht*. Dáibhí Ó Cróinín (*The Kings Depart*, 16–19) highlights the importance of shared name elements in tracking relations between the Northumbrians who visited Ireland.

I propose a new scenario, namely, that Ecgfrith's attack was linked to competition for power in the Irish Sea during the dying years of the trade in imported goods. These exotic items had sustained the political networks of several key players: the rulers of Kintyre, Brega, Dál Fiatach, and the areas north of Solway. Ecgfrith had an interest in these developments since he was overlord in the Solway Firth and the Isle of Man. Indeed, isotopic analysis of skeletons at Bamburgh and on the Isle of Man raises the possibility that individuals of southern European or North African origin travelled to these places, perhaps while engaging in trade.[154] The turbulence in the west is graphically illustrated by the burning of the Mote of Mark to the north of the Solway; I suggest that the hillfort was a casualty of power-play around the Irish Sea.[155] This period saw conflict between Dál Fiatach and Brega rulers, and bands of Britons became active in Dál Riata, among the Ulaid and in Brega from the late 670s onwards.[156] I would identify the Britons as the rulers of the Isle of Man, who were fending off challenges for control of the Island.[157] This interpretation is supported by an annal entry for 682, no doubt derived from the Iona Chronicle, which seems to link a battle of Britons against the Cruithni with a killing on the Isle of Man.[158] Ecgfrith's desire to retain control of the Island may have prompted him to challenge the most powerful of the Irish kings with maritime interests, Fínsnechta Fledach in Brega. If my suggestion is plausible, it highlights the continued role of the Isle of Man in drawing the Northumbrians into contact – or confrontation – with their Gaelic counterparts. Indeed, Northumbrian influence continued on the Isle of Man even after 684, as indicated by two rune-inscribed monuments at Kirk Maughold, which formed the head- and footstone of a tomb. They commemorate a certain Blæcmon, which is an extremely unusual name, but one found in the Bernician royal line. There are other hints of Anglo-Saxon influence, such as the possible representation of an episcopal seal on a slab at the Manx church of Maughold that commemorates a bishop.[159]

After Dunnichen, Northumbrian–Gaelic relations evolved from dominance to diplomacy. Ecgfrith was succeeded by his half-brother, Aldfrith, whose mother was Fín of Cenél nÉogain. This came as a surprise to many people, perhaps including

---

[154] Groves *et al.*, 'Mobility histories', 470; Hemer *et al.*, 'No man', 246–7; cf. Hemer *et al.*, 'Evidence of early medieval trade'. If this interpretation is correct, it may suggest gaps in the current distribution of imported goods. No Mediterranean imports are known from Man, and only a small amount of Continental E-ware, from Port y Candas and Kiondroghad: Campbell, *Continental and Mediterranean Imports*, 41, 49, 116.

[155] I am departing from the view of Laing and Longley that Northumbrians burnt the hillfort down: *The Mote of Mark*, 22, 24, 168.

[156] Britons fought Cenél Loairn in 678 and Fínsnechtae defeated Bécc Boirche of Dál Fiatach in 679: AU 678.3 (ed. and transl. Mac Airt and Mac Niocaill, 144–5); AT [677, 678] (ed. and transl. Stokes, I, 164–5); CS [674, 675] (ed. and transl. Hennessy, 104–5); CI 678.3, 679.3 (transl. Charles-Edwards, I, 162–3).

[157] *Contra* Smyth, *Warlords*, 26, 82 (disaffected Rheged warband); Fraser, *From Caledonia to Pictland*, 207; Higham, *Ecgfrith*, 204 (Dumbarton rulers).

[158] AU 682.2 (ed. and transl. Mac Airt and Mac Niocaill, 146–7); AT [681] (ed. and transl. Stokes, I, 206–7); CI 682.2 (transl. Charles-Edwards, I, 164). CS [678] (ed. and transl. Hennessy, 106–7) only includes the battle. The Manx identification is also favoured by Charles-Edwards, *Early Christian Ireland*, 433 n. 75.

[159] MM 42, 43; Trench-Jellicoe, 'A re-definition', I, 231–4; Wilson, 'Stylistic influences', 315, 317 (dating the cross of arcs design to the eighth or early ninth century); *idem, Manx Crosses*, 30–2 (noting the episcopal seal), 35. For the name Blæcmon, see Dumville, 'The Anglian collection', 30, 35.

Aldfrith himself. He had been in training for an ecclesiastical career on Iona, and his succession was not smooth; some regarded him as illegitimate.[160] Even so, Aldfrith's background facilitated negotiations with Adomnán, who visited twice in order to secure the release of the hostages that Ecgfrith had taken from Brega.[161] It is appropriate that the Old Irish wisdom text attributed to Aldfrith (in his Irish guise as Flann Fína) extols the virtue of learning over martial prowess.[162] Aldfrith concentrated on the governance of his core territory, and he is the first Northumbrian king to be named on coins. The lion on the obverse of his coins drew on both Classical models and Insular art, an appropriate symbol for a man of Aldfrith's learning.[163]

Aldfrith's decision to establish his kingdom *intra fines angustiores* 'within narrower bounds' had knock-on effects for the balance of power in Gaeldom.[164] Aldfrith retained his close relationship with Iona and Cenél nGabráin, but he could no longer offer them protection. It is no coincidence that this period saw challenges to Cenél nGabráin's status in Dál Riata in Britain. In the early eighth-century tract *Cethri prímchenéla Dáil Riata* Cenél Comgaill appear to have escaped from their position of subordinacy to Cenél nGabráin. Moreover, the tract accords Cenél Loairn, the northern Dál Riatan kindred, more prominence than Cenél nGabráin, although this may be an illusion created by the circumstances of textual transmission.[165] Cenél Loairn became increasingly dominant in the first decade of the eighth century, which explains why Cumméne's lament for Cenél nGabráin was included in an early eighth-century manuscript of *Vita Sancti Columbae*.[166] As to Ireland, the continued suspicion of Northumbrians is seen in the legal tract *Críth Gablach*, which cited the foreign invasion as an example of an emergency in which kings could issue *rechtgi* 'ordinances'.[167] Even so, Columba's people, Cenél Conaill, and the Iona community did not perform *damnatio memoriae*. Ecgfrith was said to have been buried on Iona (an uncomfortable situation for Northumbrians who expected to inter him at home) and the Iona community commemorated him in an early eighth-century martyrology.[168] Meanwhile Aldfrith's maternal kin, Cenél nÉogain, were becoming

---

[160] *Vita Sancti Cuthberti auctore anonymo* III.6 (ed. and transl. Colgrave, 104–5); *HE* IV, 24 (26); V, 12, 7 (ed. Lapidge, II, 354; III, 82–3; ed. and transl. Colgrave and Mynors, 430–1, 496–7). Wearmouth-Jarrow may have been relatively unsupportive of Aldfrith, which would have coloured Bede's presentation of the situation: Yorke, *Rex Doctissimus*, 7–11.

[161] Adomnán, *Vita Sancti Columbae* II.46 (ed. and transl. Anderson and Anderson, 178–81). One of the visits is mentioned by Bede *HE* V, 15, 1–3 (ed. Lapidge, III, 94, 96, 98; ed. and transl. Colgrave and Mynors, 504–9). The Iona Chronicle recorded the captives' return (which probably took place in 688): AU 687.5 (ed. and transl. Mac Airt and Mac Niocaill, 150–1); AT [686] (ed. and transl. Stokes, I, 210); CS [683] (ed. and transl. Hennessy, 108–9); *CI* 687.5 (transl. Charles-Edwards, I, 167).

[162] *Bríathra Flainn Fína maic Ossu* §7 (ed. and transl. Ireland, 33–4); Ó Corráin, *Clavis*, II, 1190.

[163] Gannon, *The Iconography*, 125–; cf. Grierson and Blackburn, *Medieval European Coinage* I, 166; Metcalf, 'The coinage', 153; Naismith, *Medieval European Coinage VIII*, 96.

[164] *HE* IV, 24 (26), 2 (ed. Lapidge, II, 354–5; ed. and transl. Colgrave and Mynors, 430–1).

[165] *Cethri prímchenéla Dáil Riata* (ed. Dumville, 176–82). See *ibid.*, 187 for the importance of Cenél Loairn, which is challenged by Broun, '*Cethri prímchenéla*', 66–8.

[166] Adomnán, *Vita Sancti Columbae* III.5 (ed. and transl. Anderson and Anderson, 188–9); Fraser, *From Caledonia to Pictland*, 146, 244–6, 249–53.

[167] *Críth Gablach* (ed. Binchy, lines 522–3). For further adverse reaction, especially at Armagh, see Wadden, 'Theories', 173–7.

[168] MT May 27 (ed. Best and Lawlor, 46); *Libellus de exordio* I.5 (ed. and transl. Rollason, 46–7); Ó Riain, *Anglo-Saxon Ireland*, 11–12.

increasingly powerful in the northern half of Ireland, which ensured more peaceful relations with the Northumbrians.

Aldfrith was the last great king of Northumbria's Golden Age, and so it is worth surveying the hallmarks of Northumbrian–Gaelic relations during this period. The key point is the diversity of relationships across Gaeldom; Northumbrian kings did not deal with the Gaels as a whole, but rather with particular kindreds and dynasties. The lynchpins were the dominant Dál Riata kindred Cenél nGabráin and their favoured church on Iona. This relationship dated back to the exile of the sons of Æthelfrith, and perhaps to an even earlier period. The Northumbrian expansion westwards, particularly into the Isle of Man, also antagonised the Ulaid, the Cruithni and Síl nÁeda Sláine in Brega. Yet relations with the northern Uí Néill were cordial, and this group had become dominant by the early eighth century. These well-established relationships would become strained during the eighth and ninth centuries, when new sources of Gaelic influence arose.

3

FRAGMENTATION AND OPPORTUNITY:
FROM THE EIGHTH CENTURY TO THE VIKING AGE

Northumbrian politics became more introspective during the eighth century. The kingdom was riven by internecine rivalries and the power of the nobility grew, limiting the influence of Northumbrian kings. Gaeldom was also changing: in the second quarter of the eighth century, Cenél Conaill lost its pre-eminence in the northern parts of Ireland, Síl nÁeda Sláine its dominance in the Irish Midlands, and Dál Riata was subdued by a Pictish king, Onuist son of Uurguist. Then came the Viking attack on Lindisfarne in 793, which caused shock far beyond the Northumbrian kingdom, and was soon followed by raids in the Irish Sea. These events accelerated Northumbria's disintegration: the kingdom's political makeup looked very different by the tenth century, even if the concept of a Northumbrian polity persisted. Yet this fragmentation ultimately heightened and diversified the opportunities for Gaelic influence and encroachment during the Viking Age.

Years of decline? The eighth and ninth centuries

Before exploring this apparently turbulent era, it is worth asking how changes in the source material affect our understanding of Northumbria's external relations. Bede said less about his contemporaries than he did about the Golden Age; he thought that his own generation fell short of their seventh-century forebears, and he sought to inspire improvements among his contemporaries.[1] After Bede, the sources diminish further in detail: the northern annals are laconic and the core text of the 'Chronicle of Ireland' shifted from Iona to the Irish Midlands *ca* 740. Northern Britain featured less prominently in this phase of the chronicle, even if some information filtered through from Iona and Pictland.[2] Notwithstanding these points, I would argue that there was a real decline in Northumbrian–Gaelic diplomatic contacts during the eighth century, and I would seek the reasons not only in the Northumbrian kingdom, but also in the Gaelic world.

There were already signs of weakness in the rule of Æthelfrith's line by the early eighth century. Before Aldfrith's son, Osred, could succeed to kingship, the throne was briefly seized by Eadwulf son of Ecgwulf, who came from a rival Bernician line. The Iona chronicler took an interest in Eadwulf and his son, and there are hints

---

[1] *HE* preface, 1 (ed. Lapidge, I, 94, 96; ed. and transl. Colgrave and Mynors, 2–3); Campbell, 'Bede I', 10–12, 17; Higham, *(Re-)reading Bede*, 69–70. Other factors that may have influenced *HE* include opposition to St Wilfrid's supporters (Goffart, *The Narrators*, 235–328) and reform of the Northumbrian Church (Thacker, 'Bede's ideal', 132–3, 142–50).

[2] Evans, 'Irish chronicles', 23–4, 39–42.

that they fled to Pictland.[3] Once installed in the kingship, Osred was a controversial ruler, the eminent missionary Boniface bemoaning his wantonness and attacks on the Church.[4] Osred died in a skirmish *besuðan gemære* 'south of the border' in 716. This area may be identified with the Pictish/Brittonic territory of Manaw on the Firth of Forth, which had seen conflict between Picts and Northumbrians five years earlier.[5] The dominant Pictish kingdom of Fortriu was by this time ruled by Nechtan son of Der-Ilei, who descended on his father's side from the Dál Riata kindred Cenél Comgaill.[6] Cenél Comgaill in turn enjoyed a long-running alliance with the Dumbarton Britons, and the references to *perfidia* 'treachery' in Bede's commentary on the Book of Samuel (written around the time of Osred's death) appear to be aimed at the Britons.[7] Thus the killing of Osred emerges as the result of an alliance between Fortriu, Dumbarton and Cenél Comgaill against the Northumbrians. During the following year, the Britons were at war with Dál Riata, perhaps to be identified in this instance with Cenél nGabráin, who may have supported Osred on account of their long association with his family.[8] This sequence of events has echoes of long-standing patterns of interaction and enmity between the Northumbrians and the various Dál Riata *cenéla*.

After Osred's death, the Northumbrian kingdom saw further jostling for power between the descendants of Æthelfrith and Ecgwulf. Ceolwulf, a great-grandson of Ecgwulf, was the royal dedicatee of Bede's *Historia ecclesiastica*. He was imprisoned and tonsured in 731 according to the annals added to the Moore manuscript, which contains an early copy of *Historia ecclesiastica*. Bede omitted the event from his text, perhaps because it raised tensions at his own monastery. Eventually Ceolwulf abdicated to take up an ecclesiastical life in Lindisfarne.[9] It has been suggested that the Iona chronicler, still in contact with Lindisfarne, accorded him the Gaelic pseudonym, 'Eochaid'. However, it is more likely that Eochaid was a Cenél nGabráin king who became a cleric around the time of Ceolwulf's imprisonment, both events being recorded under the same year in the Iona chronicle.[10] What the entry shows is that the Iona community maintained an interest in the Northumbrian kings.

---

3   AU 717.2, 741.7 (ed. and transl. Mac Airt and Mac Niocaill, 172–3, 194–5); AT [716] (ed. and transl. Stokes, I, 185); *CI* 717.2, 741.7 (transl. Charles-Edwards, I, 191, 213); *HR* (ed. Arnold, II, 38); *Vita Sancti Wilfridi* 59 (ed. Colgrave, *The Life*, 128–9). The lineage appears in Dumville, 'The Anglian collection', 30, 35 (where Ecgwulf may be Ecgwald, although the chronology is incorrect); for Pictish links, see Fraser, *From Caledonia to Pictland*, 265.

4   *S. Bonifatii et Lulli epistolae*, no. 73 (ed. Tangl, 152–3).

5   *HE* V, 24, 1 (ed. Lapidge, III, 186; ed. and transl. Colgrave and Mynors, 566–7); ASC D [710, 716] (ed. Cubbin, 10); ASC E [710, 716] (ed. Irvine, 35); AU 711.3, 716.1 (ed. and transl. Mac Airt and Mac Niocaill, 166–7); AT [710, 715] (ed. and transl. Stokes, I, 182, 185); *CI* 711.3, 716.1 (transl. Charles-Edwards, I, 185, 190).

6   Clancy, 'Philosopher-king'.

7   *In primam partem Samuhelis* 2, 15, 27–8 (ed. Hurst, 134); Thacker, 'Bede, the Britons', 140, 144–7.

8   AU 717.5 (ed. and transl. Mac Airt and Mac Niocaill, 172–3); AT [716] (ed. and transl. Stokes, I, 186); CS [713] (ed. and transl. Hennessy, 118–19); *CI* 717.5 (transl. Charles-Edwards, I, 191). Cenél nGabráin were not then the dominant kindred, Selbach of Cenél Loairn being pre-eminent.

9   *HE* preface; V, 23, 2 (ed. Lapidge, I, 94; III, 172, 174; ed. and transl. Colgrave and Mynors, 2–3, 558–9); *Continuations* (to 766) *s.aa.* 731, 737 (ed. Colgrave and Mynors, 572–3); Story, 'After Bede', 172–3. The Lindisfarne connection is detailed in the twelfth-century Durham text *Libellus de exordio* II.1 (ed. and transl. Rollason, 78–9).

10   AU 731.2–3 (ed. and transl. Mac Airt and Mac Niocaill, 182–3); cf. *CI* 731.2–3 (transl. Charles-Edwards, I, 203; the entries are not separated in the edition of AT [730] (ed. and transl. Stokes, I, 195). Cf. Dumville, 'On editing', 84–5; Kirby, *The Earliest English Kings*, 159 n. 36, correcting *idem*, 'King Ceolwulf', 168–73.

Ceolwulf's abdication gave an opening to Eadberht, who ruled from 737/8 to 758. He was the only eighth-century Northumbrian ruler to wield significant influence beyond his borders. Eadberht was Ceolwulf's cousin, and he was accorded his own pedigree in the Anglian collection of genealogies. The pedigree was also copied into *Historia Brittonum*, which is a mark of Eadberht's wider influence.[11] Symeon of Durham reported that Eadberht exchanged gifts with the Frankish king Pippin III, which is plausible against the broader backdrop of Northumbrian–Carolingian contacts.[12] Eadberht reinstituted an explicitly royal coinage, and a parallel coinage was issued by his brother Ecgberht, York's first archbishop. Northumbria was experiencing a bullion shortage, and earlier coins were reminted in an ambitious *renovatio monetae*.[13] The well-connected scholar Alcuin, writing later in the eighth century, viewed the regime of Eadberht and Ecgberht as *tempora felicia* 'fortunate times'.[14] Yet Eadberht's reign was not free from internal challenges: he notoriously besieged a son of Aldfrith on Lindisfarne in 750 and took Bishop Cynewulf prisoner.[15]

During Eadberht's reign the Northumbrian kingdom became embroiled once again in external conflicts. He encountered a different set of opponents from those of the seventh century, showing how far the axes of Insular politics had shifted. There is a tradition that Alpín, a mid-eighth-century Dál Riatan king, fought battles in Galloway, which is worth exploring since that region was still under Northumbrian rule. The tradition is first recorded in a version of the Scottish king-list dating to the reign of Alexander II (1214–49), where the eighth-century Alpín is confused with the ninth-century father of the renowned king Cináed mac Ailpín. This is clearly a later record because the name *Galwithia* 'Galloway' was not used for the region until the eleventh or twelfth centuries.[16] A tradition developed that Alpín was defeated by a native chieftain called Indrechtach, which is – I suggest – a result of confusion with an entry in the 'Chronicle of Ireland' for 741.[17] The entry records a battle in north-eastern Ireland, in which Dál Riata apparently faced Indrechtach, a king of the Cruithni. Later writers seem to have confused these Cruithni with the *Picti* who were said to reside in twelfth-century Galloway (*Picti* being translated *Cruithni* in Gaelic).[18]

By this time, the Northumbrians' main northern opponent was the Pictish king Onuist son of Uurguist, who had emerged from a four-way contest free of internal

---

[11] Dumville, 'The Anglian collection', 30, 36; *HB* 61 (ed. Mommsen, 205; ed. and transl. Morris, 37, 78).

[12] Story, *Carolingian Connections*, 19–26; *Libellus de exordio* II.3 (ed. Rollason, 80–3)

[13] Naismith, 'Kings', 301–7; *idem*, *Medieval European Coinage VIII*, 116–17.

[14] Alcuin, *Versus de patribus regibus et sanctis Euboricensis ecclesiae* l. 1277 (ed. and transl. Godman, *Alcuin*, 100–1).

[15] *HR s.a.* 750 (ed. Arnold, II, 39–40); *Libellus de exordio* II.2 (ed. and transl. Rollason, 78–81).

[16] King-lists D, F, I, K (ed. Anderson, 265, 271, 282, 286); cf. *ibid.*, 46, 112, 182, 195–6. Andrew of Wyntoun equated this Alpín with the father of Cináed in his *Orygynale Cronykil* (ed. Amours, IV, 172–3). I follow H. M. Chadwick, *Early Scotland*, 127 in relating the story to the earlier Alpín.

[17] Maxwell, *A History*, 37–8; Skene, *Celtic Scotland*, I, 291–2; Brooke, *Wild Men*, 59. Maxwell reports a tradition that Laicht Alpín near Lochryan marked the king's burial place.

[18] AU 741.10 (ed. and transl. Mac Airt and Mac Niocaill, 213); *CI* 741.10 (transl. Charles-Edwards, I, 213). AT only has a short entry and CS is defective. The entry's strange syntax makes it unclear whose side Indrechtach was on. However, he appears in the king-list of Dál nAraidi (a line of the Cruithni) in *The Book of Leinster* (ed. Best *et al.*, I, 193). For the Galloway *Picti*, see MacQueen, *Nynia*, 44–53, who also notes the later application of the term *kreenies* to some inhabitants of Galloway.

rivalry.[19] He exploited tensions between the Dál Riata *cenéla*, culminating in *percutio Dal Riatai* 'the smiting of Dál Riata' in 741.[20] Onuist controlled the citadel of Dunadd in Kintyre, and the Pictish boar symbol carved on the summit may be a symbol of his power. It is tempting to date the Pictish symbols on Trusty's Hill (Dumfries and Galloway, formerly Kirkcudbrightshire) to the same period, and to interpret them as a Pictish show of force in the Irish Sea.[21] This might also explain how Pictish designs began to influence sculpture at the great Manx church of Maughold.[22] Onuist's tentacles reached across Britain and Ireland: he made alliances with Irish kings and he may have reached an agreement with Æthelbald of Mercia to divide the overlordship of Britain.[23] Onuist's power was ebbing by 750, and Eadberht seized this opportunity to conquer the plain of Kyle in Ayrshire. At the end of their careers, Eadberht and Onuist co-operated in a campaign against the Dumbarton Britons (756). Even so, the Continuation of Bede contains a damning assessment of Onuist as *tyrannus carnifex* 'a tyrannical slaughterer'. The name is given in Gaelic form (*óengus*), which suggests that the information was transmitted from the Gaelic world to the Northumbrian kingdom, an incidental insight into channels of contact.[24]

The second half of the eighth century saw a bewildering array of Northumbrian kings, and this turbulence disrupted external connections. Some kings came from the line of Ecgwulf, some from collateral branches of Ida's dynasty, and others did not descend from Ida at all. One branch of Æthelfrith's line survived through a certain Oslaf, descendant of Ecgfrith, whose pedigree appears only in *Historia Brittonum*. Charles Phythian-Adams has proposed Carlisle as the base of Oslaf's line, and he characterises them as an 'Anglo-Celtic' lineage, given that they were accorded Brittonic epithets.[25] In my view, the epithets are more likely to have been added by the compiler of *Historia Brittonum*; even so, the Gwynedd-based writer's inclusion of this unique pedigree suggests that Oslaf's family had contacts with the Britons. It is plausible that they survived on the most westerly edge of the kingdom.[26]

The reign of Æthelwold Moll (759–65) heralded a new era in Northumbrian kingship, for he was a *patricius*, the head of the royal household, rather than a descendant of Ida. He first appears in a letter of Pope Paul I, which mentions Eadberht's alienation of three monasteries to 'Moll'.[27] The letter illustrates the problem of satisfying ambitious aristocrats who wielded significant power in their

---

[19] *Continuations* (to 766) *s.a.* 740 (ed. and transl. Colgrave and Mynors, 572–5); Woolf, 'Onuist son of Uurguist', 37 suggests that Onuist put forward Earnwine son of Eadberht as a candidate for Northumbrian kingship.

[20] AU 741.10 (ed. and transl. Mac Airt and Mac Niocaill, 194–5); CI 741.11 (transl. Charles-Edwards, I, 213) Fraser, *From Caledonia to Pictland*, 293–305.

[21] Forsyth and Thickpenny, 'The rock carvings', 99–100; Lane and Campbell, *Dunadd*, 20–2, 272.

[22] For Pictish-influenced stones, see Trench-Jellicoe, 'A re-definition', I, 256–7, 261–9, 279–80; Wilson, *Manx Crosses*, 43–7.

[23] *Continuations* (to 766), 750 (ed. and transl. Colgrave and Mynors, 574–5); Charles-Edwards, 'The continuation'. Dumville, 'The English', 53–4 doubts the reality of this joint high-kingship. Irish alliances are discussed by Fraser, *From Caledonia to Pictland*, 295–7.

[24] *Continuations* (to 766), 750, 761 (ed. and transl. Colgrave and Mynors, 574–7). Compare *Chronicle* (to 802) in *HR* 756, 761 (ed. Arnold, II, 40–1), which contains the Pictish form *Unust* (Forsyth, 'Evidence', 25–7).

[25] *HB* 61 (ed. Mommsen, 205; ed. and transl. Morris, 37, 78); Phythian-Adams, *Land of the Cumbrians*, 58–61, 64, 168–9.

[26] Edmonds, 'The expansion', 48.

[27] *Councils* (ed. Haddan and Stubbs III, 394–6); *English Historical Documents* I no. 184 (ed. Whitelock, 830–1).

own right.[28] Æthelwold attained the kingship by killing Eadberht's son, Oswulf. Two years later, Æthelwold faced the rebellion of a certain Oswine, who made his stand in a distant part of the kingdom: the northern annals included in *Historia regum* name the location as Eildon (the distinctive hills near Melrose).[29] The large kingdom was in danger of fragmentation, for restive nobles might build up power bases in far-flung locations.[30] Indeed, Æthelwold was eventually deposed by a council of noblemen and his tonsuring is reported in the Annals of Tigernach, an entry that probably derives from the 'Chronicle of Ireland'.[31] Another example of the newly confident nobility is Ealdorman Wada, who was involved in a conspiracy to murder King Æthelred in 796. I would identify Wada as one of the people who persuaded Osred II, a descendant of Ecgwulf, to return from exile in 792 to replace Æthelred. Osred had been in exile on the Isle of Man, and he was betrayed and captured upon his return.[32] The place-names Waddington (estate of the descendants of Wada) and Waddow (Wada's Hill) indicate that Wada's own territory lay in the Ribble Valley. This strategic location between the Pennines and the Irish Sea gave Wada ready access to the Isle of Man.[33] Wada fought against King Eardwulf near Whalley (Lancashire), also in the Ribble Valley, in 798.[34] By now, regional Northumbrian magnates were capable of taking the lead in contacts with the Gaelic world. The information about ninth-century Northumbrian kingship is fragmentary. Snippets from a northern text appear in Roger of Wendover's thirteenth-century chronicle and Symeon of Durham's *Libellus de exordio*. There are two regnal lists from twelfth-century Durham, which contain a 'reconstruction of a distant Anglo-Saxon past', in David Dumville's words.[35]

These texts sometimes contradict other source material; for example, they say nothing about a second reign of Eardwulf, which is implied by a papal letter.[36] Numismatic evidence drastically shortens the reign-length of Osberht in the 850s/60s relative to the texts, although this calculation rests on questionable assumptions about rates of coin production.[37] Up until this point, the Northumbrian 'styca' coins circulated widely despite their debasement and varied metallic content. This suggests

---

[28] Rollason, *Northumbria*, 181–2, 197.

[29] *HR* (ed. Arnold, II, 41); ASC D [761] (ed. Cubbin, 14), located the battle *æt Eadwinesclife* 'at Edwin's Cliff', which could be in the Eildon Hills.

[30] For insight into how kings dealt with this problem elsewhere, see Wickham, *Framing the Middle Ages*, 345–6.

[31] AT [763] (ed. and transl. Stokes, I, 222): *Moll rí Saxan clericatus eficitur*. Evans ('Irish chronicles', 37) suggests the entry derives from Iona. Cf. the northern annals *s.a.* 765 in *HR* (ed. Arnold, II, 43).

[32] *Chronicle* (to 802): *HR* (ed. Arnold, II, 54).

[33] *PNWY*, VI, 199; Kirby, 'The battle of Whalley', 184. The Domesday form *Widitun* (1086) is aberrant: all later forms start with Wad- (*Wadingtun* 1231 onwards).

[34] ASC D [798] (ed. Cubbin, 18); ASC E [798] (ed. Irvine, 43) (the northern recension). There is more detail in Chronicle (to 802); see (for example) *HR* (ed. Arnold, II, 59).

[35] Pagan, 'Northumbrian numismatic chronology', 4–7; Dumville, 'Textual archaeology', 45–7 (quotation at 47); Rollason, *Northumbria*, 196. Regnal lists: 'De primo Saxonum adventu'; 'Series regum Northymbrensium' (ed. Arnold, *Symeonis monachi opera omnia*, II, 376–7, 391).

[36] 'Leonis III papae epistolae' (ed. Hampe, 91–2). Eardwulf's two reigns are accepted by Kirby, *The Earliest English Kings*, 157, 196 and doubted by Yorke, *Kings*, 96. Eardwulf's coinage was unknown until 1994: Pirie, 'Earduulf'; Fitzwilliam Museum, 'Early medieval corpus', *s.n.* Eardwulf (eight specimens in 2018).

[37] For Osberht's reign, see Pagan, 'Northumbrian numismatic chronology', 7–12; Lyon, 'Ninth-century Northumbrian chronology', 31–6; nuanced by Kirby, 'Northumbria', 16–17. Methodological problems are raised by Naismith, *Medieval European Coinage VIII*, 124–5.

firm control on the part of the minting authority in York, regardless of the cutthroat dealings of the kings.[38]

As to external relations, by the mid-ninth century Cináed mac Ailpín had emerged as the dominant ruler north of the Forth. Cináed has traditionally been credited with the Gaelic conquest of Pictland, as related in the 'Chronicle of the Kings of Alba', which incorporates a late-tenth-century regnal list and other tenth- to twelfth-century material.[39] The kingdom of Alba is now thought to have emerged from a long-standing process of Gaelic–Pictish interaction, in which the Picts were as much active contributors as passive victims. Whether Cináed was a Gael or a Pict, when he died he was described as *rex Pictorum*, indicating that his powerbase lay in the east. He bolstered his position by leading numerous raids across the Forth to *Saxonia*, targeting Melrose and Dunbar.[40] This demonstrates the vulnerability of the northern-most part of the Northumbrian kingdom at a time when central rule was weakening.

There are also hints of the Scandinavian activity that would bedevil the Northumbrian kingdom during the next decade. Roger of Wendover stated that the usurper Rædwulf fought against *pagani* at *Alutthelia*, and while this is a unique and unverifiable record, Rædwulf's reign is corroborated by coins bearing his name.[41] Numismatic chronology indicates that Rædwulf reigned during the late 850s rather than 844, as Roger stated.[42] No Viking armies are known to have been circling the eastern coast of England at this time. Another possibility is that the *pagani* were based in Ireland, which saw an acceleration in Viking activity across the early ninth century. The original raiders emanated from western Norway and Vestfold, as seen from the Irish metalwork that they brought home, which was ultimately deposited in female graves.[43] Within a few decades permanent bases were being established in Dublin and elsewhere, and in the early 850s a new, powerful Scandinavian dynasty arrived on the Irish scene.[44] I suggest that they launched an exploratory campaign to northern England, travelling between the Tyne–Solway gap and York when they were intercepted. *Alutthelia* may contain the form *Al(c)lut* (miscopied), which was an early name for Bishop Auckland (Co. Durham).[45] If so, this was a foretaste of the links between Scandinavian activity in Ireland and the Anglo-Saxon kingdoms that developed during the next decade.

To sum up the discussion so far, the eighth and ninth centuries saw changes in Northumbrian dealings with the Gaelic world. Northumbrian kings were no longer overlords and tribute takers, and the decline of Æthelfrith's dynasty disrupted the

---

[38] Naismith, *Medieval European Coinage VIII*, 125–6.

[39] CKA (ed. and transl. Hudson, 148, 152); Dumville, 'The Chronicle'; Woolf, *From Pictland to Alba*, 88–93.

[40] AU 858.2 (ed. and transl. Mac Airt and Mac Niocaill, 316–17); *CI* 858.3 (transl. Charles-Edwards, I, 312); CKA (ed. and transl. Hudson, 148, 152).

[41] Roger of Wendover, *Chronica*, *s.a.* 844 (ed. Coxe, I, 282–3); 'Early medieval corpus', *s.n.* Redwulf (84 specimens).

[42] Pagan, 'Northumbrian numismatic chronology', 14 (858); Lyon, 'Ninth-century Northumbrian chronology', 36 (853); Kirby, 'Northumbria', 17–18 (848).

[43] The Insular artefacts are discussed in Wamers, 'Insular finds'; Heens-Pettersen, 'Insular artefacts'. For the purposes of the raids, see Barrett, 'What caused the Viking Age?'; nuanced by Ashby, 'What really caused the Viking Age?'.

[44] AU 841.4, 853.2 (ed. and transl. Mac Airt and Mac Niocaill, 298–9, 312–13); CS [841, 853] (ed. and transl. Hennessy, 142–3, 152–3); *CI* 841.5, 853.3 (transl. Charles-Edwards, I, 299, 309). In general see Downham, *Viking Kings*, 11–16. The Scottish dimension is stressed by Ó Corráin, 'The Vikings', although grave goods indicate that early raiders returned to Norway.

[45] Breeze, 'The battle'.

long-standing links with Cenél nGabráin. Dál Riata in Britain fell under Pictish sway, and by the mid-ninth century the kings known as *rex Pictorum* were the most powerful players north of the Forth. Meanwhile, there are hints of more localised interactions between Northumbrian magnates and their counterparts across the sea. Even in this ill-documented era, a complex and entangled picture of Gaelic–Northumbrian links is perceptible.

Scandinavian York and Dublin

A new era of contact began with the arrival of the *mycel hæðen here* 'great heathen army' on English shores in 865. The fragmentation of the Northumbrian kingdom opened up new opportunities for Scandinavian groups, and the establishment of a firm dynastic link between York and Dublin magnified pan-Insular contacts. Meanwhile the expansion of the kingdom of Alba (the incipient Scottish kingdom) increased Gaelic influence across the Forth, pointing the way to an Anglo-Scottish border that is still familiar today. This period saw a striking range of contacts and enmities between various groups in the Gaelic world and in the disintegrating Northumbrian realm.

The Great Army was a force capable of disrupting whole kingdoms. The army's movements were chronicled at Alfred's court and incorporated into the 'common stock' of the Anglo-Saxon Chronicle.[46] This account suggests that civil war eased the army's conquest of York in November 866, for King Osberht was fighting Ælle, who was *ungecyndne cyning* 'not a king by hereditary right'. The eleventh-century Durham text *Historia de Sancto Cuthberto* qualifies the chaotic impression by suggesting that Osberht and Ælle were brothers.[47] Yet numismatic evidence points to a loss of control of minting in Osberht's reign: not only was his coin output minimal, imitations were issued. Moreover, many *stycas* (including the enormous Hexham hoard of approximately 8,000 coins) were buried between the 840s and 870s, which is suggestive of turbulence. The hoards include 700 stycas buried in Kirkoswald, Cumberland (now Cumbria), and the cache of jewellery, metalworking paraphernalia and six stycas from Talnotrie, Kirkcudbrightshire (now Dumfries & Galloway). These hoards contain items suggestive of interaction with Scandinavian groups: a nicked silver trefoil brooch and abbasid dirhams, respectively.[48] Thus there were reverberations of the army's activities in the west of the Northumbrian kingdom.

The Great Army was a composite force made up of contingents that were ultimately of Scandinavian origin, and were highly mobile. Isotope analysis of selected graves and charnel deposits at Repton, the Great Army's winter encampment in 873–4, highlights their diversity. Results from a joint burial and two skulls point to Denmark as the place of origin; in contrast, a different male and a female may have

---

[46] Dumville, 'Vikings', 354; Keynes, 'The manuscripts', 539–40.
[47] *HSC* 10 (ed. and transl. South, 50–1); Rollason, *Northumbria*, 235.
[48] Hexham: Adamson, 'An account'; *idem*, 'Further account'; Durham County Council and Northumberland County Council, 'Keys to the Past' N8744. Kirkoswald: Lysons and Lysons, *Magna Britannia*, IV, ccviii; Historic England, 'Pastscape', no. 12428; Graham-Campbell, 'The dual economy', 53–4. Talnotrie: Maxwell, 'Notes on a hoard'; Canmore, ID 63576; Graham-Campbell, *Whithorn and the Viking World*, 20–6. For these and other mid-ninth-century hoards of *stycas*, see Fitzwilliam Museum, 'Checklist of Coin Hoards'.

originated around the Baltic.[49] The Great Army's winter camp at Torksey (872–3) yielded a cosmopolitan range of finds, including Anglo-Saxon dress accessories as well as metalwork from Francia and Ireland.[50] The contribution of a contingent from Ireland is especially pertinent, but has been much debated because of uncertainty surrounding the names applied to the army and its leaders. The 'Chronicle of Ireland' describes those who attacked York as *Dubgaill* ('dark foreigners' also known as *Dubgennti* 'dark heathens'), a group who first arrived in Ireland in the early 850s. The term is often interpreted as 'Danish', but such national labels are anachronistic in this period. An alternative interpretation (albeit not uniformly accepted) is that the colour terms *finn* and *dub* were euphemisms for 'old' and 'new' groups under different leadership.[51] I find it credible that the *Dubgaill* of the Great Army had Irish links since their activities ranged across the Insular world. Furthermore, several versions of the Anglo-Saxon Chronicle name one of their leaders as *Ingwær*, and he can be identified with the *Ímar* (Ívarr) who appears in the 'Chronicle of Ireland' during the period 853–64.[52] Similarly Hálfdan, Ívarr's brother, has been identified with an *Albann* mentioned in Ireland.[53] Some historians remain unconvinced by these identifications, but *Ímar*'s obituary *rex Nordmannorum totius Hibernie et Brittanie* ('king of the Northmen of all Ireland and Britain') captures the pan-Insular scope of his activity.[54]

The Great Army eventually split into different forces, and Hálfdan's group settled in Northumbria.[55] In 875 they were based on the Tyne and raided Pictland and Strathclyde; it is possible that they crossed the Tyne–Solway gap to sack Carlisle, as reported by John of Worcester.[56] Ívarr had already besieged the citadel of Dumbarton in alliance with his associate (or possibly relative) Óláfr of Laithlinn in 870, thus

[49] Budd *et al.*, 'Investigating population movement', 137–8. The radiocarbon dates of the Repton remains have been placed in the era of the Great Army, taking into account the marine reservoir effect: Jarman *et al.*, 'The Viking Great Army'.

[50] Hadley and Richards, 'The winter camp', 58–9. *HSC* 11–12 (ed. and transl. South, 50–1), using the term *Scaldingi* in reference to the Scheldt Estuary, as suggested by Woolf, *From Pictland to Alba*, 71–2; cf. McLeod, *The Beginning*, 109–71.

[51] AU 867.7 (ed. and transl. Mac Airt and Mac Niocaill, 322–3); AClon *s.a.* 865 (ed. Murphy, 142); *CI* (transl. Charles-Edwards, I, 320). AC A adds *id est cat dub gint* ('that is, the battle of the black heathens') (ed. Dumville, 12–13). Varying interpretations of the terms include Smyth, 'The black foreigners', 103–11 (old Norwegian Vikings and new Danish Vikings); Downham, 'Viking identities', 191–6 (different leadership); Etchingham, 'Names', 32–3 (criticising the 'old'/'new' translations).

[52] ASC A [878] (ed. Bately, 50); ASC B [878] (ed. Taylor, 37); ASC C 879 (ed. O'Keeffe, 61); ASC D [878] (cd. Cubbin, 27); ASC E [878] (ed. Irvine, 50); cf. *Iguuar* in Æthelweard, *Chronicon* (ed. Campbell, 35–6), which drew on the ASC. The identification goes back to Haliday, *The Scandinavian Kingdom*, 134, and is supported by Smyth, *Scandinavian Kings*, 169–94; Downham, *Viking Kings*, 21, 64–7. Just as **Anlaif* gave OE *Anlaf* and OIr *Amláib*, so *Ingwær* relates to *Ímar*.

[53] AU 875, 877 (ed. and transl. Mac Airt and Mac Niocaill, 330–3); CS 877 (ed. and transl. Hennessy, 166–7); Smyth, *Scandinavian York and Dublin*, I, 29; Downham, *Viking Kings*, 68–71, 238. For a brother of Ívarr and Hálfdan, see the ASC entries cited in n. 52.

[54] AU 873 (ed. Mac Airt and Mac Niocaill, 328–9); AFM *s.a.* 871 (ed. O'Donovan, I, 518–19); *CI* 873.3 (transl. Charles-Edwards, I, 324). Britain is not mentioned in Ívarr's obituary in CS [873] (ed. and transl. Hennessy, 164–5). For a sceptical view, see Valante, *The Vikings*, 72–5.

[55] McLeod, *The Beginnings*, 112–32.

[56] ASC A [875, 876] (ed. Bately, 49); ASC B [875, 876] (ed. Taylor, 36); ASC C (ed. O'Keeffe, 60–1); ASC D (ed. Cubbin, 26); ASC E (ed. Irvine, 50); John of Worcester, *Chronicon* (ed. and transl. Darlington and McGurk, II, 62–3).

opening up the Clyde–Forth route between Ireland and northern Northumbria.[57] Hálfdan retained close links with Ireland and died in a battle between *Dubgaill* and *Finngaill* on Strangford Lough (Co. Down).[58] Hálfdan had no known heirs whereas the sons of Ívarr became prominent in Ireland. Northumbria was largely left in the hands of puppet rulers, whose reigns are only reported in twelfth-century Durham texts. The first Scandinavian king, Guðrøðr, features in Æthelweard's late-tenth-century chronicle (based on earlier sources) and on a sole coin. *Historia de Sancto Cuthberto* depicted Guðrøðr being rescued from slavery by the abbot of Carlisle to become king, a story designed to highlight the role of St Cuthbert's community in Northumbrian politics.[59] The name 'Guðrøðr' is in fact suggestive of more exalted origins, for it was used recurrently in the dynasty of Ívarr.[60] *Historia de Sancto Cuthberto* also relates that Guðrøðr resisted a large-scale Scottish invasion, in reality presumably a raid led by a king of Alba.[61] The story is garbled, but it is credible that the northern edge of Northumbria was vulnerable, given that the Scandinavian polity was focused on York and its hinterland. The next rulers of York were called Knútr and Sigfrøðr; the latter led a Northumbrian fleet to Wessex, and he is most probably the same man as the Jarl Sigfrøðr who was in dispute with a son of Ívarr in Dublin.[62] Thus the Scandinavians of York and Dublin continued to interact even during this obscure period.

In 902 the Dubliners suffered a severe blow when the kings of Leinster and Brega joined together to expel Scandinavians from Dublin. This event is traditionally seen as the cause of Scandinavian settlement in the west of the Northumbrian kingdom, although I would argue that it was merely the beginning of a long phase of Gaelic–Scandinavian influence. Indeed, there was no full exodus from Dublin: excavations at one lower-status settlement in the city have shown that it continued to be occupied, and neighbouring Irish kings continued to extract wealth from the town, as seen in the hoards around Lough Ennell (Co. Westmeath).[63] The Dublin warriors dispersed across a wide area, including the Hebrides and possibly the Cotentin peninsula on the Continent.[64] Yet if even a portion of Dublin's ships came to the coast of what is now north-west England, they would have made a significant impact since no-one

57 The eleventh-century *Fragmentary Annals* §239 (ed. and transl. Radner, 94–5) described Óláfr and Ívarr as brothers. However, some scholars see the two as having different backgrounds, for example, Rowe, *Vikings*, 128–30, 137.

58 AU 877.5 (ed. and transl. Mac Airt and Mac Niocaill, 332–3); CS [877] (ed. and transl. Hennessy, 166–7); CI 877 (transl. Charles-Edwards, I, 327). *Cogadh Gaedhel re Gallaibh* §25 (ed. and transl. Todd, 26–7), a late witness with earlier elements, names the opponent as Bárith. He is described elsewhere as *mac Ímair*, which calls into question the relationship between Ívarr, Hálfdan and *Dubgaill* (Etchingham, '*Laithlinn*', 87).

59 Æthelweard, *Chronicon* IV.3 (ed. and transl. Campbell, 50); HSC 13 (ed. and transl. South, 52–3). The coin may have been minted south of the Humber: Grierson and Blackburn, *Medieval European Coinage I*, 321; Naismith, *Medieval European Coinage VIII*, 292.

60 Dumville, 'Old Dubliners', 87–8; Townend, *Viking Age Yorkshire*, 45.

61 HSC 33 (ed. and transl. South, 70–1); *Libellus de exordio* II.13 (ed. and transl. Rollason, 126–7).

62 AU 893.4 (ed. and transl. Mac Airt and Mac Niocaill, 348–9); Smyth, *Scandinavian York and Dublin*, I, 34; Downham, *Viking Kings*, 74, 79. For their coins, see Naismith, *Medieval European Coinage VIII*, 293. The unique *Airdeconvt* coin from the Silverdale Hoard was minted around this time: Williams, 'A new coin type'. The name may be an extended form of *Knútr*: Townend, *Viking Age Yorkshire*, 48.

63 Simpson, 'Forty years', 25; Maas, 'The Viking events', 258–62.

64 Downham, *Viking Kings*, 26–31, 83; cf. Smyth, *Scandinavian York and Dublin*, I, 61–3; Ó Corráin, 'The Vikings', 336.

had replaced the top-level rule of the Northumbrian kings. The area was controlled by local noblemen such as Elfred son of Brihtwulf, who fled east to avoid the *pirati* ('pirates', 'Vikings') when they arrived.[65] A colourful narrative in the so-called 'Fragmentary Annals of Ireland' describes how a certain Ingimund led a contingent from Dublin to Wales, from which they were driven out. Æthelflæd, lady of the Mercians, settled them near Chester, which they then proceeded to attack.[66] The 'Fragmentary Annals' were compiled from various sources, including annals, prose tales and an eleventh-century chronicle. The work was primarily structured around the reigns of kings of Tara, and the chronicler had an interest in the ruling dynasty of Osraige.[67] Nevertheless, some details are corroborated by chroniclers writing on the other side of the Irish Sea: Ingimund's presence on Anglesey is noted in a mid-tenth-century version of *Annales Cambriae*, and the restoration of Chester appears in the 'Mercian register', which was incorporated into some versions of the Anglo-Saxon Chronicle.[68]

The exiled warriors brought quantities of silver with them, as seen in the spectacular hoards they left behind. The classic example is the Cuerdale hoard, which was found on the southern bank of the River Ribble near Preston (Lancashire) in the nineteenth century. This massive treasure was buried in a lead-lined chest in *ca* 903–5, and it comprised hacksilver, ingots and over 7,000 coins (primarily of Anglo-Scandinavian origin, but also English, Arabic and Continental). Much of the bullion came from Ireland (30 per cent of the hoard's weight), and there are also freshly minted coins from York.[69] The hoard is usually interpreted as the chest of a leading warband exiled from Dublin; an alternative is that the hoard was assembled in York using copious amounts of Dublin metalwork.[70] The silver was deposited near the head of tidal navigation on the Ribble, just as other contemporary hoards were left in coastal areas or by rivers. There are caches of similar broad-band arm-rings at Red Wharf Bay in eastern Anglesey and Huxley on the River Gowy in Cheshire.[71] The Silverdale Hoard (Lancashire), discovered near Morecambe Bay in 2011, is another treasure of this era. It comprises over two hundred items in a lead chest, including 27 coins, ingots, arm-rings and hacksilver.[72] The Galloway Hoard, found even more recently near Kirkcudbright, is as yet unpublished; it is a complex and extensive find, comprising more than one deposit. The ingots and broad-band arm-rings are of the Dublin-produced types found in Cuerdale; in addition, there is Northumbrian ecclesiastical metalwork and a Carolingian cup filled with brooches and Byzantine silk. This is an extraordinary range of material and the circumstances of deposition remain to be explored.[73]

---

[65] *HSC* 22 (ed. and transl. South, 60–1).

[66] *The Fragmentary Annals* §429 (ed. and transl. Radner, 166–73).

[67] Ní Mhaonaigh, '*Caraid taraisi*', 267–9. For eleventh-century elements of the tale, see Radner, *The Fragmentary Annals*, xxii–xxxi; Downham, 'The good', 33–4, 37; Edmonds, 'History and names', 6; Ní Mhaonaigh, '*Caraid taraisi*', 276–8.

[68] AC A 902 (ed. Dumville, 14); ASC B [907] (ed. Taylor, 49); ASC C [907] (ed. O'Keeffe, 75); Wainwright, 'Ingimund's invasion', 153–4.

[69] Graham-Campbell, 'Some archaeological reflections', 344; Higham, 'Northumbria, Mercia', 27; cf. Edwards, *Vikings*, 53–68.

[70] Graham-Campbell, 'Some archaeological reflections', 343; Williams, 'The Cuerdale coins', 70–1.

[71] Redknap, 'Silver'; Sheehan, 'The Huxley Hoard'.

[72] Williams, 'A new coin type'.

[73] National Museums Scotland, 'The Galloway Hoard'; Owen, 'Galloway's Viking treasure'.

The hoards indicate that warbands with connections to Dublin were present in the west of the Northumbrian kingdom in the first decade of the tenth century. The Cuerdale contingent also had close links with York, as suggested by the package of freshly minted coins that they had recently received from the city. The Dublin–Ribble–York axis underpinned the Scandinavian force that Edward the Elder tackled at Tettenhall (near Wolverhampton) in 910 following its campaign in Mercia. The main body of the Scandinavian force was based *on Norðhymbrum*, most likely in York. The report of those slain includes names favoured by the dynasty of Ívarr, which indicates co-operation between the army based in York and the Dublin exiles.[74] The fallen warriors also included *Agmund hold* (Norse *hǫldr*, a term of high office), who may be associated with Amounderness in Lancashire. The place-name comprises either the Norse personal name *Agmundr* in the genitive and Norse *nes*, 'headland' or *Agmund* in stem form compounded with Old English *hērness*, 'area subject to authority'.[75] The name *Agmund* was not unusual, but if this identification is correct, it suggests that Scandinavian warriors had started to take lands in north-west England.[76] Others returned to action in the Irish Sea region: *gennti* 'heathens' defeated a new fleet of the Ulaid *i n-airiur Saxan* 'on the coast of the Saxons' in 913, and Rǫgnvaldr, grandson of Ívarr, fought a naval battle near the Isle of Man in 914.[77]

Scandinavian communities began to settle in north-west England and Man during this period, to judge by the appearance of richly furnished burials of Scandinavian type. These are the vestiges of a settled population, whose elaborate burial rituals involved families and the wider community.[78] While it is tempting to link the settlers with the expulsion from Dublin, isotope analysis of the Balladoole burial (Isle of Man) indicates that the deceased grew up further afield, most likely in Scandinavia. Wealthy women were also involved in the settlement, including the so-called 'Pagan Lady' of Peel Castle (Isle of Man), who had not grown up locally either.[79] Such evidence adds a new complexion to long-standing discussions about the numbers and makeup of the settlers. Since the mid-twentieth century, studies of blood groups and genetic markers have augmented the debate, but it is difficult to date patterns observed in the modern population.[80] One example is the controversy generated by the recent 'People of the British Isles' project, which found minimal evidence for a Viking-Age Scandinavian contribution to eastern England. The project's team

[74] ASC B [910] (ed. Taylor, 47); ASC C (ed. O'Keeffe, 73); ASC D [910] (ed. Cubbin, 38); Dumville, 'Old Dubliners', 88–9. I do not see a Ribble-based contingent as incompatible with a York-based force *contra* Quanrud, 'Taking sides', 79–83.
[75] Fellows-Jensen, 'Scandinavian place-names', 40; Higham, 'Northumbria, Mercia', 24; Edmonds, 'History and names', 7. For the boundaries of the territory granted by Athelstan, see Le Patourel, 'Amounderness'. The later administrative unit of Amounderness encompassed a smaller area: Farrer *et al.*, *The Victoria County History of Lancaster*, VII, 69. In *Norðleoda laga* the wergeld of the *hǫðr* is equated with that of the king's high-reeve: Liebermann, *Die Gesetze*, I, 460–1.
[76] *Agemundrenesse* 1065 (1086): DB Yorks 1L1, fol. 301v; Fellows-Jensen, 'Amounderness'. For the personal name, see Lind, *Norsk-Isländska Dopnamn*, I, 637–8.
[77] AU 913.5, 914.4 (ed. and transl. Mac Airt and Mac Niocaill, 366–7; CS [912, 913] (ed. and transl. Hennessy, 186–7).
[78] Graham-Campbell, 'The Irish Sea Vikings'; *idem*, 'The early Viking Age'.
[79] Symonds *et al.*, 'Medieval migrations', 5–7, 15–17; cf. Bersu and Wilson, *Three Viking Graves*, 1–44 (Balladoole); Freke, *Excavations*, 66–9 (Peel); Wilson, *The Vikings*, 25–8, 46–51. For the role of elite women in colonisation, see Jesch, *Women*, 75–83; for children, see Hadley and Hemer, 'Microcosms'.
[80] An early study of the Lakeland population was Roberts *et al.*, 'Genetic variation', which compared blood groups with those in Norway.

attributed a phase of admixture (population mingling) to Anglo-Saxon movement from northern Germany rather than Viking-Age migrations, but the timing allows for both.[81] In contrast, a recent study of the Wirral and West Lancashire focused on men with local surnames, and discovered that half of those sampled had a Y-chromosome type most commonly found in Norway.[82] To date, there has been no investigation of mitochondrial DNA in north-west England, which would potentially offer a point of comparison with such research in Iceland and the Faroes. Those studies are especially pertinent given that a disproportionate number of the female settlers emanated from the Gaelic-speaking world.[83] In short, while DNA studies have a role to play in broaching the scale and nature of Scandinavian settlement, they do not yet hold definitive answers. Moreover, in my view it is misleading to focus on one phase of migration, for there was constant mobility across the Irish Sea.[84]

The next recorded sequence of seaborne movements marked the end of exile for the grandsons of Ívarr. The brothers Rǫgnvaldr and Sigtryggr took their fleets to Ireland in 917, Rǫgnvaldr conquering Waterford, and Sigtryggr eventually capturing Dublin. Níall Glundub of Cenél nEógain launched a counter-attack in 919, but Sigtryggr triumphed and his victory was celebrated in skaldic verse.[85] Meanwhile, Rǫgnvaldr turned his attentions to the Northumbrian kingdom and met Constantín mac Áeda, king of Alba, in battle at Corbridge on the River Tyne (Northumberland). *Historia de Sancto Cuthberto* gives the impression that there were two battles of Corbridge, in 914 and 918, but all other texts focus on the later encounter, which had an inconclusive outcome.[86] Constantín was a grandson of Cináed mac Ailpín, and by now his kingdom was undergoing gaelicisation. He was allied with Ealdred son of Ealdwulf of Bamburgh, whose dynasty was of Northumbrian origin. While English writers did not consider the Bamburgh lords to be kings in their own right, the 'Annals of Ulster' described them as *rí Saxan tuaiscirt* 'king of the Saxons of the north'. The Armagh-based chronicle may be drawing on records from Dunkeld in Alba here, which supports the impression of interaction between the ruling dynasty of Alba and the Northumbrian house of Bamburgh.[87]

---

[81] Leslie *et al.*, 'The fine-scale genetic structure', 313, countered by Røyrvik and Kershaw, 'The "People of the British Isles" project', 1670–4; *eaedem*, 'Finding the English Vikings', 44–5.

[82] Bowden *et al.*, 'Excavating past population structures'; Redmonds *et al.*, *Surnames*, 207–9.

[83] Agnar Helgason *et al.*, 'mtDNA'; Jorgensen *et al.*, 'The origin'; Als *et al.*, 'Highly discrepant populations', critically appraised by Jesch, *The Viking Diaspora*, 35–6, cf. 57–8.

[84] Isotopic evidence supports this view. Several individuals at Black Gate cemetery, Newcastle, had moved significant distances at least three times: Hadley and Hemer, 'Microcosms', 73–5. Hadley, *The Vikings*, 2–6 surveys the debate about the scale of settlement.

[85] AU 914.4; 917.2, 4; 919.3 (ed. and transl. Mac Airt and Mac Niocaill, 368–9); CS [913, 916, 918] (ed. and transl. Hennessy, 188–91); AI 919 (ed. and transl. Mac Airt, 146–7). The poem *Darraðarljóð* (ed. Einar Ól. Sveinsson, *Brennu-Njáls saga*, ch. 157, 448–60) is placed in this context by Poole (*Viking Poems*, 122–5) and Townend ('Whatever happened', 53–5; *Viking Age Yorkshire*, 61).

[86] HSC 22, 24 (ed. and transl. South, 60–3); AU 918.4 (ed. and transl. Mac Airt and Mac Niocaill, 368–9); CKA (ed. and transl. Hudson, 150, 157); Downham, *Viking Kings*, 92–3; Woolf, *From Pictland to Alba*, 142–3.

[87] AU 913.1 (ed. and transl. Mac Airt and Mac Niocaill, 360–1); Broun, 'Dunkeld', 101–4. Cf. *Adulf mcEtulfe, king of the North Saxons* in AClon *s.a.* 928 (ed. Murphy, 149), a seventeenth-century translation of earlier annals. This may be a reference to Ealdred of Bamburgh, as suggested by Woolf, *From Pictland to Alba*, 164–5.

Later in 918, Rǫgnvaldr conquered York.[88] It is unclear who controlled York at the time; one scenario is a balance of power between several oligarchs and the archbishop.[89] Rǫgnvaldr's reign marked a new assertion of royal power, as witnessed by the new symbols on his coins, which were perhaps dynastic emblems. He was succeeded by his brother, Sigtryggr, in 921, who eventually married the sister of Athelstan of Wessex, the leading English king.[90] Sigtryggr was described as *Norðhymbra cyng* in the northern English report of his marriage, which indicates that a concept of Northumbrian power lived on, even if Sigtryggr ruled only the rump of the former kingdom.[91] The brothers ushered in an era of close dynastic links between York and Dublin.

The death of Æthelflæd, lady of the Mercians (or *regina Saxonum* 'Queen of the Saxons' according to Irish and Welsh chroniclers) assisted the stability of the York–Dublin axis.[92] Æthelflæd and her brother, Edward the Elder, had implanted fortifications along the Rivers Mersey and Irwell (in what is now north-west England) and on the coast of North Wales. In 919 the burh at Manchester was still being described as *on Norþhybrum*.[93] There were several motives for the construction of these strongholds, including the promotion of royal authority, defence against Viking attack and control of strategic route-ways.[94] At this stage, it seems that the Mercians were sealing off the area north of the Mersey, which was then fair game for the rulers of Scandinavian York and Dublin. Nicholas Higham has argued that the Mercians extended their authority even further north, to the Ribble, constructing another *burh* on a bluff overlooking the river at Penwortham.[95] This may have occurred several decades later, given that the area between Mersey and Ribble was included in the will of the Mercian Wulfric Spott (*ob. ca* 1004). Wulfric's dynasty specialised in the control of contested frontier zones.[96] In the meantime, the Ribble Valley acted as an artery of communication between York and Dublin.

By the early tenth century, Mercia was firmly attached to Wessex as part of the embryonic English kingdom. English pressure was mounting further north, and this limited interaction between the Northumbrian kingdom and Hiberno-Scandinavian Dublin. Sigtryggr's death in 927 allowed Athelstan to take power in York.[97] Athelstan subsequently met Constantín, Ealdred of Bamburgh, Hywel Dda and a certain Owain at Eamont near Penrith (Cumbria) to establish peace. While the D version of the

---

[88] The conquest of York is not listed under 918 in the chronicles: *HR* (ed. Arnold, II, 93); ASC D [923] (ed. Cubbin, 41); ASC E [923] (ed. Irvine, 54). Nevertheless, there is good reason to think that Rǫgnvaldr gained control of York in that year: Downham, *Viking Kings*, 93–4.

[89] Rollason (*Northumbria*, 214–30) accords the archbishop a more prominent role than Townend (*Viking Age York*, 58–9).

[90] Sigtryggr's departure from Dublin is reported in AU 919 [=920] (ed. and transl. Mac Airt and Mac Niocaill, 369–73); CS [920] (ed. and transl. Hennessy, 192–3). Cf. Downham, *Viking Kings*, 34. Sigtryggr's name appears on coins minted in the Five Boroughs, whereas unnamed sword/St Peter coins were being minted in York: Blackburn, 'The coinage', 338–9; Naismith, *Medieval European Coinage VIII*, 295–8, 302–3.

[91] ASC D [926] (ed. Cubbin, 41).

[92] AU 918.5 (ed. and transl. Mac Airt and Mac Niocaill, 368); AC A, B and C 918(ed. and transl. Dumville, 14–15; ed. Williams (ab Ithel), 17).

[93] ASC A [922 for 919] (ed. Bately, 69).

[94] Griffiths, 'The North-West frontier', 179–84.

[95] Higham, 'The Cheshire burhs', 213–14; Higham, 'Northumbria, Mercia', 28.

[96] Will of Wulfric Spott (ed. Sawyer, *Charters of Burton*, no. 29, 53–6); cf. Sawyer, *Anglo-Saxon Charters*, no. 1536; Insley, 'The family', 124–5.

[97] ASC D [926] (ed. Cubbin, 41).

Anglo-Saxon Chronicle identifies Owain as ruler of Gwent in south-eastern Wales, William of Malmesbury more plausibly describes him as *rex Cumbrorum* 'king of the Cumbrians', a term that I associate with the expanded kingdom of Strathclyde. The Cumbrians had a diplomatic matter to resolve with Athelstan, for they had been harbouring the Dublin ruler Guðrøðr, who had failed in a bid to take York.[98] The royal meeting occurred on the new southern boundary of the Cumbrian kingdom, which had expanded along the Roman roads through Annandale and Carlisle.[99]

Strathclyde's expansion illustrates how the vulnerable western portion of the Northumbrian kingdom was being dismembered, opening up several possible conduits of Gaelic influence. The Cumbrian kingdom has long been seen as an appanage of Alba, the nascent Scottish kingdom; however, this impression derives from John of Fordun's thirteenth-century source rather than contemporary testimony.[100] In my view, the expansion occurred in a piecemeal fashion, sometimes as a result of deals with local lords and sometimes through conquest. This enabled the kings of Strathclyde to absorb existing settlements, which resulted in a diverse cultural makeup. The Cumbrian kingdom already encompassed pockets of Gaelic–Scandinavian settlement, notably at the political centre and naval base of Govan on the Clyde.[101] It can be envisaged that the male and female group buried at Cumwhitton near Carlisle (Cumberland, now Cumbria) were connected in some way with the Cumbrian kingdom. The burials were furnished with weaponry and accoutrements from Scandinavia and the Isles, including several swords. One of these is in an originally Carolingian style but may have been manufactured in Norway; its finely decorated pommel features Insular-style decoration, including a distinctive central design that is closely paralleled by material in the Irish Sea and the Hebrides, and the sculptural motifs at Govan.[102] At first glance, this family's set of connections stands at odds with the dominance of Dublin in the traditional narrative of Scandinavian settlement in north-west England. Yet the two channels of influence were not mutually exclusive for the Hebrides were at times connected with the Dublin–York political axis.[103]

Athelstan went on to be proclaimed *rex totius Britanniae* on English coins and in charters, an indication of the scope of his ambition. In 934, he travelled through the Northumbrian kingdom and launched a naval expedition into Alba.[104] Athelstan also strengthened his control in the west in 934, as witnessed by his grant of Amounderness (an area north of the Ribble) to St Peter's church, York. The charter survives in

---

98   ASC D 926 (ed. Cubbin, 41); William of Malmesbury, *Gesta regum Anglorum* (ed. and transl. Mynors *et al.*, I, 214–15); *HR* (ed. Arnold, II, 93). For Strathclyde/Dublin co-operation, see Smyth, *Scandinavian York*, II, 156, 279–80; Higham, 'The Scandinavians', 42–5; Downham, *Viking Kings*, 165–9.

99   Edmonds, 'The emergence', 53; Clarkson, *Strathclyde*, 63–6; *contra* Kirby, 'Strathclyde', 86; Phythian-Adams, *Land of the Cumbrians*, 109–14.

100   Fordun, *Chronica gentis Scottorum* (ed. Skene, I, 163–4; II, 155). Challenged by Broun, 'The Welsh identity', 131 n. 84; *idem*, *Scottish Independence*, 215–68. Cf. Hudson 'Elech' for a further reason to doubt Scottish influence in the kingdom.

101   Edmonds, 'The expansion', 62–6.

102   Paterson *et al.*, *Shadows in the Sand*, esp. 53–67, 102. Adam Parsons has identified the parallel between the central design and Govan sculpture, among other regional parallels.

103   For example, after the Dubliners attacked Muirchertach mac Néill of Cenél nEógain he targeted the Hebrides: AU 939.3 (ed. and transl. Mac Airt and Mac Niocaill, 386–7); CS [940] (ed. and transl. Hennessy, 204–5); Etchingham, 'North Wales', 167; Downham, *Viking Kings*, 43–4.

104   *HR* (ed. Arnold, II, 124); Woolf, *From Pictland to Alba*, 158–66. For *rex totius Britanniae*, see Sawyer, *Anglo-Saxon Charters*, nos 416, 422, 430, 438, 446 and 448; Blunt, 'The coinage', 55–6; cf. Foot, *Æthelstan*, 151–5.

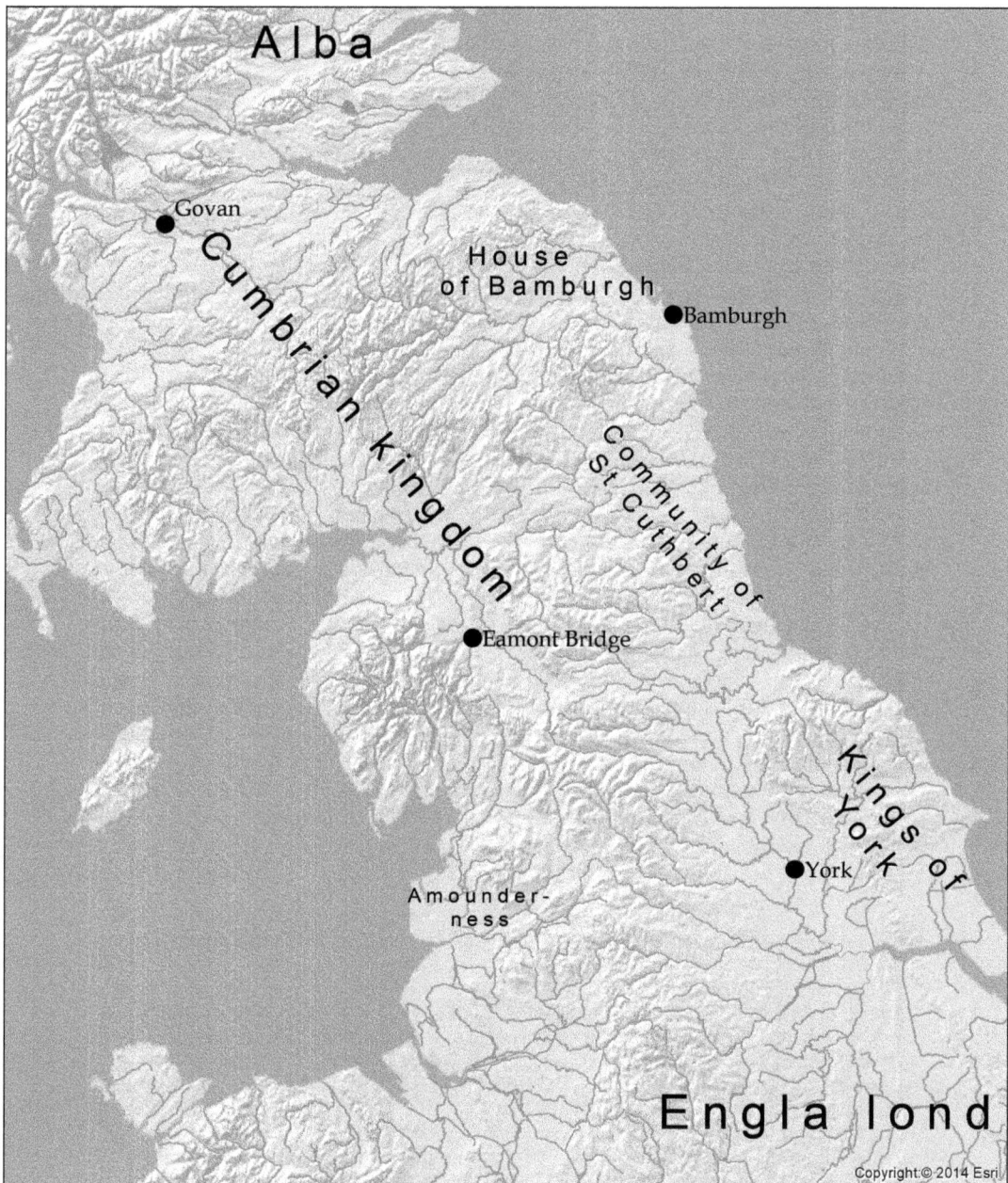

Map 2: The political geography of the royal meeting, 927

several later copies but its most recent editor, David Woodman, accepts its authenticity because it resembles products of the scribe 'Athelstan A'.[105] Strife resumed between Athelstan and the dynasty of Ívarr in 937. Óláfr son of Guðrøðr, ruler of Dublin, mounted a large campaign against Athelstan in alliance with Constantín of Alba and the Cumbrians. Athelstan achieved a crushing victory over this coalition at the battle of *Brunanburh*. The location of this battle has been a source of endless debate, a popular candidate being Bromborough on the Wirral.[106] I am more inclined to place the battle on the western than the eastern coast because Óláfr had sailed there from Dublin.[107] It would have been a dangerous and lengthy business to circumnavigate Britain, a symbolic gesture rather than a hard-headed calculation prior to a battle. After his defeat, Óláfr gathered his straggling survivors on to their ships and sailed away from *Dingesmere*, a name that may refer to the *þing* assembly site of Thingwall on the Wirral.[108] The epic battle is a suitable place to pause and consider the extent of Gaelic influence in the Northumbrian kingdom. The Scandinavian kings of Dublin were increasingly immersed in Irish politics, and their supporters will have included some who were bilingual in Gaelic and Norse. Meanwhile, Constantín of Alba brought armies of Gaelic-speakers into the Northumbrian kingdom on defensive manoeuvres; such campaigns would evolve into the Scottish raids of the eleventh century. These kings met stiff opposition from Athelstan in seeking the spoils of Northumbria's fragmentation.

Athelstan's success at *Brunanburh* was reversed upon his death in 939, when Óláfr Guðrøðsson took power in York. He left Dublin in the hands of his brother, Blákári, thus keeping the two cities in the control of one dynasty. Kevin Halloran has recently suggested that Óláfr Guðrøðsson's reign is illusory, a result of confusion with his younger contemporary, Óláfr Sigtryggsson. Yet the northern chronicle record indicates that Óláfr Sigtryggsson outlived another King Óláfr, and the shift in York's coin insignia from the raven to the triquetra/standard is suggestive of a change in rulership.[109] Óláfr Guðrøðsson died in 941 after sacking the church of St Balthere at Tyninghame on the Forth; the Viking-Age grave at the nearby church of Auldhame may belong to a high-ranking person who died in the expedition.[110] This campaign illustrates the enduring importance of the Forth–Clyde route, and also its vulnerability. Use of the route entailed co-operative relations with the house of Bamburgh and the kings of Alba.

---

[105] Sawyer, *Anglo-Saxon Charters*, no. 407; *Charters of Northern Houses* (ed. and transl. Woodman, 86–97).

[106] The Old English Brunanburh poem provides the earliest detailed account: ASC A (ed. Bately, 70–2); ASC B (ed. Taylor, 51–3); ASC C (ed. O'Keeffe, 77–9); ASC D (ed. Cubbin, 42–3). A comprehensive review of the sources is found in Livingstone, *The Battle*, 28–153. For Bromborough, see Dodgson, 'The background', 303–4, 314–15.

[107] Another proposed western location is Burnswark near the Solway: Halloran, 'The Brunanburh campaign', 144–7.

[108] For this interpretation of *Dingesmere,* see Cavill *et al.*, 'Revisiting *Dingesmere*', 29–36. The theory that Óláfr sailed around to the Humber derives from John of Worcester, *Chronicon* (ed. and transl. Darlington and McGurk, II, 392–3). Suggested battle locations that could be accessed from the Humber include the River Went, Yorkshire (Wood, 'Searching for Brunanburh', 155–8) and Lanchester (Breeze, 'Brunanburh located').

[109] ASC D [941, 944] (ed. Cubbin, 43–4); ASC E 942, 944 (ed. Irvine, 55); *HR* (ed. Arnold, II, 94); Blackburn, 'Currency under the Vikings II', 217; *contra* Halloran, 'Anlaf Guthfrithson'.

[110] *HR* (ed. and transl. Arnold, II, 94). The text's chronology is defective, but this event appears in a correctly dated entry. For the grave, see Woolf, 'A historian's view', 170.

The rulership of York between 939 and 954 is difficult to pin down because the chronicles provide inconsistent accounts, but Clare Downham has clarified the sequence of rulers.[111] The dynasty of Ívarr and the English kings vied constantly for control of York, and the Northumbrian council (especially the archbishop) had a role in selecting rulers. The matter was complicated by factionalism within Dublin, including competition between the descendants of Guðrøðr and Sigtryggr during the 940s. Dublin was under pressure from the surrounding kingdoms, notably northern Uí Néill, but there was also considerable interaction between the Dubliners and their neighbours.[112] The career of Óláfr Sigtryggsson (also known as Óláfr Cúarán) reveals the extent to which Scandinavians in Ireland had become gaelicised and Christian. He was married to Dúnlaith, daughter of Muirchertach mac Néill of northern Uí Néill, and then to Gormlaith of Leinster. The Irish poet Cináed ua hArtacáin composed a stanza in his honour, which appears at the end of some versions of 'Achall ar aicce Temair', a poem on the hill of Skreen (Co. Meath). Cináed originated in Brega and worked for Óláf's sometime ally, Congalach mac Maíle Mithig of Brega.[113] The gaelicisation of the Scandinavian leaders and warriors of Dublin will have promoted Gaelic influence in northern England, not least because the turbulent political situation entailed frequent movement between York and Dublin.

Óláfr's influence was once again curtailed by an English king. Óláfr lost the English Midland towns (the 'Five Boroughs') to Edmund, in 942. Edmund sponsored Óláfr's baptism in 943, as well as that of a rival, Rǫgnvaldr Guðrøðsson, and expelled both men a year later.[114] Edmund consolidated his power in the west by granting the Cumbrian kingdom to Máel Coluim of Alba on the basis that he would become a *midwyrhta* 'co-operator' on land and sea. This can only have been a temporary arrangement for the Cumbrians were operating independently again in 973.[115] Óláfr returned to Dublin in 945, and conducted ill-fated campaigns with Congalach, after which his old rival Blákári Guðrøðsson seized Dublin.[116] Meanwhile Edmund was assassinated and a new Scandinavian ruler, Eiríkr, took control of York. Saga writers, working several centuries later, identified him with the Norwegian Eiríkr blóðøx. The near-contemporary poem *Arinbjarnarkviða* lends some weight to this identification when it states that Eiríkr's York-based retinue included a Norwegian supporter.[117] Clare Downham has proposed an alternative identification, namely, that Eiríkr belonged to the dynasty of Ívarr and was a rival to Óláfr. The dynasty was

---

[111] Downham, 'The chronology', esp. 49.

[112] Woolf, 'Amlaíb Cuarán', 35, 39–42; Downham, *Viking Kings*, 43–8, 111–12.

[113] For the marriages of Dúnflaith and Gormflaith, see *Ban-shenchus* (ed. and transl. Dobbs, 314, 337–8); see CGH 117 c 47 (ed. O'Brien, 13) for Gormflaith's three leaps into marriage. The poem is in *The metrical dindshenchas* (ed. and transl. Gwynn), 1.46–53. Óláfr became a patron of a Columban church at Skreen; see below, 151.

[114] ASC D [942] (ed. Cubbin, 43); *HR* (ed. Arnold, II, 94). The latter wrongly dates the contest over the Five Boroughs to 940, as shown by Downham, 'The chronology', 34–8. Woolf, 'Amlaíb Cuarán', 37, notes that Edmund encouraged rivalry between Rǫgnvaldr and Óláfr.

[115] ASC A (ed. Bately, 74); ASC B (ed. Taylor, 53); ASC C (ed. O'Keeffe, 80); ASC D 945 (ed. Cubbin, 44); ASC E 945 (ed. Irvine, 55); recorded as a wasting of *Strat Clut* in AC A (ed. and transl. Dumville, 16–17); see Clarkson, *Strathclyde*, 111; Edmonds, 'The emergence', 61 for the temporary nature of the arrangement.

[116] AU 945.2, 7 (ed. and transl. Mac Airt and Mac Niocaill, 392–3); CS [944] (ed. and transl. Hennessy, 206–7); AClon *s.a.* 937 (ed. Murphy, 154); AFM [943] (ed. and transl. O'Donovan, II, 654–5).

[117] *Arinbjarnarkviða* (ed. Bjarni Einarsson, *Egils Saga*, 155–62; transl. Fell, 198–200; Townend, *Viking Age Yorkshire*, 74–8. Williams, *Eirik Bloodaxe*, 80–103 also supports this identification.

indeed suffering from factionalism at this point, and this identification would make sense of the revival of Sigtryggr's sword design for the second phase of Eiríkr's coinage.[118] Yet as far as we know, 'Eiríkr' was not one of the dynasty's favoured names, and no such individual is known to have been active in Ireland.[119]

What is not in doubt is the determination of Edmund's successor, Eadred, to expel Eiríkr. Eadred also took oaths from the men of Alba, who had an interest in the fate of Northumbria.[120] Yet the Northumbrians continued to invite in Scandinavian kings, alternating between Óláfr and Eiríkr and eventually settling on the latter. Archbishop Wulfstan of York was a prime mover in this diplomatic balancing act, and his attendance at the English court enabled him to act as a vital link between the two worlds.[121] The changes between rulers offered an opportunity for kings of Alba to raid northern Northumbria in 949 and 952. On the second occasion the army of Alba joined with the Cumbrians and the house of Bamburgh to attack the *Gaill* 'Foreigners', presumably Eiríkr's force.[122] This may explain why the near-contemporary Norse praise poem *Höfuðlausn* honours Eiríkr with the kenning *fárbjóðr Skota* 'destroyer of Scots', a reference to the inhabitants of Alba.[123] Whoever Eiríkr was, and however many reigns he enjoyed, his struggles underline the continued importance of the Gaelic kingdom to the north of the Forth.

These final manoeuvres of the kings of York and Dublin underline the pattern of Gaelic influence from two directions: beyond the Forth and across the Irish Sea. The political machinations of the 930s–50s are dizzying in their complexity, and yet it is clear that the Northumbrian council (based in York) frequently invited in kings from Dublin rather than accept the rule of southern English kings. The York–Dublin rulers were, however, weakened by internal factionalism as well as external pressure from Wessex. Meanwhile, the most northerly areas of the former kingdom were in the hands of the semi-autonomous house of Bamburgh. Their lands increasingly became the target of ambitious kings of Alba, by now a dynasty with a strongly Gaelic identity, who created the incipient Scottish kingdom.

Gaeldom and the Orbis Britanniae

The expulsion of Eiríkr from York in 954 marked the demise of the independent kingdom of York. It also spelled the end of the York–Dublin axis, a key moment in Gaelic–Northumbrian relations. Yet the circumstances of Eiríkr's death hint at the lingering importance of the Irish Sea region in Northumbrian politics. Those connections remained especially important on the coast and peninsulas of the west of the Northumbrian kingdom, which lay beyond the grasp of the English kings.

---

[118] Downham, 'Eric Bloodaxe'; *eadem, Viking Kings*, 115–20. For the coins, see Naismith, *Medieval European Coinage VIII*, 300–1.

[119] Townend, *Viking Age Yorkshire*, 76.

[120] ASC A (ed. Bately, 74); ASC B (ed. Taylor, 53); ASC C (ed. O'Keeffe, 80); ASC D 946 (ed. Cubbin, 44); ASC E 948 [946] (ed. Irvine, 55).

[121] He witnessed charters at the English court in 949, apparently during the reign of Óláfr Cúarán: Sawyer, *Anglo-Saxon Charters*, nos 544, 546, 549, 550, 552. Cf. Keynes, 'Wulfstan', 493; Downham, *Viking Kings*, 114–15.

[122] CKA (ed. and transl. Hudson, 150–1, 158) (seventh year of Máel Coluim's reign); AU 952.2 (ed. and transl. Mac Airt and Mac Niocaill, 396–7); Clarkson, *Strathclyde*, 113–16.

[123] *Höfuðlausn* (ed. Bjarni Einarsson, *Egils Saga*, 106–12; transl. Fell, 190–2). On the meaning of *Skotar*, see below 167–8.

Eiríkr was heading westwards across the pass of Stainmore when he was killed, probably en route to the Solway Firth and Ireland. The information about his death derives from Roger of Wendover, who was drawing on an earlier northern text. The murderer was Maccus son of Onlaf (Óláfr) whose name is characteristic of the Gaelic–Scandinavian world; he may have been a son of Óláfr Sigtryggsson, who no doubt harboured ambitions in York.[124] Other York notables moved towards the Isle of Man, again highlighting links to the Gaelic–Scandinavian world. These exiles deposited numerous hoards on the Island, which include a high proportion of coins minted in York.[125] A recently discovered hoard from the Furness peninsula (Cumbria) has similar features to the Manx hoards, such as cut fractions and bullion. The coins were minted mainly in the 940s and 950s, predominantly during the reign of Eadred (946–55), with the hoard being buried *ca* 955–7.[126] Thus the York exiles stayed, at least temporarily, in the west of the Northumbrian kingdom, which was not incorporated into the English Kingdom in 954.

In contrast, York was drawn into the administrative reforms that played a key role in the unification of England. One example is the coin reform instigated by Edgar in the early 970s, which imposed uniformity of production on York and all other English mints.[127] The inhabitants of York were still described as *Dene* 'Danes' in recognition of their cultural and legal distinctiveness, yet they were subject to English royal law codes.[128] Some of the greatest magnates were invited to Edgar's court, where they occasionally attested charters. In 963, three notable northerners, two described as *duces* 'ealdormen', witnessed Edgar's grant of five hides at Ballindon (Derbyshire) to a certain Æthelferth. The three were *Gunner dux* (recipient in that year of an estate at North Newbald in Yorkshire), *Myrdah dux* and an *Oslac dominus*, the future Ealdorman Oslac.[129] Myrdah is only attested on one other occasion, in 958, when he witnessed a royal diploma conveying land at Sutton (Nottinghamshire) to the see of York. His Gaelic name 'Muiredach' may indicate that he was based near the Irish Sea; if so, this is a sign that English kings were casting their eyes to the west of the Pennines.[130] On the other hand, this area does not seem to have been included in the ealdormanry based in York, to which Oslac was appointed in the mid-960s.[131] Oslac's appointment sidelined Thored son of Gunnar, who made a show of force by ravaging *westmoringa land* 'the land of the people west of the moors'

[124] *Flores Historiarum* (ed. Coxe, I, 401); cf. the historical sketch of the Northumbrian earls in *HR* (ed. Arnold, II, 197).

[125] Bornholdt Collins, 'Viking-Age coin finds', I, 74, 269–70, 334–7, 275–99; cf. Downham, *Viking Kings*, 122, 182–97.

[126] Boughton *et al.*, 'Buried wealth', 29–31; PAS LANCUM-80A302; Edmonds, 'The Furness peninsula', 30.

[127] Molyneaux, *The Formation*, 116–41; Naismith, *Medieval European Coinage VIII*, 260–1.

[128] Innes, 'Danelaw identities', 72–7; Hadley, 'Viking and native', 46–53.

[129] Brooks *et al.* (eds), 'A new charter', 141, 144–5. For Gunnar, see Sawyer, *Anglo-Saxon Charters*, no. 716 (the grant); nos 674 and 712 (witnessing).

[130] Sawyer, *Anglo-Saxon Charters*, no. 679; *Charters of Northern Houses* (ed. and transl. Woodman, 110–18). For Muiredach's base, see Brooks *et al.*, 'A new charter', 144; Bolton, *The Empire*, 113.

[131] McGuigan, 'Bamburgh', 123–4 dates Oslac's appointment to 963 rather than the usual 966.

(Westmorland).[132] Oslac's appointment replaced an earlier, looser arrangement in which York fell under the purview of the house of Bamburgh.[133]

English kings sought to influence other rulers in Britain, including their Gaelic-speaking neighbours. One aim was to curtail their co-operation with Northumbrians, and so to reduce the risk of regional separatism.[134] In 973 Edgar held a royal meeting at Chester, which was recorded in English texts and the southern Welsh continuation of *Annales Cambriae*. The Insular rulers promised to be his *efenwyrhtan ... on sœ and on lande* 'allies on sea and on land', which suggests that the meeting was something of a peace summit.[135] Twelfth-century writers amplified the impression of English dominance at Chester by adding a colourful vignette of the kings rowing Edgar on the River Dee. Taken together, the pre- and post-conquest texts mention up to eight kings, including Cináed mac Maíl Choluim, king of Alba, the Cumbrian Máel Coluim, Maccus of the Isles, and several Welsh rulers.[136] Cináed was a particularly dangerous neighbour, who was starting to encroach on lands to his south. A chronicle written during his reign reports that he led a three-pronged expedition to Stainmore, *Cluia* (which I identify with Clougha Pike near Lancaster) and Derwentwater in the Lake District. The raid touched the edges of the Northumbrian earldom (defined as *Saxonia*) and threatened Edgar's control.[137]

The accounts of the Chester meeting reveal significant shifts in Insular politics, including the emergence of a new sea-kingdom. Maccus was described as *plurimarum rex insularum* 'king of many islands' in reports of the meeting. He was the brother of Gofraid mac Arailt (Guðrøðr Haraldsson), who was accorded the title *rí Innse Gall* 'king of the Hebrides' in his obituary.[138] The brothers had a base on the Isle of Man and they extracted tribute from Anglesey at a time when it was vulnerable, its overlord Maredudd ab Owain being based in southern Wales.[139] Maccus's name is suggestive of a Gaelic–Scandinavian background, and the brothers may have had links to the dynasty of Ívarr; indeed, a Hebridean contingent assisted Óláfr Cúarán at the battle of Tara in 980.[140] Their sea-kingdom was another conduit of Gaelic influence to the fringes of the former Northumbrian kingdom, not least given their proximity to the Furness peninsula, which was sometimes defined as an island.[141]

---

[132] IV Edgar 2.1–2.2, 12, 13.1–14 (ed. Liebermann, *Die Gesetze*, I, 206–14). ASC D 966 (ed. Cubbin, 46); ASC E 966 (ed. Irvine, 58); for the raid as a result of internecine struggles in Yorkshire, see Stenton, 'Pre-conquest Westmorland', 218–19. For Westmorland's distance from the king, see Molyneaux, *The Formation*, 178; McGuigan, 'Bamburgh', 119.

[133] McGuigan, 'Bamburgh', 123–4, cf. *HR* (ed. Arnold, II, 197); *De primo Saxonum adventu* (ed. Arnold, II, 382).

[134] Molyneaux, *The Formation*, 45–7.

[135] ASC D 973 (ed. Cubbin, 46); ASC E (ed. Irvine); Ælfric of Winchester, *Vita S. Swithvni* (ed. Lapidge, *The Cult*, 606–7); AC C [973] (ed. Williams (ab Ithel), 19; ed. Gough-Cooper [c297.1]); Byrhtferth of Ramsey, *Vita S. Oswaldi* III.10 (ed. Lapidge, *Byrhtferth*, 74–5); for the nature of the meeting, see Barrow, 'Chester's earliest regatta', 84–90; Thornton, 'Edgar', 77–9.

[136] John of Worcester, *Chronicon* (ed. Darlington and McGurk, II, 422–4); William of Malmesbury, *Gesta regum* (ed. Mynors *et al.*, I, 238–40).

[137] CKA (ed. and transl. Hudson, 151, 161).

[138] AU 989.4 (ed. and transl. Mac Airt and Mac Niocaill, 418–21); AT 989 (ed. and transl. Stokes); CS 987 (ed. and transl. Hennessy, 230–1); AFM 988 [=989] (ed. O'Donovan, II, 726–7); AClon s.a. 982 (ed. Murphy, 160). Gofraid may be the *Giferth* who attended the Chester meeting: Thornton, 'Edgar', 73.

[139] AC B and C 987, 989 (ed. Williams (ab Ithel), 20–1).

[140] Downham, *Viking Kings*, 186–90; *contra* Hudson, *Viking Pirates*, 68–70.

[141] Woolf, *From Pictland to Alba*, 246; Edmonds, 'The Furness peninsula', 31.

By contrast, Irish rulers are conspicuously absent from early accounts of the Chester meeting. The *Altitonantis* charter asserts that Edgar dominated Dublin, but it is a twelfth-century forgery despite its date of 964.[142] The continued power of Óláfr Cúarán should not be underrated, and he may never have relinquished his claim to York. Óláfr's long reign finally ended at the battle of Tara, 980, in which Máel Sechnaill of the southern Uí Néill beat back the Dubliners. The aged king retired to Iona and died in 981.[143]

Towards the end of the tenth century there was an upsurge in Danish activity on the Irish Sea, which augmented Gaelic–Scandinavian influence in the former Northumbrian kingdom. A new northern fleet attacked Cheshire in 980, undermining the mint at Chester, and Gofraid mac Arailt fought a battle on the Isle of Man in 987 in alliance with *Danair*.[144] The Danish king Sveinn Haraldsson also raided the Isle of Man in 995 following his departure from south-eastern England with a hefty amount of tribute.[145] The English king Æthelred II launched an expedition to the Cumbrian kingdom and the Isle of Man in 1000, perhaps seeking to curtail further co-operation with Sveinn.[146] However, Sveinn's attention shifted to the east of the English kingdom, where he extracted tribute from Æthelred, a practice that eventually escalated into a bid for English kingship.

Meanwhile eastern Northumbria was becoming ever more integrated into England, although Æthelred's priorities lay elsewhere.[147] The fragmentation of the Northumbrian kingdom created opportunities to the south of the Forth for the kings of Alba, opening up a new channel of Gaelic influence. Their main opponents were the house of Bamburgh, who were by now firmly aligned with the English kings; indeed, the renowned warlord Uhtred of Bamburgh had married Æthelred's daughter. Uhtred famously preserved Durham from a severe Scottish raid in 1006.[148] This was reported as *bellum etir fhiru Alban 7 Saxanu* by the Irish chronicler at Armagh, who drew some of his material from Alba.[149] Taking stock at the start of the eleventh century,

---

[142] Sawyer, *Anglo-Saxon Charters*, no. 731. John, *Orbis Britanniae*, 240–1 argued that it was a much-embellished original charter.

[143] AU 980.1 (ed. and transl. Mac Airt and Mac Niocaill, 414–15; CS 978 [=980] (ed. and transl. Hennessy, 22–7); AT 980 (ed. and transl. Stokes, II, 233–4); AI 980 (ed. and transl. Mac Airt, 162–3); AFM 978 [=980] (ed. and transl. O'Donovan, II, 708–9); *The Book of Leinster* (ed. Best *et al.*, I, 98).

[144] AU 987.1 (ed. and transl. Mac Airt and Mac Niocaill, 420–1); ASC C 980 (ed. O'Keeffe, 84–5) *fram norð scipherige*; Dolley and Pirie, 'Repercussions'. Etchingham, 'North Wales', 177–8, argues that *Danair* were Danes rather than Orkneymen, as tentatively suggested by Crawford, *Scandinavian Scotland*, 66. Crawford points out that hoarding was taking place in the Hebrides and Man, which might be consistent with Orcadian tribute-taking: *The Northern Earldoms*, 120–5. The later saga account of such tribute-taking is in *Njáls saga* 86 (ed. Einar Ól. Sveinsson, 208; transl. Bayerschmidt and Hollander, 166).

[145] AC B and C (ed. Williams (ab Ithel), 21); Etchingham, 'North Wales', 177.

[146] ASC C [1000] (ed. O'Keeffe, 88); ASC D [1000] (ed. Cubbin, 50); ASC E (ed. Irvine, 63); Downham, *Viking Kings*, 167–70; Edmonds, 'The expansion', 64–5.

[147] Wulfstan II, archbishop of York, was one of Æthelred's leading statesmen: Keynes, 'Æthelred II'.

[148] This raid became conflated with a later siege (1039/40) in the tract *De obsessione Dunelmi*, which was completed in the twelfth century (ed. Arnold, *Symeonis monachi opera omnia*, I, 215–20; transl. Morris, *Marriage and Murder*, 1–5). The later siege, but not that of 1006, appears in *Libellus de exordio* III.9 (ed. and transl. Rollason, 168–9).

[149] AU 1006.5 (ed. and transl. Mac Airt and Mac Niocaill, 436–7) 'a battle between the men of Alba and the Saxons'. Meehan, 'The siege of Durham', 16–17 placed this battle in the west of Northumbria, but I prefer to identify it with the siege of Durham, as did Smyth, *Warlords*, 236.

the earls of Bamburgh looked to the English south rather than the Gaelic north for support, while the west of the Northumbrian kingdom remained open to influence from the Gaelic–Scandinavian world.

The year 1014 witnessed the famed battle at Clontarf (Co. Dublin), which had seismic effects on Insular politics. The background to the battle was the rise of Dál Cais on the margins of the *cóiced* 'fifth, province' of Munster.[150] Brían Bórama, the most famous son of Dál Cais, enhanced his power still further by taking hostages and armies from other provincial kings, eventually gaining the upper hand over the southern Uí Néill ruler, Máel Sechnaill.[151] In 1006 Brían underlined his unprecedented success by performing a circuit of Ireland, stopping at Armagh on the way, where he had been declared *imperator Scottorum* 'emperor of the Scotti'.[152] Brían's patronage of Armagh reveals how he co-opted Uí Néill heritage to support his dominance in the northern half of Ireland. In the process, power shifted away from dynasties that had dominated Gaelic–Northumbrian relations during the Golden Age. Earlier maritime history came to be reinterpreted thus, *Míniugud senchasa fer nAlban* was reconfigured in the last decade of the tenth century, at a time when Brían may have sought overlordship in the island portion of Dál Riata. The Isles were of interest to him on account of their close relationship with Dublin, which was now in his grasp.[153] Sigtryggr of Dublin (son of Óláfr Cúarán) exploited these Insular Viking links when he joined with his Leinster neighbours to foment the rebellion that eventually led to the battle of Clontarf. It is worth considering whether the Scandinavians of Northumbria were among these allies.

The most detailed account of the battle appears in *Cogad Gáedel re Gallaib*, which was written for Brían's illustrious descendant, Muirchertach Ua Briain (*ob.* 1119).[154] The text includes several references to Viking York and the Northumbrians; it is necessary to weigh up whether they reflect twelfth-century embellishments or details transmitted through earlier sources. The *Cogad* reports that the Scandinavian forces included Brodar (Bróðir) and Amlaíb (Óláfr) *mac ríg Lochlann*, two earls of *Cair*, and *Saxain tuaiscirt* 'Saxons of the north'.[155] Amlaíb appears to be an anachronistic echo of the Amlaíb who was active in the 850s–70s. Even so, an Amlaím mac Laghmaind appears in the account of Clontarf in the Annals of Ulster alongside *Brotor toisech na loingsi Lochlannaighi* 'Brodar, commander of the Lochlannic fleet', the man who slew Brían. The annalistic account was itself embroidered, but at its core lay the work of a contemporary Armagh chronicler. It is unclear where Brodar originated because the resonances of the term *Lochlann* evolved from the vague (a term for somewhere distant and Scandinavian) to the precise (a name for

---

[150] Ní Mhaonaigh, *Brian Boru*, 21–8; Duffy, *Brian Boru*, 85–91.
[151] Ní Mhaonaigh, *Brian Boru*, 40–55; Duffy, *Brian Boru*, 106–35.
[152] AU 1006.4 (ed. and transl. Mac Airt and Mac Niocaill, 436–7); AI 1006.2 (ed. and transl. Mac Airt, 178–9).
[153] Wadden, 'Dál Riata *c.* 1000', 174–6. For Brían and the Isles, cf. Etchingham, 'North Wales', 180.
[154] Ní Mhaonaigh, 'The date'. On balance I remain persuaded by this view, rather than the argument that it was produced for Donnchad mac Briain or his descendants, whether in the late eleventh or twelfth century (Duffy, *Brian Boru*, 198, 242; Casey, 'A reconsideration'). The scope of Brían's Insular ambition, as portrayed in the text, seems suited to Muirchertach's reign.
[155] *Cogadh Gaedhel re Gallaibh* §§87, 94 (ed. and transl. Todd, 150–1, 164–5).

Norway).[156] *Njáls saga* locates Bróðir off the coast of the Isle of Man, and depicts him as an apostate and a sorcerer. This colourful character sketch came through the hands of a thirteenth-century Icelandic author, who drew on a lost *Brjáns saga* (or a number of sources relating to the battle), perhaps including material composed in Dublin.[157] The *Cogad*, by contrast, links Brodar's base at *Cair* with the Saxons of the North and elsewhere the author uses the term *Cair Ebroc* (York).[158] This association is amplified by another embellished account of the battle in the sixteenth-century 'Annals of Loch Cé', which mentions warriors from *Caer Ebroc* and lists Brodar as the *jarl* of the city. Even if the author of the *Cogad* was wrong to identify Bróðir as an earl of York, it is credible that Sigtryggr enlisted warriors in that city because his father Óláfr Cúarán had once ruled there.[159] The *Cogad* contains another reference to Saxons that arguably relates to the political circumstances of 1014. Brían is said to have levied a tribute from the Saxons and the Britons, Argyll and the Lennox. These areas lay on the west coast and they may have been prey to Brían once he began to show an interest in the Irish Sea.[160] In short, the *Cogad* hints that parts of Northumbria retained Gaelic–Scandinavian links in the early eleventh century. When Brían sought to exert influence over Scandinavian communities in Ireland, those of northern England fell within his line of vision.

Shortly after the battle of Clontarf, a major change occurred in English politics, which had knock-on effects for relations between Northumbrian territory and the Gaelic–Scandinavian world. The deaths of Æthelred and his son, Edmund, gave Sveinn's son, Knútr, free rein in the kingship of England. Knútr showed increasing interest in the Irish Sea, capitalising on a power vacuum after the death of Brían Bórama. These ambitions are reflected in one of Óttarr svarti's verses for Knútr, which opens with a greeting to the Danes, English, Irish and Islanders.[161] By now Dublin had its own coinage, and whereas its moneyers had once copied Æthelred's pennies, they now copied those of Knútr. The transfer of dies need not imply a political relationship, but it is indicative of trade and cultural contacts. It is interesting that two York moneyers borrowed obverse dies from Dublin for the 'Long Cross' issue, as did another for the 'Helmet' issue.[162] This numismatic evidence complements certain unusual Gaelic personal names in Yorkshire, which indicate that members of the Northumbrian nobility were still connected with the descendants of Óláfr Cúarán.[163]

---

[156] In respect of this entry Ó Corráin favours a Scottish/Manx location ('The Vikings', 206–10). Etchingham demonstrates the Norwegian connotation from the 1050s onwards ('North Wales', 152–4). He distinguishes *Lochlann* from *Laithlinn*, which he argues had Norwegian connotations in the ninth century ('*Laithlinn*', 82–4).

[157] *Brennu-Njáls saga* ch. 155 (ed. Einar Ól. Sveinsson, 445; transl. Bayerschmidt and Hollander, 353); Hudson, 'Brjáns saga'; balanced by Ní Mhaonaigh, *Brian Boru*, 79–80, who outlines the possibility of several sources. The identification of Bróðir as an Islesman may perhaps be supported by the reference to his half-brother Conmáel in *Cogadh Gaedhel re Gallaibh* §94 (ed. and transl. Todd, 164–5), who was in the Isles contingent at the battle of Tara: AU 980.1 (ed. and transl. Mac Airt and Mac Niocaill, 414–15). Cf. Duffy, *Brian Boru*, 184.

[158] This is another borrowing of a Brittonic version of an English place-name: cf. *Cair Ebrauc*: HB 66a (ed. Mommsen, 210; ed. and transl. Morris, 40, 80).

[159] ALC (ed. and transl. Hennessy, 4–5); Duffy, *Brian Boru*, 192–4.

[160] *Cogadh Gaedhel re Gallaibh* §78 (ed. and transl. Todd, 136–7); Duffy, *Brian Boru*, 148–9; Downham, 'Scottish affairs', 93–4; Wadden, 'Dál Riata', 175.

[161] Óttarr svarti, *Lausavísur*, stanza 2 (ed. Fulk, 783); Hudson, 'Cnut', 47–8.

[162] Blackburn, 'Hiberno-Norse and Irish Sea imitations', 5.

[163] See below, 182–3.

Thus the deeply rooted connections between York and Dublin were absorbed into high-level political interchange between English and Irish kings.

The long-standing political links and tensions between Dublin and the Isle of Man were pertinent to Knútr's ambitions in the Irish Sea. The Island came under the rule of the king of Dublin, Echmarcach mac Ragnaill, in the 1020s, which may explain the transfer of a set of Dublin coin dies to Man.[164] Echmarcach most likely came from the leading dynasty of Waterford, which was engaged in a feud with the descendants of Óláfr Cúarán; this became a proxy war between their Munster and Leinster backers. Control of the city vacillated between Echmarcach and Óláfr's descendants until the son of the expansionist Leinster king Diarmait mac Maíl na mBó took power in 1052.[165] Echmarcach ended his life as king of the Rhinns of Galloway, showing that the western peninsulas of the former Northumbrian kingdom could be incorporated into Gaelic–Scandinavian sea-kingdoms.[166] In its early days Echmarcach's thalassocracy may have posed a threat to Knútr's aspirations to pan-Insular overlordship. Knútr underlined his dominance in a meeting with three kings in 1031: Mælcolm (Máel Coluim), Mælbæþe (Macbeth) and Iehmarc (Echmarcach). This group had a mutual interest in countering the Orkney earl Þórfinnr, who was threatening Knútr's interests in Norway as well as the western seaways.[167]

Turning to events on the eastern side of Britain, here Knútr's conquest of England also influenced the course of Gaelic–Northumbrian relations. Knútr took time to extract a submission from Uhtred of Bamburgh, but the two had a fractious relationship.[168] A major battle soon took place at Carham on the River Tweed, in which the Northumbrians were defeated by the Scottish king Máel Coluim II and his Cumbrian ally, Owain Foel. Several aspects of the battle are debatable, including the date and the leadership of the Northumbrian forces. I am persuaded by *Historia regum*, which places the battle in 1018 and identifies Uhtred as the Northumbrian leader.[169] The most likely scenario is that Uhtred's dispute with Knútr rendered him vulnerable to

---

[164] Dolley, *Some Irish Dimensions*; Bornholdt-Collins, 'Coinage'. Murchadh mac Diarmata sought tribute from a *mac Ragnaill* on Man in 1061: AT 1061.3 (ed. and transl. Stokes, II, 294); AFM *s.a.* 1060 (ed. and transl. O'Donovan, II, 878–90).

[165] Expulsion of Sigtryggr: AT 1036.8 (ed. and transl. Stokes, II, 268); Diarmait's family and Dublin: AU 1052.8 (ed. and transl. Mac Airt and Mac Niocaill, 488–9); AT 1052.2 (ed. and transl. Stokes, II, 284); AFM 1052. 8 (ed. and transl. O'Donovan, II, 860–1); cf. Duffy, 'Irishmen', 95–7.

[166] Marianus Scottus, *Chronicon s.a.* 1065 (ed. Waitz, 559) mentions the death of Echmarcach *rex Innarenn* on pilgrimage to Rome with Donnchad, son of Brían Bórama. Marianus was writing on the Continent but had knowledge of Insular politics thanks to his training at Movilla (Co. Down). Cf. AI 1064.5 for Donnchad's pilgrimage (ed. and transl. Mac Airt, 222–3); Duffy, 'Irishmen', 97–9.

[167] ASC E 1031 (ed. Irvine, 76); cf. ASC D (ed. Cubbin, 65). The skald Sigvatr Þórðarson also mentioned the meeting: *Lausavísur* no. 12 (ed. Fulk, 714); Hudson, 'Cnut', 60–1. For the threat of Þórfinnr, see Bolton, *Cnut's Empire*, 140–6; Crawford, *The Northern Earldoms*, 131–4.

[168] ASC C (ed. O'Keeffe, 100–3); ASC D (ed. Cubbin, 60–1); ASC E (ed. Irvine, 72–3). This section of the chronicle was written up in the 1020s. Uhtred witnessed no charters after 1015 (Sawyer, *Anglo-Saxon Charters*, no. 934); cf. 'Prosopography of Anglo-Saxon England' ('Uhtred 10').

[169] I explain my reasons in detail in 'Carham: the western perspective', 79–84. See *HR* (ed. Arnold, II, 155–6). This element of the text is drawn from the northern chronicling tradition represented by *The Chronicle of Melrose* 1018 (ed. Anderson and Anderson, 21). For the dating difficulties, see Stenton, *Anglo-Saxon England*, 418; Duncan, 'The battle of Carham'. The 1018 date is supported by a comet mentioned in Symeon of Durham, *Libellus de exordio* III.5 (ed. and transl. Rollason, 154–7); AU 1018.7 (ed. and transl. Mac Airt and Mac Niocaill, 454–5); cf. Woolf, *From Pictland to Alba*, 236.

attack from the north, leading to defeat at Carham and death shortly afterwards.[170] Historians have long debated the consequences of the battle for Anglo-Scottish relations, and in particular the fate of Lothian. Texts of the Anglo-Norman era offer two possible versions of events: either that King Edgar (*ob.* 975) gave Lothian to Cináed mac Maíl Choluim in return for his submission, or that Uhtred's successor Eadulf Cudel was forced to cede Lothian.[171] In my view, the battle opened the way for permanent dominance of Lothian by the kings of Alba (who by now might be termed the kings of Scots); the Firth of Forth is likely to have been a significant dividing line prior to that point.[172] Gaelic cultural influence would have increased in Lothian once Máel Coluim II had a firm grip on the region and made grants to Gaelic-speaking noblemen. Some Lothian nobles continued to bear Gaelic personal names down to the early twelfth century, such as the unusually named *Malbead* (Máel Bethad) de Liberton, who flourished during the reign of David I (*ob.* 1153).[173]

By the mid-eleventh century, political alignments were stabilising in the east. Everything was still to play for in the Irish Sea, and various Gaelic–Scandinavian groups circled the western parts of the former Northumbrian kingdom. It is often assumed that north-west England was incorporated into the English Kingdom after 954; the Furness hoard, however, points to close links with the Isle of Man and the dynasty of Ívarr. I have argued elsewhere that the peninsulas and river-valleys of the western coast were ruled by chieftains who might be incorporated into larger polities when the opportunity arose.[174] The earliest indication of English control in what is now North Lancashire and South Cumbria is a geld list incorporated into the Yorkshire Domesday, which names Earl Tostig as lord of a number of manors north of the River Ribble. The list must have been compiled before Tostig was expelled in 1065, and it certainly does not date from the year of the Domesday survey, 1086.[175] It may be that this area lacked the administrative structures to conduct a proper survey, which indicates that it had been incorporated into England relatively recently. Prior to this, the coastal localities were wide open to the Gaelic–Scandinavian world, which explains the presence of numerous Gaelic and Norse personal names in the geld list.[176]

A new group appeared in the Solway Firth in the mid-eleventh century: the Gall-Goídil 'foreigner Gaelic-speakers'. I am persuaded by Thomas Clancy's view that they originated in the Firth of Clyde in the tenth century, notwithstanding their

---

[170] Uhtred's death appears in the 1016 entry in ASC C (ed. O'Keeffe, 101); ASC D (ed. Cubbin, 61); ASC E (ed. Irvine, 74), but this is a retrospective strand in the chronicle, combining several events: McGuigan, 'The battle of Carham', 9–11.

[171] *De primo Saxonum adventu* (ed. Arnold, *Symeonis monachi opera omnia*, II, 382); *De obsessione Dunelmi* (ed. Arnold, I, 218; transl. Morris, *Marriage and Murder*, 3). The tenth-century cession is accepted by Whitelock, 'The dealings', 85; Stenton, *Anglo-Saxon England*, 370, but treated critically by Anderson, 'Lothian', 100–3. The twelfth-century context of these reports is explored by McGuigan, 'Neither Scotland nor England', 144–53.

[172] Woolf, *From Pictland to Alba*, 234–6, points out that Northumbrian diocesan organisation encompassed the area up to the Forth. See *HSC* 4 (ed. and transl. South, 46–7).

[173] *The Charters of David I* no. 71 (ed. and transl. Barrow, 87); Beam *et al.*, 'People of Medieval Scotland', *s.n.* Mael Bethad.

[174] Edmonds, 'The expansion', 65–6.

[175] DB Yorks 1L1, 3, 6; fol. 301v; Lewis, 'An introduction', 1–2, 8, 31–5. For Tostig's controversial earldom, see Kapelle, *The Norman Conquest*, 86–119.

[176] Edmonds, 'History and names', 11–12; see below, 183.

designation by the same name as an earlier group of Gall-Goídil in Ireland.[177] I am less convinced by the view that they originated throughout Dál Riata as a result of mixing between Gaelic speakers and Scandinavian settlers, a notion that rests partly on the uncertain equation of the historical Gall-Goídel Caittil Find with the saga character Ketill flatnefr.[178] The Gall-Goídil were Gaelic speakers who seemed in some way Scandinavian, and this cultural makeup marked them out from other peoples nearby.[179] They subsumed earlier enclaves of Scandinavian settlers in the coastal areas of south-west Scotland, including the Machars, the Dee estuary and the area near Tinwald (*Þingvöllr*, assembly place).[180] By the eleventh century, Gall-Goídil were expanding into the territory that would eventually bear their name, that is, Galloway. They were also developing a political identity: the Armagh-based 'Annals of Ulster' mention Suibne mac Cináeda *rí Gall-Gaidhel* in 1034.[181] Thus south-west Scotland was a dynamic cultural zone in which two Gaelic-speaking spheres, Dublin/Man and the Gall-Goídil, encountered Northumbrian society.

The demise of the Cumbrian kingdom, a virtually unrecorded process, offered further opportunities for movement around the Solway. This is indicated by the unusual document known as Gospatric's writ, a thirteenth-century version of a text in Old English. Gospatric opens the text by greeting his retainers and kindred *on eallun þam landann þeo weoron Combres* 'in all the lands that were Cumbrian'. He grants privileges to a certain Thorfynn in Allerdale (Cumberland, now Cumbria) and mentions the peace that he and Earl Siward had granted.[182] Gospatric may be identified with either Gospatric son of Uhtred of the house of Bamburgh (*ob.* 1064) or his relative Earl Gospatric (*ob. ca* 1073).[183] The text reveals the extraordinary cultural melting pot of the west coast, including English, Brittonic, Norse and Gaelic personal names, as well as two 'inversion compound' place-names, whose word order indicates Gaelic influence.[184] It seems that the Cumbrian kingdom was caught between the expansion of the Gall-Goídil, the Dubliners and Earl Siward; indeed, the 'Annals of Tigernach' record a ravaging of Britons by English and Dubliners in 1030.[185] By 1054 Cumbria was no longer an autonomous unit, and Máel Coluim, *regis Cumbrorum filius* 'son of the king of the Cumbrians' was set up as a puppet-king following Earl Siward's defeat of the powerful Scottish overlord Mac Bethad.[186]

---

[177] The crucial piece of evidence is a tenth-century reference to St Bláán's feast day, which locates Kingarth (Bute) in Gall-Goídil territory: MT 10 August (ed. Best and Lawlor, 62); Clancy, 'The Gall-Ghàidheil', 29–30.

[178] Jennings and Kruse, 'From Dál Riata to Gall-Ghàidheil'(note, though, 133 for Bute).

[179] Downham, 'The break-up', 197–205. Downham places their southward expansion earlier than Clancy.

[180] Fellows-Jensen, 'Scandinavians', 80–7.

[181] AU 1034.10 (ed. and transl. Mac Airt and Mac Niocaill, 472–3); AT 1034 (ed. and transl. Stokes, II, 266).

[182] *Gospatric's Writ* (ed. and transl. Woodman, *Charters of Northern Houses*, 370–1).

[183] For the son of Uhtred, see for example Kapelle, *The Norman Conquest*, 44, 249–50; for the earl, see Phythian-Adams, *Land of the Cumbrians*, 175. I surveyed the debate more fully in 'Personal names', 54–5.

[184] See below, 169–71.

[185] AT [1030] (ed. Stokes, II, 262); Broun, 'The Welsh identity', 136–7.

[186] John of Worcester, *Chronicon* (ed. Darlington and McGurk, II, 574–5); William of Malmesbury, *Gesta regum* (ed. and trans. Mynors *et al.*, I, 348–9). A. A. M. Duncan has shown that Máel Coluim was a Cumbrian, and not the future Scottish king Máel Coluim III: *The Kingship*, 37–41. On Mac Bethad's core power-base of Moray, see Woolf, *From Pictland to Alba*, 240–2, 252–63; Ross, *The Kings*, 64–127.

There was not yet, however, any certainty about the future of 'Middle Britain', and this provided opportunities for the Dubliners, the Scots and Gall-Goídil.

Taking an overview of the entire era, internal troubles wrought several shifts in Gaelic–Northumbrian political relations. In the eighth century, dynastic strife and the increasing power of the nobility prevented Northumbrian kings from taking a leading role on the Insular stage. The one exception, Eadberht, encountered a different set of alignments from the Golden Age: by now a Pictish, rather than Dál Riatan, king was the key player in northern Britain. In 867, the Scandinavian Great Army exploited Northumbria's internal tensions and catalysed its *de facto* fragmentation as well as laying the foundations of the York–Dublin axis. While York and its hinterland ultimately became part of the English realm, the northern and western edges of the former kingdom were open to intense competition from across the Irish Sea and the Firth of Forth. The nadir of Northumbrian fortunes was the high point of Gaelic influence.

4

PATHWAYS THROUGH THE PAST:
ROUTES BETWEEN THE GAELIC WORLD
AND THE NORTHUMBRIAN KINGDOM

There is a modern vogue for treading in the tracks of ancient travellers and recreating the voyages of early seafarers.[1] Cultural interaction takes place against an enduring geographical background: the strength of the tides, climatic shifts, and the paths of least resistance. So far I have elucidated the reasons why royalty, warbands, exiles and settlers moved between Gaeldom and the Northumbrian kingdom; these travellers would have encountered the intractable bogs of the Pennines and the unpredictable state of the Irish Sea. To support my case that there were varied channels of Gaelic influence on the Northumbrian kingdom, I need to show that travel was feasible in the early medieval period.

Early medieval route-ways can be faintly perceived through the fog of the fragmentary evidence. Chroniclers rarely commented on the practicalities of transport, and few administrative documents are available until the late-medieval period. Small finds and place-names help to pinpoint hubs in the transport network, while pollen diagrams from certain sites offer some insight into the effects of landscape and climate change. My strategy is to investigate Roman and late-medieval infrastructure, and to compare this information with a range of early medieval material. I then investigate each major route-way in turn, showing that a variety of links between the Northumbrian and the Gaelic world were usable, and used. In the future, it would be worthwhile to consider the choices made between these various route-ways by using GIS (Geographical Information Systems) mapping to understand visibility, the effort involved in traversing the landscape, and proximity to transport nodes.[2]

The *longue durée* perspective is well established in studies of pre-modern communication. Fernand Braudel's seminal work on the Mediterranean revealed how landscape and seascape gave rise to ingrained patterns of behaviour and modes of thinking.[3] Peregrine Horden and Nicholas Purcell have explored the Mediterranean over an extended period, and proposed two interpretations of communication: the 'interactionist' model, in which the sea provides a means of linking disparate peoples, and the 'ecologising' model, which emphasises their common environmental

---

[1] Macfarlane, *The Old Ways*. For voyages in reconstructed Viking ships, see Vikingeskibsmuseet (Roskilde), 'Viking ships sail again'; Draken Harald Hårfagre, 'Expedition America'. Havhingsten fra Glendalough (the Sea Stallion of Glendalough) sailed from Denmark to Ireland in 2007 and back again in 2008; see Bill, *Welcome on Board!*

[2] For pioneering work relating to the early medieval period, see Murrieta-Flores and Williams, 'Placing the Pillar of Eliseg', 77–90; Brookes and Huynh, 'Transport networks', 483–8.

[3] Braudel, *The Mediterranean and the Mediterranean World*, transl. Reynolds, I, 103–67; *idem, The Mediterranean in the Ancient World*, transl. Reynolds, xvi, 301.

circumstances.[4] The Irish Sea has long been compared with the Mediterranean in terms of cultural contact, and the concept of the 'Irish Sea province' has appeared in scholarship ranging from the Neolithic to the medieval period.[5] Two other maritime zones with evidence of long-term cultural contact, tempered by regional and chrono-logical diversity, are the Atlantic seaboard and the North Sea zone.[6] While maritime links could be durable, more immediate political and economic concerns deter-mined the attractiveness of an individual route-way at any given time. Indeed, Søren Sindbæk's analysis of Viking-Age trade networks has revealed how long-distance systems of exchange could become fragile and prone to collapse when one major hub failed.[7] If communication routes fluctuated in importance, this supports my over-arching argument that Gaelic influence reached the Northumbrian kingdom from several different directions.

Evidence for pre-modern transport

Two of the fastest modern routes between northern England and southern Scotland are the M6 motorway and the West Coast mainline. They run side by side through the Lune Gorge (Cumbria, formerly Westmorland), where a spectacularly narrow river valley winds around the base of the Howgill Fells. Here modern travellers follow a Roman road that was constructed along a similar line; ancient engineers made skilful use of valleys and passes in this upland terrain. Roman roads also marked out convenient approaches to coastal areas and ports through the wetlands. If the courses of Roman roads still bear traffic today, it is likely that they did so during the early medieval period.

There were three types of Roman road: major routes built by the state for military purposes; those constructed by regional government bodies such as *civitates*; and lesser roads for industry and smaller settlements.[8] The survival of roads in the first two categories would have enabled travellers to pass through the Northumbrian kingdom. Yet there remains some uncertainty about the extent of the network even in its heyday. Scholars assess the likelihood of a Roman date for a road by exam-ining its build and alignment, and investigating the relationship to forts. In recent years, LiDaR (Light Detection and Ranging) sensing has significantly amended the map of Roman roads, especially in north-west England.[9] One example of a road of uncertain date survives on the steep incline of Blackstone Edge, a trans-Pennine pass near Manchester. This substantial paved surface has been characterised as a Roman road, a packhorse way or an eighteenth-century turnpike. The groove in the middle is unique; it may have been a drainage channel or an indentation for cables to winch

---

[4] Horden and Purcell, *The Corrupting Sea*, 12–13.
[5] Pocock, 'The limits', 316; Moore (ed.), *The Irish Sea*, esp. Bowen, 'Britain', 13–28; Cummings (ed.), *A View*, 4. Halford Mackinder's concept of a 'British Mediterranean' (1902) is an early example, but was inseparable from his political views: Mackinder, *Britain*, 20; Sloan, *The Geopolitics*, 23, 35–6.
[6] Cunliffe, *Facing the Ocean*, 542, 554–7; Loveluck and Tys, 'Coastal societies'; Loveluck, *Northwest Europe*, 125, 196, 204.
[7] Sindbæk, 'The small world', 62, 65, 71.
[8] Jones and Mattingly, *An Atlas*, 165.
[9] Ratledge, 'Roman roads'.

Roman Roads shown in **bold,** other routes as dotted lines.

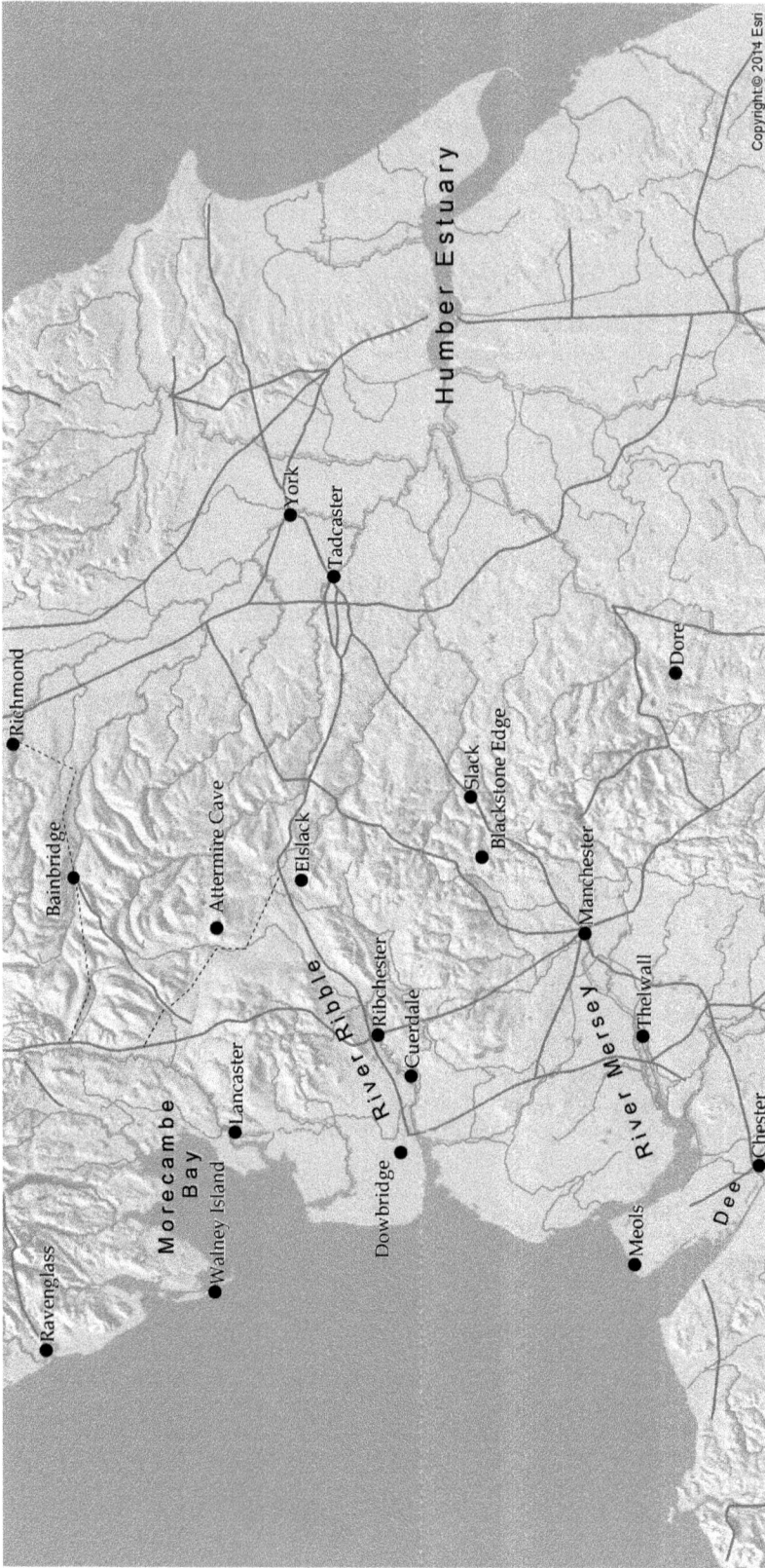

Map 3: Communication routes south of the Tyne-Solway gap

waggons up the steep incline.[10] A recent survey indicates that medieval features overlie the road cuttings, and so the paved surface cannot have been constructed as late as the eighteenth century. Moreover, at more than 4.9m/16ft from kerb to kerb the road does not resemble the narrower packhorse ways. The scale of the cuttings points to the resources and engineering skill usually associated with Roman roads.[11]

Similar uncertainties surround the ports used in the first millennium. At the Roman legionary fortress of Chester, a jetty was constructed to enable ships to dock in all tidal conditions. Grain and other supplies were shipped to Chester from the south, and they were then transported to the ports further north.[12] If similar Roman installations existed on Northumbria's west coast, they would have been decaying by the early medieval period. Nevertheless, the western coast had harbours with natural sheltered anchorages, which shallow-draught boats could have used without docking facilities.[13] Raymond Selkirk has argued that Roman engineers constructed a network of dams and pound-locks to facilitate navigation further upriver, enabling barges to access a fort as far inland as Brough via the River Eden.[14] Selkirk drew his evidence for these artificial improvements from aerial and ground surveys, which have not been substantiated by modern excavations.[15] In contrast, James Anderson's study of north-eastern England indicates that Roman supplies were brought up naturally navigable sections of rivers and then transferred to road-based transport. This system could have persisted in post-Roman times, with boats arriving into the estuaries around the Irish Sea and the Firth of Forth, and their passengers or cargo travelling overland to the Northumbrian heartlands.[16]

By comparing Roman infrastructure with the fragmentary early medieval evidence, it may be possible to pinpoint some of the routes that sustained traffic between Gaeldom and Northumbria. Reconstructions of Anglo-Saxon route-ways have tended to focus on the south and Midlands of England, where the boundary clauses in charters sometimes refer to trackways.[17] The law codes of late-seventh-century kings of Kent and Wessex reveal that roads were under the king's peace, and travellers were not supposed to stray from them lest they be considered thieves.[18] As to maintenance, the so-called *trinoda necessitas* (triple obligation) on Anglo-Saxon landowners included maintenance of bridges as well as repair of fortresses and military service.[19] There is no comparable Northumbrian legal or charter material, although Bede's *Historia ecclesiastica* and saints' Lives provide some oblique references to the logistics of travel.[20] According to Bede, King Edwin was so concerned with the good of the people that he had drinking bowls set up *iuxta*

[10] Margary, *Roman Roads*, 404 (no. 720a). For the lack of regard for wheeled traffic in some Roman infrastructure, see Poulter, *The Planning*, 14–15.
[11] Pollington, 'A new survey'; *contra* Poulter, *The Planning*, 65–6.
[12] Mason, *Roman Britain*, 118–19, 124–6, 174.
[13] Cleere, 'Roman harbours', 36–7. For some possible harbour structures at Maryport and Lancaster, see Jarrett, *Maryport*, 6–8; Wood, 'Roman Lancaster', 40.
[14] Selkirk, *The Piercebridge Formula*, 101.
[15] Lewis, 'Roman navigation', 119.
[16] Anderson, *Roman Military Supply*, 68–9.
[17] See for example Hooke, 'The reconstruction'; Pelteret, 'The roads'; Williamson, *Environment*, 89–94; Reynolds and Langlands, 'Travel *as* communication', 412.
[18] Wihtred 28; Ine 20 (ed. and transl. Attenborough, 30–1, 42–3); Cooper, 'The rise and fall', 46–9.
[19] Stevenson, 'Trinoda Necessitas', 689; Brooks, 'The development', 69–72.
[20] Rosenthal, 'Bede's Ecclesiastical History', 1–4, 13–14; Edmonds, 'The practicalities', 130. The locations of early medieval battles correspond closely to the Roman road system. See the map in Higham, *The Kingdom*, 122.

publicos transitus viarum 'near the public passages of roads'. He quotes a prover-
bial saying that a woman with a new-born child could walk from sea to sea without
harm.[21] The earliest extant, relatively realistic depiction of the Insular world is the
eleventh-century Cotton *Mappa Mundi*, which was probably compiled at Canterbury
on a Roman model. It depicts the coast more fully than inland areas, and strikingly
reveals the continued significance of Hadrian's Wall and the Solway Firth.[22] Place-
names supplement the meagre textual haul: Stratton and Stretton, for example, designate settlements that supplied services to travellers (OE *strǣt-tūn*), and are often
located by Roman roads.[23]

Archaeological material further augments the picture drawn from textual and
onomastic evidence; indeed, scholars have long thought that distributions of small
finds may reveal early route-ways. When discussing prehistoric tracks, Cyril Fox
commented: 'there was no continuous string of finds ... finds will turn up only at or
near obstacles'.[24] He went on to describe the obstacles as 'rivers, streams or marshes
... where in the Bronze Age or today (there would be) hamlets or villages'. This
raises the question of whether such clusters of artefacts simply represent settlements,
rather than transport hubs. Yet the settlements might have come into being at junctions between road and river precisely because transport benefited the inhabitants.[25]
Modern transport theory highlights linkages and nodes as the key features of infrastructure, and this concept is increasingly being applied to medieval road networks.[26]
Nodal points such as crossroads had a broader social significance in early medieval
times: they were locations where worship might take place, crosses constructed, and
outcasts buried.[27]

Suspected early medieval route-ways can also be compared with later medieval
infrastructure. From the thirteenth century onwards, roads and waterways are
mentioned in a much richer range of texts, including purveyance accounts, maps and
the reconstructed itineraries of kings and bishops. These sources reveal an increasingly elaborate network of local and inter-regional routes between the eastern and
western coasts of Britain. The legal context of road use also becomes clearer, notably
the principle that roads were rights of way rather than physical entities. Some roads
'made and maintained themselves', such as the unmetalled tracks running in parallel
with older, declining roads.[28] New highways emerged to connect recently founded
towns, mints and monasteries. Others, however, followed time-honoured prehistoric
and Roman routes, arteries of communication that had survived through the early
medieval period.[29]

The evolution of the landscape needs to be considered in any discussion of the
ease (or otherwise) of journeys between Northumbria and the Gaelic world.[30] The

---

[21] *HE* II, 16, 3 (ed. Lapidge, I, 378–9; ed. and transl. Colgrave and Mynors, 192–3).
[22] London, British Library, Cotton MS Tiberius B.V., fol. 56v; for Hadrian's Wall, see Shannon,
       Murus Ille Famosus, 31–2; for the coastal perspective, see Reynolds and Langlands, 'Travel *as*
       communication', 413.
[23] Gelling and Cole, *The Landscape*, 65, 93–4.
[24] Fox, *The Personality*, 67.
[25] Leighton, *Transport*, 154; Reynolds, 'The archaeology', 343.
[26] Hendrickson, 'A transport geographic perspective', 445.
[27] Reynolds and Langlands, 'Travel *as* communication', 419–20.
[28] Flower, *Public Works*, II, xvi (quotation); Hindle, 'Roads and tracks', 193–4; *idem*, 'Sources',
       34.
[29] Coles, 'Prehistoric roads', 10.
[30] Reynolds and Langlands, 'Travel *as* communication', 413–14.

Northumbrian kingdom encompassed a vast swathe of territory in which the land was exploited in varied ways. Oliver Rackham's classic study of the countryside placed much of the area north of the Mersey–Humber line in the 'highland' zone, which was characterised by dispersed settlement. The eastern lowlands of Yorkshire lay in the 'planned' zone, in which nucleated villages and open fields evolved, and the western coastal plain belonged to the 'ancient' zone where Romano-British field systems persisted.[31] At a more fine-grained level, the 'Fields of Britannia' project has used geology, settlement and woodland densities to identify nine regions to the south of Hadrian's Wall, of which parts of the northern uplands, western lowlands, north-east lowlands and central zone lay in the Northumbrian kingdom.[32] The Pennine range, often described as 'a backbone', is the key boundary between these different regions. The eastern areas faced the North Sea, and their settlements featured long-lasting, substantial timber structures. Such buildings were originally constructed as far north as Yeavering in the Tweed Valley, but there was a retraction of this building culture, leaving the north of the Northumbrian kingdom as part of a 'middle zone' in terms of its built environment. The western areas featured dispersed settlements and slighter, sometimes circular, buildings that had much in common with counterparts in the Gaelic and Brittonic worlds.[33]

The peaty flanks of the Pennine moors and the western coastal mosses provide a valuable resource for reconstructing changes in the environment. Cuttings taken from waterlogged soil contain preserved pollen grains, which can be analysed and sometimes radiocarbon dated. A number of palynological analyses have been carried out on sites that became part of the Northumbrian kingdom, especially near the two Roman walls.[34] These studies show that numerous phases of clearance and regeneration had occurred before the early medieval period. In southern Scotland some of the deforestation occurred during the late Iron Age, and sites along the line of the Antonine Wall generally remained clear, or were cleared for the first time, during the Roman period.[35] Some localities along Hadrian's Wall remained wooded until midway through the Iron Age, and others were cleared early in the Roman era.[36] These sites generally experienced woodland regeneration in the post-Roman period, but the date of this shift is controversial. Petra Dark has pointed to regrowth of trees shortly after Roman withdrawal, whereas Rob Collins has highlighted some stability in pollen cores during the period from the fourth to the sixth century.[37] Localities in the modern counties of Lancashire and Cumbria show a trend towards clearance for pastoral agriculture before and during the Roman periods, with some woodland regeneration in the post-Roman period. However, there is considerable variation

---

[31] Rackham, *The History*, 1–4. Compare the west/east distinction between the 'north and west province' and the 'central province' in Roberts and Wrathmell, *An Atlas*, figs 9, 10. Their third zone, the south-eastern province, lay outside Northumbria. For some early nucleated settlements, see Loveluck, *Northwest Europe*, 84–5.

[32] Rippon *et al.*, *The Fields of Britannia*, 44–56.

[33] Blair, *Building Anglo-Saxon England*, 25–31.

[34] Syntheses include Pennington, 'Vegetation history', 73–4; Ramsay and Dickson, 'Vegetational history', 147; Tipping, 'Vegetational history', 157–8; Dark, *The Environment*, 55–66, 99–114, 144–9; Wells, 'Environmental changes', 73–81.

[35] Tipping, 'The form', 32–4; Ramsay and Dickson, 'Vegetational history', 146–7.

[36] Dark, *The Environment*, 63. Fozy Moss, close to Hadrian's Wall, is an example of a site cleared in Roman times; see Dumayne, 'The effect', 220–4.

[37] Collins, *Hadrian's Wall*, 134–7; cf. Wells, 'Environmental changes', 78, 80, *contra* Dark, *The Environment*, 145–6.

within the region: a number of pollen diagrams from Lancashire and the Lake District show no increase in trees until the seventh/eighth centuries.[38] In general, there was more woodland in the western and northern parts of the Northumbrian kingdom than in the east and the Midlands of England, but woodland regeneration was patchy and varied.

A phase (or several phases) of climate change from the tenth to the twelfth century is known as the 'Medieval Warm Period'. The gradual warming of the climate facilitated the colonisation of previously marginal lands across the North Atlantic, which has a bearing on Gaelic–Scandinavian settlement on the edges of the Northumbrian kingdom.[39] Indeed, in Cumbria there has been a tendency to equate the increased exploitation of the uplands with Viking activity;[40] a reappraisal of the fall of *Quercus* (oak) values suggests, however, that upland clearances happened gradually and variably. The detailed pollen diagram from Fairsnape Fell (Lancashire) demonstrates a gradual fall in arboreal pollen suggestive of expansion or intensification of livestock breeding and increased usage of seasonal pasture over several centuries.[41] This picture is consistent with the documentary evidence available from the twelfth century onwards, which reveals a piecemeal process of assarting on the edges of fells. Indeed, Norse *þveit* 'clearing' names continued to be coined long after the Viking Age in Cumbria.[42] In southern Scotland there is less of a tendency to implicate the Vikings in environmental change; nevertheless, the exploitation of upland areas increased from *ca* 1000 AD, and new landholders, such as reformed monasteries, played a role.[43]

Climatic improvements and landscape improvements promoted population growth in areas that had previously been sparsely inhabited. This in turn had knock-on effects for the use of route-ways, especially the complex network of tracks associated with transhumance, droving and peat cutting.[44] The Domesday survey has been used to estimate England's population in 1086, although its accuracy is a subject of debate. The latest estimate is 2.5 million, based on the argument that Domesday under-recorded the population relative to twelfth-century estate surveys.[45] The density varied regionally: by late-medieval times, the population

---

[38] Examples include Valley Bog in the North Pennines and Knowsley Park in the Lancashire mosses: Mighall *et al.*, 'A record', 14, 33–4; Cowell and Innes, *The Wetlands*, 151. In general, see Pennington, 'Vegetation history', 72–3; Kenyon, *The Origins*, 68; Higham, *The Northern Counties*, 244; Rippon *et al.*, *Fields of Britannia*, 256–7, 287.

[39] Keigwin, 'The Little Ice Age', 1506–7; Crowley and Lowery, 'How warm', 53–4; Huddart and Stott, *Earth Environments*, 860–4. For the possible link to the expansion of the kingdom of Alba, see Ross, *The Kings*, 9–12. Compare expansion of cereal growing in southern and Midlands England: Williamson, *Environment*, 19–20, 42–5.

[40] Birks, 'Pollen analytical investigations', 311–12; Oldfield, 'Pollen analysis', 309.

[41] MacKay and Tallis, 'The recent vegetational history', 580; cf. Higham, 'Continuity studies', 12–18. For livestock and transhumance, see Winchester and Crosby, *England's Landscape: The North West*, 39, 104.

[42] Winchester, *Landscape*, esp. 41–2; Fellows-Jensen, 'Little Thwaite'; Whaley, *A Dictionary*, 420. Cf. the critiques of Viking expansion and landscape change in Higham, *A Frontier Landscape*, 31–5; Williamson, *Environment*, 72–80.

[43] Ramsay and Dickson, 'Vegetational history', 147; Oram, 'Trackless, impenetrable and underdeveloped?', 319–20.

[44] Winchester, *Landscape*, 5–7; Higham, *A Frontier Landscape*, 70–1; Oram, 'Trackless, impenetrable and underdeveloped?', 314–16.

[45] Hinton, 'Demography', 173, 176–7. Compare the estimate of 1.5–2.5 million in Dyer, *Making a Living*, 94–5.

exceeded twenty people per square mile (twelve per square kilometre) in much of south-eastern and midland England, but the East Riding of Yorkshire is the only northern region in this category.[46] Current (tentative) estimates for Lancashire's Domesday-era population are a mere 2,000–4,000.[47] Yet even if the edges of the Northumbrian kingdom were sparsely settled, it does not follow that travellers avoided these areas. The strategically important river-valleys and passes were vital arteries for kings, warbands and churchmen.

This broad overview of environmental developments indicates that long-standing roadways could have remained in use, and in demand. Travel times between the Northumbrian heartlands and the Gaelic world will have varied considerably depending on the type of traffic. The regular day's march, or *iustum iter* of the Roman legionaries was up to twenty Roman miles, equivalent to 18.4 miles/29.6km in the modern day. In northern Britain, the spacing of forts along Hadrian's Wall and the Antonine Wall was fairly regular at seven to eight Roman miles, which roughly equates to half a day's march between each fort. This is comparable with the fifteen-mile (24-km) range per day of Edward I's army when moving through the same territory.[48] An army might cover the distance from York to the Irish Sea via the Ribble Valley in five-and-a-half days, and a rider on horseback (travelling up to 35 miles/56km per day) reduced the trans-Pennine crossing to an excursion of just over two days.[49] These rates of travel assume good conditions, of course, and the deterioration of Roman roads would have impeded some traffic.

The waterways of the Northumbrian kingdom were also at the mercy of environmental change. Navigation on the Irish Sea depends on tidal fluctuations, the prevailing westerly or south-westerly winds and the availability of harbours. The tides push traffic from north-eastern Ireland into the Solway and around the Point of Ayre on the northern tip of Isle of Man. In the other direction, tides flow from Cumbria to the Solway, or from the Dee/Mersey area to south of Man.[50] True to form, the Solway and the Isle of Man loomed large in links between the Northumbrian kingdom and Ireland. Parts of Northumbria's western seaboard are dangerous for unwary navigators: the tidal range along the Lancashire coast is 4–6m/13–20ft greater than that of south-eastern Ireland, and rocks and sandbanks quickly become submerged.[51] Some rivers on Britain's western coast experience tidal bores, as well as floods that run off the watersheds during bad weather.[52]

The navigational challenges help to explain why no evidence of the early medieval Mediterranean and Continental trade has (so far) emerged on the eastern side of the Irish Sea north of Meols on the Wirral.[53] Detailed information about sailing routes becomes available in the late-medieval period, in the form of the Mediterranean portolan charts (depicting sea marks and havens) and the northern 'rutters' (sailing instructions). Taken together, these texts reveal that the main north/south shipping lanes ran to the west of the Isle of Man. The earliest extant English rutter, which dates from the mid-fifteenth century, directs sailors around the west side of the Irish

---

[46] Jewell, *The North–South Divide*, 96; Harris, *Shaping the Nation*, 209–10.
[47] Higham, *A Frontier Landscape*, 71–2.
[48] Benario, 'Legionary speed of march', 360; Edwards, 'The Romans', 13; Breeze, 'The placing of forts', 28. Compare Prestwich, 'The royal itinerary', 188, for Edward I's army.
[49] Margary, *Roman Roads*, 371–4 (72b); Forgeng and Singman, *Daily Life*, 215.
[50] Davies, 'The diffusion', 42–4; Cooney, 'Neolithic worlds', 147–8.
[51] Buchanan, 'The Irish Sea', 3.
[52] Kenyon, *The Origins*, 12–13.
[53] Wooding, *Communication*, 101; Campbell, *Continental and Mediterranean Imports*, 10.

Sea, using Copeland Island (Co. Down), and the Isle of Man as markers. It also gives directions from Wicklow to St David's Head and thence to Rhuddlan, but nothing for the eastern side of the Irish Sea north of Chester.[54] On the other hand, the innovative tide diagram of the Breton cartographer Guillaume Brouscon (1548) depicted *Lerpoll* (Liverpool), *Quintall* (Kendal), *Pilfout* (Piel of Fouldray, Barrow-in-Furness) and *Damfurs* (Dumfries), highlighting the significance of the Mersey, Morecambe Bay and the Solway.[55] If there was an incentive to sail from or to the eastern side of the Irish Sea region, early navigators could overcome the challenges. The prolific Neolithic axe factories of the Langdale Pikes exported their wares from Walney Island (Cumbria, formerly Lancashire) and Luce Sands (Dumfries and Galloway, formerly Wigtownshire).[56]

As to the environment of inland waterways, changes in sea-level enabled boats to move further up some estuaries and rivers in the first millennium than before or after. High-tide levels were rising throughout the Roman period, and there was a marine transgression in Lancashire around the sixth century.[57] Coastal change was, however, a localised phenomenon involving movements of channels in estuaries and inundations of sand.[58] Wigtown's medieval port was situated at the mouth of the River Bladenoch, and it has since disappeared because the river's course has shifted.[59] The early medieval coastline is hard to reconstruct following centuries of reclamation of moss and marshland, although the detailed archaeological work of the North-West Wetlands Survey has shed light on the extensive mosses of Lancashire.[60] One significant feature was the large brackish lake of Martin Mere (now mostly drained), which offered one way to transport heavy goods in the late-medieval era.[61] In their maximalist survey of late-medieval English waterways, Edwards and Hindle labelled only the Mersey, Lune, Derwent and Eden as 'major rivers' (navigable more than ten miles/16km upriver) in the north-west.[62] However, early medieval water travellers were less frequently impeded than their late-medieval counterparts, who had to contend with the wide-scale construction of mills and weirs. On balance, then, the watery landscape of western Northumbria was amenable to transport by boat.

The attractiveness of water transport also depended on ship technology. The boats used in the Irish Sea region included small flat-bottomed craft suitable for negotiating marshlands and rivers beyond the tidal limit. Fifteen examples have been

---

[54] *Sailing Directions* (ed. Gairdner, 19–20); Lester, 'The earliest English sailing directions', 333–6; Ward, 'The earliest known sailing directions', 59, 82–3.

[55] Cartwright, *Tides*, 18–19. I am grateful to Dr Bill Shannon for drawing my attention to this information.

[56] Bradley *et al.*, 'Maritime havens', 136–9, 143–6; cf. Edmonds, *The Langdales*, 25.

[57] Roman sea-levels: Waddelove and Waddelove, 'Archaeology', esp. 262–4. Transgressions: Tooley, 'Theories', 84–5; Jones, 'Archaeology and coastal change', 100, 102; Wells, 'Environmental changes', 75–8. Barlow and Shennan, 'An overview', 26–41 give a more complex picture.

[58] Dark, *The Environment*, 28–30; Griffiths, 'Medieval coastal sand inundation', 107–11.

[59] Graham, 'Some old harbours', 41, 66.

[60] Cowell and Innes, *The Wetlands*; Middleton *et al.*, *The Wetlands of North Lancashire*; Hodgkinson *et al.*, *The Lowland Wetlands*; Middleton *et al.*, *The Wetlands of South-West Lancashire*; cf. Higham, *A Frontier Landscape*, 11–16, 77, 97.

[61] Hale and Coney, *Martin Mere*, 98–124.

[62] Edwards and Hindle, 'The transportation system', 131. For a more limited picture, see Langdon, 'Inland water transport', esp. 4, although his sources (purveyance accounts) do not exist for north-west England.

recovered from around Martin Mere, including a logboat dated to 535 AD.[63] Larger, sea-going vessels were already in use in prehistoric times, as shown by the impressive, golden model of a boat with benches, oars and a mast in the Broighter Hoard, found near the coast of north-eastern Ireland.[64] *Míniugud Senchasa Fer nAlban* reveals that the *secht-sess* 'seven-bencher' was the typical ship of the Dál Riatans; it was crewed by twenty-eight men, and twenty houses would supply two of these ships for expeditions.[65] During the Viking Age, developments in ship technology further eased sea-going voyages and riverine navigation. The narrow thirty-oared warship found in a grave at Ladby (*ca* 900) was fast and highly manoeuvrable, and had a shallow draught of 1.05m/3.4ft, making estuarine raiding feasible.[66] The Dublin-built sixty-oared ship Skuldelev 2 was longer (29.3m/96ft as opposed to 21.5m/70.5ft), wider and more seaworthy on Atlantic voyages. It was built in 1042 and sunk in a blockade in Roskilde in the 1070s.[67] In addition smaller craft sailed around the islands and coast, such as the 5m/16.4ft-long ship recently found in a boat burial at Ardnamurchan.[68] A notional day's sailing might cover 72 nautical miles (133km) with favourable tides, and journeys across the Irish Sea to western Northumbria could be broken into two daylong stints by stopping on the Isle of Man.[69]

Thus water transport was a practical way to access the Northumbrian kingdom from the Gaelic-speaking lands, but how often were such voyages made? If the edges of the Northumbrian kingdom were relatively sparsely populated, merchants may not have found ready markets there. On the other hand, the Pennine uplands were yielding metal ores for which markets existed as far afield as Norway, and these must have been exported by sea.[70] Other goods could have passed through, including Whitby jet: this was a sought-after commodity in York and the Irish Sea region, even though jet-like substitutes (oil shale and lignite) could be found elsewhere in northern Britain and Ireland.[71] Those who owned ships may have supplemented their activities by fishing as well as raiding, and by the end of the first millennium there was an upturn in commercial fishing across the North Atlantic.[72] This may explain the appeal of an impressive monument at Gosforth (Cumbria, formerly Cumberland) that depicts the Norse god Thor on a fishing trip.[73] The region's waterways were also populated by the sleek vessels that conveyed armies and rulers to and from the Hiberno-Scandinavian towns.

Taken together, Roman and late-medieval infrastructure provide clues as to which route-ways were open to travellers through the Northumbrian kingdom. Environmental changes affected the use of these lines of communication, but if

---

[63] McGrail, *Logboats*, 153–6; Hale and Coney, *Martin Mere*, 70–3.

[64] McGrail, *Ancient Boats*, 186.

[65] *Míniugud Senchasa Fer nAlban* (ed. and transl. Bannerman, 47, 49); cf. Bannerman, *Studies*, 148–54.

[66] Sørensen, *Ladby*, 181–245; Williams, *The Viking Ship*, 59–63.

[67] Crumlin-Pedersen and Olsen, *The Skuldelev Ships I*, 141–92.

[68] Harris, 'Assembling places', 194.

[69] Morcken, 'Norse nautical units', 396 (defining *dægr sigling* 'day's sailing' primarily as a unit of distance rather than time); cf. Ferguson, 'Re-evaluating early medieval Northumbrian contacts', 294. Hudson (*Viking Pirates*, 17) notes that a fully laden cargo ship took 24 hours to cross from Man to Dublin in the fifteenth century.

[70] See above, 21–2.

[71] Stevens, 'Early medieval jet-like jewellery', 240, 242–3. Jet or a jet-like material was worked at Yard 2, Fishamble Street, in Dublin: Wallace, *Viking Dublin*, 291–8, 495–6.

[72] Barrett, 'The pirate fishermen'; *idem*, 'The origins of intensive marine fishing', 2419–20.

[73] Bailey, *Viking Age Sculpture*, 131–2; *Corpus II*, 108–9.

anything, the circumstances seem to have become increasingly propitious to transport by the tenth and eleventh centuries. I will now investigate the main routes running to the western coast and the far north in more detail, moving from south to north in the Northumbria kingdom.

Trans-Pennine passes and the Irish Sea

The southern edge of the Northumbrian kingdom was skirted by route-ways that led from the eastern heartlands to the Gaelic-speaking lands across the Irish Sea. The legionary fortresses of York and Chester were nodal points in the infrastructure of Roman Britain, and their significance endured into the early medieval period. York lay on the north-east bank of the River Ouse, slightly upstream from the confluence with the River Foss, which has some vestiges of Roman riverside structures. Goods were probably trans-shipped in the Humber Estuary and sent to York on lighters.[74] Several roads facilitated travel inland from York; for current purposes, the most significant are the connection to the Great North Road (Dere Street) at Aldborough, and the link to the trans-Pennine routes near Tadcaster.[75] The more southerly of these trans-Pennine routes ran to Manchester via the Roman fort at Slack (*Cambodunum*), where distinct traces of *agger* (road embankment) can still be seen. Bede named *Campodunum* as one of Edwin's *villae regiae* 'royal vills', which was burnt down and replaced by another site *in regione Loidis* 'in the Leeds region'.[76] Roman roads were attractive locations for royal vills, which underpinned the circuits of the Northumbrian kings.[77]

Manchester was a major hub in the infrastructure of northern Britain, then as now. The fort of *Mancunium* has yielded hints of sub-Roman occupation in the form of four pits parallel to a late-Roman wall.[78] Manchester lay *on Norþhymbrum* 'amongst the Northumbrians' in the early tenth century, but was precariously close to Mercian territory. Whether there was a linear boundary between the two kingdoms is a matter of debate; any such border would have evolved over the course of the seventh century.[79] A Roman road ran from York to Manchester via Doncaster, the Roman fort of Brough in the Hope Valley, and Snake Pass in the Peak District.[80] This route retained its strategic significance in the early medieval period: in 829, the Northumbrian king Eanred submitted to Ecgberht of Wessex and Mercia at Dore, which lies between this Roman road and the River Sheaf.[81] Dore is presented as

---

[74] Mason, *Roman Britain*, 126.

[75] Margary, *Roman Roads*, 416–17 (28c), 127–8 (8a).

[76] *HE* II, 14, 3 (ed. Lapidge, I, 372; ed. and transl. Colgrave and Mynors, 188–9). *Cambodunum* appears in the Antonine *Iter* II (ed. Parthey and Pinder, *Itinerarium*, 223); Rivet and Smith, *The Place-Names*, 302–4. The distances complicate the identification of *Cambodunum* with Slack; on the other hand, the fort was clearly located between Tadcaster and Manchester. I do not see a difficulty in identifying the Roman place-name with Bede's rendering (*contra* Higham, *The Kingdom*, 85–6).

[77] Charles-Edwards, 'Early medieval kingships', 28–33.

[78] Bryant *et al.*, *Roman Manchester*, 54–6.

[79] ASC A [922 for 919] (ed. Bately, 69). Here I follow Higham 'Northumbria's southern frontier' *contra* Blair, 'The Northumbrians'. Cf. Clark, 'The Northumbrian frontiers', 41–63.

[80] Margary, *Roman Roads*, 361–3 (710b, 711); Blair, 'The Northumbrians', 117–20; Higham, 'Northumbria's southern frontier', 405.

[81] ASC A *s.a.* 827 (ed. Bately, 42); B (ed. Taylor, 30); C (ed. O'Keeffe, 52); D (ed. Cubbin, 20); E (ed. Irvine, 45).

the northern edge of Mercia in a poem that celebrated Edmund's reconquest of the Five Boroughs in 942.[82] In the west, the River Mersey has a telling name (*Mærse* 1002: *(ge)mære + ēa* 'boundary river'), and Manchester stands on one of its tributaries, the River Irwell.[83] The accumulated evidence suggests that the most southerly routes between York and the west of the Northumbrian kingdom remained in use, and could have offered access to the Mercian port of Chester if the political circumstances were propitious.

Chester was the pre-eminent port of the region, and its close relationship with Dublin and Waterford lasted until at least 980. Chester's Irish-Sea connections are evident in finds of metalwork (including a Borre/Jellinge brooch that resembles a pair from High Street, Dublin) and the mixed Castle Esplanade hoard of *ca* 965, which resembles Irish and Manx hoards. Conversely, Chester-minted coins and Chester Ware have been found in quantity in Dublin. David Griffiths has suggested that the pottery contained salt produced in Cheshire, a commodity described as *salann saxanach* in one of the scenes of gluttony in the Middle Irish text *Aislinge Meic Conglinne*.[84] Chester's port remained significant until the Dee estuary began to silt up in the eleventh century. Shipping gradually transferred to the Mersey, where King John founded the borough of Liverpool in 1207.[85] Thus while the Mersey was a significant boundary of the Northumbrian kingdom, it was not a major destination for ships arriving from Ireland. Indeed, control of the Mersey's North–South crossings seems to have been as significant as movement along the river. The lowest ford offered access between Runcorn and Widnes, tides permitting, and it was watched over by the *burh* that Æthelflæd founded at Runcorn in 912.[86] Roman vessels had moored further upstream at Wilderspool, Warrington, where there was an industrial site and depot, as well as a bridge for the north–south Roman road.[87] I suggest that boats navigated even further upstream in the early medieval period; shallow-draught Viking ships may have travelled as far as Thelwall, where the modern M6 crosses the Mersey and the Manchester Ship Canal. The Old English place-name Statham (dative plural of *stæð* 'at the landing places') is located beneath the modern Thelwall Viaduct.[88] The significance for shipping helps to explain Edward the Elder's construction of a *burh* at Thelwall in 919, shortly after the brothers Rǫgnvaldr and Sigtryggr gained control of York and Dublin.[89] In the late-medieval period the head of navigation lay even further upstream at Barton-upon-Irwell, one of the Mersey tributaries. Logboats found near Barton have yielded radiocarbon dates that cluster around the twelfth century, suggesting that small craft frequently passed on these

[82] ASC A 942 (ed. Bately, 73).
[83] *PNLa*, 26.
[84] Thacker, 'Early medieval Chester', 22; Griffiths, *Vikings*, 129, 130–5. For the hoard, see Webster *et al.*, 'A Saxon treasure hoard'; Graham-Campbell, *The Cuerdale Hoard*, 11–12. For the salt, see *Aislinge Meic Conglinne* (ed. and transl. Meyer, 60–1).
[85] Marker, 'The Dee estuary', 66.
[86] Higham, 'The Cheshire burhs', 199–200, 203–4; Cox and Crosby, 'Bridging the Mersey', 124. The new 'Mersey Gateway' bridge was opened over this crossing in October 2017.
[87] Margary, *Roman Roads*, 302–3, 359, 367 (70a, 70b); Mason, *Roman Britain*, 119; Cox and Crosby, 'Bridging the Mersey', 123.
[88] *Stathum* 1284–5: Dodgson, *The Place-Names*, II, 38; Cole, 'The place-name evidence', 75. I add this reference for my father, who crossed the Thelwall daily for many years.
[89] ASC A [922 for 919] (ed. Bately, 69).

stretches of the river.[90] The road from Manchester to Chester crossed the Mersey nearby at Stretford, an Old English *strǣt* place-name.[91]

The Northumbrians lacked a busy trade centre on the Irish Sea to rival Chester. Nevertheless, Northumbrians may have been trading at Meols on the Wirral, a beach market which operated from the Iron Age until the Viking Age. A wide range of artefacts was recovered from sand dunes at Meols, and in this regard it resembles a number of other coastal sites around the Irish Sea that have yielded early medieval metalwork.[92] The site probably stood outside Chester's fiscal jurisdiction, in a territory that had been settled by Scandinavians, perhaps beginning with Ingimund's force.[93] The finds from Meols include Byzantine, Irish and Anglo-Saxon artefacts, including four Northumbrian *styca*s.[94] These copper alloy coins had a low value and circulated more widely west of the Pennines than the silver *sceatta* coins. Northumbrian traders sailed on from Meols, hugging the coastline of North Wales: a *styca* has been found at Segontium fort (Caernarfon), and there are two *styca*s as well as Anglo-Saxon and Irish metalwork at Llanbedrgoch (Anglesey), which became a Viking-Age trading centre.[95] This is as far as *styca*s travelled around the Irish Sea because their low value rendered them inappropriate for international trade.[96] It is possible that smaller, informal beach markets remain to be found under the sand dunes of south-west Lancashire, which have shifted considerably since medieval times.[97] The Norse place-name Croxteth and the English place-name Huyton refer to landing places. Huyton is located on the River Alt, which is no longer navigable, and this illustrates that water transport was easier in the past in this mossy part of Lancashire.[98]

Moving further north, the Ribble–Aire gap was an important artery of communication in Roman times. The route offered a gentle Pennine crossing through a gap created by geological faults. It was the most direct link between York and the Irish Sea, and there are strong indications that it remained a significant link to Ireland in the early medieval period. The Roman road ran from Tadcaster to a junction at *Olicana* (Ilkley), where another road arrived from Aldborough.[99] The Goldsborough hoard was discovered not far the latter road; it may have been assembled in Ireland and was buried *ca* 925. The coins are predominantly Arabic dirhams, and there are fragments of Irish penannular and pseudo-penannular brooches of types found in the Cuerdale Hoard.[100] A few years later the much larger and more coin-dominated (but

---

[90] Edwards and Hindle, 'The transportation system', 131; McGrail and Switsur, 'Medieval logboats'.

[91] *Stretford* 1212; *Stratford* 1292: *PNLa*, 32; Edwards, 'The Romans', 24.

[92] Griffiths 'The coastal trading ports'.

[93] Wainwright, 'Ingimund's invasion', 154–9; Griffiths, *Vikings*, 115.

[94] Griffiths *et al.*, *Meols*, 343.

[95] Besly, 'Few and far between', 716; Redknap, 'Viking-Age settlement', 156; cf. *idem*, 'Glitter', 302–4.

[96] Wickham, *Framing the Middle Ages*, 707 highlights the importance of local and regional exchange systems, as against the better-reported long-distance trade.

[97] Griffiths, 'Medieval coastal sand inundation', 108.

[98] Croxteth: *Crocstad* 1257: *Croxstath* 1297 (ON *krókr* 'bend' + *stǫð* 'landing place'). Huyton: *Hitune* 1086 (OE *hȳþ* 'landing place' + *tūn*). For the evidence, see *PNLa* 113–14; Cole, 'The place-name evidence', 76.

[99] Margary, *Roman Roads*, 401–3 (72a).

[100] Graham-Campbell, 'The Cuerdale hoard', 112; *idem, The Cuerdale Hoard*, 112, 234–7. For the dating, see Gareth Williams in *ibid.*, 237; cf. Williams, 'The "Northern hoards"', 461–6.

still mixed) Vale of York hoard was buried not far from the same road.[101] From Ilkley the road ran through and out of Airedale towards Elslack fort, before descending the Ribble Valley, crossing the river at Ribchester and running along the north bank.[102]

There has long been debate about how far inland the River Ribble was navigable in this period.[103] The modern tidal limit is Walton-le-Dale near Preston, where there was a site geared towards production, storage and trans-shipment of goods during the second and third centuries, and possibly later.[104] Shallow-draught Viking vessels could perhaps have proceeded further upstream than their heavily laden Roman counterparts; indeed, recent analysis of sediments in the lower Ribble Valley has revealed that there were flood inundations throughout the early medieval period.[105] The find-spot of the Cuerdale Hoard offered access to the Roman road to York (via a ford, now crossed by the M6 motorway) and can be envisaged as the temporary base of a group of Dublin exiles. It is possible that there were encampments closer to the estuary at locations such as Penwortham motte or the confluence with the River Douglas. However, the lower reaches of the river were surrounded by vast expanses of marsh and moss prior to the creation of Preston docks, which involved the straightening and deepening of the Ribble.[106] In my view travellers from Ireland to York would have sailed as far as the lower Ribble Valley and then transferred to horses or journeyed on foot to York. This may be why the Mercian and Wessex kings began to show an interest in the Ribble during the first half of the tenth century. The area was a strategic flash-point, and the failure to recover the Cuerdale Hoard suggests that its owners suffered some sort of catastrophe.

The Roman road along the Ribble continued towards the Irish Sea, and sections survive near Dowbridge Fort, Kirkham (Lancashire). The fort was founded in the first century, when the tidal waters of the Ribble estuary came closer to Dowbridge.[107] Writers have long postulated that the road continued through the mosslands of the Fylde towards a port on the Wyre Estuary, which some would identify with Ptolemy's *Setantion limen*.[108] However, recent excavations near Kirkham have found no trace of the road, and the results of LiDaR analysis are also negative.[109] If there ever was such a road, it would have fallen into disrepair after Kirkham fort was abandoned in the second century and been in a derelict state during the early medieval period.[110] Even so, there is evidence that the River Wyre was accessible to boats in the early medieval period. Skippool (*Skippoles* 1330: ON *skip* 'ship') and Todderstaffe (*Taldrestath* 1332: unknown generic + OE *stæð*) both lie near creeks that feed into the Wyre.[111]

---

[101] Williams and Ager, *The Vale of York Hoard*.

[102] Margary, *Roman Roads*, 371–4 (72b).

[103] See references in Edmonds, 'Barrier or unifying feature?', 24.

[104] Gibbons and Howard-Davis, *Excavations* (unpublished first draft).

[105] Quatermaine, *Aggregate Extraction*, 103–12.

[106] Lewis, 'Vikings', 22–5 considers these options, with particular emphasis on the River Douglas. For changes to the Ribble, see Barron, *A History*, 261–321.

[107] Howard-Davis and Buxton, *Roman Forts*, 3, 68, 77.

[108] Just, 'The Roman roads'; Thornber, 'Remarks'. For *Setantion limen*, see Ptolemy, *Geographia* II, 3.2 (ed. Nobbe, I, 68); above, 25.

[109] Middleton *et al.*, *Wetlands of North Lancashire*, 99–100, 207; Ratledge, 'Roman roads'; *contra* Margary, *Roman Roads*, 374–5 (no. 703); Lightbown, *The Dane's Pad*; Graystone, *Walking Roman Roads in the Fylde*, 65–7, noting possible traces near Puddle House Farm, Poulton-le-Fylde.

[110] Howard-Davis and Buxton, *Roman Forts*, 3.

[111] *PNLa*, 140; Edmonds, 'Barrier or unifying feature?', 27; Cole, 'The place-name evidence', 76.

Moving further north, the Lune Estuary was approached from the east by roads from Wharfedale via Bainbridge fort and from Brough-under-Stainmore. From the western end of the Stainmore route the mountain road known as High Street branched off and other roads radiated into the heart of the Lake District.[112] These trans-Pennine routes provided access to two probable Roman ports for the Irish Sea. Lancaster's fort was, as I have noted, turned into a major coastal installation in the fourth century to guard against Irish raiders.[113] Recent excavations on Castle Hill have located a corner of this robustly built fort, and beneath the hill there is an early waterfront of the River Lune, complete with a possible warehouse.[114] An inscription on an altar found upstream mentions a *numerus barcariorum* (unit of bargemen), who may have engaged in assaults on the raiders who preyed on the local coastline.[115] Several finds of Byzantine coins offer tentative hints of post-Roman occupation at Lancaster.[116] By the eleventh century, the Roman fort housed the castle and the priory, and the latter may have pre-Viking origins, given the fine collection of sculpture found there.[117] Lancaster's fort had a vast view of Morecambe Bay, where evidence has increasingly been accumulating for early medieval navigation. An intriguing (but no longer traceable) group of Roman and early medieval finds emerged at Castlehead hillfort on Morecambe Bay when it was turned into a stately home in the eighteenth century. These included Northumbrian *styca*s, which were also found close by in Merlewood Cave.[118] Castlehead was once located on an inlet that was navigable at high tide, as seen on Yates's 1786 map of Lancashire.[119] The Silverdale and Furness hoards reflect the Viking-Age significance of Morecambe Bay, and they are complemented by other, smaller finds such as the package of hacksilver and dirhams from near Carnforth.[120]

Slightly further north, the Roman site of Ravenglass was located on a platform overlooking a sheltered anchorage at the confluence of the Rivers Irt, Esk and Mite. A lead seal from the fort was impressed with the stamp of *cohors primae aeliae classicae* (first cohort of the Aelian fleet), and fragments of a diploma of a veteran of the unit, dated 158, have been found on the foreshore.[121] The Aelian fleet was formed in the Hadrianic period, and some elements of it became infantry cohorts following the building of the Wall. The cohort stationed at Ravenglass is likely to have continued its naval service on account of the site's coastal vulnerability. At the very end of the Roman period *Notitia Dignitatum* places the *cohors primae aeliae classicae* at *Tunnocelum*; this fort lay nearby if not at Ravenglass itself (which is often identified

---

[112] Margary, *Roman Roads*, 383–5, 387–9 (nos 73 & 74); Graystone, *Walking Roman Roads in Bowland*, 46–63.

[113] See above, 26; cf. Livens, 'Litus Hibernicum'.

[114] Wood, 'Roman Lancaster', 40.

[115] Collingwood and Wright, *The Roman Inscriptions* (no. 601); Shotter, 'Numeri barcariorum'; *idem* and White, *Roman Fort*, 23–7.

[116] Penney, 'Gazetteer' (1977), 47–8; *idem*, 'Gazetteer' (1978), 6. Note, however, the difficulties with the attribution of three Byzantine coins to Meols: Griffiths *et al.*, *Meols*, 342–3.

[117] *Corpus IX*, 33–54.

[118] Stockdale, *Annales Caermoelenses*, 5–6, 201–5; Metcalf, 'A topographical commentary', 378–9; Higham, *The Northern Counties*, 303.

[119] Lancashire County Council, 'Lancashire, 1786'.

[120] For a summary of this evidence, see Edmonds, 'The Furness peninsula', 28–30.

[121] Collingwood and Wright, *The Roman Inscriptions*, no. 2411; Holder, 'A Roman military diploma'; Cherry, 'The topography', 11.

with *Glannoventa*).[122] If the kings of Rheged and their Northumbrian successors required a western naval base, Ravenglass was a good candidate.[123] Eventually the channel of the River Esk became too shallow for larger boats, but a harbour still existed in the twelfth century.[124] One of the spits that shelters the former Roman port is named Drigg (*Dreg ca* 1175–99), which is analogous to a Swedish name for a portage point.[125] Viking-Age mariners may have dragged their boats over the spit into the sheltered haven.

The Roman routes between York and the Irish Sea can be compared with those on the Gough map, *ca* 1360.[126] It shows the Doncaster–Manchester and Lune Valley roads, but surprisingly not the Ribble–Aire gap, which is one of several significant routes to be excluded.[127] The map does, however, show a non-Roman trans-Pennine route (perhaps a track rather than a metalled road), which linked Settle and Richmond (North Yorkshire). There is circumstantial evidence that this route was in use during the early medieval period. A Northumbrian *sceat* has been found at Richmond, and slightly east of Settle is Attermire Cave, which has yielded five *styca*s dating between 790 and 848, as well as a *sceat* of Archbishop Ecgberht with Eadberht (737–58) and a Dorestad coin of Lothair I (840–55).[128] The cave is located in inhospitable territory half-way up a cliff, and it may have been a hiding place for traders' goods. A *sceat* of Eadberht and a *styca* have also been found on open moorland nearby at Malham, and in Malham itself.[129] Also nearby is a group of upland farmsteads that have been recently excavated and dated to the period from the seventh to the tenth century. The inhabitants of the settlement at Crummack Dale were relatively prosperous, to judge from artefacts such as a decorated glass drinking vessel and Cumbrian haematite, which raises the question of whether they benefited from their location next to a trans-Pennine pass.[130] The recently discovered settlements bear comparison with the upland settlement at Gauber High Pasture, located next to the Roman road to Lancaster, where excavators discovered four *styca*s and a bell.[131] The distribution of these sites and coins bears out David Metcalf's comparison of those passes to the rungs of a ladder that carried eastern Northumbrian goods westwards.[132]

In short, the more southerly part of the Northumbrian kingdom offered several routes to the Irish Sea. In this area, coastal trade was overshadowed by Chester, but there are indications that rivers and valleys facilitated other types of movement. In particular, the Ribble Valley played a vital role in contact between the Scandinavian settlements of York and Dublin.

[122] *Notitia Dignitatum*, Oc. XL, 52 (ed. Seeck, 212); Hind, 'Agricola's fleet', 287; Mason, *Roman Britain*, 128–9. For the fort's name cf. Shotter, *Romans and Britons*, 105–9.
[123] See above, 35; cf. Cramp, *Whithorn*, opposite fig. 2, and for royal navies in general, Haywood, *Dark Age Naval Power*, 110–12.
[124] Collingwood, 'Ravenglass', 40; Cherry, 'The topography', 11.
[125] *PNCu*, II, 376–7.
[126] Image accessed at the 'Linguistic geographies' project: http://www.goughmap.org/map/
[127] Stenton, 'The road system', 240; Millea, *The Gough Map*, 85–9.
[128] Booth, 'Sceattas in Northumbria', 79, 90; Pirie, 'Finds of "sceattas"', 74, 79; EMC (find-spot: Attermire Cave).
[129] Booth, 'Sceattas in Northumbria', 79, 94; Pirie 'Finds of "sceattas"', 74, 79; EMC (find-spot: Malham). The moorland scatter may be linked with an upland settlement: King, 'Post-Roman upland architecture', 337–8; Loveluck, Northwest Europe, 80–1.
[130] Johnson, *The Crummack Dale Project*, 65–6. I am grateful to David Johnson for highlighting the relative prosperity implied by the finds.Cf. his 'Early medieval rural settlement', 32–4.
[131] King, 'Gauber High Pasture'; *idem*, 'Post-Roman upland architecture', 338–41.
[132] Metcalf, 'A topographical commentary', 364.

The Tyne–Solway Gap

The Tyne–Solway gap offered another gentle route from the east side of Britain to the Irish Sea. The significance of this natural division between the Pennine and Cheviot Hills increased in Roman times thanks to the construction of Hadrian's Wall, the accompanying Military Way and its predecessor, the Stanegate. The Wall remained a significant feature in the landscape throughout the early medieval period, and it was strategically important to the Bernicians; it may even be where they originated.[133]

The end-points of the Tyne–Solway gap were approached by the two major north–south Roman roads. The Great North Roman road (sometimes replicated by the modern A1) would have been well used by Northumbrians who travelled from York to Durham. A mixed silver hoard of the early tenth century has recently been found along this road, at Bedale (North Yorkshire).[134] Those travelling to the Solway Firth could take a short cut over the high ground of the Stainmore pass via the fort of Bowes. A Viking-Age hoard of hacksilver and silver ingots was unearthed immediately next to the Roman road at Old Spital, Bowes Moor, in 1982.[135] Similarly, Edward I travelled between Bowes and Carlisle via Brough-under-Stainmore and Brougham in 1300.[136] The Stainmore pass rises to 417.5m/1,370ft and it can be impassable in bad weather, whereas the Tyne–Solway gap offers a gentler crossing.[137] Even so, political factors led the Scandinavian kings of York and Durham to favour the Stainmore route on occasion. The last Scandinavian king of York, Eiríkr, seems to have been attempting to reach the Solway when he was killed on Stainmore.

Turning to the River Tyne itself, in Roman times, goods entered the Tyne from the North Sea and were trans-shipped from cargo boats to barges at Arbeia (South Shields), a fort that had a post-Roman afterlife.[138] The nearby mudflats of Jarrow slake became known as *portus Ecgfridi* 'Ecgfrith's port', which implies that a royal fleet was based on the Tyne. Ian Wood has argued that Ecgfrith's fleet departed from here in 685 to fight the ill-fated battle of Nechtansmere in Pictland.[139] I suggest that the Tyne was known as *Inber in ríg* (the estuary of the king) to Gaelic speakers, on account of its royal fleet. This name appears in the ninth-century tale *Scéla Cano meic Gartnáin* as a place where the protagonist will drink ales of sovereignty, shortly after a similar description of a Pictish region.[140] The Tyne was a link to the eastern 'coastal highway', which encompassed the *emporium* at York and its long-distance trading connections, as well as offering passage towards the Continent and Rome.[141]

The River Tyne was crossed by the Great North Road at the fort and civil centre of Corbridge, which was also the start of the westbound route known as the

---

[133] Orton and Wood, *Fragments of History*, 113–14.
[134] The Yorkshire Museum, 'The Bedale Hoard'.
[135] Pickin, 'A Viking-Age silver hoard', 170–1.
[136] See above, 79; Hindle, 'Medieval roads', 88.
[137] *Iter* II and V (ed. Parthey and Pinder, *Itinierarium*, 223, 226–7); Margary, *Roman Roads*, 433–6 (82); Higham, *The Northern Counties*, 222; Phythian-Adams, *Land of the Cumbrians*, 15.
[138] Shotter, 'Numeri barcariorum'; Mason, *Roman Britain*, 140; Collins, *Hadrian's Wall*, 103–5.
[139] Symeon of Durham, *Libellus de exordio*, II, 5 (ed. and transl. Rollason, 88–9); Wood, 'Bede's Jarrow', 72–3.
[140] *Scéla Cano meic Gartnáin* (ed. Binchy, 17), lines 481–5.
[141] Cramp, *Wearmouth and Jarrow*, 219–41; Deckers, 'The maritime cultural landscape', 153. For the eastern coastal route, by which exotic goods were disseminated, see Petts, 'Coastal landscapes', 80; Loveluck, *Northwest Europe*, 188–90; Ferguson, 'Re-evaluating early medieval Northumbrian contacts', 294; Turner *et al.*, *Wearmouth and Jarrow*, 99–101.

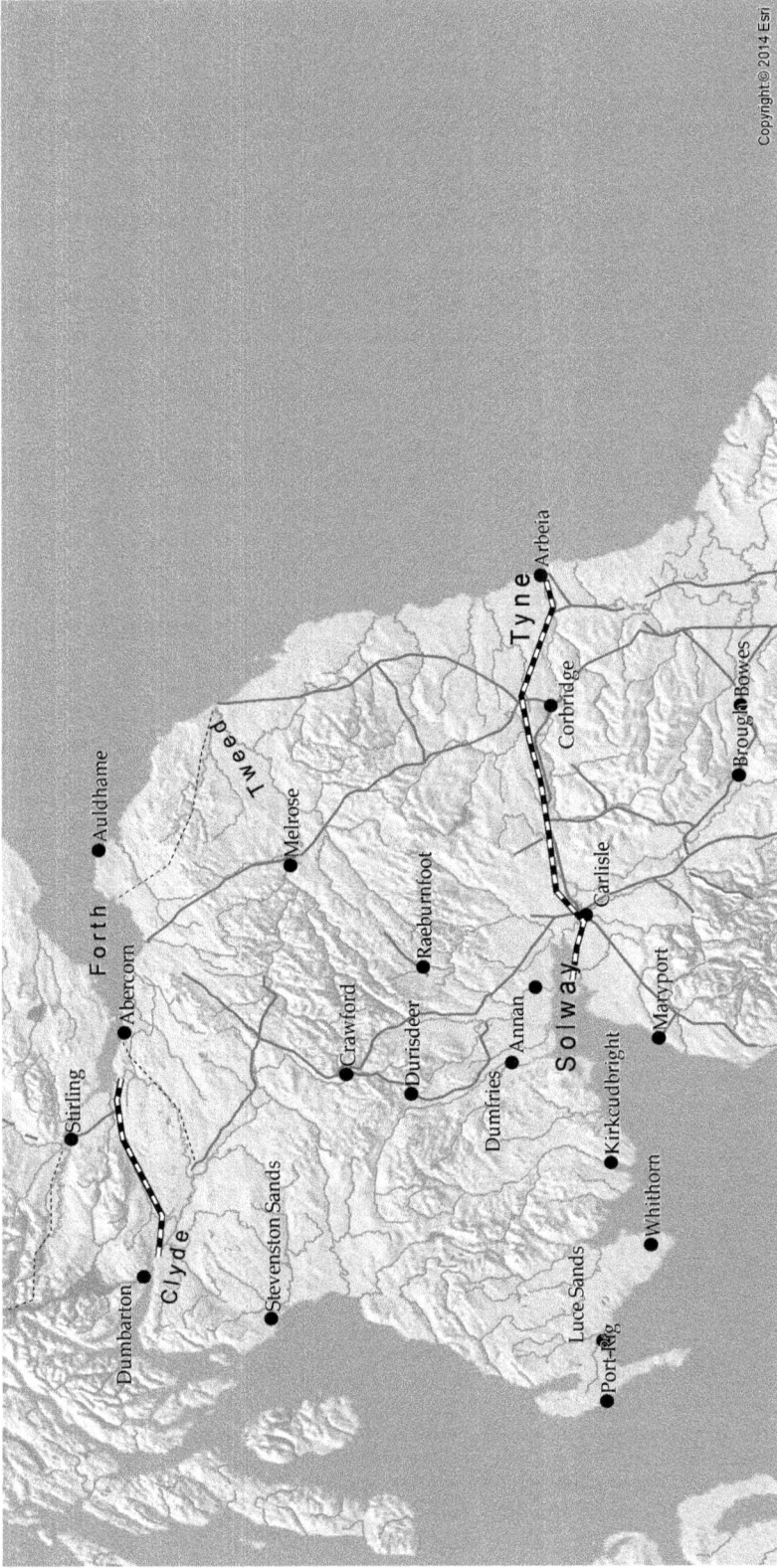

The two Roman walls are shown as heavily dotted lines, Roman roads in **bold**, other routes as lightly dotted lines (see Taylor, 'Iona abbots', 50).

Map 4: Communication routes north of the Tyne-Solway gap

Stanegate. Roman Corbridge was supplied by barges moving along the Tyne, and a large store and depot has been traced on the north bank of the river.[142] The place-name 'Corbridge' implies that the Tyne bridge was maintained in the post-Roman period, most likely through the construction of a timber crossing on top of the Roman stone piers.[143] There are indications of sub-Roman occupation at Corbridge's fort, including fifth- and sixth-century accoutrements, and the fort was subsequently used as a quarry for the minsters of Hexham and St Andrew's, Corbridge.[144] Early references to Corbridge highlight the importance of links with Ireland, as is appropriate for the terminus of a major route from the west. Visitors included Ealdwulf, bishop-elect of Mayo, in 786 and the unfortunate eleventh-century Irish slave Moriuht, who was sold at Corbridge's market. Corbridge was also the site of a major battle between Rǫgnvaldr (travelling from Ireland), the king of Alba and the house of Bamburgh in 918.[145]

The Stanegate is only patchily traceable further west, and it has been argued that its western section was barely surfaced.[146] This is ironic given that *Stanegate* means 'stone road', and indeed excavations prior to the installation of the Shell north-western pipeline in the 1990s found a cobbled road just north-east of Carlisle.[147] Slightly further north, the Military Way linked the forts of Hadrian's Wall.[148] St Cuthbert made several journeys to Carlisle along this route, on one occasion passing through a mountainous area called the *regio Æchse*, which has been identified with the area around the wall-fort of *Aesica* (Great Chesters).[149] Excavations in Carlisle have shown that the main roads into the city 'almost certainly continued to function into the medieval period and later'.[150] Small finds bear this out: they include a *sceat* and over sixty *stycas*, mostly from around the cathedral precinct, which may have been the site of a minster.[151] On one east–west road (Crown and Anchor Lane), a continuous series of metalling was discovered, along which late- and post-Roman buildings were aligned. Not all Anglo-Saxon buildings respected the plan of the late Roman town, however: at Blackfriars' Street a post-in-slot building cut across two Roman structures at some point in the post-Roman period.[152]

---

[142] Hanson *et al.*, 'The Agricolan supply-base'; Mason, *Roman Britain*, 96.

[143] *Corebricg ca* 1050: Mawer, *The Place-Names*, 52; Harrison, *The Bridges*, 101–2; Baker and Brookes, *Beyond the Burghal Hidage*, 157.

[144] Collingwood Bruce, *Handbook*, 90–9; Forster and Knowles, 'Corstopitum', 272; Collins, *Hadrian's Wall*, 102, 110, 172. The brooches detailed in Miket, 'Two Anglo-Saxon brooches' may be relevant but are possibly from Tadcaster. For the minsters, see Taylor and Taylor, *Anglo-Saxon Architecture*, I, 172–6; Richardson, 'A late pre-Conquest carving'.

[145] *HR* (ed. Arnold, I, 28); Warner of Rouen, *Moriuht* (ed. and transl. McDonough, 76–7); *HSC* 22, 24 (ed. and transl. South, 60–3).

[146] Poulter, 'The date', 54–5.

[147] Lambert, *Transect through Time*, 12–13.

[148] Margary, *Roman Roads*, 443–50.

[149] *Vita Sancti Cuthberti auctore anonymo* IV, 5 (ed. and transl. Colgrave, *Two Lives*, 116–17); Phythian-Adams, *Land of the Cumbrians*, 51–2. Colgrave's rendering (*Ahse*) is questionable, as noted by Bullough, 'A neglected early ninth-century manuscript', 118.

[150] McCarthy *et al.*, *The Roman Waterlogged Remains*, 13.

[151] McCarthy *et al.*, *A Roman, Anglian and Medieval Site*, 180–1; *idem et al.*, *The Southern Lanes*, 47–8, 118; *idem et al.*, *Castle Street*, 48–52; Zant and Howard-Davis, *The Carlisle Millennium Project*, I, 469–70; II, 686–7. On a possible association between the *sceatta* coins and ecclesiastical activity at Carlisle see Higham, *The Northern Counties*, 303.

[152] McCarthy *et al.*, *A Roman, Anglian and Medieval Site*, 70–3; compare the alignment of St Cuthbert's church with a road: McCarthy, 'Thomas', 241–56.

The maritime approach to Carlisle takes in the hazardous shallows of the Solway Firth. The entire coastline of the Solway Firth has changed significantly since medieval times, for the firth used to extend up to 2 miles/3.2km further inland.[153] It is likely that shallow-draught boats could sail to Carlisle in the first millennium, given that barges served the city in the thirteenth century.[154] The Solway coast south of Carlisle had been defended in Roman times by a system of fortlets and milecastles that was effectively an extension of Hadrian's Wall. The installations were eventually consolidated at major coastal forts such as Maryport, where evidence of sub- or post-Roman inhabitation is currently accumulating.[155] Some of the smaller coastal forts are likely to have had harbours, including Burrow Walls, which lay north of the Derwent estuary. I suggest that this harbour became attached to the ecclesiastical site at Workington, which had links to Ireland and the Cuthbertine community.[156] The harbour was located a short distance from the likely site of the minster, a typical arrangement for a coastal ecclesiastical community.[157]

I have collected a disparate body of evidence to show that the Solway Firth and the Tyne Valley were significant arteries of communication in the early medieval period, as they had been in Roman times. During Ecgfrith's reign both the Tyne Valley and Carlisle were closely linked with royalty, and it is reasonable to describe both of those areas as Northumbrian heartlands.[158] By the early tenth century, however, the Solway Firth had become a highly contested territory, which may have heightened the attractiveness of more southerly crossing places and ports.

North of the Solway

The Romans had a more ephemeral impact to the north of Hadrian's Wall than further south, and roads fell out of the hands of their Roman builders and maintainers at a relatively early stage. Even so, textual evidence illustrates that the lines of major Roman roads were still being followed in the late-medieval period. It is unclear whether the Romans had a naval strategy for the north side of the Solway, beyond deterring raiders. The maritime significance of the area is nevertheless clear, for the fast currents in the North Channel propel sailors from north-eastern Ireland into the Solway Firth.

Turning first to shipping, the north side of the Solway has experienced significant coastal changes since the Middle Ages. In general the firth's estuaries and river systems are likely to have been navigable further inland than they are today, although localised shifts of channels and sandbanks must be taken into account. Starting in the east, the harbour on the River Annan is currently at Annan itself, 2 miles/3.2km from the sea. In the nineteenth century, Annan had a larger number of vessels than any other port north of Solway.[159] Goods were originally landed on the bank, where a motte was constructed in the twelfth century. This practice

---

[153] Neilson, 'Annals of the Solway', 20–2.
[154] Phythian-Adams, *Land of the Cumbrians*, 13, cf. Higham and Jones, *Carvetii*, 44; Higham, *The Northern Counties*, 220 argues that Carlisle was reached from the sea in Roman times.
[155] Jarrett, *Maryport*, 6–8, 83–9; Higham, *The Northern Counties*, 215; Symonds, 'Maryport's mystery monuments'.
[156] Cleere, 'Roman harbours', 38; see below, 112.
[157] Deckers, 'The maritime cultural landscape'.
[158] Rollason, *Northumbria*, 50–2.
[159] Scott, *Solway Country*, 103.

is referred to in a *computus* of Edward I (1299), which reveals that the goods had come by sea from Skinburness, on the Cumbrian coast.[160] Waterborne routes across the Solway tended to avoid the mosses west of Carlisle and head for ports located further south in Cumbria, as in this case. A similar pattern of cross-Solway contacts is evident in tenth- and eleventh-century sculpture, which circumvented the head-waters of the Solway.[161]

The River Nith flows out into a more open section of the Solway Firth, and the head of navigation is currently at Dumfries. In 1186, Dumfries became a royal burgh, after several decades of Scottish royal encroachment on the lordship of Nithsdale.[162] By early modern times Dumfries had become the centre of legal trade on the Solway, as opposed to smuggling via the Isle of Man, and the channel began to be cleared and deepened from 1790 onwards.[163] Again, circumstances may have been better for early medieval boats, and the proximity of a twelfth-century motte to the head of naviga-tion suggests a similar disembarking arrangement to Annan.[164] There were several other landing places and creeks in the Nith estuary that could have been used by shal-low-draught boats in the early medieval period.[165] Further west, the River Dee had a significant port at Kirkcudbright that handled nearly as much tonnage as Dumfries in 1846.[166] The medieval town of Kirkcudbright lay on a ford across the lower Dee that was partly encircled by a tidal creek, the harbour originally being located at its mouth. The creek originally ran close to the church of St Cuthbert's, which seems to have been the site of a Northumbrian minster.[167] The remains of a furnished Viking grave have been found in the churchyard, and the lavish Galloway Viking hoard emerged not far away, although the precise location has not been disclosed.[168]

Further west again, the Machars peninsula enjoys easy inter-visibility with the Isle of Man. This was the home of the major ecclesiastical site of Whithorn, which had close links with Man and Ireland through its harbour on the Isle of Whithorn.[169] The most westerly peninsula, the Rhinns of Galloway, has a hammer-headed shape with arms stretching north and south; the latter looks onto the Ards peninsula in north-eastern Ireland. The tidal races around the Rhinns and Machars pose a chal-lenge to navigation, and early sailors sought to mitigate some of the dangers by using portages. The place-names West and East Tarbert mark the use of a short portage in order to avoid navigation around the Mull of Galloway, the element *tairbert* being *tar* 'across' + a form of the verb *beirid* 'carry', hence 'carrying/bringing' of boats.[170] Another key site was Luce Sands, where a market grew up next to a portage to Loch Ryan, from which sailors could progress safely towards the Firth of Clyde

---

[160] *Calendar of Documents relating to Scotland II* (ed. Bain, 284); Graham and Truckell, 'Old harbours', 117–17.

[161] Bailey, 'Irish Sea contacts', 18–19; Phythian-Adams, *Land of the Cumbrians*, 15. Compare Scott, *Solway Country*, 103 on later cross-Solway trade; see Winchester and Crosby, *England's Landscape: the North West*, 57 for Solway fords.

[162] Oram, *The Lordship*, 106, 196–7.

[163] Historic Environment Scotland, 'The Canmore database', ID 65521; Graham and Truckell, 'Old harbours', 124. For smuggling, see Prevost, 'The Solway smugglers', 61–5.

[164] Graham and Truckell, 'Old harbours', 123–6, 128.

[165] *Ibid.*, 123–6, 128.

[166] Scott, *Solway Country*, 103.

[167] Graham and Truckell, 'Old harbours', 131; see below,112–13.

[168] 'The Canmore database', ID 64074; Scott, 'A note', 52; Graham-Campbell, *Whithorn*, 17–18.

[169] See below, 112–13, 214; Graham, 'Some old harbours', 49–51, 56–60.

[170] eDIL, *s.v. tairbert*; MacQueen, *Place-Names in the Rhinns*, 43.

and Kintyre.[171] The prehistoric beach-market at Luce Sands remained important in the post-Roman period, yielding three penannular brooches and more than a dozen Northumbrian *styca*s.[172] The recent discovery of an Anglo-Saxon strap-end, Hiberno-Norse ring-pin and harness mount on the shore of Loch Ryan suggests there was a similar beach market at the other end of the portage.[173] The significance of the Rhinns for Irish sailors is revealed by a twelfth-century text that describes the journey of Néidne mac Adna, Ireland's most vaunted poet, from Kintyre to Ireland. Néidne visited two ports that are located in Galloway, *Rind Snóc* and *Port Ríg*.[174] The itinerary of the poet indicates that the unidentified *Rind Snóc* was the more northerly of the ports, while *Port Ríg* was an early name for Portpatrick.[175] Although the text offers a somewhat fantastical literary representation of travel, Portpatrick's role as the chief Galwegian port for Ireland is well attested from the early modern period onwards.[176] Since the name *Port Ríg* means 'king's port' it is tempting to speculate that this harbour once accommodated a Northumbrian fleet.

I now turn to the roads on which travellers could have made onward journeys from the Solway ports to eastern Northumbria. Two Roman roads ran out of Nithsdale, one via Lochmaben and Lockerbie; another via Durisdeer to Crawford. A suspected Viking grave has been found at Carronbridge, next to a cobbled section of the route through Nithsdale.[177] The longevity of these routes can be tested by comparing the references to Scottish royal pilgrimages to Whithorn in the late-fifteenth- and early sixteenth-century accounts of the Lord High Treasurer. These confirm the continued importance of the Roman road junctions at Crawford and Durisdeer.[178] Thus, even though the Roman military maintained the roads for a short time, their courses were still visible to late-medieval travellers. A number of the locations mentioned in the accounts, such as Minnigaff and Penninghame, have yielded pre-Norman sculpture and are likely to be the locations of early medieval churches.[179]

Two major Roman roads ran northwards from Carlisle and Corbridge, heading for the Firths of Clyde and Forth, respectively. These routes would have facilitated travel between the northern edges of the Northumbrian kingdom and Gaelic-speaking areas further north, including the incipient kingdom of Alba. One road is named *Derestrete* in a description of a boundary in twelfth-century Lauderdale, a name that the Cuthbertine community applied to the same road between the Rivers Tees and Wear.[180] The north-bound roads were linked by a cross-country route between Lockerbie and Newstead; the central section, which ran near the fort of Raeburnfoot, was expertly constructed in the manner of a Roman road. Another cross-country road

---

[171] Davies, 'The diffusion', 44; Bradley *et al.*, 'Maritime havens', 29–30; Griffiths, *Early Medieval Whithorn*, 6–8.

[172] Cormack, 'Northumbrian coins'; Griffiths, 'Glenluce Sands', 98–9; *idem*, *Vikings*, 110–11; EMC find-spot Glenluce.

[173] Griffiths, *Early Medieval Whithorn*, 8–9.

[174] *The Book of Leinster* (ed. Best *et al.*, IV, 815).

[175] *CPNS*, 157–8.

[176] Graham, 'Some old harbours', 56–60.

[177] Margary, *Roman Roads*, 464–6 (nos 76, 77); Maxwell, *The Romans*, 81–3; *idem*, 'The evidence', 28; Graham-Campbell, *Whithorn*, 17–18; McLeod, 'A traveller's end?'

[178] *Compota Thesaurariorum Regum Scotorum* (ed. Dickinson *et al.*), I–V. An example is James IV's overnight stay at Durisdeer in 1506–7 while on a journey to Whithorn: III, 373. Cf. Graham, 'Some old harbours, 69–73; Craig, 'The distribution', I, 36–7.

[179] Craig, 'The distribution', I, 37.

[180] *Regesta regum Scottorum* I, no. 236 (ed. Barrow, 258); *HSC* 9 (ed. and transl. South, 50–1); Oram, 'Trackless, impenetrable and underdeveloped?', 309.

ran from Crawford to the port of Cramond, a point of departure for travel across the Firth of Forth and into Pictish territory.[181] A significant number of post-Roman and Anglo-Saxon artefacts have been found at this fort, which suggests that it continued to be used during the early medieval period.[182] Some scholars have identified Cramond with Bede's *urbs Giudi*, the *urbs quae vocatur Iudeu* where Penda cornered and besieged Oswiu according to *Historia Brittonum*.[183] A potential stumbling block is Bede's application of the term *urbs* to fortified sites of non-Roman origin, although this was not a universal rule.[184] Other commentators have highlighted Bede's description of the *urbs* as *in medio sui* ('in the middle of it, the firth') as indicative of an island in the middle of the firth. Cramond Island is an attractive possibility given its tidal access to the mainland, and its similarity to the *urbs* on Clyde Rock (Dumbarton), which Bede discusses in the same passage.[185] A third possibility is that Bede was thinking of somewhere in the middle of the firths of Forth and Clyde, in which case Castle Rock, Stirling, might be a candidate. Stirling is not in fact located centrally on the isthmus, but its strategic importance is clear: it stands by the head of tides on the River Forth, where there was a ford for the Roman road that ran north of the Antonine Wall.[186] This may be one of the fords that was fortified by Cináed mac Maíl Choluim (*ob.* 995) following his raid into Northumbrian territory as far as Stainmore. That act of fortification indicates that the fords were perceived as a likely route of invasion from the south.[187] The Forth crossings were of immense strategic significance to the Northumbrians in their dealings with the Gaelic world.

The Firth of Forth also sustained ecclesiastical interactions between the Northumbrian and Gaelic worlds. Simon Taylor has shown that the names of abbots of Iona are found in numerous place-names alongside routes from Iona to Lindisfarne. Churchmen and pilgrims would have sailed into Loch Etive before following well-worn mountain passes to the crossroads at Crianlarich. They then moved southwards towards Loch Lomond and the Clyde, or south-east to the ford over the Forth at Stirling. The firth could be negotiated by boat to reach various churches on its southern edge. The tracks across the Lammermuir Hills completed the journey to Lindisfarne, and a Roman road ran to the affiliated church of Melrose.[188] There was

[181] Margary, *Roman Roads*, 455–64 (no. 7f).
[182] Cessford, 'Post-Severan Cramond'.
[183] *HE* I, 12, 1 (ed. Lapidge, I, 150; ed. and transl. Colgrave and Mynors, 40–1); *HB* 64 (ed. Mommsen, 205–8; ed. and transl. Morris, 38, 79). *Giudi* is thought to be an English rendering of *Iudeu*, the *G-* being a palatal approximant: Breeze, 'Some Celtic place-names', 59–60. For the identification with Cramond, see Blair, 'The origins', 27–8; Rutherford, '*Giudi* revisited', although the latter's case was complicated by use of the Ravenna Cosmography, as noted by Jackson, 'Varia 1', 6–7.
[184] Campbell, 'Bede's words', 101; criticised by Dunshea, 'The Brittonic kingdoms', 172–3.
[185] Fraser, 'Bede', 15–16, 21, notes problems with the Cramond Island identification but keeps it in contention. Skene, *Celtic Scotland*, I, 71, favoured Inchkeith.
[186] Graham, 'Giudi'; Jackson, 'Varia 1', 4–5. The geographical difficulties are discussed by Fraser, 'Bede', 3–9; Dunshea, 'The Brittonic kingdoms', 176–7. For the Roman road, see Margary, *Roman Roads*, 491 (no. 9a).
[187] CKA (ed. and transl. Hudson, 151, 161). *Vallavit ripas uadorum Forthin* 'he fortified the banks of the fords of the Forth'. Hudson includes a length mark on Forthín, making it a diminutive, 'little Forth'. Another option is *foirthiu*, an accusative plural of 'fords' (cf. eDIL *s.v. foirthiu*) but that would be tautologous. Watson identified these fords specifically as the Fords of Frew west of Stirling: CPNS, 52–3, 349–50. For later evidence of fords across the Forth, see McGuigan, 'Neither Scotland nor England', 149–51.
[188] Taylor, 'Seventh-century Iona abbots', esp. 49–52; compare Edmonds, 'The practicalities', 134 (fig. 7.1) for Roman roads.

a particularly significant church at Abercorn, not far from the crossing that became known as Queensferry in honour of Queen Margaret (*ob.* 1093). Abercorn served as the seat of Trumwine, the Northumbrian bishop of the Picts; he fled southwards after the disaster at Nechtansmere (685) and may have supplied Bede's information about the Firth of Forth.[189] On the eastern edge of this coastline, the elite site of Dunbar and several major churches clustered around the most northerly point of the Northumbrian North Sea coastal trading route. The church at Auldhame has recently yielded a rich mid-tenth-century Viking burial, which is suggestive of continued use of these shipping routes.[190]

There is a long-standing debate about the use of the Forth–Clyde isthmus as a portage during the Viking Age, which has significant bearing on the logistics of Northumbrian–Gaelic contact. Alfred Smyth argued that boats were transferred between York and Dublin via the Forth–Clyde portage, rather than sailed around the northern tip of Britain.[191] This would have been a portage on a grand scale, and yet it is unrecorded, and so it is worth considering the feasibility of this route. The firths of Forth and Clyde may have been navigable further inland than today, in a similar way to the Solway. Nevertheless, the land-based section of the journey would still have been extensive, given that the isthmus is currently 30 miles/55.5km across.[192] Irish kings were occasionally known to drag ships over distances as long as this: in 1065, Uí Maine and the Conmaicne dragged their boats from the sea to the Shannon in order to plunder Clonmacnoise and Clonfert, a 33-mile/53-km-long feat. Yet the denouement of this expedition reveals the difficulty of long portages, for the aggressors met resistance on the way and abandoned their ships.[193] Many portages attested in place-names, such as those on the Rhinns of Galloway, are a quarter of a mile across.[194] Neither were the famous Russian portages on the scale of the Forth–Clyde isthmus: the trade route from Staraya Ladoga to Byzantium and the Arabic world involved a portage of 2 miles/3.2km from the Lovat River to the source of the Volga.[195] Dragging or rolling a ship entailed a very considerable investment of time, energy and manpower, as shown by a 1999 reconstruction, in which hundreds of volunteers moved an 8-tonne replica Viking ship over Mavis Grind in Shetland.[196] Extraordinarily long portages such as the one undertaken by Uí Maine may have been a show of force rather than part of a routine journey.

Even if the Forth–Clyde isthmus was not a routine portage, it was a vital and well-evidenced route between Dublin and York.[197] I suggest that Dubliners berthed their ships in a harbour and trans-shipment site near the head of tidal navigation on the Clyde. The strategically important site at Govan is an obvious candidate, and

---

[189] *HE* IV, 26 (24), 2 (ed. Lapidge, II, 352; ed. and transl. Colgrave and Mynors, 428–9); Fraser, 'Bede', 5–6.

[190] Petts, 'Coastal landscapes', 81; for Auldhame, see above, 60.

[191] Smyth, *Scandinavian York and Dublin*, I, 22, 301–3.

[192] Graham-Campbell and Batey, *Vikings in Scotland*, 98. I am grateful to Alex Woolf for discussing the Forth–Clyde route with me.

[193] AFM [1065.9] (ed. and transl. O'Donovan, II, 888–9). Cf. AT [1065.1] (ed. and transl. Stokes, II, 32–3). Etchingham, 'Skuldelev 2', 84–5 discusses this and other evidence of portages in Ireland.

[194] Phillips, 'Portages', 196.

[195] Duczko, *Viking Rus*, 156.

[196] Griffiths, *Early Medieval Whithorn*, 8; 'Ship pulled by Norse power': http://news.bbc.co.uk/1/hi/uk/380273.stm (28 June 1999). For Mavis Grind in the Viking Age, see Crawford, or Mavis Grind in the Viking Age, see Crawford, Scandinavian Scotland, 26.

[197] Smyth, *Scandinavian York and Dublin*, I, 35–6, 63–4, 94–5, 108; II, 43–4, 272, 278–82.

its remarkable series of hogback stones and other sculpture reveals the openness of its inhabitants to seaborne contacts.[198] Travellers could then progress on horseback or on foot to the Firth of Forth, perhaps heading north to the Military Way in the rear of the Antonine Wall, which joined milecastles and forts in the same way as the route along Hadrian's Wall.[199] One obstacle for this scenario is that the name *Dyvelinstanes* was once applied to a street that ran down to York's waterfront, indicating that some Dublin traders arrived by ship. Yet ships carrying bulky cargoes are likely to have been sailed around the northern tip of Britain rather than dragged a substantial distance overland. The Orkney Islands would have played a crucial role as a stopping place or entrepôt, and there is evidence for both Anglo-Scandinavian and Irish contacts with Orkney.[200]

In short, those moving from the Northumbrian kingdom to the Gaelic world had a considerable choice of route-ways. Roman infrastructure underpinned both the road network and many of the ports. Major ecclesiastical sites, royal naval bases and Viking hoards were often located close to the vestiges of Roman engineering. This *longue durée* perspective helps us to understand which routes were available, but contemporary political flux may have been the decisive factor in the choice of one route-way over another. The channels of Gaelic–Northumbrian contact varied significantly across the period from the seventh to the eleventh century.

Ports and roads in Ireland and Dál Riata in Britain

Finally, it is necessary to consider the ease of journeys from the borders of the Northumbrian kingdom to the different parts of the Gaelic world. The western coast of the kingdom faced Brega, the Isle of Man and Ulaid territory, while the northernmost parts offered access to crossings over the Firth of Forth. Once travellers had voyaged across the water, they visited coastal trading sites or made onward journeys to political centres and churches.

Starting in Ireland, there were well-established lines of communication connecting ports to major sites inland. This much is clear from Cogitosus's late-seventh-century *Vita* of St Brigit, which refers to the construction of a road under the auspices of a king who mobilised labour from all of the client peoples of Leinster.[201] The vignette is included to set the scene for a miraculous diversion of a river away from the road; even so, it highlights the mechanism for maintaining infrastructure. There were various types of roads, ranging from the ceremonial highway linking Tara and Skeen to the *tóchar* 'causeway' across the bog of the Lámraige.[202] Colm Ó Lochlainn was the first scholar to map these inter-regional route-ways: he examined references to journeys in hagiographical and literary texts, place-names that refer to fords and tales of the five great highways (*sligid*).[203] His work has since been developed by

---

[198] For the nature of the site and its sculpture, see, for example, Driscoll, *Govan*, 8–13; Crawford, *The Govan Hogbacks*, 18–23.

[199] Margary, *Roman Roads*, 488–90.

[200] For the street name, see Smyth, *Scandinavian York and Dublin*, II, 236–7, 256; for navigation to and around Orkney, see Crawford, *The Northern Earldoms*, 11–14. Hudson, *Viking Pirates*, 17 indicates that a journey from Dublin to Orkney took 30 hours.

[201] Cogitosus, *Vita S. Brigitae* 30 (transl. Connolly and Picard, 23–4).

[202] *Tochmarc Étaíne* (ed. and transl. Bergin and Best, 176–9); Bhreathnach, *Ireland*, 59–60, 220–1, 226–7; Doherty, 'A road', 22–5.

[203] Ó Lochlainn, 'Roadways'.

other scholars, who have examined imported goods of the turn of the first millenium, as well as early medieval imports. The exotic goods correlate with Ó Lochlainn's map of roads and ports, especially in north-eastern Ireland, Leinster, and the Irish Midlands.[204] The resulting maps provide an indication of the routes that Northumbrian travellers encountered upon landing in Ireland.

A number of trading sites lay on the eastern coast of Ireland, facing western Northumbria. The significance of Strangford Lough (Co. Down), a sea lough that offers sheltered harbours, is revealed by both texts and archaeology. Distinctive shards of glass from an Anglo-Saxon claw beaker and palm cup have been found alongside imported pottery at Dunnyneil Island on the lough.[205] Muirchú's *Vita S. Patricii* portrays Patrick sailing from Brega to Inber Sláne near Saul, where an important Patrician church grew up on the southern edge of Strangford Lough.[206] Further south, several ports on the coast of Brega are mentioned in texts of the pre-Viking period, including Inber Colpthai on the Boyne.[207] A cemetery nearby has yielded evidence of Anglo-Saxon influence on burial practices, and these graves may be the resting places of laymen who accompanied English ecclesiastical dignitaries to Ireland.[208] Similarly, a post-built structure found at Temple Bar in Dublin resembles Anglo-Saxon examples, and this is a tantalising hint that the Liffey sustained pre-Viking contact.[209] The Isle of Man could have acted as a staging post on journeys between western Northumbrian ports and the Irish coast. Indeed, some of the exotic goods imported to north-eastern Ireland were redistributed to the Isle of Man, and perhaps to the elite sites of the Solway Firth.[210]

Northumbrian travellers might alternatively access the Gaelic world by visiting Iona. Two episodes in Adomnán's *Vita Sancti Columbae* imply that Iona was in regular contact with *Daire Calgaig* (Derry); the two places were linked by their bond with the northern Uí Néill group Cenél Conaill. The first episode concerns two Columban monks who rowed to Ireland in order to visit St Fintén, stopping at Daire Calgaig on the way.[211] The longer episode features a man who resided in Ireland while he undertook penance prescribed by Columba. Having completed his tasks, the penitent wished to return to Iona, and he sought passage on a boat that was setting sail from Derry. Yet the crew refused to take him because *non erant de monachis sancti Columbae* 'they were not of the monks of Saint Columba'. The penitent eventually obtained his passage by invoking a miracle through Columba.[212] It is not certain that St Columba had founded the church at Derry by this point, but the church had certainly come into being by the time when Adomnán was writing.[213] Iona offered access to other Hebridean islands and the Kintyre peninsula. Ships from the continent berthed at Dunadd on Kintyre, which is probably to be identified with

---

[204] Warner, 'Some observations', 269, 277; Comber, 'Trade', 82–9.

[205] McCormick and McDonald, *Excavations*, 43, 51; Campbell, *Continental and Mediterranean Imports*, 32.

[206] Muirchú, *Vita*, I 11 (ed. and transl. Bieler, *The Patrician Texts*, 84–5).

[207] Muirchú, *Vita*, I 14 (ed. and transl. Bieler, *The Patrician Texts*, 78–9); Charles-Edwards, *Early Christian Ireland*, 16; Bhreathnach, 'The medieval kingdom', 411–12.

[208] O'Brien, 'Contacts', 98; *eadem*, *Post-Roman Britain*, 182–3.

[209] Simpson, 'Pre-Viking and early Viking-Age Dublin', 61.

[210] Campbell, *Continental and Mediterranean Imports*, 73.

[211] Adomnán, *Vita Sancti Columbae* I.2 (ed. and transl. Anderson and Anderson, 18–23); cf. Lacey, *Cenél Conaill*, 141.

[212] Adomnán, *Vita Sancti Columbae* II.39 (ed. and transl. Anderson and Anderson, 158–61).

[213] Sharpe, *Adomnán*, 29.

Adomnán's *caput regionis* 'chief place of the region'.[214] Northumbrian dignitaries such as St Oswald and King Oswiu used Iona as their stepping stone to the rest of the Gaelic world.

In summary, I have shown that roads and ports connected the Gaelic world and the western and northern areas of the Northumbrian kingdom. It is worth reflecting on the frequency with which the routes were used, for travel was not open to everyone in this period. Major ecclesiastical communities often had their own harbours, and some even enjoyed the services of semi-professional sailors.[215] The Northumbrian kings kept royal fleets on the eastern and western coasts, and they sought to control key harbours, not merely to protect against attack but also to take tolls from traders. This is the implication of a scene in the tenth-century text *Betha Adamnáin* where the Northumbrian coastguards are dispatched to meet St Adomnán upon his arrival.[216] There has long been a debate about the extent to which kings and their administrators controlled major trading sites, and a comparison between Chester and Meols suggest that they had varying levels of success.[217] The relative ease of water transport in western Northumbria meant that smaller creeks and peninsulas offered routes of entry for Irish and Manx traders who sought to operate more freely. The collapse of the Northumbrian kingdom in the late ninth century opened major estuaries such as the Ribble to Viking activity, eventually facilitating the dynastic link between York and Dublin. Thus social, political and economic factors governed the selection of an itinerary from the various available options. The variety of these routes supports my argument that Northumbrian–Gaelic contacts flowed along diverse channels.

[214] Adomnán, *Vita Sancti Columbae* I.28 (ed. and transl. Anderson and Anderson, 54–5). Fraser, *From Caledonia to Pictland*, 243, suggests that the site might equally be identified with Dunollie on Oban Bay, closer to Iona.

[215] Wooding, *Communication*, 96; Edmonds, 'The practicalities', 131.

[216] *Betha Adamnáin* (ed. and transl. Herbert and Ó Riain, 12–13, 54–7).

[217] In general see Hodges, *Dark Age Economics*, esp. 54; McCormick, *The Origins*, 639–69. For greater emphasis on the merchants, see Loveluck, *Northwest Europe*, 204–6; for Meols, see Griffiths *et al.*, *Meols*, 404–5.

5

A GOLDEN AGE OF ECCLESIASTICAL CONTACTS

In the popular imagination, Northumbrian–Gaelic interaction is often associated with the atmospheric site of Lindisfarne. The tidal island, at once remote from the mainland and yet visible from Bamburgh, seems to evoke the spirit of 'Celtic Christianity'.[1] Lindisfarne's community enjoyed theological, intellectual and artistic interchanges with their counterparts elsewhere in the Insular world and beyond. These cultural connections arose from the travels of churchmen, skilled craftspeople and manuscripts. In this chapter, I examine ecclesiastical links from the perspective of Church organisation, and I explore how the northern and western edges of the Northumbrian kingdom sustained ecclesiastical relations.

My geographical focus lends itself to a study of churches and their networks. No manuscripts have survived from the west and north of the kingdom, which rules out consideration of artistic and intellectual exchanges. Even so, it is worth reflecting on recent research into those topics in order to place my study in its broader cultural context. During the earliest phases of interaction, Irish churchmen helped to devise an alphabet for Old English, most likely to assist Anglo-Saxons who were studying in Ireland. The Northumbrian tradition of glossing manuscripts in the vernacular may owe something to this tutelage in Ireland, where the vernacular was written at an early stage.[2] Budding Northumbrian scholars flocked to churches associated with the *Romani*, a group who had adopted the dating of Easter that was current in Rome. These churches were located in the south of Ireland, creating a strikingly different pattern of contact from the more northerly political links that I have explored. Northumbrian students resided at churches such as St Berrihert's Kyle, Toureen Peacaun (Co. Tipperary) and Tulach Léis na Saxan (Tullylease, Co. Cork), where the English name 'Berechtuine' appears on an intricately carved slab.[3] Another important community was Ráith Máelsigi (identified with Clonmelsh in Leinster) from which the Northumbrian Willibrord launched a mission to Frisia.[4] Texts passed from this part of Ireland to Northumbria; for example, Dáibhí Ó Cróinín has traced the

[1] For this concept, see above, 20.
[2] Ó Néill, 'The origins', 21; cf. Ó Néill, '*Romani* influences'. For interchange between Latin and the Irish and English vernaculars, compare Warntjes, *The Munich Computus*, lxxv–lxxvi; Wright, *The Irish Tradition*, esp. 33–5, 59–67. For vernacular glossing in Ireland, see Johnston, *Literacy*, 53–5 and in Northumbria, Jolly, *The Community*, 9–10.
[3] Okasha and Forsyth, *Early Christian Inscriptions*, 121–3, 253–5, 325–6; Charles-Edwards, 'The east cross'; Edmonds, 'The practicalities', 143–4; Stancliffe, 'The Irish tradition', 32. 'Berechtuine' features the epenthetic vowel, a Northumbrian feature.
[4] *HE* III, 27, 3; V, 10, 1–2 (ed. Lapidge, II, 168, 170; III, 56, 58; ed. and transl. Colgrave and Mynors, 312–15); Ó Cróinín, 'Rath Melsigi'; Fanning, 'Appendix'. For the Continental context, cf. Palmer, Anglo-Saxons, 63–5.

movement of a computistical collection to Aldhelm in Wessex and thence to Bede.[5] Aldhelm was a well-connected scholar who had been to Ireland and enjoyed a close friendship with the Northumbrian royal exile Aldfrith, a bond arguably forged on Iona.[6] By the end of the seventh century the intellectual cultures of Ireland, Iona and several Anglo-Saxon kingdoms were closely interwoven.[7]

Art history sheds further light on the circulation of manuscripts across the Insular world, notably the lavish Gospel Books of the late seventh and early eighth centuries. There has been much debate about where they were produced: broadly speaking, the manuscripts exhibit some characteristics of production in Ireland or Iona, and others that may reflect Northumbrian origins.[8] To take one example, the Book of Durrow is constructed from quinions (groups of five leaves) and has a single column of text, as do the earliest Irish manuscripts. The images are drawn from the material culture of Ireland and the Brittonic world (such as enamelled metalwork), Anglo-Saxon animal ornament and Pictish beasts.[9] The range of inspiration perhaps points most strongly to Iona, but diverse influences were circulating throughout the Insular world.[10] Continental churches were another nexus of stylistic and manuscript transmission, as seen in Echternach's manuscripts.[11] This brief excursion into art and manuscript history reveals the vigour of Insular and Continental cultural contacts.

In the absence of this rich body of manuscript evidence, other information must be used to explore ecclesiastical links in the west and north of the Northumbrian kingdom.[12] The writings of Bede are informative; yet Bede's attitude to the Gaelic world was not necessarily representative of other Northumbrian writers. Three distinct views arose in the wake of the Synod of Whitby in 664, where the calculation of the date of Easter was resolved. One party left Northumbria because they adhered to St Columba's teachings on Easter; another adopted the Roman Easter calculation while honouring the Columban legacy; and a third equated the older Easter practices with the Quartodeciman heresy.[13] Bede's attitude may have evolved over time, for he reported the papal condemnation of the Quartodeciman heresy among the Scotti in *Chronica maiora* (composed in 725), whereas he omitted this

---

5 Ó Cróinín, 'The Irish provenance', esp. 242–3; cf. Wallis, *Bede*, lxxii–lxxiii.
6 Aldhelm, *Epistola ad Acircium* (ed. Ehwald, 479–80; transl. Lapidge and Herren, 31–46). For their link with Iona, see Lapidge, 'The career', 22–30, whereas Yorke, 'Adomnán', 42 suggests they met in Ireland.
7 Note, for example, the relationship between the canonical collection Theodore's penintential, compiled by a Deiran, and Cummian's penitential, a text of the *Romani*: *Penitential* (ed. Finsterwalder, *Die Canones*, 239–334); *Poenitentiale Cummiani* (ed. and transl. Bieler, 108–35); Charles-Edwards, 'The penitential', 156–8; Flechner, 'The making', 129–30; *idem*, 'An Insular tradition', esp. 44–6.
8 For example, compare views of Durham Cathedral Library MS A.II.10: Brown in Verey, *The Durham Gospels*, 42–9; Ó Cróinín, 'Pride and prejudice', 361–2; Netzer, 'Willibrord's scriptorium', 204–5; Brown, *The Lindisfarne Gospels*, 47–8. For the difficulties of ascribing manuscripts to specific churches, see David Dumville's sceptical treatment of the Lindisfarne scriptorium: *A Palaeographer's Review*, 76–80, 129–30.
9 Dublin, Trinity College, MS 57, fol. 3v (carpet page); fol. 191v (lion); fol. 192v (John carpet page); Lowe, *Codices Latini Antiquores*, II, no. 273.
10 A recent discussion of the matter is Netzer, 'The Book of Durrow'; cf. Ó Corráin, *Clavis*, I, 53–6.
11 Netzer, *Cultural Interplay*, 4–8; Ó Corráin, *Clavis*, I, 477–82.
12 Gameson, 'Northumbrian books', 43, and see 75–83 for a list of Northumbrian manuscripts.
13 Stancliffe, *Bede, Wilfrid*, 1–12; cf. Richter, *Ireland*, 149; Charles-Edwards, *Early Christian Ireland*, 320, 336; *idem*, 'Wilfrid', 244–8. For the contrast with the Britons, see Stancliffe, *Bede and the Britons*, 18.

detail from *Historia ecclesiastica* (731).[14] Bede came to see Saint Áedán and his pupil Ceadda (Chad) as embodiments of Gregory the Great's pastoral ideal.[15] This presentation of Gaelic-speaking churchmen can be compared with the late-seventh/ early eighth-century *Vita Sancti Cuthberti* by an anonymous Lindisfarne monk and Eddius Stephanus's *Vita Wilfridi*.[16] In Ireland, a handful of Latin hagiographical texts date from the same period, and vernacular Lives start to emerge in the tenth century.[17] These texts sometimes depict the travels of saints and the churches they founded, which provide oblique insights into relations between churches at the time of writing.[18]

In this chapter I examine three groups of churches whose interactions illustrate the links between Northumbrian clerics and their counterparts in Gaeldom. What emerges is the wide range of locations involved and the length of time for which different churches remained in contact. In some cases, these links continued during the Viking Age and beyond.

Church organisation in the Northumbrian and Gaelic worlds

Early medieval churches forged connections – both institutional and informal – that transcended political boundaries. Historians have weighed up the balance between such far-flung connections and more territorially coherent spheres of influence. The debate has focused primarily on Church organisation in Ireland, but it is worth considering how churches in the west and north of the Northumbrian kingdom fit into the picture.

Widespread ecclesiastical connections were prominent in Kathleen Hughes's influential study of the early Irish Church (1966). She argued that the original unit of organisation was the episcopal *paruchia*, which was coterminous with the *túath*. This unit offered an alternative to the *civitas*, which underpinned the bishop's see in formerly Roman areas.[19] The system was apparently ill-adapted to Ireland's decentralised society, and so dispersed monastic federations (which Hughes termed *paruchiae*) came to the fore instead.[20] Columba's churches epitomised the far-flung

---

[14] *Chronica maiora* §541 in *De temporum ratione* (ed. Jones, 525; transl. Wallis, *Bede*, 228); Higham, *(Re-)reading Bede*, 122–4, 128–43. For debate about the way in which Bede presented the Irish contribution to Northumbrian Christianity, compare Pepperdene, 'Bede's *Historia Ecclesiastica*' with McCann, '*Plures de Scottorum regione*', 23–5.

[15] *HE* III, 28, 3 (ed. Lapidge, II, 174, 176; ed. and transl. Colgrave and Mynors, 316–17); Thacker, 'Bede and the Irish', 37–8, 43–4, 49–50, drawing on *idem*, 'Bede's ideal', 137–46.

[16] *Vita S. Cuthberti auctore anonymo* (ed. and transl. Colgrave, *Two Lives*); *Vita Sancti Wilfridi* (ed. and transl. Colgrave).

[17] Sharpe, *Medieval Irish Saints' Lives*, 18–26; Ó Corráin, *Clavis*, I, 261–8, 274–90, 336.

[18] A church disputed between three communities is mentioned in Tírechán, *Collectanea*, 22.4 (ed. and transl. Bieler, *The Patrician Texts*, 140–1); cf. Charles-Edwards, *Early Christian Ireland*, 11–12. The nature of these hagiographical relationships (ranging from dependence to transient alliances) is considered by Bitel, *Isle of the Saints*, 194–207; Mac Shamhráin, *Church and Polity*, 26–7, 171, 185–92; Firey, 'Cross-examining the witness', 42.

[19] Hughes, *The Church*, 50. Her usage of *paruchia* drew on Kenney, *Sources*, 291–2, 329. For episcopal organisation in the *túath*, see Charles-Edwards, *Early Christian Ireland*, 244–5, 248.

[20] Hughes, *The Church*, 39, 79–90, 132–3, cf. Ó Cróinín, *Early Medieval Ireland*, 166–70. Contemporary examples of the application of the term *paruchia* to a monastic federation were collected by Mac Shamhráin, *Church and Polity*, 168–72, although some are rejected by Etchingham, *Church Organisation*, 124.

federation; his ecclesiastical communities comprised a *familia*, a spiritual family that transcended boundaries of kin and kingdom.[21] An ecclesiastical traveller who moved from one territory to another, and especially overseas, was undertaking *peregrinatio*. This potentially dangerous practice had ascetic connotations and was therefore prized by the ecclesiastics of the era. The legal category of *deorad Dé* 'exile for God' distinguished the *peregrini* from the legally disadvantaged *muirchuirthe* 'one thrown up by the sea'.[22]

More recently, scholars have placed weight on bishops' roles and territorial jurisdiction. The reappraisal began with Richard Sharpe's 1984 article, which highlighted the continued significance of bishops. Colmán Etchingham has since accumulated much evidence for the application of the term *paruchia* to bishops' pastoral jurisdictions.[23] In Etchingham's view, there was a single, diverse system of organisation encompassing monastic, episcopal and temporal elements, and this could accommodate dispersed *familiae* as well as contiguous groups of churches.[24] By the seventh century the most influential Irish churches housed monks (in the strict sense), a bishop and secular clergy, and they offered pastoral care to their tenants (*manaig*).[25] A question remains about the role of small churches in pastoral care, such as the *mineclais na túaithe* 'small church of the *túath*' that appear in the eighth-century tract *Ríagal Phátraic*. Small churches are relatively well-attested archaeologically and (in some areas) architecturally in Ireland.[26]

Turning to the Northumbrian kingdom, John Blair's influential model of pre-Viking English ecclesiastical organisation focuses on minsters (Old English *mynster*, from Latin *monasterium*). While the terminology is monastic, minsters were multi-functional, sustaining ordained clergy alongside monks and playing a major role in pastoral care.[27] In his letter to Bishop Ecgberht of York, Bede suggested that bishops could conduct their episcopal activities from minsters, a flexible model that resembles the great Irish churches.[28] The 'minster hypothesis' has been criticised for downplaying the episcopal dimension, for bishops would have consecrated

---

[21] Sharpe, 'Some problems', 244–5. It has been suggested that the *familia Iae* was normally the brethren of Iona itself, whereas *familia Coluim Cille* could sometimes apply to the wider network: Etchingham, *Church Organisation*, 127. However, the Iona chronicle embedded in the 'Chronicle of Ireland' applied the term *familia Iae* to Columban churchmen who lived in Pictland: AU 717.4 (ed. and transl. Mac Airt and Mac Niocaill, 172–3); CS [717] (ed. and transl. Hennessy, 94–5); *CI* 717 (transl. Charles-Edwards, I, 191).

[22] Charles-Edwards, 'The social background', 52–4. Clare Stancliffe has shown that the concept of 'white martyrdom' related to asceticism in general, rather than *peregrinatio* specifically: 'Red, white and blue martyrdom', 38–40.

[23] Sharpe, 'Some problems', 230–70; cf. Hughes, *The Church*, 68–70. Etchingham, 'The implications', 141–53; *idem, Church Organisation*, 23–31, 106–25.

[24] Etchingham, *Church Organisation*, 27–8, 90–3, 126–30.

[25] *Ibid.*, 250–62; *idem*, 'Pastoral provision', 82–3; Stancliffe, 'The Irish tradition', 24–5.

[26] *Ríagal Phátraic* (ed. and transl. O'Keeffe, 220). For a variety of views about the relationship between these *minecailsi* and the wider laity, see Etchingham, *Church Organisation*, 252–3; Swift, 'Early Irish priests', 26–31. Ó Carragáin ('Cemetery settlements', 349–50; *Churches in Medieval Ireland*, 226–7) has highlighted the numbers of archaeologically attested local churches in Ireland compared with Anglo-Saxon England.

[27] Blair, *The Church*, 135–41; Foot, *Monastic Life*, 5–10, 172–84.

[28] Bede, 'Epistola', 9–10 (ed. Plummer in *Venerabilis Baedae Opera Historica*, II, 412–14); Blair, *The Church*, 108–11.

clergy to serve the lay population and overseen the behaviour of monks.[29] There is, however, a consensus that local churches were few and far between in the pre-Viking period, and in this respect Anglo-Saxon England contrasts with Ireland.[30] One explanation is the larger and apparently more centralised nature of Anglo-Saxon kingdoms, where distribution of lands to churches could be carefully controlled. The western and northern parts of Northumbria had regional rulers akin to petty kings, but they were drawn into ceremonies to celebrate royal endowments of monasteries such as Ripon.[31]

These differences notwithstanding, Columba's *familia* may have influenced the development of dispersed groups of churches in Anglo-Saxon England. Aldhelm depicted the abbots of Wilfrid's churches as *dilecti alumni* 'beloved foster-children', a phrase reminiscent of *familia*.[32] Henry Mayr-Harting has suggested that Wilfrid learned 'the value and efficacy of a monastic confederation' during his time at Lindisfarne.[33] This mode of organisation was not unique, for Máel Rubai, abbot of the renowned church of Bangor in north-eastern Ireland, founded an offshoot at Applecross on the northern edge of Dál Riata in Britain.[34] Sarah Foot has identified several models of ecclesiastical contact: dispersed houses linked by their founder (such as Iona/Lindisfarne); friendships and intellectual connections; and minsters with dependencies, whether located far afield or in localised clusters.[35] These models highlight the potential diversity of Northumbrian-Gaelic ecclesiastical relations, and I will explore this point further by considering three major churches: Lindisfarne, York and Whithorn.

Iona and Lindisfarne

The close connection between Iona and Lindisfarne dates back to King Oswald's vision of St Columba on the eve of the battle of Heavenfield (633/4). Following his victory, Oswald founded a church at Lindisfarne and he sought its first bishop from Iona. He eventually received Áedán, a man of modest habits and strength of character, and the two worked together to Christianise the Northumbrian kingdom.[36] The longevity of the link has been debated: if the Synod of Whitby did not sever ties, it is assumed that Viking raids did. I argue that Iona's influence endured into the Viking Age, and that churches in the west and north of the kingdom nurtured these ties.

---

[29] Cambridge and Rollason, 'Debate'. Blair accepted that the role of bishops should not be underestimated but countered other criticisms in his 'Debate'. Another point at issue was whether mother parishes equate to minsters, broadly accepted by Palliser ('Review', 214), whereas Rollason ('Monasteries', 69–70) remained sceptical.

[30] Ó Carragáin, 'Cemetery settlements', 348–52.

[31] Blair, *The Church*, 75; *Vita Sancti Wilfridi* 17 (ed. and transl. Colgrave, *The Life*, 36–7).

[32] Aldhelm, *Epistola* XII (ed. Ehwald, 501; transl. Lapidge and Herren, 169). Cf. Blair, *The Church*, 97.

[33] Mayr-Harting, *The Coming of Christianity*, 78, 167 (quotation); cf. John, 'The social and political problems', 50; Roper, 'Wilfrid's landholdings', 66–7. Foot, *Monastic Life*, 265–8 notes that Irish influence might have been mediated by Continental models.

[34] AU 673.7, 722.1, 802.5 (ed. and transl. Mac Airt and Mac Niocaill, 140, 142, 176); AT [673.4], 722.1 (ed. and transl. Stokes, I, 33, 45); CS [669] (ed. and transl. Hennessy, 102–3); *CI* (transl. Charles-Edwards, I, 160, 195, 263); MacLean, 'Maelrubai', 173–6.

[35] Foot, *Monastic Life*, 251–82.

[36] *HE* III, 3, 1; III, 5, 3 (ed. Lapidge, II, 24, 40; ed. and transl. Colgrave and Mynors, 218–19, 228–9). Áedán replaced an earlier Iona bishop, whose mission was unsuccessful.

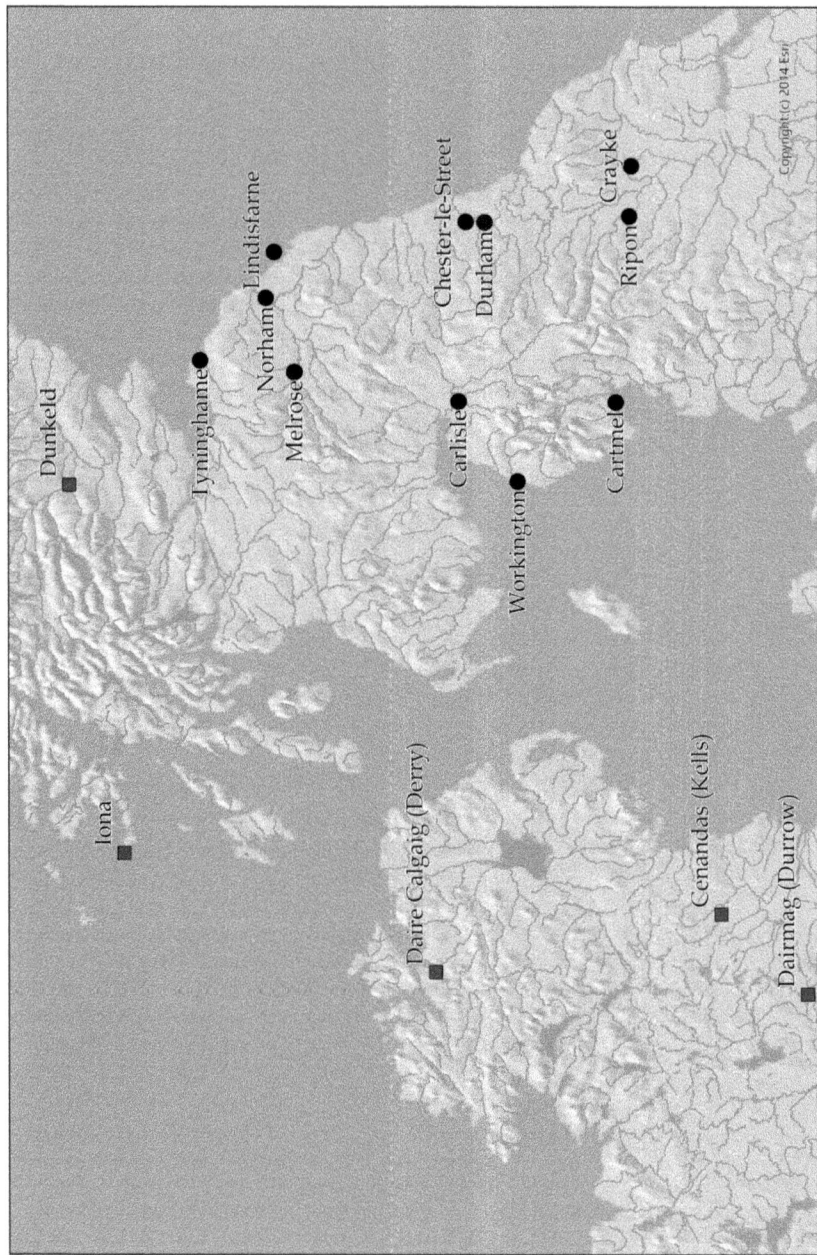

Map 5: The Cuthbertine community and the Columban familia

● The Cuthbertine churches

■ The Columban *familia*

Map labels:
Dunkeld
Iona
Tyninghame
Lindisfarne
Norham
Melrose
Chester-le-Street
Durham
Carlisle
Workington
Cartmel
Ripon
Crayke
Daire Calgaig (Derry)
Cenandas (Kells)
Dairmag (Durrow)

Copyright (c) 2014 Esri

Lindisfarne's organisation bore Iona's imprint from the time of its foundation onwards. The island was an unusual choice of episcopal seat since it lacked a Roman past; the earlier missionary Paulinus had, by contrast, been based in the Roman provincial centre of York. Moreover, as Bede relates, Lindisfarne was ruled by an abbot rather than a bishop, a pattern that replicated Iona's organisation.[37] Lindisfarne belonged to the wider Columban *familia*, and the abbot of Iona conducted visitations of Northumbria, just as he did the Columban churches in Ireland.[38] Lindisfarne's first three bishops were sent directly from Iona, and they were well connected with the wider network of the Columban *familia*.[39] The bishops drew inspiration from Ireland and Iona in order to balance the demands of their pastoral role with their contemplative activities.[40]

Iona was tied to its affiliated churches through familial links, for many of the personnel belonged to Columba's kindred, Cenél Conaill of the northern Uí Néill.[41] Of the early Lindisfarne bishops, only Áedán's genealogy is recorded, and it does not suggest Cenél Conaill affinities. The *Martyrology of Donegal* linked Áedán with a segment of the Fothairt of Leinster and the church of Scattery Island in the Shannon:

> Aedhan mac Lughair. Do shliocht Eachdhach Finn Fuath nairt o bhfuil Brighit dó. Epscop ó Inis Cathaig, acus ó Inis Medh-coit i niarthar thuaiscert Saxan mbecc, acus dia oilithre do choidh Aedhán co hInis Medcoit.

> Áedán son of Lugar. He was of the race of Eochaid Finn Fothart from whom Brigit descends. He was bishop at Inis Cathaig (Scattery Island) and at Inis Medcoit (Lindisfarne) in the north-west of Little Saxonland. Áedán went to Inis Medcoit on his pilgrimage.[42]

I suggest that the seventeenth-century compilers of the Donegal martyrology confused Áedán of Lindisfarne with Áedán, bishop of Ferns. The Irish Life of Senán of Scattery Island, which has potentially tenth-century elements, indicates a link between the two churches when it asserts that Senán attained the abbacy of Ferns.[43] Confusion between the two Áedáns may have arisen because Lindisfarne was sometimes named *Ferna*, as seen in Cuthbert's obituary in the 'Annals of the Four Masters'.[44] It is possible, then, that Áedán shared the northern background of the other leading Iona brethren. As to Bishop Fínán of Lindisfarne, he is described in his

---

37 *Vita Sancti Cuthberti auctore Beda* 16 (ed. and transl. Colgrave, 208–9); Stancliffe, 'The Irish tradition', 26.

38 This is suggested by Abbot Ségéne's personal contact with King Oswald: see Adomnán, *Vita Sancti Columbae* I.1 (ed. and transl. Anderson and Anderson, 91–2); Charles-Edwards, *Early Christian Ireland*, 250, 316. Herbert, *Iona*, 45, 48–51 suggests that the abbot of Iona conducted a visitation of Irish dependencies in 661, 673 and 692.

39 Fínán and Colmán were sent *a Scottis* and *a Scottia*, respectively: *HE* III, 25, 1, 3; IV, 4, 1 (ed. Lapidge, II, 142, 146, 220; ed. and transl. Colgrave and Mynors, 294–7, 346–7).

40 Stancliffe, 'Cuthbert', 36–40; *eadem*, 'The Irish tradition', 26.

41 For example, Columba's cousin Laisrén, prior of Durrow: Adomnán, *Vita Sancti Columbae* I.29 (ed. and transl. Anderson and Anderson, 56–7); Herbert, *Iona*, 33, 36–40, 43, 46–7, 57–8, 60, 66, 74, 79, 310–11.

42 *The Martyrology of Donegal* (ed. O'Donovan *et al.*, 230–1). I have slightly amended the translation.

43 *Betha Senáin* (ed. and transl. Stokes, *Lives of Saints*, 61–2, 208); for the dating, see Kenney, *Sources*, 364.

44 AFM 686.4 (ed. and transl. O'Donovan, I, 293).

annalistic obituary as *filius Rimedo*, 'son of Rímid'.[45] Fínán is likely to have been the son of the powerful king Colmán Rímid of Cenél nÉogain, the other leading northern Uí Néill dynasty. At the time, Cenél nEógain were allied with Cenél nGabráin, Iona's patrons in Dál Riata.[46]

Lindisfarne added to the already widespread Columban *familia* by founding churches in the Northumbrian kingdom. Melrose (Scottish Borders, formerly Roxburghshire) was located in a bend of the River Tweed. The church had been founded by the year of St Áedán's death (651), when Cuthbert entered the community. The abbot, Eata, had been a pupil of Áedán at Lindisfarne, and the prior was Boisil, whose name suggests an origin in the Gaelic-speaking world. His cult was celebrated at St Boswells near Melrose, which is located by the River Tweed en route to Iona.[47] One of Melrose's later inhabitants was the visionary Dryhthelm, who came from *Incuneningum*, most likely Cunninghame in Ayrshire.[48] Eata also founded Ripon (North Yorkshire), and Cuthbert went with him to act as guest-master. Ripon, like Melrose, lay on the edge of territory that had only recently been conquered from Brittonic kings.[49] Lindisfarne's tendrils were spreading into the distant parts of the Northumbrian kingdom, and Gaelic influence along with them.

The Synod of Whitby (664) is often seen as a breaking point in the relations between Iona and Lindisfarne. This seminal debate saw the Northumbrians replace the Easter calculation taught by St Columba with that favoured in Rome. Theodore, archbishop of Canterbury, also had major changes afoot for the Northumbrian bishopric, which was broken into three dioceses (Lindisfarne, Hexham and York).[50] The bishops of Lindisfarne ceased to be drawn from Iona, although they often came from Lindisfarne's federation; for example, Bishops Eata and Æthelwald had been abbots of Melrose.[51] They belonged to the wing of the Northumbrian Church that accepted the change of Easter observance while continuing to respect the Columban legacy. Indeed, the Synod of Whitby did not put an end to links between Northumbria and Iona, as Kathleen Hughes conclusively demonstrated.[52] Lindisfarne had ceased to be subject to Iona, but its community retained an affinity with the mother house. This could be seen as a relationship of *filiatio* rather than *subiectio*, to borrow Kassius Hallinger's terminology for ecclesiastical federations on the Continent.[53]

---

[45] AU 660.1 (ed. and transl. Mac Airt, 132–3); AT [659.1] (ed. and transl. Stokes, I, 45–6); CS [656] (ed. and transl. Hennessy, 94–5); *CI* (transl. Charles-Edwards, I, 151).

[46] See above, 35.

[47] *HE* III, 26, 2; IV 25 (27), 1 (ed. Lapidge, II, 162, 164, 356, 358; ed. and transl. Colgrave and Mynors, 308–9, 430–3); *Vita S. Cuthberti auctore anonymo* III.1; *Vita S. Cuthberti auctore Beda* 6, 16 (ed. and transl. Colgrave, 94–5, 172–3, 206–7). Cf. Ireland, 'Boisil'; Kirby, 'Cuthbert', 52; McCann, 'Cuthbert and Boisil', 76. For St Boswells, see Taylor, 'Seventh-century Iona abbots', 49.

[48] *HE* V, 12, 1 (ed. Lapidge, III, 68; ed. and transl. Colgrave and Mynors, 488–9).

[49] *HE* III, 25, 3 (ed. Lapidge, II, 148; ed. and transl. Colgrave and Mynors, 298–9); *Vita S. Cuthberti auctore Beda* 7–8 (ed. and transl. Colgrave, 174–9); Stephen, *Vita Wilfridi* 8, 17 (ed. and transl. Colgrave, 16–19, 34–37).

[50] *HE* III, 28, 1; IV, 12, 3 (ed. Lapidge, II, 172, 256, 258; ed. and transl. Colgrave and Mynors, 315–17, 370–1); Stephen, *Vita Wilfridi*, 24 (ed. and transl. Colgrave, 48–51).

[51] *HE* IV, 25 (27), 1; V, 12, 7 (ed. Lapidge, II, 356; III, 82; ed. and transl. Colgrave and Mynors, 430–1, 496–7). Cf. *Vita S. Cuthberto auctore Beda* ch. 30 (ed. and transl. Colgrave, 254–5) for Æthelwald, see Blair, *The Church*, 84–5.

[52] Hughes, 'Evidence', 63–6; cf. Bullough, 'The missions', 94–5; Campbell, 'The debt', 340–6; Cramp, 'Northumbria and Ireland', 199; Stancliffe, 'The Irish tradition', 35–40.

[53] Hallinger, *Gorze-Cluny*, 736–46; cf. Herbert, *Iona*, 44–5; Sharpe, 'Some problems', 245–6.

During the later seventh century, Northumbrian scholars gravitated to the churches of the *Romani* in the southern half of Ireland, not merely to Iona. There was some overlap between the *Romani* and the wing of the Northumbrian Church that cherished the Columban legacy. St Ceadda, a former pupil of Áedán, travelled to Ireland and resided with his fellow Northumbrian Ecgberht, presumably at Ráith Máelsigi.[54] The first bishop of Lindisfarne after the Synod of Whitby was Tuda, who had been educated in the south of Ireland.[55] Tuda died shortly afterwards and was buried at the monastery of *Pægnalæch*, which has long been identified with Whalley (Lancashire), although the distortion of the name poses significant difficulties.[56] Another individual who sought to reconcile the new Easter customs and the Columban heritage was St Cuthbert. He is more certainly linked with the west of the kingdom because he made annual visits to St Herbert, who dwelt on an island in Derwentwater. Cuthbert also made trans-Pennine journeys to fulfil his pastoral role once he became bishop of Lindisfarne in 685 (having swapped with Eata, who assumed responsibility for Hexham).[57] Bede's prose *Vita Cuthberti* records that there was a *monasterium* in Carlisle, whose abbess was the sister of the Northumbrian Queen Iurminburg. The queen herself resided in the city while her husband, Ecgfrith, fought at Nechtansmere. Iurminburg may have chosen to support Cuthbert's activities in preference to those of Wilfrid, whom she had denounced.[58]

St Cuthbert's links with Carlisle were later elaborated by the Cuthbertine community, who were custodians of the saints' relics and patrimony. This is apparent in *Historia de Sancto Cuthberto*, whose date has been much discussed. I see it as an eleventh-century compilation that incorporated a considerable amount of earlier material, including records of estates.[59] The *Historia* states that King Ecgfrith gave St Cuthbert the city of Carlisle along with land in a fifteen-mile radius around it, in addition to Crayke near York.[60] This information is echoed in a forged charter of the twelfth century, which purports to record grants of land to St Cuthbert at Carlisle and Crayke.[61] The charter is connected with Durham's brief phase of episcopal jurisdiction in Carlisle, which was challenged by plans to create an independent bishopric of Carlisle.[62] Even so, the formula used to describe the grant of lands in a circuit is unusual: *Adiecit civitatem quae vocatur Luel, quae habet circuitu .xv. miliaria*, 'he

---

[54] *HE* IV, 3, 6 (ed. Lapidge, II, 216, 218; ed. and transl. Colgrave and Mynors, 344–5).

[55] *HE* III, 26, 2; III, 27, 1 (ed. Lapidge, 162, 168; ed. and transl. Colgrave and Mynors, 308–9).

[56] Compare the forms *Wagele* in ASC E 664 (ed. Irvine, 30) and *Pagele* in an Anglo-Norman list of resting places: Rollason, 'A list', 69–70. Lewis, 'Was St Tuda buried at Whalley?'; Breeze, 'Where Were Bede's *Uilfaresdun* and *Paegnalaech*?', 190–1, suggesting Wawne (East Riding).

[57] *Vita Sancti Cuthberti auctore anonymo* IV.9; *Vita Sancti Cuthberti auctore Beda* 28 (ed. and transl. Colgrave, 124–5, 248–51); *HE* IV, 26 (28), 4 (ed. Lapidge, II, 366; ed. and transl. Colgrave and Mynors, 436–7); Tudor, 'St. Cuthbert', 67–8.

[58] *HSC* 5 (ed. and transl. South, 46–7); *Vita Sancti Cuthberti auctore Beda* 27 (ed. and transl. Colgrave, 242–3); Stephen, *Vita Wilfridi* 24 (ed. and transl. Colgrave, 48–51).

[59] Craster, 'The patrimony', 177–8 placed the initial composition in the tenth century. A potential eleventh-century interpolation was highlighted by Simpson: 'The King Alfred/St Cuthbert episode', 398–9. In contrast, South (*Historia de Sancto Cuthberto*, 14–36) dates the whole text to the eleventh century, and Crumplin ('Rewriting history', 34–41, 62–72) sees it is a composite text compiled from the tenth century onwards.

[60] *HSC* 5 (ed. and transl. South, 46–7). In *PNCu*, I, iii, xxii this area is identified with the parish of St Cuthbert Without.

[61] Sawyer, *Anglo-Saxon Charters*, no. 66 (ed. and transl. Woodman, *Charters*, 348–9).

[62] *Regesta regum Anglo-Normannorum* I, nos 463, 478 (ed. Davis with Whitwell, 113, 115); Sharpe, 'Symeon as pamphleteer'; McGuigan, 'Neither Scotland nor England', 200–1.

(Ecgfrith) added the city that is called Carlisle, which has a circumference of fifteen miles'. This formula is paralleled in seventh-century charters issued to Bobbio and Stavelot-Malmedy, Irish foundations on the Continent. Thus it is likely that the charter and the *Historia* draw on an earlier record of the grant that was influenced by precedents in Gaeldom.[63]

The Cuthbertine community acquired other lands in the west of the kingdom, according to the *Historia*. King Ecgfrith reportedly granted an estate at Cartmel (near Morecambe Bay) to St Cuthbert, along with some Britons.[64] There are indeed references to Britons in the local place-names Birkby Hall and Walton Hall, which mention *bretar* (ON 'Britons') and *w(e)alas* (OE 'Britons') respectively.[65] Brittonic culture would have been relatively enduring in this area thanks to contact with Brittonic-speaking kings on the Isle of Man.[66] In the Domesday survey, Cartmel's estate was named *Cherchebi*, a Norse place-name that was applied to settlements owned by a church.[67] The most likely candidate for this minster is Heversham, whose abbot fled from the *piratae* to the Cuthbertine church of Norham-on-Tweed in the early tenth century.[68] Tilred may be the man who became bishop of Chester-le-Street (by then the base of the Cuthbertine community) in 915.[69] A further indication of Cuthbertine influence in the west is the presence of a relic of the saint's hair at a monastery near the River Dacre. The community must have acquired this relic after Cuthbert's translation in 698.[70] The Dacre in question used to be identified with a place near Ripon, but excavations at Dacre (Cumbria, formerly Cumberland) have revealed many attributes of an early medieval ecclesiastical establishment.[71] Dacre's community must have had close personal links with Cuthbert's community to obtain a bodily relic.

Just as Lindisfarne had estates near the Irish Sea, so it acquired more northerly lands. The *Historia* indicates that the core endowments (beyond Lindisfarne itself) lay between the rivers Tweed, Till and Breamish, including the areas known as Islandshire and Norhamshire.[72] The *Historia* lists two large landholdings north of the Tweed: the land between the rivers Adder and Leader (Berwickshire), save the estates of the church of Coldingham, and the lands between the Lammermuirs and Eskmouth belonging to the *monasterium* of St Balthere (Baldred) at Tyninghame. Lindisfarne must have acquired Tyninghame's lands during the eighth century or

---

[63] The formula appears in the Lombard king Agilulf's grant to Columbanus, and in subsequent texts (ed. Richter, *Bobbio*, 14–18). They were altered in transmission but contain some original formulae. Cf. Wormald, *Bede and the Conversion*, 17; Blair, *The Church*, 222–3.

[64] *HSC* 6 (ed. and transl. South, 48–9). South translates *dedit ei rex Ecgfrith terram quae vocatur Cartmel et omnes Brittani cum eo* as 'King Ecgfrith and all the Britons with him gave him (Cuthbert) the territory of Cartmel' because masc/neuter *eo* cannot refer to *terram*. Nevertheless, the word order suggests that *eo* refers to the land, not Ecgfrith. Perhaps a scribal error is responsible for confusion between *eo* and *ea*.

[65] *Britby*, *Walletun* 1086: DB Yorks (ed. Faull and Stinson, 1L1; ed. Williams and Martin, fol. 301v); *PNLa*, 196, 224; cf. Crowe, 'Cartmel'.

[66] Edmonds, 'The Furness peninsula', 21–3.

[67] DB Yorks (ed. Faull and Stinson, 1L1; ed. Williams and Martin, fol. 301v); Pickles, *Power*, 31–2.

[68] *HSC* 21 (ed. and transl. South, 58–61).

[69] *Libellus de exordio* II.16 (ed. and transl. Rollason, 132–3); Tudor, 'St. Cuthbert', 75 n. 26.

[70] *HE* IV, 32, 1 (ed. Lapidge, II, 282; ed. and transl. Colgrave and Mynors, 446–9).

[71] Leech and Newman, 'Excavations at Dacre'.

[72] *HSC* 4 (ed. and transl. South, 42–3); Craster, 'The patrimony', 178–9.

later since Balthere died in 756.[73] Tyninghame also appears in a list of *mansiones* that belonged to the bishopric of Lindisfarne at the start of Eardwulf's bishopric (854). The list was inserted into the twelfth-century texts *Historia regum* and the *Chronica* of Roger of Howden. Apart from a generalised claim to all of the churches between Tweed and Tyne, the list comprises church sites, including major minsters such as Carlisle, Melrose, Coldingham and Abercorn.[74] There are three ways in which the list might be interpreted: as a reflection of a 'monastic federation' on the Iona model;[75] as a description of a consolidated Bernician diocese (the *mansiones* being places where the bishop had a residence);[76] and as an insight into increased landholdings in the tenth or eleventh century, following the demise of other minsters.[77] These explanations may be compatible: Melrose and Carlisle, for example, had links with Lindisfarne prior to the consolidation of the Bernician diocese.[78] What is clear is that Lindisfarne's influence progressively increased in the area between Tweed and Forth, an area that was crucial to inter-action with Iona.[79]

In the early eighth century, the Iona community changed their method of calcu-lating Easter, a development that revivified links between Iona and its Northumbrian offshoots. The change had been afoot for some time: Adomnán reformed his Easter observance during a visit to the Northumbrian King Aldfrith, who had been a *sapiens* 'ecclesiastical scholar' on Iona.[80] The Northumbrian churchman Ecgberht completed Iona's conversion to the new Easter dating in 716.[81] This was the period when information about Northumbrian (and especially Lindisfarne) saints was entered into a copy of the 'Martyrology of Jerome' that was kept at Iona. The text eventually arrived at Tallaght, and attained something approaching its current form in the early ninth century.[82] Ecgberht also helped the nobleman Eanmund to found a new daughter house from Lindisfarne (the location is unidentified). Around a century later, Æthelwulf portrayed life at this monastery in his poem *De Abbatibus*. Ecgberht's links with Iona and Ireland may explain the presence of a highly skilled scribe and illuminator named Ultán (a Gaelic name).[83]

Ecgberht had close associations with Lindisfarne's former daughter houses at Ripon and Melrose, which helped to reinvigorate their links with Iona. Shortly before the Synod of Whitby, there had been a rupture in the Columban tradition at Ripon, when the church was granted to St Wilfrid. Abbot Eata and others *qui Scottos sequebantur* 'who followed the Scotti' refused to change their practices,

---

[73] *HSC* 4 (ed. and transl. South, 42–3). For Balthere's death, see the York annals in *HR* (ed. Arnold, II, 41).

[74] *HR* (ed. Arnold, II, 101); *Chronica magistri Rogeri de Houedene* (ed. Stubbs, I, 45); Aird, *St Cuthbert*, 16. The general claim is described as a later addition by Woolf, 'The diocese', 233–4.

[75] Craster, 'The patrimony', 179–80; Rollason, *Northumbria*, 133.

[76] Woolf, *From Pictland to Alba*, 81–3; *idem*, 'The diocese', 235–6 (defining *mansio*).

[77] Aird, *St Cuthbert*, 16; South, *HSC*, 80.

[78] *HR* (ed. and transl. Arnold, II, 94).

[79] Taylor, 'Seventh-century Iona abbots'.

[80] *HE* V, 15, 1 (ed. Lapidge, III, 94; ed. and transl. Colgrave and Mynors, 504–7); V, 21, 14 (ed. Lapidge, III, 162, 164; ed. and transl. Colgrave and Mynors, 550–1); cf. *Vita Sancti Cuthberti* II.46 (ed. and transl. Anderson and Anderson, 178–81). For Aldfrith, see above, 42–3.

[81] *HE* V, 22, 1–2 (ed. Lapidge, III, 166, 168, 170; ed. and transl. Colgrave and Mynors, 552–5).

[82] MT 18 March (ed. Best and Lawlor, 24); Ó Riain, *Anglo-Saxon Ireland*, 4–13. On the date-range, cf. Dumville, 'Félire Óengusso', 43–4.

[83] Æthelwulf, *De Abbatibus* VIII (ed. and transl. Campbell, 18–23).

and they retreated to Melrose.[84] Ecgberht's network soothed these divisions: one of Ecgberht's companions had served Prior Boisil, and he experienced a vision of Boisil while residing with Ecgberht's community in Ireland.[85] By associating Melrose with Ecgberht's community, Bede subtly elided any lingering sensitivities surrounding the Easter practices of Boisil and his fellow monks from Iona.[86] As to Ripon, it is interesting that the bodies of Ecgberht and Wihtberht rested there along with Wilfrid. This information appears in a list of saints' resting places known as *Secgan*, which dates from the eleventh century in its current form but contains a ninth-century element.[87] Wihtberht was a member of Ecgberht's cohort in Ireland before he embarked on the mission to Frisia. He later returned to Ireland, where he acted as a guarantor of Adomnán's law, *Cáin Adomnáin,* and was venerated at several Irish churches.[88] There are signs of Ripon's revival of interest in its Columban heritage in the eighth century. Abbot Sléibíne of Iona (*ob. ca* 767) visited the church, and St Cuthbert's followers resided there before they relocated from Chester-le-Street to Durham in the later tenth century.[89] Another hint is found in the *Vita S. Kentigerni* by the late-twelfth-century author Jocelin of Furness. Jocelin notes that Ripon had a crosier of St Columba, which had reportedly been conveyed to the church by St Kentigern.[90] Whatever the story's veracity, it suggests that Jocelin gleaned from his northern English sources that Ripon housed a Columban relic.[91]

Lindisfarne's federation continued to grow in the ninth century, when Bishop Ecgred (*ob.* 845) founded a new monastery at Norham-on-Tweed. The endowment included two estates in Jedburgh, a strategically important area near the confluence of the Rivers Teviot and Tweed.[92] Ecgred transported the wooden church of Áedán, and the relics of Cuthbert and Ceolwulf (*ob.* 765), to the new site. *Secgan* confirms that Cuthbert's body rested at Norham, a reference that most likely belongs to the

---

84 *HE* III, 25, 3 (ed. Lapidge, II, 146–9; ed. and transl. Colgrave and Mynors, 298–9). *Vita Wilfridi* 8 (ed. and transl. Colgrave, 16–19) mentions the gift to Wilfrid but not the prior occupants; *Vita Sancti Cuthberti auctore Beda* 8 (ed. and transl. Colgrave, 180–1) gives no specific reason for Eata's departure.

85 *HE* V, 9, 2 (ed. Lapidge, III, 52; ed. and transl. Colgrave and Mynors, 476–7); Kirby, 'Cuthbert', 50; Ziegler, 'The Ripon connection?'.

86 McCann, 'Cuthbert and Boisil', 76–82, noting that these sensitivities may explain Boisil's absence from *Vita Sancti Cuthberti auctore anonymo*.

87 Rollason, 'A list', 62–8. McGuigan, 'Neither Scotland nor England', 77–8, calls into question the ninth-century element, but I remain convinced.

88 Rollason, 'A list', 89; Blair, 'A handlist', 532, 559–60; *HE* V, 9–10 (ed. Lapidge, III, 50–62; ed. and transl. Colgrave and Mynors, 474–85). For Wihtbert's cult, see the eleventh-century notes to *Félire Óengusso: Martyrology of Oengus* 8 December (ed. Stokes, 256–9). The 'Ichtbricht epscop' who was a guarantor of *Cáin Adomnáin* used to be identified with Ecgberht: Ní Dhonnchadha, 'The guarantor list', 180, 193–4. However, Ó Cróinín, 'Rath Melsigi', 24–6, argues that he was Wihtberht.

89 Hughes, 'Evidence', 55–6, citing the Chartres MS of *Historia Brittonum; Libellus de exordio* III.1 (ed. and transl. Rollason, 144–5).

90 Jocelin of Furness, *Vita Kentigerni*, 39–40 (ed. Forbes, 229–232); Gardner, 'Kentigern', 1–7, 20–2.

91 Jackson, 'The sources', 279–80, 310, 340–1. For other Columban staffs, see Bourke, 'Insignia Columbae II'. The detail about Ripon's crosier is omitted from the version of this tale in the fifteenth-century *Breviarium Aberdonense* (ed. Blew, II, *pars hiemalis*, fols xxvii v–xxx r); cf. MacQuarrie, 'The career', 16; *idem, The Saints*, 135–6.

92 *HSC* 9 (ed. and transl. South, 48–51).

ninth-century stratum of the text.[93] The reference to Áedán indicates that Lindisfarne continued to promote the Columban legacy in Northumbria.

Taken as a whole, the two centuries from the 630s to the 830s witnessed significant changes in the relationship between the Columban *familia* and the Northumbrian kingdom. What began as an institutionalised relationship between Iona and Lindisfarne became a more informal connection founded on the Columban heritage. The expansion of the Cuthbertine community towards the northern and western edges of the Northumbrian kingdom helped to foster these common interests.

The Columban familia *and the Cuthbertine community in the Viking Age*

The Viking Age has often been portrayed as a time of dramatic change for the churches of the Insular world. There were shifts in patterns of episcopal affiliation, landholding and patronage. These changes were partly the result of Viking raids, but also a response to broader developments in landownership and politics. The ties between the Columban and Cuthbertine churches were not severed during this period; rather, they continued to evolve against the changing backdrop.

The ninth century saw changes in the Columban *familia*, and I propose that these developments affected Lindisfarne. In 807–14 a new church was built at Cenanas (Kells, Co. Meath), which lay in southern Uí Néill territory.[94] Several decades later, some Columban relics were moved to Kells and to the newly built church of Dunkeld in Pictland.[95] These developments create the impression that Iona was losing influence, yet there is no firm evidence that Columba's *comarbae* (*heres*, heir) was permanently based at Kells until 1007.[96] Abbot Diarmait of Iona remained an influential figure in Ireland, especially in the ascetic *céli Dé* movement.[97] That said, the ninth century was a period of instability for the Columban *familia*, and in 878 Columba's shrine was moved to Ireland in flight from the *Gaill*.[98] I have argued elsewhere that the trigger was the raids of Hálfdan into Pictland from his base on the Tyne, and that similar problems encouraged the Cuthbertine community to follow suit.[99]

---

[93] Rollason, 'A list', 68, 87 (using the name *Ubbanford* for Norham). Here I follow Jolly, *The Community*, 19 and diverge from McGuigan, 'Neither Scotland nor England', 58–81 and Woolf, 'The diocese', 233, who suggest that Cuthbert's relics could have rested at Norham until the eleventh century.

[94] AU 807.4, 814.9 (ed. and transl. Mac Airt and Mac Niocaill, 262–3, 270–1); CS [807, 814] (ed. and transl. Hennessy, 126–7); CI 807.4, 814.10 (transl. Charles-Edwards, 268, 273); Herbert, *Iona*, 68–9.

[95] Indrechtach brings relics to Ireland: AU 849.7 (ed. and transl. Mac Airt and Mac Niocaill, 308–9); CI 849.10 (transl. Charles-Edwards, 306). This entry is omitted from the briefer CS. For the removal of relics to Pictland, see CKA (ed. and transl. Hudson, 148, 152); Bannerman, '*Comarba Coluim Chille*', 42–4; Dumville, *The Churches*, 20–1, esp. n. 53. For the significance of corporeal relics in Ireland, see Wycherley, *The Cult*, 69–72.

[96] Clancy, 'Iona, Scotland', 111–14, 117–18, 120 discusses Iona's role in Dunkeld's foundation. For the seat of the *comarbae*, see Clancy, 'Iona v. Kells', esp. 90 *contra* Herbert, *Iona*, 74–82; Bannerman, '*Comarba*'. David Dumville ('Máel Brigte') has drawn attention to the significance of Raphoe (Co. Donegal) during this period, which is another indication that the transfer of the headship was complex.

[97] Clancy, 'Iona, Scotland'.

[98] AU 878.9 (ed. and transl. Mac Airt and Mac Niocaill, 334–5); CS [878] (ed. and transl. Hennessy, 166–7); CI 878.10 (transl. Charles-Edwards, 328).

[99] Edmonds, 'St Cuthbert', esp. 7–11.

The Cuthbertine community was also changing in the ninth century. There is a dearth of contemporary information and a danger in over-reliance on retrospective, post-Norman descriptions of the situation. Broadly speaking, the community was now composed largely of hereditary priests (perhaps alongside a more strictly monastic group), who looked after St Cuthbert's relics, lands and people (the *haliwerfolc*). Once Hálfdan had set up camp on the Tyne, the community uprooted St Cuthbert's shrine and embarked on a seven-year period of wanderings, eventually settling at Chester-le-Street *ca* 883.[100] During this phase of exile, the community attempted to send their saint to Ireland, as reported in *Historia de Sancto Cuthberto*.[101] The episode relates that Bishop Eardwulf of Lindisfarne and Abbot Eadred of Carlisle removed Cuthbert's relics from Lindisfarne and eventually arrived at *Derunt muthe* (the mouth of the River Derwent, Cumbria). They placed the holy body in a boat and started to sail to Ireland while the saint's people wept, lamenting the loss of their patron. A miraculous storm whipped up, and three waves turned into blood as they washed over the boat, prompting the group to return to shore.

The *Historia*'s version of events is not straightforward, for it is influenced by the Old Testament account of the Exodus.[102] Yet some of the details ring true, given our knowledge of Cuthbertine landholdings. David Rollason has argued that the community did not wander randomly; rather they toured their dependent estates, in the manner of some Continental communities exiled by Viking raids.[103] The Cuthbertine community had a long-standing association with Carlisle, as already noted, and Abbot Eadred is described elsewhere in the *Historia* as *abbas de Luercestre* 'abbot of Carlisle'.[104] Alex Woolf has suggested that the former Roman city of Carlisle temporarily became the seat of the combined see of Lindisfarne/Hexham in the 870s.[105] Further south along the Cumbrian coast, on the south side of the Derwent estuary, St Michael's church at Workington has yielded several high-quality pieces of pre-Viking sculpture as well as some coffined burials of this era. These are pointers to the site of a minster, which may have had its own port at the former Roman fort of Burrow Walls on the north side of the Derwent.[106]

The storm eventually drove the saint's boat to Whithorn, according to Symeon of Durham's early twelfth-century *Libellus de exordio*.[107] There are indications that St Cuthbert's cult was well-established in the vicinity of Whithorn by this time. Reginald of Durham related that Ailred of Rievaulx visited the community of

---

[100] This picture derives from eleventh- and twelfth-century texts, which were informed by the descendants of the coffin-bearers: Aird, *St Cuthbert*, 116–19. For Chester-le-Street, see Jolly, *The Community*, 15–36.

[101] *HSC* 20 (ed. and transl. South, 58–9); compare *HR*, *s.a.* 875 (ed. Arnold, II, 82); *Libellus de exordio* II.6 (ed. and transl. Rollason, 100–1, 104–5).

[102] Exod. 4.9; 7.17–18; commented on explicitly in *Miracula* (ed. Arnold, *Symeonis monachi opera omnia*, I, 237); *Libellus de exordio* II.11 (ed. and transl. Rollason, 114–15). The illustrated version of the *Miracula* in Oxford, University College, MS 165, p. 143 appears on the front cover.

[103] Rollason, 'The wanderings', 50. I discuss Continental communities in 'St Cuthbert', 16.

[104] *HSC* 13 (ed. and transl. South, 52–3).

[105] Woolf, *From Pictland to Alba*, 81. Woolf suggests that the combined bishopric also included Whithorn, but if so, this was temporary. By the tenth century, Whithorn was functioning as the centre of a smaller bishopric focused on the Machars peninsula: Hill, *Whithorn*, 53.

[106] *Corpus II*, 11, 154–7, now augmented by material from the more recent excavations, as described in Paterson, 'The sculptural fragments'. Cf. Edmonds, 'Barrier or unifying feature?', 25–6; *eadem*, 'The practicalities', 146.

[107] *Libellus de exordio* II.11–12 (ed. and transl. Rollason, 114–15; 118–21).

Cuthbrictis khirche (Kirkcudbright) in 1164.[108] They were observing St Cuthbert's festival, and the festivities turned high-spirited when a bull was brought to the churchyard to be baited. Some of the churchmen voiced their disapproval of this activity on the basis that it would violate St Cuthbert's sanctuary.[109] Another relevant twelfth-century text is *Libellus de Ortu Sancti Cuthberti*, which relates the tradition of St Cuthbert's birth in Ireland. Thomas Clancy has identified one of the author's informants, Bishop Alanus, with Gille Aldan of Whithorn.[110] The young Cuthbert is said to have travelled from Ireland to *(regio), quae Rennii vocatur, in portu qui Rintsnoc dicitur*, 'to the region called Rhinns in the port which is called Rintsnoc'.[111] He voyaged in a stone currach, which could still be seen at Rintsnoc at the time of writing. These texts provide seemingly independent testimony to the veneration of Cuthbert in Galloway.[112]

The *Libellus* also sheds further light on the links between the Cuthbertine federation and Ireland. The text asserts that Cuthbert had been born at Kells, which seems most unlikely given that Bede placed Cuthbert's childhood near Melrose; nevertheless, the tradition offers insight into Cuthbert's cult at Kells. The story of Cuthbert's birth is credited to Eugenius bishop of Ardmore, who had himself been born and raised at Kells. He noted *ab incolis locus illius nativitatis ostenditur*, 'the place of his birth is pointed out by the inhabitants [of Kells]'.[113] I suggest that St Cuthbert's cult developed at Kells around the time when the saint's body was despatched to Ireland. Kells was a very appropriate destination because it had recently acquired relics of St Columba.

There is further support for this theory in the mid-tenth-century text *Betha Adamnáin*, which sought to bolster Kells's prestige by recounting the achievements of St Adomnán.[114] The author reveals considerable knowledge of Northumbria when he relates Adomnán's quest to retrieve hostages after Ecgfrith's raid on Brega. This episode was circulating widely in Ireland thanks to the Middle Irish translation of Bede's *Historia ecclesiastica*, but *Betha Adamnáin*'s version contains unique information about the saint's journey.[115] Once Adomnán arrived on the shore of the *Saxain Tuaiscirt* ('Saxons of the North', Northumbrians), he drew a circle in the sand,

---

[108] Reginald of Durham, *Libellus de Admirandis*, chs 84–5 (ed. Raine, 177–9).

[109] The Anglian cross-head may add weight to the idea of an Anglo-Saxon minster here, but it is not certain that it was always at Kirkcudbright: Brooke, 'The Northumbrian settlements', 305–6.

[110] *Libellus de Ortu* preface (ed. Raine, 64); Clancy, 'Magpie hagiography', 218, 220, 222.

[111] *Rennii* is a Latinised form. The -*nn* could be rendered -*nt* in Irish or -*nd* in Scottish Gaelic: Jackson, *The Gaelic Notes*, 140, 150.

[112] *Libellus de Ortu*, 14 (ed. Raine, 74); Clancy, 'Magpie hagiography', 222. Sharpe suggested that the writer was a monk of Durham in 'Were the Irish annals known', 137–9. However, Thomas Clancy argues that the *Libellus de Ortu* is too divergent from the style of Symeon and Reginald of Durham to have been written there: Clancy, 'Magpie hagiography', 227–9.

[113] *Libellus de Ortu*, 12 (ed. Raine, 72).

[114] *Betha Adamnáin* 12 (ed. and transl. Herbert, 54–7). The date of the work (961 x 965) was determined through examination of content and linguistic features, see *ibid.*, 4–8 and Herbert, *Iona*, 153–69. The upper limit was partly dictated by the text's lack of allusion to Dál Cais, though this may have been deliberate: Breatnach, 'Léirmheas: Betha Adamnáin'. Another reviewer has suggested that the report of the attack on Brega 684 was an allusion to a Scandinavian raid on Kells in 970: Ó Briain, 'Léirmheasanna/ Reviews: Betha Adamnáin', 157–8. Thus a later date for the text can be envisaged, but it can still be placed in the mid to late tenth century.

[115] Ní Chatháin, 'Bede's Ecclesiastical History' (only a fragment survives). It is cited as *Stáir Bhéid* ('Bede's History') in *The Fragmentary Annals* §166 (ed. and transl. Radner, 56–7); cf. Ní Mhaonaigh, '*Caraid tairisi*', 274–5.

which became an island and acted as a safe haven while the Saxons tried to prevent him from landing. This miracle so impressed his adversaries that they granted the hostages to him.[116] As Patrick Wadden has noted, Exodus shaped the depiction of Adomnán's journey, and the name for Adomnán's landing place (*Trácht Romra*) recalls the Red Sea.[117] This allusion is, however, compatible with the idea that *Trácht Romra* was based on real-life experience; indeed the description of its tidal range resembles the Solway Firth.[118] I suggest that *Betha Adamnáin* and *Historia de Sancto Cuthberto* both portray a route across the Irish Sea that was plied by the communities of Lindisfarne and Kells.

Once the Cuthbertine community had settled at Chester-le-Street, they remained open to Irish learning, as well as absorbing new influences from the contemporary reform movement in Southumbria. As Karen Louise Jolly has shown, they acquired a service book from southern England and augmented it with texts and commentary, some of which have Irish affinities.[119] These scholarly resources reflect the community's heritage; is it also possible that they were receiving texts from Kells? *Historia de Sancto Cuthberto* and *Betha Admamnáin* share the concept of using a saint's Life to explore a church's dependencies and assets, an idea that was routine in Irish hagiography.[120] The *Historia* incorporates records of land transactions, which are similar to those preserved in the margins of the Durham *Liber Vitae*, another practice that is unusual in an English context.[121] Two of the Durham memoranda are reminiscent of the 'Latin charter tradition' of Ireland, Scotland, Wales, Brittany in that they were recorded in a precious manuscript, in the third person, with sanction clauses (although no witness lists). It may be no coincidence that the Book of Kells contains a substantial body of vernacular property records of this type.[122]

The Cuthbertine and Columban federations remained conscious of their common heritage during the Viking Age. There were ongoing contacts between the two groups of churches, which involved the movement of churchmen and perhaps also the circulation of texts. The estates in the west and north of the Northumbrian kingdom facilitated journeys between these two great ecclesiastical federations. I now turn to a different church, York, to ascertain whether this picture is representative.

York: a cosmopolitan city

At first glance, York's ecclesiastical community appears unlikely to have forged bonds with churches in the Gaelic-speaking world. Wilfrid was the second bishop of York, and his animosity towards Iona's Easter customs is notorious. Yet York's

---

[116] See above, 43. The tale was subsequently elaborated in Conchubranus's *Vita Monennae* I.14–15 I.15 (ed. Esposito, 215–16). I discuss this further in my 'Irish hagiographical representations'.
[117] Wadden, '*Trácht Romra*'.
[118] Cf. Ó Corráin, 'The Vikings', 316.
[119] Durham Cathedral Library MS A.IV.19; Jolly, *The Community*, 118, 125–6, 174, 179, 183, 197, 211.
[120] The Anglo-Norman points of comparison offered by South (*HSC*, 12–14, 25–36) post-date the *Historia*.
[121] Woodman, *The Charters*, 317; *idem*, 'Charters, Northumbria', 46–7.
[122] The classic work is Davies, 'The Latin-charter tradition'. For Kells, see *The Irish Charters* (ed. O'Donovan); Herbert, 'Charter material'. Dauvit Broun has questioned the coherence of the group of so-called 'Celtic charters': *The Charters*, 38–40. For Frankish parallels, see Hodge, 'When is a charter not a charter?', 130–2.

intermittent connections with churches in Ireland and Dál Riata in Britain emerge in three ways: Wilfrid's profession of authority for the northern parts of Britain and Ireland; York's authority over the bishops of Mag nÉo (Mayo); and the tradition that *céli Dé* 'clients of God' dwelt in York. York's bishops, and later archbishops, wielded great influence throughout Northumbria, and their interests in the west of the kingdom would have facilitated contacts with Ireland.

Wilfrid's career was notoriously turbulent. He rose to prominence through a formidable display of rhetoric at the Synod of Whitby, 664, and was elected to the Northumbrian bishopric. While he was away on the Continent seeking consecration, Ceadda was installed in his place; Archbishop Theodore eventually resolved the matter in favour of Wilfrid. A decade later, Wilfrid was expelled after an altercation with Ecgfrith. He sought redress from Pope Agatho in Rome, professing authority for the northern halves of Ireland and Britain, as well as the islands in between.[123] In the meantime, Archbishop Theodore rationalised diocesan organisation by dividing the Northumbrian bishopric in three. When Wilfrid was eventually allowed to return, he was appointed bishop of York, and after a further period of exile he ended his career as bishop of Hexham.

Wilfrid's claim to episcopal authority in the northern parts of Britain and Ireland affected the Columban *familia*; Wilfrid wanted 'York to be the new, orthodox Iona'.[124] One obstacle was that Iona had its own bishops, even if they are only attested sporadically.[125] Uncertain instances include Dorbbéne, who attained the *kathedra* of Iona in 713 (perhaps a term that connotes episcopal status);[126] Cillíne Droichtech, whose epithet may be a literal translation of Latin *pontifex*;[127] and Abbot Fergna's description as a bishop in late-medieval notes on the Martyrology of Gorman.[128] A Bishop Conamail acted as a guarantor of *Cáin Adomnáin* in 697, and he may be the Conamail who became abbot of Iona in 704.[129] One certain example of a bishop of Iona is his fellow guarantor of *Cáin Adomnáin*, Coeddi. This man, who has an unusual English name, was described as *episcopus Iae* in his obituary in 712.[130] Whether or not Iona had a regular episcopal succession, the continuing interchange of personnel between the Columban *familia* and Northumbria will have attracted Wilfrid's interest. Clare

---

[123] *HE* V, 19, 9 (ed. Lapidge, III, 122; ed. and transl. Colgrave and Mynors, 524–5); *Vita Wilfridi* esp. 53 (ed. and transl. Colgrave, 108–16).

[124] Charles-Edwards, *Early Christian Ireland*, 432–3.

[125] Márkus, 'Iona', 123–4. For Iona bishops of the tenth century, see Etchingham, *Church Organisation*, 186.

[126] AU 713.5 (ed. and transl. Mac Airt and Mac Niocaill, 168–9); AT [713.6] (ed. and transl. Stokes, I, 23); *CI* 713.5 (transl. Charles-Edwards, 187); Herbert, *Iona*, 58 n. 6; Etchingham, *Church Organisation*, 92.

[127] Bourke, 'Cillíne Pontifex'. For Cillíne's obit, in which he is described as an anchorite of Iona, see AU 752.1 (ed. and transl. Mac Airt and Mac Niocaill, 206–7); AT 752.1 (ed. and transl. Stokes, I, 29); *CI* 752 (transl. Charles-Edwards, I, 223).

[128] Bourke, 'Fergna Epscop'. *Félire Húi Gormáin*, 2 March (ed. Stokes, 46–7). For Fergna's obit, in which he is described as abbot of Iona, see AU 623.1 (ed. Mac Airt and Mac Niocaill, 112–13); AT [624.1] (ed. and transl. Stokes, I, 21); *CS* [623] (ed. and transl. Hennessy, 76–7); *CI* 623.1 (transl. Charles-Edwards, I, 132).

[129] Ní Dhonnchadha, 'The guarantor list', 180, 191–2; Márkus, 'Iona', 128–9. For Conamail's obit, see AU 710.1 (ed. and transl. Mac Airt and Mac Niocaill, 166–7); AT [710.1] (ed. and transl. Stokes, I, 33); CS 706 (ed. and transl. Hennessy, 116–17); *CI* 710.1 (transl. Charles-Edwards, I, 184).

[130] AU 712.1 (ed. and transl. Mac Airt and Mac Niocaill, 168–9); AT [712.1] (ed. and transl. Stokes, I, 34); *CI* 712 (transl. Charles-Edwards, I, 185); Ní Dhonnchadha, 'The guarantor list', 191.

Stancliffe has shown that Wilfrid was hostile not only to Iona's Easter practices but also towards the Columban inheritance in its entirety.[131]

In Ireland, Wilfrid's ambitions encroached on the spheres of jurisdiction claimed by Armagh and Kildare. Unlike Iona, those churches sought to establish authority throughout the whole of Ireland, not merely the northern half.[132] Armagh may have aspired to influence elsewhere in the Irish Sea region, as hinted at by Muirchú's *Vita Sancti Patricii*, which was written towards the end of the seventh century. Muirchú ascribes the conversion of Mac Cuill, a future bishop of the Isle of Man, to Patrick.[133] The text was written in the aftermath of the raid on Brega, and this episode helped to bolster Armagh against the spread of Northumbrian ecclesiastical authority across the Irish Sea.[134] Northumbrian contacts with the Isle of Man are apparent on several inscriptions at the major church site of Maughold, including the design on the monument that honours Irneit, bishop of the Island (or the Isles?).[135] Once again, the Island emerges as a key part of Northumbrian–Gaelic relations.

Aside from the episcopal dimension, Wilfrid's minsters fostered links with Irish churches. Willibrord entered Ripon as a child oblate and subsequently studied at Ecgberht's community of Ráith Máelsigi in Ireland.[136] At this stage Ripon was treated as one of Wilfrid's personal monasteries, rather than an episcopal possession of York, although it had become one of the archbishop of York's estates by the tenth century.[137] Ripon had recently acquired churches and estates in the west of the kingdom, which could have facilitated the connections with Ireland. The Deiran sub-ruler Alhfrith granted churches and estates from which Brittonic churchmen had fled *iuxta Rippel et Ingaedyne et in regione Dunutinga et Incaetlaevum in caeterisque locis*. These places have been traditionally identified as Dent in western Yorkshire, Yeadon near Leeds, Catlow in the Ribble Valley and lands next to the River Ribble.[138] Ian Wood has questioned the Yeadon identification on the basis that Britons are more likely to have been resident west of the Pennines by this time, although other scholars allow for the survival of Brittonic culture in the former kingdom of Elmet.[139] Ripple in Worcestershire has been proposed as an alternative identification for *Rippel*, but in my view Ribblesdale is a more natural adjunct to the other Pennine lands.[140] Ribchester's Roman fort offered a suitable base for an early medieval ecclesiastical community, as is shown by early medieval sculpture and metalwork.[141] The place-names Bispham (*Biscopham* 1086 'bishop's settlement'), Kirkham (*Chicheham* 1086 'church settlement') and Preston (*Prestune* 1086

[131] Stancliffe, *Bede, Wilfrid*, 10–21.
[132] *Liber Angeli* 28 (ed. and transl. Bieler, *Patrician Texts*, 188); Cogitosus, *Vita S. Brigitae*, preface to ch. 4 (transl. Connolly and Picard, 11).
[133] Muirchú, *Vita S. Patricii*, I.23 (ed. and transl. Bieler, 102–7).
[134] For Armagh's reaction to the raid, see Wadden, 'Theories', 173–7. On the Mac Cuill episode in relation to Armagh's interests across the Irish Sea, see Howlett, *Muirchú Moccu Macthéni*, 180–3; Wycherley, *The Cult*, 89–90.
[135] See above, 42.
[136] *HE* III, 13, 1–3 (ed. Lapidge, II, 74, 76, 78; ed. and transl. Colgrave and Mynors, 252–5); *Vita Wilfridi* 26 (ed. and transl. Colgrave, 52–3); Ó Cróinín, 'Rath Melsigi', 22–5.
[137] Sawyer, *Anglo-Saxon Charters*, no. 1461 (ed. Woodman, *Charters*, 139–41, 147–8).
[138] *Vita Wilfridi* 17 (ed. and transl. Colgrave, 36–7); Cox, 'The place-names', 18.
[139] Wood, 'Anglo-Saxon Otley', 24; compare Jones, 'Some donations', 30–6 (noting that Yeadon appeared in a tenth-century list of lands around Otley belonging to Archbishop Oswald of York).
[140] Sims-Williams, 'St Wilfrid', 180–3.
[141] The presence of a -*p*- in the rendering of the river name is not unique, cf. Domesday's *inter Ripam et Mersham*: *PNLa*, 65.

'settlement of the priests') point to a major complex of ecclesiastical landholdings along the Ribble.[142] Wilfrid's lands may also have encompassed the Lune Valley, although here the evidence rests solely on sculptural correspondences and church dedications.[143] A large number of churches (twenty-three) are dedicated to the saint in the former Northumbrian kingdom. A considerable proportion of these dedications postdate the twelfth century, when there was renewed interest in, and reworking of, the hagiography of Wilfrid. Others may be early dedications to the founder saint, including Preston and Ribchester.[144] If these tentative identifications of Wilfrid's lands are accepted, Ripon emerges as the owner of several trans-Pennine passes and some coastal estates.

The archbishopric of York (as it was after 735) maintained links with another Irish church, Mag nÉo na Saxan (Mayo). After the Synod of Whitby, Bishop Colmán of Lindisfarne took a group of followers to Iona, and they then travelled on to Ireland, founding a monastery at Inis Bó Finne (Inishbofin, Co. Galway). Colmán established a second community at Mayo in which the Saxon monks who had accompanied him were housed.[145] Just as Colmán was a bishop, so his successors at Inishbofin and Mayo held this office, as recorded in the Iona chronicle embedded in the 'Chronicle of Ireland'.[146] After the core text of the chronicle moved to Ireland *ca* 740, the bishops of Mayo ceased to be recorded. There are, however, indications that one particular Mayo figure, St Gerald (*ob.* 732), was held in high esteem on both sides of the Irish Sea. He may be among the figures known as Garuald or Geruald whose names are recorded in the ninth-century core of the Durham *Liber Vitae*. This text most likely derives from Wearmouth-Jarrow and includes a wide range of people associated with the Northumbrian Church.[147] Gerald's name also appears in the *Martyrology of Tallaght* and a ninth-century Irish litany of saints.[148] Subsequent references to the consecration of bishops of Mayo appear in the northern annals incorporated into the *Historia regum*.[149] The last-known bishop was Ealdwulf, who was consecrated in 786; like his forebears, he had an English name.

York's archiepiscopal oversight of Mayo was presumably based on the status of its founder, Colmán, as a former bishop of Lindisfarne. Yet there was a hiatus in relations until the Mayo community adopted Roman Easter customs, which had

---

[142] *PNLa*, 146, 152, 156.

[143] Clark, 'Wilfrid's lands?'.

[144] For the twelfth century, see Hayward, 'St Wilfrid of Ripon', esp. 17–21. The medieval dedication evidence is given in Farrer *et al.*, *Victoria County History of Lancaster*, II, 160; VII, 72–91; VIII, 123, 187. Hornby is listed as St Margaret in Ecton, *Thesaurus*, 586, but the medieval priory was dedicated to St Wilfrid. As to Ribchester, the presence of the feast of St Wilfrid in the dating clause of a deed of 1370 suggests that this was the medieval dedication: Smith and Short, *The History*, 47, citing a deed from the Towneley MSS: Lancashire Archives DDTO.

[145] *HE* IV, 4, 1–2 (ed. Lapidge, 220, 22; ed. and transl. Colgrave and Mynors, 348–9).

[146] Mayo: AU 732.6, 773.5 (ed. and transl. Mac Airt and Mac Niocaill, 184–5, 226–7); AT [732.4] (ed. and transl. Stokes, I, 47); *CI* 732.5, 773.5 (transl. Charles-Edwards, I, 204, 239). Inishbofin: AU 676.1, 713.1 (ed. and transl. Mac Airt and Mac Niocaill, 142–3, 168–9); *CI* 676.1, 713.1 (transl. Charles-Edwards, I, 161, 187).

[147] *Durham Liber Vitae*, fols 18v1, 38v1, 22v1, 27r1, 28r1, 29v1, 34v1, 38r1, 39r1 (ed. Rollason and Rollason, I); for the core material, see below, 173.

[148] MT 12 March (ed. Best and Lawlor, 22); *The Book of Leinster* (ed. Best *et al.*, VI, 1699) (lines 52198–9). For the date of the litany, see Hughes, 'On an Irish litany'; cf. the later Life of Gerald discussed by Ní Mhaonaigh, 'Of Saxons', 417–26.

[149] *HR* (ed. Arnold, II, 44–5, 51); cf. Chadwick, 'Mayo', 194–5.

occurred before Bede finished writing his *Historia ecclesiastica* in 731.[150] After that, the archbishop's jurisdiction entailed communication back and forth between Mayo and York. Alcuin, at one stage a member of York's clerical school, wrote letters to the community of Mayo referring to the many monks who had visited York.[151] His participation in contemporary links with Ireland makes an interesting contrast with his rendition of the earlier history of Northumbrian conversion, in which Áedán and the Iona monks were virtually overlooked.[152]

The ultimate fate of the York–Mayo link is obscure; even so, there are hints that York's cathedral community remained in contact with the Gaelic world during the Viking Age. One intriguing pointer is the presence of *céli Dé* 'clients of God' in York. These *céli Dé* have received little attention since the nineteenth century, when they tended to be romanticised as eremitical Iona monks, or even a band of 'Celtic druids'.[153] The references cannot be accepted at face value since they appear only in late-medieval texts associated with St Leonard's hospital. There are two possible contexts for the tradition of *céli Dé* in York, which are not mutually exclusive. The first is that a twelfth-century writer equated the pre-reform churchmen of York with the contemporary Scottish *céli Dé*; the second is that the concept of *céli Dé* arrived in York through early medieval connections with Ireland.

The York *céli Dé* appear in the foundation account of St Leonard's Hospital, which is preserved in the first volume of the hospital's fifteenth-century cartulary.[154] The account begins with Athelstan crowning Constantín as king of Scots; Constantín rebelled and ravaged Northumbria, prompting Athelstan to launch a campaign northwards. Athelstan called in at the important Yorkshire churches of Beverley and York en route, and promised to honour them upon his return. York's churchmen are termed *ministri* but we are told that they were called *colidei* in Athelstan's time. Athelstan was impressed that the *colidei* cared for a large number of poor people, and he granted them renders of thraves (a unit of grain) known as Petercorn. The *colidei* later established a hospital for the poor on a site donated by William the Conqueror and assigned the thraves for its upkeep. William Rufus donated a new site, on which the hospital still stood at the time of writing, and King Stephen founded a church there in honour of St Leonard. The cartulary was compiled in the fifteenth century, when there was still a preoccupation with renders of thraves. The collection of Petercorn was becoming increasingly difficult, and the troubles culminated in the East Riding rebellion of 1469. After this, Edward IV rescinded the right to collect thraves and compensated the hospital.[155] However, it does not follow that the account of the *colidei* and their thraves was fabricated in the fifteenth century. Rather, the account seems to have reached its current form

---

[150] *HE* IV, 4, 1–2 (ed. Lapidge, II, 220, 22; ed. and transl. Colgrave and Mynors, 348–9); Orschel, 'Mag nÉo na Sacsan', 90.

[151] Alcuin, *Epistola* 2 (ed. Dümmler, *Epistolae Karolini aevi II*, 445–6).

[152] In the relevant section of his poem on the church of York, Alcuin devotes attention to Oswald. Áedán only appears when Alcuin retells a story from Bede: *Versus de patribus regibus et sanctis Euboricensis ecclesiae* line 291 (ed. and transl. Godman, *Alcuin*, 28–9).

[153] Higgins, *The Celtic Druids*, 194–6; Jamieson, *An Historical Account*, 256. A more scholarly discussion is found in Reeves, *On the Céli-dé*, 58–61.

[154] London, British Library Cotton MS Nero D iii, fol. 7r–v; printed in *Monasticon Anglicanum* (ed. Dugdale, VI, 608–9). This volume covered general charters and holdings in York; another covered estates in the West and East Ridings; and the third is now lost. See Carpenter, *The Cartulary*, I, xxxix.

[155] Cullum, *Cremetts and Corrodies*, 7.

in the twelfth century, given that it ends with quotations from papal confirmations, the last dated to 1173.

The term *céli Dé* was meaningful in a twelfth-century context because of the controversy over the suffragan status of Scottish bishops in the archbishopric of York. York's need for suffragan bishops clashed with King David I's campaign to secure a pallium for an archbishopric of St Andrews. David's efforts were unsuccessful, but later in the twelfth century the Scottish bishops were accorded a direct relationship with the Pope, bypassing York.[156] Any writer based in twelfth-century York, especially one in an institution closely linked with the cathedral, would have been attuned to the arguments for supremacy over the Scottish bishops. Such writers were no doubt aware of the group of churchmen known as *céli Dé* based at St Andrews. During the era of Church reform, each *céle Dé* was given the option of joining the Augustinians or keeping his prebend for life, yet the community was remarkably tenacious and remained closely linked with the bishop and the king.[157] The York writer may have been inspired by the contemporary *céli Dé* at St Andrews when seeking a term to describe the pre-Norman York canons. In this case, the *colidei* would merely be a quirk of terminology and provide no real insight into early medieval York and its ecclesiastical links.

On the other hand, the generous endowment of Petercorn (confirmed soon after the Conquest) points to an early practice of collecting thraves for the poor, even if the hospital owed its site to a post-conquest royal grant.[158] Moreover, the foundation account implies that the term *colidei* was somewhat old-fashioned by the twelfth century. The word occurs in a different form, *kelidenses*, in the presentment of a jury in 1246, which concerned the right of appointment to the mastership of St Leonard's Hospital. The jury reported that the *kelidenses* had asked William the Conqueror for a new site to tend the sick and infirm and assigned thraves to support it.[159] The story cannot have been copied from the foundation account since the name-forms are different. Another striking phrase in the foundation account is *rex totius Britanniae*, which appears in Athelstan's charters during the relevant part of his reign.[160] Thus I would argue that the author of the account had access to some tradition or written record of *céli Dé* in pre-conquest York, and applied this term to the pre-Norman clerics of the cathedral.

How was the concept of *céli Dé* transmitted to York? The city enjoyed links with Ireland in the first half of the tenth century through the rulers of Scandinavian York and Dublin, who eventually reached an accommodation with the archbishops. There was a specifically ecclesiastical dimension to these tenth-century relations, as Victoria Whitworth has suggested in her appraisal of a cross-head at St Mary Castlegate. This monument features a ring-head, bosses and crouching animals, all of which have parallels in Ireland and western Scotland.[161] One channel of contact was the Cuthbertine community, who held an estate at Crayke in order to facilitate visits to York.[162] The parish of St Mary Castlegate may have fostered the cult of St

---

[156] Broun, *Scottish Independence*, 141–4; Oram, *Domination*, 344.
[157] Barrow, 'The cathedral chapter'; Taylor, 'From *Cinrigh Monai*', 31–2.
[158] *Early Yorkshire Charters* (ed. Farrer and Clay, I, 117–18 (William II's grant of the site), 141–2 (confirmation of thraves)); Rees Jones, *York*, 35 (grant from the crown fee); Palliser, *Medieval York*, 78, 109 (Petercorn).
[159] Rollason, *Sources*, 200–1; Page, *The Victoria County History of York Volume III*, 336.
[160] See above, 58, 60.
[161] Whitworth, 'A cross-head'; York St Mary Castlegate 3, *Corpus III*, 98–9.
[162] *HSC* 5 (ed. and transl. South, 47–8); DB Yorks 3Y10, Bi1; fols 304v, 381r.

Cuthbert, even if it was not formally affiliated to the community. An inscription in Latin and Old English records the building of the church and its dedication to Christ and various saints, one of which (though incomplete) is usually interpreted as Cuthbert.[163] Abbot Diarmait of Iona (*ob. ca* 832) has been identified as an influential mover in the *céli Dé*, and as the individual who brought their tenets to Britain.[164] Thus, information about the movement might have passed through the Columban *familia* to Northumbria.

I propose that the use of the term in York relates to the reputation that *céli Dé* developed for tending the poor and sick. There has been much debate about the nature of the *céli Dé* movement, with recent commentators contending that they were not a religious order, more a collection of like-minded, ascetically inclined and high-status individuals.[165] By the tenth century, certain groups of *céli Dé* were becoming associated with care of the poor and sick.[166] In 921 Guðrøðr ua Ímair plundered Armagh: *7 na taigi aernaighi do anacal lais cona lucht de cheilibh De 7 di lobraibh* 'and he spared from destruction the prayer-houses with their complement of céli Dé and sick'.[167] This is not a one-off association; for example, another leading *céle Dé* was Conn na mBocht, who died in 1032 as head of *céli Dé* in Clonmacnoise, and whose epithet suggests an association with the poor.[168]

I envisage the following scenario: in the early tenth century, the clerics of St Peter's church in York had a desire to improve their care for the disadvantaged. They drew inspiration from *céli Dé* communities in Ireland, becoming aware of their work through channels such as the Columban/Cuthbertine link. The York clerics looked to King Athelstan to help support their new initiative, and he was happy to lend his patronage at a time when he sought to strengthen his position in the North.[169] Notwithstanding its later authorship and transmission, the foundation account of St Leonard's Hospital offers an insight into York's links with the Gaelic world.

Whithorn's renown in the Insular world

Finally I turn to Whithorn, which was one of the best known of the Northumbrian churches, and surely the best located for contact with Ireland, the Isle of Man and Argyll. Rather than build up a widespread federation, Whithorn's community developed informal friendships and a reputation for scholarship. Elsewhere, I have gathered evidence of Whithorn's renown by examining Irish saints' Lives and martyrologies.[170] I will summarise the discussion here, first outlining briefly my method and aims. I am not seeking to establish the nature of Whithorn in the fifth and sixth centuries (when the saints' Lives are set) nor to discover whether the church referred to as 'Rosnat' was genuinely located at Whithorn. Rather, I view the

---

[163] *Corpus III*, York St Mary Castlegate 7; Rollason, *Sources*, 176–7. The Cuthbertines had land in York (DB Yorks C2; fol. 298v), which has been identified as either the parish of St Mary Castlegate (for example Aird, *St Cuthbert*, 19) or All Saints, Pavement.

[164] Clancy, 'Iona, Scotland'.

[165] Lambkin, 'Blathmac' (emphasising the legal dimension); Etchingham, *Church Organisation*, 339–60; Follett, *Céli Dé in Ireland*, 1–65.

[166] Haggart, 'The *céli Dé*', 21–2.

[167] AU 921.4 (ed. and transl. Mac Airt and Mac Niocaill, 372–3).

[168] AFM 1031.16 (ed. and transl. O'Donovan, II, 824–5).

[169] The grant of Amounderness to York also dates to the year of the Scottish expedition, 934: see above, 58, 60.

[170] Edmonds, *Whithorn's Renown*.

texts as windows on the time when they were composed, and on the development of Whithorn's reputation from the eighth century to the eleventh.[171] Over the centuries, Irish writers began to associate (and confuse) Whithorn with a number of other churches that were located in Britain. This is testimony to Whithorn's significant reputation, which overshadowed that of many other churches in Britain.

Whithorn's founding saint was Ninian, whose life and works have generated much scholarly interest.[172] Thomas Clancy has argued that the man behind Ninian's cult was Uinniau, a man of letters who lived during the sixth century. Uinniau's cult also underpinned that of St Finnian in Ireland, and Uinniau's background has provoked much debate.[173] Clancy argues that Ninian developed a distinct cult under the aegis of Northumbrian Whithorn, when *Uinniau* was incorrectly rendered *Ninniau*.[174] One obstacle is that the Northumbrian brethren are unlikely to have misspelt the name of their patron saint, and James Fraser's solution (transmission through Hexham) has not met with universal support.[175] This debate is of interest since it raises the possibility of pre-Northumbrian links between Whithorn and Ireland. However, my analysis begins with the Northumbrian texts of the eighth century.

Bede relates that St Nynia was a Briton who received instruction in Rome and launched a mission to the southern Picts. His see was dedicated to St Martin and it was known as *Candida Casa* (*hwīt-ærna* in English) because it had a stone church.[176] Whithorn became an episcopal see once again under the Northumbrians, and Bishop Pehthelm was one of Bede's correspondents.[177] Bede presents Whithorn as a Roman-influenced, orthodox institution, in keeping with its place in the Northumbrian ecclesiastical hierarchy.[178] This background was significant in a Pictish context, for King Nechtan son of Der-Ilei had adopted Roman Easter customs under the guidance of Bede's own abbot, Ceolfrith.[179] Furthermore, it was necessary to distance Nynia from the Britons' error in calculating Easter.[180] In reality, Whithorn may have been a culturally diverse institution that benefited from the Britons' long-standing links across the Irish Sea. Seventh-century inscriptions hint at these interactions, as does

---

[171] For this reason I do not accept Andrew Breeze's challenges to my Whithorn Lecture (see 'Reviews'). Breeze focuses on the original location of Rosnat whereas I place the texts in their contemporary context. If, as I suggest, a Cornish saint became confused with St Nynia, this does not rule out Breeze's argument that Rosnat was Old Kea in Cornwall.

[172] Broun, 'The literary record', 143.

[173] Clancy, 'The real St Ninian'. For debate about Uinniau, see, for example, Ó Riain, 'Finnio and Winniau'; Dumville, 'St. Finnian'. Further references are given in Edmonds, *Whithorn's Renown*, 30 n. 23.

[174] Clancy, 'The real St Ninian', 23–7. The **Uinno-* element in the name means 'white', and Pamela O'Neill has linked this meaning with the names Whithorn and *candida casa*: 'Six degrees', 263–7.

[175] Fraser, 'Northumbrian Whithorn', 54. Barrow remained unconvinced in *Saint Ninian*, 9.

[176] *HE* III, 4, 1 (ed. Lapidge, II, 30, 32; ed. and transl. Colgrave and Mynors, 222–3).

[177] *HE* V, 23, 4 (ed. Lapidge, III, 176; ed. and transl. Colgrave and Mynors, 558–61). For Pehthelm as an informant, see *HE* V, 13, 4; V, 18, 1 (ed. Lapidge, III, 90, 106; ed. and transl. Colgrave and Mynors, 502–3, 512–13); Chadwick, 'St. Ninian', 10–19.

[178] Fraser, 'Northumbrian Whithorn', 42–9; *idem, From Caledonia to Pictland*, 71, 100.

[179] *HE* V, 21, 1–16 (ed. Lapidge, III, 134–66; ed. and transl. Colgrave and Mynors, 532–53).

[180] *AC* A, B and C *s.a.* 768 (ed. and transl. Dumville, 21), here drawing on North Welsh information, as discussed by Charles-Edwards, *Wales and the Britons*, 350. For the other Britons, see *HE* V, 15, 1 (ed. Lapidge, III, 94; ed. and transl. Colgrave, 504–5); cf. Stancliffe, *Bede and the Britons*, 24–5.

the cult of St Martin, which was not merely popular on the Continent but also in the Gaelic world.[181]

Another text that sheds light on eighth-century Whithorn is *Miracula Nynie Episcopi*. This poem survives alongside a hymn for Nynia in a Continental manuscript, which contains material compiled by Alcuin.[182] Alcuin had written to the community of Whithorn and he received some poems in return. It has been suggested that Alcuin or his students wrote the *Miracula* poem in York, working with the material provided by the Whithorn community.[183] The poem portrays Nynia as a bishop who established monasteries where the brethren lived communally.[184] This suggests Whithorn was an ecclesiastical site with diverse functions, a type of institution familiar in the Northumbrian kingdom and in Ireland. Nynia is also praised as *praeclarus doctor in orbe* 'a teacher famous in the world'.[185] This is high praise from Alcuin's circle, and it suggests that Whithorn had built up a reputation for scholarship. Indeed, St Boniface sent a letter to Bishop Pehthelm seeking advice on canon law, which confirms that Whithorn was a place of learning.[186]

Many of the *Miracula*'s stories appear in a slightly altered form in the twelfth-century *Vita Niniani* by Ailred of Rievaulx. These two texts must have had a common source, but its nature is controversial. One option is that it was a *Vita* composed at pre-Northumbrian Whithorn; alternatively, the *Vita* may belong to the Northumbrian period, which would account for the presence of an English place-name in Ailred's *Vita*.[187] One episode that is unique to Ailred's text relates how one of Ninian's pupils committed a misdemeanour and escaped in a half-finished boat, using Ninian's staff to plug the holes miraculously.[188] The boy is said to have been making for *Scotia*, which would mean the core of the Scottish kingdom by Ailred's time, but in his eighth-century source it would be a reference to Ireland.[189] In this episode, then, we glimpse what may have been routine sailings between Whithorn and Ireland.

Next I examine texts of Hiberno-Latin origin that refer to Whithorn or Nynia. The first is a saint's Life entitled *De servo Dei Finano*, which was collected by John of Tynemouth, the itinerant assembler of saints' Lives, in the fourteenth century. His version of the text derives from the Tironensian–Benedictine house of Kilwinning, Ayrshire, which was established between 1162 and 1188. The Life elucidates the origins of Kilwinning's patron, Finanus *Wallico nomine* 'called in Welsh' Winnin.[190] Reformed houses often commissioned new hagiography to shed light on obscure founder saints, and some writers sought texts from Ireland to assist them.[191] Scholars

---

[181] Mullins, 'Trouble', 113–16; see below, 200–1 for the inscriptions.
[182] Bamberg, Staatsbibliothek, Misc. patr. 17. Strecker, 'Zu den Quellen'; Levison, 'An eighth-century poem'; Chadwick, 'St. Ninian', 24–6. For authorship at York, see Lapidge, 'Aediluulf', 166–7.
[183] Alcuin, *Epistola* 4 (no. 273) (ed. Dümmler, *Epistolae Karolini aevi* II, 431).
[184] *Miracula* 3, 7 (ed. Strecker, 947, 951–2; transl. W. MacQueen, in J. MacQueen, *St Nynia*, 92, 99).
[185] *Miracula* 1 (ed. Strecker, 945; transl. W. MacQueen, 88).
[186] *Councils* (ed. Haddan and Stubbs, III, 310).
[187] MacQueen, *St Nynia*, 4–11, 79–85; compare Clancy, 'The real St Ninian', 6–7; Fraser, 'Northumbrian Whithorn', 40–4.
[188] *Vita Niniani*, 10 (ed. Forbes, *Lives*, 19–21, 151–3).
[189] MacQueen, *St. Nynia*, 84–5, cf. Boyle, 'Saint Ninian', 66.
[190] *De Servo Dei Finano* (ed. Horstmann, I, *Nova Legenda Anglie*, 444–7).
[191] One example is Geoffrey of Burton's use of Conchubranus's Life of Monenna to write the Life of St Modwenna of Burton: *Vita Sancte Modwenne*, preface (ed. and transl. Bartlett, 2–3).

have long suspected that *De servo Dei Finano* is based on a much earlier Life of St Finnian of Mag mBili (Movilla, Co. Down), which also underpinned the Life of Frediano of Lucca.[192] One difficulty is the absence of references to Movilla, although the text betrays a detailed knowledge of north-eastern Ireland. This omission can be explained as the work of the twelfth-century compiler, who substituted his own church of Kilwinning for Movilla. Another obstacle is that Finanus is linked with Dál nAraide, a dynasty of the Cruithni, rather than being accorded his usual Dál Fiatach pedigree.[193] The context may be an attempt by Dál nAraide to claim the renowned church of Movilla; if so, the text fits most comfortably during the high-point of Dál nAraide's power, the seventh or eighth centuries.[194] In my view, *De servo Dei Finano* preserves an eighth-century text written from the perspective of north-eastern Ireland.

I will focus on the portion of the text that describes Finnian's education at *magnum monasterium* 'the great monastery', a site that scholars have long identified with Whithorn.[195] Finnian was first entrusted to Bishop Colmán, who may be identified with the saint of Druim Mór (Dromore, Co. Down).[196] Colmán was unable to chastise his student, and so Finnian went to Cóelán, abbot of Nendrum, but he felt unworthy to take on such an excellent pupil.[197] At that moment, ships arrived from Britain bearing the holy Bishop Nennio and he took Finnian back to *magnum monasterium* to study. While *magnum monasterium* is not explicitly identified with Whithorn, there are strong indications that the author had this location in mind. First, the name *Nennio* is surely an attempt to represent *Nynia* or its Brittonic equivalent.[198] The affectionate form *Monenn* appears on Nynia's feastday, 16 September, in the *Martyrology of Tallaght*, albeit erroneously associated with the saint of Cluain Conaire. Here the diminutive *–ia(u)* suffix has been replaced by the affectionate *mo–* suffix.[199] In *De servo Dei Finano*, Nennio is described as *sanctissimus pontifex* 'a very holy bishop', just as eighth-century Northumbrian writers emphasised Nynia's role as a bishop. Irish writers were attuned to the importance of episcopal status, and the inclusion of Nennio's title was meaningful.[200] The significance of episcopal status tells against an identification of *magnum monasterium* with any church that lacked a bishop in the eighth century.[201] Moreover, the story is an example of the Irish

---

[192] Société des Bollandistes, *Bibliotheca Hagiographica Latina*, no. 3175; Sperber, 'Lives', 88.

[193] *De servo Dei Finano*, line 16 (ed. Horstmann, I, 444); Sperber, 'Lives', 88. *Corpus genealo-giarum sanctorum Hiberniae* 136.1, 423, 662.140 (ed. Ó Riain, 23, 64, 96) gives the saint's Dál Fiatach genealogy.

[194] Edmonds, *Whithorn's Renown*, 15; cf. Sperber, 'Lives', 88–9.

[195] *De servo Dei Finano*, lines 32–40 (ed. Horstmann, I, 444–5); for an early example of the identification, see Maxwell, *A History*, 46. More recently, see Hamlin, *Ninian*, 9–10.

[196] Reeves, *Ecclesiastical Antiquities*, 304–5.

[197] For the identification of Cóelán with Nendrum's founder saint, Mochaoi, see *ibid.*, 144, 188–9 and discussion in Towill, 'Saint Mochaoi', 105–6.

[198] Andrew Breeze does not take the Nennio–Nynia equation into account in his review of my Whithorn lecture, nor does he discuss the eighth-century, north-eastern Irish context of the episode. He highlights the reference to Nennius *qui Mancennus dicitur, de Rosnacensi monasterio*, but this is in a twelfth-century text, the Life of St Eógan of Ardstraw.

[199] Russell, 'Patterns'. For Brittonic name forms, see Gough-Cooper, 'Some notes', 5–10. I discuss the martyrological evidence in more detail in *Whithorn's Renown*, 17–21.

[200] Etchingham, *Church Organisation*, 69–72.

[201] As far as I am aware, Saints Mawgan/Meugan were not identified as bishops in the pre-Norman period, which is an obstacle for the identification of these saints with the Nennio of *magnum monasterium* (Breeze, 'Rosnat', 46–7).

hagiographical topos in which meetings between saints reflect the hierarchy of their churches.[202] Finnian's church (Movilla) is portrayed as the leading church of this part of Ireland, yet on a par with *magnum monasterium* in Britain. Both Nendrum and Movilla housed bishops in the seventh century, but here there is a pointed remark about Cóelán's of Nendrum's lack of episcopal status:[203]

> (Caelán) dixit: "Iste meus nunquam erit discipulus: vere enim in caelo et in terris honore et merito lunge me precellit. Nam episcopus erit, sapientia clarus et religione ac sanctitate conspicuus"[204]

> Caelán said: "this boy will never be my disciple, for he far excels me in honour and merit in heaven and earth. For he will be a bishop, bright in wisdom and illustrious in religion and holiness."

In short, the author of *De servo Dei Finano* was immersed in the ecclesiastical relations of north-eastern Ireland and located just a short sea-crossing from Whithorn. He may even have read the early *Vita* of Nynia since *De servo Dei Finano* and the *Vita Niniani* share a very similar episode relating to a king called Tuathal/Tudval.[205] His work shows an awareness of Whithorn's founder saint, its episcopal status and reputation of a centre of learning.

Another version of the tale of Finnian's education is found in the Irish *Liber Hymnorum*. This work survives in two manuscripts of the eleventh or early twelfth centuries. The relevant hymn, attributed to St Mugint, begins *parce domine, parce populo tuo*, a quotation from the Book of Joel. The prayer is prefaced by a text in Latin and Irish that describes the pupils who studied under St Mugint at Futerna. They included Finnian and a princess called Drusticc, who unsuccessfully tried to inveigle Finnian into helping her to seduce another pupil, Rióc.[206] The tale is an elaboration of a story in *De servo Dei Finano*, in which a princess tempts a pilgrim at *magnum monasterium*.[207] Drusticc is an unusual Pictish name, which hints at a story that originated some time before the eleventh century; it is tempting to compare the Pictish carvings at Trusty's Hill.[208]

The preface explicitly identifies Mugint's school as Whithorn. It starts: *Mugint fecit hunc hymnum hi Futerna* 'Mugint composed this hymn in *Futerna*'.[209] This is a Gaelicised version of the Anglian name *hwīt ærne*: F had been substituted for W by analogy with the incorporation of words beginning with W into Irish. The name *Futerna* also appears in the extensive commentary that was added to Óengus's martyrology. The writer seeks to explain the identity of a St Finnia commemorated

---

[202] See n. 101, above.

[203] We lack a full record of these bishops on account of the patchy annalistic record: Etchingham, 'The bishops'.

[204] *De servo Dei Finano,* lines 23–39 (ed. Horstmann, I, 444–5).

[205] *Vita Niniani*, ch. 4 (ed. Forbes, 10–13, 144–5); *De servo Dei Finano*, lines 30–44 (ed. Horstmann, I, 446–7); Wilson, 'St Ninian', 170; *idem*, 'St. Ninian: Irish evidence', 141, 143. I prefer the idea of textual interchange to the notion that this episode was associated with an early cult of Uinniau.

[206] *The Irish Liber Hymnorum* (ed. Bernard and Atkinson, I, 22–4). Cf. the translation and commentary in MacQueen, *St Nynia*, 41–4.

[207] *De servo Dei Finano* (ed. Horstmann, I, 445).

[208] MacQueen, *St Nynia*, 41, 44.

[209] I have checked that Futerna appears in both manuscripts: Dublin, Trinity College MS 1441, fol. 4r; Dublin, University College, MS Franciscan A2, p. 19.

on 28 September: *alii dicunt combad hé dobeth i Futerna isna Rannaib* 'some say it is he who used to be in Futerna in the Rhinns'.[210] The commentator was working at Armagh in the eleventh century, and he had access to numerous sources, including a version of the *Liber hymnorum*.[211] His phrase 'Futerna in the Rhinns' betrays up-to-date knowledge of Whithorn's political backdrop. By this time, the Machars peninsula was dominated by Echmarcach mac Ragnaill (*ob.* 1064/5), who was termed *rex Innarenn* 'king of the Rhinns' at the time of his death.[212]

While the identification of *Futerna* with Whithorn is clear, the name of the teacher, *Mugint* is more difficult to explain. The name appears to derive from the Old Welsh *Moucan*, which became *Meugan* in Middle Welsh.[213] I suggest that eleventh-century Irish scholars equated the two saints, perhaps because of their British background, and because of the vague resemblance of Meugan's *orationes Moucani* to Mugint's hymn.[214] The eleventh-century commentators frequently weighed up whether a saint in one location was identical to another. This process is also apparent in the twelfth-century Life of St Eógan of Ardstraw, which mentions *vir sanctus ac sapiens Nennyo, qui Maucennus dicitur* 'a holy and wise man, Nennio, who is called Maucennus'.[215] Eógan was one of several northern and north-eastern saints who was said to have studied at a monastery called *Rosnat*, just as their neighbour, Finnian, had travelled to *magnum monasterium*. The epithets applied to *Rosnat*, and perhaps the place-name itself, may link the school with a monastery in Cornwall or South Wales rather than Whithorn.[216] This is a different matter, however, on the point of reference for *magnum monasterium* in the much earlier text that underpins *De servo Dei Finano*. Further consideration of the circulation of information about *Rosnat* must await detailed study and dating of these later hagiographical works.[217]

The accumulated evidence indicates that Whithorn's community remained in communication with counterparts in north-eastern Ireland from the eighth century until the eleventh century. Irish authors praised Whithorn's school and its episcopal status. As I discuss later, archaeological evidence indicates that Whithorn suffered a set-back in the late ninth century. It re-emerged in the tenth century as the centre of Church organisation in the Machars peninsula and enjoyed renewed links with Ireland.[218] The nearby Norse place-name *Bysbie* 'settlement of the bishop' (*Biskeby* 1305) indicates that Whithorn remained the seat of a bishop, and it was still

[210] *Félire Óengusso* (ed. Stokes, 212–13); cf. Etchingham, 'North Wales', 161.

[211] Ó Riain, *Feastdays*, 173–203. Brief versions of the story of Drusticc also appear in one manuscript of the commentary on *Félire Óengusso* (ed. Stokes, 238–9), and the tract on saints' mothers: *Corpus genealogiarum sanctorum Hiberniae*, 722.100 (ed. Ó Riain, 180).

[212] See above, 68.

[213] The *-n* to *-nt* may represent a hypercorrection based on the shift of the endings of verbs in the present tense third person plural from *-n* to *-nt*. If so, the Irish scholar was using a text from Wales or Cornwall. I am grateful to Paul Russell for advice on this point.

[214] Howlett, '*Orationes Moucani*'; Edmonds, *Whithorn's Renown*, 25–6.

[215] *Vita sancti Eogani episcopi Ardstratensis* (ed. Heist, *Vitae Sanctorum*, 400). For the date of the text, see Flanagan, *The Transformation*, 15.

[216] See, for example, Wilson, 'St Ninian and Candida Casa', 181–5 (South Wales); Thomas, '*Rosnat*' (Tintagel); Breeze, '*Rosnat*' (Old Kea).

[217] For thirteenth-century features in two relevant Lives, those of Tigernach of Clones and Enda of Aran, see Sharpe, *Medieval Irish Saints' Lives*, 393, 398.

[218] See below, 195, 214, 217.

perceived as such by Irish writers.[219] These literary contacts do not suggest institutional and hierarchical relationships, but rather the passage of students, scholars and texts between Whithorn and Ireland.

Throughout this chapter, I have traced a range of Gaelic–Northumbrian ecclesiastical contacts that involved churches in the west and north of the kingdom. The Cuthbertine community retained an affiliation to the Columban *familia* long after the Synod of Whitby, even if this was no longer a relationship of dependency. By the tenth century, the Cuthbertine community was forging links with the new Columban centre at Kells. Meanwhile, York's cathedral community had become aware of the reputation of the *céli Dé* for care of the poor, and they sought to emulate this activity. Further west, Whithorn was renowned as an episcopal seat and school among writers based in north-eastern Ireland. The variety of ecclesiastical contacts adds weight to my broader argument that Gaelic–Northumbrian interaction was diverse and enduring.

---

[219] Oram, 'Scandinavian settlement'. Hoddom was an alternative seat of a bishop, but this is only indicated by Jocelin of Furness's twelfth-century *Vita Kentigerni*, 33 (ed. Forbes, 219); cf. Oram, *The Lordship*, 83–4.

6

SAINTS AND SEAWAYS IN THE VIKING AGE

The voyages of saints across the Irish Sea seem to epitomise early medieval cultural contacts. Church dedications were once thought to reveal movements of churchmen during the so-called 'Age of the Saints', the shadowy period between the fifth century and the seventh. Scholars now take a more complex view, acknowledging the numerous chronological layers in a saint's cult. In this chapter, I contend that the foundation of new churches during the Viking Age underpinned the transmission of saints' cults from the Gaelic world to the Northumbrian kingdom. I disentangle evidence of Viking-Age devotion from the late-medieval veneration of Gaelic saints in the area. The resulting pattern supports the argument that I have developed so far, namely, that Gaelic influence arrived in the Northumbrian kingdom from a variety of directions and over a lengthy period of time.

The study of church dedications raises two formidable problems: it can be difficult to identify the medieval dedication of a church, and it is hard to know how a church came to be dedicated to a specific saint, in an era before formal dedication ceremonies became routine. These difficulties have spawned a long and venerable tradition of *Patrozinienforschung*, or researching dedications, across Europe.[1] There have long been ceremonies relating to the consecration of the church building and its dedication to God. From the fourth century onwards, an additional patron might be honoured, and this gave rise to what is now commonly described as a 'church dedication'.[2] Medieval bishops performed three related ceremonies: the dedication of the church, the consecration of the altar and the enclosure of relics.[3] The role of relics in the foundation of churches is attested in both Ireland and the Northumbrian kingdom. When Bishop Colmán left Lindisfarne, he selected some relics of Saint Áedán, and transported them to the church that he founded at Inis Bó Finne (Inishbofin, Co. Mayo).[4]

It is questionable whether all of the churches that were dedicated to Gaelic saints in the west of the Northumbrian kingdom held corporeal relics, given their number. Indeed, the Council of Chelsea (816) made provision for churches to be consecrated in the absence of relics, by sealing the Eucharist in the altar. The Council emphasised the role of the bishop in consecration ceremonies, in line with Archbishop

---

[1] Dorn, 'Beiträge zur Patrozinienforschung' and Delahaye, 'Loca Sanctorum' give insights into earlier work.

[2] Binns, *Dedications*, 3, noting that in strict terms a church is dedicated to God.

[3] Muncey, *A History*, 41–7; Orme, *English Church Dedications*, 4–5.

[4] AU 668.3 (ed. and transl. Mac Airt and Mac Niocaill, 138–9); AT [667] (ed. and transl. Stokes, I, 160); CS [664] (ed. and transl. Hennessy, 100–1); *CI* 668.4 (transl. Charles-Edwards, I, 157). Cf. *HE* IV, 4, 1 (ed. Lapidge, II, 220, 222; ed. and transl. Colgrave and Mynors, 346–9); Wycherley, *The Cult*, 113–27.

Wulfred of Canterbury's broader assertion of episcopal rights.[5] Again, the peripheral areas of the Northumbrian kingdom may have fallen short of this standard during the Viking Age, when there was significant disruption to the Northumbrian dioceses. Even in southern England, where some dioceses were more stable, a significant number of churches had not been formally consecrated by the twelfth century.[6] The diffuse nature of episcopal authority in parts of the Northumbrian kingdom may also have affected decisions about who was considered a saint; papal canonisation was primarily a phenomenon of the eleventh century onwards.[7] In short, the church dedications that I investigate in this chapter may reflect the informal devotion of the local community rather than an officially sanctioned cult. As such, they have the potential to shed light on cultural influence on sectors of society that were rarely touched by high-level political and ecclesiastical connections.

This potential can only be unlocked if the medieval dedication of a church can be established. The Reformation curtailed aspects saints' cults in northern England and southern Scotland, and knowledge of saints' dedications was sometimes lost.[8] Nicholas Orme's work on Devon has revealed that around 30 per cent of church dedications have changed since the medieval period, and estimates for other parts of England range from 20 to 25 per cent.[9] The first comprehensive lists of church dedications emerged in the eighteenth century at the hands of John Ecton, who compiled information relating to the values and taxes of parishes in 1535. A decade later, Browne Willis published surveys of cathedrals and associated parishes in England and Wales, including their dedications.[10] While these works remain useful sources of information, they do not distinguish between medieval and more recent dedications. The same is true of the later compilations by Frances Arnold-Forster, James Mackinlay and Francis Bond, which gather church dedications of varying dates in order to understand the influence of particular saints.[11] There is a need to compile medieval evidence for church dedications, an enormous task that will remain only partially complete while significant bodies of evidence (such as late-medieval wills) remain unpublished.[12] Fortunately, in the early twentieth century several scholars compiled medieval material pertaining to church dedications in the diocese of Carlisle and the county of Lancashire.[13] As to Scotland, the 'Database of dedications to saints in medieval Scotland' provides a thorough survey of material relating to any particular cult or dedication.[14] Another source of information about saints' cults is 'hagiotoponyms', that is, place-names that contain saints' names. Such place-names

---

5 Council of Chelsea 816 §2 (ed. Haddan and Stubbs, *Councils*, III, 580); Cubitt, *Anglo-Saxon Church Councils*, 194; Blair, *The Church*, 123.
6 Orme, *English Church Dedications*, 5.
7 Kemp, *Canonization and Authority*, 36–59.
8 In some areas, consecration and rogation ceremonies survived or were revived; see Walsham, *The Reformation*, 252–73.
9 Orme, *English Church Dedications*, xli; cf. Jones, *Saints in the Landscape*, 43–4.
10 Ecton, *Liber Valorum et Decimarum* (1711; 2nd edn 1723); Willis, *Survey of Cathedrals* (1727–30); *idem*, *Parochiale Anglicanum* (1733); Ecton, *Thesaurus Rerum Ecclesiasticarum* (1742) (incorporating work of Willis).
11 Arnold-Forster, *Studies* (1899); Mackinlay, *Ancient Church Dedications (1910–14)*; Bond, *Dedications* (1914). For deficiencies in this approach, see Levison, 'Medieval church-dedications', 63–5, 72–3; Butler, 'Church dedications', 48–9.
12 Jones, *Saints in the Landscape*, 9.
13 Farrer *et al.*, *The Victoria County History of Lancaster*; C & G. There is a list of dedications (without dated attestations) for Northumberland in Gregory, 'Dedication names', 381–3.
14 http://saints.shca.ed.ac.uk/.

are prolific in both south-west Scotland and north-west England. Scotland is well served by the 'Saints in Scottish place-names' database, and English examples are mostly covered by the works of the English Place-Name Survey.[15]

Once a pre-Reformation dedication has been identified, there remains the challenge of identifying when it became established within the medieval period. In this chapter, I argue that some Gaelic saints' dedications became established in the former Northumbrian kingdom during the tenth and eleventh centuries. This era witnessed the foundation of numerous 'proprietary churches', that is, local churches under the control of lay lords. The fragmentation of the Northumbrian kingdom opened up various links with Ireland, the Isles and the kingdom of the Scots, and these cultural influences can be detected in saints' dedications. I illustrate this point by examining saints' cults that flourished in Dublin, north-eastern Ireland and Dál Riata in Britain in turn.

Chronology and Transmission

The spread of Celtic saints' cults across the seaways has long attracted interest, yet the Viking Age has rarely been seen as a time when saints' cults flourished. I therefore begin by investigating the likely mechanisms for transmitting cults from the Gaelic world to the Northumbria kingdom. In the process, it is necessary to consider broader developments in Church organisation for, as Wilhelm Levison noted long ago: 'the increase in the number of churches naturally spread the custom of the dedication to a patron saint'.[16]

In his pioneering essay on Welsh saints, Rice Rees contended that the saints themselves founded the churches that bear their names, and that these churches predated those dedicated to universal saints.[17] Early and mid-twentieth-century scholars, notably E. G. Bowen, developed the idea that the distribution of churches associated with saints of Ireland and western Britain reflected early seaborne contacts. While Bowen's work related primarily to Wales, it also had a bearing on Northumbria's western coastline, which features in some of his maps.[18] Wilhelm Levison criticised this approach on the basis that cults tended to be based around the tombs of the saints rather than their lifetime activities. He suggested that some dedications to Irish and Welsh saints post-dated the seventh century, and this impression is borne out by analyses of south-west Britain, where these cults continued to spread in the tenth century and the Norman era.[19] Owen Chadwick further argued that dedications to martyrs and apostles were the norm elsewhere in Western Europe, and that a Welsh

---

[15] http://saintsplaces.gla.ac.uk/; *PNCu*; *PNWe*. Saints' names appear in place-names across Europe, as discussed by Delehaye, 'Loca Sanctorum', 43 ff., but the examples considered here are distinctive because they are combined with an item of vocabulary referring to a holy place. The studies of dedications in Scottish place-names found throughout *CPNS* remain valuable.

[16] 'Medieval church-dedications', 64.

[17] Rees, *An Essay* (1836), esp. 26–76. Note xii 'the churches were so called not so much because they were dedicated to the saints, as because they were founded by them'.

[18] For early twentieth-century scholarship see, for example, Crawford, 'Western seaways'; Bowen, *The Settlements*. Other examples are cited by Wooding, 'The figure', 9. Relevant maps include those of churches dedicated to St Kentigern and St Donnán in Bowen, *The Settlements*, 77; *idem*, *Saints, Seaways and Settlements*, 75.

[19] Pearce, 'The dating'; Jankulak, *The Medieval Cult*, 139–45.

preference for local holymen would have been unusual.[20] Bowen in fact admitted that dedications might have emerged in later times, and he highlighted the cult of St Brigit in particular in this respect.[21]

I would not rule out the possibility that a local saint's cult became established during the fifth and sixth centuries. In Ireland, the identity of an *érlam*, the founder or patron of a church, typically a saint, remained significant long after the era of foundation. The kindred of the *érlam* retained rights to the property and ecclesiastical office, and many of these saints appear in genealogical collections. The significance of *érlama* may explain why a considerable number of early Irish churches were dedicated to local patrons rather than universal saints, which counters Chadwick's concern about the lack of dedications to universal saints in Wales.[22] Yet Chadwick's point is relevant to the Northumbrian kingdom, where church founders tended to honour martyrs and apostles. This is despite the fact that saints Columba and Patrick appear in the Old English martyrology, a ninth-century Mercian compilation.[23] The sole known exception to the pattern of dedication to universal saints is the church that the community of *Scythlescester* founded on the site of King Ælfwald's murder (788), dedicating it to saints Cuthbert and Oswald.[24]

The concept of a fifth- or sixth-century origin for some saints' dedications also hinges on the interpretation of 'hagiotoponyms', that is, place-names that incorporate saints' names. A pertinent debate surrounds a group of *llan-* names in Ceredigion that may – according to one view – contain Irish saints' names in Welsh forms.[25] In the Northumbrian kingdom, hagiotoponyms are most prolific in Galloway, where there are considerable numbers of place-names featuring Gaelic *cill-* and Norse *kirkja*. Scholars used to associate the *cill-* (earlier *cell*) names with the pre-Northumbrian period, viewing them as one of several place-name elements that attested settlement from Ireland in the fifth century.[26] If that were the case, the *cill-* names would indicate that there had been very significant Irish influence north of the Solway prior to the expansion of the Northumbria kingdom.[27] Yet several scholars have called into question the notion of a sixth-century migration from Ireland to Galloway, noting that the relevant place-names could have been coined in later centuries.[28] Indeed, *cill-* remained a productive place-name element in eastern Scotland in the seventh century, and in Argyll as late as the fifteenth century.[29] As to south-western Scotland, a number of *cill-* names replaced earlier place-names in

[20] Levison, 'Medieval church-dedications', 69–72 (on St Ninian); Chadwick, 'The evidence', 175–7.
[21] See, for example, Bowen, *The Settlements*, 6–9; idem, *Saints, Seaways and Settlements*, 81; idem, 'The cult'.
[22] Charles-Edwards, '*Érlam*'; Wycherley, *The Cult*, 161–3. For genealogies and a preference for dedications to local saints (with exceptions such as Michael and Mary), see Ó Riain, 'Conservation', 360.
[23] *The Old English Martyrology*, 17 March, 9 June (ed. Rauer, 64–5, 114–15).
[24] *HR* (ed. Arnold, II, 52); Levison, *England and the Continent*, 259–85.
[25] Ó Riain ('The saints') has promoted an Irish origin, which Jankulak, ('Carantoc', 142–8) has disputed this in some cases. She has also highlighted later mechanisms of transmission of saints' cults from Ireland to Wales.
[26] MacQueen, 'Kirk- and Kil-'; idem, 'The Gaelic speakers', 17–18, 26; idem, *Place-Names in the Rhinns*, 46, 57; idem, *Place-Names of the Wigtownshire Moors*, 68–9, 75–83. Cf. Nicolaisen, *Scottish Place-Names*, 166–8.
[27] See the valuable lists in MacQueen, 'The Gaelic speakers', 19–24.
[28] See below, 159–60.
[29] Taylor, 'Place-names'; Clancy, 'Gaelic', 366; Butter, 'St Munnu', 32–8.

kirk- in the late medieval and early modern periods.[30] Moreover, some *cill-* names were coined afresh in late medieval times, such as Killantringan ('the church of St Ringan/Ninian') in Portpatrick, Ballantrae and Colmonell parishes. The place-name appears along pilgrimage routes to Whithorn, and is likely to reflect the late-medieval zenith of St Ninian's cult.[31]

As the Northumbrian kingdom expanded westwards, it absorbed existing churches and perhaps also their dedications. Some significant churches may have had multiple clergy, such as the *sacerdotes* Viventius and Mavorius, who were commemorated on a sixth-century monument at Kirkmadrine (Wigtownshire, now Dumfries and Galloway).[32] The place-name *eccles* (Brittonic *eclēs*, borrowed from Latin *ecclesia*) signifies a pre-existing church, and these names occur in association with early administrative units in both Lancashire and southern Scotland.[33] There is insufficient evidence to gauge the distribution of churches within the Brittonic kingdoms. It is possible that there were local cemeteries and churches controlled by kin groups, given that these are known from diverse parts of the early Insular world.[34] The evidence of pre-Northumbrian church dedications is similarly slim, the only certain example being the dedication to St Martin of Tours at Whithorn. St Martin's cult spread rapidly on the Continent and attracted interest amongst the Irish and the Britons.[35] There are faint hints of more localised cults; for example, *Sanctus Elfin* (or his church) held one carucate of land in Warrington at the time of the Domesday Survey.[36] Points of comparison include the churches of St Probus at *Lanprobi* near Sherborne (Dorset) and St Tegan at Landican on the Wirral, which were incorporated in Wessex and Mercia, respectively, during the seventh century.[37] St Tegan's cult is obscure, but there is a chance he may be identical to the Irish saint Tagán, in which case the possibility of early Irish influence on church dedications cannot be ruled out.[38]

As I have noted, ecclesiastical organisation in the Northumbrian kingdom revolved around minsters rather than local churches.[39] There may not have been much scope for new church dedications beyond the churches founded in honour of the universal

---

[30] Grant, 'A reconsideration', 98.

[31] MacQueen, 'The Gaelic speakers', 19, 25, 28–9; cf. Brooke, 'Kirk-compound place-names', 58, 60, 64–7 for the late-medieval dating of some *cill-* names in the area.

[32] *CIIC*, 516.

[33] Barrow, *The Kingdom of the Scots*, 53; Higham, *The Kingdom*, 101; Charles-Edwards, *Wales and the Britons*, 611.

[34] Davies, *An Early Welsh Microcosm*, 58–9; Pryce, 'Pastoral care', 58–60; Ó Carragáin, 'Church buildings', 91–2, 97, 111. The debate about 'undeveloped' cemeteries is discussed below, 193.

[35] *HE* III, 4, 4 (ed. Lapidge, II, 30; ed. and transl. Colgrave and Mynors, 222–3); Levison, 'Medieval church-dedications', 75; Mullins ('Trouble', 119–22) also notes evidence for early veneration of St Martin in Ireland and among the Columban *familia* more broadly.

[36] DB Chesh, 8, 7; fol. 265r. The name Elffin is a Brittonic rendering of *Alpinus*, and it appears in genealogies of the North Britons, such as Rhun ap Arthgal of Dumbarton's pedigree in the tenth-century Harleian genealogies (ed. Bartrum, *Early Welsh Genealogical Texts*, 10).

[37] *Lanprobi* was associated with a grant of King Cenwalh (642–72), which appears in a later list of royal grants to Sherborne: Finberg, *The Early Charters*, 155; *idem*, 'Sherborne', 98. Landican is recorded as Landechene in DB Chesh R3, 1; fol. 269v; cf. Dodgson, *The Place-Names*, IV, 266–7. The first letter of the saint's name will have been mutated (*t > d*).

[38] Ó Riain, *A Dictionary*, 569. Cf. Kiltigan, Co. Laois: Carrigan, *History and Antiquities*, II, 223–4; Kiltegan, Co. Wicklow (Celltagain, 1179): Price, *The Place-Names*, I, 111. There is also a Llandegan in Pembrokeshire: Baring-Gould and Fisher, *Lives*, II, 279–85.

[39] See above, 102–3.

saints at the minsters. For this reason, it is unlikely that churches were dedicated to Gaelic saints during the heyday of the Northumbrian kingdom. The exceptions may be the Iona saints associated with minsters on the route to Lindisfarne; in these cases, the saints' cults would have been nurtured throughout the early medieval period and eventually recorded as a dedication.[40] The dedication to St Balthere at Tyninghame and some of the St Wilfrid dedications in Lancashire may have arisen in this way.[41]

I propose that the diversity of saints' dedication increased during the Viking Age, when landowners began to found new churches on their estates. These may be defined as 'proprietary churches', in this context meaning especially the property of a layman and his kin, rather than of an abbot and his community.[42] If such churches were in short supply during the heyday of the Northumbrian kingdom, there would have been an upsurge in foundations once minsters started to lose their grasp of large estates. The reasons for the break-up of minster estates are complex, and include the growth of a buoyant market in land transactions and the encroachment of secular interests on minsters themselves. These developments allowed patronage to be devoted to small churches, which served a restricted constituency, and this informal organisation was eventually regularised into a parochial system.[43] Scandinavian settlers are implicated in these changes (even if they were not the main catalyst), and new landowners of Scandinavian origin sought to found churches once the process of conversion was under way.[44] The distribution of pre-Viking and Viking-Age sculpture in north-west England indicates that at least half of the minsters remained in use alongside the new foundations. In addition to the presence of sculpture at some new sites, there was also a very considerable increase in the amount of sculpture at each site.[45] This tendency towards the proliferation of sculpture is also seen in south-western Scotland and the Isle of Man.[46]

The foundation of new churches, or co-option and transformation of old ones, provided an opportunity for saints' cults to be transmitted from the Gaelic world to the Northumbrian kingdom. I propose that Scandinavian settlers who converted to Christianity in Dublin's hinterland, the Isle of Man and the Hebrides brought saints' cults to north-west England and south-west Scotland. The Gall-Goídil introduced another layer of saints' cults from their base around the Firth of Clyde in the eleventh century. W. G. Collingwood long ago broached the idea that mobile groups of Scandinavian extraction were responsible for disseminating saints' cults.[47] In the Insular world, Gaelic saints' cults might be transmitted rather than cults of Scandinavian saints. There are only a limited number of dedications to St Olaf in the Hebrides, and one to St Clement (an early martyr held dear by Scandinavian

---

[40] Taylor, 'Seventh-century Iona abbots'; Blair, 'A saint for every minster?'. Blair points out that the evidence for local saints is better in tenth-century southern England than in the North because of the hagiographical activity associated with the tenth-century Reform.

[41] St Balthere/Baldred's dedication at Tyninghame is attested in a charter of *ca* 1550: 'Database of dedications', EN/EW/2388. His association with the minster goes back to the eighth century; see above, 108–9.

[42] Wood, *The Proprietary Church*, 3–4.

[43] Blair, *The Church*, 291–323.

[44] Hadley, 'Conquest, colonisation'; cf. Blair, *The Church*, 292–5, for a qualified view.

[45] Bailey, *Viking Age Sculpture*, 80–1; Blair, *The Church*, 311.

[46] This is especially the case now that Ross Trench-Jellicoe ('A redefinition') has reclassified a number of 'pre-Scandinavian' Manx stones as belonging to the Viking Age.

[47] Collingwood and Rogers, 'Lost churches', 292–4; Collingwood and Graham, 'Patron saints', 11–12; Collingwood, 'Christian Vikings'.

Christians), and all of these seem relatively late.[48] The Icelandic settlement history *Landnámabók* reveals that some of the Hebridean settlers were devotees of St Columba. Örlyggr Hrappson, the foster-son of a Hebridean bishop, founded a church in honour of St Columba at Mount Esja, and one version of the text refers to another church dedicated to Columba at Innríholmur in Akranes.[49] *Landnámabók* is a twelfth-/thirteenth-century compilation, but the absence of these dedications from later ecclesiastical records suggests that they arose during the settlement period (870–930s) and were subsequently lost.[50]

One challenge to understanding the adoption of saints' cults by Scandinavians in the Insular world is that no missions are recorded to the settlers in Ireland or western Scotland. Óláfr Cúarán and his kinsman Rǫgnvaldr Guðrøðsson, for example, were baptised in England, as a result of an alliance with King Edmund. Óláfr was not isolated from Irish and Hebridean Christians, however: he married two Irish wives (Dúnlaith of Cenél nEógain and Gormlaith of Laigin) and he spent the last months of his life on Iona.[51] Lesley Abrams's distinction between conversion and Christianisation is relevant to the adoption of Gaelic saints' cults by Scandinavian voyagers. Conversion often ensued from specific events, such as Óláfr Cúarán's acceptance of baptism; Christianisation, on the other hand, ensued from the assimilation of Scandinavian settlers into the native populace. Christianisation occurred over an extended period, during which old beliefs and customs fused with Christian practices, and it was facilitated by everyday interactions that rarely received attention from chroniclers.[52] Just as Óláfr Cúarán had Irish wives, so those lower down the social scale may have married Irish women and adopted the preferred cults of their families. The children of these marriages would have helped to mediate the complex transition from paganism to Christianity.[53] Christianisation would have been accelerated by the survival of churches and priests, and indeed the relatively prolific local churches of pre-Viking Ireland seem to have survived and thrived in Scandinavian-settled areas of Ireland.[54] In the Hebrides, some major and influential institutions attracted the patronage of Scandinavian settlers, notably Iona. This point is significant because Iona is attested as an episcopal seat during the 970s, a prerequisite for the ordination of priests.[55] Indeed, some of the chapels in the Isles seem to have originated as Viking-Age estate churches; the recently excavated Speke Keeill

---

[48] Crawford, 'The dedication'; Abrams, 'Conversion and the Church', 177–8. The dedication to St Olaf at Wasdale Head (Cumbria) is modern: Bailey, *The Vikings*, 40.

[49] *Landnámabók* (ed. Jakob Benediktsson, 52–5, 66; transl. Hermann Pálsson and Edwards, 22–4).

[50] Marner, 'Irish saints', 150–3, nuancing Cormack, *The Saints*, 15, 92.

[51] Iona: AT [978] (ed. and transl. Stokes, II, 233). Marriages: *Ban-shenchus* (ed. and transl. Dobbs, 314, 337–8); *CGH* 117 c 47 (ed. O'Brien, 13) (Gormlaith's three leaps into marriage). See above, 61; Woolf, 'Amlaíb Cuarán', 41–2 and in general Abrams, 'The conversion of the Scandinavians'; *eadem*, 'Conversion and the Church', 179–80.

[52] Abrams, 'The conversion of the Danelaw'.

[53] For the involvement of non-Scandinavian wives in conversion, see Jesch, *Women*, 102–4; for children, see Hadley and Hemer, 'Microcosms', 66–7.

[54] Ó Carragáin, 'Cemetery settlements', 333–4, 347, 357–8. The abandonment of some sites in Kerry contrasts with continuity in Co. Dublin.

[55] Mugrón *ab Iae, scriba optimus atque suí-epscop na Trí Rand* 'abbot of Iona, excellent scribe, and pre-eminent bishop of the Three Parts': AR [979] (ed. Gleeson and Mac Airt, 171); AFM 978.1 (ed. and transl. O'Donovan, II, 708–9). The interpretation of the *trí rand* is discussed by Etchingham, *Church Organisation*, 186 (suggesting Ireland, Scotland, Man); Clancy, 'Iona v. Kells', 99 (Dublin, the Isles and Man). For Iona and church survival in general, see Jennings, 'Iona'; Abrams, 'Conversion and the Church', 167.

on the Isle of Man, for example, dates to the tenth century, even if it was based on an earlier cemetery. Carl Marstrander famously proposed that there was a correspondence between keeills and treens (administrative units), a system that developed fully through the foundation of estate churches by Scandinavian settlers.[56]

The twelfth century witnessed another flourishing of Gaelic saints' cults in northern England and southern Scotland. This phenomenon impacted on the hagiographical genre, for Anglo-Norman writers sought out Irish hagiography as part of a quest for the origins of pre-conquest saints. They incorporated Irish saints' Lives into the hagiography of saints venerated in England; for instance, Geoffrey of Burton based his Life of St Modwenna of Trent partly on the eleventh-century *Vita* of Monenna of Killevy (Co. Armagh).[57] Some Anglo-Norman hagiographers wrote Lives of Irish saints, an example being Lawrence of Durham's *Vita S. Brigidae*.[58] The literary activity coincided with the fixing of parish boundaries, the foundation of permanent church buildings and the consolidation of parochial revenues. According to R. K. Rose's classic study, Anglo-Norman lords reinvigorated local churches in north-west England following a period of abeyance in the Viking Age. They dedicated these new churches to Gaelic and Brittonic saints in a bid to integrate into local society.[59] I would argue that Rose has underrated the survival of minster churches and foundation of proprietary churches in the tenth and eleventh centuries. In my view, Gaelic saints' cults had been gestating in the area since the Viking Age, only to be developed further in the late-medieval period.

This point can be illustrated by examining the cult of St Brigit. A considerable number of medieval dedications are attested across the former Northumbrian kingdom (see Table 1).[60]

The map and table illustrate that the cult of St Brigit flourished on the western edge of the region. There are, however, obstacles to detecting Viking-Age veneration among the many churches and chapels in the list. Many chapels north of the Solway bear the name Kirkbride or Kilbride, and some will have been founded when efforts were made to improve access to pastoral care in large parishes during the late-medieval period. The names of the chapels would have been formed by analogy with pre-existing place-names in the region. The place-name *Kirklebride* illustrates the late and confused nature of this process: this name, which is first attested in 1593, had acquired two words for church, *kirk* and *cill*.[61] It is therefore necessary to examine the parochial status of the Kirkbrides, and identify relatively early dedications, in order to trace potentially early centres of Brigit's cult. Only the churches

---

[56] Marstrander, 'Treen og keeill' – note that at 337 he suggested that smaller keeills might be pre-Viking. For the Isle of Man, see the recent excavations at Speke Keeill, although it is not clear how representative this site is: Wessex Archaeology, 'Speke Keeill', 21–2. Cf. Crawford, *Scandinavian Scotland*, 167, 180–1 for the Northern and Western Isles.

[57] Bartlett, 'Cults', 69–71; *Conchubrani Vitae Sanctae Monennae* (ed. Esposito); Geoffrey of Burton, *Life and Miracles* (ed. Bartlett).

[58] *Vita sanctae Brigidae* (ed. Heist, *Vita Sanctorum Hiberniae*, 1–37). A letter survives between Lawrence and Ailred of Rievaulx concerning this work: Hoste, 'A survey', 263–5.

[59] Rose, 'Cumbrian society'. Compare the developments in southern Scotland.

[60] For the following tables and maps, I cite only church and chapel dedications and names up to *ca* 1500. I cover the territory of the Northumbrian kingdom *ca* 800, and so I exclude Renfrewshire and Lanarkshire. I am grateful to Michael Ansell for sharing his maps of *kirk*- names with me.

[61] Grant, 'A reconsideration', 105–9. For chapel foundation, see Oram, 'Parishes and churches', 211–12; Thomas, *The Parish*, 51–86 (here defined as 'dependent chapels'). Excavations at Brydekirk (Annan) support a late-medieval date for this chapel: Crowe, 'Excavations at Brydekirk'.

Table 1: Medieval dedications to St Brigit

Church	Medieval status	Date of first attestation	Source	Secondary reference
Beckermet St Bridget, Cumberland	Parish church	1262	*Register of the Priory* (ed. Wilson), 131	C & G, 17
Brydekirk (Annan, Dumfriesshire)	Parish church	1507	Place-name: *Bridechapell*	J-F, 1
Bridekirk, Cumberland	Parish church	1212/ ca 1210	*Register* (ed. Prescott, 502)/ Place-name: *Bridekirke*	C & G, 18 / *PNCu*, II, 283
Brydischapell (Lochmaben, Dumfriesshire)	Chapel	1517	Place-name: *Brydischapell*	'Saints in Scottish place-names'
Kilbride (now Kirkbride, Kirkcudbright)	Chapel	1456	Place-name: *Kilbride*	Brooke, 'Kirk-compound', 69
Kilbride (Stewarton, Ayrshire)	Chapel	1315–21	Place-name: *Kilbryde*	'Database of dedications'
Kirkbride (Anwoth parish, Kirkcudbrightshire)	Chapel	1534	Place-name: *Mekill Kyrkebride*	'Saints in Scottish place-names'
Kirkbride (Blaiket, Kirkcudbrightshire)	Parish church	1164 × 1175	*Liber cartarum Sancte Crucis* (ed. Innes, 69)	Brooke, 'Kirk-compound', 69; 'Database of dedications' EN/ EW/3539
Kirkbride, Cumberland	Parish church	1163	Place-name: *Chirchebrid*	*PNCu*, 144
Kirkbride (Durisdeer, Dumfriesshire)	Parish church	1274	Place-name: *Kyrkbrid*	'Saints in Scottish place-names'*
Kirkbride (Keir, Dumfriesshire)	Chapel	1320 / 1522	Place-name: *Brydeburgh*; Kirkbridis	J-F, 67
Kirkbride (Kirkcolm, Wigtownshire)	Chapel	1462	Exchequer Rolls	Brooke, 'Kirk-compound', 70
Kirkbride (Kirkmabreck, Wigtownshire)	Chapel	1406 / 1534	Unpublished MSS / Place-name: *Litil Kyrkbryde*	M'Kerlie, *Lands*, IV, 275 / 'Saints in Scottish place-names'
Kirkbride (Kirkmaiden, Wigtownshire)	Chapel	1545	Place-name: *Kirkbryd*	'Saints in Scottish place-names'
Kirkbride (Maybole, Ayrshire)	Parish church	1194	Place-name: *Kirkebride*	'Saints in Scottish place-names'

Kyrkbride (Kirkatrick Iuxta, Dumfriesshire)	Chapel	1355–6	Place-name: *Kyrkbride*	Fraser, *The Annandale Family Book*, I, 10–11
Polchillebride (Colvend, Kirkcudbrightshire)	Chapel noted in burn name	1175 × 1185	Place-name: *Polchillebride* Register (ed. Grainger and Collingwood), 99–100.	Livingston, 'The Lanes'; Clancy pers. comm; Brooke, 'The Deanery' 54**
Sanquhar (Dumfriesshire)	Parish church	1519	Confirmation in mortmain: *in ecclesia parochiali S. Brigide de Sanquhare*	'Database of dedications', EN/ JD/644
Sundrum (Ayrshire)	Chapel	1329	Comptum: *capelle Sancte Brigide* (ablative)	'Database of dedications', EN/ EW/3

* Is this Kirkbride to be identified with the *ecclesia beati Brigide de Wintertonegan in valle Niht* that appears in a 1227 charter of Affrica of Nithsdale? See 'Database of dedications', EN/ JD/2281.

** Colvend is listed as a possible St Brigit dedication in Brooke, 'The deanery', 65. There is no medieval dedication evidence for the parish church. For the place-name, see Livingston, 'The Lanes', 4.

at Blaiket, Maybole and the unidentified *Wintertonegan* meet the criteria north of the Solway.[62] They were given to religious houses in the twelfth and early thirteenth centuries by the kinsmen Uhtred of Galloway and Duncan of Carrick, and by Affrica, lady of Nithsdale. These individuals descended from the rival dynasties of Galloway and Nithsdale, both of which originated among the Gall-Goídil.[63] The clerics based at these three churches may have disseminated the cult to newly founded chapels in their parishes. Alternatively, some of the late chapel dedications may reflect the Douglas family's influence on the area in the fourteenth and fifteenth centuries; they had a strong affinity with Brigit, as illustrated by the dedication at Douglas parish church (Lanarkshire).[64]

South of the Solway, Beckermet is a good candidate for Viking-Age devotion to Brigit given the presence of Viking-Age monuments there. Indeed, the church also has a high-quality, early ninth-century monument featuring an inscription, and there is another collection of Viking-Age sculpture at Beckermet St Johns.[65] I propose that Beckermet was a Northumbrian minster, which was divided into two proprietary

[62] None of these has current parochial status: Kirkbride was united with Maybole parish soon after 1571; Blaiket had been incorporated into Urr parish by the fourteenth century; and Kirkbride in Upper Nithsdale was divided between Durrisdeer and Sanquhar in 1732: Cowan, *The Parishes*, 118; Brooke, 'The deanery', 54.

[63] Uhtred grants Blaiket to Holyrood in 1164 × 1175: *Liber cartarum Sancte Crucis* no. 69 (ed. Innes, 69); Duncan grants Maybole to North Berwick: *Carte monalium de Northberwic* no. 120 (ed. Innes, 30–1); Affrica, lady of Nithsdale grants Wintertonegan church to Glasgow: *Registrum episcopatus Glasguensis* no. 142 (ed. Innes, I, 120). For her dynasty, see my 'Names on the Norman edge' (forthcoming).

[64] Bowen, 'The cult', 41–2; MacQueen, 'The Gaelic speakers', 25; 'Database of dedications' EN/ JD/546 (an attestation of the dedication at Douglas in 1506).

[65] *Corpus II*, 57–61, 54–7.

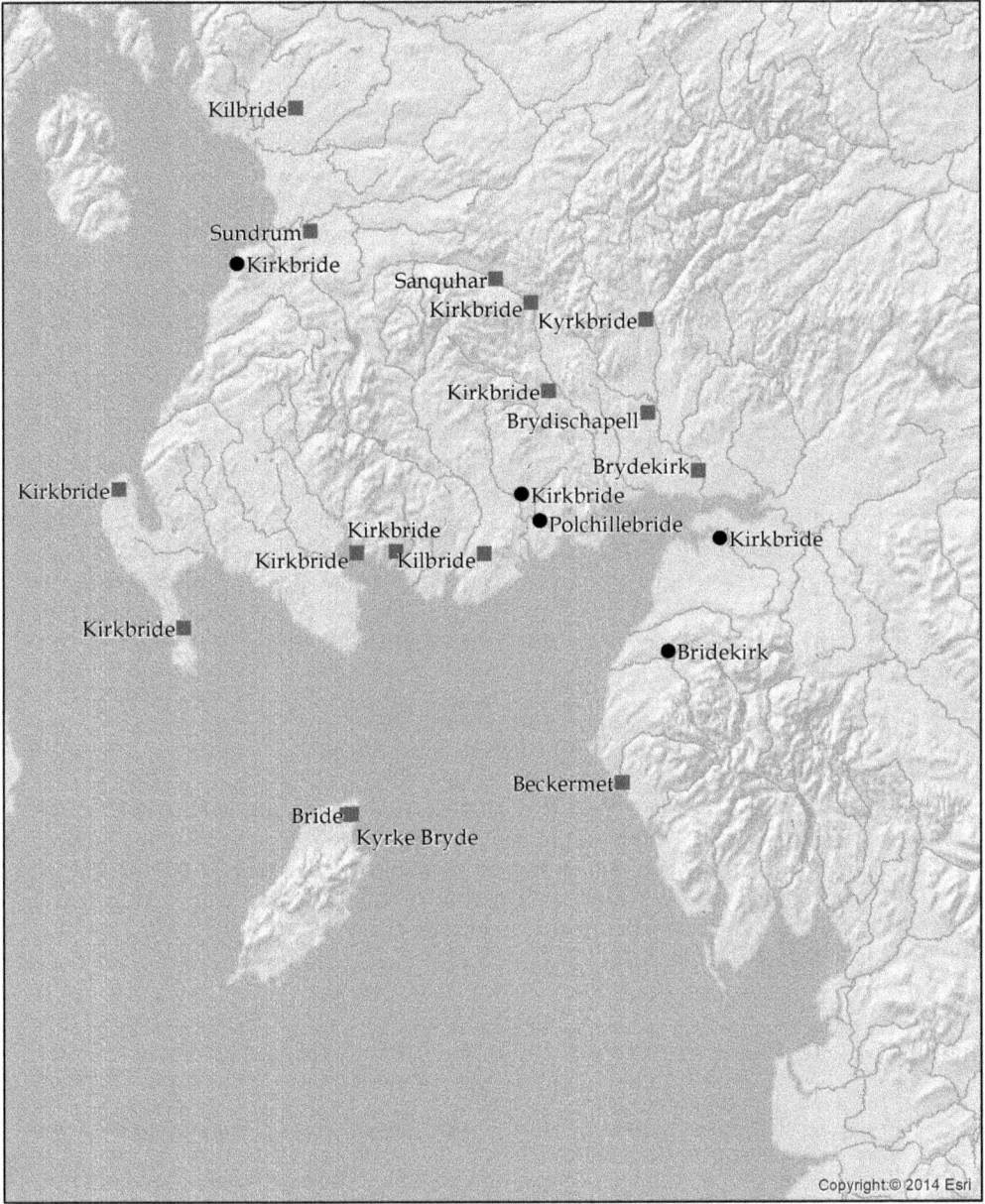

Kilbride

Sundrum
●Kirkbride

Sanquhar
Kirkbride   Kyrkbride

Kirkbride
Brydischapell

Brydekirk

Kirkbride   ●Kirkbride
●Polchillebride

Kirkbride
Kirkbride   Kilbride   ●Kirkbride

Kirkbride

Kirkbride
●Bridekirk

Beckermet

Bride
Kyrke Bryde

Copyright:© 2014 Esri

● St Brigit dedications attested up to *ca* 1250

■ St Brigit dedications attested from *ca* 1250 to 1550

Map 6: the cult of St Brigit on the eastern side of the Irish Sea to ca *1550*

churches during the Viking Age. One preserved the minster church's dedication to St John and the other acquired a new dedication to Brigit. West Kirby on the Wirral offers a parallel for a Brigit-dedicated church with an impressive collection of Viking-Age sculpture.[66] Kirkbride in Cumberland lacks early sculpture, but I suggest that the name was coined during the main era of inversion-compound formation, the eleventh century. The parish community of Kirkbride preserved a Gaelic hypocoristic version of the saint's name, 'Brydock' (featuring the *-óc* suffix), which must have been formed by Gaelic-speakers.[67] The place-name Bridekirk, on the other hand, may date from the end of Norse speech in the twelfth century; the parish looks like a creation of that period, complete with a stone church and a fine font featuring an unusual runic inscription. It is possible that this parish was carved out of the much larger parish of Brigham, which also has a Brigit dedication, albeit one that is first attested in the eighteenth century.[68]

Brigit's cult might have arrived in the Solway region through various channels. Her chief church was Kildare, which promoted the cult through a series of early hagiographical works.[69] Veneration of St Brigit also accompanied the distribution of her people, the Fothairt, but although early hagiography features a story in which this people led British travellers to Brigit, no similar hint of Northumbrian contact exists.[70] There are churches dedicated St Brigit in the Hebrides, the Orkneys and around the Firth of Clyde, the likely place of origin of the Gall-Goídil.[71] Despite the uncertainty concerning the route(s) of transmission, I have demonstrated that the saint was venerated in the west of the former Northumbrian kingdom during the Viking Age. I will now seek to trace such connections more precisely by investigating localised cults.[72]

Dublin and its hinterland

Dublin was a major source of influence on the former Northumbrian kingdom, down to 954 and beyond. By the eleventh century, the urban centre of Dublin depended on an extensive hinterland, and I aim to show that saints' cults were transmitted from that area to the Isle of Man and western Northumbria. The cult of St Santán is particularly illustrative because it was so localised, developing only in four (possibly five) locations across the Irish Sea.[73]

---

[66] The dedication is mentioned in the context of a dispute between Basingwerk Abbey and St Werburgh's, Chester, over the church in 1279: *The Chartulary* 514 (ed. Tait, 295–6); *Corpus IX*, 133–6. I discuss West Kirby and the churches dedicated to St Brigit in north-eastern Wales in my 'Irish saints' cults' (forthcoming).

[67] *Contra* Arnold-Forster, *Studies*, II, 158, who suggested it was a local name for the saint. For inversion compounds, see below, 169–71.

[68] Barnes and Page, *The Scandinavian Runic Inscriptions*, 285 (Middle English words in runic alphabet); C & G, 18: Brigham had a chantry dedicated to St Mary in the fourteenth century; I suggest there was a double dedication with St Brigit.

[69] Sharpe, '*Vita S. Brigidae*'.

[70] Charles-Edwards, 'Early Irish saints' cults', 82–6.

[71] MacKinlay, *Ancient Church Dedications*, 119–21, 130; 'Saints in Scottish place-names'.

[72] In what follows I have mainly focused on saints with localised cults rather than including a comprehensive examination of Gaelic saints' cults in the Northumbrian kingdom. For a broader survey, see Edmonds, 'Hiberno-Saxon and Hiberno-Scandinavian influence', I, 166–218; II, 23–33.

[73] I cover this cult in more detail in my 'Saints' cults', 45–52.

Table 2: Medieval dedications to saints associated with Dublin's hinterland and Leinster

Church	Medieval status	Date of first attestation	Source	Secondary reference
Bassenthwaite, Cumberland (St Bega)	Parish church	1291	*Taxatio*, 1291 (*Behokirk*)*	C & G, 17
Dunbar, East Lothian (St Baye)	Collegiate church	1419	Papal supplication	'Database of dedications', EN/EW/4210
Killochan (Ayrshire) (St Onchú)	Chapel	1504–5	Place-name: *Killounquhane*	Paterson, *History of the County*, 136
Kirksanton, Cumberland (St Santán)	Chapel	1086 (1065)	DB Yorks, 301v	C & G, 24
St Bees, Cumberland (St Bega)	Parish church	*ca* 1125	*Register of the Priory* (ed. Wilson), 27–8	C & G, 17–18

* '*Taxatio* database', *s.n.* Bassenthwaite.

Santán was the patron of Kirksanton church in Cumbria (formerly Cumberland), which lies on the coast in the shadow of the prominent navigational feature Black Combe. Kirksanton was located in the seigniory of Millom, which is part of an area now known by the Norse name Copeland (*kaupaland* 'bought land'). Such blocks of land seem to have changed hands as going concerns during the Viking Age.[74] St Santán's cult is first attested here in a section of the Yorkshire Domesday thought to derive from a geld list of 1065. The name is rendered *Santacherche*, in which the second element is likely to be a rendering of Norse *kirkja* (rather than English *cirice*) in Domesday orthography.[75] The next reference to the place-name is *Kirkesantan* (1152), a form featuring 'inversion-compound', or Gaelic-influenced, word order. This may suggest continued interaction between Norse- and Gaelic-speakers in the locality down to the twelfth century.[76] By the thirteenth century, Kirksanton was a chapel of Millom parish church, which had the advantage of being located next to a castle. Two pieces of tenth- or eleventh-century sculpture are built into the walls of Millom parish church, but these may have been brought from elsewhere in the parish.[77] A fragment of a cross-shaft features a distinctive Stafford knot with diamond-shaped tie, a design otherwise encountered in Galloway and the Isle of Man.[78] The Isle of Man is the only other area in which St Santán's cult is celebrated outside Ireland. The dedication of the parish church of Kirk Santon to St Santán is first attested in 1291, and the saint is celebrated on one of the days associated with the Irish St Santán.[79]

---

[74] *SSNNW*, 115, 290, 293, 300; Winchester, 'The multiple estate', 90.
[75] DB Yorks, fol. 301v; 1L6. For the orthography, see Fellows-Jensen, 'Scandinavians in Dumfriesshire', 90; Grant, 'A reconsideration', 103; for the geld list, see above 69.
[76] *PNCu*, II, 415–16.
[77] Winchester, *Landscape*, 25; *Corpus II*, 133.
[78] Bailey, 'Manx patterns', 187–8; *idem*, *Viking Age Sculpture*, 223.
[79] Beam *et al.*, 'People of Medieval Scotland', 5/1/0. The place-name is attested in post-medieval sources: Kneen, *The Place-Names*, 133; *PNIOM* V, 224.

Feasts of St Santán were celebrated in Ireland on 9 May and 10 June, according to the early ninth-century *Martyrology of Tallaght*.[80] Santán also appears in the saints' genealogies, which are thought to have been compiled in response to the production of hagiographical works in the eleventh century. He is presented as a bishop who had two saintly brothers: Bishop Sanctán (presumably a doublet) and Bishop Lethnán. The genealogies assign him a British father, either a certain King Canton or Samuel Cendisel (known as Sawyl Penuchel in Welsh genealogies). His mother was a princess of the Ulaid:[81]

> Epscop Santain et epscop Sanctain et epscop Lethnain tri meic Cantoin ríg Bretan. It é filet i Cill Epscuip Santain.
> Bishop Santán and Bishop Sanctán and Bishop Lethnán, three sons of Canton, king of Britons. It is they who are in Cell Epscuip Santain.

> Deichter ingen Muridaig Mundeirg ríg Ulad mathair Matóc & Epscoip Santain m. Samuel Chendisil.
> Deichter daughter of Muiredach Muinderg king of the Ulaid, mother of Matóc and Bishop Santán son of Samuel Cennísel.

The name Santán seems to combine the Brittonic word for a saint with a diminutive suffix, thus illustrating the saint's perceived British background.[82] Molly Miller argued that St Santán was a Briton who grew up near Kirksanton (Cumberland) in the sixth century, and that his cult was later transmitted to Ireland. Yet it seems unlikely that this church dedication would be preserved throughout the Northumbrian era, and the place-name Kirksanton is instead suggestive of Gaelic–Scandinavian influence.[83] Pádraig Ó Riain has suggested another possible Brittonic origin for Santán's cult in Ireland, namely, that he was originally identical to St Samson of Dol, who was active in the vicinity of Dublin.[84] In my view, Santán's cult developed in Ireland and was then brought to the Isle of Man and the coast of Cumberland in the Viking Age.

Bishop Santán was venerated at *Cell Epscuip Santain*, also known as Kilnesantan or St Ann's Chapel, in the parish of Tallaght (Co. Dublin). This church must have become associated with the bishop at a relatively early date since it was mentioned in the saints' genealogies. The church appears in an obituary in the Annals of the Four Masters for 952: *Caoncomhrac, abb Cille h-Easpuicc Sanctáin & Sruthra*.[85] Santán is also associated with Cell dá Lés in Leinster, which has been identified with Templelusk, Arklow.[86] Kilnesantan was located within the *Dyflinnarskíri*, the area of Dublin's hinterland that lay under the political sway of the Hiberno-Scandinavian city. This explains how the cult could be transmitted across the Irish Sea because Dublin, Man and what is now Cumbria were all part of the Gaelic–Scandinavian world. These links are likely to date to the late tenth or eleventh century, by which

---

[80] MT 9 May, 10 September (ed. Best and Lawlor, 41, 49); Ó Riain, *A Dictionary*, 547; Ó Riain, 'The Tallaght martyrologies'. On the date-range, cf. Dumville, 'Félire Óengusso', 43–4.

[81] *Corpus Genealogiarum Sanctorum Hiberniae* 669.3 (112), 722.76 (177). Sawyl (but not Santán) appears in *Early Welsh Genealogical Tracts* (ed. Bartrum 12, 56, 69, 72).

[82] Ó Riain, 'Samson', 322.

[83] Miller, 'The commanders', 106–10. I argue further against this interpretation by reference to the Welsh genealogical evidence in my 'Saints' cults', 48–9.

[84] Ó Riain, 'Samson', 320–3.

[85] AFM 952 (ed. and transl. O'Donovan, II, 668–9).

[86] *Chartularies of St. Mary's Abbey* (ed. Gilbert, I, 118, 120); Hogan, *Onomasticon*, 664.

time the urban centre had established relationships of protection and clientage with the surrounding rural area.[87] Arklow was probably not part of *Dyflinnarskíri*, but it was a Scandinavian settlement and benefited from the seaborne links between Dublin and Waterford.[88] This picture is complicated by the existence of another Kirkesantan, also rendered *Ceall Santáin*, which was the location of a castle built by John de Courcy in Ulaid.[89] It is tempting to suggest that that John de Courcy's followers rendered the place-name in a form familiar from their home territory of Copeland, Cumbria.[90] Santán may have been venerated in north-eastern Ireland because of the perceived kinship of certain Ulster saints with those associated with the major Leinster church of Glendalough.[91] Santán's cult appears to have originally been focused in Dublin and Leinster, and then to have travelled to north-eastern Ireland and across the Irish Sea.

This picture of Dublin's influence is supported by an examination of the cult of St Bega. The dedication is first attested in the foundation charter of the Benedictine priory of St Bees (Cumbria), dating to the mid-1120s.[92] The reformed community apparently engaged in the well-worn quest for their patron saint's origins, producing a *Vita* that presented Bega as an Irish princess. The *Vita* relates that Bega's beauty was renowned, and so she attracted an offer of marriage from a Norwegian prince. Having pledged herself to the service of God, Bega surreptitiously escaped with the help of a protective bracelet and went to the Cumbrian coast, where she established a hermitage. This section of the story has parallels with the Norwegian hagiography of St Sunniva, and the *lectiones* on St Medana of Kirkmaiden on the Rhinns, which is suggestive of a tale circulating in a Gaelic–Scandinavian milieu.[93] The Life goes on to relate that Bega eventually moved to Hartlepool before dying at Hackness.[94] This section of the story conflates St Bega with Begu, a nun who features in Bede's *Historia Ecclesiastica*.[95] The author of the *Vita* of St Bega indeed notes the discovery of Begu's body at Hackness in the 1100s.[96]

The *Vita* shows the hallmarks of an Anglo-Norman reformed community exploring various sources to elucidate the origins of an obscure patron saint. There is, however, evidence that the cult and a substantial ecclesiastical community already existed before the foundation of St Bees priory. The cartulary copy of the foundation charter records various witnesses, including a man called Gille Beccóc. This is a Gaelic patronal name meaning 'devotee of St Beccóc', which indicates that the cult was already celebrated in the locality. The saint's name is 'Becc' (or possibly

---

[87] Bradley, 'The interpretation', 53–62; Valante, 'Dublin's economic relations'.

[88] Here I follow Etchingham, 'Evidence', against Bradley, 'The interpretation', 56–7.

[89] Reeves, *Ecclesiastical Antiquities* 74, 324.

[90] AU2 1197.1 (ed. and transl., Hennessy and Mac Carthy, II, 225–6); Reeves, *Ecclesiastical Antiquities*, 74, 324; cf. Duffy, 'The first Ulster plantation' for the origins of John's followers.

[91] Mac Shamhráin, *Church and Polity*, 66–8.

[92] *The Register of St. Bees* (ed. Wilson, 27–8) – a cartulary copy of the charter.

[93] Downham, 'St Bega', 39; for Sunniva, cf. Rekdal, 'Parallels'; 'Vikings and saints', 260–3; for St Medana: *Breviarium Aberdonense*, pars estiva fols. clviii–clix.

[94] *Vita et Miracula S Bege Virginis* (ed. Wilson, *Register*, 497–520). The Life survives in British Library Cotton MS Faustina BIV, a manuscript from Holm Cultram Abbey, but it is widely thought to be the work of a member of the St Bees community (though see Last, 'St. Bega', 62, who ascribes the work to Everard of Holm Cultram).

[95] *HE* IV, 23, 8 (ed. Lapidge, II, 328; ed. and transl. Colgrave and Mynors, 412–15).

[96] Todd, 'St. Bega', 30–1 notes that the discovery of Begu's body at Hackness probably prompted the incorporation of Bede's account into the Life of Bega.

the unrelated Bécc) with a hypocoristic *–óc* suffix.[97] The settlement was known as *Kirkebibeccoch* (ecclesiastical settlement of Beccóc) in the 1200s.[98] A substantial collection of high-quality, Viking-Age sculpture supports the idea that a significant pre-Norman church was located here, as does the size and complexity of the mother parish of St Bees.[99]

There are several other definite and possible dedications to St Bega across northern Britain. The parish church of Bassenthwaite has no pre-Norman remains, but its Norse name *Behokirk* indicates that its congregation celebrated Bega's cult by the twelfth century. St Bega is one candidate for the identification of St Baya, a female recluse on Little Cumbrae in the Firth of Clyde. The neighbouring island of Great Cumbrae has an elaborate slab that features designs reminiscent of sculpture in the vicinity of St Bees. This indicates that maritime routes connected communities between these two opposite ends of the Cumbrian kingdom.[100] Another medieval dedication to a St Baye is found at Dunbar, near the Firth of Forth. There is, however, scope for confusion with Bede's Begu, given the popularity of another Northumbrian female saint, Æbbe, in this part of the kingdom.[101] A final possibility is Kilbucho in Peeblesshire, but here the place-name forms are less persuasive.[102]

St Bega's Irish origins have been the subject of considerable debate. W. G. Collingwood and T. H. B. Graham suggested that the cult was based on the Scandinavian practice of swearing on arm-rings, for the Old English word for ring (*bēah*) resembled the saint's name.[103] Yet the Scandinavian settlers who transmitted the arm-ring tradition knew Bega's name in the Gaelic form, Beccóc, which bears little relation to the Norse word for ring (*baugr*). A number of saints who bore names featuring the element *Becc* (or *Bécc*) may instead be considered candidates for the origin of the cult. Mo Bhéccóc, patron of Toureen Pecaun, County Tipperary, and Kilpeacaun, County Limerick, bore a similar name to the patroness of St Bees.[104] Yet later traditions reveal that Mo Bhéccóc was male, unlike St Bega.[105] The only female Irish saint who may share a name with Cumbria's Beccóc is St Beccnat. Clare Downham has noted that Beccnat is the base name Becc with a female *–nat* suffix; if this were replaced with the hypocoristic *–óc* suffix, the name 'Beccóc' would result.[106] In the corpus of Irish saints' genealogies, Beccnat was tied to the Leinster-based dynasty Dál Messin Corb, who were associated with the major church of Glendalough. Her chief church, Cell Becnatán, seems to have been located in County Wexford.[107] Her

---

[97] Todd, 'St. Bega', 28–9; Last, 'St. Bega', 57–8; Barrow, 'Northern English society', 8. See below, 183–4, for patronal names. I think this is a personal name, not an epithet, and that the *Coremac* listed before *Gille Beccóc* was a separate individual (who also had a Gaelic name).

[98] *PNCu*, II, 430–1.

[99] *Corpus II*, 145–69; Todd, 'The pre-conquest church'.

[100] *Breviarium Aberdonense*, 2 November (ed. MacQuarrie, 262). The slab is discussed in Fisher, *Early Medieval Sculpture*, 72.

[101] Mackinlay, *Ancient Church Dedications*, 192; Perry, *Castle Park Dunbar*, 286–7.

[102] 'Saints in Scottish place-names': *Kilbevhoc* 1204; *Kilbocho* 1560.

[103] C & G, 15–16. The argument derives ultimately from a suggestion made by Wilson, *Register of St. Bees*, xxxiii–iv. Its merits are discussed by Downham, 'St. Bega', 35–7.

[104] AU 690.4 (ed. and transl. Mac Airt and Mac Niocaill, 152–3).

[105] Gwynn and Hadcock, *Medieval Religious Houses: Ireland*, 393–4.

[106] Downham, 'St. Bega', 37.

[107] *Corpus Genealogiarum Sanctorum Hiberniae*, 181/14 (31). Mac Shamhráin (*Church and Polity*, 182, 206, 215 n. 6) has noted that there are two Kilbegnets, one in County Roscommon and the other in County Wexford; the latter is most likely to have been Cill Becnatán because of the Leinster-oriented nature of Becnat's cult.

cult was also celebrated on Dalkey Island, which lay within Scandinavian Dublin's sphere of influence.[108] One obstacle to identifying Beccnat with Bega and Beya is that the saints' days do not correspond. Beccnat's day was 12 November whereas Bega's day was celebrated on 31 October.[109] However, 31 October is the day on which Begu of Hackness died, and it is possible that Begu's feast day supplanted St Beccnat's day.

Turning north of the Solway, the place-name Killochan in Ayrshire is also suggestive of links with Dublin and Leinster. This saint's cult gave rise to the local surname MacClannachan (and its variants), which derives from Mac Gille Onchan.[110] These names commemorate St Onchú (Onchan is the genitive).[111] There are two possible candidates for this Onchú: a saint from County Clare, and the Onchú who gathered relics of the saints at Cluain Mór Máedóic in Co. Carlow. Given the pattern of connections that I have already traced, I am inclined to associate Onchú with the Leinster saint.[112] Similarly, I suggest that St Cóemgen of Glendalough was commemorated in the guise of St Cwyfan or Cwyfien in north-eastern Wales. The twelfth-century core of *Bonedd y Saint*, the Welsh saints' pedigrees, assigns Cwyfan a local background. One late-medieval Welsh genealogist, however, linked him with Glendalough, and the correspondence between their feast days suggests that his intuition was correct.[113] It is significant that Maen Achwyfan, a great stone monument, bears his name. This eleventh-century stone cross exhibits links with the areas around the Irish Sea region in its abstract designs.[114] Glendalough was located in the Wicklow Mountains, some way beyond the *Dyflinnarskíri*, yet as time went on the urban centre interacted to a greater degree with this mountainous zone.[115] By the twelfth century, a church dedicated to St Cóemgen was located just to the south of the defended Hiberno-Scandinavian town of Dublin.[116] Again, the eleventh century seems to be a likely time for the transmission of this saint's cult.[117]

It is worth asking whether Northumbrian saints' cults travelled along the same channels in the opposite direction. The veneration of St Cuthbert at Cell mo Chudric (Kilmahuddrick) in County Dublin is one possible example. A brief chronicle included in the annals of St Mary's, Dublin, reported the tradition that Cell mo Chudric was Cuthbert's birthplace.[118] The place-name includes the name 'Cuthberht' in a form featuring the cognate *briht* for *be(o)rht* 'bright', as is the case in the place-name Kirkcudbright.[119] Cell mo Chudric lay near Cluain Dolcáin

---

[108] O'Reilly, 'Notes', 201; Downham, 'St. Bega', 38.

[109] Mac Shamhráin, *Church and Polity*, 215 n. 6; Forbes, *Kalendars*, 166, cf. 276–8.

[110] Black, *Surnames*, 469; 'Saints in Scottish place-names'. I am grateful to Professor Thomas Clancy for highlighting this saint's cult.

[111] See *PNIOM* IV, 411 for Onchan on Man, although the form 'Conchan' may relate to a different saint.

[112] MT 8 February (ed. Best and Lawlor). The eleventh-century scholia on *Félire Óengusso* (ed. and transl. Stokes, 70–1) makes the link with Cluain Mór Máedóic. See Ó Riain, *A Dictionary*, 108 for the saint in Co. Clare.

[113] *Early Welsh Genealogical Tracts* (ed. Bartrum, 62). I make this argument in more detail in my 'Irish saints' cults'.

[114] Edwards, *A Corpus III*, 366–71.

[115] Mac Shamhráin, *Church and Polity*, 79, 81, 86, 90, 136–7, 143 n. 7, 145–8 for a minimalist reading of Scandinavian links. Etchingham, 'The Viking impact' allows for more interaction.

[116] Clarke, 'Christian cults', 151.

[117] For Maen Achwyfan, see Edwards, *A Corpus*, III, 366–71.

[118] *Chartularies* (ed. Gilbert, II, 287–92); Stancliffe, 'The Irish tradition', 32.

[119] Campbell, *Old English Grammar*, §305. Kirkcudbright is first attested as *Cuthbrictis Khirche* in Reginald of Durham, *Libellus de admirandis beati Cuthberti* 85 (ed. Raine, 179), relating to a visit of Ailred of Rievaulx in 1164.

(Clondalkin), which was a dependency of Glendalough.[120] During the Viking Age, Clondalkin drew added importance from the presence of a Scandinavian settlement known as *dún Amhlaimh* 'Olaf's fort'.[121] Local churches were already densely distributed in County Dublin in the pre-Viking period, and the hypocoristic *mo-* form in *Mo Chudric* was mainly productive during the seventh and eighth centuries.[122] One possibility, then, is that Cuthbert's cult reached the area through the high-level ecclesiastical connections of the Northumbrian Golden Age.[123] Even so, local churches in the area continued to receive investment throughout the tenth and eleventh centuries, as seen in the stone monuments known as Rathdown slabs. The patrons may even have had exposure to sculptural traditions in the west of the Northumbrian kingdom, to judge by the designs they used.[124] The church of Kilmacud in County Dublin is also reputed to have been dedicated to St Cuthbert, although the place-name is less convincing.[125] The presence of Cuthbert's cult on the Isle of Man can be inferred from the name MacGilcobraght, which was borne by families in the townships of Leodest, Smeall beg and Brausta (Kirkandreas parish) and first recorded in the early sixteenth century.[126] The townships lie five miles from Ballacuberagh, a place-name that implies a Cuthbertine dedication at the former keeill.[127] Thus it is possible that the transmission of Cuthbert's cult westwards reflects links between Dublin and Man during the Viking Age.

To summarise, I have examined several saints' cults that reveal close links between Dublin, Man and the west of the former Northumbrian kingdom. While it is true that the fame of certain Leinster saints spread far and wide (including to Argyll and the Hebrides),[128] the cults that I have examined include several that were relatively obscure and localised. I propose that Scandinavian settlers came into contact with functioning churches in the Dublin area and subsequently transmitted their cults to the Isle of Man and Northumbria. There they took over pre-existing institutions or formed new ones, dedicating them to their chosen saints. The distribution of the cults indicates that this process took place in the late tenth and eleventh centuries. This contact might have taken place through the same channels as the creation of great sea-kingdoms, such as that of Echmarcach mac Ragnaill (*ob.* 1064/5), or through the localised Irish-Sea links that continued after the fall of York (954).

---

[120] *Chartularies* (ed. Gilbert, I, xxi, 173); Mac Shamhráin, *Church and Polity*, 125, 142 n. 3.

[121] AU 867.8 (ed. and transl. Mac Airt and Mac Niocaill, 322–3). On this Scandinavian settlement, see Downham, *Viking Kings*, 21.

[122] Russell, 'Patterns'.

[123] Cuthbert is one of the Lindisfarne saints who appears in the Martyrology of Tallaght: MT 20 March (ed. Best and Lawlor, 25).

[124] In general, see O'Brien, 'Churches'. For pre-Viking churches, see Boazman, 'Hallowed by saints'. The Rathdown slabs are covered by Healy, *Pre-Norman Grave-slabs*, 49–61, 70–1, 82–100. For Northumbrian links, see Ó hEailidhe, 'The Rathdown slabs', 75–88, drawing comparisons with Aspatria (Cumberland) and Craignarget (Wigtownshire) although Bailey and Cramp (*Corpus II*, 53) are more sceptical.

[125] Local tradition connected the old church at Kilmacud with Cuthbert: O'Hanlon, *Lives*, III, 862–3.

[126] *Manorial Roll* (ed. Talbot, 73–4).

[127] Kneen, *Place-Names*, 503; *PNIOM*, II, 285; Kermode and Bruce, *Manx Archaeological Survey*, III, 36. Another possible Cuthbertine church is Keeill Poogeragh (Lezayre): *PNIOM*, III, 409.

[128] MacLean, 'Knapdale dedications'.

Saints of north-eastern Ireland

A different web of connections underpins the dedications to saints of north-eastern Ireland in the vicinity of Whithorn. It must be admitted that the transmission of these saints' cults is difficult to date, and possible contexts range from the sixth century until the sixteenth. Even so, I have shown that Whithorn remained a significant ecclesiastical centre during the eleventh century, and it continued to capture the attention of Irish writers.[129] These literary contacts may have made some impact in terms of church dedications on the ground.

Although St Nynia's cult had literary vitality at Northumbrian Whithorn, no dedications to the saint survive in 'early' place-name forms near Whithorn. Thomas Clancy has explained this phenomenon by pointing to the relative abundance of dedications to St Finnian, a saint most readily associated with Movilla (Co. Down) in this context. Clancy has suggested that Nynia and Finnian were ultimately identical, both cults deriving from that of an early and influential saint, Uinniau.[130] It is worth asking whether the transmission of St Finnian's cult to what is now south-western Scotland could have been multi-layered.[131] Indeed, I have already noted that there were at least two phases of interchange between the hagiography of St Finnian of Movilla and texts written in south-western Scotland. The first is the parallels between Finnian's Life (in the form *De servo Dei Finano*) and *Miracula Nynie episcopi*; the second is the borrowing of the Life by the Tironensian community of Kilwinning.[132] It is worth asking whether any of the church dedications fill in the gap between those two phases of contact.

The Finnian dedications divide into two groups: those featuring Gaelic name forms, and those with Brittonic forms. The Gaelic forms come down to us in late place-names such as Chapel Finian, Mochrum (first attested in the seventeenth century, even though the building is earlier) and *Killingeane* (1649), which may represent a form like *Cill Fhinnéin*.[133] Brittonic speakers, by contrast, preferred the form (G)uinnin, where the /w/ sound is represented by *gu* orthography, as was the case elsewhere in the Brittonic world. One explanation for the popularity of this cult in south-western Scotland is that *Guinnin* is the local manifestation of the sixth-century St Uinniau.[134] Another possibility is that Finnian's cult was (re-)transmitted to the area from Ireland and adopted by Brittonic speakers several centuries later. They could have transformed the Gaelic name *Finnén* (a version of Finbarr/Finnian) to *Guinnin* if they knew that Brittonic /gw/ or /w/ was the equivalent of Gaelic /f/. Scribes at Armagh made this equation when they transformed *hwīt ærne* into *Futerna*.[135] Some of the dedications to St (G)uinnin lay on the edge of the Cumbrian kingdom, where Brittonic and Gaelic speakers were mingling in the eleventh and twelfth centuries.

---

[129] See above, 120–6.

[130] Clancy, 'The real St Ninian', 11–20. The paucity of Ninian dedications was first noted by Chadwick, 'St. Ninian', 46. For one possible example see Boyle, 'Saint Ninian', 65.

[131] Ó Riain, 'St. Finnbarr', 73 argued that Finnian's cult may not have been vibrant, given the apparent lack of a Life of Finnian. If it is correct to identify *De seruo Dei Finano* as that text, then wider influence becomes possible.

[132] See above, 122–3.

[133] Chapel Finian: Symson, *A Large Description*, 54; Clancy, 'The real St Ninian', 17. Killingeane: MacQueen, 'Kirk- and Kil-', 149.

[134] Clancy, 'The real St Ninian', 17–18; cf. *idem*, 'Scottish Saints', 411–12. For late variation in the use of the *gu* orthography, see Russell, 'Scribal (in)consistency'.

[135] This is more similar to Watson's interpretation in *CPNS*, 83. For Futerna, see above, 124–5.

Kirkgunzeon by the Solway (*Cherchwinni*, 1159–81) is one example.[136] That said, the dedications to St Winnin in south-western Scotland considerably exceed those to St Finnian, which suggests that the cult was spreading internally rather than repeatedly being refreshed from Ireland.

Cóelán or Mochaoi of Nendrum is another saint who appears in the Whithorn episode in *De servo Dei Finano*. E. S. Towill noted that several churches in south-western Scotland were dedicated to St Mochaoi of Nendrum, and he suggested that their dedications reflected an early alliance between that church and Whithorn.[137] Yet some of Towill's Mochaoi dedications can be attributed to other saints. Kirkmahoe, Dumfriesshire is likely to commemorate Mungo/Kentigern since the latter saint was recorded as its patron in the fourteenth century; *Mochohe* was a Gaelic nickname for Kentigern.[138] St Mochaoi can also be confused with Saints Mochutu, Mochua and Machutus.[139] Nevertheless, the name 'Machutus' is relevant for current purposes because it was also the Latin appellation of the Manx saint Maughold. Proximity suggests that the latter saint was the Machutus to whom Wigtown parish church and a chapel in the Rhinns are dedicated.[140] The spread of the Manx saint's cult to Galloway might be attributed to the later medieval period, for Maughold's miracle-working spring was still visible at the time when Jocelin of Furness was writing.[141] However, the major church at Maughold also had an extensive network of overseas contacts during the pre-Viking period and Viking Age, as its sculptural affinities attest.[142] Killumpha (Kirkmaiden parish), a place-name first attested in 1548, seems to contain the name of St Imchad.[143] The eleventh-century commentary on *Félire Óengusso*, written at Armagh, located her church at Cell Droichit in Arda Ulad, the Ards peninsula (Co. Down), close to Nendrum.[144] Another place-name in the Rhinns, Barnultoch (*Barnulte* 1623), may be related to contacts with north-eastern Ireland since it means *barr nan Ultach* 'height of the Ulaid'.[145]

The final saint to be examined in relation in north-eastern Ireland is St Patrick. Armagh had become his chief church by the seventh century, and his body was located at Sabal (Saul) in County Down.[146] Some of the churches dedicated to Patrick (whether formally or informally) were dependencies of Armagh. Yet not all Patrician dedications arose in this way, especially outside Ireland.[147]

---

[136] *Register*, 120 (ed. Grainger and Collingwood, 99).

[137] Bowen, *Saints and Seaways*, 73; Towill, 'Saint Mochaoi', 108–11, esp. map on 109.

[138] Jackson, 'Sources', 302.

[139] Although Towill claimed that Mochaoi was the patron of Kirkmahoe, Dumfriesshire, Mackinlay attributed the dedication of this church to St Mochua: Mackinlay, *Ancient Church Dedications*, 135.

[140] Mackinlay, *Ancient Church Dedications*, 104 also lists eastern Scottish possibilities. The parish church's dedication is first attested in 1325: 'Saints in Scottish place-names'.

[141] Jocelin, *Vita Patricii* §§132–4 (ed. Sperber and Bieler).

[142] See above, 42, 48, 116.

[143] *CPNS*, 166–7; Mac Queen, 'Kirk- and Kil-', 144; *idem, Place-Names of the Rhinns*, 47–8.

[144] *Félire Óengusso* 8 January (ed. Stokes, 212–13). For the location of the church, cf. AFM 1149 (ed. and transl. O'Donovan, II, 1088–9).

[145] Maxwell, *The Place-Names*, 31; *CPNS*, 184.

[146] Muirchú, *Vita S. Patricii*, II.5–6 (ed. and transl. Bieler, 116–17); Charles-Edwards, *Early Christian Ireland*, 65.

[147] Mac Shamhráin, *Church and Polity*, 38–9.

Table 3: Medieval dedications to St Patrick

Church	Medieval status	Date of first attestation	Source	Secondary reference
Aspatria? (Cumberland)	Parish	*ca* 1160	Place-name: *Aspatric* (NB not a church name)	*PNCu*, II, 262[*]
Bampton Patrick (Westmorland)	Parish	1362	*Testamenta Karleolensia*, 68	C & G, 17[**]
Heysham (Lancashire)	Parish	1280s	*Coucher Book* (ed. Atkinson, II, 281)	N/A
Kirkpatrick Durham (Kirkcudbrightshire)	Parish	1274	Place-name: *Kyrkepatric Durrant*	Brooke, 'Kirk-compound', 70
Kirkpatrick Fleming (Dumfriesshire)	Parish	1204	Place-name: *Kirkepatric*	'Saints in Scottish place-names'
Kirkpatrick Irongray (Kirkcudbrightshire)	Parish	1274	Place-name: *Kyrkpatric Cro*	Brooke, 'Kirk-compound', 70
Kirkpatrick Juxta (Dumfriesshire)	Parish	1274	Place-name: Kirkpatrik juxta Moffet	'Saints in Scottish place-names'
Lambley (Northumberland)	Nunnery/parish	1201	Dugdale, *Monasticon Anglicanum*, IV, 305–8	Hodgson *et al.*, *A History II*, 93
Ousby (Cumberland)	Parish	1300	Cal IPM, 28 Edward I, 494	C & G, 25
Patrick Brompton (Yorkshire)	Parish	1230	*Yorkshire Deeds* (ed. Brown, 124)	Edmonds, 'Personal names', 60
Patrington (Yorkshire)	Parish	1487	Testamentary burial	Poulson, *The History*, II, 448

[*]   The church dedication is not attested until the eighteenth century: C & G, 17.
[**]   The Patrick dedication here is medieval. By contrast, the dedication of Preston Patrick is first attested in the eighteenth century, and the medieval dedication was to St Gregory: C & G, 25.

The distribution of dedications implies two main sources of influence for St Patrick's cult. The more northerly dedications correspond very closely to the main axis of the expanded kingdom of Strathclyde, as Thomas Clancy has noted. Clancy has drawn attention to the early medieval textual evidence that links Dumbarton Rock with St Patrick, and he has suggested that this association dates back before the siege of the site by Óláfr and Ívarr in 870. The cult would have spread southwards as the kingdom expanded in the early tenth century, and this would fit with the earliest possible date for the coining of *kirk*-compound names.[148] In support of the association between the cult of Patrick and the kingdom of Strathclyde/Cumbria, I have pointed to the adoption of the Brittonic patronal name *Gospatric* by the house of Bamburgh. The name first appears in this dynasty in the mid-eleventh century, with Gospatric,

---

[148] Clancy, 'The cults', 26–32; idem, 'The big man', 15.

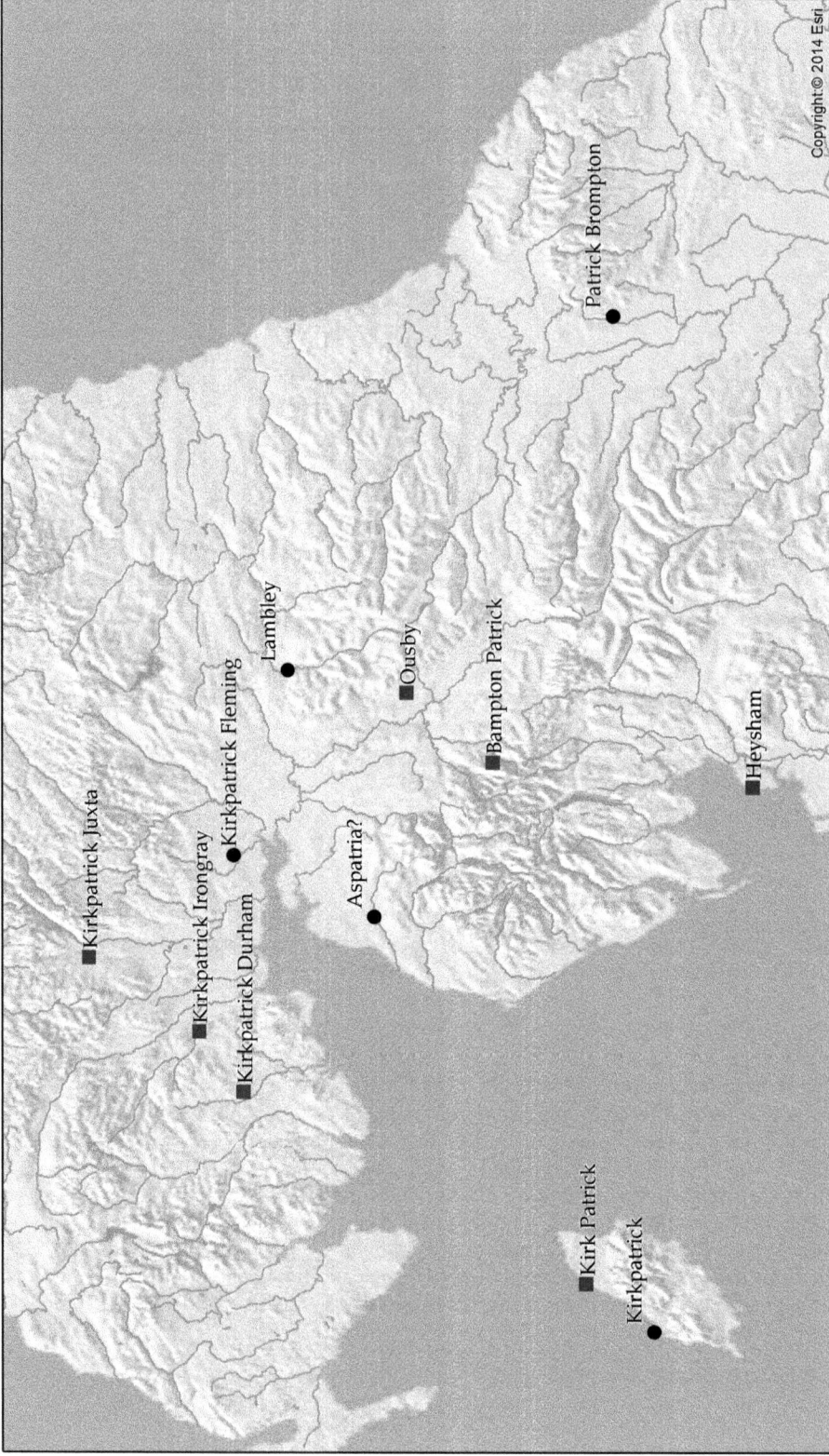

Map 7: *The Cult of St Patrick on the eastern side of the Irish Sea to ca 1550*

- ● St Patrick dedications attested by *ca* 1250
- ■ St Patrick dedications attested from *ca* 1250 to 1550

Labels on map:
Patrick Brompton
Lambley
Ousby
Bampton Patrick
Heysham
Aspatria?
Kirkpatrick Fleming
Kirkpatrick Juxta
Kirkpatrick Irongray
Kirkpatrick Durham
Kirk Patrick
Kirkpatrick

Copyright© 2014 Esri

son of Uhtred (d. 1064).[149] I have argued that he and his nephew, Earl Gospatric, were instrumental in the assumption of power in the former Cumbrian kingdom. Their names signify a close link with the polity, both in terms of the Brittonic naming practice and the saint.[150] The patronal name *Gospatric* adds to the evidence for veneration of Patrick in the former Northumbrian kingdom during the eleventh century.

I have suggested that Patrick's cult appealed to another group of people resident in and around the kingdom, namely, Gaelic–Scandinavian communities. St Patrick's chapel at Heysham had been part of an Anglo-Saxon minster, and was transformed in the Viking Age into a church with lay graveyard; the sparse grave goods suggest that at least some of the community had links to the Insular Scandinavian world.[151] Similarly, the church dedicated to St Patrick at Patrick Brompton lies in a Scandinavian-settled area of Wensleydale. The landholder in 1066 was a certain *Ghilepatric* (Gille Pátraic), who had a Gaelic patronal name.[152] That Patrick's cult thrived among Gaelic–Scandinavians is shown by the fact that the saint was mentioned alongside Malachy and Adomnán on a runestone from Keeill Woirrey, Isle of Man.[153] As to links with Dublin, Jocelin of Furness related that the Scandinavian community of Dublin adopted Christianity under the aegis of St Patrick.[154] A version of Dublin's conversion legend also exists in *Lebor na Cert*, an early twelfth-century compilation, which details the authority that the most powerful king in Ireland (based at that time in Munster) had throughout Ireland. The poem itself emanates from the late eleventh century, when Armagh was promoting its claims to the bishopric of Dublin, in the face of Canterbury; it seems to have found an audience in Dublin as well as Armagh itself.[155] The success of the cult in the former Northumbrian kingdom is likely to reflect its appeal to the culturally diverse communities of the region.

Saints of Argyll and the Hebrides

The final group of saints' cults emanated from areas further north in the Gaelic world. They include several saints associated with the Columban *familia*, which raises the possibility that there is a pre-Viking dimension to the transmission of these cults to the Northumbrian kingdom. Furthermore, the cult of Columba continued to thrive in the twelfth century and beyond under the aegis of the kings of Scots. Yet I suggest that the mobile world of the Viking Age was also responsible for spreading an interest in Columba and his associates, as we have already seen in the case of Örlygg's church in Iceland.

---

[149] *HR* (ed. Arnold, II, 199, 209); 'De obsessione' (ed. Arnold, I, 219).

[150] Edmonds, 'Personal names', 46–51. One of these men is the Gospatric of the famous writ: see above, 70. I suspect (but cannot prove) that a link to the house of Bamburgh explains the dedication of Lambley nunnery in Tynedale to St Patrick and St Mary.

[151] See below, 189, 204.

[152] DB Yorks, 6–29.

[153] If the Malachy commemorated on the stone was the Irish archbishop and saint who died in 1148, the stone's inscription would postdate the period with which the current chapter is concerned, but it nevertheless attests Patrick's cult. Cf. Kermode, *Manx Crosses*, 212–13.

[154] Jocelin, *Vita Patricii* (ed. Sperber and Bieler).

[155] *Lebor na Cert* (ed. Dillon, 114–19). For comments on the chronology of the relationship with Jocelin's text, see Dumville, 'St Patrick'; Breatnach and Boyle, 'Senchas Gall Átha Clíath'; Ní Mhaonaigh, '*Caraid tairisi*', 270–1.

Table 4: Medieval dedications to saints of the Columban familia

Church	Medieval status	Date of first attestation	Source	Secondary reference
Abbey St Bathans, Berwickshire (Báithíne)	Parish church	1250	*Registrum de Dunfermlyn* no. 313 (ed. Innes, 205)	'Saints in Scottish place-names'
Bothans, Lothian (Báithíne)	Parish church*	1421	Place-name: *Bothanis* 1421	'Saints in Scottish place-names'
Casterton, Westmorland (Columba)	Chapel	1356	Farrer, *Records,* II, 331	C & G, 19
Kirkcolmonell, Ayrshire (Colmán Elo)	Parish church	1179	*Registrum episcopatu Glasguensis,* no. 51 (ed. Innes, 42–4)	'Saints in Scottish place-names'
Kirkcormack (Kelton), Kirkcudbrightshire (Cormac ua Liatháin)	Former parish church	1172 × 1174	*Regesta Regum Scottorum,* II, (ed. Barrow, 213–14)	Brooke, 'Kirk-compound', 69
Nether Cramond, Lothian (Columba)	Parish church	1478	RMS, II, 295	'Database of dedications'
St Boswells, Roxburghshire (Boisil)	Former parish church	1447	Place-name: *St Bessils chapel*	'Saints in Scottish place-names'
St Colmonell's Church (Urr), Kirkcudbrightshire (Colmán Elo)	Former parish church	1164	*Liber cartarum Sancte Crucis* (ed. Innes, 169)	Brooke, 'The deanery', 53
St Colmonell's church (Buittle), Kirkcudbrightshire (Colmán Elo)	Chapel	1381	Charter in favour of Sweetheart Abbey: M'Kerlie, *Lands,* III, 234	Brooke, 'The deanery', 65
Topcliffe, Yorkshire (Columba)	Parish church	1303	*Yorkshire Deeds* (ed. Brown, 123).	Gardner, 'Kentigern', 18
Warcop, Westmorland (Columba)	Parish church	1206 × 1217	*English Episcopal Acta Carlisle* no. 16 (ed. Smith, 12)	C & G, 27 (citing later references)

*   The parish church of Yester (aka Bothans) is now dedicated to St Cuthbert.
** St Columba's churchyard, Lindisfarne, is first attested at the end of the sixteenth century, see O'Sullivan, 'The plan', 140.

St Columba was venerated by the monks who travelled from Iona to Lindisfarne, and his cult will have been fostered in closely associated churches such as Ripon. It is worth asking to what extent Columban veneration survived the aftermath of the Synod of Whitby (664). Bede relates that Alhfrith, Oswiu's son, had been instructed by Wilfrid:

> huius doctrinam omnibus Scottorum traditionibus iure praeferandam sciebat. Unde ei etiam donauerat monasterium XL familiarum in loco qui dicitur Inhrypum; quem uidelicet locum paulo ante eis qui Scottos sequebantur in possessionem monasterii

dederat, sed quia illi postmodum data sibi optione magis loco cedere quam suam mutare consuetudinem uolebant, dedit eum illi, qui dignam loco et doctrinam haberet et uitam.

whose teaching he preferred to all the traditions of the *Scotti* and had therefore given him a monastery of forty hides in the place called Ripon. He had presented the site a short time before to those who followed the ways of the *Scotti*; but because, when given the choice, they preferred to renounce the site rather than change their customs, he gave it to one who was worthy of the place both by his doctrine and his way of life.[156]

The regime change may have dented Columba's cult, although I have already shown that consciousness of Ripon's Columban heritage revived in the eighth century. It is possible that the nearby dedication of Topcliffe-on-Swale reflects a cult that dated back to the days of the Iona mission, as suggested by Walter Bower in his fifteenth-century *Scotichronicon*.[157] Yet there is no evidence of a pre-Viking church at Topcliffe itself, whereas there is a well-preserved tenth-century wheelhead cross, a type redolent of the Irish Sea (indeed it closely parallels an example at Brigham, Cumberland).[158] A Gaelic–Scandinavian lord may, therefore, have founded the church at Topcliffe in a similar way to the proprietary churches west of the Pennines. Indeed, the Columban cult not only flourished among the Scandinavians of the Hebrides, but also those of Dublin. Óláfr Cúarán endowed Skreen, a Columban church on the edge of his sphere of influence, before he was defeated at the Battle of Tara in 980. Ripon could also have cultivated Columban connections further north, which would explain how information about both Topcliffe and Ripon ultimately reached Bower. Indeed, Scotton 'settlement of the Scots' is located near Ripon on the great Roman road to the north, and a certain Máel Coluim 'devotee of Columba' (a popular name in Scotland) was based at nearby Little Ouseburn in 1086.[159]

Similarly I would identify two chronological layers in Columba's cult in Warcop (Westmorland). This church was in the hands of a certain Torfin (Norse Þorfinnr) in the twelfth century. At the start of the thirteenth century, Torfin's daughters granted the church of Warcop to the Praemonstratensian house of Easby in Richmondshire (Yorkshire), a district in which they also held lands. The family also founded a chapel dedicated to St Columba on their lands in Casterton (Westmorland). Thus Columba had become the favoured patron of a family that was at least partly of Scandinavian ancestry, to judge by their choice of personal names.[160] The pre-existing cult may have sparked the interest of Scottish clerics during the twelfth-century phase of Scottish rule in Westmorland. A tradition associated with the church of Dunblane (Stirlingshire) portrays St Bláán (Blane) of Bute raising a young boy named Columba from the dead, and being granted lands in northern England (including Appleby,

---

[156] *HE* III, 25, 3 (ed. Lapidge, II, 146, 148; ed. and transl. Colgrave and Mynors, 296–9).
[157] Walter Bower, *Scotichronicon* III.42 (ed. and transl. MacQueen and MacQueen, II, 121). At III.30 (ed. and transl. MacQueen and MacQueen, 81). Bower mentioned the story of the Ripon crosier, which Kentigern had exchanged with Columba; see above, 110.
[158] Lang, *Corpus VI*, 214; compare Bailey and Cramp, *Corpus II*, 77.
[159] Bhreathnach, 'The documentary evidence'; *eadem*, 'Columban churches', 11, 14; above, 178.
[160] *English Episcopal Acta: Carlisle* 16 (ed. Smith, 12); *Records (ed. Farrer and Curwen,* II, 326–7). The family also used the Norse names Copsi and Arkill.

most likely in Westmorland).[161] Thus there were two different phases of influence on the Columban cult in Westmorland, emanating from different parts of the Gaelic world. It is worth noting that the communities of both Ripon and Casterton knew Columba in the Gaelic form 'Colum Cille'.[162]

Saints Báithéne and Boisil were closely associated with the Columban church, being an abbot of Iona (*ob. ca* 600) and an influential monk of Melrose (*ob.* 661), respectively. The dedications of churches at Abbey St Bathans and St Boswells are attested in the medieval period, and the place-name of Bothans (Yester) is suggestive of St Boisil, although the modern dedication is to St Cuthbert. The cults of these saints would have been fostered at an early stage, and they eventually yielded church dedications, in a similar way to saints Balthere and Wilfrid. Abbey St Bathans and Bothans lie along a routeway across the Lammermuirs to the Firth of Forth, which would have been used by those travelling between Iona and Lindisfarne. Also located along this route is Bunkle (Gaelic *bun chill*), which had become attached to the bishopric of Dunkeld by the twelfth century.[163] Dunkeld also controlled the church dedicated to St Columba at Nether Cramond, which underlines how late-medieval Scottish clerics formalised and amplified ecclesiastical links that dated back to the Northumbrian Golden Age.

In the Solway region, communities venerated several other saints associated with the Columban federation. The place-name Kirkcolm, a former parish church in the north of the Rhinns, seems to contain Columba's name. However, the early attestations reveal that the dedicatee was in fact St Cumméne, the abbot of Iona who wrote the first known Life of St Columba.[164] Cumméne himself was reputedly the subject of a hagiographical work by Everard of Holm Cultram, but the evidence for this is late and controversial.[165] Two churches in Galloway and one in Ayrshire (Kirkcolmonell) are dedicated to St Colmán Elo; the other known dedication to the saint outside Ireland is Kilcalmonell in Kintyre.[166] Adomnán gave Colmán the designation *moccu Sailni*, which suggests he belonged to the Dál Sailni of northeastern Ireland. He became a pupil of St Columba and eventually founded the church of Lann Elo (Lynally, Co. Offaly), from which he gained his epithet.[167] The dedicatee of Kirkcormack is probably Cormac ua Liatháin, an associate of St Columba, and a well-known *peregrinus*.[168] This identification cannot be proven

---

[161] Walter Bower, *Scotichronicon* XI.21 (ed. Taylor and Watt, VI, 60–1). I am very grateful to Gilbert Márkus for drawing this to my attention.

[162] Jocelin of Furness, *Vita Kentigerni*, ch. 40 (ed. Forbes, 231–2); *Records* (ed. Farrer and Curwen, II, 325). It is surprising that there are no Columban churches in Dumfriesshire and Galloway, save a chapel in Caerlaverock whose dedication is attested in the eighteenth century: Chalmers, *Caledonia*, III, 321.

[163] Taylor, 'Seventh-century Iona abbots', 46–7. The 'Abbey' element refers to the future site of a Cistercian nunnery.

[164] The earliest place-name form, *Kyrcum* (1275) is ambiguous, but papal letters of 1395 refer to the church as *ecclesia Sancti Cummin*: Brooke, 'Kirk-compound place-names', 61, 70, *contra* Mackinlay, *Ancient Church Dedications*, 48.

[165] Fordun's *Scotichronicon* is usually cited as the source of information about Everard's hagiographical activities, but a search reveals no such statement. The reference appears in the controversial work of the seventeenth-century writer Thomas Dempster: Hardy, *Descriptive Catalogue*, II, 225–6.

[166] 'Saints in Scottish place-names'; Brooke, 'The deanery', 53, 65.

[167] Adomnán, *Vita Sancti Columbae* I.5, III.12 (ed. and transl. Anderson and Anderson, 222–3).

[168] Adomnán, *Vita Sancti Columbae* I.6, II.42 (ed. and transl. Anderson and Anderson, 28–31, 166–74); MacQueen, 'Gaelic Speakers', 22.

because a number of saints were called Cormac.[169] However, Kirkcormack was transferred from Iona's jurisdiction to that of Holyrood Abbey, along with the church of Colmanell (Urr), which supports the idea that these churches were associated with a Columban *milieu*.[170] This reference to Iona's ownership is significant because it demonstrates a formal ecclesiastical connection. I have suggested that Gaelic saints' dedications generally arose more informally, through the affinity of lay patrons with a cherished saint.

The two final dedications that I discuss do not belong to the Columban *familia*, but they nevertheless illustrate links with more northerly parts of the Gaelic world. Two chapels called Kildonan (in Stoneykirk parish, Wigtownshire and Colmonell, Ayrshire) are first mentioned in the post-medieval period but the identity of their saint is clear: St Donnán was a sixth-century Irish missionary, who founded a church on Eigg. He achieved some measure of fame as a result of the fact that he and his followers were martyred by pirates, an event commemorated in the 'Chronicle of Ireland'.[171] The eleventh-century commentary on *Félire Oengusso* reveals that St Donnán's cult continued to thrive on Scotland's western seaboard. These notes recast the martyrdom of the saint and his followers as the plot of a queen who was angered by their arrival *in Gallgaidelu* 'among the Gall-Goídil' since they disturbed her sheep.[172] Similarly, the 'Martyrology of Tallaght' included *Blaani episcopi Cind Garad i nGallgaedelaib* '(feast) of Bláán, bishop of Kingarth in Gall-Goídil' as the first entry for 10 August.[173] The entry appears to belong to the phase of the text that emerged at Tallaght in the early ninth century; to some, however, this seems uncomfortably early for the use of the term Gall-Goídil on Scotland's western seaboard. Another option might be to see this as a tenth-century addition that was worked into the main body of the text.[174] As Thomas Clancy has argued, the martyrological references indicate that the Gall-Goídil of western Britain formed around the Firth of Clyde, and were only gradually moving into what is now Galloway by the eleventh century.[175] St Bláán is commemorated at Kirkblane in Caerlaverock parish, which is attested as *ecclesia sancti Blaani* in 1165.[176] Gall-Goídil seem to have had a special affinity with Bláán and Donnán, which explains how these cults were transmitted to Galloway and Nithsdale.

In this chapter, I have demonstrated that many of the Gaelic saints' cults of north-western England and south-western Scotland date back to the tenth and eleventh centuries. I have proposed a mechanism by which many of these cults took root during the Viking Age, namely, foundation of proprietary churches and the transformation

---

[169] *Corpus Genealogiarum Sanctorum Hiberniae* (ed. Ó Riain, 273).

[170] *Regesta Regum Scottorum*, II (ed. Barrow, 213–14). Cf. Brooke, 'Desnes Cro', 63; Oram, *The Lordship of Galloway*, 10–11.

[171] AU 617.1 (ed. and transl. Mac Airt and Mac Niocaill 108–9); *CI* 617.1 (transl. Charles-Edwards, I, 129).

[172] *Félire Óengusso 17* April (ed. Stokes, 114–17). The accusative plural –*u* ending indicates that the people are still being described here, rather than a territory.

[173] MT (ed. Best and Lawlor, 62).

[174] Dumville, '*Félire Óengusso*', 39; Clancy 'The Gall-Ghàidheil', 30, argues that any such addition must have been made by the early tenth century.

[175] MT 10 August (ed. Best and Lawlor, 62); see above, 69–71.

[176] *Liber S. Marie de Calchou* no. 11(ed. Innes, 11); *CPNS*, 164–5. Another Kilblane is attested in the nineteenth century in Kirkmahoe parish: 'Saints in Scottish place-names'. A Gille Blááin witnessed a grant of Ralph son of Dunegal of Nithsdale in 1135 × 1185: 'People of Medieval Scotland database', 3/34/1. I am grateful to Thomas Clancy for drawing these references to St Bláán to my attention.

of minsters to local churches. I have traced a complex web of relationships between communities based in the west of the former Northumbrian kingdom and their counterparts in Gaeldom. These connections fall into three broad categories: links with Dublin's hinterland; north-eastern Ireland; and the Columban *familia*. There are hints of other influences too: lingering interest in the Northumbrian Church; veneration of specific saints among the Gall-Goídil; and renewed interest from Scottish clerics during the twelfth century. The church dedications fully demonstrate the diversity of links between the Northumbrian kingdom and the Gaelic world.

7

MEDIEVAL MULTILINGUALISM:
GAELIC LINGUISTIC INFLUENCE IN
THE NORTHUMBRIAN KINGDOM

The political, ecclesiastical and cultural interactions that I have outlined so far brought speakers of different languages into contact. In this chapter, I investigate the evidence for Gaelic linguistic influence in the Northumbrian kingdom, tracing several different channels and chronological contexts. Bede's famous depiction of King Oswald's collaboration with Bishop Áedán provides some insight into the theme:

> atque eius ammonitionibus humiliter ac libenter in omnibus auscultans, ecclesiam Christi in regno suo multum diligenter aedificare ac dilatare curauit. Ubi pulcherrimo saepe spectaculo contigit, ut euangelizante antistite, qui Anglorum linguam perfecte non nouerat, ipse rex suis ducibus ac ministris interpres uerbi existeret caelestis; quia nimirum tam longo exilii sui tempore linguam Scottorum iam plene didicerat.

> and humbly and willingly in all cases giving ear to his (Áedán's) admonitions, he (the king) industriously applied himself to build and extend the Church of Christ in his kingdom; wherein, when the bishop, who was not skilful in the English tongue, preached the gospel, it was most delightful to see the king himself interpreting the word of God to his commanders and ministers, for he had perfectly learned the language of the *Scotti* during his long banishment.[1]

Bede's portrayal of this partnership drew on biblical models of Christian kingship and a Gregorian vision of the episcopal life.[2] Oswald's translation of the sermon was in line with St Paul's approach: 'If I do not know the meaning of the language, I shall be a foreigner to the speaker and the speaker a foreigner to me.'[3] The portrayal of Oswald and Áedán as Gaelic speakers seems realistic given that both men had spent time in Argyll and Ireland, but how common was this experience in the Northumbrian kingdom? Did the two men belong to a wider Gaelic-speaking community, or were they members of a small, mobile group of noblemen and clerics?[4]

There is a burgeoning scholarship on medieval multilingualism, which tackles the theme from various angles. Scholars have studied texts in search of terms

---

[1] *HE* III, 3, 2 (ed. Lapidge, II, 26, 28; ed. and transl. Colgrave and Mynors, 220–1).
[2] See below, 33.
[3] I Cor. XIV.10–11. The Vetus Latina and Vulgate contain the word *barbarus* (for Greek βάρβαρος) which is translated 'barbarian' in the Douay–Rheims version; see *Vetus Latina Database*; *Biblia Sacra Vulgata* (ed. Weber and Gryson, 127). Modern translations, such as the Revised Standard Version and the New International Version, render βάρβαρος as 'foreigner'.
[4] For the influences on Bede's evidence presentation of multilingualism, see Scharer, 'The role of language'; Hall, 'Interlinguistic communication', 43–55.

borrowed from other languages, and analysed the circumstances in which vocabulary was borrowed or adapted.[5] The influence of texts composed in different linguistic milieus is a topic of enduring interest, as noted already in relation to *Cogad Gáedel re Gallaib* and the postulated *Brjáns saga*, a lost Norse text that was later incorporated into *Njáls saga*. There are, indeed, indications that several texts relating to the battle of Clontarf were circulating in the Norse-speaking world.[6] The role of Latin as an intermediary between scholars who spoke different vernacular languages has drawn attention, as have vernacular glosses on Latin texts.[7] Historians have studied attitudes to speakers of different languages, and analysed the social contexts in which multilingualism developed. Medieval communities could make themselves understood by using interpreters (professional or otherwise) or a *lingua franca*.[8] In the mercantile world of the Irish Sea and the North Atlantic, Norse could have become that *lingua franca*, command of the language being something of a badge of identity for traders and urban communities, who were unified as much by occupational as ethnic affinities.[9] Norse could have been a mediator between speakers of English and Irish during the Viking Age, while Latin remained a universal point of connection between literate individuals.

The lack of extant texts and manuscripts from western and northern Northumbria poses a problem. Some of the textual approaches to multilingualism – such as the study of glosses – are not available in our area. One of the few extant texts from western Northumbria, Gospatric's writ, features a rich mixture of personal and place-names, as well as the unique term *wassenas* (Brittonic *gwas* 'servant' plus both Brittonic and English plural endings). Place-names are the main source of information about linguistic interaction in the area, but few are attested as early as Gospatric's writ (an eleventh-century text in a thirteenth-century copy).[10] The twelfth century is the documentary horizon for much of southern Scotland and northern England, and some minor names are first attested as late as the nineteenth century. It is therefore difficult to know when a name might have been coined. In a multilingual area there might have been several different names for a place, and yet the scribe selected only one, based on his own linguistic preferences.[11] Another obstacle to onomastic study is the lack of full place-name surveys for certain areas, which means that some early forms remain to be collected and some etymologies unknown.[12] That said, the place-names of northern England and southern Scotland remain an enduring source of fascination because of their extraordinary variety.

[5] Richard Dance has highlighted the role of literary register in the use of borrowed Norse terms in Middle English: 'English in contact', 1732–4. Matthew Townend has broached the question of 'dialect congruity' in relation to English and Norse: *Language and History*, 45–5.

[6] See above, 67.

[7] O'Brien, *Reversing Babel*, 79, 100–1, 215–16; Ní Mhaonaigh, 'Of Bede's "five languages"', 100–1, and 116–17 for the shift to the vernacular in ninth-century Ireland; Johnston, *Literacy and Identity*, 54.

[8] Attitudes are discussed in Putter, 'Multilingualism', 88–9; for mechanisms of communication, see O'Brien, *Reversing Babel*, 80, 87, 105, 125; Crick, 'The "English"', 223–37; cf. Bullock-Davies, *Professional Interpreters*, 18.

[9] In general, see Hsy, *Trading Tongues,* 1–9. For the occupational identity of Gaelic–Scandinavian merchants, see Downham, 'Coastal communities', 369–73.

[10] *Gospatric's Writ* (ed. and transl. Woodman, *Charters*, 370–1); Breeze, 'Old English *wassenas*'.

[11] Townend, 'Viking Age England', 98; Edmonds and Taylor, 'Languages and names', 162.

[12] The current state of scholarship on place-names in the area is surveyed in Edmonds and Taylor, 'Languages and names', 141–2.

In this chapter, I seek to relate the onomastic picture to the broader historical context. This endeavour is fraught with problems, for there is no agreement about how to interpret distributions of place-name elements in relation to political developments. A classic instance is the debate surrounding the scale of Scandinavian settlement during the Viking Age. Some scholars have viewed the density of Norse place-names as an indicator of large-scale rural colonisation, whereas others have suggested that the language of the warrior elites could have percolated down the social strata over time, leading to gradual changes in place-names.[13] A recent approach to the problem is to combine DNA evidence with analysis of linguistic shifts. Such research has sometimes suffered from a lack of chronological precision, but a recent study based on a sample of men bearing long-standing local surnames in the Wirral has yielded promising results. Around half of the group had a male ancestor with a Y-chromosome type found in Norway.[14]

It is worth considering how Gaelic speakers intermingled with this population of Scandinavian settlers. Gaelic-speaking women apparently married Scandinavian settlers in Ireland and the Isles, and then moved on to new colonies, as the mitochondrial DNA analyses of the Faroes and Iceland suggest. Judith Jesch has recently highlighted how women such as these could have played an influential role in the linguistic makeup of the North Atlantic diaspora.[15] If they were able to impart the 'mother tongue' to their children, this would have ensured continuity of Gaelic speech in western Northumbria for at least a generation. The famous episode in *Laxdœla saga* in which the Irish princess Melkorka discloses that she has taught her Icelandic-born son Óláfr to speak Irish is illustrative of this process, even if the tale was recorded some centuries later.[16] The women who forged new lives in the North Atlantic included those who had been captured and conveyed as slaves, Melkorka being an example.[17] This episode raises the possibility that slaves – both male and female – were involved in the Scandinavian settlement of the Northumbrian kingdom. Command of different languages may have been a matter of social status and gender as much as politics. Even so, circumstances changed over time, and by the mid-eleventh century Irish kings such as Diarmait mac Maíl na mBó of Leinster were in the ascendant in the Irish Sea. It is no surprise that Dublin and the Isle of Man were becoming increasingly gaelicised by this time.[18]

By the eleventh century, speakers of four languages (English, Norse, Gaelic and Brittonic) were mingling in the west of the former Northumbrian kingdom.[19] While many aspects of the area's linguistic history remain obscure, it has much to contribute to the theme of medieval multilingualism. I will show that the influences on Gaelic speech in Northumbria varied from locality to locality, and across

---

[13] Compare Sawyer, 'The density'; *idem, The Age*, 123–31, 154–76 (minimalist interpretation) with Stenton, 'The historical bearing'. Both of these models have been applied to other situations of language contact: Weinreich, *Languages in Contact*, 3, 59–60, 78–8, 83–110; Thomason and Kaufman, *Language Contact*, 10, 43–4, 67–8, 95–6, 122–4.

[14] The chronological problems are evident in Cavalli-Sforza, *Genes, Peoples and Languages*, 133–72. For the surname-based approach, see Redmonds *et al., Surnames*, 207–10.

[15] Jesch, 'Speaking like a Viking', 53–4; *eadem, The Viking Diaspora*, 91.

[16] *Laxdaela saga* (ed. Einar Ól. Sveinsson, 22–5; transl. Magnus Magnusson and Hermann Pálsson, 68).

[17] Wyatt, *Slaves*, 153–4.

[18] Ní Mhaonaigh, 'Perception and reality', 141–2 on the literary dimension; see below, 183–4 for personal names.

[19] Murison, 'Linguistic relationships', 73.

different social contexts. This interpretation adds further weight and nuance to my overarching argument that Gaelic influence was enduring and varied in the Northumbrian kingdom.

Pre-Viking linguistic contacts

The Northumbrian Golden Age was a high point of Gaelic political influence; by contrast, the Gaelic place-names ascribed to the sixth and seventh centuries have been the subject of much debate. Even so, the relatively rich textual material provides some insight into linguistic relations in the kingdom, especially the eastern areas. The textual evidence indicates that Gaelic was used in specialised spheres, including the Church and at court.

Bede famously depicted Oswald as ruling all of the *nationes* and *prouinciae* of Britain, which was divided among speakers of four different languages. Earlier Bede had written of five languages in Britain (including Latin), and he drew a comparison with the Pentateuch, revealing that his depictions of languages were influenced by the Bible.[20] In his commentary on Acts, Bede discussed the Pentecost miracle, in which the apostles spoke in tongues, while listeners of various nationalities heard the wonders of God proclaimed in their own languages. He suggested that this prefigured the linguistic diversity of the Church when it had spread across the world.[21] In his commentary on Genesis, he alluded to the Pentecost miracle, noting that it enabled people of diverse languages to understand one another and praise God in an identical faith.[22] Another type of linguistic symbolism is seen in Bede's depiction of the Synod of Whitby: just as there were two views about Easter dating, so two separate groups spoke in Gaelic and English, with Bishop Cedd acting as interpreter.[23] Bede's writings include several insights into communication between Gaelic and English speakers, and hint at various degrees of bilingualism. Oswald was fully bilingual in Gaelic and English, having spent many years in Dál Riata; Áedán was a Gaelic-speaker who did not yet know the English language *perfecte*; and Oswald's *duces* and *ministri* heard the bishop preach in Gaelic, but required an English translation.[24]

Preaching involved oral communication, but literate clerics from Gaelic and Northumbrian backgrounds also interacted on the page. The alphabet devised for Old English bears traces of Irish influence, and it may have been developed in the Irish churches that hosted émigré Northumbrian scholars.[25] One revealing example of multilingual scholarship is an eighth-century Latin commentary on the psalms that includes twenty-six Irish and five Old Northumbrian glosses written into the

---

[20] *HE* I, 1, 3; III, 6, 1 (ed. Lapidge, I, 114; II, 42; ed. and transl. Colgrave and Mynors, 16–17, 230–1).

[21] Acts II.1–13; Bede, *Expositio actuum apostolorum* II.3–4 (ed. Laistner, 16–17; transl. Martin, 29).

[22] Gen. XI.1–9; Bede, *In principium Genesis* III.11.8–9b (ed. Jones, 155–62; transl. Kendall, 231–8); Stanton, 'Linguistic fragmentation', 20–3; Hall, 'Interlinguistic communication'.

[23] *HE* III, 25, 4 (ed. Lapidge, II, 148; ed. and transl. Colgrave and Mynors, 298–9); Hall, 'Interlinguistic communication', 44–8, noting that Latin was not used as a *lingua franca* here.

[24] *HE* III, 3, 2 (ed. Lapidge, II, 26, 28; ed, and transl. Colgrave and Mynors, 220–1). This episode bears out the view of M. Görlach ('Celtic Englishes?', 30) that preaching would be conducted in English. Yet the use of an interpreter suggests that Gaelic was also being used in the Northumbrian kingdom.

[25] Ó Néill, 'The origins', 20–2.

text. The Northumbrian glosses had been copied by a scribe who did not under-stand them, and so speakers of Irish and English may not have been working side by side in this case. This situation contrasts with the Continental church of Echternach, which attracted both English and Irish scholars from Willibrord's mission base, Ráith Máelsigi in Ireland.[26] Communication between the *literati*, often through a Latin intermediary, was facilitated (and reflected) by the development of an 'Insular system of scripts'. This was a hierarchy of scripts for different functions, and while the chronology of and influences on its development have sparked much discussion, the Irish background was formative.[27] Northumbrian–Gaelic ecclesiastical interaction also made its mark on the English language. A number of rarely attested words in Old English are likely to have been borrowed from Old Irish in an ecclesiastical context. The Old English *ancra, ancor* ('anchorite') derives ultimately from Latin *anacho-reta*, and entered English via Old Irish *ancharae*.[28] The Northumbrian churches are good candidates for this linguistic interaction, as indicated by the term *cursung* (in the sense 'punishment'), which may have been influenced by the Old Irish verbal noun *cúrsagad*. This term appears in the tenth-century, Old Northumbrian glosses on the Lindisfarne Gospels and the related glosses on the Rushworth/Macregol Gospels.[29]

The impact of such high-level ecclesiastical interaction on the Northumbrian people is worth considering. Indeed, early medieval missionaries debated the desirability of integrating into the local community by speaking its language and adopting its customs.[30] One pointer to the wider impact of the Gaelic language is the presence of potentially early Gaelic place-names in the vicinity of churches dedicated to Iona saints; the local community must have accepted and perpetuated such names. One example is *Bunkle* (Bonkel 1275), *bun chell* 'church at the foot (of the Lammermuirs)', which lay near the church of St Baíthéne (Abbey St Bathans).[31] A gaelicised form of the Brittonic name Melrose (*Mailros*) appears in the anonymous *Vita* of Cuthbert from Lindisfarne, as well as Bede's works. Bede no doubt adopted the form from the Lindisfarne text, and it is possible that it was also circulating orally in the Columban *familia*.[32]

---

[26] Vatican Library Pal. Lat. 68. McNamara, 'Ireland and Northumbria'; Ó Néill, 'Old English bron-degur'. Cf. Ó Cróinín, 'The Old Irish and Old English glosses' for Echternach manuscripts.

[27] See, for example, the debates around the two phases of Insular half-uncial. Compare T. J. Brown, *A Palaeographer's View*, 196–8, 201–20, with Dumville, *A Palaeographer's Review*, esp. 41–57, further discussed by M. Brown, 'Writing', 148–52.

[28] Förster, 'Altenglisch *stōr*', 51–2; Campbell, *Old English Grammar*, 220. Cf. eDIL *s.v. ancharae*; Bosworth and Toller, *An Anglo-Saxon Dictionary, s.vv. āncor, āncra; eidem, Supplement, s.v. āncora*. For other possible loans from Old Irish, see Förster, 'Keltisches Wortgut', 142–62; Breeze, 'Seven types', 176–7; Durkin, *Borrowed Words*, 79–80.

[29] eDIL, *s.v. cúrsagaid*; Bosworth and Toller, *An Anglo-Saxon Dictionary*, 175; *eidem, Supplement*, 136; Thomson, 'Aldrediana V', 31–2; Breeze, 'Celtic etymologies', 287–9. See the gloss on Luke XX.47: *Codex Lindisfarnensis* (ed. Kendrick *et al.*, fol. 191v); Ross and Stanley, 'Index', 73; *The Macregol Gospels* (ed. Tamoto, 233). There were two glossators of the Macregol Gospels; the glossator of Luke was working in a Northumbrian dialect.

[30] Wood, *The Missionary Life*, 258–60. Compare more modern missions: Mufwene, *The Ecology*, 63–4; Hall, 'Interlinguistic communication', 63, 71–2.

[31] Taylor, 'Seventh-century Iona abbots', 43–9.

[32] *Vita Sancti Cuthberto auctore anonymo* II.4, III.1 (ed. and transl. Colgrave, *Two Lives*, 82–3, 94–5); Bede, *Vita Sancti Cuthberti* 6, 25 (ed. and transl. Colgrave, 172–3, 239–40); Jackson, *Language and History*, 326–7. *HE* III, 26, 2; IV, 25 (27), 1 (ed. Lapidge, II, 164, 356; ed. and transl. Colgrave and Mynors, 308–9, 430–5).

What of the church at the end of this well-trodden route, Lindisfarne itself? The place-name may feature Brittonic *lindo-* ('pool'), while the second element is often interpreted as Old English *farena* (genitive of *faran* 'travellers'). The *Lindisfaran* were the inhabitants of Lindsey, the area south of the Humber.[33] Richard Coates has suggested instead that Áedán and his followers coined the Gaelic name *Lindis-ferann* ('land by the lake-stream').[34] One difficulty with the Gaelic etymology is that the Iona monks knew Lindisfarne by another name, *insula/inis Medgoit*, which derived from the Brittonic *(insula) Medcaut*.[35] If Áedán had invented a new name for the island, it is surprising that his Iona colleagues did not use it. Another potentially Gaelic name on Lindisfarne is 'The Lough', a freshwater lake, whose name may derive from Gaelic *loch*.[36] An alternative explanation is that 'Lough' is related to the dialect word *low*, which derives from Brittonic *luch* (Modern Welsh *llwch*). The element was borrowed into Old Northumbrian as *luh* and used to gloss Latin *fretum* ('stream') and *stagnum* ('lake') in the Lindisfarne Gospels.[37] The development of the word is reflected in the early records of St Mary's Loch and the Loch of the Lowes in Selkirkshire, which begin as the *luhes*, then become the *louʒhes* and later the *lowes*.[38] A final candidate is Beal, which is located opposite Lindisfarne and resembles Scottish Gaelic *beul* ('mouth'; Old Irish *bél*).[39] However, early forms such as *Behulle* (1248) have been interpreted as 'bee-hill'.[40] Thus a cluster of ecclesiastical Gaelic place-names has yet to be demonstrated around Lindisfarne.[41]

Turning westwards, there are many more Gaelic place-names to investigate, and these are likely to have formed over a lengthy period. John MacQueen, in a pioneering study, suggested that some were coined in the sixth century, following a migration from north-eastern Ireland.[42] He placed many names in *cill-* 'church' in the pre-Viking period, suggesting that Gall-Goídil were unlikely to form such

---

[33] Watts, *The Cambridge Dictionary*, 374; Green, *Britons and Anglo-Saxons*, 242–52. English speakers would have adopted the name before assimilation of *-nd-* to *-nn-*, i.e. by the early seventh century: Sims-Williams, *The Celtic Inscriptions*, 78–81, 283, 290; for earlier dating, see Jackson, *Language and History*, 511–13.

[34] *Lindis, lind* ('pool') + suffix: Coates, 'The significances', 76–8; *idem*, 'Un-English reflections'. Alan James has suggested Brittonic *lind-es* (*BLITON* II, *lïnn*). For *ferann*, see eDIL, *s.v.*

[35] AU 632.4 (ed. and transl. Mac Airt and Mac Niocaill, 116–17); AT [631] (ed. and transl. Stokes, I, 142); CS (ed. and transl. Hennessy, 82–3); *CI* 632 (ed. Charles-Edwards, I, 138). For Medcaut, see *HB* 63, 65 (ed. Mommsen, 206, 208; ed. and transl. Morris, 38–9, 79–80). Coates suggests that the name derives from Latin *medicata (insula)*, 'healing island': 'Un-English reflections', 241; modified by Breeze, '*Medcaut*'.

[36] Ekwall, *English River-Names*, 264–5; Coates, 'Un-English reflections', 242, 250, 255.

[37] Ross and Stanley, 'Index', 112; Förster, 'Keltisches Wortgut', 130–2; *BLITON* II, *s.v. luch*.

[38] Williamson, 'The non-Celtic place-names', 108. The form *lough* is found in early modern forms of the dialect word, e.g. the Lindisfarne *freshwater loughe*, recorded on John Speed's map of 1611/ 12 (Coates, 'Un-English reflections', 259) and the Forest of Lowes, which Leland spelt 'Forest of *Loughes*' (mid-sixteenth century): Mawer, *The Place-Names*, 137; Smith, *English Place-Name Elements*, II, 27. Modern forms such as St Mary's Loch have been influenced by Scottish Gaelic *loch*.

[39] eDIL, *s.v. bél*.

[40] Thomas Clancy has drawn my attention to this place-name. For the topographically problematic 'bee-hill', see Mawer, *The Place-Names*, 14.

[41] For another possible Gaelic ecclesiastical name in England, see Richard Coates and Andrew Breeze's derivations of Bede's *Domnoc*: Coates, '*Domnoc/Dommoc*'; Breeze, 'Bede's *Civitas Domnoc*'.

[42] MacQueen, 'Welsh and Gaelic'. His arguments were taken up and amplified by W. F. H. Nicolaisen in, for example, 'Gaelic place-names'.

names on account of their pagan background.[43] I have already argued, however, that Christianised Scandinavians from Ireland and the Isles disseminated some of the saints' cults attested by *cill-* names in the late tenth and eleventh centuries.[44] The other place-name elements thought to be diagnostically early were *slew* in the sense 'hill' (Scottish Gaelic *sliabh*), and *carraig* 'rock', which cluster in the Rhinns of Galloway. The distribution of *sliabh* names in Scotland seemed to mirror the extent of Dál Riatan territory, and so it was argued that there was a similar migration to the Rhinns in the fifth or sixth centuries.[45] Simon Taylor's revised distribution map of *slew-* place-names has cast doubt on this early stratum of Gaelic in Galloway, for the names are not restricted to Dál Riata. Moreover, some of the names are compounded with later-medieval place-name elements; Taylor has therefore suggested that the dense cluster of *slew-* names in the Rhinns emerged as a result of later connections with north-eastern Ireland and the Isle of Man.[46] While Taylor's interpretation has not won universal approval, I find it convincing because it tallies with linguistic similarities between Galloway, Man and north-eastern Ireland that had become evident by the late-medieval period.[47] Indeed, other Gaelic place-names in Galloway date to this era, such as the *bal-* (Scottish Gaelic *baile*) place-names, some of which refer to the holdings of twelfth-century monasteries.[48] The dating limits for the flourishing of Gaelic in Galloway are now the eleventh century (following the expansion of Gall-Goídil) until the sixteenth or seventeenth century. That period mostly falls outside the scope of this book, although I will touch on evidence for the expansion of Gall-Goídil.[49]

Norse place-name evidence

I will now focus on the Viking Age, and consider Norse place-name evidence for Gaelic–Scandinavian influence in the Northumbrian kingdom. Place-names coined in Norse do not provide evidence for Gaelic speech; nevertheless, they may indicate cultural influence from the Gaelic world. Scholars have long thought that Gaelic speakers travelled in the wake of Norwegian settlers; for example, A. H.

---

[43] MacQueen, 'The Gaelic speakers', 18–26. W. F. H. Nicolaisen supported an early date for many of the *cill-* names: *Scottish Place-Names*, 166–8.

[44] See above, 133–4.

[45] Nicolaisen, '*Slew-* and *sliabh*'; idem, *Scottish Place-Names*, 51–9. For the varying senses of *sliabh* across Scotland, see Fraser, 'Mountain, hill or moor?'.

[46] Taylor, 'The element *sliabh*'; idem, '*Sliabh*'. Compare Ó Mainnín, 'The mountain names', 43. Broderick, *PNIOM*, VII, 343-5, lists forty *slieau* names on Man. While he allows for some having been coined early on, he also suggests that the element remained productive into relatively recent times. It is possible that analysis of the *carraig* names will reveal similar results. For *carraig* in the Isle of Man, see Broderick, 'Creag and carraig'.

[47] See 5, above. Taylor's interpretation has not been accepted by Nicolaisen ('Gaelic *sliabh* revisited') or MacQueen (*Place-Names of the Wigtownshire Moors*, 69), but it is supported by Clancy, 'Gaelic', 363–4; Livingston, 'Gaelic in Galloway', 86. For Galloway's similarity to Man and north-eastern Ireland in the matter of eclipsis, see Ó Maolalaigh, 'Place-names as a resource', 29–30.

[48] MacQueen, 'Gaelic speakers', 30; Oram, *The Lordship of Galloway*, 244–5; Clancy, 'Gaelic', 368–72. Livingston, 'Gaelic in Galloway', 89–90 offers reasons to date some farm names to the fourteenth century or later. Compare the rich naming tradition in the late-medieval documents explored by McWhannell, '*Gaill*', 95–108.

[49] Clancy, 'The Gall-Ghàidheil'; Lorimer, 'The persistence'.

Smith observed that Gaelic loanwords appeared alongside Norwegian 'test words' (words considered diagnostic of Norwegian influence) in Allertonshire, Yorkshire North Riding, where Danish features were lacking.[50] In more recent times certain Norwegian and Danish 'test words' have been discarded, and the fundamental distinction between Norwegian and Danish spheres of activity has been called into question.[51] The linguistic implications of this debate have not yet been fully explored, and so I shall avoid discussing Norse place-names as a whole, focusing rather on those that suggest a background in the Gaelic world. These place-names have provoked a different debate about the settlers' provenance: scholars once spoke only of 'Irish' features, but Gillian Fellows-Jensen and Alison Grant have argued strongly in favour of a Hebridean dimension.[52] I do not see these two spheres of activity as mutually exclusive, and I shall argue that Gaelic influence reached our area from a variety of directions.

The provenance of certain groups of Scandinavian settlers is apparent from the use of Norse terms borrowed from Gaelic, which appear in place-names and dialect. These include Norse *kapall* (from Old Irish *capall* 'pack horse'), which yielded the Cumbrian dialect term *capple* (for example, Capplebeck, *Caypilbecmire ca* 1300).[53] The Old Irish term *coirce* 'oats' was borrowed into Norse as *korki* and occurs in various minor place-names in Lancashire.[54] The terms *kapall* and *korki* also occur in Iceland and the Faroes at locations such as Korkadalur in Mykines.[55] The term *kross* 'cross' was borrowed from Old Irish *cros*, and it is found throughout the North Atlantic area, although its popularity in north-west England is partly down to its borrowing into Middle English.[56] The Norse spoken in the North Atlantic was therefore tinged by Gaelic influence, and the loanwords might have been brought to north-west England from anywhere in the Atlantic diaspora. That said, Cumbrian dialect preserves a few specialised Gaelic terms not otherwise known in Norse, such as Old/Middle Irish *gerrán* (*garran*, 'gelding') and *tendál* (*teanlay*, 'bonfire').[57] These terms indicate direct contact with Gaelic-speaking regions, not merely participation in a broad North Atlantic Norse-speaking continuum.

The element that best encapsulates the borrowing of Gaelic terms into Norse is *ǽrgi* (from Old Irish *áirge* 'herd of cattle, summer milking place').[58] The term is of interest because it appears in both northern England and south-western Scotland, where the place-names were coined in Norse and Gaelic respectively.[59] This disparity highlights the variation in Gaelic linguistic influence across the former Northumbrian kingdom.[60] It seems unlikely that many, if any, of the *airy* place-names in south-

[50] *PNNY*, xxvii.
[51] For example, the form *hulm* for ON *holmr* had been designated Danish, but Fellows-Jensen has highlighted scribal and dialectal variation: *SSNNW*, 313–16; cf. Kenyon, *The Origins*, 129–30. For the broader argument, see Downham "'Hiberno-Norwegians'".
[52] E.g. *SSNNW*, 319–21; Grant, 'A new approach', 73.
[53] Smith, *English Place-Name Elements*, I, 2; *PNCu*, II, 456.
[54] Wainwright, *Scandinavian England*, 267.
[55] Lockwood, 'Some traces'; Matras, 'Korkadalur'; Jesch, *The Viking Diaspora*, 111.
[56] Ellwood, *Lakeland*, xv, 54; Smith, *English Place-Name Elements*, I, 114.
[57] Gilgarran (*Gillegarran* 1230): *PNCu*, II, 375; Wright, *The English Dialect Dictionary*, VI, *s.v. teanlay*; cf. eDIL *s.vv.* gerrán, tendál.
[58] eDIL, *s.v. áirge*; Kelly, *Early Irish Farming*, 40, 44. For early discussions, see Colley March, 'The Place-Names', 89–96; Ekwall, *Scandinavians*, 74–87.
[59] The form *ǽrgi* is discussed in Fellows-Jensen, 'Common Gaelic *áirge*', 68.
[60] There are approximately twenty-eight names; see Megaw, 'The Manx "eary"', 345; Grant, 'Scandinavian place-names', 368.

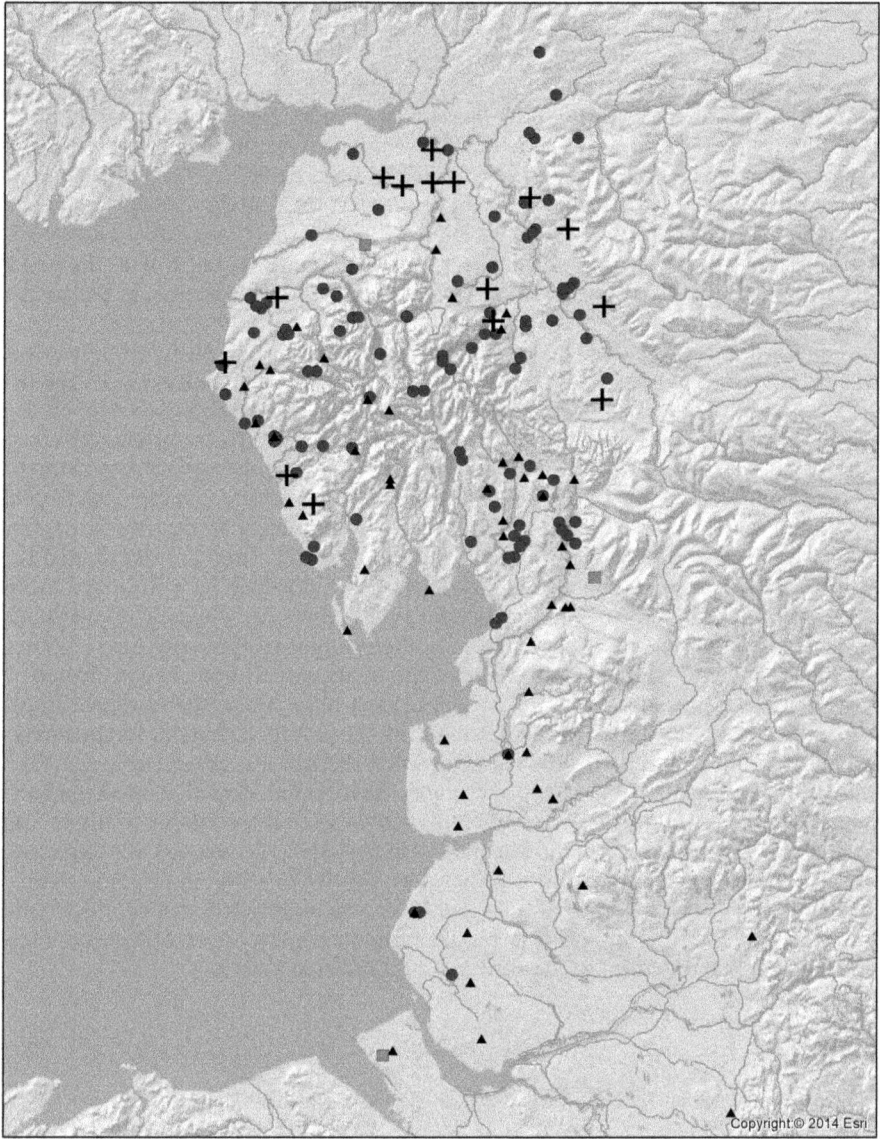

Map 8: Place-names in north-west England that are indicative of Gaelic influence

western Scotland date back to the pre-Viking period, given that *cill-*, *carraig* and *slew-* names are now interpreted as later coinages. Some of the *airy* place-names were demonstrably coined in the tenth century or later; for example, Airyhemming (Old Luce) and Areeming (Kirkpatrick Durham) feature the Norse personal name *Hemingr*, which is unlikely to have arrived in the area before the tenth century.[61] There are no Norse *ærgi* place-names in south-western Scotland, even though some of the Gaelic *airy* names are located amidst clusters of Norse place-names.[62] The names of south-western Scotland share some place-name elements with their Manx counterparts, indicating continued contact and parallel developments in the northern Irish Sea region down to the late medieval period.[63]

The chronology of the northern English *ærgi* names is more straightforward because they were coined in Norse, which was spoken in the area between the tenth and twelfth centuries. The place-names *Ergone* (Argam) and *Ergune* (Arkholme) in the Yorkshire Domesday must have been coined when Old Norse grammar was still understood, for they feature the dative plural *-um* ('at the shielings').[64] Transhumance endured in some localities until the early seventeenth century, but the term *ærgi* did not remain in use in local dialects.[65] There are approximately eighty-five *ærgi* names in northern England, including minor and field names.[66] They are distributed most densely in the north-west, with several outliers in Yorkshire East Riding, Cheshire and Lincolnshire. The distribution resembles other markers of Gaelic–Scandinavian influence; for example, the place-name Coldman Hargos (*Colemanergas* 1119) in the North Riding features *ærgi* plus the Gaelic personal name Colmán and is located near Commondale (*Colemandale* 1273).[67] The closest parallels to the northern English *ærgi* names are the nineteen *ærgi* names in the Faroe Islands.[68] Excavations at Ergidalur (Suðuroy) in the 1960s confirmed that the site was occupied in the Viking Age; more recently, Viking-Age structures have been identified at Argisbrekka (Eysturoy) and on Fugloy.[69] Shielings remained in use on the Faroes until the intensification of sheep farming in the late medieval period.[70] The window for the creation of *ærgi* place-names on the Faroes is therefore similar to northern England, whereas the *eary* and *airy* place-names of Man and Galloway mainly reflect a later flourishing of Gaelic speech. This supports my broader contention that several phases of Gaelic influence affected the west of the former Northumbrian kingdom.

---

[61] MacQueen, *Place-Names in the Rhinns*, 39; Grant, 'Scandinavian place-names', 109, 368. Cf. Clancy, 'Reviews', 90–1.

[62] Oram, 'Scandinavian Settlement', 133–5, 139–40; *idem, The Lordship*, 249, 276.

[63] Megaw, 'The Manx "eary"', 333–5.

[64] Argam (East Riding): *Ergone* DB Yorks 1E26, SETu5; fols 301r, 382r; *Ergum* 1162–75: *PNEY*, 108. It is now deserted, but a nearby farm bears the place-name; see Darby and Maxwell, *The Domesday Geography*, 174. Arkholme (Lancashire): *Ergune* DB Yorks 1L3; fol. 301v; *Argum* 1196: *PNLancs*, 180; *SSNNW*, 52, 61, 326. For the Domesday orthography, see Fellows-Jensen, *Scandinavian Settlement Names in Yorkshire*, 86.

[65] Winchester, *The Harvest*, 84; English Heritage, 'Shielings'.

[66] Fellows-Jensen, 'A Gaelic–Scandinavian loanword', 19–20; *eadem*, 'Old Faroese', 92.

[67] *PNNY*, 148; Ekwall, *Scandinavians*, 84; Smith, 'Some aspects', 46–7. For the distribution, see Smith, *English Place-Name Elements*, II, map 11; Edmonds, 'History and names', 9–10.

[68] For the distribution, see Matras, 'Gammelfærøsk *ærgi*'. Eighteen examples are listed in Dahl, 'Um ærgistaðir', 362–3. The place-name Eyrgislág has since been identified in Fugloy: Matras *et al.*, 'A Viking-Age shieling', 204.

[69] Dahl, 'Um ærgistaðir'; *idem*, 'The Norse settlement', 71; Mahler, *Sæteren ved Argisbrekka*; Matras *et al.*, 'A Viking-Age Shieling', 202–7.

[70] Mahler, *Sæteren ved Argisbrekka*, 412–32, 479–97.

The location where Scandinavians borrowed the Gaelic term *áirge* is significant because it would help us to identify a channel of Gaelic–Scandinavian influence to the Northumbrian kingdom. Relatively few *áirge* place-names are known in Ireland, and all of them are outside areas of Scandinavian settlement.[71] Despite the rarity of *áirge* place-names, it is possible that Scandinavian townsfolk encountered this term itself in neighbouring rural areas of Ireland. A Middle Irish tale describes St Máel Ruain of Tamlacht (Tallaght, Co. Dublin) visiting his *áirge* on Slíab Mairgge (Slievemargy, Co. Laois), closer to Dublin's hinterland.[72] The paucity of *áirge* place-names in Ireland may reflect the narrow senses of the modern Irish term *áirí* ('summer milking place' and 'herd'). The term did not develop the broader sense 'shieling' as it did in western Scotland because *búaile* fulfilled this function instead.[73] The Isle of Man may be a more likely location for the borrowing of *áirge* into Norse. The Manx word *eary* denotes both herd and mountain pasture, and it appears in over forty place-names.[74] Eleanor Megaw proposed a pre-Viking origin for some of these names; others are clearly later coinages, such as Aryhorkell ('*Þorkell*'s eary', Michael parish).[75] The shieling known as 'Block Eary' has been dated to the twelfth century, the period of Scandinavian rule on the Island, but there are only four possible candidates for Norse *ærgi* names.[76] The Gaelic names are much more numerous and include examples in the thirteenth-century abbeyland bounds.[77] It has been suggested that transhumance was practised by Gaelic-speaking women, who tended to milk cows at the summer pastures.[78] If so, this supports the argument that there was considerable survival of Gaelic speech on the Island.

The Hebrides and adjacent coastline seem to offer the most likely location for the borrowing of the term since both Gaelic *àirigh* place-names and Norse *ærgi* names occur there.[79] The modern distribution of Gaelic *àirigh* names is, however, a misleading guide to Viking-Age circumstances since the practice of taking livestock to the *àirigh* continued down to the mid-twentieth century on some islands.[80] Scottish Gaelic *àirigh* developed the broad senses 'hill-pasture' and 'summer residence for

---

[71] Breandán Ó Cíobháin has provided five examples in Matras *et al.*, 'A Viking-Age shieling', 209. Others may be as yet unrecorded; Aalen ('Clochans', 41) noted: 'local tradition preserves many unrecorded names and among these "buaile", "airghe" and "macha" are frequent elements'.

[72] Matras *et al.*, 'A Viking-Age shieling', 209; 'Story of Máel Ruain' (ed. Best, 34).

[73] *Búaile* originally designated a cattle-pen or byre: eDIL, *s.v. búaile*. For transhumance, see Williams and Robinson, 'The Excavation', 29.

[74] Kelly, *The Manx Dictionary*, 70. For a list of the place-names, see Megaw, 'The Manx "eary"', 327, 343–4.

[75] Megaw, 'The Manx "eary"', 329, 333. Aryhorkell is now called Eary Kelly; see *PNIOM* II,18, 68–9.

[76] For the Scandinavian context of transhumance on Man, see Gelling, 'Shielings'; *idem*, 'Medieval shielings', 158, 161–2,171, whereas Quine, 'A reconsideration' has stressed the Insular context. The four place-names are Sliddary, Block Eary, Gredary and Tramsarie: *PNIOM* I, 160; III, 310; IV, 397, 420.

[77] *Cronica regum Mannie et Insularum* (ed. and trans. Broderick, fol. 53r, fol. 54r); Quine, 'A reconsideration', I, 79, 233.

[78] Megaw, 'The Manx "eary"', 339. For women at Hebridean shielings, see Newton, *Warriors of the Word*, 175, 309; Currie, 'Àirighean'.

[79] As argued for the Faroes by Matras, 'Gammelfærøsk *ærgi*'; Fellows-Jensen, 'Common Gaelic *áirge*', 69–71.

[80] Dòmhnallach, 'An Àirigh'; Currie, 'Àirighean'. One example of a late *àirigh* name is Àirigh Fhionnlaigh in Carloway, Lewis, which local tradition dates to 1890: Cox, *The Gaelic Place-names*, 121, 153.

herdsmen and cattle', which explains its popularity in place-names.[81] The Norse *ærgi* names may offer a better insight into Viking-Age circumstances, and they cluster in specific localities, notably the Outer Hebrides and the arc of territory around Glenelg and Ardnamurchan on the mainland. This mainland area is a likely location for Norse-speakers to have borrowed the Gaelic term *áirge* because it lay at the northern edge of Dál Riata and continued to be populated by some Gaelic-speakers during the Viking Age. There are numerous examples of Gaelic *àirigh* as well as some Norse *ærgi* names, such as Smirisary in Moidart.[82] Yet it is very unlikely that this sparsely populated area generated all of the Scandinavian settlers who dispersed to the Faroes, north-west England, the far north of Scotland and the Outer Hebrides. Rather, I suggest that the term travelled with a mobile population of Norse-speakers who had direct or indirect links to the Highlands and Islands. The terms then circulated among the wider Norse-speaking population in areas such as Caithness and north-west England.[83]

The second point of debate is why the term was borrowed from Gaelic; what function did it fulfil for Norse-speakers? Transhumance was well established in Norway and was exported from there to the North Atlantic colonies.[84] Other Norse shieling terms were available to Norse-speakers, namely, *sætr*, *skáli* and *sel*, and eventually Northern Middle English *skaling* and *schele*.[85] This raises the question of whether the *ærgi* sites differed from other sites associated with transhumance. In northern England, *ærgi* sites are generally distributed below the altitude that is customary for summer grazing (600ft/183m), whereas *sætr* and *skáli* sites are located in remote locations on the Lakeland massif.[86] Did the *ærgi* have a specialised function for which a Gaelic term was considered appropriate? Gillian Fellows-Jensen has suggested a parallel with the Scandinavian *heimseter*, an intermediate spring shieling, yet a number of Manx and Hebridean *eary* and *àirigh* sites were located too far from home to fulfil this purpose.[87] I suggest that the meaning of the term *ærgi* remained close to its Old Irish roots ('herd', 'milking place') during the Viking Age. This view draws inspiration from Mary Higham's examination of the *ærgi* sites in the Forest of Bowland (Lancashire/Yorkshire). Several of these became vaccaries, that is, specialised stock-rearing and dairy-producing enterprises.[88] One example is Beatrix (Batherarghes 1343, featuring ON personal name Bǫvarr), a vaccary that was used for the lord's stock in the medieval period.[89] Mary Higham suggested that the vaccaries had ancient roots and were taken over by Gaelic–Scandinavian settlers who had become familiar with the stock-leasing system in Ireland.[90] Cattle had social

---

[81] Dwelly, *The Illustrated Gaelic–English Dictionary*, s.v. *àiridh*.

[82] Smirisary: ON *smjǫr* + *ærgi* ('butter shieling'): Macbain, *Place-names*, 291; Fellows-Jensen, 'Common Gaelic *áirge*', 70. For Gaelic survival in Moidart, see Jennings and Kruse, 'From Dál Riata', 143.

[83] Cf. Ekwall, *Scandinavians*, 87. For Caithness, see Macbain, *Place-names*, 290–1; cf. Henderson, *The Norse Influence*, 164–5.

[84] Austad *et al.*, 'An overview', 11–12; Albrethsen and Keller, 'The use'.

[85] Whyte, 'Shielings', 105; English Heritage, 'Shielings'.

[86] Whyte, 'Shielings', 105–8; Whaley, *A Dictionary*, 388.

[87] Quine, 'A reconsideration', I, 266–70 *contra* Fellows-Jensen, 'A Gaelic–Scandinavian loanword', 23–5; *eadem*, 'Common Gaelic *áirge*', 71–2.

[88] Higham 'The "Erg" place-names', 10–14; cf. *eadem*, 'Pre-Conquest settlement', 122–4.

[89] *PNWY*, VI, 211; Ekwall, *Scandinavians*, 83. Beatrix carried the stock of the duke of Lancaster, King Henry VI, by 1422: see Whitaker, *An History*, I, 344; Cunliffe Shaw, *The Royal Forest*, 375–7. Bǫvarr's main settlement was nearby Badresbi: DB Yorks, 30W37, fol. 380v.

[90] For cattle in the north-west, see Whyte, 'Shielings', 114; Winchester, *The Harvest*, 18.

as well as economic significance in the medieval Gaelic-speaking world, for lords leased cattle to their clients, and clients provided cattle tribute in return.[91] Even in the more extreme landscape of the Faroes, the *ærgi* was part of a broad-based system of farming including cattle, which was eventually displaced by intensive sheep farming.[92] I propose that Scandinavian settlers sought to dominate cattle-rearing systems in Ireland or Argyll, and thereby became familiar with the practice of summer grazing on the *àirge*. I have dwelt on the *ærgi*/airy names because they are crucial to the debate about provenance of Gaelic–Scandinavian settlers, and because they reveal different phases of Gaelic influence either side of the Solway.

Table 5: Settlement names referring to Írar, Íras, Skotar *and* Scottas

Place-name	First attestation	Date	Source
Ireby (Cumberland)	Irebi	*ca* 1160	*PNCu*, II, 299–300
Ireby	Irebi	1086	*PNLa*, 183
Irton*	Yrton	*ca* 1225	*PNCu*, II, 402
Irby	Erberia/Irreby	*ca* 1096–1101	Dodgson, *The Place-Names*, IV, 264–5
Irton (Yorkshire, Pickering)	Iretune	1086	*PNNR*, 101–2
Irton (Yorkshire, Birdforth)	Iretone	1086	*PNNR*, 193
Irby Manor (Yorkshire)	Irebi	1086	*PNNR*, 218
Irby upon Humber (Lincolnshire)	Iribi	1086	Cameron, *The Place-Names*, V, 124–5
Irby in the Marsh (Lincolnshire)	Irebi	*ca* 1115	Cameron, *A Dictionary*, 70
Ireton Farm (Derbyshire)	Iretune	1086	*PNDerbys*, II, 508–9
Kirk Ireton (Derbyshire)	Hiretune	1086	*PNDerbys*, II, 381
Scotby (Cumberland)	Scoteby	1130	*PNCu*, I, 163
Scotton (Lincolnshire)	Scottun	1060–6	Cameron, *A Dictionary*, 101
Scotton (Yorkshire)	Scottune	1086	*PNNR*, 133

* This name has been explained as a formation from the name of the River Irt (e.g. *PNCu*, I, 17). The river name is suspected to be Brittonic, but I prefer to see the river name as a back formation from the settlement name.

Another type of Norse place-name sheds light on these connections, that is, names referring to *Írar* 'Irish people' and *Skotar* 'Scottish people'. The distinction is worth investigating since it implies that two separate Gaelic groups were active in the area. As noted previously, the Latin term *Scotti* and vernacular equivalents originally denoted Gaelic-speakers in general, but they became restricted to inhabitants of the kingdom of Alba during the tenth century. Scotby near Carlisle

[91] Kelly, 'Cattle in ancient Ireland'. Compare Newton, *Warriors of the Word*, 37–8, 134–5, 138–40, 151, 186–7, 324–5 for the Highlands.
[92] Dahl, 'The Norse settlement', 71; Fellows-Jensen, 'Old Faroese *ærgi*', 94; Arge, 'Viking and medieval settlement', 615.

(*Scoteby* 1130) was indeed linked with the core of the Scottish kingdom, for David I, king of Scots, received rent from a mill there.[93] I have already suggested that Scotton near Ripon was an equivalent place-name coined in English, which signified links with the kingdom of Alba.[94] The Norse term *Írar* and the rare Old English term *Íras* seem to have emerged in response to the narrowing of Scottish terminology. These terms were sometimes restricted to Ireland; for example, an Old English homily by Ælfric (*ob. ca* 1010) describes St Fursey as *geond eal Yrrland and Scōtland* ('over all Ireland and Scotland') *bodiende betwux Yrum and Scottum* ('preaching between the Irish and the Scots').[95] The distinction raises the question of how Manx people and Hebrideans would be designated, for terms such as *Suðreyingar* do not appear in place-names. It is significant that Ireland and the incipient Scottish kingdom seem to have dominated the perceptions of outsiders.[96] The Ireby and Scotby place-names help to balance the Highland and Islands background of the *ærgi* names, highlighting a wide range of Gaelic influences in Viking-Age northern England.

The place-names shed light on the provenance of the settlers, but to what extent were these groups gaelicised? Mary Higham observed that Ireby names tend to occur on relatively marginal land, such as upland slopes or marshes, which supports the idea that they signified minority groups.[97] The term *Írar* could denote both native Irish and Scandinavians who had been based in Ireland, and it is difficult to distinguish between these possible meanings.[98] Kirk Ireton and Little Ireton in Derbyshire are located in areas that were dominated by English-speakers, and so the place-names may have signified a small group of Scandinavian settlers from the Gaelic world.[99] In contrast, there is considerable evidence for the settlement of the Wirral peninsula by Scandinavians from Ireland, all of whom might have been designated *Írar* in the sense of people who had come from Ireland. It is possible, then, that this Irby must commemorate a group of Irish speakers who travelled in the midst of the wider group of Scandinavian settlers.[100] Other minorities may have moved as part of the broader groups that we now designate 'Scandinavian settlers', such as displaced groups of Britons. The Domesday entry for the large and valuable manor of Northallerton is intriguing since the outliers included a *Bretebi* (now Birkby) and it had jurisdiction over an *Irebi* (a deserted village by Irby Manor).[101] These settlements may date back to the early tenth century, whereas the Furness peninsula (Cumbria, formerly Lancashire) experienced more enduring links to the Gaelic–Scandinavian world. The place-name Ireleth in Furness (*Íra* + *hlíð* 'slope of the Irishmen') could have been

---

[93] *Charters of King David I* (ed. Barrow, 89–90), charter dated 1136 × 1141; *PNCu*, I, 163.

[94] See above, 151.

[95] Bosworth and Toller, *An Anglo-Saxon Dictionary*, 246. The text is quoted from Ælfric, *Catholic Homilies* (ed. Godden, 197, cf. 366). For further examples, see Milfull and Thier, 'Anglo-Saxon perceptions', 215–21.

[96] For terms applied to islanders, see Jesch, *Ships and Men*, 77–8. The excerpts from skaldic verse in Hines, *Old-Norse Sources*, 26–8 refer to a range of Insular peoples.

[97] Higham, 'Scandinavian settlements'.

[98] Hines, *Old-Norse Sources*, 21.

[99] *PNDerbys*, I, xxxiii, xxxvi; II, 381, 508–9.

[100] The earliest place-name form *Erberia* shows confusion with OE *byrig*: *SSNNW*, 33; Dodgson, *The Place-Names*, IV, 264–5.

[101] *PNNY*, 218; *SSNY*, 31. Movements of Britons are discussed in *SSNY*, 21, 189, 246; James, 'A Cumbric diaspora', esp. 191–3.

coined as late as the twelfth century.[102] In short, the Ireby and Ireton names highlight considerable variation in the chronology and intensity of Gaelic influence across northern England.

Place-names coined by Gaelic speakers

The discussion of *Írar* and *Skotar* has opened up the possibility that Gaelic–Scandinavian settlement involved Gaelic-speaking groups as well as the more dominant Norse-speaking community. I now turn to an examination of place-names that were coined in Gaelic by communities with a partly Scandinavian background. Some of these names emerged no earlier than the eleventh century, which adds further weight to my argument that parts of the Northumbrian kingdom remained in contact with Gaelic speakers at that late stage. Indeed, the eleventh century was a time when Gaelic flourished across the Irish Sea region, for the gaelicisation of the Hiberno-Scandinavian and Manx communities was under way. Meanwhile, the increasingly confident Gaelic dynasty of Alba turned their attention southwards.[103] I suggest that these developments affected the place-names of the former Northumbrian kingdom.

I will start by considering the unusual group of place-names known as 'inversion compounds'. These names feature word order familiar to Celtic speakers, that is, generic plus specific: Kirksanton, for example, is *kirkja* 'church' plus the saint's name. The word order favoured by Norse speakers is specific plus generic, which would result in *Santonkirk*. While the syntax of the inversion compounds is rooted in the Gaelic world, the vocabulary is varied, and Norse elements often feature. For this reason, Eilert Ekwall suggested that the inversion compounds had been coined by Norse-speakers who had spent time in Ireland.[104] Alison Grant has reviewed this suggestion in light of recent advances of linguistic theory, and she has persuasively argued that the inversion compounds were in fact coined by Gaelic speakers who were learning Norse as their second language. She sees these people as part-way through a process of transition towards the prestigious culture of their Norse-speaking lords.[105] Half of the inversion compounds contain Gaelic personal names, some of which are diminutives (nicknames), indicating a community immersed in Gaelic naming practices. One example is *Hovedh Kellan*, ON *hǫfuð* 'high land' plus Gaelic personal name Cellán/Ciallán, featuring the *-án* diminutive.[106]

Grant's interpretation leaves one problem unsolved, namely, the way in which the distribution of the inversion compounds differs from that of the *ærgi* names. The latter have a more southerly distribution, being focused on areas such as the Forest of Bowland as well as Pennine valleys such as Wensleydale and as far east as Arram, East Riding (*Argun* in 1086). In contrast, the inversion compounds occur around the Solway region, along the Eden Valley and around Morecambe Bay. There are only four possible examples from Yorkshire, one of which also features the element *ærgi* (Arrathorne, North Riding: *Ergthorn* 1259).[107] The differing

---

[102] *PNLa*, 205: *Irlid* 1190, *grangiam de Ireleyth* 1200; SSNNW, 138; see Edmonds, 'The Furness peninsula' for the enduring links between Furness and the Gaelic–Scandinavian world.
[103] Clancy, 'Gaelic', 391.
[104] Ekwall, *Scandinavians*, 51–5.
[105] Grant, 'A new approach', 77–81.
[106] *PNWe*, I, 140; Grant, 'A new approach', 80.
[107] Smith, 'Irish influence', 51–5; *PNNR*, 158, 240–1.

geographical spreads of these two name-types raise the suspicion that they reflect distinct phases of Gaelic influence.

David Parsons has recently offered a persuasive answer to this conundrum, namely, that the inversion compounds reflect a later wave of Gaelic speakers who moved into the region. They would have encountered Norse speakers who were already resident, and so learnt Norse as their second language.[108] Parsons suggests that this wave of Gaelic speakers emanated mainly from the north, and he has proposed two possible channels: the expansion of Gall-Goídil in the eleventh century, and the phase of Scottish rule under David I (*ob.* 1153).[109] I find the first explanation highly persuasive; the second less so. The eleventh-century Gospatric's writ already includes two inversion compounds: *bek Troyte* (ON *bekkr* 'river' plus personal name Truite) and *poll Þaðæn* (the dialect term *poll* 'pool', plus a second element perhaps based on Norse *vað* 'ford').[110] Parsons has pointed to three places with the Gaelic etymology *ceann monaidh* 'head of the moor' in north-west England and Yorkshire, and I would add Kinmont in Dumfriesshire to the list. The word *monadh* 'moor' occurs in Scottish Gaelic, but not Irish or Manx, and it derives from a Brittonic or Pictish term comparable to Welsh *mynydd*.[111] This does not, however, preclude the possibility that the newly arrived Gaelic speakers adapted a Brittonic *penmynydd* name south of the Solway.[112] The northerly clusters of inversion compounds relate convincingly to an extension of Gall-Goídil influence across the Solway. A more southerly group of inversion compounds clusters around Morecambe Bay, and in my view they are more likely to reflect links with the Isle of Man, given the ease of sailing from the Furness peninsula to Man. Indeed, several inversion compounds appear in the late-thirteenth-century Manx 'Abbeyland bounds', including *toftar Asmund*, which recurs in other texts with reversed word order.[113] The Isle of Man also has *kirk*-compounds, which are a specialised type of inversion compound with a distinctive distribution.[114] I am not suggesting that the inversion compounds were formed on Man and exported to Morecambe Bay; rather, that the process of gaelicisation on the Isle of Man spilled out across the Irish Sea.

One point that the scholarship has not yet fully addressed is the relationship between the inversion compounds and the other speech communities of what is now north-west England. The place-name Tarn Wadling (*Terwathelan* 1285) encapsulates these complex interactions since it features a Norse generic (*tjǫrn* 'tarn') and the Brittonic specific *gwyddelan*, which is a diminutive of the term *gwyddyl* 'Irishman'.[115] English elements are rare, but Seatoller (*Settaller* 1563) may feature

---

[108] Parsons, 'On the origin', 136.

[109] *Ibid.*, 138–9.

[110] 'Gospatric's writ' (ed. Woodman, *Charters*, 370), cf. Parsons, 'On the origins', 134.

[111] Parsons, 'On the origin', 128, noting Kinmont (Cumberland), Kinmond (Westmorland) and Kilmond (North Riding).

[112] *BLITON* II, *mönïd, pen(n)*. Other *pen* names (such as Penrith) will have survived in Brittonic place-names because Gaelic influence was localised.

[113] Gelling, 'The place-names', 172–3; *Cronica regum Mannie et Insularum* (ed. and transl. Broderick, fol. 53r–fol. 54v.

[114] Gelling, 'The place-names', 172 suggested the names were imported from south-west Scotland, but this view is based on a late dating of the 'Abbeyland bounds'. For *kirk*-names, see in general Grant, 'A reconsideration'.

[115] *PNCu*, II, 202.

ON *sætr* + OE *alor* (summer pasture of the alder tree).[116] Elsewhere I have suggested that the inversion compounds may have arisen in the midst of a *Sprachbund*, that is, a situation where numerous languages are spoken but no single tongue is dominant. This eventually leads to the development of similar grammatical features among all of the languages.[117] The push towards Celtic word order came not only from the Gaelic speakers, but also from Brittonic speakers, some of whom had moved into the area when it became part of the Cumbrian kingdom in the early tenth century.[118] The extraordinary minor name *Trerankelborhan* in Westmorland indicates Brittonic involvement since it is most probably a Brittonic **trev* name incorporating an existing English place-name in *burgæsn* 'burial place' and the Norse personal name *Hrafnkell*.[119] That Gaelic speakers encountered Brittonic speakers in the area south of Solway is suggested by the gaelicisation of what appear to be Brittonic *glyn-* 'valley' names to the Gaelic form *glenn*. An example is Glenridding (*glenredyn* 1292), which includes Brittonic *rhedyn* 'bracken'.[120] Thus it is possible to detect Gaelic influence on both Brittonic and Norse speakers.

There are several instances of place-names that were coined afresh in Gaelic south of the Solway. Ravenglass (*rengles*, ca 1180) appears to contain Gaelic *rann* 'division of land' + Gaelic personal name *Glass*.[121] Other examples include Drumleaning, Dunmallard and Torkin, all of which are located in the same areas as the inversion compounds. There are also simplex names such as Knock (Westmorland), from *cnocc* 'hillock'.[122] These names are not numerous, but when set alongside the inversion compounds they reveal the presence of Gaelic speakers south of Solway in the eleventh century. Our knowledge of political history in this area is slim; it seems to have been a border region of the Cumbrian kingdom that came under Northumbrian rule by the mid-eleventh century.[123] Gall-Goídil and Manx families may have arrived in the area through intermarriage or localised land-grabs in a zone devoid of firm rule. This illustrates the danger of seeking to relate linguistic history to rulership, a point borne out by studies of multilingual communities elsewhere in Europe. As Julia Smith observes 'we must appreciate the linguistic diversity of early medieval Europe'.[124]

The Gaelic place-names of south-eastern Scotland are more intelligible in relation to politics, for they seem to reflect the southward expansion of Alba, the nascent Scottish kingdom. Indeed, Gaelic names might be preserved through their inclusion

---

[116] *PNCu*, II, 352. Whaley, *A Dictionary*, 302 has suggested that OE *alor* replaced ON *elri(r)*. Grant, 'A reconsideration', 73, has noted the incorporation of existing English place-names into inversion compounds.

[117] Alex Woolf first made the comparison with the Balkan *Sprachbund*, in *From Pictland to Alba*, 154, and the idea has been considered further by O'Brien, *Reversing Babel*, 84; Clancy, 'Gaelic', 387. For my application of the concept to inversion compounds, see Edmonds and Taylor, 'Languages and Names', 166.

[118] Edmonds, 'The expansion', 55–9. James ('A Cumbric diaspora?') has suggested that Brittonic speakers moved for economic reasons.

[119] *PNWe*, I, 53; Edmonds and Taylor, 'Languages and names', 167.

[120] *PNWe*, II, 222. Whaley, *Dictionary*, 132–3, 400 has highlighted the importance of the *glen* names.

[121] *PNCu*, II, 425.

[122] *PNCu*, I, 119, 188; *PNWe*, II, 114, 215. For a preliminary list, see Parsons, 'On the origin', 146–7. I have added Dunmallard, Another additional name, Mellbreak, is mentioned by Whaley: *A Dictionary*, xxiii, 233–4.

[123] See above, 70–1.

[124] Smith, *Europe*, 26–7 (quotation at 27); Wickham, *The Inheritance*, 272–3.

in the records of Scottish court and Church circles. Alnmouth (Northumberland) appears in a Scottish king-list in the form *Inveralden* (featuring Gaelic *inber* 'river-mouth'), and that name might have survived had the area been permanently annexed to the kingdom of the Scots.[125] Bedrule (Roxburghshire) is first recorded in Celtic word order as *Rulebethok* in 1280, the elements being a river name and the female name *Bethóc*.[126] The landholder was Bethóc, daughter of Domnall Bán, king of Scots (*ob.* 1099), successively wife of Uhtred of Tynedale and Radulf of Nithsdale. This is a notable case of language change on the estate of a female landholder, who presumably settled her own clients there.[127] Such people would have coined both settlement names and minor names that appear ephemerally in the record. One example is *Aldenisslauer* (*Allt an eas labhair* 'burn of the loud waterfall') in Eddleston, Peeblesshire.[128] Other Gaelic-speaking landholders gained lands in Lothian and the former Cumbrian kingdom, although many estates remained in the hands of their Northumbrian lords.[129]

This survey of place-name evidence has revealed that the eleventh century was the high-point of Gaelic linguistic influence on the former Northumbrian kingdom. Gaelic speakers spread southwards across the Solway and eastwards from the Isle of Man, encountering a complex mixture of Norse, Brittonic and English speakers. Meanwhile Gaelic-speaking landowners and retainers were acquiring lands in Lothian through Scottish expansion. The eleventh-century layer of Gaelic influence has been little appreciated until recently, and it adds to my view that Gaelic influence accelerated during the Northumbrian kingdom's demise.

Gaelic personal names

My final category of onomastic evidence is personal names. A Gaelic personal name can be borne by someone who is not a Gaelic speaker; even so, the names betray something of the cultural background of the families who selected them. I will provide a brief survey of sources for Gaelic personal names before focusing my attention on the names in the Yorkshire Domesday survey. This body of material has rarely been explored as a source of information about Gaelic influence in what is now northern England, and yet it strengthens the picture of links with Gaeldom during the eleventh century.

First, it is necessary to consider how personal names may be used to shed light on medieval cultural contact. Here I define a personal name as an individual's first or only name, which was often given at birth or baptism, or occasionally assumed later

---

[125] King-list F (*Inneraldan*); king-list I (*Inveraldan*) (ed. Anderson, *Kings*, 276, 284). Anderson dated this note to the early twelfth century: *ibid.*, 52. Cf. Edmonds and Taylor, 'Languages and names', 162.

[126] *Regesta regum Scottorum IV pt 1* (ed. Neville and Simpson, 151); Compare *Bethocrulle* (1306 × 1329): *CPNS*, 134.

[127] Edmonds, 'Names on the Norman edge' (forthcoming).

[128] *Registrum episcopatus Glasguensis* no. 173 (ed. Innes, I, 142); *CPNS*, 135; Nicolaisen, 'Gaelic place-names', 20–5. For some further instances, see Edmonds, 'Names on the Norman edge' (forthcoming). More examples are found in Milne, *Gaelic Place-Names*, but that volume is over a century old and does not cite early forms of the place-names, which reduces the validity of the etymologies.

[129] The process of re-naming was still ongoing in the twelfth century. Barrow noted that the earls of Fife held land in East Lothian by that time: *The Kingdom*, 123.

in life.[130] It is worth asking whether medieval families chose Gaelic names because of their Gaelic linguistic background, or for other reasons. Cecily Clark observed that the linguistic background of a name often became irrelevant once it had been adopted by a family or community: 'the meaning of name is always extra-linguistic, that of a personal name being primarily a social one'.[131] In her investigation of the name 'William', Clark was able to show how a name spread through family groups, networks of lords and clients and eventually godparents and parish priests.[132] Matthew Townend's exploration of Norse personal names in Yorkshire has similarly revealed how names spread through family connections, rather than through fashion.[133] Wives might transmit the names of their male relatives, although female personal names were often selected from a different, more conservative, pool.[134] These factors help to explain the notable mixture of names on the runic inscription on the eleventh-century 'Mal Lumkun' cross (Michael, Isle of Man), which features the Gaelic male names Dubgall and Máel Lomchon, the Gaelic name Máel Muire (apparently female in this context), and Norse Aþisl.[135] Personal names are, then, a helpful source of information about the cultural background and family connections of those who dwelt in the Northumbrian kingdom.

Before turning to the more copious record of Gaelic names in the Viking Age, I will briefly review the evidence for Gaelic personal names in pre-Viking Northumbria. My discussion of churches in the 'Golden Age' has already touched on a number of churchmen with Gaelic names who were chiefly, if not exclusively, associated with Lindisfarne.[136] The ninth-century core of the Durham *Liber Vitae* includes at least fifteen individuals with Gaelic names among the lists of people to be commemorated. There are not as many as might be expected in a record from Lindisfarne; the alternative attribution to Wearmouth-Jarrow might help to explain the relative paucity.[137] Another possible explanation is that compilation was based on lists that dated from the 680s onwards, that is, after the end of the formal link between Lindisfarne and Iona. By the eighth century, Cenél nGabráin (with whom the Northumbrians enjoyed a special relationship) were suffering declining fortunes, and this would explain why no Dál Riatans appear in the list of kings, whereas their Pictish overlords are listed.[138] Several of the Gaelic-named individuals can be identified and were alive in the eighth century, namely, Bresal, abbot of Iona (*ob.* 801),

---

[130] I have avoided the term 'Christian name' because some of the Scandinavian population were pagan during the early Viking Age. See Redmonds, *Christian Names*, xiv.

[131] Clark, 'Socio-economic status', 101.

[132] Clark, 'Willelmus rex?'; compare Wilson, *The Means of Naming*, 84, for the European perspective.

[133] Townend, *Scandinavian Culture*, 7; *idem*, *Viking Age Yorkshire*, 96–8.

[134] Clark, 'Women's names'.

[135] MM 130; Kermode, *Manx Crosses*, 195–9; Wilson, *Manx Crosses*, 132–3. It is difficult to ascertain the precise family relationships between the group because of grammatical difficulties; see Olsen, 'Runic inscriptions', 216; Page, 'The Manx rune stones', 234–5.

[136] Adomnán of Coldingham is an example outside Lindisfarne and its associated churches: *HE* IV, 23 (25) (ed. Lapidge, II, 342–50; ed. and transl. Colgrave and Mynors, 420–7).

[137] The two possibilities have been weighed up by Briggs, 'Nothing but names', 63–5, who prefers Lindisfarne. I only include a brief discussion of the Gaelic names in the Durham *Liber Vitae* because they have been thoroughly analysed by other scholars: Dumville, 'Gaelic and other Celtic names'; Russell, 'Celtic names'; *idem*, '"Ye shall know them"'.

[138] Briggs, 'Nothing but names', 82 has expressed surprise at the lack of Dál Riata kings; for the background to my explanation, see above, 47–8.

Augustín abbot of Bangor (*ob.* 780), and Ultán, the scribe praised in *De Abbatibus*.[139] The Gerald who appears in the *nomina abbatorum gradus praesbyteratus* is likely to be identified with the bishop of Mag nÉo na Sacsan/Mayo (d. 732).[140] Two of the other name forms are notable because they are phonetic renderings: *Salfach* for Selbach, and *Failfi* for Failbe (where medial –b- is pronounced /v/).[141] This suggests that the names were pronounced by Gaelic speakers when they were being written into the original lists, and so people competent in the language must have been visiting the Northumbrian kingdom during the eighth century.[142] Such ecclesiastical links persisted into the ninth and tenth centuries, as I have already shown, and this is borne out by the appearance of the name *Myredah* (Muiredach) in an Anglian runic inscription on a late-ninth- or early tenth-century cross-shaft at Alnmouth (Northumberland). The monument is closely linked with sculpture of Lindisfarne and Chester-le-Street.[143]

I will now examine evidence from the Viking Age, including a Norse runic inscription that has recently been discovered at Sockburn (County Durham). It features the Gaelic name Máel Muire and the formula *X reisti kross þenna eptir Y* 'X raised this cross in memory of Y', which is familiar from the Isle of Man.[144] The inscription hints at the use of Gaelic personal names among Norse-speakers, an impression strengthened by Norse place-names containing Gaelic personal names. Several *bý*-compounds featuring Gaelic personal names appear in the Yorkshire Domesday (and so must have been coined by the eleventh century), including Melmerby near Ripon, which contains *Máel Muire*. The Yorkshire Domesday also records *Difgelibi* (Duggleby, East Riding: *Dubgall*) and *Fechesbi* (Fixby, West Riding: *Fíacc*), and around fifteen further examples of Norse place-names featuring Gaelic personal names are attested in Yorkshire records down to the fourteenth century.[145] They may be compared with place-names in north-west England, including another Melmerby near Penrith (*Malmerbi*, 1201), as well as the very numerous examples of Gaelic names in inversion compounds.[146] One reason for caution is that a number of the -*bý* names in the Eden Valley and the Solway region were formed as late as the twelfth century, and indeed the Gaelic-named Glassán of Glassonby was alive in the

---

[139] *Durham Liber Vitae*, 18v1(45); 18r1(26); 21v1(49) (ed. Rollason and Rollason, I). AU 780.11; 801.4 (ed. and transl. Mac Airt and Mac Niocaill, 234–5, 256–7); AClon [773] (ed. Murphy, 122); *CI* 780.11, 801.4 (transl. Charles-Edwards, I, 245, 262). Briggs has suggested that Saebercht represented Sóerbergg, the name of an abbot of Clonmacnoise ('Nothing but names', 83 n. 134). Russell does not accept this as a Celtic name: 'The names', 5 n. 4.

[140] *Durham Liber Vitae*, 18v1(8) (ed. Rollason and Rollason, I); AU 732.5 (ed. and transl. Mac Airt and Mac Niocaill, 184–5); AT [731] (ed. and transl. Stokes, I, 196). I think this identification is likely, for the origins of the name 'Garalt' in Ireland are mysterious; see Chadwick, 'Bede, St Colmán', 196. No comparable English name appears in 'The prosopography of Anglo-Saxon England'.

[141] *Durham Liber Vitae*, 21v1(25); 35r1(57) (ed. Rollason and Rollason, I); Russell, 'The names', 39.

[142] The visitors need not have been the individuals whose names appear in the manuscript, but rather those who wished to commemorate them.

[143] *Corpus I*, 161–2. I am very grateful to Victoria Whitworth for drawing this to my attention.

[144] Gunn *et al.*, 'A new runic inscription'; Jesch, *The Viking Diaspora*, 188.

[145] *PNER*, 124; *PNWR*, III, 35; *PNNR*, 255; Smith, 'Irish Influence', 46–50; Fellows-Jensen, *Scandinavian Settlement Names in Yorkshire*, 25–6, 33.

[146] *PNWe*, II, 230; Ekwall, *Scandinavians*, 67–72; Grant, 'A new approach', 80.

reign of Henry I.[147] Several scholars have described the personal names as distinctively Scottish, but in fact all of these examples are attested in Ireland and the Isle of Man.[148] Sockburn's locality might have been a meeting place between for those travelling from the Irish Sea region and the Scottish kingdom, given its location near the eastern terminus of the Stainmore route at Scotch Corner, where it meets Dere Street, the great route to the north.

Another source of information about Gaelic personal names during this period is the reverse legends of late Anglo-Saxon coins. A major reform of coinage took place towards the end of the reign of Edgar (*ob.* 975), after which mint-signatures began to be listed consistently, as well as moneyers' names. At this point it becomes possible to localise the activities of the moneyers (with the caveat that they were not always resident at the mints),[149] as well as to date their issues to a particular reign.[150] The names are accessible thanks to Veronica Smart's compilations of names and groupings into linguistic categories.[151] Gaelic names are not found at mints in southern England, but there are a few possible examples in the Midland towns of the Five Boroughs, including the unusual Cristðegn (a translation of *Gilla-Crist*?).[152] Gaelic names appeared recurrently at Chester, starting in the reign of Athelstan with the moneyer Mældomen (Máel Domnaig), and continuing until the Gilla-Críst who was prolific during the regencies and reigns of the sons of Cnut, approximately 1036–42.[153] The only mint in the former Northumbrian kingdom was York, and in the earlier tenth century it seems to have had an unusual organisation under one 'overlord moneyer', which means that fewer moneyers' names were recorded.[154] Norse names became increasingly prominent among York moneyers later in the century, accounting for three-quarters of the names by the reign of Æthelred.[155]

Gaelic names were less numerous than Norse names among York moneyers, but they recurred throughout the period. The reformed issues of Edgar, Edward the Martyr and Æthelred featured several examples including *Beaniene*, an attempt at a phonetic rendering of Bénén, with a palatalised central -*n*-. Another phonetic rendering is Cieolog for *Cellach*, or alternatively *Cellóc*, where the C is palatalised.[156]

---

[147] Edmonds, 'Names on the Norman edge' (forthcoming). Cf. Roberts, 'Late bý- names', *contra* Fellows-Jensen in *SSNNW*, 22–5, who saw the place-names as tenth-century formations in which the personal names were later replaced.

[148] For the proposed Scottish origin, see Smyth, *Scandinavian York and Dublin*, I, 81; Fellows-Jensen, 'Anthroponymical specifics', 52; Grant, 'A new approach', 72. The 'Mal Lumkun' inscription discussed above features Máel Muire and Dubgall, and Fíacc appears on an inscription at Kirk Braddan (MM 135). For an Irish example, see Gilla Míchíl mac Gillai Cholmáin of Laigin *CGH* 123 c 32 (ed. O'Brien, 62).

[149] Smart, 'Moneyers ... 973–1016', 211–13.

[150] *Ibid.*, 193–4. I have used the dates on the Fitzwilliam Museum's 'Early medieval corpus' website.

[151] I also include more recent additions, which can be traced in her indices to SCBI as well as the EMC: Smart, *Cumulative Index of Volumes 1–20*; *Cumulative Index of Volumes 21–40*.

[152] Dolley, 'OE *Christðegn'; Smart, 'Moneyers ... 973–1016', 239.

[153] SCBI 5 (Pirie, *The Grosvenor Museum I*, 267); 18 (Galster, *Royal Collection, Part IV*, 190–1); 36 (Kluge, *State Museum, Berlin*, 786); 40 (Talvio, *Royal Coin Cabinet*, 163–6).

[154] Blunt *et al.*, *Coinage*, 221–2.

[155] Smart, 'Scandinavians, 178–9, 183.

[156] As Smart points out ('Moneyers ... 973–1016', 230–1), the rendering is not entirely successful since OE *ci* was pronounced [tʃ]. Cellóc is closest to the form on the coin, and is attested in the saint's name Mochellóc, but Cellach is much better evidenced: *Corpus Genealogiarum Sanctorum Hiberniae* 704.191 (ed. Ó Riain, 135); *CGH* (ed. O'Brien, 538–40).

Table 6: York moneyers with Gaelic names, 973–1066

Mint signature	Name-form	Normalised form	Type and reign of issue	SCBI reference (vol. and coin no.)/EMC reference
York	Beaniene	Index II: p. 43: Bénéne (OIr < Lat Benignus)	Edward the Martyr Small Cross 975–8/9	21: xlvi; Grueber, *A Catalogue Vol. 2*, 193
" "	Beolan	Béollán	Edward the Martyr Small Cross 975–8/9 (PASE Beolan 2)	4: 820; 29: 513; EMC 2002.0158; EMC1004.082 EMC 1029.0513
" "	Beolan	" "	Æthelred First Hand 979–85 (PASE Beolan 1)	2: 812; EMC 1002.0812
" "	Beo[]	" " (PASE Beolan 2)	Edward the Martyr Small Cross 975–8/9	9: 430; EMC: 1009.043
	Beollan	" " (PASE Beolan 1)	Æthelred First Small Cross 978–9	11: 61; EMC: 1011.0061
" "	Cielog (Gieolog)	Cellach	Æthelred First Small Cross 978–9	21: xlvi; Hill, 'A find of coins', 161
" "	Crinan	Crínán	Cnut Pointed Helmet 1023–9	13: 585–8; 21: 153–5; 25: 837; 29: 625; 37: 258; 45: 134; 51: 781
" "	Dvfacan	Dubacán	Harold Jewel Cross 1036–8	18: 85; 40: 649
" "	Dvfeoam	" "	" "	40: 650
" "	Fællan	Fáelán	Æthelred First Hand 979–85	Grueber, *A Catalogue Vol. 2*, 215
" "	Giole	Goll? Gille?	Æthelred First Hand 979–85	50: 293
" "	Golla	Goll	Æthelred Crux 991–7	7: 246; 11: 73
" "	Crvcan/ Crucan	Grúcán (Grúagán)	Cnut Pointed Helmet 1023–9	13: 589; 25: 838; 29: 626
			Cnut Short Cross 1029–36	2: 958; 6: 681; 9: 732; 13: 590–604; 17: 348; 21: 196–9; 25: 878; 29: 656–7; 45: 155; 51: 921–2 (29 coins)
" "	Grvrn/ Grurn	" "	Cnut Pointed Helmet 1023–9	13: 699–703; 21: 156–8; 29: 627; 51: 786

" "	Grvcan	" " "	Cnut Pointed Helmet 1023–9	13: 696; 21: 171
			Cnut Short Cross 1029–36	13: 697–8
" "	Crvcann	" " "	Harold Jewel Cross 1036–8	1: 803; 18: 83; 40: 648
" "	Crvca	" " "	" " "	EMC 2004.0250
" "	Crvcan	" " "	" " "	18: 81–2; 40: 646–7
" "	Crucan	" " "	" " "	EMC 1996.0244

The Old Norse name *Íri*, which appears in both Æthelred and Cnut's reigns, seems to refer to Ireland.[157] In the later Anglo-Saxon period, Old Norse names continued to predominate, but Gaelic names also occurred, including the prolific Crínán. The rare name Grucán appears on several issues in various forms, and this name also occurs in the Yorkshire Domesday.[158] *Dubucán* provides further evidence of phonetic rendering since the form *Dufacan* shows medial -*b(h)*- represented appropriately by -*f*-. The moneyers' names strengthen the picture of ongoing communication between York and the Irish Sea region following the collapse of the York–Dublin axis in 954.

My final category of evidence is the Gaelic personal names recorded in Domesday Book. The Domesday commissioners arrived in Yorkshire in 1086, and sought information about current landholders as well as their predecessors *tempore Regis Edwardi* (at the time of King Edward, 1066). The Domesday survey offers a wealth of information about naming practices in eleventh-century Yorkshire, but the text also has pitfalls for scholars of personal names. Domesday landholders tend to be represented only by their forenames, and it is difficult to ascertain how many people bore the same name.[159] This problem is less acute, however, for Gaelic personal names, which were relatively unusual in a Yorkshire context. The Yorkshire Domesday has three main sections: the main text; the *clamores*, or disputes; and the so-called 'Summary', which is itself a composite text. The main text is organised by fief whereas the Summary is arranged geographically for the most part, and there are some discrepancies between these two sections.[160] Such inconsistencies arose because the Summary was composed at an early stage in the Domesday survey, probably in York, whereas the main text was compiled and abbreviated in the Exchequer.[161] The main text of the Yorkshire survey shows signs of hasty compilation and experimentation on the part of the Exchequer scribe, which may account for some unusual orthography.[162] *Crave*, or Craven (including Amounderness in Lancashire) is excluded from the three ridings of Yorkshire and

---

[157] Lind, *Norsk–Isländska Dopnamn*, 656; Smart, 'Moneyers … 973–1016', 229; *eadem*, 'Moneyers … 1017–42', 250; *eadem*, 'Scandinavians, Celts', 178, 182–3. Cf. 'The prosopography of Anglo-Saxon England' Ire 1 & 2.

[158] DB Yorks, 29W2; fol. 330v.

[159] Lewis, 'Joining the dots'. The 'Prosopography of Anglo-Saxon England: Domesday' now greatly facilitates such analyses.

[160] Palliser, 'An introduction', 9–10.

[161] Roffe, 'The Yorkshire summary'.

[162] Roffe, 'Domesday Book'.

given a more cursory treatment. The Amounderness material seems to be reliant on a geld list from 1065, as Chris Lewis has argued.[163]

The personal names of the Yorkshire Domesday survey are disproportionately Norse in origin: the ratio of Norse names to others is 70:30, the highest of any English county.[164] Gaelic names were far less numerous: the map depicts the fifty-one lands in *Eurvicscire* held by men with nineteen different Gaelic personal names, the vast majority of whom had lost their lands by 1086.[165] A very striking distribution emerges, which indicates that Gaelic names were selected for specific reasons, and had not become part of the general name stock.[166] No Gaelic personal names are recorded in the south of England and only a handful in Lincolnshire and Cheshire.[167] There is a cluster of lands associated with Gaelic-named landowners in the hundred of Lonsdale (now part of Lancashire and Cumbria), despite the fact that this area received only perfunctory treatment. Another cluster is found in the valleys of Swaledale and Wensleydale, while Airedale has a reasonable spread. The distribution of Gaelic personal names in Domesday coincides very closely with the major communication routes between York and Dublin, and the distribution of place-names featuring the term *ærgi*.

The first Gaelic personal name to be considered is Máel Coluim, 'devotee of St Columba'. A man named *Malcolun* held one of the 'lands of the king's thanes' in 1086; the Domesday scribe often mistook final 'm' for 'n'.[168] He held Little Ouseburn (West Riding), which had previously belonged to Ormr and Maccus, and lay beside Dere Street. The name *Maccus*, which derives from the Gaelic word *macc*, 'son', is attested among Gaelic–Scandinavian communities.[169] Another man named Máel Coluim may be represented by the forms *Alcolm* and *Alcolme*. This Máel Coluim held lands at Thornton-in-Craven, Earby and 'another Earby' (West Riding), next to the trans-Pennine route through the Ribble–Aire gap.[170] The name *Máel Coluim* rarely occurred in medieval Ireland, but it was strongly associated with the royal dynasty of Alba.[171] The name was also borne by 'devotees of Columba' elsewhere in Scotland; for example, several men named Máel Coluim dwelt near the monastery at Deer (Aberdeenshire), which was dedicated to Drostán and Columba.[172] No doubt the name remained popular in the vicinity of Iona, and so it is possible that the Domesday landholders named Máel Coluim were descendants of Islesmen who settled in Yorkshire under the aegis of the dynasty of Ívarr. This suggestion is supported by the fact that the Yorkshire Domesday *clamores*, 'disputes', mention 'Norman filius Malcolumbe'. The personal name Norman (Norðmaðr) was often given to men of Scandinavian extraction.[173] The long-standing association of Ripon

---

[163] For Craven, see Palliser, 'An Introduction', 4. For the geld list, see Lewis, 'An introduction', 1–2, 8, 31–5.

[164] Parsons, '*Anna, Dot, Thorir …*'.

[165] Glúniairn's complex estate in Wensleydale is counted as one landholding for the purposes of this figure, but the component parts of the estate are shown as dots on the map. Cf. Table 7.

[166] The same was true in the twelfth century: Postles, *The North*, 55.

[167] DB Chesh 14.11; 26.12; fols 266v, 267v; *Domesday Book: Lincolnshire* (ed. Morgan and Thorn, T5; 27.25, 33; 25.1; ed. and transl. Williams and Martin, fols 337r, 358r, 356r).

[168] As in several renderings of *Ergum*, see above, n. 164.

[169] DB Yorks, 29W14; 330v; Thornton, 'Hey Macc!'

[170] DB Yorks, 30W19–21; 332r.

[171] Ó Corráin and Maguire, *Gaelic Personal Names*, 129.

[172] *The Gaelic Notes* (ed. and transl. Jackson, 31–2, 34–5).

[173] DB Yorks, CE23; CW26; 373r, 374r.

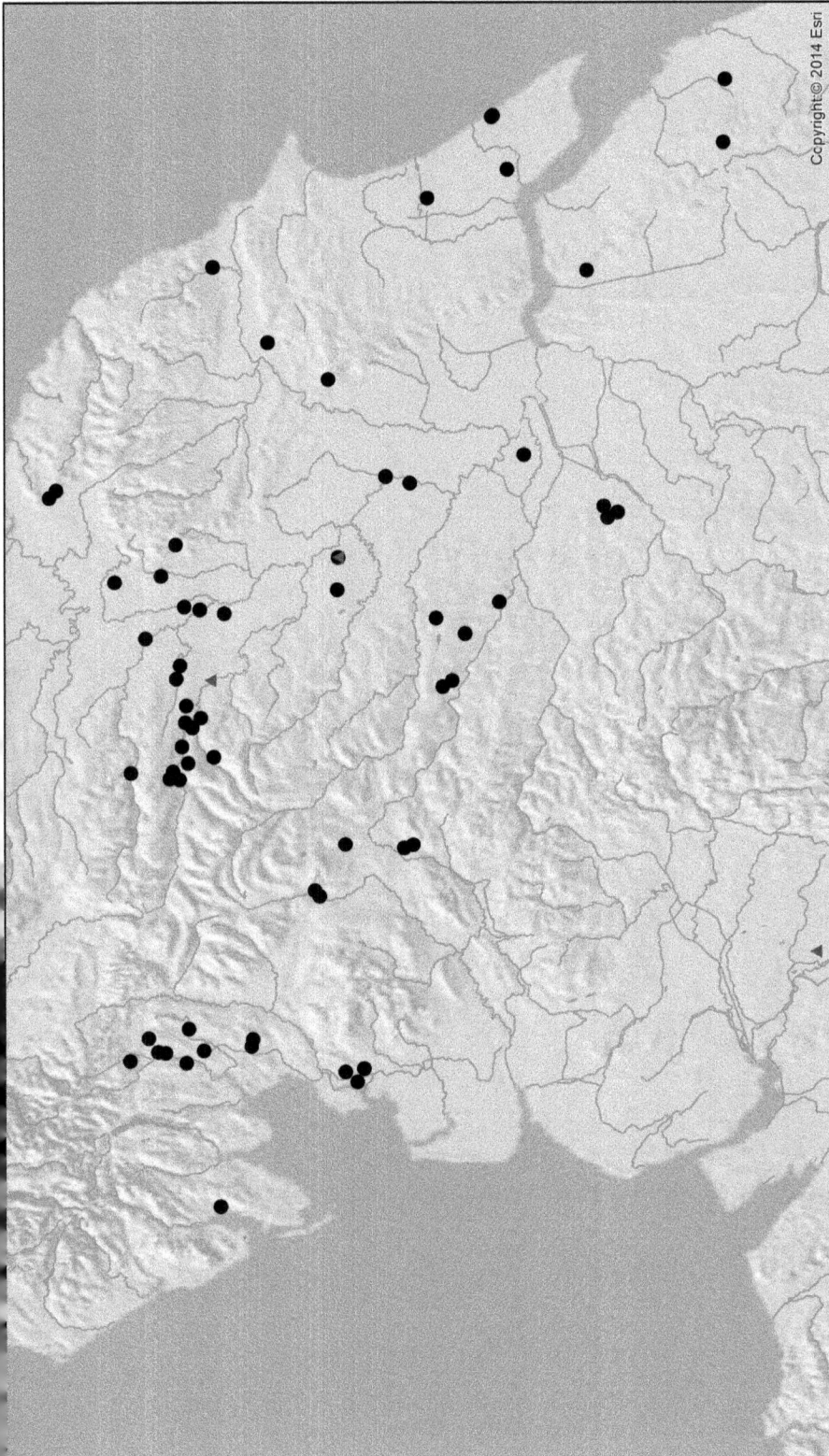

● Gaelic names in 1066

▲ Gaelic names in 1086

Map 9: Gaelic personal names in the Yorkshire Domesday

Table 7: Gaelic names represented in the Yorkshire Domesday

Domesday name form	Normalised Middle Irish form (my identification)	Domesday reference	Domesday folio no.	Identification by Smith, 'Irish Influence', with pp.	Identification by von Feilitzen, with pp.
Alcolm(e)	Máel Coluim	30W19–21	332r	Obscure: 40–1	Obscure: 143
Claman[a]	Error for ON Kalman, from Irish Colmán	1W38	301v	Irish Clamán: 41	Error for ON Kalman: 216
Crin[b]	Crín	6N74	311r	Crín: 41	Crín: 219
Doneuuald	Domnall	6N119	312r	Domnall: 41	/
*Duuan	Dubán	1L8	302r	/	Dubán: 226
Duglel	Dubgall	1N133	301r	Dubhghall: 41–2	Dubhghall: 226
Fech[c] / Feg	Fíacc	30W1 / 30W31	332r / 332r	Fíacc: 42	Fíacc or ON Feigr
Finegal	Findgall	6N11	309r	Finghall: 251	Finghal: 42
Ghilander	Gilla Anndrais	13N12	323r	Gilleandrais: 261	Gilleandrais: 43
Ghilemicel / Ghilemichel / *Gilemichel	Gilla Míchil	1N135 / 30W39 / 1L7	301r / 332r / 302r	Gillemicel: 261	Gillemicel: 42
Ghilepatric / Gilepatric	Gilla Pátraic	6N28, 87, 94, 99, 102 / 6N90	309v, 311r–v / 311r	Gillepatric: 261	Gillepatric: 42
Gilli[d] / Ghile / Ghilla	ON Gilli, from Old/ early Middle Irish Gilla	1E46 / 6N29 / 6N131, 137–8	301r / 309v / 312r–v	ON Gilli, from Irish Gilla: 42	ON Gilli, from Irish Gilla: 261
Glunier	Middle Irish epithet Glún-iairn	1W13, 18–19, 29; 6N92; 9W14, 16, 39–40; 10W39; 30W30	298r, 301r–v, 311r–v, 315r–v, 320r, 332r	Gluniairn: 43	Glúniairnn: 262
Grucan	Grucán[e]	29W2	330v	Possibly an Irish name cognate with Old Welsh Guorcein: 43	Probably Irish; precise etymology uncertain: 276
Macus	Maccus (from Irish macc, 'son')	14E48; 29W14	325r, 330v	An Irish or Welsh name: 44	Old Cornish maccos: 323

Magbanec[f]	Irish macc, 'son' + Welsh epithet pennog	1N18–19	300r	Irish macc + Bennacht: 45	Irish 'the son of Benedict': 323
(Norman filius) Malcolumbe Malcolun	Máel Coluim	CE23; CW26 / 29W14	373r, 374r / 330v	Maelcolumban; Maelcoluim: 45	Maelcolumban: 323
Melmidoc	Máel Máedóc	1N123	300v	Maelmaedhog; 45	Maelmaedhog: 323
Meurdoch Murdac Murdoc	Muiredach	C14 / 14E3 / 14E34, 53	298r / 323v / 324v, 325r	Muiredach: 45	Muiredach: 331
Sudan	Suthain[g]	6N156	313r	Irish *Suthain, found as the second element of Máel Suthain: 46	Perhaps linked to Old Irish suthain, 'eternal': 377

a   I am not persuaded by Smith's suggestion that this form represents clamán, a diminutive of a Gaelic personal name linked with clam, 'wretched'. The Domesday forms of Gaelic personal names are generally phonetic renderings. The medial -m- in clamán would have been pronounced /v/, so one would expect the Domesday form to be clauan (as in the form Duuan for Dubán). Von Feilitzen's identification of Claman with Old Norse Kalman assumes a scribal error, but in other respects the Domesday form matches the pronunciation of the name Kalman. This Norse name ultimately derived from Irish Colmán. See, for example, Landnámabók (ed. Jakob Benediktsson, 62): Kalman var ok irskr, 'Kalman was also Irish'.

b   This name is usually found in the diminutive form Crínán, but the form Crín is represented in a twelfth-century section of the Durham Liber Vitae (fol. 46r). See Russell, 'The names', 37. The name must have originated as an epithet meaning 'withered': eDIL s.v. Crín. The names Crínán and Crín are found throughout Northern Britain, but rarely in Ireland. For several examples, see Woolf, From Pictland to Alba, 249–52. The name Crínán also appears in a runic inscription on the Isle of Man, for which see Holman, Scandinavian Runic Inscriptions, 113–14.

c   The suggestion that these forms represent Old Norse feigr, 'death-bound', was first made by Ekwall in Scandinavians, 83. The word feigr was used as a by-name, but not as a personal name, in Scandinavia: Fellows-Jensen, Scandinavian Personal Names, 81. In contrast, the Gaelic personal name Fíacc was fairly prevalent in Ireland during the tenth and eleventh centuries. See, for example, the numerous examples in CGH (ed. O'Brien, 635–6). The lands associated with Fech and Feg were Giggleswick and Langcliffe. The name also occurs in two Yorkshire place-names in the vicinity: Fixby (Fechesbi in 1086) and Feizor (Fegesargh in the twelfth century): PNWR, III, 35; VI, 226.

d   This name ultimately derives from Irish gilla ('servant, land'), which was used to form patronal names such as Gilla Míchil. The simplex name Gilla was used by Insular Scandinavian communities: O'Brien, 'Names', 229.

e   Cf. the obituary of Maelbrighde Ua Grugáin, AFM 1265 (ed. O'Donovan, III, 396–7).

f   The first element represents Irish macc, 'son'. Smith's suggestion that this is the Irish name 'Maol Beannachta' is problematic because of the lack of the final -a (representing the genitive) in Magbanec.

g   The word suthain is generally used as an adjective meaning 'eternal', but is also attested as a substantive meaning 'long-lived person': eDIL, s.v. suthain. The word was not used as a personal name among medieval Gaelic-speakers, but it did appear as the second element of the name Máel-suthain. The form Suthain is attested in various northern English place-names (for which see Ekwall, Scandinavians, 44), and in the Durham Liber Vitae (for which see Russell, 'The names', 42). I suggest that these forms derived from the name Máel-suthain, which was shortened by analogy with the Máel- compounds that feature a saint's name as their second element.

with the Iona mission, and the increasing interest of Scottish clerics in that heritage, may have helped to perpetuate the name.

Another *máel-* name can be linked more strongly to Ireland. *Melmidoc* (Máel Máedóc) shared the estate of Welbury (North Riding) with a certain *Fredgist* (Friðgestr) in 1066.[174] Welbury is located to the east of Swaledale, very close to Irby. The name *Máel Máedóc* occurred more frequently in Leinster: it appears in the gene-alogies of Fothairt and Dál Messin Corb, for example.[175] This is not surprising, for Leinster was the centre of the cults of two saints named Máedóc. The cult of Máedóc of Ferns was favoured by Uí Chennselaig of southern Leinster, but interest in the cult spread north-eastwards during a revival of Uí Chennselaig power in the mid-eleventh century. The cult of St Máedóc of Cluain Mór was associated with Uí Dúnlainge, whose territory extended towards Dublin's hinterland during the tenth and eleventh centuries.[176] Thus, the name Máel Máedóc might have been brought to Yorkshire by an Irishman from Leinster or by a Hiberno-Scandinavian who had spent time on the edge of Dublin's hinterland. The name adds to the picture that I have already drawn of the popularity of Leinster saints in areas of Gaelic–Scandinavian settlement.[177]

The name rendered *Glunier* by the main scribe has lost its final *-n*, in common with some other names in Great Domesday.[178] *Glunier* represents the Gaelic name *Glúniairn*, which is a translation of the Scandinavian name *Járnkné*, 'iron knee'. The Gaelic version of the name must have originated among Gaelic–Scandinavian communities that had some bilingual members. Two men named *Glúniairn* were active in Ireland; one lived during the ninth century, and the other was the son of Óláfr Cuarán, king of Dublin and one-time king of York. This second Glúniairn (*ob.* 989) later became king of Dublin in his own right.[179] The high standing of the name *Glúniairn* in the dynasty of Ívarr may explain the adoption of the name by Uí Dúnlainge and Uí Fháeláin of Leinster.[180] The name *Glúniairn* may have also influenced the unusual appellation 'Mac Íarainn' given to a king of Uí Enechglaiss, as Colmán Etchingham has noted.[181] These dynasties were all located in the vicinity of the Hiberno-Scandinavian settlements at Dublin and Arklow. It is surely signif-icant that the Domesday officials always recorded Glúniairn's name in its Gaelic form, even though the Norse version would have been more widely understood in Yorkshire. I suggest that the Gaelic version continued to be used because of its pres-tigious associations with Hiberno-Scandinavian leaders. The Glúniairn of Yorkshire Domesday may have been related to Glúniairn, son of Óláfr Cuarán; this association with the dynasty of Ívarr would help to explain how Glúniairn's family managed to amass so many estates in Yorkshire. That Glúniairn was indeed in the top rank of Yorkshire noblemen is suggested by the appearance of *Glonieorn f. Heardulf* among the Northumbrian worthies who rebelled against Earl Tostig in 1065.[182] Glúniairn owned a house in York, as well as an estate in the Vale of York, while his other

---

[174] DB Yorks, 1N123; 300v.
[175] *CGH*, 126 b 1 (ed. O'Brien, 85).
[176] Mac Shamhráin, *Church and Polity*, 97, 133, 214.
[177] See above, 138–44.
[178] Von Feilitzen, *The Pre-Conquest Personal Names*, 262.
[179] Downham, *Viking Kings*, 26, 29, 252–3, 267.
[180] *Corpus Genealogiarum Sanctorum Hiberniae*, 117 d 1; 117 c 51 (ed. Ó Riain, 13–14); AT 1041, 1070 (ed. and transl. Stokes, II, 100, 133).
[181] Etchingham, 'Evidence', 120.
[182] John of Worcester, *Chronicon* (ed. Darlington and McGurk, II, 330–1).

lands were grouped in three clusters on the edge of the Pennines.[183] The southern-most group clustered around the junction of Dere Street and the road running west-wards to Blackstone Edge; further north, he was in charge of lands in Airedale,[184] and he possessed an unusually large and valuable manor in Wensleydale. Presumably the value of this land lay in its proximity to the Roman road that leads towards Morecambe Bay.[185] I suggest that Glúniairn's Gaelic-Scandinavian ancestor was entrusted with these strategic clusters of lands because they overlooked the major communication routes between York and Dublin. Glúniairn's family must have remained in charge of the lands after the fall of the kingdom of York in 954, and no doubt members of the family intermarried with other high-ranking Northumbrians.

Finally, turning to the west, fewer personal names were recorded in the 1065 geld list because lands tended to be listed under one chief settlement. Even so, several Gaelic names appear in the Domesday survey for Amounderness under Tostig's manor of *Hougun*, which was located on and around the Furness penin-sula.[186] The landowners had the Old English names Earnwulf and Clibert (the latter being a distinctively northern name) and the Old Norse names Ormr, Þorfinnr, Þórulfr and Ulfr.[187] Chris Lewis has suggested grounds for identifying Þorfinnr and Ormr with major Yorkshire landholders.[188] The Gaelic names are *Machern* (which I would derive from Mac Íarainn); *Duvan* (Dubán, rendered phonetically); and *Gillemichel* (Gille Míchíl).[189] These men had lands around Morecambe Bay and the Kent Valley, areas that were strategically important for communication across the Irish Sea. *Mac Íarainn* is rare, but attested among Uí Enechglais, who were based in the vicinity of the Hiberno-Scandinavian port of Arklow. *Dubán* is found among the Gaelic–Scandinavian settlers of Iceland, and *Gille Míchíl* is chiefly (if not exclusively) associated with areas north of the Solway.[190] There could be no better illustration of the mixture of Gaelic influences in the Northumbrian kingdom by the mid-eleventh century.

It is worth reflecting on the significance of these Gaelic personal names as evidence for broader historical developments. Eilert Ekwall and many later scholars assumed that Scandinavian settlers brought Gaelic personal names to the west of the Northumbrian kingdom in the early tenth century; in that case the names would have persisted down to the eleventh century through family tradition.[191] I would argue, however, that the names reflect ongoing connections between the Furness peninsula and the Irish Sea region down to *ca* 1065. Gaelic personal names only became popular among Gaelic-Scandinavian communities in the mid- to late-tenth century, and the name *Gille Míchíl* belongs to a type of name that is not attested until

---

[183] DB Yorks, ed. Faull and Stinson, C12; 1W29; 298r; 301v.

[184] DB Yorks, 1W13, 1W17, 1W18, 1W19, 9W14, 9W16, 30W30; 301r, 315r, 332r.

[185] DB Yorks, 6N92; 311r–v.

[186] For the location of *Hougun* (dative plural of ON *haugr* 'at the mounds'), see Farrer *et al.*, *Victoria County History of Lancaster* I, 289 n. 3; Fellows-Jensen, *SSNNW*, 131.

[187] 'Prosopography of Anglo-Saxon England'; *Durham Liber Vitae* (ed. Rollason and Rollason, II, 51).

[188] Lewis, 'Introduction', 33–4; Fellows-Jensen, *Scandinavian Personal Names*, 204–6, 302, 317, 321–7.

[189] I discussed the *ch*- orthography for /k/ above, 139.

[190] Etchingham, 'Evidence', 120; *Landnámabók* (ed. Jakob Benediktsson, 176–7; transl. Pálsson and Edwards, 66); 'People of medieval Scotland database', *s.n. Gille Míchíl*.

[191] Ekwall, *Scandinavians*, 66–72.

that time.[192] Furthermore, I have suggested that the highly unusual name Glúniairn reflects the persistence of high-level dynastic links between York and Dublin down to the early eleventh century. Óláfr Cúarán and his descendants may have cherished their glorious past in York for longer than is apparent in the texts.

As a whole, the linguistic evidence shows a trend towards ever-increasing Gaelic influence in the Northumbrian kingdom during the early medieval period. The 'Golden Age' may have been the high point of ecclesiastical contact, but the Gaelic language seems to have been restricted to specialised uses in churches and at court. Norse speakers put down roots in the tenth century, and Gaelic–Scandinavians from Ireland and the Isles were one element among them. I would not claim that they were the dominant group; indeed, the terminology of social organisation was entirely Norse.[193] During the eleventh century, however, a new wave of Gaelic-speakers moved into the Northumbrian kingdom from various directions: the Solway, the Isle of Man and the Scottish kingdom. These almost entirely unrecorded movements left multi-layered traces in the onomastic record, as Gaelic speakers met Brittonic and Norse speakers, as well as the English-speaking culture of the Northumbrian kingdom.

[192] Ó Cuív, 'Personal names', 11–12.
[193] Andersen, *Det siste norske landnåmet*, 62–117.

8

MOVEMENT AND MATERIAL CULTURE
IN THE NORTHUMBRIAN AND GAELIC WORLDS

Material culture has long been seen as a rich source of information about interaction across the Irish Sea.[1] The relationship between peoples, artefacts and structures is, however, fraught with problems, and the association of style and identity has been the subject of much debate. In this chapter I will not seek to identify 'Gaelic' or 'Northumbrian' material culture, for there was a great deal of variation within the areas inhabited by those peoples. Rather, I trace contacts between specific localities, institutions or social groups.

A comprehensive study of material culture is impossible within the constraints of the book. My main aim in this chapter is to compare and contrast several aspects of material culture with other categories of source material, to test whether they bear out my picture of enduring and varied links between Gaeldom and the Northumbrian kingdom. I will focus on three types of material: ecclesiastical sites, sculpture and portable metalwork. These categories of evidence have the potential to shed light on trends noted elsewhere in the book. Ecclesiastical sites may (or may not) bear out the picture of an upsurge in proprietary churches during the Viking Age, and sculpture has the potential to reveal both high-level ecclesiastical links and the affinities of lay patrons. Personal effects such as dress accoutrements are, by contrast, portable, and may reflect the networks of other social groups (traders, for example). In future, it would be illuminating to augment these case studies with other material, such as the Galloway Hoard, which promises to deepen our understanding of contacts between the Northumbrian kingdom and Gaeldom.[2]

First, I ask how archaeological material can shed light on cultural interaction. The idea of tracing movements of people through distributions of material culture was once a mainstay of the 'culture-historical school', which sought to date phases of material culture in northern and western Europe by reference to the Middle East and the Mediterranean.[3] In the mid-twentieth century, radiocarbon dating upset the relative chronologies that had been developed through this 'diffusionist' approach.[4] Meanwhile, the archaeologist Gustaf Kossinna associated Germanic peoples with specific artefacts, while downplaying external influences, a discredited approach with nationalist connotations.[5] The aftermath of the Second World War swept away

---

[1] See, for example, Moore (ed.), *The Irish Sea Province.*
[2] See below, 54.
[3] Trigger, *A History*, 167. For a seminal example, see Childe, *The Dawn*, esp. 322–40, although Childe ultimately became more interested in economic and technological influences, as seen in his article 'Restrospect', cf. Trigger, *A History*, 244, 250–63.
[4] Renfrew, *Before Civilisation*, esp. 20–68.
[5] Kossinna, *Die Herkunft*, 4: *Kulturgebiete sind Volksgebiete* 'cultural areas are tribal areas'; cf. Veit, 'Ethnic concepts', 36–42; Wood, *The Modern Origins*, 246–8.

these ideas regarding the origins of peoples and their relationship to material culture and language. From the 1960s onwards, the 'New' or 'processual' Archaeology focused on internal innovations and adaptations, rather than cultural contact.[6] By contrast, the 'post-processual' archaeology of the 1980s explored the ways in which material culture can be purposefully manipulated to influence social relations.[7] Artefacts were understood to shape differences between groups, rather than simply reflecting those differences. Consequently it is no longer possible to read off patterns of cultural influence from distributions of artefacts, in the manner of the culture-historical school.[8]

These broader developments in archaeology have coincided with, and influenced, reappraisals of medieval ethnic identity. It is now recognised that medieval peoples could select aspects of their appearance to emphasise their shared consciousness, as well as their difference from other groups.[9] Thus the correlation between artefacts and peoples is far from straightforward; there is a 'complex pattern of overlapping material-culture distributions relating to the repeated realization and transformation of ethnicity in different social contexts'.[10] A relatively new area of enquiry is the relationship between material culture and other identities, such as gender, status, locality or age.[11] Studies of nation and culture have often focused on male-dominated spheres, but there is now recognition that women played an active role in cultural interaction. In some contexts they became the bearers of tradition, as manifested in kin relations as well as language, dress and customs.[12]

A key challenge is pinpointing at what level group identities or places of origin became visible in material culture. The term 'Gaelic' has proved a fruitful way to look at both the thought-world of medieval authors and linguistic influences, yet it is problematic to assume a correlation between speech communities and distributions of artefacts.[13] It cannot be claimed that a common material culture encompassed the territories inhabited by Gaelic speakers; indeed, dissimilarities between the material cultures of Argyll and Dál Riata in Ireland have prompted scepticism of the Dál Riatan origin story.[14] Furthermore, material culture was sometimes deployed to mark and foster specific group identities within Gaeldom; for example, the inhabitants of Hiberno-Scandinavian towns expressed their cultural distinctiveness through urban

---

[6] Tallgren, 'The method', is an early critique of the culture-historical approach. Classic works of the 'New Archaeology' include Binford, 'Archaeology', 218–19; Clarke, 'Archaeology', 14, discussed by Trigger, *A History*, 206, 244–88, 313–19.

[7] Hodder, *Reading the Past*, 11–13; Trigger, *A History*, 348–57.

[8] Hodder, 'Economic and social stress'; *idem, Reading the Past*, 2–3, 8; Shennan, 'Archaeological "cultures"'.

[9] See above, 3. In the context of archaeology, see Lucy, 'Ethnic and cultural identities', 91, 96–7; Curta, 'Some remarks', 172–3; *idem*, 'Medieval archaeology', 539; Jones, *The Archaeology*, 3; Pohl, 'Telling the difference', 40.

[10] Jones, *The Archaeology*, 124.

[11] Díaz-Andreu and Lucy, 'Introduction', 9; Lucy, 'Ethnic and cultural identities', 105–6; Curta, 'Medieval archaeology', 542.

[12] Effros, 'Dressing conservatively', 173–84; Hakenbeck, *Local, Regional and Ethnic Identities*, 143. For the ascription of the role of 'cultural reproducers' to some women, see Yuval-Davis, *Gender and Nation*, 23, 39–67. See below, 216–17.

[13] Lucy, 'Ethnic and cultural identities', 92; cf. Zvelebil, 'At the interface'.

[14] Campbell, 'Were the Scots Irish?'; Ian Armit has suggested that further investigation of Argyll's settlement archaeology is required to verify the apparently stark contrast: 'Irish–Scottish connections', 2.

building styles.[15] Conversely, specific practices acquired varied associations: mound burial might recall the Scandinavian homelands; or be seen as a feature of the Isle of Man and what is now Cumbria; or as a pagan practice.[16] I have already traced instances of localised contacts, as well as links between specific institutions, and I will pursue the material culture with the same focus. This is not, then, a full survey of material culture in the Northumbrian kingdom. I will focus on attributes that are suspected of being linked with different parts of the Gaelic world.

Ecclesiastical sites

To begin, I will explore several early medieval church sites that have features suggestive of links with Ireland, the Isles and Argyll. The search for these characteristics has been a recurring theme since Charles Thomas's work in the second half of the twentieth century. He sought to identify Irish attributes in the Solway area through criteria such as slab-shrines, small timber chapels and curvilinear enclosures.[17] He was working at a time when the Rhinns of Galloway were thought to have been settled from Ireland in the early sixth century; the recent reappraisal of this migration opens up consideration of later influences.[18] The matter has continued to attract interest, for Ann Hamlin made comparisons between the ecclesiastical archaeology of Galloway and that of north-eastern Ireland.[19] More recently still, Nicola Toop has designated the Rhinns and Machars a 'western zone' in terms of its monumentality.[20]

First, I will briefly assess the state of knowledge about the early medieval churches in the west and north of the Northumbrian kingdom, before reviewing features that may be diagnostic of Irish influence. The renowned ecclesiastical complex at Whithorn dominates the literature because it has undergone a complex series of investigations. These began with nineteenth- and mid-twentieth-century work to the east of the priory church, which was presumed to be the site of the principal early medieval church.[21] Peter Hill carried out the most extensive campaign of excavations between 1984 and 1991, focusing on a flank of the hill south of the priory. This work discovered stark changes in building styles and material culture during the period from the sixth century to the eleventh.[22] In subsequent years, York Archaeological Trust undertook excavations elsewhere on the hill, clarifying the relationship between the settlement zone and the area of burials to the south.[23] Most recently, Adrián Maldonado and Katherine Forsyth have raised the question of whether Whithorn was in fact a monastic site in its earliest incarnation, for its quantities of imported pottery

[15] Wallace, 'The archaeological identity', esp. 47–64; Downham, 'Living on the edge', 35–6; Griffiths, *Vikings*, 127.
[16] Griffiths, 'Settlement and acculturation', 127, 133–4; Downham, 'Coastal communities', 375–6.
[17] Thomas, *The Early Christian Archaeology*, 41–3, 58, 72–4, 142.
[18] *Ibid.*, 88; see above, 160–1.
[19] Hamlin, *Ninian and Nendrum*, ed. Fry, esp. 14–15. Ann Hamlin's Whithorn lecture was originally delivered in 2001, and published posthumously in 2014.
[20] Toop, 'Northumbria', 94.
[21] Radford, 'Excavations at Whithorn, 1949', esp. 106–19; *idem*, 'Excavations at Whithorn: final report'.
[22] Hill, *Whithorn*, 8–10.
[23] Pollock, *Whithorn 6*; Clarke, 'Seeking St Ninian'; McComish and Petts, *Archaeological Investigations*. Meanwhile, Headland Archaeology have analysed late-medieval graves that were uncovered in the mid-twentieth century: Lowe, *'Clothing for the Soul Divine'*.

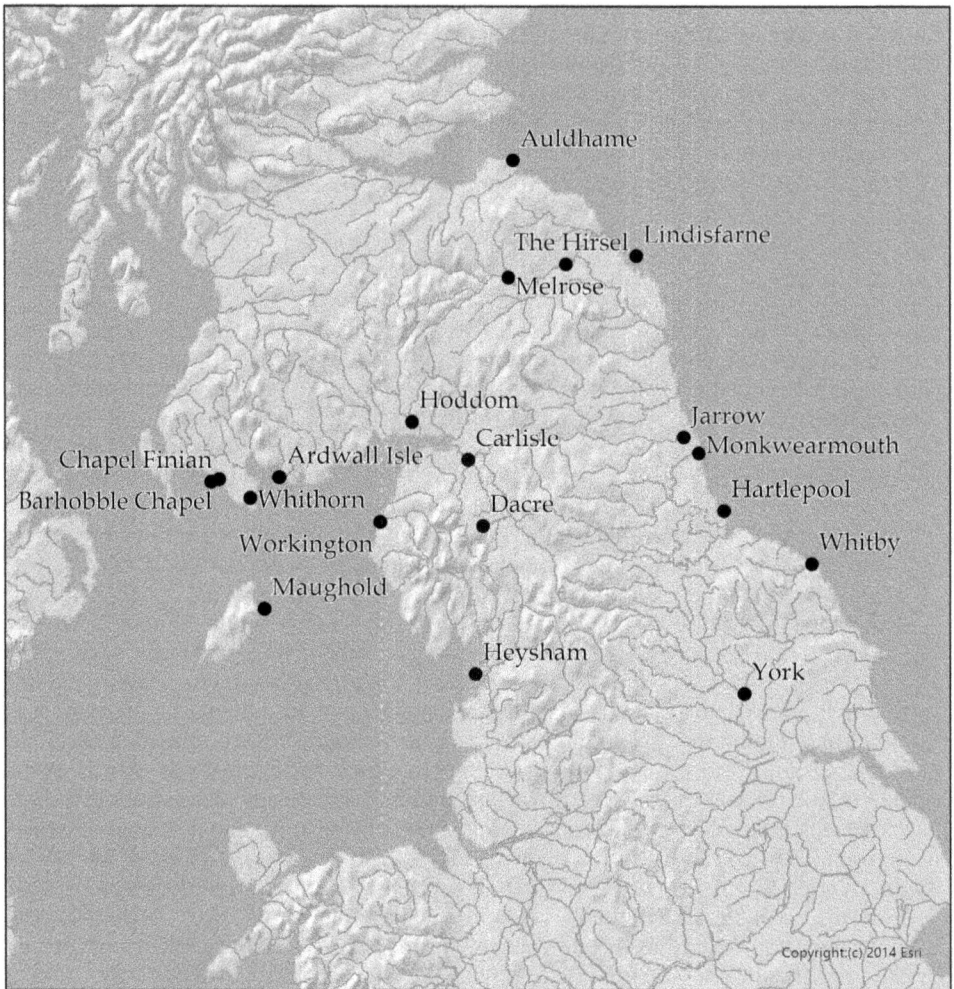

Map 10: Sites mentioned in Chapter 8

and glass resemble those at high-status secular sites.[24] Whatever the early origins of the site, a shrine complex had been installed by the seventh century.[25] Another major ecclesiastical site has been investigated further east along the Solway, at Hoddom (Dumfries and Galloway, formerly Dumfriesshire). In 1991, quarrying prompted excavation of an enclosure, and a number of early medieval domestic buildings were

---

[24] I am grateful to these scholars for sharing their views at the highly productive 'Whitfest' in Glasgow in 2008. Their ongoing work is cited at: http://www.whithorn.com/timeline/christian-settlement/. Ewan Campbell has also stressed Whithorn's uniqueness among the high-status sites that enjoyed these imports: *Continental and Mediterranean Imports*, 117, as has Márkus, *Conceiving the Nation*, 100–1.

[25] Hill, *Whithorn*, 89, 103–4 110–11, 114, 134–43, 148.

discovered.[26] As to Cumbria, during the 1980s the early monastery at Dacre was partially uncovered, and an area of Carlisle Cathedral was excavated prior to the construction of a new treasury, revealing Viking-Age graves.[27]

Several smaller churches have been investigated, notably Ardwall Isle, where Charles Thomas conducted excavations in the mid-1960s. His work revealed a cemetery focused on a shrine and a small timber church, which was later reconstructed in stone.[28] Portions of the buildings at Chapel Finian and Barhobble Chapel (Dumfries and Galloway, formerly Wigtownshire) and Kirkmirran (formerly Dumfriesshire) have been explored, and Ruthwell churchyard has undergone small-scale excavation.[29] The ruined chapel of St Patrick at Heysham (Lancashire) has been excavated, along with a graveyard to the south.[30] The nave of St Michael's Church, Workington, suffered a serious fire in 1994, and subsequent archaeological work uncovered two phases of early medieval graves enclosed by a ditch.[31] In the more northerly parts of the Northumbrian kingdom, excavations at Auldhame have uncovered a single-chamber church that probably replaced a seventh-century building, as well as evidence for a literate monastic culture.[32] The unicameral drystone church at the Hirsel (Berwickshire) was founded as a proprietary church in the tenth or eleventh century.[33]

In order to weigh up the cultural affinities of these churches, I will consider parallels from neighbouring areas, including the heartlands of the Northumbrian kingdom. Excavations have taken place at several major monastic sites in eastern Northumbria, including sites that were closely linked with Iona in their early days. Lindisfarne's plan can only be tentatively reconstructed as yet, although recent geophysical work has identified features that may clarify the route of the *vallum*. Furthermore, ongoing excavations to the east of the priory church have revealed an early medieval cemetery and a new name-stone. Separate excavations on a promontory to the south have unearthed remains of a church made of gleaming sandstone.[34]

---

[26] Lowe *et al.*, 'New light'; *idem, Excavations at Hoddom*. For earlier excavations, see RCAHMS, *Seventh Report*, 93–4; Radford, 'Hoddom', 180–1.

[27] Dacre: Leech and Newman, 'Excavations at Dacre', 87–93; *eidem* (eds), *The Early Christian Monastery* (forthcoming). I am grateful to Rachel Newman for allowing me to view this work in draft. Carlisle: McCarthy, 'The origins', 36–8; *idem et al.*, 'Were there Vikings in Carlisle?', 139–44; *idem et al.*, 'A post-Roman sequence'. An up-to-date synthesis of ecclesiastical sites in the north-west will feature in the new North-West Regional Research Framework. In the meantime, see Newman *et al.*, 'The early medieval period: resource assessment' (2004).

[28] Thomas, 'An Early Christian cemetery', esp. 130–1. An earlier version of this report is also available: *idem*, 'Ardwall Island'.

[29] Radford, 'The excavations'; Crowe, 'An excavation at Kirkmirran'; *idem*, 'Excavations at Ruthwell'; Cormack, 'Barhobble'.

[30] Potter and Andrews, 'Excavation and survey'.

[31] Flynn, 'Excavations at St. Michael's'; McCarthy and Paterson, 'A Viking-Age site'. I am grateful to Adam Parsons for information about the two phases of early medieval burial at the site, and showing me the excavation report while it was forthcoming: Zant and Parsons, *St Michael's Church, Workington*.

[32] Crone and Hindmarch, *Living and Dying*, 14–18, 136–8.

[33] Cramp, *The Hirsel Excavations*, 49–50, 72–4.

[34] For earlier work, see O'Sullivan, 'The plan'; the recent geophysics is discussed in Petts, 'Expanding the archaeology', 303–6. For ongoing excavations east of the priory, see Casswell, 'Lindisfarne', 3, 13–14 and the project website: https://digventures.com/lindisfarne/. The newly uncovered church lacks dating evidence but is suspected to be from the late-seventh or eighth century. See Carlton, 'Archaeological excavations', and the project website: http://www.peregrinilindisfarne.org.uk/community-archaeology-group/.

The double houses (male and female communities) of Whitby and Hartlepool had links with Lindisfarne through Abbess Hild.[35] The excavations at Whitby took place before the advent of modern recording techniques, but yielded a wealth of cross fragments, imported pottery and metalwork.[36] More recent work at Hartlepool unearthed sequences of timber and stone-footed domestic buildings as well as metalworking apparatus.[37] Excavations to the south of St Peter's church, Monkwearmouth and St Paul's church, Jarrow have uncovered cemeteries and impressive structures built of stone and mortar, roofed with lead and lit by stained-glass windows.[38] Northumbrian stone architecture can be further explored at the intact church of St John, Escomb (Co. Durham), which dates back to the late-seventh or eighth century.[39]

There is an increasing body of evidence for ecclesiastical sites and architecture in the Gaelic world. A number of major Irish churches have undergone partial excavation, ranging from early twentieth-century work at Nendrum to recent excavations prior to road-building at Clonfad (Co. Westmeath).[40] The most comprehensive excavations of ecclesiastical sites have taken place in the west of Ireland, and there has also been much consideration of the major complex at Armagh.[41] Tomás Ó Carragáin's recent reappraisal of early Irish church buildings adds further dimensions to the evidence drawn from excavations.[42] On the other side of the North Channel, Iona has undergone a series of investigations, although it is hard to reconstruct an overall picture of the site.[43] A project is currently exploring the archive from Charles Thomas's excavations in the 1950s and 1960s, which promises to clarify the nature of the *vallum* 'boundary'.[44] Another monastery with Columban links has been excavated at Portmahomack in eastern Pictland.[45] Maughold, the chief monastery of the Isle of Man, had four subsidiary keeills in addition to the main church, although it is unclear when all of these structures were built. There is also an impressively large collection of sculpture, of which the earliest pieces date from the seventh century, and the majority to the Viking Age.[46] Thus it is necessary to proceed with caution when comparing churches from the edges of the

[35] *HE* IV, 21, 2–4 (ed. Lapidge, II, 318–22; ed. and transl. Colgrave and Mynors, 236–8).

[36] Peers and Radford, 'The Saxon monastery'; White, 'Finds from the Anglian monastery'; Cramp, 'A reconsideration', 64–73.

[37] Daniels, 'The Anglo-Saxon monastery'.

[38] Cramp, 'Excavations at the Saxon monastic sites', 31–7, 45–50; *eadem*, *Wearmouth and Jarrow*, esp. 91–109, 187–230.

[39] Taylor and Taylor, *Anglo-Saxon Architecture*, I, 234–8.

[40] Lawlor, *The Monastery*; Stevens, 'A monastic enclosure site'; O'Sullivan *et al.*, *Early Medieval Ireland*, 140. Modern developments in infrastructure and construction have increased the numbers of excavated settlements in Ireland, as highlighted by Bhreathnach, *Ireland in the Medieval World*, 17.

[41] O'Sullivan *et al.*, *Early Medieval Ireland*, 139–40. For Armagh, see Hamlin and Lynn (eds), *Pieces of the Past*, 57–61; Aitchison, *Armagh*.

[42] Ó Carragáin, *Churches*.

[43] Reece, *Excavations in Iona*; McCormick, 'Iona: the archaeology'; O'Sullivan, 'Iona: archaeological investigations'.

[44] Iona Research Group, 'Charles Thomas excavations': https://ionaresearchgroup.arts.gla.ac.uk/index.php/projects/charles-thomas-excavations-1956-1963/.

[45] Carver, *Portmahomack*.

[46] Kermode and Bruce, *The Manx Archaeological Survey*, I (report 4), 10–28. Early pieces of sculpture include the slab of Bishop Irneit, discussed above at 116. Trench-Jellicoe, 'A re-definition', has re-dated some pieces to the Viking Age. I have benefited from hearing Andrew Johnson speak about his ongoing work on the Manx keeills.

Northumbrian kingdom with their counterparts. No normative model of a 'Gaelic', 'Irish' or 'Northumbrian' church is available since the ecclesiastical culture of these territories was diverse, and our knowledge of it is partial. However, the evidence is sufficient to enable comparison between Northumbrian churches and those in the Hebrides, the Isle of Man and Ireland.

One striking feature of early ecclesiastical sites is the enclosures. They served spiritual needs, demarcating zones of particular sanctity and separating the sacred world from secular society. Graveyards might be defined by smaller enclosures, while larger, perhaps multiple, boundaries encircled major ecclesiastical establishments.[47] Descriptions of the biblical city offered a common source of inspiration for the layout of Irish and English churches,[48] although the form and fabric of their enclosures could vary considerably. Curvilinear enclosures have long been seen as a feature of Irish or Brittonic churches, in contrast to the rectilinear enclosures of some major Anglo-Saxon monasteries.[49] The evidence is of variable quality, for few enclosures have been dated in the same way as the backfill of Hartlepool's curvilinear *vallum*, which yielded bone radiocarbon-dated to the seventh century.[50] Nevertheless, there are sufficient examples to assess whether Irish and Anglo-Saxon enclosures differed in shape.

The archetypal Irish ecclesiastical site was surrounded by multiple circuits, as shown by the illustration of a monastery in the Book of Mulling. This depiction may be somewhat removed from reality since it was influenced by Continental drawings; nevertheless, it illustrates the ideal of the circular enclosure.[51] Multiple circuits facilitated the separation of zones that contained different levels of holiness, as the *Collectio Canonum Hibernensis* relates.[52] The three cashels (stony walls) that surround Nendrum seem to replicate this ideal on the ground, and recent excavations at Clonfad have revealed parts of two curving ditches dating from the earliest monastic phase.[53] As to inspiration from the secular world, circular enclosures and buildings had once been widespread across Europe, but they gradually waned and were then revived in sixth-century Ireland in the form of the *ráith* 'ring-fort'.[54] Among the Britons, circular structures persisted alongside rectilinear forms inspired by Roman architecture.[55] This may also be true of the western parts of the Anglo-Saxon kingdoms, and indeed the Northumbrian elites wrested oval-shaped hillforts from

---

[47]   Petts, 'Cemeteries and boundaries', 26.
[48]   Blair, 'Anglo-Saxon minsters', 231, 235–46; *idem, The Church*, 196–8; Doherty, 'The monastic town', 46–7.
[49]   Thomas, *The Early Christian Archaeology*, 41–3.
[50]   Daniels, 'The Anglo-Saxon monastery', 161–2, 168, 184, 207. For enclosures on aerial photographs, see Norman and St Joseph, *The Early Development*, 95–112; Aitchison, *Armagh*, 211–33.
[51]   Nees, 'The colophon drawing'.
[52]   *Collectio Canonum Hibernensis* 44.5 (ed. Wasserschleben, *Die irische Kanonensammlung*, 202); Doherty, 'The monastic town', 54; Bitel, *Isle of the Saints*, 61 and n. 10; Ó Carragáin, *Churches*, 58–9.
[53]   Lawlor, *The Monastery*, 95–101; Jope, *An Archaeological Survey*, 293–4; Stevens, 'A monastic enclosure site', 9–11; O'Sullivan *et al.*, *Early Medieval Ireland*, 145–8.
[54]   There has been debate about the dating of the ring-forts; here I follow Stout, *The Irish Ringfort*, 24–9; O'Sullivan *et al.*, *Early Medieval Ireland*, 322. For their links between ring-forts and church sites, see Bitel, *Isle of the Saints*, 59–61; Edwards, *The Archaeology*, 106.
[55]   Blair, *The British Culture*, 16–17; *idem, Building Anglo-Saxon England*, 35.

the Britons.[56] The Irish, and to a lesser extent the Britons, were 'the last inhabitants of a circular world', but it was in Ireland that those forms persisted most strongly.[57]

In Northumbria, the circuits of holy land at the Cuthbertine churches of Crayke and Carlisle recall the Irish idea of sacred space, and the zone of sanctuary at Wetheral (Cumbria) is comparable to the Irish *termonn*.[58] Curvilinear enclosures are found at a broad range of ecclesiastical sites, including local churchyards.[59] The small church and cemetery complex at Ardwall Isle was surrounded by an oval, stone-faced bank, and a Roman-era oval enclosure is located close to the renowned Northumbrian cross at Ruthwell (Dumfries and Galloway, formerly Dumfriesshire).[60] At nearby Hoddom, a D-shaped enclosure had been purpose-built to extend a boundary formed by the River Annan. The man-made features must have been constructed by the mid-seventh century, given radiocarbon dating of charcoal over the palisade and the earliest fill deposits in the ditch.[61] Similarly, the monastery at Melrose was surrounded by a meander in the River Tweed that was joined together by a man-made enclosure, replicating the island setting of its mother house, Lindisfarne.[62] In cases such as Melrose and Ardwall, the curvilinear enclosures are in keeping with Irish connections; Ruthwell, however, reminds us that there were also local sources of inspiration.

The correspondence between rectilinear enclosures and Anglo-Saxon minsters seems more straightforward. Some prominent Anglo-Saxon ecclesiastical communities were founded within Roman forts, including St Peter's church at York, the forerunner to York minster. York's status as the capital of *Britannia Inferior*, as well as a fourth-century episcopal centre, resonated with Paulinus's mission and the later archbishops.[63] Roman walls were attractive to ecclesiastical communities of all sizes since they helped to demarcate sacred space from the outside world.[64] *Romanitas* was particularly meaningful to communities associated with St Wilfrid, including the churches founded within the forts at Ribchester and possibly Lancaster (Lancashire).[65]

---

[56] Blair, *The British Culture*, 22; *idem*, *Building Anglo-Saxon England*, 35–8. For the hillfort at Dunbar, see *Vita Sancti Wilfridi* 38 (ed. and transl. Colgrave, 76–7); Alcock, *Kings and Warriors*, 213–14. The double-house of *urbs Coludi* was once identified with a promontory fort: Thomas, *The Early Christian Archaeology*, 35–6; Blair, 'Anglo-Saxon minsters', 233, n. 27; *idem*, *The Church*, 198, 268–70. Recent discoveries of an enclosure and artefacts suggest, however, that the monastery was located closer to Coldingham Priory: Stronach, 'The Anglian monastery', 397–8, 415–19.

[57] Edwards, *The Archaeology*, 17–19. For the quotation, see Bradley, *The Idea of Order*, 215.

[58] For *termonn*, see *eDIL*, *s.v.*; Doherty, 'The monastic town', 56–8; Stalley, 'Ecclesiastical architecture', 717. For Carlisle, Crayke and Wetheral, see Blair, *The Church*, 222–3 and above, 107–8.

[59] O'Sullivan, 'Curvilinear churchyards'.

[60] Thomas, 'An Early Christian cemetery', 130, 143; Crowe, 'Excavations at Ruthwell', 40, 45–7.

[61] Crowe, 'Looking for a monastery'; Lowe, 'New light', 12–5; *idem*, *Excavations at Hoddom*, 10, 18–21, 32–8, 171–2, 186–90.

[62] Canmore ID 55629; RCAHMS, *An Inventory*, II, 323 (no. 620); Thomas, *The Early Christian Archaeology*, 35–6.

[63] *HE* II, 14, 1 (ed. Lapidge, I, 368–71; ed. and transl. Colgrave and Mynors, 186–9); Palliser, *Medieval York*, 16, 19. David Rollason has highlighted sub-Roman ecclesiastical discontinuity, noting for example that the fourth-century church would have been located outside the fort, rather than on the site of the minster: *Northumbria*, 77–8.

[64] Blair, *The Church*, 196; Bell, 'Churches on Roman buildings'. At 14–17, Bell notes that there is a cluster of churches built in former Roman forts around the western end of Hadrian's Wall.

[65] Lancaster: Shotter and White, *Roman Fort*, 3, 23–7; *Corpus IX*, 215–33 (Lancaster St Mary 1–29, Vicarage Field 1–3). Ribchester: *ibid.*, 236–7 (Ribchester 1–2). Links between Wilfrid and the Ribble and Lune Valleys are suggested by Clark, 'Wilfrid's lands', 30 and above 116–17.

Ecclesiastical communities could replicate Roman rectilinear layouts even when they were founded outside forts, as was the case at Jarrow. Nearby forts such as *Arbeia* were ready sources of building stone, while grid-planning techniques could be learnt from continental contacts.[66] Roman Britain did not have the monopoly on rectilinear enclosures, however, for one is also suspected at Iona, and recent excavations suggest that it was purpose-built for the early monastery.[67] Overall, then, enclosures had cultural and theological resonances, but they are not a failsafe indicator of the origins of ecclesiastical influences in the Northumbrian kingdom.

To illustrate this point in more detail, it is worth exploring the evolution of Whithorn's enclosures. The earliest boundary was a curvilinear ditch, which encircled the area in which the ruined cathedral currently stands; an enlarged version underlay a Northumbrian hall.[68] This enclosure was not traced during recent excavations at Whithorn, and so its shape and extent are somewhat uncertain.[69] The inner zone was subsequently re-planned in a rectilinear format, a development dated to the Northumbrian period by coin losses.[70] The rectilinear layout was in turn superseded, and new curvilinear ditches were laid out alongside new buildings for Hiberno-Scandinavian craft-workers.[71] At first sight the development of Whithorn's plan supports the notion that Northumbrians imposed rectilinear layouts. Yet the minster continued to be surrounded by a curvilinear outer boundary until the early Viking Age.[72] This boundary was slight and ephemeral in contrast to the substantial works seen at other major ecclesiastical sites.[73]

Other aspects of ecclesiastical sites hint more strongly at connections with the Gaelic world. In Anglo-Saxon England, saints' bodies tended to rest in the main church, whereas in Ireland and on Iona, shrines provided a separate focus for relics.[74] Ardwall Isle had an underground cavity that was probably covered by slabs, as well as a timber church next to a rectilinear 'corner-post' shrine.[75] The complex was transformed by a stone church and a new phase of burials, a change that apparently occurred under Northumbrian control, although there are Irish

---

[66] Cramp, 'Excavations at the Saxon monastic sites', 44; *eadem*, 'St Paul's church', 28–35, esp. 30; *eadem*, *Wearmouth and Jarrow*, 26, 207, 359; Blair, *Building Anglo-Saxon England*, 148–9.

[67] The rectilinear layout is suggested by RCAHMS, *Argyll*, 36–9. A prehistoric origin was posited by McCormick *et al.*, 'Excavations at Iona', 80, 104. However, the Iona Research Group has recently dated the lowest fill of one section to AD 580–660: 'Excavations on Iona, 2017'. Investigations of the *vallum* in the 1950s and 1960s are discussed by Campbell and MacIver, 'Excavations at Iona Abbey', 14–15, 42–4, 96.

[68] Hill, *Whithorn*, 28–9, 31, 69, 76–9, 91–3.

[69] McComish and Petts, 'Archaeological excavations', 185.

[70] Hill, *Whithorn*, 112, 135–6.

[71] *Ibid.*, 190–1, 199; 186; 201–33.

[72] *Ibid.*, 31, 33, 111–12, 133, 181, 207, 218.

[73] Petts, 'Cemeteries and boundaries', 30.

[74] Ó Carragáin, *Churches*, 71–2. Blair, *The Church*, 145 distinguishes between prestigious minsters with above-ground coffins, and minsters where founder-saints remained in their original graves.

[75] Thomas, 'An Early Christian cemetery', 141–2, 167–9. Thomas placed the slab-shrine and earliest burials before the church. Tomás Ó Carragáin has challenged this sequence of 'undeveloped' to 'developed' cemeteries in respect of Ireland: *Churches*, 67. At Ardwall, the lack of dating evidence makes it uncertain whether any burials preceded the church. On the affinities of the shrines, see Thomas, *The Early Christian Archaeology*, 141–4, 150–60; cf. Cramp, *Whithorn*, opposite fig. 6.

parallels for this development.[76] Whithorn also had a rectangular structure marked with crosses, which was aligned with a mortuary enclosure and a circular structure that may have been a shrine.[77] This phase of the site is dated to the seventh century because it coincided with the importation of E-ware pottery. The log-coffin burial rite was also introduced at this point; it has a few parallels in northern and western Britain, but in this location it could potentially have been inspired by burial practices in Ireland.[78] Following Northumbrian takeover, the possible circular shrine was initially accommodated within an oratory complex, and was only demolished during late-eighth-century rebuilding.Other organisational changes reflect the relationship of the church to its community, such as the establishment of a children's graveyard.[79] Further east, stone fragments from Jedburgh and Ancrum belonged to a house-shaped shrine that was inspired by continental examples or Irish slab-shrines; one suggestion is that it was the shrine of St Boisil. The double vinescroll decoration derives from the Northumbrian repertoire of the eighth century.[80] At all three of these sites, there are hints that traditions from Ireland and Iona were mingling with those of the Northumbrian heartlands.

Turning to the fabric of churches, it is worth asking whether there were distinctive building styles in the Northumbrian kingdom and the Gaelic world. This is implied by Bede's statement that Fínán's church at Lindisfarne was constructed *more Scottorum* 'in the manner of the *Scotti*' in oak and thatch, whereas Jarrow's stone buildings were built *more Romanorum* 'in the manner of the Romans'.[81] Bede's depiction was to some extent symbolic, linking Roman-style stone edifices to the Easter-dating current in Rome.[82] Nevertheless, his characterisation is not unique, for Conchubranus described a wooden church as built *more Scoticarum* in his eleventh-century *Vita Monennae*.[83] In Ireland, mortared stone churches were indeed uncommon until the tenth century, although drystone buildings were constructed in specific areas. The *dairthech* 'oak house; wooden church' was the typical form, and it could be lavishly built.[84] The early *damliac* 'stone church' at Duleek (Co. Meath) lay in reach of the Irish Sea, hence it may have been inspired either by Northumbrian stone-built churches or by sub-Roman structures in western Britain.[85] Armagh's *oratorium lapideum* 'stone oratory' was recorded in 789; it

---

[76] Thomas, 'An Early Christian cemetery', 131–41. Thomas compared the timber to stone sequence at Church Island (Co. Kerry): O'Kelly, 'Church Island', 58–9, 61–6, 115–20, 128.

[77] Hill, *Whithorn*, 92–6. The shrine interpretation is disputed by Maldonado, 'Burial', 21 on the basis of stratigraphy.

[78] *Ibid.*, 103–15; Clarke, 'Seeking St Ninian', 24. The log-coffin rite is discussed in Maldonado, 'Burial', 16.

[79] Hill, *Whithorn*, 37–8, 134–50, 167–72; Maldonado, 'Burial', 9.

[80] RCAHMS, *An Inventory*, I, 207–8; Radford, 'Two Scottish shrines', 43–7; Thomas, *The Early Christian Archaeology*, 147–50; Cramp, 'The Anglian sculptures', 281.

[81] *HE* III, 25, 1 (ed. Lapidge, II, 142; ed. and transl. Colgrave and Mynors, 294–5).

[82] Gem, 'Towards an iconography', 1–9; *idem*, 'Architecture', 29–56.

[83] Conchubranus, *Vita Monennae* III, 12 (ed. Esposito, 237; ed. Ulster Society for Medieval Latin Studies, 446–7); cf. Reeves, *The Life*, 177–8, n. e.

[84] Radford, 'The earliest Irish churches', 1–2; Hamlin, 'The study', 118; Stalley, 'Ecclesiastical architecture', 715; Ó Carragáin, *Churches*, 56.

[85] Macdonald, 'Notes on monastic archaeology', 306–7 (Northumbrian influence); Ó Carragáin, *Churches*, 60–1 (Whithorn); O'Keeffe, *Romanesque Ireland*, 68–9. This *damliac* is first mentioned in Tírechán's late-seventh-century *Collectanea*, 27.(3) (ed. and transl. Bieler, *The Patrician Texts*, 146–7).

conveyed an appropriate sense of *Romanitas* for an ecclesiastical community that had relics of Roman martyrs.[86]

On the other side of the Irish Sea, there was some variation in ecclesiastical architecture, as seen at Whithorn. The site already had a stone church (not yet located), which St Nynia is reputed to have founded in honour of St Martin.[87] The excavations of the 1980s uncovered a subsidiary complex between the inner and outer boundaries, comprising a clay burial chapel and two timber churches.[88] The timber buildings conform to the double-square ground plan known from other Anglo-Saxon buildings. Even so, the westernmost building incorporated a pre-Northumbrian shrine, showing some accommodation of the existing ritual layout.[89] The church was subsequently enlarged and elaborated, and it was rebuilt with stone footings after a fire *ca* 845, in the same way as domestic buildings at other Northumbrians sites.[90] The burial chapel had clay walls that facilitated its function as a morgue, as well as window glass comparable to other Northumbrian minsters.[91] Although the structures on this sector of the site were rectilinear, there was a reversion to the original sub-oval, wattle-walled buildings during the Viking Age. It is possible that these styles had never ceased to be used, and that only the grandest buildings in the minster had been reconfigured.[92]

So far I have explored buildings at renowned and extensive ecclesiastical complexes; I now turn to the smaller sites. At Ardwall Isle, the small timber church was replaced by a larger structure built from rubble masonry and bonded with clay. The unicameral plan, the length to breadth ratio and the western entrance are all in keeping with Irish churches, as is the gable finial.[93] In the Northumbrian kingdom, finials have only been found at Lastingham and Lythe, whose communities had affinities with Lindisfarne through their founders, Cedd and Hild.[94] Clay-bonded churches are known in Ireland, and another point of comparison is St Ronan's chapel, Iona, which was constructed between the eighth and twelfth centuries.[95] At Auldhame, an early timber church was replaced by a unicameral building

[86] AU 789.8 (ed. and transl. Mac Airt and Mac Niocaill, 244–5); *CI* 789.3 (transl. Charles-Edwards, I, 253). Material is missing from AT and CS at this point. Ó Carragáin, *Churches*, 63–5, details the accumulation of architectural references to Rome at Armagh. More generally, see Aitchison, *Armagh*, 207–8.
[87] *HE* III, 4, 1 (ed. Lapidge, II, 30; ed. and transl. Colgrave and Mynors, 222–3); Radford, 'Excavations at Whithorn, 1949', 107–19; *idem*, 'Excavations at Whithorn: final report', 181.
[88] Hill, *Whithorn*, 134, 136, 141–4, 164–70.
[89] *Ibid.*, 89, 103–4 110–11, 114, 134–43, 148. For the plan, see also James *et al.*, 'An early medieval building tradition', 186.
[90] Hill, *Whithorn*, 136, 144, 146, 148, 151–2, 162, 164; for Cumbrian parallels with the church's plan, see Cramp, *Whithorn*, penultimate page of text. For stone footings, see Hartlepool: Daniels, 'The Anglo-Saxon monastery', 175–81, 204–5; Whitby: Rahtz, 'Appendix C', 461; Cramp, 'A reconsideration', 65–6; Dunbar: Perry, *Castle Park, Dunbar*, 67, 73–6; Hoddom: Lowe, *Excavations at Hoddom*, 183.
[91] Hill, *Whithorn*, 165; Cramp, 'The early medieval window glass', 326–9.
[92] Clark, 'The Northumbrian frontiers', 152–226; Blair, *The British Culture*, 21–2; *idem*, *Building Anglo-Saxon England*, 47.
[93] Thomas, 'An Early Christian cemetery', 131–8. As Blair notes (*The Church*, 376 n. 24) the dating evidence at Ardwall is inferential, resting partly on the funerary monuments.
[94] Thomas, 'An Early Christian cemetery', 157–8; *Corpus III*, 171–2 (Lastingham 9); *Corpus VI*, 26–7, 167 (Lythe 37). Lythe was most likely linked with Whitby. For Irish finials, see Ó Carragáin, *Churches*, 42–6.
[95] O'Sullivan, 'Excavation of an early church', 332–5. For examples in the north of Ireland, see Swift, 'Irish ecclesiastical influence', 217.

with footings of earth-bonded rubble and a timber superstructure. It was probably constructed between the mid-eighth and mid-ninth centuries, and 'we need look no further than Ireland and western Scotland for the source of inspiration'.[96] At Heysham (Lancashire), two mortared churches stood in an east–west alignment, St Peter's in a hollow and St Patrick's on a headland overlooking the Irish Sea. Their doorways were constructed in 'Escomb style' with long-and-short jambs, a classic Northumbrian building method.[97] On the other hand, the earliest church of St Patrick was a small single-celled structure with a doorway in the west wall, like many in Ireland and Scotland. This building is associated with small rock-cut graves to the east and west, which are best explained as reliquaries; the presence of a shrine chapel in a group of churches is again in tune with western Britain and Ireland.[98] A bird-headed stone retrieved from a grave at Heysham resembles the finials from Lythe and Lastingham, although it was carved on only one face, and a more plausible interpretation is that it belonged to a high-backed chair.[99] The bird decoration recalls a stone from Minnigaff (Kirkcudbrightshire, now Dumfries and Galloway), for which Irish parallels can be suggested.[100]

The tenth and eleventh centuries saw the foundation of new local churches, as well as the rebuilding of older structures in stone. John Blair has traced this process in an English context, and inspiration could also be found on the Isle of Man.[101] The timber church at Barhobble was replaced by a building made of large split stones packed with rubble and bonded with clay.[102] The clay-bonding technique was used locally (as at Ardwall Isle), and also in Manx keeills such as Ballakilley, which has been interpreted as a proprietary church of the eleventh century.[103] There are also Manx parallels for Barhobble's distinctive south doorway and its tapering altar, which contained bones (presumably relics) that have been radiocarbon-dated to the mid-thirteenth century. Barhobble's stone building was probably constructed in the late eleventh or twelfth century, for it lay under a thirteenth-century occupation layer and was superimposed on burials radiocarbon-dated to the earlier eleventh century.[104] The parallels between Barhobble and Manx keeills suggest that expertise was being shared across the Irish Sea in order to replace earlier church buildings.

Just over a mile away stands Chapel Finian, a small but ambitious structure with mortared walls that were plastered externally. It has been interpreted as a church that

---

[96] Crone and Hindmarch, *Living and Dying*, 16, 49–50, 137 (quotation). There were early unicameral churches in Wales, but none in stone until the twelfth century: Pritchard, 'The origins', 249–53. At the Pictish ecclesiastical complex on the Isle of May, the timber church was replaced with stone in the tenth/eleventh century: James and Yeoman, *Excavations*, 176–7.

[97] Taylor and Taylor, *Anglo-Saxon Architecture*, I, 312–17.

[98] Potter and Andrews, 'Excavations at Heysham', 62–6, 74–6, 87–8. The doorway was moved to the south wall when the building was extended. Cf. Petts and Turner, 'Early medieval church groups', 294.

[99] Cramp, 'The sculpture'; *Corpus IX*, 207 (Heysham 12).

[100] See below, 202–3.

[101] Blair, *The Church*, 375–6.

[102] Cormack, 'Barhobble', 23–4, 43; compare the timber to stone transition at Kirkmirran (Dumfriesshire): Crowe, 'An excavation at Kirkmirran', 59, 62.

[103] Cormack, 'Barhobble', 15, 45–6; for a list of clay-bonded keeills, see Swift, 'Irish ecclesiastical influence', 224. For Ballakilley, see Bruce, *The Manx Archaeological Survey*, II (report 6), 10.

[104] Cormack, 'Barhobble', 14–22, 43, 45. Compare the altar at Cabbal Pherick: Kermode *et al.*, *The Manx Archaeological Survey*, I (report 3), 5, and an altar at the clay-bonded church at Raholp (Co. Down): Bigger, 'Some notes', 124. For the relics, see Thomas, *The Parish*, 152.

was founded for pilgrims seaborne or on foot during the tenth or eleventh century.[105] Chapel Finian's proportions are consistent with those of Irish churches, and it has *antae* (protrusions at the end of the walls), which are diagnostically Irish features.[106] Tomás Ó Carragáin has suggested that *antae* had symbolic resonances: they originated as representations of Roman buildings in wood, and then became skeumorphic features on stone churches. By the eleventh century, Irish churches were increasingly being built without *antae*, but where they persisted, they created the impression of a long history.[107] *Antae* have only been located at a handful of sites outside Ireland, each of which has Irish connections, including Iona and Glastonbury.[108] Another possible candidate is the proprietary church at the Hirsel (Berwickshire).[109] Nearer to Chapel Finian is the complex, multi-period ecclesiastical site of Peel Island on the Isle of Man. In the 1960s, St Patrick's Church, Peel, was excavated, revealing that the earliest building on the site had *antae*. It stood in alignment with a round tower, another distinctively Irish building-type; together the two features can be dated to the tenth or eleventh century.[110] At this church, as with its Irish counterparts, *antae* were formed by the north and south walls extending past the gable end. In contrast, at Chapel Finian the east and west walls protrude and there are two central *antae*-like features, which are unparalleled in Ireland. Did the architect of Chapel Finian wish to evoke Irish churches, without fully understanding how *antae* should be positioned?

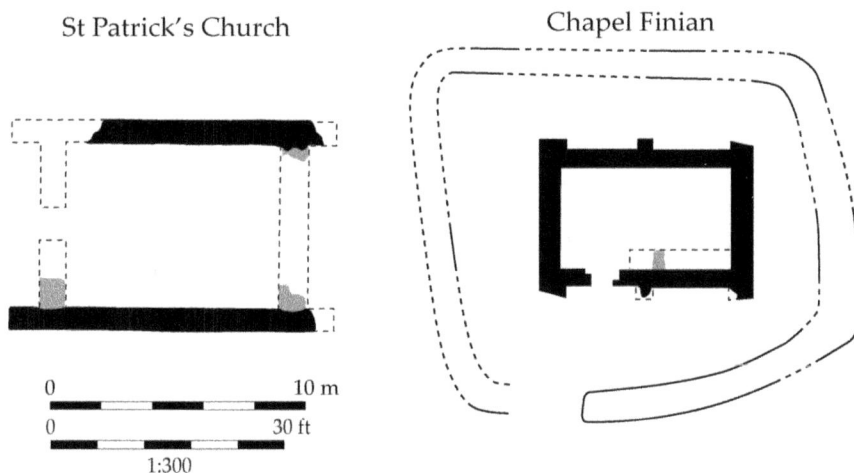

Figure 1: Plans of St Patrick's Church, Peel, and Chapel Finian (Illustration by Adam Parsons after plans in Radford, 'The excavations' and 'St Patrick's Church')

---

[105] Radford, 'The excavations at Chapel Finnian', 29, 39–40; Thomas, *The Parish*, 122–3. Cf. Cramp, *The Hirsel Excavations*, 23.

[106] Leask, *Irish Churches*, I, 55–6; O'Keeffe, *Romanesque Ireland*, 69–70; Harbison, 'Early Irish churches', 622–4; Ó Carragáin, *Churches*, 31–3.

[107] Ó Carragáin, *Churches*, 26–32, 87, 113, 147.

[108] Hamlin, 'The study', 131; Radford, 'The earliest Irish churches', 3; Ó Carragáin, *Churches*, 87.

[109] Cramp, *The Hirsel Excavations*, 50, 314. The *antae* could only be subtly traced at the end of two walls on account of a later building phase.

[110] Cubbon, 'The early Church', 278–80; Radford, 'St Patrick's Isle, Peel', 386–8; Freke, *Excavations*, 13, 132–3.

In sum, then, while Bede's distinction between building *more Scottorum* and *more Romanorum* remains problematically stark, ecclesiastical sites reveal a variety of connections between Northumbrian and Gaelic spheres. These include distinctive features such as *antae* and shrines. There were also shared developments in church building around the Solway from the tenth century onwards.

Sculptural contact

During early medieval times, Northumbria and the Gaelic world abounded in stone sculpture. It offers insight into an array of influences, and can be described as 'cross-cultural' in terms of form and decoration.[111] The emergence of stone-working among the Northumbrians partly reflects the appeal of Rome's monumental traditions, as disseminated through missions despatched by the Pope. Meanwhile, the free-standing crosses of Northumbria and Ireland had a common source of inspiration on Iona. While sculpture was primarily the preserve of the Church, its images offered an educational guide for the illiterate, and skilfully sculpted monuments enjoyed a wide audience. One side of the Ruthwell Cross may have been intended for the edification of local lay Christians, while the other was aimed at a monastic community.[112] By the tenth century, networks of patronage were broadening, as lay lords invested in sculpture in the Solway area. Sculpture therefore offers insights into a range of cultural contacts during the Golden Age and the Viking Age.

How did designs travel from one monument to another, and what did this mean in terms of cultural contact? Since sculptured stones were rarely portable, shared motifs emerged through the movements of sculptors, motif-pieces and templates, or other artistic media.[113] The late-ninth or tenth-century cross from Alnmouth (Northumberland) was signed by one *Myredah* 'Muiredach', the bearer of a Gaelic name. The layout, key patterns and interlace of this cross are closely linked with the Cuthbertine community at Lindisfarne and Chester-le-Street.[114] It is worth asking how close the parallels between designs need to be in order to qualify as evidence of contact. Berechtuine's slab from Tullylease (Co. Cork) features a distinctive cross that closely resembles the cross on folio 26v of the Lindisfarne Gospels. The similarity may simply reflect a common background in the Insular artistic repertoire; even so, Lindisfarne's broader network remains a possible channel of transmission. The key pattern that fills Berechtuine's cross appears on sculpture related to Lindisfarne, as well as at Portmahomack in Pictland, which had Columban associations.[115]

Sculptors and their styles flowed through several channels. An ecclesiastical *familia* might disseminate distinctive sculptural traditions through its affiliated churches. For example, a cross-head from Mayo has been identified as a Northumbrian form, while

---

[111] Bailey, *England's Earliest Sculptors*, 44–57; Hawkes, 'East meets west', 42–5, 54 (quotation); see below, 201.

[112] Meyvaert, 'A new perspective'; cf. Bailey, *Viking Age Sculpture*, 81–5.

[113] Bailey, 'Irish Sea contacts', 11, 30–1; *idem*, *Viking Age Sculpture*, 242–54; Cramp, *Early Northumbrian Sculpture*, 1.

[114] *Corpus I*, 161 (Alnmouth); Bailey, *England's Earliest Sculptors*, 87–90.

[115] Okasha and Forsyth, *Early Christian Inscriptions*, 120–3. Henderson and Okasha have highlighted the differences between the slab and the Gospel book: 'The Early Christian inscribed and carved stones', 15–17, 22–4, 34. Compare Carver, *Portmahomack*, 126, 142, 154–5; Maddern, *Raising the Dead*, 181–2. For Berechtuine, see above, 41.

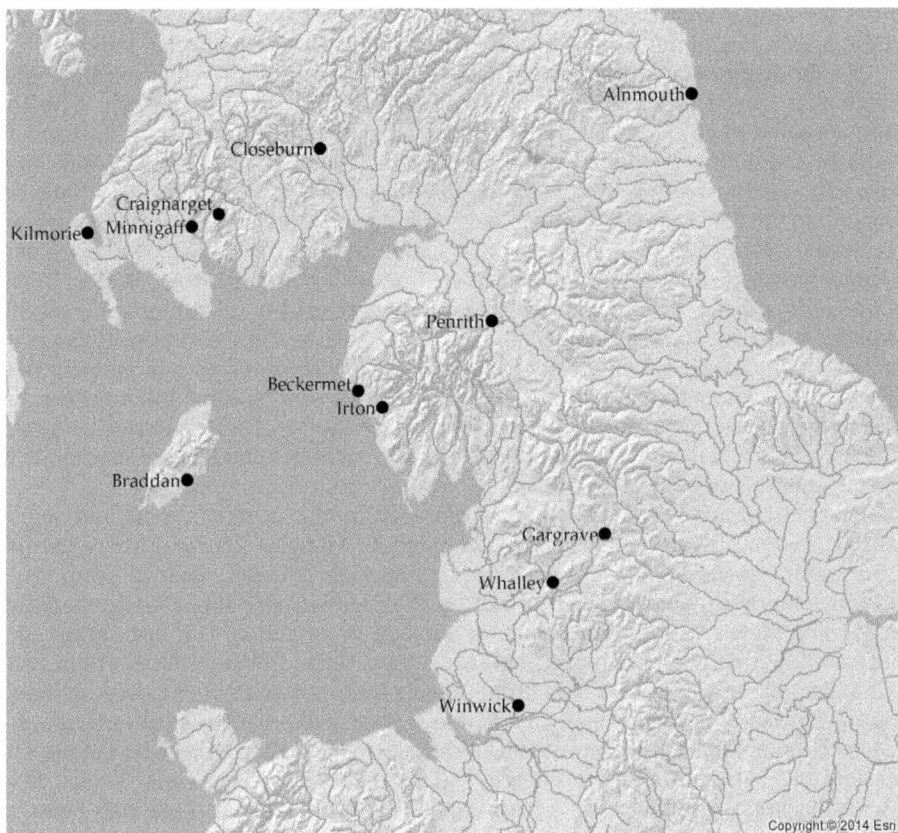

Map 11: Monuments mentioned in Chapter 8

its leonine decorations are reminiscent of Iona crosses.[116] Episcopal influence may have played a role in the dissemination of the vinescroll ornament epitomised by Acca's Cross at Hexham.[117] Alternatively, a sculptor, or school of sculptors, could confine their activities to a specific kingdom or region.[118] One master-craftsman on the Isle of Man claimed *kaut kirþi þana auk ala imaun* 'Gautr carved this and all in Man'.[119] His style was indeed influential, although the long-lived nature of Manx sculpture must mean that other sculptors took over once Gautr hung up his chisel. Practical considerations determined a monument's form and ornamentation: Manx slate was better suited to cross-slabs than free-standing crosses. There was also significant cross-influence between stonework and long-lost wooden carvings, which can sometimes be detected in skeuomorphic features.[120] While the surviving monuments are only a portion of what once existed, there is a wealth of evidence

[116] Hawkes, 'An iconography of identity?', 271–2.
[117] *Corpus I*, 174–6 (Hexham 1); Cramp, *Early Northumbrian Sculpture*, 7–8 and 14 n. 23.
[118] Sidebottom, 'Viking-Age stone monuments', 217–31.
[119] Michael 74 (MM101); Kermode, *Manx Crosses*, 149–53; Wilson, *Manx Crosses*, 131, 161.
[120] Bailey, *England's Earliest Sculptors*, 105–6; Kelly, 'The heart of the matter', 107, 116, 129.

from the Insular world. I will therefore focus on several case studies, and compare these pieces of sculpture with other evidence of Gaelic–Northumbrian links.

At the beginning of the period, Chi-Rho monograms offer one example of a motif that spread through seaborne contacts. The six-bar Constantinian Chi-Rho first appeared in Britain in the fourth century and it survived on memorial stones in western and northern Britain.[121] The example in St Ninian's Cave near Whithorn is best explained as a reflex of cross-Solway contact with Maryport's fort.[122] A four-bar version of the Chi-Rho was disseminated from the Continent to the Irish Sea region, as seen at Kirkmadrine (Dumfries and Galloway, formerly Wigtownshire), and Drumaqueran (Co. Antrim), as well as in Cornwall and north-west Wales.[123] The Chi-Rho symbols evolved into compass-drawn cross-of-arcs and hexafoil motifs, which are rare in Northumbrian sculpture.[124] One such symbol, still bearing the hook of the Rho, appears above the inscription *loci Petri Apustoli* on a monument near Whithorn.[125] The reference to St Peter is suggestive of a Northumbrian milieu, but the script is earlier than the eighth century. The cross-of-arcs belongs to the culture of the Irish Sea, and the mention of St Peter's *locus* calls to mind the late-seventh-century Kilnasaggart stone (Co. Armagh).[126]

Compass-drawn designs remained popular in the northern Irish Sea region during the era of Northumbrian encroachment. At Maughold (Isle of Man), the two 'Blæcmon' stones feature crosses-of-arcs alongside Anglian runic inscriptions.[127] A fragmentary monument from Nendrum (Co. Down) also has a compass-drawn motif and an inscription that was once thought to be runic. The inscription is in fact written in Insular decorative capitals, a style well known in the Northumbrian kingdom, and its presence at Nendrum reflects Irish-Sea contact.[128] Compass-drawn motifs appeared more informally as graffiti or scratched ornamentation at Barhobble Chapel, Whitekirk (East Lothian) and Whithorn, where they appear on paving laid around the Northumbrian-era church.[129] The collection of memorial stones from Ardwall Isle also hints at the mingling of different traditions. One slab bears an encircled equal-armed cross under which the English name 'Cuthgar' is inscribed in Insular half-uncial lettering.[130] The slab's layout and dimensions resemble memorial stones from western Britain and Ireland rather than the name-stones of Lindisfarne

---

[121] Thomas, *The Early Christian Archaeology*, 106–10; Trench-Jellicoe, 'The Skeith Stone'.

[122] Maryport plaque: Collingwood and Wright, *Roman Inscriptions of Britain I*, no. 856 (285). St Ninian's Cave: Canmore ID 63133; Thomas, *The Early Christian Archaeology*, 11, 100–1; Forsyth, 'The Latinus stone', 23–4, 28, 30–6.

[123] Thomas, *The Early Christian Archaeology*, 100, 107; Hamlin, 'A Chi-Rho-carved Stone'; Edwards, 'Chi-Rhos'.

[124] Thomas, *The Early Christian Archaeology*, 120–1; Lionard, 'Early Irish grave-slabs', 110–12. Trench-Jellicoe discusses two examples from Monkwearmouth that are in relief and presently of uncertain date: 'The Skeith Stone', 502; *Corpus I*, 133–4 (Monkwearmouth 28 and 29).

[125] *CIIC* I, no. 520 (498).

[126] Craig, 'The distribution', I, 99–100; Charles-Edwards, *Wales and the Britons*, 146. For the epigraphy, see Forsyth, '*Hic memoria perpetua*', 127–30 (sixth century); Tedeschi, *Congeries Lapidum*, I, 298 (seventh century). For Kilnasaggart, see *CIIC* II, no. 946 (114–15).

[127] See above, 42.

[128] Charles-Edwards, 'Reading the Nendrum "rune-stone"' *contra* Lawlor, *The Monastery*, 70.

[129] Cormack, 'Barhobble', 64–5; Lowe, *Angels, Fools and Tyrants*, 34; Craig, 'The sculptured stones', 439–40; Hill, *Whithorn*, 104–5, 114, 150, 186–7, 197–8.

[130] Thomas, 'An Early Christian cemetery', 153–5. A smaller secondary inscription features the same name.

and Hartlepool.[131] However, the use of a name in the nominative (as opposed to the genitive) and the pocked technique of carving fit best in a Northumbrian milieu.[132] In the far west of the kingdom, then, there was accommodation between the monumentality of the northern Irish Sea region and the styles of the Northumbrian heartlands.[133]

The free-standing cross was the seminal development of eighth-century sculpture in Northumbria, Ireland and the Hebrides. It is no coincidence to find impressive crosses in all three areas: King Oswald was inspired by the Iona community to set up a wooden cross before the battle of Heavenfield, and such monuments will have inspired the surviving stone versions.[134] Their sculptors drew on a common repertoire of abstract decoration derived from manuscripts and metalwork. Within a Northumbrian context, manuscript-derived styles were most prevalent at Lindisfarne and other churches in the far north.[135] In contrast, Hexham and Jarrow favoured vine scroll, a style that was less characteristic of Ireland or Iona (whereas it thrived in Pictland).[136] The sculptors of Wearmouth-Jarrow, no doubt inspired by models imported by Benedict Biscop, depicted drapery and human figures in a naturalistic Roman fashion.[137] A highly accomplished example is the Ruthwell Cross's depiction of Paul and Anthony breaking bread, which alludes to a practice that was current on Iona. This scene relates to a panel that recalls the *Agnus Dei* chant for breaking bread, a liturgical innovation in Rome; this is a reminder of the complex cross-cultural world that underpinned the cross's iconography.[138] Another characteristic of Anglo-Saxon crosses is their proportions: a tall, narrow pillar topped by a small, unringed head. In Irish and Hebridean crosses, there is no break between the shaft and the head, and rings sometimes encircle the head in the form widely known as the 'Celtic cross'.[139]

Notwithstanding these distinctive features, it is difficult to isolate diagnostic features of influence from, say, the Columban *familia* or Ireland. This is because so much of the artistic repertoire, and the thought-world lying behind the iconography of crosses, was shared throughout the Insular world. I will therefore approach the question of specific influences through two case studies. One of the most highly decorated crosses in the west of the Northumbrian kingdom stands at Irton (Cumbria, formerly Cumberland). The broad faces are covered with panels of abstract ornament surrounded by interlace, which lend the monument a noticeably different appearance from crosses such as Ruthwell and Bewcastle. The narrow sides are decorated with vinescrolls, as is typical on Northumbrian crosses, although Irton's designs show considerable creativity. The cross-head is of the type found in simpler form at Ardwall Isle, and the monument's proportions are in line with

[131] Maddern, *Raising the Dead*, 1–15.
[132] Thomas, 'An Early Christian cemetery', 155–6; Craig, 'The distribution', I, 98, 183–4; II, 281–2; Okasha, *A Handlist*, 48.
[133] Toop, 'Northumbria', 90–4, 100–1.
[134] Cramp, *Early Northumbrian Sculpture*, 6; Kelly, 'The heart of the matter', 106, 139; see above, 00.
[135] Allen and Anderson, *The Early Christian Monuments*, II, 428–9; Stevenson, 'The Inchyra stone', 46–7 (Tyninghame); *Corpus I*, plate 265 (Aberlady); Cramp, 'The artistic influence', 225–6; Edwards, 'Abstract ornament', 113–15; Ó Carragáin, 'The Ruthwell Cross', 119–20.
[136] Henry, *Irish High Crosses*, 14; Cramp, 'The artistic influence', 225.
[137] Cramp, *Early Northumbrian Sculpture*, 2–4.
[138] Ó Carragáin, 'The Ruthwell Cross', 117–18; *idem*, 'Ruthwell and Iona'.
[139] Ó Riordáin, 'The genesis', 108–14; Kelly, 'The relationships', 220–2.

ninth-century Northumbrian sculpture.[140] Turning to specific aspects of decoration, one of the broad faces featured an inscription (now illegible), which separated two panels of interlace. The interlace on the upper panel may be manuscript-derived; the double-stranded interlace on the lower panel was irregular and had not been constructed on a grid.[141] On the other broad face, there is a chequerboard panel with sunken cross-lets, which are paralleled on Irish crosses, though these too may be inspired by Insular manuscripts and metalwork more broadly.[142] Two spiral-termi-nalled crosses closely resemble motifs on a broken cross-head from Clonca (Co. Donegal).[143] The knotwork borders have parallels on Pictish slabs, on St Oran's cross, Iona, and on one of the tall crosses at Sandbach (Cheshire). It is worth noting that the other Sandbach cross features a depiction of the Virgin and Child that was based on models circulating in Columban churches. The simpler twist border on the other side of the Irton Cross closely resembles the cross-shaft at Closeburn (Dumfries and Galloway, formerly Dumfriesshire).[144] T. D. Kendrick long ago commented that 'the main inspiration of the Irton ornamental style is Irish',[145] although it could be said that Irton's decoration resembles works from across the Insular world. Rosemary Cramp has recently described the cross as 'specifically Cumbric' and 'carved by someone who knew the worlds up and down the west coast'.[146] The place-names Irton 'settlement of the Irishmen' and Ravenglass (Gaelic: 'Glass's division of land') indicate that Gaelic links were to become an increasingly important part of this maritime environment.[147]

The second stone that merits discussion is the unusual monument from Minnigaff, which I have already mentioned in connection with the bird-head stone from Heysham. The monument's form is unique, and it may be an internal fitment rather than a cross.[148] One face features a small bird standing on top of a cross, the second a man, and the third a bird that covers the entire face. The face featuring the cross alludes to Christ's crucifixion, which is represented by the five wounds on the cross-head and the eagle, which calls to mind the ascension. The other two faces depict the symbols of the evangelists Matthew and John.[149] The limbless man closely resembles the image of Matthew on fol. 21v of the Book of Durrow; his oval face and almond-shaped eyes are comparable to figural representations more generally in

[140] *Corpus II*, 115–17; compare Cramp, *Grammar*, xvi (type B10); Thomas, 'An Early Christian cemetery', 151–8.
[141] *Corpus II*, 116; Cramp, *Grammar*, xxxix–xlii.
[142] *Corpus II*, 117; compare Henry, *La sculpture irlandaise*, 103–4.
[143] Harbison, *The High Crosses*, I, 44–5; III, fig. 123; Henry, *La sculpture irlandaise*, 108; Lionard, 'Early Irish grave slabs', 106–9.
[144] Allen and Anderson, *The Early Christian Monuments*, II, 216–17 (Cossins), 300–1 (Meigle 5), 384–5 (Iona 3), 436 (Closeburn). More recent analyses are: Fisher, *Early Medieval Sculpture*, 131 (Iona); Craig, 'The distribution', I, 220–2 (Closeburn); *Corpus IX* (Sandbach Market Square 2), 118; Hawkes, *The Sandbach Crosses*, 132. For the Virgin and Child, see *ibid.*, 141–3; *Corpus IX*, 24.
[145] Kendrick, *Anglo-Saxon Art*, 202.
[146] Cramp, 'Crosses of the Cumbrian coast', 63–7.
[147] See above, 167, 171. The place-names most likely post-date the Irton Cross, but could be contemporary with a ring-headed cross from the parish: *Corpus IX*, 117–18 (Irton 2).
[148] Craig, 'The distribution', I, 192–5; II, 326–31. For a second stone from Minnigaff, see Allen and Anderson, *The Early Christian Monuments*, II, 476–7.
[149] Bailey, *Ambiguous Birds* (no page numbering).

Figure 2: The Irton Cross (© Corpus of Anglo-Saxon Stone Sculpture, photographer T. Middlemass)

Irish art, such as the Moone high cross and the metalwork head from Arnside.[150] On the strength of these parallels, a date in the eighth or ninth century seems likely for the Minnigaff stone.[151] A context for this unusual decoration may be found in ecclesiastical links between Ireland and the Machars peninsula, via Whithorn.

---

[150] Collingwood, 'The early crosses', 227 described the style of the faces as 'Gaelic'. Compare Henry, *La sculpture irlandaise*, 146; Harbison, *The High Crosses*, I, 154–6; III, figs 509, 514; Bailey, *Ambiguous Birds* (no page numbering); Alexander, *Insular Manuscripts*, 30–2 (fig. 14). For the Arnside head, see below, 212.

[151] Craig, 'The distribution', I, 195 *contra* Collingwood, 'The early crosses', 228 (eleventh-century dating).

I have considered the monuments from Minnigaff and Irton in relative isolation, which makes it hard to assess whether they are representative of broader trends. They are not unique: at Beckermet St Bridget, close to Irton, recent excavations have unearthed a fragment with a metalwork-inspired boss that originally formed the centre of a cross-head. Decorated bosses appear on monuments in Ireland and Pictland, and also at Lindisfarne and associated churches, where they are a reflex of the enduring connection with Iona.[152] Such monuments stand out from much of the Northumbrian corpus, paying testimony to specific channels of cultural contact. Beckermet and Irton are unrecorded in the fragmentary textual record, and so the sculpture offers welcome insight into their connections.

Northumbrian sculptural styles transformed during the Viking Age. Regional schools of sculpture emerged amidst the political fragmentation and the break-up of once-great minster estates. At Lindisfarne and Durham, the Cuthbertine community perpetuated their manuscript-derived sculptural styles, and absorbed influences from Jarrow while they were based at Chester-le-Street.[153] Meanwhile, stylised versions of Northumbrian decorative traditions persisted in Yorkshire and on the coast of north-west England, sometimes mingling with new art-styles brought from Scandinavia. There were also new forms of monument, notably the hogback grave-marker, which also appeared at Govan in the heart of the kingdom of Strathclyde and along the Firth of Forth.[154] A renowned example is the Heysham hogback, which is adorned with elaborate depictions of Norse mythology, in common with a number of other crosses in northern England and the Isle of Man.[155] Hogback stones, however, can no longer be seen as a 'colonial monument' of Scandinavian settlement, for they were adorned with a versatile mixture of Insular and Scandinavian art-styles.[156]

On the eastern side of the Irish Sea, the quantity of sculpture increased significantly during the tenth century. Thanks to the foundation of proprietary churches, monuments were now being commissioned by rural magnates and urban merchants.[157] Where once pagan elites had buried their dead in impressively furnished mound burials, they now diverted their investment to funerary monuments at churches.[158] There was no such proliferation of sculpture in Ireland, where high crosses continued to be the preserve of exalted ecclesiastical and royal patrons.[159] This difference in patronage explains why it is difficult to trace parallels between Northumbrian and Irish sculpture during the Viking Age. There are a few exceptions to this rule, such as the small hogback tombstone at Castledermot (Co. Kildare), which is unique in Ireland.[160] Conversely, the ring-headed crosses that suddenly proliferated in the west of the Northumbrian kingdom were influenced by Irish and Hebridean high crosses.[161] Otherwise, sculptural evidence does not tell the same tale about Irish influence as texts, place-names and metalwork. The stones do, however, reveal a

---

[152] I thank Daniel Elsworth for information about the Beckermet boss. See now Cramp, 'Crosses of the Cumbrian coast', 57–9; *eadem*, '"Heads you lose"', 17–18.

[153] *Corpus I*, 27, 31–2; Cramp, 'The artistic influence', 227–8.

[154] Lang, 'The hogback'; Crawford, *The Govan Hogbacks*.

[155] Bailey, *Viking Age Sculpture*, 101–42; Kopár, *Gods and Settlers*, 3–56.

[156] Williams, 'Citations in stone'.

[157] Bailey, *Viking Age Sculpture*, 254–5; Stocker, 'Monuments and merchants'.

[158] Abrams, 'The conversion of the Danelaw', 35–6; Griffiths, 'Settlement and acculturation', 133–4;

[159] Bailey, 'Irish Sea contacts', 13, 28–30; Edwards, *The Archaeology*, 167.

[160] Lang, 'The Castledermot hogback'. Compare the Rathdown slabs, discussed above, 144.

[161] Bailey, *Viking Age Sculpture*, 70–1.

wealth of other seaborne contacts, links that are also seen in saints' dedications, architecture and place-names. The sculptural evidence is copious for the Viking Age, and has been extensively discussed by scholars. I will briefly survey the evidence for specific channels of contact, before focusing on several pertinent monuments.

Sculpture reveals a vibrant network of links between the Cumbrian coast and the Isle of Man. This is despite the fact that the Island's stone is best suited to slabs, whereas free-standing crosses and hogbacks predominate in Cumbria. On the western Cumbrian plain, two regional schools developed, chiefly deriving their ornament from earlier local monuments. They were the 'Beckermet School', whose main interlace pattern featured Stafford knots, and the 'Spiral Scroll School', which favoured a stylised plant scroll, stopped-plait interlace and a distinctive design on the cross-head.[162] A monument from Maughold (Isle of Man) features large crosses that are surrounded by abstract ornament, including Cumbrian spiral-scroll and stopped-plait.[163] Meanwhile, the Stafford knots of the Beckermet School appear on a stone from Braddan which – tellingly – is carved from St Bees sandstone from Cumbria. A second stone from Braddan has a shaped head and Cumbrian-style knotwork.[164] The traffic in motifs was not one-way, for a Manx 'link-lock twist' motif decorates a circle-headed cross-head from Aspatria.[165] The arrival of Manx styles on the Cumbrian coast is contextualised by the excavations at St Michael's church, Workington. Here the inhumations fall into two broad phases: a seventh- to ninth-century group, including coffined burials, and an early eleventh-century group including stone-lined coffins.[166] There is some pre-Viking sculpture from the site, including an architectural fragment inscribed with a name, but the majority of stones date from the Viking Age.[167] They include fragments of cross-shafts featuring spiral-scroll- and Beckermet-school designs, portions of a hogback, and fragments of two circle-headed crosses.[168] The cross-head was formerly attached to a shaft that was decorated with Borre ring-chain and ribbon-animals in the Scandinavian Mammen art-style. The Mammen style is rarely encountered on sculpture in northern England, but it is found on Manx sculpture, including a free-standing cross from Braddan.[169] The Workington excavations raise interesting questions about dating, for the monuments tend to be placed in the tenth century, whereas the radio-carbon dates of the burials cluster in the early eleventh century. There are historical contexts for continued links between the Cumbrian kingdom and the Isle of Man at that time.[170]

A separate regional school developed north of the Solway, with its epicentre in the minster of Whithorn. 'Whithorn School' carvings were generally confined to the Machars peninsula, and their distribution reflects the emergence of a parish

---

[162] Bailey, *Viking Age Sculpture*, 194–206; *Corpus II*, 33–40.

[163] Kermode, *Manx Crosses*, 172–3 (Maughold 72, MM98).

[164] Kermode, *Manx Crosses*, D5 (MM146); 70 (MM78); Bailey, 'Irish Sea contacts', 25–6. For the imported stone, see Trench-Jellicoe, 'A re-definition', I, 72–3.

[165] *Corpus II*, 50–1 (Aspatria 1); Bailey, 'Irish Sea contacts', 23–5.

[166] Zant, 'The stratigraphic sequence', 11–28.

[167] *Corpus II*, 154, 157 (Workington 1, 7 and 8).

[168] *Corpus II*, 155–8 (Workington 3, 4, 6). For the hogback, see Paterson, 'The sculptural fragments', 78–81.

[169] *Corpus II*, 155–6 (Workington 3); Bailey, *Viking Age Sculpture*, 57. Compare Thorleif's Cross, Braddan (Braddan 108, MM135): Kermode, *Manx Crosses*, 203–5; Wilson, *Manx Crosses*, 91–3.

[170] Adam Parsons drew the dating of the sculpture to my attention. See above, 65 for links between the Cumbrian kingdom and Man in 1000.

system under Whithorn's aegis.[171] There are no specific connections between the Whithorn School and Manx sculpture, and few comprehensive parallels across the Solway. One hint is the now-lost monument at Knockcross on the south side of the firth, which resembled a Whithorn School cross.[172] The Spiral Scroll and Beckermet schools had subtle influence further afield; for example, a slab from Great Cumbrae features a Stafford knot pattern with pellets alongside an Anglo-Scandinavian ribbon-animal.[173] The expansion of the kingdom of Strathclyde may have facilitated the voyages of sculptors or their patrons between the Cumbrian coast and the Firth of Clyde. Two distinctive slabs from the Rhinns reveal further evidence of cross-Solway contacts that circumvented the Whithorn School. A slab from Craignaret features an idiosyncratic collection of motifs that closely resembles the slab from Aspatria (Cumberland, formerly Cumbria).[174] The distinctive slab from Kilmorie features a 'hammer-head' cross, a type well-known south of Solway. It depicts a cup and vine pattern (an allusion to the Eucharist) on one face, and the other face portrays the crucifixion as well as birds and smithing tools.[175] One possible interpretation of this scene is an allusion to the legend of Sigurðr; if so, this cross-slab links with other monuments that show the reception of the Sigurðr stories in a Christian context in Man and north-west England.[176]

Many of the Viking-Age monuments discussed so far belong to the world of the local church, and therefore reflect how lay patrons wished to commemorate the dead.[177] Sculpture also hints at the continuity of high-level ecclesiastical links, as Victoria Whitworth has argued in relation to crosses in Yorkshire. She has examined a ring-headed cross from St Mary Castlegate, York, as well as the impressive cross from Stonegrave, and presented parallels in Ireland and western and northern Britain.[178] A similar set of connections may lie behind three outstanding monuments to the west of the Pennines. The first is a large ring-head cross from Winwick near Warrington, of which two arms and the centre of the head survive. The fret patterns on the head, the shape of the head, the figures with bells, and the decorated boss (paralleled by the cross-head from St Mary Castlegate) recall monuments associated with the Columban *familia*.[179] Secondly, a stone from Penrith closely resembles Irish copper-alloy crucifixion plaques; these followed a specific format, depicting Christ on the cross, the spear- and sponge-bearers and angels.[180] There has been much debate about their dates, with

[171] Collingwood, 'The early crosses', 218–27; Craig, 'Pre-Norman sculpture', 53; *idem*, 'The sculptured stones', 435–6.
[172] Elsworth, 'Knockcross, Bowness-on-Solway'.
[173] Fisher, *Early Medieval Sculpture*, 9, 71–2. For instances where sculptors in south-west Scotland may have been responding to the Beckermet and Spiral Scroll schools, see *Corpus II*, 38, 40.
[174] Craig, 'The distribution', III, 50–4, 92–102. For the Aspatria slab, see *Corpus II*, 52–3 (Aspatria 5a–b).
[175] Bailey, 'Irish Sea contacts', 19; Craig, 'Pre-Norman sculpture', 51–2; *idem*, 'The distribution', III, 92–102; Bailey, *Ambiguous Birds* (no page numbering). For hammer-heads, see Bailey, *Viking Age Sculpture*, 182–3.
[176] Collingwood, *Northumbrian Crosses*, 92 (tentative suggestion); Thompson, *Dying and Death*, 168. More generally, see Kopár, *Gods and Settlers*, 29–56.
[177] Kopár, *Gods and Settlers*, 197–201.
[178] Whitworth, 'A cross-head', commenting on St Mary Castlegate 3 (*Corpus III*, 98–9) *eadem*, 'with book and cross'.
[179] *Corpus IX*, 254–9.
[180] *Corpus II*, 140–2 (Penrith 11); Bailey, 'Irish Sea contacts', 30.

some suggestions ranging from *ca* 900 to 1100.[181] The Penrith sculptor could have copied a plaque that arrived as Viking-Age plunder; this is one possible context for a crucifixion plaque recently discovered near Kirkcudbright.[182] Alternatively, and perhaps more likely given its use as a model for sculpture, the metal plaque could have travelled through ecclesiastical channels. In Ireland, such plaques were mounted on large processional crosses made from wood.[183] This type of cross was known in the Northumbrian kingdom, as seen in eighth-century fragments from Dumfriesshire, but its vinescroll ornament differs radically from the later Irish examples.[184]

The final monument to be discussed stands at Whalley in Lancashire. Three impressive (if not complete) crosses stand in the churchyard, and have done so for centuries, if not in their exact current location; there are also numerous fragments of sculpture. Two of the crosses bear highly stylised designs of a local type, whereas the other is very different, featuring small panels that contain abstract ornament (especially key patterns) and scenes featuring haloed figures.[185] T. D. Kendrick described this cross as 'Celtic' because its small, square panels closely resembles Welsh and Irish crosses. There are numerous examples in Ireland, such as the South Cross at Castledermot (Co. Kildare), and the layout appears on tenth- or eleventh-century crosses in Wales, notably Maen Achwyfan (Flintshire, north-east Wales) and Penmon (Anglesey). Those two Welsh crosses display an eclectic range of seaborne influences, including the distinctive circle-heads of Cheshire and patterns such as ring-knot and Borre ring-chain that flourished on the Cumbrian coast and the Isle of Man. Maen Achwyfan and the nearby Meliden cross-shaft feature figural ornament from Scandinavian mythology, while one of the Penmon crosses depicts the Temptation of St Anthony, a theme on Irish high crosses.[186] One argument against Kendrick's designation is that there are similar panels on the Irton Cross, and so the panel arrangement was already in use in the Northumbrian kingdom. As noted, however, the Irton Cross itself displays a varied range of Insular influences, including patterns with Irish and Ionan backgrounds.

Some specific features of the Whalley Cross provide further indications of Irish-Sea influence. The square panel of key-pattern also appears on the underside of an arm of the Winwick cross-head, and in a simpler form on Maen Achwyfan and on a contemporary cross-shaft from nearby Meliden in north-eastern Wales.[187] The *orans* 'praying' figure on the east face of the Whalley cross has an oval-shaped head, a halo, and is flanked by serpents. While the *orans* figure was a widespread borrowing from Late Antique art, figures of very similar type (albeit lacking the

[181] Bourke, 'The chronology'; Johnson, 'Irish crucifixion plaques', 105. Richard Bailey has compared an aspect of the crucifixion scene on the Penrith plaque with the tenth-century Gosforth Cross: *Corpus II*, 142; 101–2 (Gosforth 1).
[182] Canmore ID1027614; Blackwell, 'Kirkcudbright: metal detector find'.
[183] Bourke, 'The chronology', 178; Johnson, 'Irish crucifixion plaques', 98, an argument now bolstered by Murray, 'Irish crucifixion plaques', 290–2. Cf. Kelly, 'The heart of the matter', 136–43.
[184] Wegner, 'The Dumfriesshire mounts', 70. It has been postulated that these fragments were plunder (*ibid.*, 72).
[185] *Corpus IX*, 242–4. For the location of the crosses, see Taylor, *The Ancient Crosses*, 74–6.
[186] Kendrick, *Late Saxon and Viking Art*, 63; Harbison, *The High Crosses*, I, 37–41 II, figs 105, 107; Edwards, *A Corpus III*, 221–31 (Penmon 1–3), 359–62 (Meliden 1), 366–71 (Whitford 2 = Maen Achwyfan).
[187] Edwards, *A Corpus III*, 361–2 (Meliden 1), 369, 371 (Whitford 2 = Maen Achwyfan).

Figure 3: Whalley Cross 1 (© Dr Ross Trench-Jellicoe, from the Corpus of Anglo-Saxon Stone Sculpture)

halo and serpents) appear on the Castledermot South Cross and other Irish high crosses.[188] The pose, dress and framing of the Irish examples resemble the Whalley figure more closely than other examples in the Northumbrian kingdom, such as the *orans* figure on a cross shaft from Masham.[189] Other panels on the Whalley Cross point eastwards and northwards: for example, a backward-turning quadruped and a bird have parallels in Viking-Age art throughout northern England.[190] The size of Whalley's parish and its extensive sculpture collection hint that it was a significant minster in the Ribble Valley, an artery between York and Dublin. Whalley is not the only church along this route with sculpture that hints at western and eastern links. Gargrave (West Yorkshire), located in the Ribble–Aire gap, has a hammer-headed cross and a circle-head of the Cumbrian type.[191]

In this consideration of sculptural evidence, I have focused on stones that show Irish, Hebridean and Manx influences. Many other monuments in the Northumbrian kingdom were rooted in local styles or artistic influences that emanated from the south or the east. The sculptural evidence sometimes complements the picture drawn from textual evidence, particularly in relation to the enduring connection between the Cuthbertine and Columban churches. Sculpture also offers insights into a barely recorded but clearly complex pattern of links around the Solway. Sculptors and patrons travelled along the same routes as armies, settlers and traders, and they also forged their own networks.

Metal dress accessories

In contrast to sculpture, dress accessories were highly portable. They may have travelled when they were pinned to clothes, or perhaps arrived through trade; they shed light on a relatively wide range of individuals in terms of gender and occupation. The number of early medieval objects recovered from the west and north of the Northumbrian kingdom has increased significantly in recent years. This is thanks in part to the popularity of metal-detecting, and improvements in the recording of metal-detected finds, such as the Portable Antiquities Scheme.[192] Chance finds lack the secure (and potentially datable) context of artefacts recovered from excavations, such as the combs that have recently been explored so fruitfully in relation to cultural contact across the North Atlantic.[193] On the other hand, metalwork has a wide geographical distribution, notwithstanding some regional differences in rates of detection and reporting.[194] I will consider small items of metalwork found both

---

[188] Harbison, *The High Crosses*, II, figs 105, 107. For other examples, see Roe, 'The *orans*', 218–21.
[189] *Corpus VI*, 172 (Masham 3).
[190] *Corpus IX*, 244, citing, for example, Lowther 6 for the bird (*Corpus II*, 131) and Halton-on-Lune 1 for the quadruped (*Corpus IX*, 179).
[191] *Corpus VIII*, 155–9 (Gargrave 2 and 5).
[192] The Portable Antiquities Scheme (PAS) covers areas where the Treasure Act 1996 applies. The different laws in Scotland mean that all finds must be reported to the Treasure Trove Unit, which issues annual reports: https://treasuretrovescotland.co.uk/reports-and-minutes/.
[193] Ashby, 'Combs, contact and chronology', 14–18, 24–5.
[194] For Scotland, note the comments of Campbell, 'Anglo-Saxon/Gaelic interaction', 257–8; Blackwell, 'A reassessment', 26–7. Dumfries and Galloway is relatively well represented, according to Bailie, *Assessment*, 10, 33. In England, the density of finds is greatest in the east and the south, although there are some hotspots in the north-west: Richards *et al.*, 'Anglo-Saxon landscape', section 2.4.2.1.

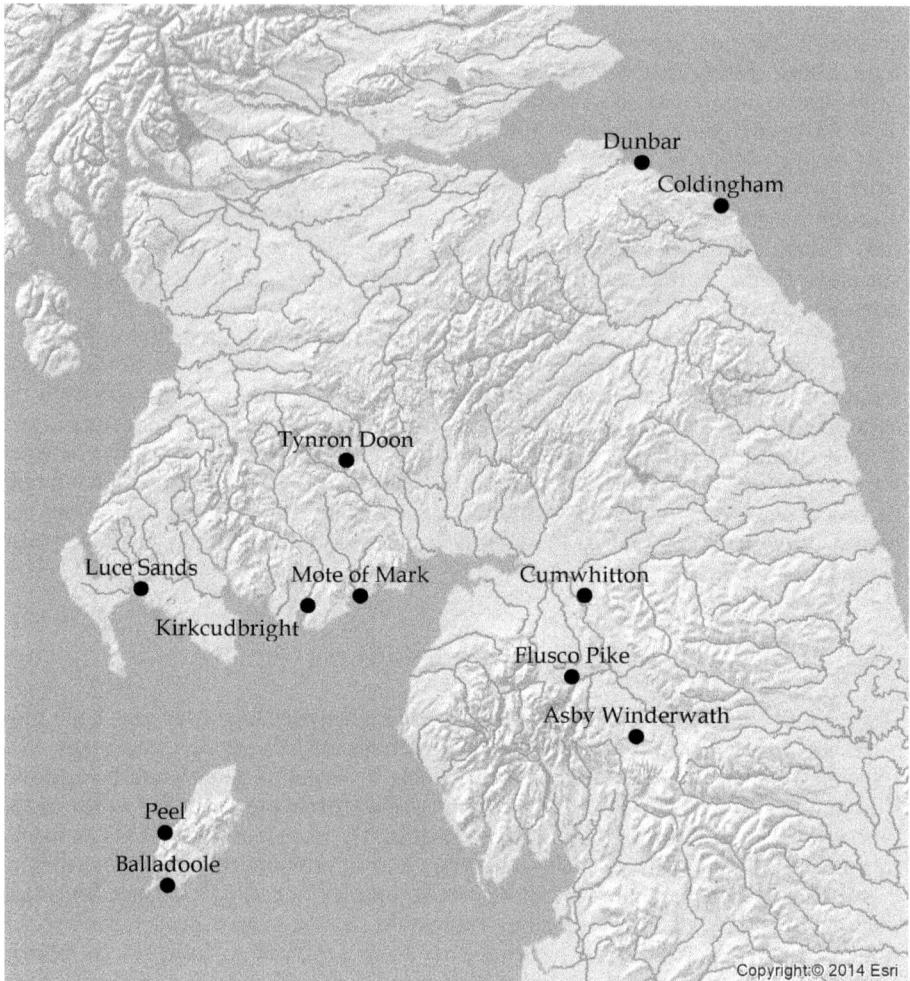

Map 12: Metalwork mentioned in Chapter 8

through detecting and excavation, as well as some objects in museums. Again, rather than provide a comprehensive study, I will focus on items that were manufactured in, or influenced by, places in the Gaelic world, and ask how they augment the picture drawn from other evidence.[195]

In the post-Roman period, the elites of the Irish Sea region focused their activities on hillforts, where metalworking took place alongside feasting.[196] One object shared across the sea was the penannular brooch, which could be worn (in different ways) by women or men. While rulers may have helped to disseminate the brooches, these items had complex connotations; indeed, eighth-century Irish legal tracts link

---

[195] For a thorough and comprehensive examination of Anglo-Saxon metalwork in Scotland, see Blackwell, 'A reassessment'.

[196] See above, 13.

brooches with status rather than political affiliation.[197] Identifying the place of manufacture is complicated, given that pennanular brooches originated in Britain and then developed further in Ireland, Argyll and Pictland.[198] Nevertheless, a zoomorphic brooch from Mealsgate (Cumberland, formerly Cumbria) closely resembles Irish examples, and the animal-headed pair from Glenluce may have come from the Dál Riatan citadel of Dunadd.[199] Penannular brooches were also made and used on the edges of the Northumbrian kingdom, as seen in the metalworking paraphernalia uncovered at the Mote of Mark.[200] This was an elite centre from which fine metalwork was distributed to retainers and their female relatives in the Solway area, as seen by the roundel from Keswick (Cumbria, formerly Cumberland), which closely parallels a mould at the Mote of Mark.[201] The workshop manufactured pins that may have been used in female dress, including a style of thistle-headed pin that was familiar on both sides of the Irish Sea.[202] The Mote of Mark's metalworkers also started to copy Anglo-Saxon zoomorphic interlace and axe-blade mounts, but these new influences augmented rather than displaced the existing styles.[203]

Anglo-Saxon metalwork involved the distinctive techniques of *cloisonné* (gold and garnet work) and filigree (gold wire work). Such products were increasingly in demand among the warrior elites around the edges of the Northumbrian kingdom. A gold and garnet sword mount from East Linton (Lothian) dates from the early seventh century and must have remained in use for some time since it had been repaired. It shares features with St Cuthbert's pectoral cross, which was most likely created in Northumbria; a fragmentary piece from Dunbar and a mount from Auldhame may also belong to this northern *cloisonné* tradition.[204] A gold filigree disc from Tynron Doon (Dumfries and Galloway, formerly Dumfriesshire) and a filigree-decorated sword handle reputed to come from Cumberland also date to the seventh century.[205] Personal contacts helped to disseminate such prestigious Anglo-Saxon items to the North Britons, and these networks also encompassed the Gaelic world. The craft of filigree entered the metalworking repertoire in Ireland and Dál Riata in Britain in

---

[197] For example, *Críth Gablach* (ed. Binchy, line 346).

[198] Fowler, 'Celtic metalwork', 132–3; Laing, *A Catalogue*, 3–5. The gender of the brooch-wearers is explored by Blackwell, 'Individuals', 18–19. In Ireland they were worn by both women and men, but there are hints that in Scotland, like Anglo-Saxon England, they were associated more with female dress.

[199] These are Type F, which may have originated in the Severn estuary: Ó Floinn, 'Patrons and politics', 2–8. For Mealsgate, see Fowler, 'Celtic metalwork', 138; Kilbride-Jones, *Zoomorphic Penannular Brooches*, no. 154 (143); O'Sullivan, 'Sub-Roman and Anglo-Saxon finds', 32. Glenluce: Fowler, 'Celtic metalwork', 106–7, 139; Laing, *A Catalogue*, nos 75–7 (63–4). Dunadd: Newman, 'Further notes', 147–8. There is a third penannular brooch from Luce Sands: Rynne, 'A bronze ring-brooch', 99–113; Laing, *A Catalogue*, no. 43 (56).

[200] Curle, 'Report on the excavation', 140–51; Laing and Longley, *The Mote of Mark*, 59–60.

[201] O'Sullivan, 'Two early medieval mounts', 146–7; the mount resembles the concentric layout of no. 194 and three-strand interlace of no. 201 in Laing, *A Catalogue*, 94–7.

[202] Laing, 'People and pins', 60; *idem*, 'The Mote of Mark', 104. Compare the style of thistle-headed pin with a mould from Lough Faughan crannog: Collins, 'Excavations', 59. Similar pins were manufactured further north at Buiston Crannog (Crone, *The History*, 138–51, 165–6) and have been found locally at Tynron Doon: Williams, 'Tynron Doon', 113–14.

[203] Graham-Campbell, 'The Mote of Mark', 49–50 *contra* Laing, 'The Mote of Mark', 103–4; cf. Close-Brooks, 'The Mote of Mark', 50–1.

[204] Coatsworth, 'The pectoral cross', 294–5; Perry, *Castle Park, Dunbar*, 113–14; Blackwell, 'Copper alloy', 53–7; *eadem*, 'A reassessment', 190–2.

[205] Wilson, *Anglo-Saxon Ornamental Metalwork*, 17–19, 139–40; Williams, 'Tynron Doon', 106, 111–12; O'Sullivan, 'Sub-Roman and Anglo-Saxon finds', 28–32.

the seventh century, before being augmented with new techniques.[206] Further west at Whithorn, material culture underwent an overhaul in the eighth century under Northumbrian influence. John Blair has identified a relatively uniform Anglo-Saxon 'minster culture' consisting of styli, tweezers, keys and pins, which is richly represented at sites in eastern England as well as at Whithorn.[207] Similarly, the finds at Auldhame on the Firth of Forth include pins and a glass inkpot, and the Dacre excavations yielded a stylus.[208] Only a select few artefacts hint at Whithorn's continued links across the Irish Sea, including ball-headed silver and iron pins found in a late Northumbrian building and a rubbish dump.[209]

Even if the dress items associated with Northumbrian minsters betray little influence from the Gaelic world, the high arts of metalwork and manuscript decoration were a key element of Insular or 'Hiberno-Saxon' art. This style arose from a fusion of many influences during the seventh and early eighth centuries, and it was 'richly diverse both in its sources and in the variety of the responses to the available models and traditions'.[210] There long been debate about where the style originated; indeed, experimentation seems to have taken place in a variety of locations. A key location was Dunadd, where excavations yielded items of Anglo-Saxon manufacture as well as moulds for items inspired by Anglo-Saxon metalwork, including a bird-headed brooch from Northumbria.[211] Metalworkers were also trialling Anglo-Saxon techniques at secular centres among the Ulaid and in Brega, areas that were involved in the Irish-Sea nexus.[212] At Hartlepool, a metalwork mould reveals the cross-influences between different artistic media: it was decorated with a lamb blowing a trumpet that resembles evangelist symbols in the Book of Durrow and the Lindisfarne Gospels.[213] Several 'Hiberno-Saxon' objects are known from the edges of the Northumbrian kingdom; it is unclear, however, whether they were used in ecclesiastical settings or conveyed through Viking raiding and trading. The disembodied metalwork heads from Arnside and Furness had originally adorned Irish ecclesiastical metalwork and were reused as weights during the Viking Age.[214] Another find in this category is the chip-carved copper alloy plaque from Rerrick (Dumfries and Galloway, formerly Kirkcudbrightshire), which had been pierced for reuse.[215] The ecclesiastical context is more evident in the case of two now-lost items: a copper-alloy roundel featuring interlace and zoomorphic motifs from Ribchester,[216] and a gilt cup or horn mount found under the chancel of Brougham church (Cumberland, now Cumbria). The

---

[206] Whitfield, 'Motifs and techniques', esp. 78; *eadem*, 'The filigree', 118–22.
[207] Blair, *The Church*, 135–41, 203–4, 206–12; Hill, *Whithorn*, 161, 164, 373–4, 378, 386–7.
[208] Campbell, 'Glass', 58–60; Newman and Leech, *The Early Christian Monastery* (forthcoming).
[209] Hill, *Whithorn*, 180–1, 192, 363, 398–9, 418.
[210] Neuman de Vegvar, *The Northumbrian Renaissance*, 168.
[211] Lane and Campbell, *Dunadd*, 93, 114–18, 150–1, 241, 245–7, 273–4; Campbell, 'Anglo-Saxon/ Gaelic interaction', 259–62; Ó Floinn, 'Irish metalwork', 244–5.
[212] Ó Floinn, 'Irish metalwork', 251. Françoise Henry had placed the origins of Hiberno-Saxon art in Ireland ('On some Early Christian objects', 53–4, 62–3) but James Graham-Campbell re-dated one of the key pieces of evidence to the ninth century: 'The Lough Ravel, County Antrim brooch', 55–6.
[213] Daniels, 'The Anglo-Saxon monastery', 186–9.
[214] Cramp, *Whithorn*, centrespread, describes the piece as 'Anglo-Celtic'; Bu'Lock, 'The eighth-century bronze boss', 77 connects the Ribchester boss with Viking activity; Clement with Youngs, 'A bronze bowl mount'; Laing, *Catalogue*, no. 248 (40).
[215] Graham-Campbell and Whitfield, 'A mount'.
[216] Laing, *Catalogue*, no. 258 (111–12).

mount was decorated with double-strand interlace that merged with stylised depictions of three winged men in Pictish style. [217]

Turning again to dress items, Anglo-Saxon 'Trewhiddle style', with its distinctive zoomorphic ornament, was becoming popular on the edges of the Northumbrian kingdom by the ninth century. It appeared most frequently on strap-ends, which prevented the ends of belts and straps from fraying and were used in male and female dress. Strap-ends were lost in quantity during this period, providing an insight into regional styles.[218] Distinctive Northumbrian decoration emerged, including strap-ends featuring large-eared, looping animals that emanated from a workshop in York. Its products travelled across the Pennines to locations such as Asby Winderwath and Hale, near the River Mersey.[219] There was another workshop at Carlisle, where two fragments of a strap-end mould were found in a timber-lined pit, depicting a Trewhiddle-style animal surrounded by interlace. Finished strap-ends of this type are known from nearby at Wetheral (Cumberland, formerly Cumbria) and also from more easterly locations such as Coldingham.[220] Other Trewhiddle-style strap-ends have been found in West Lancashire, in locations across Cumbria, and in south-west Scotland.[221] They were made in various grades of material (copper-alloy, lead and silver); those from Asby Winderwath seem to shed light on the 'everyday lives of people' since they accompanied agricultural ironwork.[222] The strap-ends show the prevalence of styles that ultimately looked east but were sometimes filtered through a regional workshop in the west of the Northumbrian kingdom.

During the Viking Age, a new, more robust type of strap-end was adopted from the Carolingian world. Novel forms of ornamentation emerged, such as the ring-and-dot pattern, which developed in Anglo-Scandinavian communities and became popular in the Irish Sea region and the Hebrides.[223] At the Cumwhitton cemetery, four of the graves yielded buckles and/or strap-ends that were products of the same workshop. One pair of strap-ends had a distinctive ribbed feature, which appears on items found elsewhere in the Irish-Sea region at Peel (Isle of Man), Dublin and Carlisle Cathedral, as well as in parts of the Danelaw.[224] The Cumwhitton belt-fittings are notable for their combination of ring-and-dot ornament with boss-capped rivets, a mixture only otherwise found on two strap-ends from Workington. This bossed decoration was another fashion of the Irish Sea and the Isles, featuring on belt sets

[217] Way, 'The tombs'; Bailey, 'A cup-mount', esp. 178–80; Laing, *A Catalogue*, no. 242 (105–6); O'Sullivan, 'Sub-Roman and Anglo-Saxon finds', 35–6.

[218] Owen-Crocker, *Dress*, 64–5, 132.

[219] Thomas, 'Strap-ends', 40 (in general); Edwards, 'A group' (Asby); Philpott, 'Recent Anglo-Saxon finds', 196–8 (Hale).

[220] Thomas, 'Strap-ends', 40 (in general); Taylor and Webster, 'A late Saxon strap-end mould', 180; McCarthy *et al.*, *Roman and Medieval Carlisle*, 118 (Carlisle mould); O'Sullivan, 'Sub-Roman and Anglo-Saxon finds', 36 (Wetheral); Blackwell, 'A reassessment', 179–80 (Coldingham).

[221] Edwards 'An Anglo-Saxon strap-end' (Shap); PAS, LANCUM-BD5768 (Cockermouth); LANCUM-720FEB (Longtown, resembling one from Bamburgh); LANCUM-61D655 (Kirkby Ireleth); LANCUM-0A8081 (Dalton); LANCUM-5F92B7 (another from Shap); LANCUM-E4D0E7 (another from Carlisle); LANCUM-87F0D7 (Burscough); Blackwell, 'A reassessment', 180–3 (Glenluce, Holywood). Graham-Campbell, *Whithorn*, 23 (Talnotrie).

[222] Edwards, 'A group', quotation at 141.

[223] Thomas, 'Strap-ends', 42–4.

[224] Paterson *et al.*, *Shadows*, 147–9. For the other finds, see Graham-Campbell, 'Tenth-century graves', 90 (Peel); Harrison and Ó Floinn, *Viking Graves*, 161–2 (Dublin, Golden Lane); McCarthy and Paterson, 'A post-Roman sequence', 213–14 (Carlisle). The style reached the Danelaw: see Thomas, 'Strap-ends', 44; *idem*, 'Anglo-Scandinavian metalwork', 249.

from Carlisle, Cnip (Lewis) and Auldhame, and bridle mounts in the finely furnished burials from Balladoole (Isle of Man) and Kiloran Bay (Colonsay).[225] Meanwhile, Scandinavian communities in Ireland were wearing strap-ends featuring roundels and interlace panels, of which an example has recently been found in Burton-in-Kendal, and there is a buckle in this style from Whithorn.[226] The variety of decoration seen in the west of the Northumbrian kingdom indicates that it was an entrepôt between the Irish-Sea region and the Danelaw.

Dublin's craftspeople developed a range of distinctive dress accessories, which spread to parts of the Insular world and the North Atlantic. One such item was the ringed pin, which originated in Ireland and featured a swivelling ring that was inserted into the perforated head.[227] By the ninth century, the plain-ringed, loop-headed form had become especially popular, and it was adopted by Hiberno-Scandinavian communities. A great number of these pins have been found in datable layers during excavations in Dublin, the most prevalent types being the plain-ringed polyhedral-headed and loop-headed types. Viking-Age ringed pins spread from Dublin to the Hebrides, the Northern Isles and across the North Atlantic, reflecting 'a general diffusion of Viking fashions in dress ornament arising out of the movement in trade and settlement'.[228] Some of the ringed pins belonged to Viking-Age graves, such as the ship burial at Balladoole, Isle of Man and three graves in the Cumwhitton cemetery (Cumbria, formerly Cumberland).[229] Ringed pins have also been unearthed from graves at churches, such as the furnished burial from Kirkcudbright, north of the Solway. The ringed pins from Kirkmirran and the foundations of Brigham church (Cumbria, formerly Cumberland) may once have belonged to graves.[230] An array of ringed pins has been found at the beach market at Meols, indicating that they may have been worn or exchanged by traders.[231] Indeed, ringed pins have also been discovered at the trading sites of Llanbedrgoch (Anglesey), Coppergate (York) and Chester.[232] Whithorn attracted a settlement of craftworkers during the late tenth and eleventh centuries, and its inhabitants had links with Dublin, as seen in the presence of a ringed pin among other aspects of material culture.[233]

The urban community of Dublin acquired jewellery crafted elsewhere in Ireland, which in turn spread across the Irish Sea. These items include the 'bossed penannular' brooches and the ostentatious 'thistle' brooches. The former had terminals featuring raised metal bosses, which were influenced by a range of Irish, Anglo-Saxon and Pictish decorative influences. The latter featured criss-crossed 'brambled' terminals that originated in Ireland under Pictish influence during the

---

[225] Paterson *et al.*, *Shadows*, 148; Paterson with Parsons and Howard-Davis, 'Early medieval finds', 48–51 (Workington); McCarthy *et al.*, 'Were there Vikings in Carlisle?', 144; McCarthy and Paterson, 'A post-Roman sequence', 217 (Carlisle); Walton Rogers, 'The copper alloy belt set', 60–2 (Auldhame); Bersu and Wilson, *Three Viking Graves*, 19–26; Paterson, 'Insular belt-fittings', 129–30 (Kiloran Bay); Steinforth, *Die Wikingergräber*, 63, 111.
[226] Hill, *Whithorn*, 371; PAS, LANCUM 2AD712; cf. Thomas, 'Anglo-Scandinavian', 246.
[227] Fanning, *Viking Age Ringed Pins*, 15, 52–4.
[228] Fanning, 'Some aspects', 327–9, 330 (quotation); *idem*, *Viking Age Ringed Pins*, 25–36, 52.
[229] Bersu and Wilson, *Three Viking Graves*, 43 (Balladoole); Paterson *et al.*, *Shadows*, 142–4; Steinforth, *Die Wikingergräber*, 63, 111.
[230] Cowen, 'A catalogue', 184; Crowe, 'An excavation at Kirkmirran', 59, 60; Edwards, *Vikings*, 20, 37.
[231] Griffiths, *Vikings*, 112–13; *idem et al.*, *Meols*, 67–9.
[232] York: Mainman and Rogers, *Craft, Industry*, 2580–2 (seven ringed pins, loop-, baluster- and polyhedral-headed); Llanbedrgoch: Redknap, 'Viking-Age settlement', 156–64; Chester: Lloyd-Morgan, 'The artefacts', 27.
[233] Hill, *Whithorn*, 51–2, 195–7, 369–70.

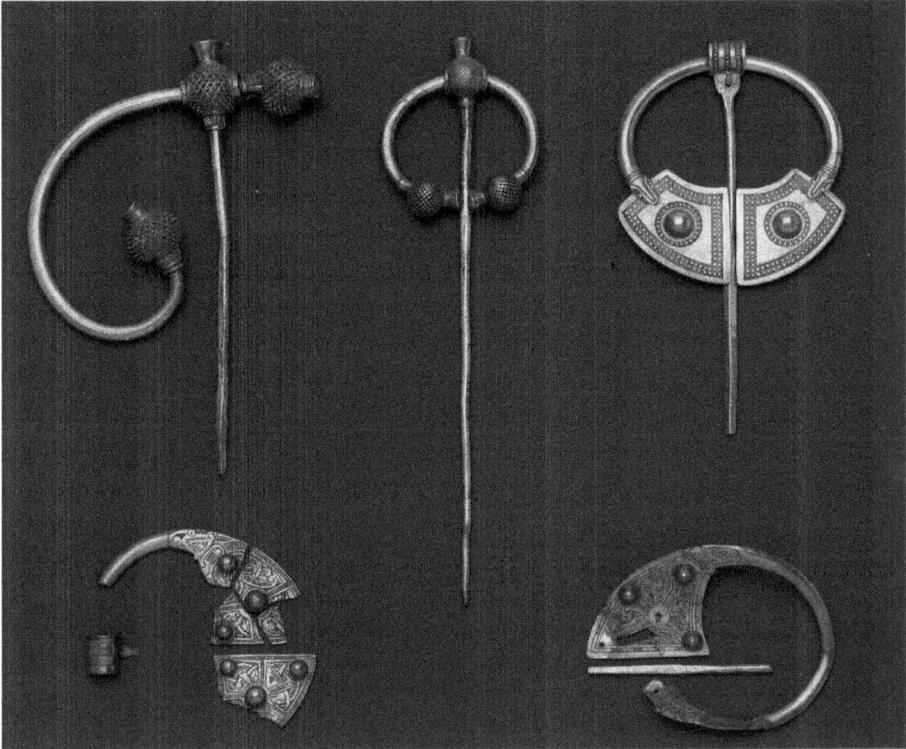

Figure 4: Penannular brooches found at Flusco Pike in 1989 (© Trustees of the British Museum)

ninth century.[234] Both types of brooch came into the hands of Hiberno-Scandinavian leaders and were turned into hacksilver, as seen in the Cuerdale Hoard.[235] There were at least seven complete brooches in the hoard from Flusco Pike near Penrith prior to ploughing damage, including two magnificently large thistle brooches. A runic *fuþark* is inscribed on the reverse of one of the bossed penannular brooches, which indicates that it belonged to a Norse-speaking owner. The hoard is hard to reconstruct because various portions of it were found during the years 1785, 1830 and 1989, along with another (possibly contemporary) deposit found in 2005. Even so, the prevalence of complete brooches and the lack of coins and hacksilver sets it apart from the Cuerdale Hoard.[236] The enormous size of the thistle brooches suggests

---

[234] Graham-Campbell, 'Bossed penannular brooches', 43–6. Johnson points to Irish as well as Anglo-Saxon precursors for the networks of bosses in 'The development', 327–31. For thistle brooches, see Graham-Campbell, 'Two groups', 115–24.

[235] Graham-Campbell, 'Bossed penannular brooches', 40–2 challenged the view that they were manufactured in Dublin or north-west England, for which see Johansen, 'Bossed penannular brooches', 114. For the fragments in the Cuerdale Hoard, see Graham-Campbell, *The Cuerdale Hoard*, 112–16, 220–2.

[236] *Idem, The Cuerdale Hoard*, 115, 230–3, 263–5. Hacksilver found nearby in 2005 most likely belongs to a separate, if contemporary, deposit: The British Museum, *Treasure Annual Report 2005/6*, no. 310.

a ceremonial role, and the collection might be tentatively linked with the movement of a delegation of Hiberno-Scandinavian leaders.[237]

The Flusco Pike hoard brings the discussion of dress accessories back to where it began, with penannular brooches. These brooches travelled across the Irish Sea in the early seventh and the early tenth centuries, and it is worth asking what sort of contacts and networks lay behind their movements. A silver penannular brooch and an Anglo-Saxon or Scandinavian sword from Carronbridge (Dumfries and Galloway) may represent the last resting place of a cosmopolitan 'lone traveller'.[238] He was not alone in moving across the Irish Sea, however: I have discussed other items that were manufactured in parts of the Gaelic world and transported on the dress of travellers or in their treasure chests. An alternative, and perhaps more pervasive, form of cultural influence might have led to the manufacture of such items in the Northumbrian kingdom. As a point of comparison, Jane Kershaw has distinguished between jewellery that was imported from Scandinavia to the Danelaw, and items produced in English workshops in emulation of Scandinavian styles.[239] The Mote of Mark offers the best evidence for local production of Irish-Sea styles in an area that was becoming Northumbrian in the seventh century. Two centuries later, the Carlisle workshop instead looked east for the inspiration behind its Trewhiddle-style strap-ends. It is, however, also a candidate for the production of the Cumwhitton strap-ends, which had affinities across the Irish Sea as well as in the Danelaw.

A variety of social groups helped to disseminate objects and styles; the splendid brooches in the Flusco Pike hoard may have belonged to the highest-ranking Hiberno-Scandinavian leaders, whereas the Cumwhitton cemetery most likely repre-sents a prosperous, regionally important family (potentially two generations).[240] Cumwhitton also opens up consideration of gender in relation to cultural contact, given that two of the graves were furnished with items generally associated with women, and the other four with more typically male assemblages.[241] One of the female graves contained a pair of oval brooches, of which over 4,000 examples have been found across the Scandinavian world, including eighty or more from Britain and Ireland. The Cumwhitton pair belonged to the late-ninth/tenth-century 'P51' style, and there was also a shattered oval brooch of the earlier 'Berdal' style. The brooches and weaponry indicates that this group, most likely a family, ultimately originated in Norway or the Northern Isles, developing links across the Insular world along the way.[242] By wearing oval brooches, at least one of the women perpetuated the tradi-tions of the homelands, a role shared with her counterparts in the Danelaw who wore Scandinavian and Anglo-Scandinavian jewellery.[243] In theory it was possible for Gaelic-speaking women to adopt such dress styles, depending on social status

---

[237] Edwards, *Vikings*, 33–6; Graham-Campbell, 'The northern hoards', 223–5.

[238] Owen and Welander, 'A traveller's end?', esp. 767–9. Graham-Campbell has defined the brooch as an Irish/Pictish hybrid: 'National and regional identities', 34–5.

[239] Kershaw, *Viking Identities*, 38–40, 133–43; cf. Thomas, 'Anglo-Scandinavian metalwork', 240–2.

[240] Paterson *et al.*, *Shadows*, 173.

[241] *Ibid.*, 53–122. It should be noted that some of the artefacts in Grave 2 were not gender-specific and there was no osteoarchaeological evidence for comparison: *ibid.*, 75. For this problem more generally, see Jesch, *The Viking Diaspora*, 88–9.

[242] Paterson *et al.*, *Shadows*, 125–30. In general, see Kershaw, *Viking Identities*, 96–101; Jesch, *The Viking Diaspora*, 94–7.

[243] Kershaw, *Viking Identities*, 157–78.

and the nature of their relationship with a family who wore Scandanavian styles.[244] Yet even when women were wearing this archetypal Scandinavian costume, Insular accessories could be incorporated, such as the bossed belts in female graves at Cumwhitton and Cnip, Lewis.[245] Thus relatively prosperous and mobile women helped to spread objects and styles around the Gaelic–Scandinavian world.

Finally, it is worth reflecting on the types of material culture that I have been unable to cover in this chapter, but which are pertinent to Northumbrian–Gaelic links. Rural settlements are notoriously difficult to locate, and in western Britain they were often built in ways that left little archaeological trace.[246] Exceptions include the crannog, an artificial island settlement that flourished in Dál Riata in Britain, in Ireland and on the far north-western edge of the Northumbrian kingdom.[247] A very different set of farmsteads with rubble footings were occupied from the seventh to the tenth centuries high up near the source of the River Ribble (North Yorkshire). The occupants of the settlement at Crummack Dale in Ribblesdale were relatively prosperous, to judge from artefacts such as a decorated glass drinking vessel, and they may have benefited from their location next to a trans-Pennine pass.[248] Closer to the sea, the excavations at Bryant's Gill in Kentmere have yielded evidence of a structure with distinctive dumps of fire-cracked stones, a feature of Scandinavian settlements in the North Atlantic, as well as buildings at Whithorn and in Dublin.[249] Turning to a different type of evidence, pottery is a rich source of evidence for cultural contact, as the imported wares of the sixth and seventh centuries vividly show.[250] The absence of these wares in north-west England is striking: it is unclear whether this reflects genuine lack of contact with the trade, or a dearth of excavated hillforts. Reports of the now-lost material from Castlehead hillfort near Grange-over-Sands (Cumbria) sound tantalisingly similar to sites north of the Solway.[251] Later on, the discovery of Souterrain Ware at Whithorn is indicative of the presence of crafts-people from north-eastern Ireland in the tenth century.[252]

To conclude, ecclesiastical sites, sculpture and portable metalwork illustrate several phases of interaction between Ireland, other Gaelic-speaking territories and Northumbria. It is impossible to estimate the relative strength of the different cultural influences because many of the sites have undergone only limited excavation. The changing balance between Irish-influenced, Northumbrian and Hiberno-Scandinavian styles is best represented at Whithorn, and other sites and stray finds hint at shifts

---

[244] The enslaved Irish princess Melkorka was made to dress in fine clothes by her Scandinavian male owner according to a saga account: *Laxdæla saga*, ch. 12 (ed. Einar Ólafur Sveinsson, 22–5).

[245] Paterson *et al.*, *Shadows*, 70–1; *eadem*, 'Insular belt-fittings', 129–30. There may also be a female grave with a belt at Workington: Paterson with Parsons and Howard-Davis, 'Early medieval finds', 48–9.

[246] Blair, *Building Anglo-Saxon England*, 30–4, 48, 70, 156–9. The new North-West Regional Research Framework will provide an up-to-date overview of this topic. In the meantime, see Newman *et al.*, 'The early medieval period: resource assessment' (2004).

[247] Crone, *The History*. For crannogs in Ireland, see O'Sullivan *et al.*, *Early Medieval Ireland*, 58–62.

[248] See, for example, Johnson, *The Crummack Dale Project*, 65–6; *idem*, *Excavation*, 4, 11–12, 35–6. See above, 87.

[249] Dickinson, 'Bryant's Gill'; cf. Blair, *Building Anglo-Saxon England*, 283.

[250] Campbell, *Continental and Mediterranean Imports*, esp. 125–39; Toolis and Bowles, *The Lost Dark Age Kingdom*, 125–9.

[251] Stockdale, *Annales Caermoelenses*, 5–6, 201–5.

[252] Campbell, 'The hand-built Dark Age pottery', in Hill, *Whithorn*, 358.

in material culture over the centuries. The analysis of material culture underlines the acceleration of links with the Gaelic-speaking and Gaelic–Scandinavian world towards the end of the Viking Age. It also highlights the great variety of connections, from long-range, high-level ecclesiastical relationships to closer ties across the Solway Firth.

CONCLUSION:
INDIVIDUALS AND INFLUENCES

In this book, I have followed early medieval travellers as they plied the seas and traversed the roads between the Gaelic-speaking world and the Northumbrian kingdom. The prime movers included kings and churchmen of the stature of King Oswald and St Adomnán, as well as the nameless yet well-travelled individual buried by the Roman road at Carronbridge in Nithsdale. The journeys of individuals, families and communities lie behind the rather abstract concept of 'Gaelic influence'. I have demonstrated that Gaelic-speaking and Gaelic–Scandinavian groups had a long-lasting and dynamic impact on the Northumbrian kingdom, not only during its heyday, but most especially during its disintegration. In this final section, I draw out themes that cut across the various types of source material, and I highlight topics that would benefit from future research.

The intrepid individuals lacked a map to guide them in their travels: landmarks, seamarks, place-names and personal guides took on a greater importance than they have today. By the eleventh century, when Gaelic influence was reaching its peak in the west and north of the former kingdom, a monk in the distant south of England was sketching out the basis of a *mappa mundi*. This work of 1025–50 is valuable since it contains the first reasonably realistic medieval representation of Britain and Ireland although – like many modern maps – it is no objective representation of the world.[1] In common with many *mappae mundi*, Jerusalem appears in the centre and Britain and Ireland on the edge, surrounded by ocean. This perception was informed by classical concepts and models (this map potentially having been based on a Roman original), as well as the significance of the biblical lands to ecclesiastical scholars.[2] The Northumbrian kingdom is nowhere to be seen; Hadrian's Wall remains the dominant feature of the region, and Cumbria gets an unexpected mention.[3] Nonetheless, some aspects of the map chime with the discussion of travel in this volume. Islands are remarkably prominent – indeed northern Britain seems to evaporate into a great number of them – and the Isle of Man takes up most of the Irish Sea. The Island has emerged as a key link between the Northumbrian kingdom and the Gaelic world, despite its underrepresentation in texts. I have suggested a Manx role in the circumstances leading to the Northumbrian attack on Brega, 684, and I have traced archaeological, linguistic and dedicatory evidence for localised movements between Man, Morecambe Bay and the Solway. Looking across to Ireland, a prominent place on the map is Armagh, in keeping with its importance to rulers such as Brían Bórama, described as *imperator Scottorum* in the Book of Armagh. The

---

[1] Cotton MS Tiberius B.V.1, fol. 56v, viewed online: https://www.bl.uk/collection-items/anglo-saxon-world-map.

[2] Hiatt, '"From Hulle"', 134–6; Foys, 'The virtual reality', 3–6.

[3] Bill Shannon has argued that the somewhat indistinct writing near the Wall is a garbled rendering of *murus pictus* 'the Pictish wall': *Murus ille famosus*, 32. I am grateful to Dr Shannon for drawing my attention to *Camri*. Cf. McGurk, 'The Mappa Mundi', 80, 86–7.

219

map captures something of the political dynamic that stimulated Gaelic influence during the eleventh century.

Maps are a snapshot in time, creating the impression of a static landscape that determined human activity. I have traced some *longue durée* aspects of communication between Gaeldom and the Northumbrian kingdom, including the constraints that landscape placed on route-ways across the Pennines and the Southern Uplands. The Forth-Clyde isthmus, the Tyne-Solway gap and the Ribble-Aire gap were strategically important for the Northumbrian kings and the rulers of York and Dublin. During the early medieval period there were no technological advances to reduce overland travelling times (a five-and-a-half day excursion being the best-case scenario for a journey between York and the Irish Sea) and some modern-day commuters on the M62 would attest that the crossing is still not easy. On the other hand, a phase of climatic warming from the tenth to the twelfth centuries had dramatic effects on the exploitation of previously marginal landscapes across the North Atlantic. The uplands of the Northumbrian kingdom were no exception, as the many 'clearing' place-names in Norse *þveit* and Brittonic *llanerch* attest. I have argued that these circumstances offered new opportunities in upland areas to settlers from Gaelic-speaking or Gaelic-Scandinavian communities, which is another reason why the eleventh century was a high-point of Gaelic influence in the Northumbrian kingdom.

The patterns of allegiance to community and polity were also dynamic. They affected (and complicate) the terminology that runs through the book: Gaelic and Northumbrian. I began by situating terms such as *Goídil* and *Scotti*, *Norðanhybre* and *Angli* in the thought-world of early medieval writers. Their biblical and classical learning led them to conceptualise the world in terms of *gentes* 'peoples' and to view cultural interaction in terms of the relationships between peoples. Yet the names of *gentes* and their territories were responsive to political change, both in terms of the labels that writers used for their own people and those for their neighbours. One example is the shift in the remit of the term *Alba*, which originally referred to the island of Britain. In the ninth and tenth centuries Gaelic scholars increasingly applied the term to the area between Forth and Spey, the core of the kingdom of Alba.[4] Meanwhile, English and Norse writers started to restrict 'Scottish' terminology to this kingdom, no longer using it for Gaelic-speakers as a whole. This in turn created a vacancy for a term for the Irish, hence the emergence of *Íras* and *Írar* in chronicles and skaldic verse, terms based on the Irish word for Ireland: *Ériu*. The terminological shifts bear the imprint of political change at the top, but they do not necessarily capture the lower-level identities that influenced cultural interaction at a more localised level. I have traced several such links across short sea-crossings including the Firth of Forth, the North Channel and between the Furness peninsula and the Isle of Man.

These localised connections push at the limits of what modern scholars can glean from their evidence, and sometimes there are discrepancies. Chronicles give no indication of the persistence of the York-Dublin link beyond 954; nowhere is it written that Óláfr Cuarán continued to harbour ambitions in York. Yet some of York's late-tenth and eleventh-century moneyers had Gaelic names, and others borrowed dies from Dublin. The Gaelic names in the Yorkshire Domesday underline the connection, and I have suggested that the prominent Yorkshire magnate Glúniairn was related to Óláfr Cuarán's descendants. This 'tale of two cities' had an epilogue: the fall of York to the English kings may have ended the strongly political connection, but familial

---

[4]   Broun, *Scottish Independence*, 71–98.

and economic links continued.[5] Neither could the role of Gall-Goídil in spreading the Gaelic language in the Solway region be guessed from the bare chronicle evidence. Turning to material culture, Richard Bailey has long argued that Irish links are muted in the sculpture of north-west England, perhaps because of differences in church organisation and patronage on either side of the Irish Sea. By contrast, links with Dublin are emerging ever more strongly from the silver hoards found recently on the eastern side of the Irish Sea (Huxley, Silverdale and the Galloway hoard).

Not only did this complex pattern of interactions involve regional and chrono-logical variation, there is also evidence of social diversity among the groups travel-ling to the Northumbrian kingdom. I explored three types of material culture, each shedding light on contacts between different groups: affluent laypeople (female as well as male), top-level ecclesiastical contacts, and the lay congregations of propri-etary churches (who were dedicating their churches to Gaelic saints). Trade is hard to detect in the west of the Northumbrian kingdom, magnificent hoards notwith-standing. The only mint was in York, and so those wishing to do business in western Northumbria either had to come with their coins ready-prepared or use other means of exchange. There was a beach market at Luce Sands, but no evidence of a major urban centre where one might be expected (Carlisle?). The most northerly trading sites on the eastern side of the Irish Sea were at Chester and Meols: did they satisfy traders' needs?[6] The question can be set in the broader European context: by the eighth century, the North Sea trading system was flourishing.[7] It may be that long-distance traders were attracted to Northumbria's eastern coast, while those on the west coast focused on localised movements of goods.[8] On the other hand, new techniques of isotope analysis have revealed that metal ores were mined in the Northumbrian uplands and exported to Norway. We have not yet identified all of the goods that were being traded around the Irish Sea.

This exciting finding leads on to another point, which is that new techniques hold the promise of filling in more gaps in this picture of Gaelic influence in the Northumbrian kingdom. The texts that I have consulted have revealed a complex and detailed picture of interactions: the Northumbrians initially dealt with Cenél nGabráin in Dál Riata and Cenél Conaill among Uí Néill. By the mid-eighth century, Cenél Conaill had lost its pre-eminence and Dál Riata had been subsumed by the Pictish king Onuist son of Uurguist. This elaborate picture of high-political inter-actions emerges from texts such as chronicles, but such sources rarely refer to the roles of women in these cultural contacts. Place-names may shed some light on their contribution, given that the linguistic dynamics in a family were – and still are – strongly influenced by the 'mother tongue'.[9] Increasingly, strontium isotope analysis is shedding light on the mobility of diverse groups, including women and children.[10] While it is often not possible to determine an individual's background with precision, this approach has the potential to clarify the level of movement in and out of the Irish Sea region.[11] Such developments pose challenges for those attempting interdiscipli-nary work, in that it is increasingly difficult to attain 'disciplinary adequacy' in all

---

[5] The title of Charles Dickens's book was used in a review article by Ray Page: 'A tale'.
[6] Griffiths *et al.*, *Meols*.
[7] McCormick, *Origins*, 12, 563–4, 609.
[8] Wickham, *Framing*, 697 observes that small-scale exchange could operate *ad hoc*.
[9] Jesch, *The Viking Diaspora*, 91.
[10] Hadley and Hemer, 'Microcosms of migration'.
[11] Hemer *et al.*, 'Evidence'; Hemer *et al.*, 'No Man'; Symonds *et al.*, 'Medieval migrations'.

relevant fields.[12] Nevertheless, new techniques may unlock dimensions of medieval cultural contact that previously lay hidden.

Finally, it is worth taking stock of the broader significance of this study. I have made the case that Northumbrian history is best studied in its Insular context. There is increasing awareness of this approach in early medieval history, and the study of central medieval 'Middle Britain' is flourishing, as is the interest in links across the Irish Sea.[13] Insular history is itself painted on a broader European and global canvas, and there is scope for comparing the framework of Gaelic–Northumbrian contact with cultural interaction elsewhere.[14]

In the year 875, when St Cuthbert's community left its ancient seat of Lindisfarne and wandered to the coast of the Irish Sea, it may have seemed that the Golden Age of ecclesiastical links was truly at an end. The Great Heathen army was disrupting kingdoms and churches, and the presence of a contingent from Ireland ensured that its activities reverberated across the Insular world. The main message of this book is that a complex and ever-changing web of connections linked the Northumbrian and Gaelic-speaking peoples. These contacts were by no means restricted to the voyages of churchmen; they also encompassed warbands, diplomats and enterprising families. The fall of the Northumbrian kingdom led to the acceleration and diversification of Gaelic influence.

[12] Repko, *Interdisciplinary Research*, 60, 193–224.
[13] Stringer and Winchester (eds), *Northern England and Southern Scotland*.
[14] See above, 21.

BIBLIOGRAPHY

Manuscripts

Cambridge, University Library, Kk. 5. 16, viewed online at: http://cudl.lib.cam.ac.uk/view/ MS-KK-00005-00016/1
Dublin, Trinity College, MS 1441, viewed online at: http://digitalcollections.tcd.ie/home/
— MS 57 (The Book of Durrow), viewed online at: http://digitalcollections.tcd.ie/home/
Dublin, University College, MS Franciscan A2, viewed online at:
'Irish Script on Screen', https://www.isos.dias.ie/
Durham Cathedral Library, MS A.IV.19, viewed online at: https://www.durhampriory.ac.uk/ list-of-digitised-durham-priory-library-books/
London, British Library, Cotton MS Tiberius B.V, viewed online at:https://www.bl.uk/ collection-items/anglo-saxon-world-map
— Cotton MS Nero D iii (Register of St Leonard's Hospital, vol. 1)
Oxford, University College, MS 165
Vatican Library, Pal. lat. 68, viewed online at: https://digi.vatlib.it/view/bav_pal_lat_68

Primary Sources

AHLQVIST, Anders (ed.), *The Early Irish Linguist*, Commentationes Humanarum Litterarum 73 (Helsinki, 1982).
AMOURS, F. J. (ed.), *The Original Chronicle of Andrew of Wyntoun*, 6 vols (Edinburgh, 1903–14).
ANDERSON, Alan Orr (transl.), *Early Sources of Scottish History*, 2 vols (Edinburgh, 1922; repr. Stamford, 1990).
— and Marjore Ogilvie ANDERSON (eds), *The Chronicle of Melrose from the Cottonian Manuscript, Faustina B.IX in the British Museum. A Complete and Full-size Facsimile in Collotype* (London, 1936).
— and Marjorie Ogilvie ANDERSON (ed. and transl.), *Adomnán's Life of Columba*, 2nd edn (Oxford, 1991).
ARNOLD, Thomas (ed.), *Symeonis monachi opera omnia*, Rolls ser. 75, 2 vols (London, 1882–5).
ATKINSON, J. and J. BROWNBILL, *The Coucher Book of Furness Abbey*, 2 vols. in 6 (Chetham, new ser., ix, xi, xiv, lxxiv, lxxvi, lxxviii, 1886–1919).
ATTENBOROUGH, F. L. (ed. and transl.), *The Laws of the Earliest English Kings* (Cambridge, 1922).
BAIN, Joseph, *Calendar of Documents relating to Scotland II AD 1272–1307* (Edinburgh, 1884).
BANNERMAN, John (ed. and transl.), 'Senchus Fer nAlban', in *idem, Studies*, 41–7.
BARNEY, Stephen A. *et al.* (transl.), *The Etymologies of Isidore of Seville* (Cambridge, 2006).
BARROW, G. W. S. (ed.), *Regesta regum Scottorum I: The Acts of Malcolm IV King of Scots 1153–65* (Edinburgh, 1965).
— (ed.), *Regesta regum Scottorum II: The Acts of William I, King of Scots, 1165–1214* (Edinburgh, 1971).
— (ed. and transl.), *The Charters of David I: The Written Acts of David I, King of Scots, 1124–53 and of his son Henry Earl of Northumberland, 1139–52* (Woodbridge, 1999).

BARTLETT, Robert (ed. and transl.) Geoffrey of Burton, *Life and Miracles of St. Modwenna* (Oxford, 2002).

BARTRUM, P. C., *Early Welsh Genealogical Tracts* (Cardiff, 1966).

BATELY, Janet (ed.), *The Anglo-Saxon Chronicle: A Collaborative Edition, 3 MS A* (Cambridge, 1986).

BAYERSCHMIDT, Carl F. and Lee M. HOLLANDER (transl.), *Njáls Saga* (New York, 1955).

BERGIN, O. and R. I. BEST, 'Tochmarc Étaíne', *Ériu* 12 (1938), 137–96.

BERNARD, J. H. and J. ATKINSON (eds), *The Irish Liber Hymnorum Volume I: Text and Introduction* (London, 1898).

BEST, R. I. (ed.), 'Story of Mael Ruain of Tallaght' (ed.), in J. P. Fraser *et al.* (eds), *Irish Texts I* (London, 1931), 34–5.

— and Hugh Jackson LAWLOR (eds), *The Martyrology of Tallaght* (London, 1931).

— *et al.* (eds), *The Book of Leinster: formerly Lebar na Núachongbála*, 6 vols (Dublin, 1954–83).

BHREATHNACH, Edel, and Kevin MURRAY (eds), '*Baile Chuinn Chétchathaig*: edition', in Bhreathnach (ed.), *The Kingship*, 73–94.

BIELER, Ludwig (ed. and transl.), *The Irish Penitentials* (Dublin, 1963).

— (ed. and transl.) *The Patrician Texts in the Book of Armagh* (Dublin, 1979).

BINCHY, D. A. (ed.), *Críth Gablach* (Dublin, 1941).

— (ed.), *Scéla Cano meic Gartnáin* (Dublin, 1963).

BIRT, Theodor (ed.), 'De consulatu Stilichonis', in *idem* (ed.), *Claudii Claudiani Carmina*, MGH Auctores antiquissimi 10 (Berlin, 1892), 189–233.

Bjarni Einarsson (ed.), *Egils Saga* (London, 2003).

BLEW, W. J. (ed.), *Breviarium Aberdonense* (2 vols., London, 1854).

BRAMLEY, K. A. *et al.* (eds), *Gwaith Llywelyn Fardd I ac Eraill*, Cyfres Beirdd y Tywysogion II (Cardiff, 1994).

BRODERICK, George (ed. and transl.), *Cronica regum Mannie et Insularum* (Douglas, 1996).

BROMWICH, Rachel (ed. and transl.), *Trioedd Ynys Prydein: The Triads of the Island of Britain*, 4th edn (Cardiff, 2014).

BROOKS, Nicholas *et al.* (eds), 'A new charter of King Edgar', *Anglo-Saxon England* 13 (1984), 137–55.

BROWN, William (ed.), *Yorkshire Deeds (volume 1)* (Leeds, 1909).

BURGESS, Richard, 'The Gallic chronicle of 452: a new critical edition with a brief introduction', in Ralph W. Mathisen and Danuta Shanzer (eds), *Society and Culture in Late Antique Gaul* (Aldershot, 2001), 52–82.

BYRNE, Francis John (ed. and transl.), 'Clann Ollaman Uaisle Emna', *Studia Hibernica* 4 (1964), 54–94.

CAMPBELL, A., Chronicon Æthelweardi: *The Chronicle of Æthelweard* (London, 1962).

— (ed. and transl.), *De Abbatibus* (Oxford, 1967).

CARPENTER, David X. (ed.), *The Cartulary of St Leonard's Hospital York: Rawlinson Volume*, 2 vols (Woodbridge, 2015).

CHARLES-EDWARDS, T. M. and Fergus KELLY (eds), *Bechbretha: an Old Irish Law-Tract on Bee-Keeping* (Dublin, 1983).

— (ed. and transl.), *The Chronicle of Ireland*, 2 vols (Liverpool, 2006).

CLANCY, J. P., 'Taliesin (late sixth century)', in Thomas Owen Clancy (ed.), *The Triumph Tree: Scotland's Earliest Poetry, 550–1350* (Edinburgh, 1998), 79–93.

COLGRAVE, Bertram (ed. and transl.), *The Life of Bishop Wilfrid by Eddius Stephanus* (Cambridge, 1927).

— (ed. and transl.), *Two Lives of Saint Cuthbert. A Life by an Anonymous Monk of Lindisfarne and Bede's Prose Life* (Cambridge, 1939; repr. New York, 1969).

— (ed. and transl.), *The Earliest Life of Gregory the Great by an Anonymous Monk of Whitby* (Lawrence KS, 1968).

— and R. A. B. MYNORS (ed. and transl.), *Bede's Ecclesiastical History of the English People* (Oxford, 1969).

CONNOLLY, S. and J.-M. PICARD (transl.), 'Cogitosus' Life of St. Brigit: content and value', *Journal of the Royal Society of Antiquaries of Ireland* 117 (1987), 11–27.

COXE, H. O., *Rogeri de Wendover Chronica, sive Flores Historiarum*, 5 vols (London, 1841–4).

CUBBIN, G. P., *The Anglo-Saxon Chronicle: A Collaborative Edition, 6 MS D* (Cambridge, 1996).

DARLINGTON, R. R. and P. MCGURK, *The Chronicle of John of Worcester*, 3 vols (Oxford, 1995–).

DAVIS, H. W. C. with R. J. WHITWELL, *Regesta regum Anglo-Normannorum, 1066–1165*, *vol. I* (Oxford, 1913).

DICKINSON, T. *et al.* (eds), *Compota Thesaurariorum Regum Scotorum. Accounts of the Lord High Treasurer of Scotland*, 13 vols (Edinburgh, 1877–1978).

DILLON, Myles (ed. and transl.), *Lebor na Cert*, ITS 46 (Dublin, 1962).

DOBBS, Margaret E. (ed. and transl.), 'The history of the descendants of Ír', *Zeitschrift für celtische Philologie* 13 (1921), 308–59; 14 (1923), 44–144.

— 'The Ban-shenchus', *Revue Celtique* 47 (1930), 283–339.

DUGDALE, William (ed.), *Monasticon Anglicanum*, ed. John Caley, 8 vols (Farnborough, 1970).

DÜMMLER, Ernst (ed.), *Epistolae Karolini Aevi II*, MGH *Epistolae* 4 (Berlin, 1895).

DUMVILLE, David N. (ed.), '*Cethri Prímchenéla Dáil Riata*', *Scottish Gaelic Studies* 20 (2000), 170–91.

— *Annales Cambriae, A.D. 682–954: Texts A–C in Parallel* (Cambridge, 2002).

EHWALD, Rudolf (ed.), *Aldhelmi opera*, MGH *Auctores antiquissimi* XV (Berlin, 1919).

Einar Ól. Sveinsson (ed.), *Laxdæla saga* (ed.), Íslenzk fornrit 5 (Reykjavík, 1934).

— *Brennu-Njáls saga*, Íslenzk Fornrit 12 (Reykjavík, 1954).

ESPOSITO, Mario (ed.), 'Conchubrani Vita Sanctae Monennae', *PRIA* 28C (1910), 202–51.

FARRER, William and Charles Travis CLAY (eds), *Early Yorkshire Charters*, 12 vols, Yorkshire Archaeological Soc. extra ser. (1914–65).

FARRER, William and John F. CURWEN (eds), *Records relating to the Barony of Kendale*, 3 vols (Kendal, 1923–6).

FAULKES, Anthony (transl.), *Færeyinga saga* (Dundee, 2016).

FELL, Christine (transl.), *Egils Saga* (London, 1975).

FERGUSON, R. S. (ed.), *Testamenta Karleolensia. The Series of Wills from the Pre-Reformation Registers of the Bishops of Carlisle* (Kendal, 1893).

FINSTERWALDER, P. W. (ed.), *Die Canones Theodori Cantuariensis und ihre Überlieferungsformen* (Weimar, 1929), 239–334.

FORBES, A. P. (ed. and transl.), *Lives of S. Ninian and S. Kentigern*, The Historians of Scotland 5 (Edinburgh, 1874).

FRESCOLN, Wilson (ed.), *Guillaume le Clerc: The Romance of Fergus* (Philadelphia PA, 1983).

FULK, R. D., 'Lausavísur', in Whaley (ed.), *Poetry*, 698–737.

GAIRDNER, James (ed.), *Sailing Directions for the Circumnavigation of England ... from a 15th Century MS* (London, 1889).

GILBERT, J. T. (ed.), *Chartularies of St. Mary's Abbey Dublin*, Rolls ser. 80, 2 vols (London, 1884).

GLEESON, Dermot and Seán MAC AIRT (eds), 'The Annals of Roscrea', *PRIA* 59 C (1957–9), 137–80.

GODDEN, Malcolm (ed.), *Ælfric's Catholic Homilies: The Second Series Text* (Oxford, 1979)

GODMAN, Peter (ed. and transl.), *Alcuin: The Bishops, Kings and Saints of York* (Oxford, 1982).

GRAINGER, F. and W. G. COLLINGWOOD (eds), *Register and Records of Holm Cultram*, CWAAS Record ser. 7 (Kendal 1929).

GWYNN, Edward John, *The Metrical Dindshenchas: Text, Translation and Commentary* (Dublin, 1903).

HADDAN, Arthur West and William STUBBS, *Councils and Documents relating to Great Britain and Ireland*, 3 vols (Oxford, 1869–78).

HAMPE, K. (ed.), 'Leonis III papae epistolae X', in E. Dümmler (ed.), MGH *Epistolae Karolini Aevi III* (Berlin, 1899), 85–104.

HARDY, Thomas Duffy (ed.), *Descriptive Catalogue of Materials relating to the History of Great Britain* (London, 1857).

HAYCOCK, Marged (ed. and transl.), *Prophecies from the Book of Taliesin* (Aberystwyth, 2013).

HEIST, W. W. (ed.), *Vitae Sanctorum Hiberniae esc Codice olim Salmanticensi nunc Bruxellensi*, Subsidia Hagiographica 25 (Brussels, 1965).

HENNESSY, William M. (ed. and transl.), *Chronicum Scotorum*, Rolls ser. 46 (London, 1866).

— (ed. and transl.), *The Annals of Loch Cé* (London, 1871).

— and B. MAC CARTHY (eds), *Annala Uladh: Annals of Ulster*, 4 vols (Dublin, 1887–1901).

HERBERT, Máire and Pádraig Ó RIAIN (eds), *Betha Adamnáin* (London, 1988).

Hermann Pálsson and Paul EDWARDS (transl.), *The Book of Settlements: Landnámabók* (Winnipeg, 1972)

The Holy Bible, King James Version. Cambridge Compact Reference Edition (Cambridge, 1994).

The Holy Bible, New International Version (London, 1979; repr. 2000).

HOOD, A. B. E. (ed. and transl.), *St Patrick: His Writings and Muirchú's Life* (Chichester, 1978).

HORSTMANN, Carl (ed.) *De Servo Dei Finano et Confessore*, in *idem* (ed.), *Nova Legenda Anglie* (Oxford, 1901), 444–7.

HUDSON, Benjamin T. (ed. and transl.), 'The Scottish chronicle', *The Scottish Historical Review* 77 (1998), 126–61.

HURST, D. (ed.), *In primam partem Samuhelis libri IIII* in *Bedae Venerabilis Opera Pars II: Opera exegetica*, CCSL 119 (Turnhout, 1962), 5–272.

INNES, Cosmo (ed.), *Liber cartarum Sancte Crucis* (Edinburgh, 1840).

— *Registrum de Dunfermlyn* (Ediburgh, 1842).

— *Registrum episcopatus Glasguensis*, 2 vols (Edinburgh, 1843).

— *Liber S. Marie de Calchou* (Edinburgh, 1846).

— *Carte monalium de Northberwic* (Edinburgh, 1847).

IRELAND, Colin A. (ed. and transl.), *Old Irish Wisdom attributed to Aldfrith of Northumbria: an Edition of Bríathra Flainn Fína maic Ossu* (Tempe AZ, 1999).

IRVINE, Susan (ed.), *The Anglo-Saxon Chronicle: A Collaborative Edition, 7 MS E* (Cambridge, 2004).

JACKSON, Kenneth Hurlstone (ed. and transl.), *The Gaelic Notes in the Book of Deer* (Cambridge, 1972).

Jakob Benediktsson (ed.), *Íslendingabók. Landnámabók*, Íslenzk fornrit 1 (Reykjavík, 1968).

JONES, C. W. (ed.), *Libri quatuor in principium Genesis*, in *Bedae venerabilis opera. Pars II, opera exegetica*, Corpus Christianorum Series Latina 118a (Turnhout, 1967).

— *De temporum ratione liber*, *Bedae Venerabilis Opera Pars VI: Opera Didascalia 2*, CCSL 123 B (Turnhout, 1977).

— *De temporibus*, *Bedae Venerabilis Opera Pars VI: Opera Didascalia 3*, CCSL 123 C (Turnhout, 1980), 585–611.

KENDALL, Calvin B., *On Genesis. Bede*, Translated Texts for Historians 48 (Liverpool, 2008).

— and Faith WALLIS, *Bede, On the Nature of Things and On Times*, Translated Texts for Historians 56 (Liverpool, 2010).

KENDRICK, T. D. *et al.* (eds), *Codex Lindisfarnensis*, 2 vols (Basle, 1956–60).

KOCH, John T. (ed. and transl.), *The Gododdin of Aneirin: Text and Context from Dark-Age Britain* (Cardiff, 1997).

LAISTNER, M. L. W. (ed.), *Bedae Venerabilis expositio actuum apostolorum et retractatio* (Cambridge MA, 1939).

LAPIDGE, Michael, (ed. and transl.) 'Vita S. Swithvni', in *idem, The Cult of St Swithun* (Oxford, 2003), 590–610.

— 'The career of Aldhelm', *Anglo-Saxon England* 36 (2007), 15–69.

— *Byrhtferth of Ramsey: The Lives of St Oswald and St Ecgwine* (Oxford, 2009).
— and Michael HERREN (transl.), *Aldhelm: The Prose Works* (Ipswich, 1979).
— (ed.) and André CRÉPIN (transl.), *Histoire Ecclésiastique du Peuple Anglais*, 3 vols (Paris, 2005).
LEWIS, Christopher (ed.), *The Cheshire Domesday*, Alecto County Edition of Domesday (London, 1991).
LIEBERMANN, F. (ed.), *Die Gesetze der Angelsachsen*, 3 vols (Halle, 1903–16).
LINDSAY, W. M. (ed.), *Isidori Hispalensis Episcopi etymologiarum sive originum libri xx*, 2 vols (Oxford, 1911).
MAC AIRT, Seán (ed. and transl.), *The Annals of Inisfallen* (Dublin, 1951).
MAC AIRT, Seán and Gearóid MAC NIOCAILL (ed. and transl.), *The Annals of Ulster (to A.D. 1131)* (Dublin, 1983).
MACALISTER, R. A. Stewart (ed. and transl.), *Lebor Gabála Érenn: The Book of the Taking of Ireland*, ITS 34–5, 39, 41, 44, 5 vols (Dublin, 1932–42).
MCDONOUGH, C. J. (ed. and transl.), *Moriuht: A Norman Latin Poem from the Early Eleventh Century* (Toronto, 1995).
MACQUEEN, John and Winifred MACQUEEN (ed. and transl.), Walter Bower, *Scotichronicon* vol. II (Edinburgh, 1989).
Magnus Magnusson and Hermann Pálsson (transl.), *Laxdaela saga* (Harmondsworth, 1969).
MARTIN, Lawrence T. (transl.), *The Venerable Bede: Commentary on the Acts of the Apostles* (Kalamazoo MI, 1989).
MEYER, Kuno (ed. and transl.), *Aislinge Meic Conglinne: The Vision of MacConglinne* (London, 1892).
— (ed.) 'The Laud genealogies and tribal histories', *Zeitschrift für celtische Philologie* 8 (1912), 291–338.
— (ed.) 'The Laud synchronisms', *Zeitschrift für celtische Philologie* 9 (1913), 471–85.
— (ed.), *Über die älteste irische Dichtung I: Rhythmische alliterierende Reimstrophen* (Berlin, 1913).
MOMMSEN, Theodor (ed.), 'Historia Brittonum cum additamentis Nennii', in *idem* (ed.), *Chronica Minora saec. IV. V. VI. VII. 3*, MGH Auctores Antiquissimi 13 (Berlin, 1898), 111–222.
— 'Chronica maiora', in *De temporum ratione*, in *idem* (ed.), *Chronica Minora saec. IV. V. VI. VII. 3*, MGH Auctores Antiquissimi 13 (Berlin, 1898), 247–327.
MORGAN, Philip and Alexander R. RUMBLE (eds), *Domesday Cheshire* (Chichester, 1978).
— and Caroline THORN (eds), *Domesday Book: Lincolnshire*, Domesday Book 31 (1 vol in 2, Chichester, 1986).
MORRIS, C. J. (transl.), *Marriage and Murder in Eleventh-Century Northumbria: A Study of 'De obsessione Dunelmi'*, Borthwick Papers 82 (York, 1992).
MORRIS, John (ed. and transl.), *Nennius: British History, and the Welsh Annals* (London, 1980).
MÜLLER, E. (ed.), *Nithardi historiarum libri IIII*, MGH Scriptores rerum Germanicarum 44 (Hanover, 1907).
MURPHY, Denis (ed.), *The Annals of Clonmacnoise being Annals of Ireland from the Earliest Period to A.D. 1408* (Dublin, 1896).
MYNORS, R. A. B., *William of Malmesbury: Gesta regum Anglorum*, 2 vols (Oxford, 1998).
NOBBE, Karl Friedrich August (ed.), *Claudii Ptolemaei Geographia*, 3 vols (Lepizig, 1843–5).
O'BRIEN, M. A., *Corpus genealogiarum Hiberniae I* (Dublin, 1962).
Ó CUÍV, Brian (ed.), 'A poem in praise of Raghnall, king of Man', *Éigse* 8 (1955–7), 283–301.
O'DONOVAN, John (ed.), *The Irish Charters in the Book of Kells* (Dublin, 1846).
— (ed. and transl.), *Annála Ríoghachta Éireann: Annals of the Kingdom of Ireland by the Four Masters from the Earliest Period to the Year 1171* (Dublin, 1849).
— *et al.* (eds), *The Martyrology of Donegal: A Calendar of the Saints of Ireland* (Dublin, 1864).
O'KEEFFE, J. G., 'The Rule of Patrick', *Ériu* 1 (1904), 216–24.

O'KEEFFE, Katherine O'Brien, *The Anglo-Saxon Chronicle: A Collaborative Edition, 5:MS C* (Cambridge, 2001).
Ólafur Halldórsson (ed.), Færeyinga saga, Íslenzk Fornrit 25 (Reykjavik, 2006).
O'RAHILLY, Cecile (ed.), *Táin Bó Cúalnge: From the Book of Leinster* (Dublin, 1967).
O'RAHILLY, Cecile (ed.), *Táin Bó Cúailnge: Recension I* (Dublin, 1976).
Ó RIAIN, Pádraig (ed.), *Corpus genealogiarum sanctorum Hiberniae* (Dublin, 1985).
OWEN, D. D. R. (transl.), *Fergus of Galloway, Knight of King Arthur* (London, 1991).
PARTHEY, G. and M. PINDER (eds), *Itinerarium Antonini Augusti* (Berlin, 1848).
PLUMMER, Charles (ed.), *Lives of Saints from the Book of Lismore* (Oxford, 1890).
— *Venerabilis Baedae Opera Historica*, 2 vols (Oxford, 1896).
— (ed. and transl.), *Bethada Náem nÉrenn*, 2 vols (Oxford, 1922).
PRESCOTT, John Eustace (ed.), *The Register of the Priory of Wetherhal* (Kendal, 1897).
RADNER, Joan (ed. and transl.), *The Fragmentary Annals of Ireland* (Dublin, 1978).
RAINE, James (ed.), Reginald of Durham, *Libellus de admirandis Beati Cuthberti virtutibus quae novellis patratae sunt temporibus* (Surtees Society 1, 1834).
— (ed.), *Libellus de ortu Sancti Cuthberti*, in idem, *Miscellanea Biographica* (Surtees Soc. 8, 1838), 63–87.
RAUER, Christine (ed. and transl.), *The Old English Martyrology* (Cambridge, 2013).
REEVE, Michael D. (ed.) and Neil WRIGHT (transl.), *Geoffrey of Monmouth: The History of the Kings of Britain* (Woodbridge, 2007).
ROLFE, John C. (ed. and transl.), *Ammianus Marcellinus: History*, 3 vols (Cambridge MA, 1939).
ROLLASON, David (ed. and transl.), *Libellus de exordio atque procursu istius hoc est Dunhelmensis Ecclesie* (Oxford, 2000).
— and Linda ROLLASON (eds), *The Durham Liber Vitae*, 3 vols (London, 2007).
SAWYER, P. H. (ed.), *Charters of Burton Abbey*, Anglo-Saxon Charters 2 (London, 1979).
SCHOLZ, Bernhard Walter (transl.), *Carolingian Chronicles* (Ann Arbor MI, 1970).
SEECK, Otto (ed.), *Notitia Dignitatum accedunt Notitia Urbis Constantinopolitanae et Laterculi Prouinciarum* (Berlin, 1876).
SHARPE, Richard (transl.), *Adomnán of Iona: Life of St Columba* (London, 1995).
SKENE, William F. (ed.), *The Four Ancient Books of Wales*, 2 vols (Edinburgh, 1868).
— (ed.), John of Fordun, *Chronica gentis Scottorum*, 2 vols (Edinburgh, 1871–2).
SMITH, David M. (ed.), *English Episcopal Acta 30: Carlisle 1133–1292* (Oxford, 2005).
SOUTH, Ted Johnson (ed. and transl.), *Historia de Sancto Cuthberto* (Cambridge, 2002).
SPERBER, Ingrid, and Ludwig BIELER (eds), Jocelin of Furness, *Vita S. Patricii*, available in online searchable edition at: Anthony Harvey and Angela Malthouse (eds), Royal Irish Academy Archive of Celtic-Latin literature (2nd development and expanded edition, ACLL-2), http://www.brepolis.net
STOKES, Whitley (ed. and transl.), *Lives of Saints: From the Book of Lismore* (Oxford, 1890).
— (ed. and transl.), *Félire Húi Gormáin: The Martyrology of Gorman*, Henry Bradshaw Society 9 (London, 1895).
— (ed. and transl.), 'Annals of Tigernach', *Revue Celtique* 16 (1895), 374–419; 17 (1896), 6–33, 119–263, 337–420; 18 (1897), 9–59, 150–97, 267–303; repr. 2 vols (Felinfach, 1993).
— (ed. and transl.), *Félire Óengusso céli Dé: The Martyrology of Oengus the Culdee*, Henry Bradshaw Society 29 (London, 1905).
STRECKER, Karl, 'Rhythmi computistici', MGH *Poetae Latini Aevi Carolini* 4.2 (Berlin, 1896).
— 'Miracula Nynie episcopi', in MGH *Poetae Latini Aevi Carolini* 4.3 (Berlin, 1923), 944–62
STUBBS, William (ed.), *Chronica magistri Rogeri de Houedene*, Rolls ser., 4 vols (London, 1868–71).
TAIT, James (ed.), *The Chartulary or Register of the Abbey of St Werburgh, Chester*, Chetham Society new ser. 82 (Manchester, 1923).
TALBOT, T. (ed.), *Manorial Roll of the Isle of Man 1511–1551* (Oxford, 1924).
TAMOTO, Kenichi (ed.), *The Macregol Gospels or the Rushworth Gospels* (Amsterdam, 2013).
TANGL, M. (ed.), *S. Bonifatii et Lulli epistolae*, MGH *Epistolae selectae* 1 (Berlin, 1916).

TAYLOR, Simon (ed.), *The Anglo-Saxon Chronicle: A Collaborative Edition, 4 MS B* (Cambridge, 1983).

— and D. E. R. WATT (ed. and transl.), Walter Bower, *Scotichronicon*, vol. IX (Edinburgh, 1990).

TIERNEY, J. J. (ed. and transl.), *Dicuil: Liber de mensura orbis terrae* (Dublin, 1967).

TODD, James Henthorn (ed.), *Leabhar breathnach annso sis: The Irish Version of the Historia Britonum of Nennius* (Dublin, 1848).

— (ed.), *Cogadh Gaedhel re Gallaibh: The War of the Gaedhil with the Gaill*, Rolls ser. 48 (London, 1867).

TOWNEND Matthew and R. D. FULK (eds), 'Lausavísur', in Diana Whaley (ed.), *Poetry from the Kings' Sagas 1: From Mythical Times to c. 1035* (Turnhout, 2012), 783.

ULSTER SOCIETY FOR MEDIEVAL LATIN STUDIES (ed. and transl.), 'The Life of St Monenna by Conchubranus', *Seanchas Ardmhacha* 9 (1978–9), 250–73; 10 (1980–2), 117–41, 426–54.

WAITZ, Georg, 'Mariani Scotti Chronicon', in Georg Heinrich Pertz (ed.), MGH *Scriptores* V (Hannover, 1844), 481–568.

WALLIS, Faith (transl.), *Bede: The Reckoning of Time* (Liverpool, 1988; repr. 2004).

WARNTJES, Immo (ed. and transl.), *The Munich Computus: Text and Translation* (Stuttgart, 2010).

WASSERSCHLEBEN, H. (ed.), *Collectio Canonum Hibernensis, Die irische Kanonensammlung* (Leipzig, 1885).

WEBER, Robert and Robert GRYSON (eds), *Biblia Sacra Vulgata*, 5th edn (Stuttgart, 2007).

WHITE, Nora (ed. and transl.), *Compert Mongáin and Three Other Early Mongán Tales* (Maynooth, 2006).

WHITELOCK, Dorothy (transl.), *The Anglo-Saxon Chronicle: A Revised Translation* (London, 1961).

— (transl.) *English Historical Documents I c.500–1042*, 2nd edn (London, 1979).

WILLIAMS, A. and G. H. MARTIN, *The Yorkshire Domesday*, Alecto County Edition of Domesday 31, ed. A. Williams and G. H. Martin (London, 1992).

— *The Lincolnshire Domesday*, ed. and transl. A. Williams and G. H. Martin (London, 1992).

WILLIAMS, Ifor (ed.), *Canu Aneirin* (Cardiff, 1938).

— (ed.), *The Poems of Taliesin*, transl. J. E. CAERWYN WILLIAMS (Dublin, 1968).

WILLIAMS (ab Ithel), John (ed.), *Annales Cambriae*, Rolls ser. 20 (London, 1860).

WILSON, James (ed.), *The Register of the Priory of St. Bees*, Surtees Society 126 (Durham, 1915).

WINTERBOTTOM, Michael (ed. and transl.), *The Ruin of Britain and other Works: Gildas* (London, 1978).

WOODMAN, David (ed. and transl.), *The Charters of Northern Houses*, Anglo-Saxon Charters 16 (Oxford, 2012).

ZANGEMEISTER, C., Orosius, *Libri historiarum adversum paganos*, 2 vols (Vienna, 1882).

Secondary Works

AALEN, F. H. A., 'Clochans as transhumance dwellings in the Dingle Peninsula, Co. Kerry', *Journal of the Royal Society of Antiquaries of Ireland* 94 (1964), 39–45.

ABRAMS, Lesley, 'The conversion of the Scandinavians of Dublin', *Anglo-Norman Studies* XX (1997), 1–30.

— 'Edward the Elder's Danelaw', in Higham and Hill (eds), *Edward the Elder*, 128–43.

— 'The conversion of the Danelaw', in James Graham-Campbell *et al.* (eds), *Vikings and the Danelaw: Selected Papers from the Proceedings of the Thirteenth Viking Congress* (Oxford, 2001), 31–44.

— 'Conversion and the Church in the Hebrides in the Viking Age: a very difficult thing indeed', in Ballin Smith *et al.* (eds), *West Over Sea*, 169–94.

— 'King Edgar and the Danelaw', in D. Scragg (ed.), *Edgar King of the English 959–75: New Interpretations* (Woodbridge, 2008), 171–91.

— 'Diaspora and identity in the Viking Age', *Early Medieval Europe* 20 (2012), 17–38.

ADAMSON, John, 'An account of the discovery, at Hexham, in Northumberland, of a brass vessel, containing a number of the Anglo-Saxon coins called stycas', *Archaeologia* 25 (1834), 279–310; repr. in *Archaeologia Aeliana*, 1st ser. 3 (1844), 77–108.

— 'Further account of the Anglo-Saxon coins, called stycas, recently discovered at Hexham, in the county of Northumberland', *Archaeologia* 26 (1836), 346–8; repr. in *Archaeologia Aeliana*, 1st ser. 3 (1844), 109–11.

Agnar Helgason *et al.*, 'mtDNA and the Islands of the North Atlantic: estimating the proportions of Norse and Gaelic ancestry', *American Journal of Human Genetics* 68 (2001), 723–37.

AHLQVIST, Anders, 'Remarks on the question of dialects in Old Irish', in Jacek Fisiak (ed.), *Historical Dialectology: Regional and Social* (Berlin, 1988), 23–38.

AIRD, W. M., *St Cuthbert and the Normans: The Church of Durham, 1071–1153* (Woodbridge, 1998).

AITCHISON, N. B., *Armagh and the Royal Centres in Early Medieval Ireland: Monuments, Cosmology and the Past* (Woodbridge, 1994).

ALBRETHSEN, Svend E. and Christian KELLER, 'The use of the sæter in medieval Norse farming in Greenland', *Arctic Anthropology* 23 (1986), 91–107.

ALCOCK, Lesley, 'Was there an Irish Sea culture-province in the dark ages?', in Moore (ed.), *The Irish Sea Province*, 55–65.

— *Kings and Warriors, Craftsmen and Priests in Northern Britain AD 550–850* (Edinburgh, 2003).

ALEXANDER, Jonathan James Graham, *Insular Manuscripts, 6th to 9th Century* (London, 1978).

ALLEN, J. R. and J. ANDERSON, *The Early Christian Monuments of Scotland* (Edinburgh, 1903).

ALLEN, Valerie and Ruth EVANS, *Roadworks: Medieval Britain, Medieval Roads* (Manchester, 2016).

ALS, Thomas D. *et al.*, 'Highly discrepant proportions of female and male Scandinavian and British Isles ancestry within the isolated population of the Faroe Islands', *European Journal of Human Genetics* 14 (2006), 497–504.

ANDERSEN, P. S., *Det siste norske landnåmet i Vesterled: Cumbria-nordvest England* (Oslo, 2006).

ANDERSON, Benedict, *Imagined Communities: Reflections on the Origin and Spread of Nationalism* (London, 1983).

ANDERSON, James D., *Roman Military Supply in North-East England: An Analysis of and Alternative to the Piercebridge Formula*, BAR British ser. 224 (Oxford, 1992).

ANDERSON, Marjorie Ogilvie, 'Lothian and the early Scottish kings', *Scottish Historical Review* 39 (1960), 98–112.

— *Kings and Kingship in Early Scotland* (Edinburgh, 1973).

ARGE, Símun V., 'The Landnám in the Faroes', *Arctic Anthropology* 28.2 (1991), 101–20.

— *et al.*, 'Viking and medieval settlement in the Faroes: people, place and environment', *Human Ecology* 33 (2005), 597–620.

ARMIT, Ian, 'Irish–Scottish connections in the first millennium AD: an evaluation of the links between Souterrain Ware and Hebridean ceramics', *PRIA* C 108 (2008), 1–18.

ARMSTRONG, A. M. *et al.*, *The Place-Names of Cumberland*, 3 vols, English Place-Name Society 20–2 (Cambridge, 1950–2).

ARNOLD, Matthew, *On the Study of Celtic Literature* (London, 1867).

ARNOLD-FORSTER, Frances, *Studies in Church Dedications, or England's Patron Saints*, 3 vols (London, 1899).

ASHBY, Steven P., 'Combs, contact and chronology: reconsidering hair combs in Early-Historic and Viking-Age Atlantic Scotland', *Medieval Archaeology* 53 (2009), 1–33.

— 'What really caused the Viking Age? The social content of raiding and exploration', *Archaeological Dialogues* 22 (2015), 89–106.

AUSTAD, I. *et al.*, 'An overview of Norwegian summer farming', in R. G. H. Bunce *et al.* (ed.), *Transhumance and Biodiversity in European Mountains* (Wageningen, 2004), 7–23.

AYRES-BENNETT, Wendy, *A History of the French Language through Texts* (London, 1996).

BAILEY, Bill, *The Vikings, Wasdale Head and their Church* (Wasdale, 2002).

BAILEY, Richard N., 'Manx patterns on sculpture of the Norse period at Stanwix and Millom', *TCWAAS*, 2nd ser. 60 (1960), 187–8.

— 'A cup-mount from Brougham, Cumbria', *Medieval Archaeology* 21 (1977), 176–80.

— *Viking Age Sculpture in Northern England* (London, 1980).

— 'Irish Sea contacts in the Viking Period: the sculptural evidence', in G. Fellows-Jensen and N. Lund (eds), *Tredie tværfaglige Vikingesymposium Københavns Universitet 1984* (Højbjerg, 1984), 1–36.

— *Ambiguous Birds and Beasts: Three Sculptural Puzzles in South-West Scotland*, Whithorn Lecture 4 (Stranraer, 1996).

— *England's Earliest Sculptors* (Toronto, 1996).

— *Corpus of Anglo-Saxon Stone Sculpture Volume IX: Cheshire and Lancashire* (Oxford, 2010).

— and Rosemary CRAMP, *Corpus of Anglo-Saxon Stone Sculpture Volume II: Cumberland, Westmorland and Lancashire North-of-the-Sands* (Oxford, 1988).

BAKER, John, 'Old English *sæta* and *sætan* names', *Journal of the English Place-Name Society* 46 (2015), 45–81.

— and Stuart BROOKES, *Beyond the Burghal Hidage: Anglo-Saxon Civil Defence during the Viking Age* (Leiden, 2013).

BAKER, Malcolm, 'Medieval illustrations of Bede's Life of St Cuthbert', *Journal of the Warburg and Courtauld Institutes* 41 (1978), 16–49.

BALDWIN, John R. and Ian WHYTE (ed.), *The Scandinavians in Cumbria* (Edinburgh, 1995).

BALLIN SMITH, Beverley *et al.* (eds), *West over Sea: Studies in Scandinavian Sea-borne Expansion and Settlement before 1300. A Festschrift in Honour of Dr Barbara Crawford* (Leiden, 2007).

BANHAM, Debby, 'Insular agricultures: comparisons, contrasts, connections', in Clayton *et al.* (eds), *England, Ireland, and the Insular World*, 29–40.

— and Rosamond FAITH, *Anglo-Saxon Farms and Farming* (Oxford, 2014).

BANNERMAN, John, *Studies in the History of Dalriada* (Edinburgh, 1974).

— '*Comarba Coluim Chille* and the relics of Columba', *Innes Review* 44 (1993), 14–47.

BARING-GOULD, Sabine and John FISHER, *The Lives of the British Saints* (London, 1908).

BARNES, Michael P. and R. I. PAGE, *The Scandinavian Runic Inscriptions of Britain* (Uppsala, 2006).

BARRETT, James, 'What caused the Viking Age?', *Antiquity* 82 (2002), 671–85.

— 'The pirate fishermen: the political economy of a maritime society', in Ballin Smith *et al.* (eds), *West over Sea*, 299–340.

— 'The origins of intensive marine fishing in medieval Europe: the English evidence', *Proceedings of the Royal Society B: Biological Sciences* 271 (2004), 2417–21.

BARRON, J., *A History of the Ribble Navigation* (Preston, 1938).

BARROW, G. W. S., 'The cathedral chapter of St Andrews and the culdees in the twelfth and thirteenth centuries', *Journal of Ecclesiastical History* 3 (1952), 23–39.

— 'Northern English society in the twelfth and thirteenth centuries', *Northern History* 4 (1969), 1–28.

— 'The pattern of lordship and feudal settlement in Cumbria', *Journal of Medieval History* 1 (1975), 117–38.

— *The Kingdom of the Scots: Government, Church and Society from the Eleventh to the Fourteenth Century*, 2nd edn (Edinburgh, 2003).

— *Saint Ninian and Pictomania*, Whithorn Lecture 12 (Stranraer, 2004).

BARROW, Julia, 'Chester's earliest regatta? Edgar's Dee-rowing revisited', *Early Medieval Europe* 10 (2001), 81–93.

BARTH, Frederik, 'Introduction', in *idem* (ed.), *Ethnic Groups and Boundaries: the Social Organization of Culture Difference* (Bergen/Oslo, 1969), 9–38.

BARTLETT, Robert, 'Cults of Irish, Scottish and Welsh saints in twelfth-century England', in Smith (ed.), *Britain and Ireland*, 67–86.

BASSETT, Steven (ed.), *The Origins of Anglo-Saxon Kingdoms* (Leicester, 1989).

BAXTER, Stephen *et al.* (eds), *Early Medieval Studies in Honour of Patrick Wormald* (Farnham, 2009).

BELL, Tyler, 'Churches on Roman buildings: Christian associations and Roman masonry in Anglo-Saxon England', *Medieval Archaeology* 42 (1998), 1–18.

BELLHOUSE, R. L., 'Roman sites on the Cumberland coast 1968–1969', *TCWAAS*, 2nd ser. 70 (1970), 9–47.

— *Roman Sites on the Cumberland Coast: A New Schedule of Coastal Sites*, CWAAS Research ser. 3 (Kendal, 1989).

BENARIO, Herbert W., 'Legionary speed of march before the battle with Boudicca', *Britannia* 17 (1986), 358–62.

BERGA, Tatjana, *SCBI 45: Latvian Collections: Anglo-Saxon and Later British Coins* (Oxford, 1996).

BERGIN, Osborn, 'Varia I', *Ériu* 12 (1938), 215–35.

BERSU, Gerhard and David M. WILSON, *Three Viking Graves in the Isle of Man* (London, 1966).

BESLY, Edward, 'Few and far between: mints and coins in Wales to the middle of the thirteenth century', in Barrie Cook and Gareth Williams (eds), *Coinage and History in the North Sea World, c. AD 500–1250: Essays in Honour of Marion Archibald* (Leiden, 2006), 701–20.

BHREATHNACH, Edel, 'The documentary evidence for pre-Norman Skreen, County Meath', *Ríocht na Midhe* 9 (1996), 37–45.

— 'Temoria: caput Scotorum?', *Ériu* 47 (1996), 67–88.

— 'Columban churches in Brega and Leinster: relations with the Norse and the Anglo-Normans', *Journal of the Royal Society of Antiquaries of Ireland* 129 (1999), 5–18.

— '*Níell cáich úa Néill nasctar géill*: the political context of *Baile Chuinn Chétchathaig*', in *eadem* (ed.), *The Kingship*, 49–68.

— 'The medieval kingdom of Brega', in *eadem* (ed.), *The Kingship*, 410–22.

— (ed.), *The Kingship and Landscape of Tara* (Dublin, 2005).

— *Ireland in the Medieval World AD 400–1000: Landscape, Kingship and Religion* (Dublin, 2014).

BIGGER, Francis Joseph, 'Some notes on the churches of Saint Tassach of Raholp and Saint Nicholas of Ardtole, and their surroundings in the Barony of Lecale in Down', *Journal of the Royal Society of Antiquaries of Ireland* 6 (1916), 121–35.

BILL, Jan, *Welcome on Board! The Sea Stallion from Glendalough, a Viking Longship Recreated* (Roskilde, 2007).

BINCHY, D. A., *Celtic and Anglo-Saxon Kingship*, The O'Donnell Lectures for 1967–8 (Oxford, 1970).

BINFORD, Lewis, 'Archaeology as anthropology', *American Antiquity* 28 (1962), 217–25.

BINNS, Alison, *Dedications of Monastic Houses in England and Wales, 1066–1216* (Woodbridge, 1989).

BIRKS, H. J. B., 'Pollen analytical investigations at Holcroft Moss, Lancashire, and Lindow Moss, Cheshire', *Journal of Ecology* 53 (1965), 299–314.

BIRLEY, Eric, 'The Roman fort at Moresby', *TCWAAS*, 2nd ser. 48 (1948), 42–72.

BITEL, Lisa M., *Isle of the Saints: Monastic Settlement and Christian Community in Early Ireland* (Ithaca NY and London, 1990).

— *Women in Early Medieval Europe, 400–1100* (Cambridge, 2002).

BLACK, George, *The Surnames of Scotland: Their Origin, Meaning and History* (New York, 1943).

BLACKBURN, Mark, 'Hiberno-Norse and Irish Sea imitations of Cnut's Quatrefoil issue', *British Numismatic Journal* 66 (1966), 1–20.

— 'The coinage of Scandinavian York', in R. A. Hall *et al.* (eds), *Aspects of Anglo-Scandinavian York* (York, 2004), 325–49.

— 'Currency under the Vikings. Part II: the two Scandinavian kingdoms of the Danelaw, c. 895–954', *British Numismatic Journal* 76 (2006), 204–26.

BLACKWELL, Alice, 'Kirkcudbright: metal detector find', *Discovery and Excavation in Scotland*, new ser. 16 (2015), 58.

— 'Individuals', in David Clarke *et al.* (eds), *Early Medieval Scotland: Individuals, Communities and Ideas* (Edinburgh, 2015), 3–67.

— 'Copper alloy', in Crone and Hindmarch, *Living and Dying*, 53–8.

— 'A reassessment of the Anglo-Saxon artefacts from Scotland: material interactions and identities in early medieval northern Britain' (Unpublished University of Glasgow PhD thesis, 2018).

BLAIR, [W.] John, 'Anglo-Saxon minsters: a topographical review', in *idem* and Sharpe (eds), *Pastoral Care before the Parish* (Leicester, 1992), 226–66.

— 'Debate: ecclesiastical organization and pastoral care in Anglo-Saxon England', *Early Medieval Europe* 4 (1995), 193–212.

— 'A saint for every minster? Local cults in Anglo-Saxon England', in Thacker and Sharpe (eds), *Local Saints and Local Churches*, 455–94.

— 'A handlist of Anglo-Saxon saints', in Thacker and Sharpe (eds), *Local Saints and Local Churches*, 495–565.

— *The Church in Anglo-Saxon Society* (Oxford, 2005).

— (ed.), *Waterways and Canal-building in Medieval England* (Oxford, 2007).

— *The British Culture of Anglo-Saxon Settlement*, H. M. Chadwick Memorial Lecture 24 (Cambridge, 2013).

— *Building Anglo-Saxon England* (Princeton NJ, 2018).

BLAIR, Peter Hunter, 'The origins of Northumbria', *Archaeologia Aeliana,* 4th ser. 25 (1947), 1–51; repr. in his *Anglo-Saxon Northumbria*, III.

— 'The Northumbrians and their southern frontier', *Archaeologia Aeliana,* 4th ser. 26 (1948), 98–126, repr. in his *Anglo-Saxon Northumbria*, IV.

— 'The boundary between Bernicia and Deira', *Archaeologia Aeliana,* 4th ser. 27 (1949), 46–59; repr. in his *Anglo-Saxon Northumbria*, V.

— 'The *Moore Memoranda* on Northumbrian history', in Cyril Fox and Bruce Dickins (eds), *The Early Cultures of North-West Europe* (Cambridge, 1950), 245–57; repr. in his *Anglo-Saxon Northumbria*, VI.

— 'Some observations on the "Historia regum" attributed to Symeon of Durham', in Chadwick (ed.), *Celt and Saxon*, 63–118.

— ed. Michael Lapidge, *Anglo-Saxon Northumbria* (London, 1984).

BLUNT, Christopher, 'The coinage of Athelstan, 924–939: a survey', *British Numismatic Journal* 42 (1974), 35–160.

— and Michael DOLLEY, *SCBI 2: University College Reading* (London, 1969).

— *et al.*, *Coinage in Tenth-Century England: From Edward the Elder to Edgar's Reform* (Oxford, 1989).

BOARDMAN, Steve *et al.* (eds), *Saints' Cults in the Celtic World* (Woodbridge, 2009).

— and Eila WILLIAMSON (eds), *The Cult of Saints and the Virgin Mary in Medieval Scotland* (Woodbridge, 2010).

BOAZMAN, Gillian, 'Hallowed by saints, coveted by kings: Christianity and early medieval social organisation in Rathdown, Co. Dublin', in Tomás Ó Carragáin and Sam Turner, *Making Christian Landscapes in Atlantic Europe* (Cork, 2016), 21–54.

DEN BOEFT, Jan *et al.*, *Philological and Historical Commentary on Ammianus Marcellinus XXVII* (Leiden, 2009).

BÖHME, H. W., 'Das Ende der Römerherrschaft in Britannien und die angelsächsische Besidelung Englands im 5. Jahrhundert', *Jahrbuch des Römisch-Germanischen Zentralmuseums in Mainz* 33 (1986), 469–574.

BOLTON, Timothy, *The Empire of Cnut the Great: Conquest and the Consolidation of Power in Northern Europe in the Early Eleventh Century* (Leiden, 2009).

— and Jón-Viðar Sigurðsson (eds), *Celtic–Norse Relationships in the Irish Sea in the Middle Ages 800–1200* (Leiden, 2014).

BOND, Francis, *Dedications and Patron Saints of English Churches: Ecclesiastical Symbolism, Saints and their Emblems* (London, 1914).

BONNER, Gerald *et al.* (eds), *St Cuthbert: his Cult and Community* (Woodbridge, 1989).

BOOTH, J., 'Sceattas in Northumbria', in D. Hill and D. M. Metcalf (eds), Sceattas in England and on the Continent: The Seventh Oxford Symposium on Coinage and Monetary History, BAR British ser. 128 (Oxford, 1984), 71–111.

BORNHOLDT-COLLINS, Kristin, 'Viking-Age coin finds from the Isle of Man: a study of coin circulation, production and concepts of wealth', 2 vols (Unpublished University of Cambridge PhD thesis, 2003).

— 'Coinage', in Duffy and Mytum (eds), *A New History of the Isle of Man Volume 3*, 411–65.

BOSWORTH, Joseph, *An Anglo-Saxon Dictionary based on the Manuscript Collections of the late Joseph Bosworth*, ed. T. Northcote Toller (Oxford, 1898).

— *An Anglo-Saxon Dictionary based on the Manuscript Collections of the late Joseph Bosworth: Supplement*, ed. T. Northcote Toller (Oxford, 1921).

BOUGHTON, Dot *et al.*, 'Buried wealth of the Norse of the North-West', *Current Archaeology* 264 (March 2012), 26–31.

BOURKE, Cormac, 'The chronology of Irish crucifixion plaques', in Spearman and Higgitt (eds), *The Age of Migrating Ideas*, 175–81.

— 'Insignia Columbae II', in *idem* (ed.), *Studies in the Cult*, 173–83.

— *Studies in the Cult of St. Columba* (Dublin, 1997).

— 'Cillíne Pontifex', *Innes Review* 49 (1998), 77–80.

— 'Fergna Epscop', *Innes Review* 51 (2000), 68–71.

BOWDEN, Georgina R. *et al.*, 'Excavating past population structures by surname-based sampling: the genetic legacy of the Vikings in northwest England', *Molecular Biology and Evolution* 25 (2008), 301–9.

BOWEN, E. G., *The Settlements of the Celtic Saints in Wales* (Cardiff, 1954).

— '"Britain and the British Seas"', in Moore (ed.), *The Irish Sea Province*, 13–28.

— 'The cult of St Brigit', *Studia Celtica* 8–9 (1973–4), 33–47.

— *Saints, Seaways and Settlements in the Celtic Lands* (Cardiff, 1977).

BOWLUS, Charles R., 'Ethnogenesis: the tyranny of a concept', in Gillett (ed.), *On Barbarian Identity*, 241–56.

BOYLE, A., 'Saint Ninian: some outstanding problems', *Innes Review* 19 (1968), 57–70.

BRADLEY, John, 'The interpretation of Scandinavian settlement in Ireland', in *idem* (ed.), *Settlement and Society in Medieval Ireland: Studies Presented to Francis Xavier Martin* (Kilkenny, 1988), 49–78.

BRADLEY, Richard, *The Idea of Order: The Circular Archetype in Prehistoric Europe* (Oxford, 2012).

— *et al.*, 'Maritime havens in earlier prehistoric Britain', *Proceedings of the Prehistoric Society* 82 (2016), 1–35.

BRAUDEL, Fernand, *The Mediterranean and the Mediterranean World in the Age of Philip II*, transl. Siân Reynolds, 2 vols (London, 1975).

— *The Mediterranean in the Ancient World*, ed. Roselyne de Ayala and Paule Braudel, transl. Siân Reynolds (London, 2002).

BREATNACH, C., 'Léirmheas: Betha Adamnáin. The Irish Life of Adamnán', *Éigse* 26 (1992), 177–87.

BREATNACH, Liam, 'Poets and poetry', in Kim McCone and Katharine Simms (eds), *Progress in Medieval Irish Studies* (Maynooth, 1996), 65–77.

— and Elizabeth BOYLE, 'Senchas Gall Átha Clíath: aspects of the cult of Patrick in the twelfth century', in J. Carey *et al.* (eds), *Sacred Histories: A Festschrift for Máire Herbert* (Dublin, 2015), 22–55.

BREEZE, Andrew, 'Old English *wassenas* "retainers" in Gospatric's writ', *Notes and Queries* 237 (1992), 272–5.

— 'Celtic etymologies for Old English *cursung* "curse", *gafeluc* "javelin", *stær* "history", *syrce* "coat of mail", and Middle English *clog(ge)* "block, wooden shoe", *cokkunge* "striving", *tirven* "to flay", *warroke* "hunchback"', *Notes and Queries*, 238 (1993), 287–97.

— 'The origin of the name *Deira*', *Transactions of the Yorkshire Dialect Society* 19.2 (1997), 35–9.

— 'Seventh-century Northumbria and a poem to Cadwallon', *Northern History* 38 (2001), 145–52.

— 'Seven types of Celtic loanword', in *The Celtic Roots*, ed. Filppula *et al.*, 175–81.

— 'The battle of Alutthelia in 844 and Bishop Auckland', *Northern History* 39 (2002), 124–5.

— 'Some Celtic place-names of Scotland: Ptolemy's *Verubium Promontorium*, Bede's *Urbs Giudi*, Mendick, Minto, and Panlathy', *Scottish Language* 23 (2004), 57–67.

— 'Bede's *Civitas Domnoc* and Dunwich, Suffolk', *Leeds Studies in English*, new ser. 36 (2005), 1–4.

— 'Where were Bede's Uilfaresdun and Paegnalaech?', *Northern History* 42 (2005), 189–91.

— '*Medcaut*, the Brittonic name of Lindisfarne', *Northern History* 42 (2005), 187–8.

— 'Three Celtic toponyms: Setantii, Blencathra, and Pen-y-Ghent', *Northern History* 43 (2006), 161–5.

— '*Scéla Cano meic Gartnáin*, Fiachna son of Báitán, and Bamburgh', in C. Ó Baoill and N. R. McGuire (eds), *Caindel Alban: Fèill-Sgrìobhainn do Dhòmhnall E. Meek, Scottish Gaelic Studies* 24 (2008), 87–95.

— 'Rosnat, Whithorn and Cornwall', *TDGNHAS* 83 (2009), 43–50.

— 'Reviews: Whithorn's Renown ...', *TDGNHAS* 84 (2010), 164.

— 'The names of Rheged', *TDGNHAS* 86 (2012), 51–62.

— 'Brunanburh located: the battlefield and the poem', in Michiko Ogura and Hans Sauer (eds), *Aspects of Medieval English Language and Literature* (Berlin, 2018), 61–80.

BREEZE, David J., 'The placing of the forts on Hadrian's Wall', *Archaeologia Aeliana*, 5th ser. 46 (2017), 21–39.

— and Brian DOBSON, *Hadrian's Wall*, 4th edn (London, 2000).

BRIGGS, Elizabeth, 'Nothing but names: the original core of the Durham *Liber Vitae*', in David Rollason *et al.* (eds), *The Durham Liber Vitae and its Context* (Woodbridge, 2004), 63–85.

BRODERICK, George, *Placenames of the Isle of Man*, 7 vols (Tübingen, 1994–2005).

— 'Creag and carraig in Manx Place-names', *Ainm* 2 (1987), 141–3.

BROOKE, Daphne, 'Kirk-compound place-names in Galloway and Carrick', *TDGNHAS*, 3rd ser. 58 (1983), 56–71.

— 'The deanery of Desnes Cro and the church of Edingham', *TDGNHAS*, 3rd ser. 62 (1987), 48–65.

— 'The Northumbrian settlements in Galloway and Carrick: an historical assessment', *PSAS* 121 (1991), 295–327.

— *Wild Men and Holy Places: St. Ninian, Whithorn and the Medieval Realm of Galloway* (Edinburgh, 1994).

BROOKES, Stuart and Hoai Nguyen HUYNH, 'Transport networks and towns in Roman and early medieval England: an application of PageRank to archaeological questions', *Journal of Archaeological Science* 17 (2018), 477–90.

BROOKS, Nicholas, 'The development of military obligations in eighth- and ninth-century England', in Clemoes and Hughes (eds), *England before the Conquest*, 69–84.

— 'The formation of the Mercian kingdom', in Bassett (ed.), *The Origins*, 159–70; repr. in his *Anglo-Saxon Myths*, 61–77.

— *Bede and the English* (Jarrow Lecture, 1999).

— 'The English origin myth', in his *Anglo-Saxon Myths*, 79–89.

— *Anglo-Saxon Myths: State and Church 400–1066* (London, 2000).

— 'English identity from Bede to the millennium', *Haskins Society Journal* 14 (2004), 33–51.

— *et al.*, 'A new charter of King Edgar', *Anglo-Saxon England* 13 (1984), 137–55.

BROUN, Dauvit, 'The literary record of St. Nynia – fact or fiction', *Innes Review* 42 (1991), 143–50.

— 'The origin of Scottish identity', in Stringer *et al.*, *Nations, Nationalism and Patriotism*,

35–55.

— *The Charters of Gaelic Scotland and Ireland in the Early and Central Middle Ages*, Quiggin Lecture 2 (Cambridge, 1995).

— 'Dunkeld and the origins of Scottish identity', *The Innes Review* 48 (1997), 112–24; repr. in *idem* and Clancy (eds), *Spes Scotorum*, 95–111.

BROUN, Dauvit, *The Irish Identity of the Kingdom of the Scots in the Twelfth and Thirteenth Century* (Woodbridge, 1999).

— 'The Welsh identity of the kingdom of Strathclyde c.900–c.1200', *Innes Review* 55 (2004), 111–80.

— 'Attitudes of *Gall* to *Gaedhel* in Scotland before John of Fordun', in *idem* and MacGregor (eds), Mìorun Mòr nan Gall, 49–82.

— and Martin MacGregor (eds), Mìorun Mòr nan Gall, *'The Great Ill-Will of the Lowlander?' Lowland Perceptions of the Highlands, Medieval and Modern* (Glasgow, 2007).

— *Scottish Independence and the Idea of Britain: From the Picts to Alexander III* (Edinburgh, 2007).

— '*Cethri prímchenéla Dáil Ríata revisited*', in John Carey *et al.* (eds), *Sacred Histories: A Festschrift for Máire Herbert* (Dublin, 2015), 63–72.

BROWN, George Hardin, 'Bede's neglected commentary on Samuel', in DeGregorio (ed.), *Innovation and Tradition*, 121–42.

BROWN, Keith, 'British history: a sceptical comment', in Asch (ed.), *Three Nations*, 49–82.

BROWN, Michelle, *The Lindisfarne Gospels: Society, Spirituality and the Scribe* (London, 2003).

— 'Writing in the Insular world', in Gameson (ed.), *The Cambridge History of the Book*, 121–66.

BROWN, T. J., *A Palaeographer's View*, ed. Janet Bately *et al.* (London, 1993).

BRYANT, S. *et al.*, *Roman Manchester: A Frontier Settlement* (Manchester, 1986).

BUCHANAN, R. H., 'The Irish Sea: the geographical framework', in M. McCaughan and J. Appleby (eds), *The Irish Sea: Aspects of Maritime History* (Belfast, 1989), 1–18.

BUDD, Paul *et al.*, 'Investigating population movement by stable isotope analysis: a report from Britain', *Antiquity* 78 no. 299 (2004), 127–41.

BUGGE, Alexander, *Vesterlandenes indflydelse, i Vikingetiden* (Oslo, 1905).

BU'LOCK, J. D., 'The eighth-century bronze boss from Ribchester, Lancashire', *Transactions of the Lancashire and Cheshire Antiquarian Society* 78 (1975), 75–8.

BULLOCK-DAVIES, Constance, *Professional Interpreters and the Matter of Britain* (Cardiff, 1965).

BULLOUGH, Donald A., 'The missions to the English and Picts and their heritage (to *c.* 800)', in Löwe (ed.), *Die Iren und Europa*, II, 80–98.

— 'A neglected early ninth-century manuscript of the *Vita S. Cuthberti*', *Anglo-Saxon England* 27 (1998), 105–38.

BUTLER, Lawrence, 'Church dedications and the cult of Anglo-Saxon saints in England', in *idem* and R. K. Morris (eds), *The Anglo-Saxon Church: Papers on History, Architecture and Archaeology in Honour of Dr H. M. Taylor* (London, 1986), 44–50.

BUTTER, Rachel, 'St Munnu in Ireland and Scotland', in Boardman and Williamson (eds), *The Cult of Saints*, 21–42.

BYRNE, Francis John, 'Tribes and tribalism in early Ireland', *Ériu* 22 (1971), 128–66.

— *Irish Kings and High-Kings* (London, 1973).

CAMBRIDGE, E. and D. ROLLASON, 'Debate: the pastoral organisation of the Anglo-Saxon Church: a review of the "Minster Hypothesis"', *Early Medieval Europe* 4 (1995), 87–104.

CAMERON, Kenneth, *The Place-Names of Derbyshire*, 3 vols, English Place-Name Society 27–9 (Cambridge 1959).

— *The Place-Names of Lincolnshire*, 6 vols in 7, English Place-Name Society 58, 64–6, 71, 73, 77 (Nottingham, 1985–2001).

— *A Dictionary of Lincolnshire Place-Names* (Nottingham, 1998).

CAMPBELL, A., *Old English Grammar* (Oxford, 1959).

CAMPBELL, Ewan, 'The hand-built Dark Age pottery', in Hill, *Whithorn*, 358.

— 'Were the Scots Irish?', *Antiquity* 75 (2001), 285–92.
— *Continental and Mediterranean Imports to Atlantic Britain and Ireland, AD 400–800* (York, 2007).
— 'Anglo-Saxon/Gaelic interaction in Scotland', in Graham-Campbell and Ryan (eds), *Anglo-Saxon/Irish Relations*, 253–63.
— 'Glass', in Crone and Hindmarch, *Living and Dying*, 58–60.
CAMPBELL, James, 'Bede', in T. A. Dorey (ed.), *Latin Historians*, 159–90; repr, in his *Essays* as 'Bede I', 1–27.
— 'Bede's words for places', in P. H. Sawyer (ed.), *Names, Words and Graves: Early Medieval Settlement*, 34–54; repr, in his *Essays*, 99–119.
— *Essays in Anglo-Saxon History* (London, 1986),
— 'The debt of the early English Church to Ireland', in Próinséas Ní Chatháin and Michael Richter (eds), *Irland und die Christenheit: Bibelstudien und Mission* (Stuttgart, 1987), 332–46.
— 'Comparing early medieval polities in Britain and Ireland', in Baxter *et al.* (eds), *Early Medieval Studies*, 47–63.
CANNY, Nicholas, 'The attempted anglicization of Ireland in the seventeenth century: an exemplar of "British history"', in Asch (ed.), *Three Nations*, 49–82.
CAREY, John, *The Irish National Origin-Legend: Synthetic Pseudohistory*, Quiggin Pamphlets on the Sources of Mediaeval Gaelic History 1 (Cambridge, 1994).
— 'In search of Mael Muru Othna', in Purcell *et al.* (eds), *Clerics, Kings and Vikings*, 429–39.
CARLTON, Richard, 'Archaeological excavations on Lindisfarne Heugh', in *Peregrini Lindisfarne: An Anthology* (Holy Island, 2017), 117–25.
CARRIGAN, William, *The History and Antiquities of the Diocese of Ossory*, 4 vols (Dublin, 1905).
CARTWRIGHT, David Edgar, *Tides: A Scientific History* (Cambridge, 1999).
CARVER, Martin, *et al.*, *Portmahomack on Tarbat Ness* (Edinburgh, 2016).
CASEY, Denis, 'A reconsideration of the authorship and transmission of *Cogad Gáedel re Gallaib*', *PRIA* 113C (2013), 139–61.
CASEY, P. J., 'The end of garrisons on Hadrian's Wall: an historico-environmental model', in D. F. Clark *et al.* (eds), *The Later Roman Empire Today* (London, 1993), 69–80.
— 'The end of fort garrisons on Hadrian's Wall', in Françoise Vallet and Michel Kazanski (eds), *L'Armée Romaine et les Barbares du IIIe au VIIe siècle* (Rouen, 1993), 259–68.
— 'The end of the Roman army in Wales and the Marches', in Barry C. Burnham and Jeffrey L. Davies (eds), *Roman Frontiers in Wales and the Marches* (Aberystwyth, 2010), 62–6.
CAVALLI-SFORZA, Luigi, *Genes, Peoples and Languages* (London, 2000).
CAVILL, Paul, 'The battle of Brunanburh in 937: battlefield despatches', in Harding *et al.* (eds), *In Search of Vikings*, 95–108.
— *et al.* 'Revisiting *Dingesmere*', *Journal of the English Place-Name Society* 36 (2003–4), 25–36.
CESSFORD, Craig, 'Post-Severan Cramond: a late Roman and early historic British and Anglo-Saxon religious centre?', *The Heroic Age*, 4 (2001), http://www.heroicage.org/issues/4/Cessford.html
CHADWICK, Hector Munro, *The Origin of the English Nation* (1907; repr. Washington DC, 1983).
— *Early Scotland* (Cambridge, 1949).
CHADWICK, Nora K., 'St. Ninian: a preliminary study of sources', *TDGNHAS*, 3rd ser. 27 (1950), 9–53.
— (ed.), *Studies in Early British History* (Cambridge, 1943; repr. 1959).
— (ed.), *Studies in the Early British Church* (Cambridge, 1958).
— (ed.), *Celt and Saxon: Studies in the Early British Border* (Cambridge, 1963).
— 'Prefatory note' and 'Introduction', in *eadem* (ed.), *Celt and Saxon*, v–vi; 1–19.
— 'Bede, St Colmán and the Irish abbey of Mayo', in *eadem* (ed.), Celt and Saxon, 186–205.
CHADWICK, Owen, 'The evidence of dedications in the early history of the Welsh Church', in N. K. Chadwick (ed.), *Studies in Early British History* (Cambridge, 1954), 173–88.

CHALMERS, G., *Caledonia: or an Account, Historical and Topographic, of North Britain*, 3 vols (London, 1807–24).

CHARLES-EDWARDS, G., 'The east cross inscription from Toureen Peacaun: some concrete evidence', *Journal of the Royal Society of Antiquaries of Ireland* 132 (2002), 114–26.

CHARLES-EDWARDS, G., 'Reading the Nendrum "rune-stone"', in McErlean and Crowthers (eds), *Harnessing the Tides*, 396–404.

CHARLES-EDWARDS, T. M., 'The social background to Irish *peregrinatio*', *Celtica* 11 (1976), 43–59.

— 'Bede, the Irish and the Britons', *Celtica* 15 (1983), 42–52.

— 'Early medieval kingships', in Bassett (ed.), *The Origins*, 28–39.

— *Early Irish and Welsh Kinship* (Oxford, 1993).

— 'Language and society among the Insular Celts, AD 400–1000', in M. J. Green (ed.), *The Celtic World* (London, 1995), 703–36.

— 'The penitential of Theodore and the *Indicia Theodori*', in Michael Lapidge (ed.), *Archbishop Theodore: Commemorative Studies on his Life and Influence* (Cambridge, 1995), 141–74.

— 'The continuation of Bede, *s.a.* 750: high-kings, kings of Tara and "Bretwaldas"', in A. P. Smyth (ed.), *Seanchas: Studies in Early and Medieval Irish Archaeology, History and Literature in Honour of Francis John Byrne* (Dublin, 1999), 137–45.

— *Early Christian Ireland* (Cambridge, 2000).

— '*Érlam*: the patron saint of an Irish church', in Thacker and Sharpe (eds), *Local Saints and Local Churches*, 267–90.

— 'The making of nations in Britain and Ireland in the early middle ages', in Ralph Evans (ed.), *Lordship and Learning: Studies in Memory of Trevor Aston* (Woodbridge, 2004), 11–37.

— 'Early Irish saints' cults and their constituencies', *Ériu* 54 (2004), 79–102.

— 'The province of Ulster in the early middle ages', in C. J. Lynn and J. A. McDowell (eds), *Deer Park Farms: The Excavation of a Raised Rath in the Glenarm Valley, Co. Antrim* (Belfast, 2011), 40–60.

— *Wales and the Britons, 350–1064* (Oxford, 2012).

— 'Wilfrid and the Celts', in N. J. Higham (ed.), *Wilfrid: Abbot, Bishop and Saint: Papers from the 1300th Anniversary Conference* (Donington, 2013), 243–59.

— 'Celtic kings: 'priestly vegetables?', in Baxter *et al.* (eds), *Early Medieval Studies*, 65–80.

CHERRY, J., 'The topography of the site', in T. W. Potter, *Romans in North-West England: Excavations at the Roman Forts of Ravenglass, Watercrook and Bowness on Solway*, CWAAS Research Series 1 (Kendal, 1979), 11.

CHILDE, V. Gordon, *The Dawn of European Civilization*, 6th edn (London, 1957; repr. 1976).

— 'Retrospect', *Antiquity* 32 (1958), 69–74.

CHURCH, Mike J. *et al.*, 'The Vikings were not the first colonizers of the Faroe Islands', *Quaternary Science Reviews* 77 (2013), 228–32.

CLANCY, Thomas Owen, 'Iona, Scotland and the Céli Dé', in B. E. Crawford (ed.), *Scotland in Dark Age Britain* (Aberdeen, 1996), 111–30.

— 'The real St Ninian', *Innes Review* 52 (2001), 12–25.

— 'Scottish saints and national identities in the early Middle Ages', in Thacker and Sharpe (eds), *Local Saints*, 397–421.

— 'Magpie hagiography in twelfth-century Scotland: the case of *Libellus de Nativitate Sancti Cuthberti*', in J. Cartwright (ed.), Celtic Hagiography and Saints' Cults (Cardiff, 2003), 216–31.

— 'Philosopher-king: Nechtan mac Der-Ilei', *Scottish Historical Review* 83 (2004), 125–49.

— 'The Gall-Ghàidheil and Galloway', *Journal of Scottish Name Studies* 2 (2008), 19–50.

— 'The cults of saints Patrick and Palladius in early medieval Scotland', in Boardman *et al.* (eds), *Saints' Cults*, 18–41.

— 'The big man, the footsteps and the fissile saint: paradigms and problems in the study of Insular saints' cults', in Boardman and Williamson (eds), *The Cult of Saints*, 1–20.

— 'Gaelic in medieval Scotland: advent and expansion', *Proceedings of the British Academy*

167 (2010), 349–92.

— 'Iona v. Kells: succession, jurisdiction and politics in the Columban *familia* in the later tenth century', in Edmonds and Russell (eds), *Tome*, 89–101.

— 'Reviews: John MacQueen, *Place-Names in the Rhinns of Galloway and Luce Valley ... Place-Names of the Wigtownshire Moors and Machars*', *Journal of Scottish Name Studies* 6 (2012), 87–96.

— 'The kingdoms of the north: poetry, places, politics', in Woolf (ed.), *Beyond the Gododdin*, 153–76.

CLARK, Cecily, 'Women's names in post-conquest England: observations and speculations', *Speculum* 53 (1978), 223–51; repr. in her *Words, Names and History*, 117–43.

— 'Willelmus rex? vel alius Willelmus?', *Nomina* 11 (1987), 7–33; repr. in her *Words, Names and History*, 280–98.

— 'Socio-economic status and individual identity: essential factors in the analysis of Middle English personal-naming', in Words, Names and History, 100–13.

— Words, Names and History: Selected Writings of Cecily Clark, ed. P. Jackson (Woodbridge, 1995).

CLARK, Felicity Helen, 'The Northumbrian frontiers, *c.*500–*c.*800' (Unpublished Oxford University DPhil thesis, 2010).

— 'Wilfrid's lands? The Lune Valley in its Anglian context', in Linda Sever (ed.), *Lancashire's Sacred History* (Stroud, 2010), 147–64.

CLARK, Grahame, 'The invasion hypothesis in British archaeology', *Antiquity* 40 (1966), 172–89.

CLARKE, Amanda, 'Seeking St Ninian and his legacy: excavations at Whithorn', *Interim: Bulletin of the York Archaeological Trust* 22 no. 2 (1997), 17–27.

CLARKE, David, 'Archaeology: the loss of innocence', *Antiquity* 47 (1973), 6–18.

CLARKE, Howard B., 'Christian cults and cult centres in Hiberno-Norse Dublin and its hinterland', in A. Mac Shamhráin and C. Thomas (eds), *The Island of St. Patrick: Church and Ruling Dynasties in Fingal and Meath, 400–1148* (Dublin, 2004), 140–58.

— et al. (eds), *Ireland and Scandinavia in the Early Viking Age* (Dublin, 1998).

CLARKSON, T. J., *The Men of the North: The Britons of Southern Scotland* (Edinburgh, 2010).

— *Strathclyde and the Anglo-Saxons in the Viking Age* (Edinburgh, 2014).

CLAYTON, Mary *et al.*, *England, Ireland, and the Insular World: Textual and Material Connections in the Early Middle Ages*, Essays in Anglo-Saxon Studies 7 (Tempe AZ, 2017).

CLEERE, H., 'Roman harbours in Britain south of Hadrian's Wall', in *idem* and J. du Plat Taylor (eds), *Roman Shipping and Trade: Britain and the Rhine Provinces*, Council for British Archaeology Research Reports 24 (London, 1978), 36–40.

CLEMENT, Morag with Susan YOUNGS, 'A bronze bowl mount found at Arnside', in M. Clement, 'Recent acquisitions and reported finds to Kendal Museum', *TCWAAS*, 3rd ser. 3 (2003), 235–6.

CLOSE-BROOKS, J., 'The Mote of Mark and Celtic interlace', *Antiquity* 50 (1976), 50–1.

COATES, Richard, 'The significances of Celtic place-names in England', in Filppula *et al.* (eds), *The Celtic Roots*, 47–85.

— '*Domnoc/Dommoc*, Dunwich and Felixstowe', in *idem* and Breeze, *Celtic Voices*, 234–40.

— 'Un-English reflections on Lindisfarne', in *idem* and Breeze, *Celtic Voices*, 241–59.

— and Andrew BREEZE, *Celtic Voices, English Places: Studies of the Celtic Impact on Place-Names in England* (Stamford, 2000).

COATSWORTH, Elizabeth, 'The pectoral cross and portable altar from the tomb of St. Cuthbert', in Bonner *et al.* (eds), *Saint Cuthbert*, 294–5.

— *Corpus of Anglo-Saxon Stone Sculpture Volume VIII: Western Yorkshire* (Oxford, 2008).

COHEN, Jeffrey Jerome, 'Introduction: infinite realms', in *idem* (ed.), *Cultural Diversity in the British Middle Ages: Archipelago, Island, England* (Basingstoke, 2008), 1–16.

COLE, Ann, 'The place-name evidence for water transport in early medieval England', in Blair (ed.), *Waterways*, 55–84.

COLES, J.M., 'Prehistoric roads and trackways in Britain: problems and possibilities', in

Fenton and Stell (eds), *Loads and Roads*, 1–21.

COLEMAN, Janet, *Ancient and Medieval Memories: Studies in the Reconstruction of the Past* (Cambridge, 1992).

COLLEY MARCH, H. 'The place-names Twistle, Skip and Argh', *Transactions of the Lancashire and Cheshire Antiquarian Society* 8 (1890), 72–96.

COLLINGWOOD, R. G., *Autobiography* (London, 1939).

COLLINGWOOD, R. G. and J. N. L. MYRES, *Roman Britain and the English Settlements* (Oxford, 1936).

— and R. P. WRIGHT, *Roman Inscriptions of Britain. Vol. 1, Inscriptions on Stone* (Oxford, 1965).

COLLINGWOOD, W. G., *The Likeness of King Elfwald: A Study of Northumbria and Iona at the start of the Viking Age* (Kendal, 1917).

— 'The early crosses of Galloway', *TDGNHAS*, 3rd ser. 10 (1922), 205–31.

— 'Christian Vikings', *Antiquity* 1 (1927), 172–80.

— *Northumbrian Crosses of the Pre-Norman Age* (London, 1927).

— 'Ravenglass, Coniston and Penrith in ancient deeds', *TCWAAS*, 2nd ser. 29 (1929), 39–48.

— and J. ROGERS, 'Lost churches in the Carlisle diocese', *TCWAAS*, 1st ser. 15 (1898–9), 288–302.

— and T. H. B. GRAHAM, 'Patron saints of the diocese of Carlisle', *TCWAAS*, 2nd ser. 25 (1925), 1–27.

COLLINGWOOD BRUCE, J., *Handbook to the Roman Wall*, ed. C. Daniels, 13th edn (Newcastle, 1978).

COLLINS, A. E. P., 'Excavations in Lough Faughan Crannog, Co. Down', *Ulster Journal of Archaeology* 81 (1951–2), 45–81.

COLLINS, Rob, *Hadrian's Wall and the End of Empire: The Roman Frontier in the 4th and 5th Centuries* (New York, 2012).

— and Lindsay ALLASON-JONES (eds), *Finds from the Frontier: Material Culture in the 4th–5th Centuries* (York, 2010).

COLLS, Robert, 'The new Northumbrians', in *idem* (ed.), *Northumbria: History and Identity*, 151–77.

— 'Gaelic and Northumbrian: separatism and regionalism in the United Kingdom, 1890–1920', in Joost Augusteijn and Eric Storm (eds), *Region and State in Nineteenth-Century Europe: Nation-Building, Regional Identities and Separatism* (London, 2012), 172–91.

— (ed.), *Northumbria: History and Identity 547–2000* (Chichester, 2007).

COMBER, Michelle, 'Trade and communication networks in early historic Ireland', *Journal of Irish Archaeology* 10 (2001), 73–92.

COONEY, Gabriel, 'Neolithic worlds; islands in the Irish Sea', in Vicki Cummings and Chris Fowler (eds), *The Neolithic of the Irish Sea: Materiality and Traditions of Practice* (Oxford, 2004), 145–59.

COOPER, Alan, 'The rise and fall of the Anglo-Saxon law of the highway', *Haskins Society Journal* 12 (2002), 39–69.

CORMACK, Margaret, *The Saints in Iceland. Their Veneration from the Conversion to 1400* (Brussels, 1994).

CORMACK, W. F., 'Northumbrian coins from Luce Sands, Wigtownshire', *TDGNHAS*, 3rd ser. 42 (1965), 149–50.

— 'Barhobble, Mochrum. Excavation of a forgotten church site in Galloway', *TDGNHAS*, 3rd ser. 70 (1995), 1–114.

COULSTON, J. C. N., 'Military equipment of the "long" 4th century on Hadrian's Wall', in Collins and Allason-Jones (eds), *Finds from the Frontier*, 50–63.

COWAN, Ian B., *The Parishes of Medieval Scotland* (Edinburgh, 1967).

COWELL, R. W. and J. B. INNES, *The Wetlands of Merseyside* (Lancaster, 1994).

COWEN, J. D., 'A catalogue of objects of the Viking period in Tullie House Museum, Carlisle', *TCWAAS*, 2nd ser. 34 (1934), 166–87.

COX, B., 'The place-names of the earliest English records', *Journal of the English Place Name Society* 8 (1975–6), 12–66.

COX, Richard A. V., *The Gaelic Place-names of Carloway, Isle of Lewis: their Structure and Signficance* (Dublin, 2002).

COX, Patricia and Alan G. CROSBY, 'Bridging the Mersey again', *Transactions of the Historic Society of Lancashire and Cheshire* 165 (2017), 123–6.

CRAIG, D. J., 'The distribution of pre-Norman sculpture in south-west Scotland: provenance, ornament and regional groups' (Unpublished Durham University PhD thesis, 1992).

CRAIG, D. J., 'Pre-Norman sculpture in Galloway: some territorial implications', in R. D. Oram and G. P. Stell (eds), *Galloway*, 45–62.

— 'The sculptured stones', in Hill, *Whithorn*, 433–41.

CRAIGIE, W. A., 'Gaelic words and names in the Icelandic Sagas', *Zeitschrift für celtische Philologie* 1 (1897), 439–54.

— 'Gaels in Iceland', *Revue Celtique* 20 (1899), 247–64.

CRAMP, Rosemary, *Early Northumbrian Sculpture*, Jarrow Lecture (1965).

— 'Excavations at the Saxon monastic sites of Wearmouth and Jarrow, Co. Durham: an interim report', *Medieval Archaeology* 13 (1969), 21–64.

— 'St Paul's church, Jarrow', in Peter Addyman and Richard Morris (eds), *The Archaeological Study of Churches* (London, 1976), 28–35.

— 'The Anglian sculptures from Jedburgh', in O'Connor and Clarke (eds), *From the Stone Age*, 269–84.

— *Corpus of Anglo-Saxon Stone Sculpture Volume 1: County Durham and Northumberland*, 2 vols (Oxford, 1984).

— 'Northumbria and Ireland', in Szarmach (ed.), *Sources*, 185–201.

— 'The artistic influence of Lindisfarne within Northumbria', in Bonner *et al.* (eds), *St Cuthbert*, 213–28.

— *Grammar of Anglo-Saxon Ornament: A General Introduction to the Corpus of Anglo-Saxon Stone Sculpture* (Oxford, 1991) (originally part of *Corpus I*).

— 'Anglo-Saxon settlement', in J. C. Chapman and H. C. Mytum (eds), *Settlement in North Britain 1000BC–AD1000*, BAR British ser. 118 (Oxford, 1993), 263–97.

— 'A reconsideration of the monastic site of Whitby', in Spearman and Higgitt (eds), *The Age of Migrating Ideas*, 64–73.

— *Whithorn and the Northumbrian Expansion Westwards*, Whithorn Lecture 3 (Stranraer, 1994).

— 'The sculpture', in Potter and Andrews, 'Excavations at Heysham', 106–9.

— 'The early medieval window glass', in Hill, *Whithorn*, 326–9.

— 'The Northumbrian identity', in Hawkes and Mills (eds), *Northumbria's Golden Age*, 1–11.

— *Wearmouth and Jarrow Monastic Sites Volume I* (Swindon, 2005).

— *The Hirsel Excavations* (London, 2014).

— 'Crosses of the Cumbrian coast in the pre-Viking Age', in David Shotter and Marion McClintock (eds), *Exploring Antiquities and Archaeology in the North West: Essays in Commemoration of the Life and Works of Ben Edwards* (Kendal, 2018), 49–73.

— '"Heads you lose"', in Eric Cambridge and Jane Hawkes (eds), *Crossing Boundaries: Interdisciplinary Approaches to the Art, Material Culture, Language and Literature of the Early Medieval World: Essays presented to Professor Richard Bailey OBE* (Oxford, 2017), 15–22.

CRASTER, H. H. E., 'The patrimony of St Cuthbert', *English Historical Review* 69 (1954), 177–99.

CRAWFORD, Barbara E., *Scandinavian Scotland* (Leicester, 1987).

— (ed.), *Scandinavian Settlement in Northern Britain* (London, 1995).

— 'The dedication to St Clement at Rodil, Harris', in *eadem* (ed.), *Church, Chronicle and Learning in Medieval and Early Renaissance Scotland* (Edinburgh, 1999), 105–18.

— *The Govan Hogbacks and the Multi-Cultural Society of Tenth-Century Scotland*, Govan lecture (Glasgow, 2005).

— *The Northern Earldoms: Orkney and Caithness from AD 870 to 1470* (Edinburgh, 2013).

CRAWFORD, O. G. S., 'Western seaways', in L. Buxton (ed.), *Custom is King: Essays presented to R. R. Marrett* (London, 1936), 181–200.

CRICK, Julia, 'The "English" and the "Irish" from Cnut to John: speculations on a linguistic interface', in Tyler (ed.), *Conceptualizing Multilingualism*, 217–37.

CRONE, Anne, *The History of a Scottish Lowland Crannog: Excavations at Buiston, Ayrshire* (Edinburgh, 2000).

— and Erlend HINDMARCH, *Living and Dying at Auldhame, East Lothian. The Excavation of an Anglian Monastic Settlement and Medieval Parish Church* (Edinburgh, 2016).

CROSBY, Alan G., *Leading the Way: a History of Lancashire's Roads* (Preston, 1998).

CROWE, C. J., 'A note on white quartz pebbles found in Early Christian contexts on the Isle of Man', *Proceedings of the Isle of Man Natural History and Antiquarian Society* 8.4 (1982), 413–15.

— 'Looking for a monastery at Hoddom', *Popular Archaeology* 4.6 (December 1982), 34–6.

— 'Cartmel: the earliest Christian community', *TCWAAS*, 2nd ser. 84 (1984), 61–6.

— 'Excavations at Brydekirk, Annan 1982–4', *TDGNHAS*, 3rd ser. 59 (1984), 33–40.

— 'An excavation at Kirkmirran, Dalbeattie', *TDGNHAS*, 3rd ser. 61 (1986), 55–62.

— 'Excavations at Ruthwell, Dumfries, 1980–4', *TDGNHAS*, 3rd ser. 62 (1987), 40–7.

CROWLEY, Thomas J. and Thomas S. LOWERY, 'How warm was the Medieval Warm Period?', *Ambio: A Journal of the Human Environment* 29 (2000), 51–4.

CRUMLIN-PEDERSEN, Ole and Olaf OLSEN, *The Skuldelev Ships I: Topography, Archaeology, History, Conservation and Display* (Roskilde, 2002).

CRUMPLIN, Sally, 'Rewriting history in the cult of St Cuthbert from the ninth to the twelfth centuries' (Unpublished University of St Andrews PhD thesis, 2005).

CUBITT, Catherine, *Anglo-Saxon Church Councils, 650–850* (Leicester, 1995).

CUBBON, A. M., 'The early Church in the Isle of Man', in Pearce (ed.), *The Early Church*, 257–82.

CULLUM, P. H., *Cremetts and Corrodies: Care of the Poor and Sick at St Leonard's Hospital*, Borthwick Paper 79 (York, 1991).

CUMMINGS, Vicki, *A View from the West: The Neolithic of the Irish Sea Zone* (Oxford, 2009).

CUNLIFFE, Barry, *Facing the Ocean: The Atlantic and its Peoples 8000 BC – AD 1500* (Oxford, 2001).

CUNLIFFE SHAW, R., *The Royal Forest of Lancaster* (Preston, 1956).

CURLE, A. O., 'Report on the excavation in September 1913, of a vitrified fort at Rockcliffe, Dalbeattie, known as the Mote of Mark', *PSAS* 48 (1913–14), 125–68.

CURTA, Florin, 'Some remarks on ethnicity in medieval archaeology', *Early Medieval Europe* 15 (2007), 159–85.

— 'Medieval archaeology and ethnicity: where are we?', *History Compass* 9 (2011), 537–48.

CURTIS, L. P., *Anglo-Saxons and Celts: A Study of Anti-Irish Prejudice in Victorian England* (Berkeley CA, 1968).

DAHL, Sverri, 'Um ærgistaðir og ærgitoftir', *Fróðskaparrit* 18 (1970), 361–8.

— 'The Norse settlement of the Faroe Islands', *Medieval Archaeology* 14 (1970) 60–73.

DANCE, Richard, 'English in contact: Norse', in A. Bergs and L. J. Brinton (eds), *English Historical Linguistics: An International Handbook*, Vol. 2, Handbooks of Linguistics and Communication Science 34.2 (Berlin and New York, 2012), 1724–37.

DANIELS, R., 'The Anglo-Saxon monastery at Church Close, Hartlepool, Cleveland', *Archaeological Journal* 145 (1988), 158–210.

DARBY, H. C. and I. S. MAXWELL, *The Domesday Geography of Northern England* (Cambridge, 1962).

DARK, K. R., 'A sub-Roman re-defence of Hadrian's Wall', *Britannia* 23 (1992), 111–20.

— and S. P. DARK, 'New archaeological and palynological evidence for a sub-Roman reoccupation of Hadrian's Wall', *Archaeologia Aeliana*, 5th ser. 24 (1996), 57–72.

DARK, Petra, *The Environment of Britain in the First Millennium A.D.* (London, 2000).

DAVIES, Margaret, 'The diffusion and distribution patterns of the megalithic monuments of the Irish Sea and North Channel coastlands', *Antiquaries Journal* 26 (1946), 38–60.

DAVIES, R. Rees, 'The peoples of Britain and Ireland 1100–1400 I: identities', *Transactions of the Royal Historical Society*, 6th ser. 4 (1994), 1–20.

— *The First English Empire: Power and Identities in the British Isles, 1093–1343* (Oxford, 2000).

DAVIES, Wendy, *An Early Welsh Microcosm: Studies in the Llandaff Charters* (London, 1978).

— 'The Latin-charter tradition in western Britain, Brittany and Ireland in the early mediaeval period', in Dorothy Whitelock *et al.* (eds), *Ireland in Early Medieval Europe: Studies in memory of Kathleen Hughes* (Cambridge, 1982), 258–80.

— 'The myth of the Celtic Church', in Nancy Edwards and Alan Lane (eds), *The Early Church in Wales and the West* (Oxford, 1992), 12–21.

— and Hayo VIERCK, 'The contexts of Tribal Hidage: social aggregates and settlement patterns', *Frühmittelalterliche Studien* 8 (1974), 223–93.

DECKERS, Pieterjan, 'The maritime cultural landscape of early medieval Northumbria: small landing places and the emergence of coastal urbanism', in Barrett (ed.), *Maritime Societies*, 138–55.

DEGREGORIO, Scott, 'Introduction: the New Bede', in *idem* (ed.), *Innovation and Tradition*, 1–10.

— (ed.), *Innovation and Tradition in the Writings of the Venerable Bede* (Morgantown WV, 2006).

— (ed.), *The Cambridge Companion to Bede* (Cambridge, 2010).

DELEHAYE, H., 'Loca Sanctorum', *Analecta Bollandiana* 48 (1930), 1–64.

DÍAZ-ANDREU, Margarita and Sam LUCY, 'Introduction', in *eaedem* (eds), *The Archaeology of Identity*, 1–12.

— and Sam LUCY (eds), *The Archaeology of Identity: Approaches to Gender, Age, Status, Ethnicity and Religion* (London, 2005).

DICKINSON, Steve, 'Bryant's Gill, Kentmere: another "Viking period" Ribblehead?', in Baldwin and Whyte (eds), *The Scandinavians in Cumbria*, 83–8.

DOCKRAY-MILLER, Mary, 'Old English has a serious image problem', *JSTOR Daily* 3 May (2017), https://daily.jstor.org/old-english-serious-image-problem/

DODGSON, J. McN., 'The background of Bruanburh', *Saga Book* 14 (1957), 303–16.

— *The Place-Names of Cheshire*, 5 vols, EPNS 44–8, 54 (Nottingham, 1970–81).

DOHERTY, Charles, 'The monastic town in early Ireland', in H. B. Clarke and Anngret Simms (eds), *The Comparative History of Urban Origins in Non-Roman Europe: Ireland, Wales, Denmark, Germany, Poland and Russia from the Ninth to the Thirteenth Century*, BAR International Series 255, 2 vols (Oxford, 1985), I, 55–63.

— 'A road less travelled: the terminology of roads in early Ireland', in Purcell *et al.* (eds), *Clerics, Kings and Vikings*, 21–30.

DOLLEY, Michael, 'OE *Christðegn – An unsuspected instance of early Middle Irish influence on name-giving', *British Numismatic Journal* 36 (1967), 40–5.

— *SCBI 11a: University Collection, Reading: Anglo-Saxon and Norman Coins* (London, 1969).

— *Some Irish Dimensions to Manx History* (Belfast, 1976).

— and Elizabeth J. PIRIE, 'Repercussions on Chester's prosperity of the Viking descent on Cheshire in 980', *British Numismatic Journal* 34 (1963), 39–44.

DÒMHNALLACH, Dòmhnall, 'An Àirigh', *Gairm* 6 (1953), 176–9.

DORN, J., 'Beiträge zur Patrozinienforschung', *Archiv für Kulturgeschichte* 13 (1917), 9–49, 220–55.

DOWNHAM, Clare, 'The chronology of the last Scandinavian kings of York, AD 937–954', *Northern History* 40 (2003), 27–51.

— 'Eric Bloodaxe – axed? The mystery of the last Scandinavian king of York', *Mediaeval Scandinavia* 14 (2004), 51–77.

— 'The good, the bad and the ugly': portrayals of vikings in the "Fragmentary Annals of Ireland"', in Erik Kooper (ed.), *The Medieval Chronicle 3* (Leiden, 2004), 28–40.

— 'Living on the edge: Scandinavian Dublin in the twelfth century', in Ballin Smith *et al.* (eds), *West over Sea*, 33–52.

— *Viking Kings of Britain and Ireland: The Dynasty of Ívarr to A.D. 1014* (Edinburgh, 2007).

— 'St. Bega – myth, maiden or bracelet? An Insular cult and its origins', *Journal of Medieval History* 33 (2007), 33–42.
— '"Hiberno-Norwegians" and "Anglo-Danes": anachronistic ethnicities and Viking-age England', *Mediaeval Scandinavia* 19 (2009), 139–69.
— 'Viking identities in Ireland: it's not all black and white', *Medieval Dublin* 11 (2011), 185–201.
DOWNHAM, Clare, 'Religious and cultural boundaries between Vikings and Irish: the evidence of conversion', in Jenifer Ní Ghradaigh and Emmett O'Byrne (eds), *The March in the Islands of the Medieval West* (Leiden, 2012), 15–34.
— 'The break-up of Dál Riata and the rise of the Gallgoídil', in Howard B. Clarke and Ruth Johnson (eds), *The Vikings in Ireland and Beyond: Before and After the Battle of Clontarf* (Dublin, 2015), 189–205.
— 'Coastal communities and diaspora identities in Viking Age Ireland', in James Barrett and S. J. Gibbon (eds), *Maritime Societies of the Viking and Medieval World* (Leeds, 2015), 369–83.
— 'Scottish affairs and the political context of *Cogadh Gaedhel re Gallaibh*', in Christian Cooijmans (ed.), *Traversing the Inner Seas: Contacts and Continuity in and around Scotland, the Hebrides and the North of Ireland* (Edinburgh, 2017), 86–106.
DRISCOLL, S. T., 'The New Medieval Archaeology: theory vs. history', *Scottish Archaeological Review* 3 (1984), 104–9.
— *Govan from Cradle to Grave*, Govan Lecture (Glasgow, 2004).
DUCZKO, Wladyslaw, *Viking Rus: Studies on the Presence of Scandinavians in Eastern Europe* (Leiden, 2004).
DUDRIDGE, Glen, 'Reworking the World System paradigm', *Past and Present* 238, supplement 13, *The Global Middle Ages* (2018), 297–316.
DUFFY, Seán, 'Irishmen and Islesmen in the kingdoms of Dublin and Man, 1052–1171', *Ériu* 43 (1992), 93–133.
— 'The first Ulster plantation: John de Courcy and the men of Cumbria', in T. Barry *et al.* (eds), *Colony and Frontier in Medieval Ireland: Essays Presented to J. F. Lydon* (Edinburgh, 2000), 1–27.
— *Brian Boru and the Battle of Clontarf* (Dublin, 2013).
— and Harold MYTUM (eds), *A New History of the Isle of Man Volume 3: Medieval Period, 1000–1406* (Liverpool, 2015).
DUMAYNE, L., 'The effect of the Roman occupation on the environment of Hadrian's Wall: a pollen diagram from Fozy Moss, Northumberland', *Britannia* 25 (1994), 217–24.
DUMVILLE, David N., 'A new chronicle fragment of early British history', *English Historical Review* 88 (1973), 312–14.
— 'The Anglian collection of royal genealogies and regnal lists', *Anglo-Saxon England* 5 (1976), 23–50.
— 'Kingship, genealogies and regnal lists', in P. H. Sawyer and I. N. Wood (eds), *Early Medieval Kingship* (Leeds, 1977), 72–104.
— 'On the North British section of the *Historia Brittonum*', *Welsh History Review* 8 (1977), 345–54.
— 'On editing and translating medieval Irish chronicles: the *Annals of Ulster*', *Cambridge Medieval Celtic Studies* 10 (1985), 67–86.
— 'Textual archaeology and Northumbrian history subsequent to Bede', in Metcalf (ed.), *Coinage*, 43–55.
— 'The Tribal Hidage: an introduction to its texts and their history', in Bassett (ed.), *The Origins*, 225–30.
— 'St. Patrick and the Scandinavians of Dublin', in *idem* (ed.), *Saint Patrick*, 259–64.
— (ed.), *Saint Patrick, A.D. 493–1993* (Woodbridge, 1993).
— 'Ireland and Britain in *Táin Bó Fraích*', *Études Celtiques* 32 (1996), 175–87.
— '*Cath Fedo Euin*', *Scottish Gaelic Studies* 27 (1996), 114–27.
— *The Churches of North Britain in the First Viking Age*, Whithorn Lecture 5 (Stranraer, 1997).

— *A Palaeographer's Review* (Kansai, 1999).
— 'St. Finnian of Movilla: Briton, Gael, Ghost?', in Proudfoot (ed.), *Down: History and Society*, 71–84.
— 'The Chronicle of the Kings of Alba', in Taylor (ed.), *Kings, Clerics and Chronicles*, 73–86.
— 'Ireland and North Britain in the earlier middle ages: contexts for *Míniugud Senchusa Fher nAlban*', in Ó Baoill and McGuire (eds), *Rannsachadh na Gàidhlig 2000*, 181–212.
— '*Félire Óengusso*: problems of dating a monument of Old Irish', *Éigse* 33 (2002), 19–48.
— 'Old Dubliners and New Dubliners in Ireland and Britain: a Viking-Age story', in Seán Duffy (ed.), *Medieval Dublin* 6 (2004), 78–93.
— 'Gaelic and other Celtic names in the ninth-century Northumbrian *Liber Vitae*: some problems and implications', *Scottish Gaelic Studies* 22 (2006), 1–26.
— 'Mael Brigte mac Tornáin, pluralist coarb (†927)', *Journal of Celtic Studies* 4 (2004), 97–116; repr. in his *Celtic Essays, 2001–7*, 2 vols (Aberdeen, 2007), 137–58.
— 'The English in inter-ethnic *imperium* in the early Middle Ages: a mid-eighth-century case study', in his *Anglo-Saxon Essays, 2001–2007* (Aberdeen, 2007), 47–54.
— 'Vikings in Insular chronicling', in Stefan Brink and Neil Price (eds), *The Viking World* (London, 2008), 350–67.
— 'Political organisation in Dál Riata', in Edmonds and Russell (eds), *Tome*, 41–52.
— 'Did Ireland exist in the twelfth century?', in Purcell *et al.* (eds), *Clerics, Kings and Vikings*, 115–26.
DUNCAN, Archibald A. M., 'Bede, Iona, and the Picts', in R. H. C. Davis *et al.* (eds), *The Writing of History in the Middle Ages: Essays Presented to Richard William Southern* (Oxford, 1981), 1–42.
— 'The battle of Carham, 1018', *Scottish Historical Review* 55 (1976), 20–8.
— *The Kingship of the Scots 842–1292: Succession and Independence* (Edinburgh, 2002).
DUNSHEA, Philip M., 'The Brittonic kingdoms of the "Old North"' (Unpublished University of Cambridge PhD thesis, 2012).
— 'The meaning of *Catraeth*: a revised early context for *Y Gododdin*', in Woolf (ed.), *Beyond the Gododdin*, 81–114.
DURKIN, Philip, *Borrowed Words: A History of Loanwords in English* (Oxford, 2014).
DWELLY, Edward, *The Illustrated Gaelic–English Dictionary* (Berwick on Tweed, 1901–11; repr. Glasgow, 1994).
DYER, Christopher, *Making a Living in the Middle Ages: The People of Britain 850–1520* (New Haven CT, 2002).
ECTON, John, *Liber Valorum & Decimarum, being an Account of such Ecclesiastical Benefices in England and Wales*, 2nd edn (London, 1723).
— *Thesaurus Rerum Ecclesiasticarum: being an Account of the Valuations of all the Ecclesiastical Benefices in the several Dioceses of England and Wales* (London, 1742).
EDMONDS, Fiona, 'Hiberno-Saxon and Hiberno-Scandinavian influence in the west of the Northumbrian kingdom: a focus on the Church', 2 vols (Unpublished Oxford University DPhil thesis, 2006).
— 'Barrier or unifying feature? Defining the nature of water transport in the early medieval north-west', in Blair (ed.), *Waterways*, 21–36.
— 'Personal names and the cult of Patrick in eleventh-century Strathclyde and Northumbria', in Boardman *et al.* (eds), *Saints' Cults*, 42–65.
— *Whithorn's Renown in the Early Medieval Period: Whithorn, Futerna and magnum monasterium*, Whithorn Lecture 16 (Stranraer, 2009).
— 'The practicalities of communication between Northumbrian and Irish churches *c.*635–735', in Graham-Campbell and Ryan (eds), *Anglo-Saxon/Irish Relations*, 129–50.
— 'History and names', in Graham-Campbell and Philpott (eds), *The Huxley Viking Hoard*, 3–12.
— 'The Furness peninsula and the Irish Sea region: cultural interaction from the seventh century to the twelfth', in Clare Downham (ed.), *Jocelin of Furness. Essays from the 2011 Conference* (Donington, 2013), 17–44.
— 'St Cuthbert, St Columba and Ireland: movements of relics in the 870s', in Colm Ó Baoill

and Nancy R. McGuire (eds), *Rannsachadh na Gàidhlig* 6 (2013), 1–29.

— 'Saints' cults and Gaelic–Scandinavian influence around the Cumberland coast and north of the Solway Firth', in Timothy Bolton and Jón-Viðar Sigurðsson (eds), *Celtic–Norse Relationships*, 39–64.

— 'The emergence and transformation of medieval Cumbria', *Scottish Historical Review* 93 (2014), 195–216.

EDMONDS, Fiona, 'The expansion of the kingdom of Strathclyde', *Early Medieval Europe* 23 (2015), 43–66.

— 'H. M. Chadwick and *Early Scotland*', in Michael Lapidge (ed.), *H. M. Chadwick and the Study of Anglo-Saxon, Norse, and Celtic in Cambridge, Cambrian Medieval Celtic Studies* 69/70 (2015), 199–214.

— 'Carham: the western perspective', in McGuigan and Woolf (eds), *The Battle of Carham*, 79–94.

— 'Names on the Norman Edge: the persistence of Gaelic names in Middle Britain', in Andrew Jotischky and Keith Stringer (eds), *Norman Expansion: Landscapes of Power and Identity* (forthcoming).

— 'Irish hagiographical representations of the raid on Brega, 684' (forthcoming).

— 'Irish saints' cults in north-eastern Wales' (forthcoming).

— and Simon TAYLOR, 'Languages and names', in Stringer and Winchester (eds), *Northern England and Southern Scotland*, 137–72.

— and Paul RUSSELL (eds), *Tome: Studies in Medieval Celtic History and Law in honour of Thomas Charles-Edwards* (Woodbridge, 2011).

EDMONDS, Mark, *The Langdales: Landscape and Prehistory in a Lakeland Valley* (Stroud, 2004).

EDWARDS, B. J. N., *Vikings in North-West England: The Artifacts* (Lancaster, 1992).

— 'The Romans and before', in Crosby (ed.), *Leading the Way*, 1–28.

— 'A group of pre-Conquest metalwork from Asby Winderwath', *TCWAAS*, 3rd ser. 2 (2002), 127–8.

— 'An Anglo-Saxon strap-end from Shap', *TCWAAS*, 2nd ser. 3 (2003), 231–33.

EDWARDS, J. F. and B. P. HINDLE, 'The transportation system of medieval England and Wales', *Journal of Historical Geography* 17 (1991), 123–34.

EDWARDS, Kevin J. and Douglas B. BORTHWICK, 'Peaceful wars and scientific invaders: Irishmen, Vikings and palynological evidence for the earliest settlement of the Faroe Islands', in Sheehan and Ó Corráin (eds), *The Viking Age*, 66–79.

EDWARDS, Nancy, *The Archaeology of Early Medieval Ireland* (London, 1990).

— 'Abstract ornament on early medieval Irish crosses: a preliminary catalogue', in Ryan (ed.), *Ireland and Insular Art*, 111–17.

— (ed.), *The Archaeology of the Early Medieval Celtic Churches* (Leeds, 2009).

— *A Corpus of Early Medieval Inscribed Stones and Stone Sculpture in Wales. Volume III, North Wales* (London, 2013).

— 'Chi-Rhos, crosses and Pictish symbols: inscribed stones and stone sculpture in early medieval Wales and Scotland', in *eadem et al.* (eds), *Converting the Isles II: Transforming Landscapes of Belief in the Early Medieval Insular World* (Turnhout, 2017), 381–407.

EDWARDS, Owen Dudley *et al.*, *Celtic Nationalism* (London, 1968).

EFFROS, Bonnie, 'Dressing conservatively: women's brooches as markers of ethnic identity?', in Julia Smith and Leslie Brubaker (eds), *Gender and the Transformation of the Roman World* (Cambridge, 2004), 165–84.

EKWALL, Eilert, *Scandinavians and Celts in the North-West of England* (Lund, 1918).

— *The Place-Names of Lancashire* (Manchester, 1922).

— *English River-Names* (Oxford, 1928).

ELLIOT, W., 'Prehistoric, Roman and Dark Age Selkirkshire', in J. M. Gilbert (ed.), *Flower of the Forest. Selkirk: A New History* (Selkirk, 1985), 9–18.

ELLIS, Steven G., 'The collapse of the Gaelic world, 1450–1650', *Irish Historical Studies* 31 (1999), 449–69.

ELLWOOD, Thomas, *Lakeland and Iceland, being a Glossary of Words in the Dialect of*

Cumberland, Westmoreland and North Lancashire (London, 1895).

ELSWORTH, Daniel, 'Knockcross, Bowness-on-Solway: rediscovered, but still lost', *TCWAAS*, 3rd ser. 16 (2016), 248–52.

— 'The extent of Strathclyde in Cumbria: boundaries and bought land', *TCWAAS*, 3rd ser. 18 (2018), 87–104.

ENRIGHT, Michael J., *Iona, Tara and Soissons: The Origin of the Royal Anointing Ritual* (Berlin, 1985).

ETCHINGHAM, Colmán, 'Evidence of Scandinavian settlement in Wicklow', in Ken Hannigan and William Nolan (eds), *Wicklow: History and Society* (Dublin, 1994), 113–23.

— 'The implications of *paruchia*', *Ériu* 44 (1993), 139–62.

— *Church Organisation in Ireland AD 650–1000* (Maynooth, 1999).

— 'North Wales, Ireland and the Insular Viking zone', *Peritia* 15 (2001), 145–87.

— 'Pastoral provision in the first millennium: a two-tier service?', in FitzPatrick and Gillespie (eds), *The Parish*, 79–91.

— 'The bishops of Nendrum: a note', in McErlean and Crothers (eds), *Harnessing the Tides*, 315–21.

— '*Laithlinn*, "Fair Foreigners" and "Dark Foreigners": the identity and provenance of Vikings in ninth-century Ireland', in Sheehan and Ó Corráin (eds), *The Viking Age*, 80–8.

— 'The Viking impact on Glendalough', in Charles Doherty *et al.* (eds), *Glendalough: City of God* (Dublin, 2011), 211–22.

— 'Names for the Vikings in Irish annals', in Timothy Bolton and Jón-Viðar Sigurðsson (eds), *Celtic–Norse Relationships*, 23–38.

— 'Skuldelev 2 and Viking-age ships and fleets in Ireland', in Purcell *et al.* (eds), *Clerics, Kings and Vikings*, 79–90.

EVANS, Nicholas, 'The calculation of Columba's arrival in Britain in Bede's *Ecclesiastical History* and the Pictish king-lists', *Scottish Historical Review* 87 (2008), 183–205.

— *The Present and the Past in Medieval Irish Chronicles* (Woodbridge, 2010).

— 'The Irish chronicles and the British to Anglo-Saxon transition in seventh-century Northumbria', in Juliana Dresvina and Nicholas Sparks (eds), *The Medieval Chronicle VII* (Amsterdam, 2011), 15–44.

— 'Irish chronicles as sources for the history of northern Britain, A.D. 660–800', *Innes Review* 69 (2018), 1–48.

EVISON, Martin Paul, 'All in the genes? Evaluating the biological evidence of contact and migration', in Hadley and Richards (eds), *Cultures in Contact*, 277–94.

FANNING, Thomas, 'Appendix – Some field monuments in the townlands of Clonmelsh and Garryhundon, Co. Carlow', in Ó Cróinín, 'Rath Melsigi', 43–9.

— 'The Hiberno-Norse pins from the Isle of Man', in Fell *et al.* (eds), *The Viking Age*, 27–36.

— 'Some aspects of the bronze ringed pin in Scotland', in O'Connor and Clarke (eds), *From the Stone Age*, 342–42.

— *Viking Age Ringed Pins from Dublin* (Dublin, 1994).

FARLEY, Julia and Fraser HUNTER, *Celts: Art and Identity* (London, 2015).

FARMER, D. H., 'A note on the origin, purpose and date of University College, Oxford, MS 165', in Baker, 'Medieval illustrations', 46–9.

FARRER, W. *et al.*, *The Victoria History of the County of Lancaster*, 8 vols (London, 1906–14).

FAULL, Margaret L. and Marie STINSON (eds), *Domesday Book: Yorkshire*, Domesday Book 30, 2 vols (Chichester, 1986).

FELL, Christine *et al.* (eds), *The Viking Age in the Isle of Man: Select Papers from the Ninth Viking Congress* (London, 1983).

FELLOWS-JENSEN, Gillian, *Scandinavian Personal Names in Lincolnshire and Yorkshire* (Copenhagen, 1968).

— *Scandinavian Settlement Names in Yorkshire* (Copenhagen, 1972).

— 'A Gaelic–Scandinavian loan-word in English place-names', *Journal of the English Place-Name Society* 10 (1977–8), 18–25.

— 'Common Gaelic *áirge*, Old Scandinavian *ærgi* or *erg*?', *Nomina* 4 (1980), 67–74.

— 'Scandinavian settlement in the Isle of Man and North-West England: the place-name evidence', in Fell *et al.* (eds), *The Viking Age*, 37–52.
— 'Anthroponymical specifics in place-names in *–bý* in the British Isles', *Studia Anthroponymica Scandinavica* 1 (1983), 45–60.
— *Scandinavian Settlement Names in the North-West* (Copenhagen, 1985).
— 'Amounderness and Holderness', *Namn och Bygd* 78 (1990), 23–30.
— 'Scandinavians in Dumfriesshire and Galloway: the place-name evidence', in Oram and Stell (eds), *Galloway*, 77–95.
— 'Scandinavian place-names of the Irish Sea Province', in Graham-Campbell (ed.), *Viking Treasure*, 31–42.
— 'Little Thwaite, who made thee?', *Proceedings of the Nineteenth International Congress of Onomastic Sciences*, 3 vols (Aberdeen, 1998), II, 101–6.
— 'Old Faroese *ærgi* yet again', in *Eivindarmál: heiðursrit til Eivind Weyhe*, Annales Societatis Scentiarum Færoensis 32 (Tórshavn, 2002), 89–96.
FENTON, A. and G. STELL (eds), *Loads and Roads in Scotland and Beyond: Road Transport over 6000 Years* (Glasgow, 1984).
FERGUSON, Christopher, 'Re-evaluating early medieval Northumbrian coastal contacts and the "coastal highway"', in Petts and Turner (eds), *Early Medieval Northumbria*, 283–302.
FILPPULA, Markku *et al.* (eds), *The Celtic Roots of English* (Joensuu, 2002).
FINBERG, H. P. R., *The Early Charters of Devon and Cornwall* (Leicester, 1953).
— 'Sherborne, Glastonbury and the expansion of Wessex', *Transactions of the Royal Historical Society* 3 (1953), 101–24.
FIREY, Abigail, 'Cross-examining the witness: current research in Celtic monastic history', *Monastic Studies* 14 (1983), 31–49.
FISHER, Ian, *Early Medieval Sculpture in the West Highlands and Islands* (Edinburgh, 2001).
— 'Cross-currents in North Atlantic sculpture', in Mortensen and Arge (eds), *Vikings and Norse*, 160–6.
FITZPATRICK, Elizabeth and Raymond GILLESPIE (eds), *The Parish in Medieval ad Early Modern Ireland: Community, Territory and Building* (Dublin, 2006).
FLANAGAN, Marie Therese, *The Transformation of the Irish Church in the Twelfth Century* (Woodbridge, 2010).
FLECHNER, Roy, 'The making of the Canons of Theodore', *Peritia* 17–18 (2003), 121–43.
— 'An Insular tradition of ecclesiastical law: fifth to eighth centuries', in Graham-Campbell and Ryan (eds), *Anglo-Saxon/Irish Relations*, 23–46.
— 'The Chronicle of Ireland: then and now', *Early Medieval Europe* 21 (2013), 422–54.
FLEMING, Robin, *Britain after Rome: The Fall and Rise 400 to 1070* (London, 2010).
FLOWER, C. T., *Public Works in Mediaeval Law*, 2 vols, Selden Society 32, 40 (London, 1915, 1923).
FLYNN, P., 'Excavations at St. Michael's, Workington', *Church Archaeology* 1 (1997), 43–5.
FOLLETT, Westley, *Céli Dé in Ireland: Monastic Writing and Identity in the Early Middle Ages* (Woodbridge, 2006).
FOOT, Sarah, 'The making of *Angelcynn*: English identity before the Norman Conquest', *Transactions of the Royal Historical Society* 6 (1996), 25 49.
— *Monastic Life in Anglo-Saxon England* (Cambridge, 2006).
— *Æthelstan: the First King of England* (New Haven CT, 2011).
FORBES, A. P., *Kalendars of Scottish Saints* (Edinburgh, 1878).
FORGENG, Jeffrey L. and Jeffrey L. SINGMAN, *Daily Life in Medieval Europe* (London, 1999).
FÖRSTER, Max, 'Keltisches Wortgut im Englischen: eine sprachliche Untersuchung', in Heinrich Böhmer *et al.* (eds), *Texte und Forschungen zur englischen Kulturgeschichte, Festgabe für Felix Liebermann* (Halle, 1921), 119–242.
— 'Altenglisch *stōr*, ein altirisches Lehnwort', *Englische Studien* 70 (1935–6), 49–54.
FORSTER, Robert Henry and William Henry KNOWLES, 'Corstopitum: a report on the excavations in 1908', *Archaeologia Aeliana*, 3rd ser. 6 (1910), 302–424.
FORSYTH, Katherine, 'Evidence of a lost Pictish source in the *Historia Regum Anglorum* of

Symeon of Durham', in Taylor (ed.), *Kings, Clerics and Chronicles*, 19–32.

— '*Hic memoria perpetua*: the early inscribed stones of southern Scotland in context', in Sally M. Foster and Morag Cross (eds), *Able Minds and Practised Hands: Scotland's Early Medieval Sculpture in the 21st Century* (Leeds, 2005), 113–34.

— 'The Latinus stone: Whithorn's earliest Christian monument', in Jane Murray (ed.), *St Ninian and the Earliest Christianity in Scotland*, BAR British ser. 483 (Oxford, 2009), 19–41.

— and Cynthia THICKPENNY, 'The rock carvings', in Toolis and Bowles, *The Lost Dark Age Kingdom*, 83–102.

FOWLER, Elizabeth, 'Celtic metalwork of the fifth and sixth centuries A.D.: a reappraisal', *Archaeological Journal* 120 (1963), 98–160.

FOX, Cyril, *The Personality of Britain: its Influence on Inhabitant and Invader in Prehistoric and Early Historic Times*, 4th edn (Cardiff, 1959).

FOYS, Martin, 'The virtual reality of the Anglo-Saxon *mappamundi*', *Literature Compass* 1 (2003), 1–17.

FRAME, Robin, *The Political Development of the British Isles, 1100–1400* (Oxford, 1990).

FRANTZEN, Allen J., and John D. NILES, 'Anglo-Saxonism and medievalism', in *eidem* (eds), *Anglo-Saxonism and the Construction of Social Identity* (Gainesville FL, 1997).

FRASER, I. A., 'Mountain, hill or moor? An examination of Gaelic *sliabh* in the place-names of the Western Isles of Scotland', in W. F. H. Nicolaisen (ed.), *Proceedings of the XIXth International Congress of Onomastic Sciences* (Aberdeen, 1998), 119–26.

FRASER, James E., 'Northumbrian Whithorn and the making of St Ninian', *Innes Review* 53 (2002), 40–59.

— 'Strangers on the Clyde: Cenél Comgaill, Clyde Rock and the bishops of Kingarth', *Innes Review* 56 (2005), 102–20.

— '*Dux Reuda* and the Corcu Réti', in Wilson McLeod *et al.* (eds), *Cànan & Cultar/Language & Culture: Rannsachadh na Gàidhlig 3* (Edinburgh, 2006), 1–9.

— 'Bede, the Firth of Forth, and the location of *Urbs Iudeu*', *Scottish Historical Review* 87 (2008), 1–25.

— *From Caledonia to Pictland: Scotland to 795* (Edinburgh, 2009).

— 'St Patrick and barbarian northern Britain in the fifth century', in Hunter and Painter (eds), *Late Roman Silver*, 15–27.

FRASER, William, *The Annandale Family Book of the Johnstones, Earls and Marquises of Annandale*, 2 vols (Edinburgh, 1894).

FREEMAN, E. A., 'The latest theories on the origin of the English', *The Contemporary Review* 29 (1877), 36–51.

— *The History of the Norman Conquest of England, its Causes and Results*, 3rd edn, 8 vols (Oxford, 1877).

FREEMAN, Philip, *Ireland and the Classical World* (Austin TX, 2001).

FREKE, David, *Excavations on St Patrick's Isle, Peel, Isle of Man, 1982–88* (Liverpool, 2002).

FRODSHAM, Paul and Colm O'BRIEN (eds), *Yeavering: People, Power and Place* (Stroud, 2005).

GALSTER, Georg, *SCBI 4: Royal Collection of Coins and Medals, National Museum, Copenhagen, Part I: Ancient British and Anglo-Saxon Coins before Æthelred II* (London, 1964).

— *SCBI 7: Royal Collection of Coins and Medals, National Museum. Copenhagen, Part II. Anglo-Saxon Coins: Æthelred II* (London, 1966).

— *SCBI 13: Royal Collection of Coins and Medals, National Museum, Copenhagen, Part IIIa* (London, 1970).

— *SCBI 18: Royal Collection of Coins and Medals, National Museum, Copenhagen, Part IV* (London, 1972).

GAMESON, Richard (ed.), 'Northumbrian books in the seventh and eighth centuries', in *idem* (ed.), *The Lindisfarne Gospels*, 43–83.

— (ed.), *The Lindisfarne Gospels: New Perspectives* (Leiden, 2017).

GANNON, Anna, *The Iconography of Early Anglo-Saxon Coinage, Sixth to Eighth Centuries* (Oxford, 2003).

GARDINER, Mark, 'An early medieval tradition of building in Britain', *Arqueología de la Arquitectura* 9 (2012), 231–46.

GARDNER, Rex, 'Kentigern, Columba, and Oswald: the Ripon connexion', *Northern History* 35 (1999) 1–26.

GEAKE, Helen, *The Use of Grave-Goods in Conversion-Period England, c.600–c.850*, BAR British ser. 261 (Oxford, 1997).

GEARY, Patrick J., 'Ethnic identity as a situational construct', *Mitteilungen der Anthropologischen Gesellschaft in Wien* 113 (1983), 15–26.

— *The Myth of Nations: The Medieval Origins of Europe* (Princeton NJ, 2002).

Geiriadur Prifysgol Cymru: a Dictionary of the Welsh Language, 4 vols (Cardiff, 1950–2002).

GELLING, Margaret, 'The place-names of the Isle of Man', *Journal of the Manx Museum* 7 no. 86 (1970), 130–9; no. 87 (1971), 168–75.

— 'Norse and Gaelic in medieval man: the place-name evidence', in Davey (ed.), *Man and Environment*, 251–64.

— and Margaret COLE, *The Landscape of Place-Names* (Stamford, 2000; repr. 2003).

GELLING, P. S., 'Shielings in the Isle of Man', *Journal of the Manx Museum* 6 no. 77 (1960–1), 123–5.

— 'Medieval shielings in the Isle of Man', *Medieval Archaeology* 6–7 (1962–3), 156–72.

GEM, Richard, 'Towards an iconography of Anglo-Saxon architecture', *Journal of the Warburg and Courtauld Institutes* 46 (1983), 1–18.

— 'Architecture of the Anglo-Saxon Church, 735 to 870: from Archbishop Ecgberht to Archbishop Ceolnoth', *Journal of the British Archaeological Association* 146 (1993), 29–66.

GERMAN, Gary D., 'Britons, Anglo-Saxons and scholars: 19th century attitudes towards the survival of Britons in Anglo-Saxon England', in Tristram (ed.), *The Celtic Englishes II*, 347–74.

GERRARD, James, *The Ruin of Roman Britain: an Archaeological Perspective* (Cambridge, 2013).

GILLETT, Andrew, 'Was ethnicity politicized in the earliest medieval kingdoms?', in *idem* (ed.), *On Barbarian Identity*, 85–121.

— (ed.), *On Barbarian Identity: Critical Approaches to Ethnicity in the Early Middle Ages* (Turnhout, 2002).

GILLINGHAM, John, *The English in the Twelfth Century: Imperialism, National Identity and Political Values* (Woodbridge, 2000).

GOETZ, Hans-Werner, 'Concepts of realm and frontiers from late antiquity to the early middle ages: some preliminary remarks', in Walter Pohl *et al.* (eds), *The Transformation of Frontiers from Late Antiquity to the Carolingians* (Leiden, 2001), 73–82.

GOFFART, Walter A., *The Narrators of Barbarian History (A.D. 550–800): Jordanes, Gregory of Tours, Bede, and Paul the Deacon* (Notre Dame IN, 1988, repr. 2005).

— *Barbarian Tides: The Migration Age and Later* (Philadelphia PA, 2006).

GÖRLACH, Manfred, 'Celtic Englishes?', in Tristram (ed.), *Celtic Englishes I*, 27–54.

GOUGH-COOPER, Henry, 'Some notes on the name "Ninian"', *TDGNHAS* 72 (1997), 5–10.

GRABOWSKI, Kathryn, and David DUMVILLE, *Chronicles and Annals of Medieval Ireland and Wales* (Woodbridge, 1984).

GRAHAM, A., 'Giudi', *Antiquity* 33 (1959), 63–5.

— 'Some old harbours in Wigtownshire', *TDGNHAS*, 3rd ser. 54 (1979), 39–74.

— and A. E. TRUCKELL, 'Old harbours in the Solway Firth', *TDGNHAS*, 3rd ser. 52 (1976–77), 109–42.

GRAHAM-CAMPBELL, James, 'Two groups of ninth-century Irish brooches', *Journal of the Royal Society of Antiquaries* 102 (1972), 113–28.

— 'The Lough Ravel, County Antrim brooch and others of ninth-century date', *Ulster Journal of Archaeology* 36 (1973), 52–7.

— 'Bossed penannular brooches: a review of recent research', *Medieval Archaeology* 19

(1975), 33–47.
— 'The Mote of Mark and Celtic interlace', *Antiquity* 50 (1976), 48–51.
— 'Some archaeological reflections on the Cuerdale hoard', in Metcalf (ed.), *Coinage*, 329–44.
— (ed.) *Viking Treasure from the North-West: The Cuerdale Hoard in its Context* (Liverpool, 1992).
— 'The Cuerdale hoard: comparisons and context' in *idem* (ed.), *Viking Treasure*, 107–15.
— 'The Irish Sea Vikings: raiders and settlers' in T. Scott and P. Starkey (eds), *The Middle Ages in the North-West* (Oxford, 1995), 59–83.
— 'The early Viking Age in the Irish Sea area', in Clarke *et al.* (eds), *Ireland and Scandinavia*, 102–28.
— 'The dual economy of the Danelaw', *British Numismatic Journal* 71 (2001), 49–59.
— *Whithorn and the Viking World*, Whithorn Lecture 8 (Stranraer, 2001).
— 'The northern hoards: from Cuerdale to Bossall/Flaxton', in Higham and Hill (eds), *Edward the Elder*, 212–29.
— 'National and regional identities: the "glittering prizes", in Redknap *et al.* (eds), *Pattern and Purpose*, 27–38.
— *The Cuerdale Hoard and related Viking-Age Silver and Gold from Britain and Ireland in the British Museum* (London, 2011).
— and Colleen BATEY, *Vikings in Scotland: an Archaeological Survey* (Edinburgh, 1998).
— and Michael RYAN (eds), *Anglo-Saxon/Irish Relations before the Vikings*, Proceedings of the British Academy 157 (London, 2009).
— and Niamh WHITFIELD, 'A mount with Hiberno-Saxon chip-carved animal ornament from Rerrick, near Dundrennan', *TDGNHAS* 67 (1992), 9–27.
— *et al.*, 'Tenth-century graves: the Viking-Age artefacts and their significance', in Freke (ed.), *Excavations on St Patrick's Isle, Peel*, 83–99.
GRANT, Alexander and Keith STRINGER, 'Introduction: the enigma of British history', in *idem* and Stringer (eds), *Uniting the Kingdom?*, 3–11.
— and Keith STRINGER (eds), *Uniting the Kingdom? The Making of British History* (London, 1995).
GRANT, Alison, 'A new approach to the inversion compounds of north-west England', *Nomina* 25 (2002), 65–90.
— 'Scandinavian place-names in northern Britain as evidence for language contact and inter-action' (Unpublished Glasgow University PhD thesis, 2003).
— 'A reconsideration of the *kirk*-names in south-west Scotland', *Northern Studies* 38 (2004), 97–121.
GRAYSTONE, Philip, *Walking Roman Roads in Bowland* (Lancaster, 1992).
— *Walking Roman Roads in the Fylde and the Ribble Valley* (Lancaster, 1996).
GREEN, Thomas, *Britons and Anglo-Saxons: Lincolnshire AD 400–650* (Lincoln, 2012).
GREGORY, John V., 'Dedication names of ancient churches in the counties of Durham and Northumberland', *Archaeological Journal* 42 (1885), 370–83.
GRIERSON, Philip and Mark BLACKBURN, *Medieval European Coinage I: The Early Middle Ages, Fifth to Tenth Centuries* (Cambridge, 1986).
GRIFFITHS, David, 'The coastal trading ports of the Irish Sea', in Graham-Campbell (ed.), *Viking Treasure*, 63–72.
— 'The North-West frontier', in Higham and Hill (eds), *Edward the Elder*, 167–87.
— 'Glenluce Sands, Wigtownshire/ Meols, Cheshire', in R. Cowie and D. Hill (eds), *Wics and Emporia: the Early Medieval Trading Centres of Europe* (Sheffield, 2001), 98–9.
— 'Settlement and acculturation in the Irish Sea region', in Hines *et al.* (eds), *Land, Sea and Home*, 125–38.
— 'Sand dunes and stray finds: evidence for pre-Viking trade?', in Graham-Campbell and Ryan (eds), *Anglo-Saxon/Irish Relations before the Vikings*, 265–80.
— *Vikings of the Irish Sea: Conflict and Assimilation AD 790–1050* (Stroud, 2010).
— *Early Medieval Whithorn: The Irish Sea Context*, Whithorn Lecture 21 (Stranraer, 2014).
— 'Medieval coastal sand inundation in Britain and Ireland', *Medieval Archaeology* 59 (2015), 103–21.

— et al., *Meols: The Archaeology of the North Wirral Coast* (Oxford, 2007).

GROVES, S. E. et al., 'The Bowl Hole early medieval cemetery at Bamburgh, excavations 1998 to 1999', *Archaeologia Aeliana*, 5th ser. 38 (2009), 105–22.

GROVES, S. E. et al., 'The Bowl Hole burial ground; a late Anglian cemetery in Northumberland', in J. Buckberry and A. Cherryson (eds), *Burial in Later Anglo-Saxon England, c. 650 to 1100 AD* (Oxford, 2010), 114–25.

— 'Mobility histories of 7th–9th century AD people buried at early medieval Bamburgh, Northumberland, England', *American Journal of Physical Anthropology* 151 (2013), 462–76.

GRUEBER, Herbert A. and Charles Francis KEARY, *A Catalogue of English Coins in the British Museum: Anglo-Saxon Series Volume 2, Wessex and England to the Norman Conquest* (London, 1893).

GRUFFYDD, R. Geraint, 'Canu Cadwallon ap Cadfan', in Rachel Bromwich and R. Brinley Jones (eds), *Astudiaethau ar y Hengerdd* (Cardiff, 1978), 25–43.

GUNSTONE, A. J. H., *SCBI 17: Midland Museums: Ancient British, Anglo-Saxon and Norman Coins* (London, 1971).

GUYONVARC'H, Christian, 'L'anthroponyme irlandais *Setanta* et les *Setantii*', *Ogam: Tradition celtique* 13 (1961), 592–9.

GWYNN, A. and R.N. HADCOCK, *Medieval Religious Houses: Ireland* (Harlow, 1970).

HADLEY, Dawn M., 'Conquest, colonisation and the Church: ecclesiastical organisation in the Danelaw', *Historical Research* 69 (1996), 109–28.

— *The Northern Danelaw: its Social Structure, c.800–1100* (Leicester, 2000).

— 'Viking and native: re-thinking identity in the Danelaw', *Early Medieval Europe* 11 (2002), 45–70.

— *The Vikings in England: Settlement, Society and Culture* (Manchester, 2006).

— and K. A. HEMER, 'Microcosms of migration: children and early medieval population movement', *Childhood in the Past* 4 (2011), 63–78.

— and Julian D. RICHARDS (eds), *Cultures in Contact: Scandinavian Settlement in England in the Ninth and Tenth Centuries* (Turnhout, 2000).

— and Julian D. RICHARDS, 'The winter camp of the Viking Great Army, AD 872–3, Torksey, Lincolnshire', *The Antiquaries Journal* 96 (2016), 23–67.

HAGGART, Craig, 'The *céli Dé* and the early medieval Irish church: a reassessment', *Studia Hibernica* 34 (2006–7), 17–62.

HAKENBECK, Susanne, *Local, Regional and Ethnic Identities in Early Medieval Cemeteries in Bavaria* (Borgo San Lorenzo, 2011).

HALE, W. G. and Audrey CONEY, *Martin Mere: Lancashire's Lost Lake* (Liverpool, 2005).

HALIDAY, Charles, *The Scandinavian Kingdom of Dublin* (Dublin, 1884).

HALL, Alaric, 'Interlinguistic communication in Bede's *Historia ecclesiastica gentis Anglorum*', in *idem et al.* (eds), *Interfaces between Language and Culture in Medieval England: A Festschrift for Matti Kilpiö* (Leiden, 2010), 37–80.

HALLINGER, Kassius, *Gorze-Cluny: Studien zu den monastischen Lebensformen und Gegensätzen im Hochmittelalter* (Rome, 1950).

HALLORAN, Kevin, 'The Brunanburh campaign: a reappraisal', *Scottish Historical Review* 84 (2005), 133–48.

— 'Anlaf Guthfrithson at York: a non-existent kingship?', *Northern History* 50 (2013), 180–5.

HALSALL, Guy, *Barbarian Migrations and the Roman West, 376–568* (Cambridge, 2003).

— *Worlds of Arthur: Facts and Fictions of the Dark Ages* (Oxford, 2013).

HAMLIN, Ann, 'A Chi-Rho-carved stone at Drumaqueran, Co. Antrim', *Ulster Journal of Archaeology* 35 (1972), 22–8.

— 'The study of early Irish churches', in Ní Chatháin and Richter (eds) *Irland und Europa*, 117–26.

— *Ninian and Nendrum: Whithorn and the Early Church in East Ulster*, ed. Malcolm Fry, Whithorn Lecture 10 (Stranraer, 2014).

— and C. LYNN (eds), *Pieces of the Past: Archaeological Excavations by the Department of the Environment for Northern Ireland 1970–1986* (Belfast, 1988).

HAMMOND, Matthew, 'Ethnicity and the writing of medieval Scottish history', *The Scottish Historical Review* 85 (2008), 1–27.

— 'Domination and conquest? The Scottish experience in the twelfth and thirteenth centuries', in Seán Duffy and Susan Foran (eds), *The English Isles: Cultural Transmission and Political Conflict in Britain and Ireland, 1100–1500* (Dublin, 2013), 68–83.

HAMP, Eric P., 'On notable trees', *Bulletin of the Board of Celtic Studies* 30 (1983), 42–4.

HANDLEY, Mark, 'The origins of Christian commemoration in Late Antique Britain', *Early Medieval Europe* 10 (2001), 177–99.

HANSON, W. S. *et al.*, 'The Agricolan supply-base at Red House, Corbridge', *Archaeologia Aeliana*, 5th ser. 7 (1979), 1–98.

HARBISON, Peter, 'Early Irish churches', in Löwe (ed.), *Die Iren und Europa*, II, 618–29.

— *The High Crosses of Ireland: An Iconographical and Photographic Survey* (3 vols, Bonn, 1992).

HARDING, Stephen *et al.* (eds), *In Search of Vikings: Interdisciplinary Approaches to the Scandinavian Heritage of North-West England* (London, 2015).

HARDY, T. D., *Descriptive Catalogue of Materials Relating to the History of Great Britain and Ireland*, Rolls Series 26, 3 vols (London, 1862–71), II, 225–6.

HARRIS, Gerald, *Shaping the Nation: England 1360–1461* (Oxford, 2005).

HARRIS, Oliver J. T. *et al.*, 'Assembling places and persons: a tenth-century Viking boat burial from Swordle Bay on the Ardnamurchan peninsula, Scotland', *Antiquity* 91 (2016), 191–206.

HARRISON, David Featherstone, *The Bridges of Medieval England: Transport and Society 400–1800* (Oxford, 2004).

HARRISON, Stephen and Raghnall Ó FLOINN, *Viking Graves and Grave-goods in Ireland* (Dublin, 2015).

HASTINGS, Adrian, *The Construction of Nationhood: Ethnicity, Religion and Nationalism* (Cambridge, 1997).

HAWKES, Jane, 'An iconography of identity? The cross-head from Mayo Abbey', in Colum Hourihane (ed.), *From Ireland Coming: Irish Art from the Early Christian to the Late Gothic Period and its European Context* (Princeton NJ, 2001), 261–75.

— *The Sandbach Crosses: Sign and Significance in Anglo-Saxon Sculpture* (Dublin, 2002).

— 'East meets West in Anglo-Saxon sculpture', in Clayton *et al.* (eds), *England, Ireland and the Insular World*, 41–61.

— and Susan MILLS, *Northumbria's Golden Age* (Stroud, 1999).

HAYWARD, Paul, 'St Wilfrid of Ripon and the Northern Church in Anglo-Norman historiography', *Northern History* 49 (2012), 11–36.

HAYWOOD, John, *Dark Age Naval Power: A Reassessment of Frankish and Anglo-Saxon Seafaring Activity* (Hockwold-cum-Wilton, 1991).

HEALY, Patrick, *Pre-Norman Grave-slabs and Cross-incised Stones in the Dublin Region* (Dublin, 2009).

HEENS-PETTERSEN, Aina Margrethe, 'Insular artefacts from Viking-Age burials from mid-Norway: a review of contact between the Trøndelag and Britain and Ireland', *Internet Archaeology* 38 (2014): http://intarch.ac.uk/journal/issue38/heenpettersen_toc.html

HEMER, K. A. *et al.*, 'Evidence of early medieval trade and migration between Wales and the Mediterranean region', *Journal of Archaeological Science* 40 (2013), 2352–9.

— 'No Man is an island: evidence of pre-Viking migration to the Isle of Man', *Journal of Archaeological Science* 52 (2014), 242–9.

HENDERSON, George, *The Norse Influence on Celtic Scotland* (Glasgow, 1910).

HENDERSON, Isabel and Elisabeth OKASHA, 'The Early Christian inscribed and carved stones of Tullylease, Co. Cork', *Cambridge Medieval Celtic Studies* 24 (1992), 1–36.

— 'The Early Christian inscribed and carved stones of Tullylease, Co. Cork: addendum', *Cambrian Medieval Celtic Studies* 33 (1997), 1–36.

HENDRICKSON, Mitch, 'A transport geographic perspective on travel and communication in Angkorian Southeast Asia (ninth to fifteenth centuries AD)', in Reynolds (ed.), *The Archaeology*, 444–57.

HENG, Geraldine, *The Invention of Race in the European Middle Ages* (Cambridge, 2018).
HENRY, Françoise, *La sculpture irlandaise pendant les douze premiers siècles de l'ère chrétienne*, 2 vols (Paris, 1933).
— *Irish High Crosses* (Dublin, 1964).
HENRY, Françoise, 'On some Early Christian objects in the Ulster Museum', *Journal of the Royal Society of Antiquaries of Ireland* 95 (1965), 51–63.
HERBERT, Máire, *Iona, Kells, and Derry: The History and Hagiography of the Monastic Familia of Columba* (Oxford, 1988).
— 'Charter material from Kells', in Felicity O'Mahony (ed.), *The Book of Kells. Proceedings of a Conference at Trinity College Dublin* (Aldershot, 1994), 60–77.
— 'Sea-divided Gaels? Constructing relationships between Irish and Scots *c.* 800–1169', in Brendan Smith (ed.), *Britain and Ireland 900–1300: Insular Responses to Medieval European Change* (Cambridge, 1999), 87–97.
— '*Rí Éirenn, Rí Alban*, Kingship and identity in the ninth and tenth centuries', in Simon Taylor (ed.), *Kings, Clerics and Chronicles in Scotland, 500–1297* (Dublin, 2000), 62–72.
HIATT, Alfred, '"From Hulle to Cartage": maps, England and the sea', in Sebastian I. Sobecki (ed.), *The Sea and Englishness in the Middle Ages: Maritime Narratives, Identity and Culture* (Cambridge, 2011), 133–58.
HIGGINS, Godfrey, *The Celtic Druids* (London, 1829).
HIGGITT, John, 'Anglo-Saxon painted lettering at St Patrick's Chapel, Heysham', in Sharon Cather *et al.* (eds), *Early Medieval Wall Painting and Painted Sculpture in England*, BAR British ser. 216 (Oxford, 1990), 31–40.
HIGHAM, Mary C., 'The "Erg" place-names of northern England', *Journal of the English Place-Name Society* 10 (1977–8), 7–17; repr. in Alan G. Crosby (ed.), *Of Names and Places: Selected Writings of Mary Higham* (Bristol, 2007), 1–10.
— 'Scandinavian settlements in north-west England, with a special study of Ireby names', in Crawford (ed.), *Scandinavian Settlement*, 195–205.
— 'Pre-conquest settlement in the Forest of Bowland', in Baldwin and Whyte (eds), *The Scandinavians in Cumbria*, 119–33.
HIGHAM, N. J., 'Continuity studies in the First Millennium A.D. in North Cumbria', *Northern History* 14 (1978), 1–18.
— 'The Scandinavians in North Cumbria: raids and settlement in the later ninth to mid-tenth centuries', in Baldwin and Whyte (eds), *The Scandinavians*, 37–51.
— *The Northern Counties to AD 1000* (London, 1986).
— 'The Cheshire burhs and the Mercian frontier to 924', *Transactions of the Lancashire and Cheshire Antiquarian Society* 85 (1988), 193–222.
— 'Northumbria, Mercia and the Irish Sea Norse, 893–926', in Graham-Campbell (ed.), *Viking Treasure*, 21–30.
— *The Kingdom of Northumbria AD 350–1100* (Stroud, 1993).
— *English Conquest: Gildas and Britain in the Fifth Century* (Manchester, 1994).
— *A Frontier Landscape: The North West in the Middle Ages* (Macclesfield, 2004).
— 'Northumbria's southern frontier: a review', *Early Medieval Europe* 14 (2006), 391–418.
— *(Re-)reading Bede. The* Ecclesiastical History *in Context* (London, 2006).
— *Ecgfrith: King of the Northumbrians, High-King of Britain* (Donington, 2015).
— and B. JONES, *The Carvetii* (Gloucester, 1985).
— and D. H. HILL (eds), *Edward the Elder 899–924* (London, 2001).
HIGHLEY, Christopher, *Catholics Writing the Nation in Early Modern Britain and Ireland* (Oxford, 2008).
HILL, George F., 'A find of coins of Eadgar, Eadweard II, and Æthelred at Chester', *The Numismatic Chronicle*, 4th ser. 20 (1920), 141–65.
HILL, Peter, *Whithorn and Saint Ninian: The Excavations of a Monastic Town, 1984–91* (Stroud, 1997).
HILLS, Catherine, *Origins of the English* (London, 2003).
HIND, J. G. F., 'Agricola's fleet and the Portus Trucculensis', *Britannia* 5 (1974), 285–8.
— '*Elmet and Deira* – forest names in Yorkshire?', *Bulletin of the Board of Celtic Studies* 28

(1978–80), 541–52.

HINDLE, Brian Paul, 'Medieval roads in the diocese of Carlisle', *TCWAAS*, 2nd ser. 77 (1977), 83–95.

— 'Roads and tracks', in L. Cantor (ed.), *The English Medieval Landscape* (London, 1982), 192–217.

— 'Sources for the English medieval road system', in Allen and Evans, *Roadworks*, 33–50.

HINES, John, *The Scandinavian Character of Anglian England in the pre-Viking Period*, BAR British ser. 124 (Oxford, 1984).

— 'Philology, archaeology and the *adventus Saxonum vel Anglorum*', in Alfred Bammesberger and Alfred Wollmann (eds), *Britain 400–600: Language and History* (Heidelberg, 1990), 17–36.

— 'The becoming of the English: identity, material culture and language in early Anglo-Saxon England', *Anglo-Saxon Studies in Archaeology and History* 7 (1994), 49–59.

— *Old-Norse Sources for Gaelic History*, Quiggin Pamphlets on the Sources of Mediaeval Gaelic History 5 (Cambridge, 2002).

— *Voices in the Past: English Literature and Archaeology* (Cambridge, 2004).

— *et al.* (eds), *Land, Sea and Home: Proceedings of a Conference on Viking Period Settlement at Cardiff, July 2001* (Leeds, 2004).

HINTON, David, 'Demography: from Domesday and beyond', *Journal of Medieval History* 39 (2013), 146–78.

HOBSBAWM, E. J., *Nations and Nationalism since 1780: Programme, Myth, Reality* (Cambridge, 1990).

HODDER, Ian, 'Economic and social stress and material cultural patterning', *American Antiquity* 44 (1979), 446–54.

— *Reading the Past: Current Approaches to Interpretation in Archaeology* (Cambridge, 1986).

HODGE, Arkady, 'When is a charter not a charter? Documents in non-conventional contexts in early medieval Europe', in Jonathan Jarrett and Allan Scott McKinley (eds), *Problems and Possibilities of Early Medieval Charters* (Turnhout, 2013), 127–49.

HODGES, Richard, *Dark Age Economics: The Origins of Towns and Trade A.D. 600–1000* (London, 1982).

HODGKINSON, David *et al.*, *The Lowland Wetlands of Cumbria* (Lancaster, 2000).

HODGSON, John *et al.*, *A History of Northumberland in Three Parts*, 3 vols in 8 (Newcastle, 1820–40).

HODGSON, Nicholas, 'The Notitia Dignitatum and the later Roman garrison of Britain', in V. A. Maxfield and M. J. Dobson (eds), *Roman Frontier Studies 1989* (Exeter, 1991), 84–92.

HOGAN, Edmund, *Onomasticon Goedelicum Locorum et Triborum Hiberniae et Scotiae* (Dublin, 1910).

HOGG, A. H. A., 'Llwyfenydd', *Antiquity* 80 (1946), 210–11.

HOGG, Richard M., 'Old English dialectology', in Ans van Kemenade and Bettelou Los (eds), *The Handbook of the History of English* (Malden MA, 2006), 395–416.

— *A Grammar of Old English: Volume 1, Phonology* (Malden MA, 2011).

HOLDER, P. A., 'A Roman military diploma from Ravenglass, Cumbria', *Bulletin of the John Rylands Library* 79 (1997), 3–42.

HOLMES, Catherine and Naomi STANDEN, 'Introduction: towards a Global Middle Ages', *Past and Present* 238, supplement 13, *The Global Middle Ages* (2018), 1–44.

HOOKE, Della, 'The reconstruction of ancient route-ways', *The Local Historian* 12.5 (1977), 212–20.

HOPE-TAYLOR, Brian, *Yeavering: an Anglo-British Centre of Early Northumbria* (London, 1977).

HORDEN, Peregrine and Nicholas PURCELL, *The Corrupting Sea: a Study of Mediterranean History* (Oxford, 2000).

HORN, T. C. R. and Harry RITTER, 'Interdisciplinary history: a historiographical review', *The History Teacher* 19 (1986), 427–48.

HOSTE, A. 'A survey of the unedited work of Lawrence of Durham', *Sacris Erudiri* 11

(1960), 249–65.

HOWARD-DAVIS Christine and Kath BUXTON, *Roman Forts in the Fylde: Excavations at Dowbridge, Kirkham* (Lancaster, 2000).

HOWLETT, David, '*Orationes Moucani*: early Cambro-Latin prayers', *Cambridge Medieval Celtic Studies* 24 (1992), 55–74.

— *Muirchú Moccu Machthéni's* 'Vita Sancti Patricii': *Life of St Patrick* (Dublin, 2006).

HSY, Jonathan, *Trading Tongues: Merchants, Multilingualism and Medieval Literature* (Columbus OH, 2013).

HUDDART, David and Tim STOTT, *Earth Environments: Past, Present and Future* (Chichester, 2010).

HUDSON, Benjamin T., '*Elech* and the Scots in Strathclyde', *Scottish Gaelic Studies* 15 (1988), 145–9.

— 'Cnut and the Scottish kings', *English Historical Review* 107 (1992), 350–60; repr. in *idem*, *Irish Sea Studies*, 60–70.

— 'Knútr and Viking Dublin', *Scandinavian Studies* 66 (1994), 319–35; repr. as 'Cnut and Viking Dublin', in *idem*, *Irish Sea Studies*, 47–59.

— 'Brjáns saga', *Medium Ævum* 71 (2002), 241–68; repr. in *idem*, *Irish Sea Studies*, 143–71.

— *Viking Pirates and Christian Princes: Dynasty, Religion and Empire in the North Atlantic* (Oxford, 2005).

— *Irish Sea Studies* (Dublin, 2006).

HUGHES, Kathleen, 'On an Irish litany of pilgrim saints', *Analecta Bollandiana* 77 (1959), 305–31.

— *The Church in Early Irish Society* (London, 1966).

— 'Evidence for contacts between the Churches of the Irish and English from the Synod of Whitby to the Viking Age', in Clemoes and Hughes (eds), *England before the Conquest*, 49–67.

— *Early Christian Ireland: Introduction to the Sources* (London, 1972).

— *Celtic Britain in the Early Middle Ages: Studies in Welsh and Scottish Sources*, ed. David N. Dumville (Woodbridge, 1980).

— 'The Celtic Church: is this a valid concept?', *Cambridge Medieval Celtic Studies* 1 (1981), 1–20.

HUNTER, Fraser, *Beyond the Edge of the Empire – Caledonians, Picts and Romans* (Rosemarkie, 2007).

— 'Hillfort and Hacksilber: Traprain Law in the late Roman Iron Age and early historic periods', in *idem* and Painter (eds), *Late Roman Silver*, 3–10.

— and Kenneth Painter (eds), *Late Roman Silver: The Traprain Treasure in Context* (Edinburgh, 2013).

INNES, Matthew, 'Danelaw identities', in Hadley and Richards (eds), *Cultures in Contact*, 65–88.

INSLEY, Charles, 'The family of Wulfric Spott: an Anglo-Saxon marcher dynasty?', in David Roffe (ed.), *The English and their Legacy: Essays in Honour of Ann Williams* (Woodbridge, 2012), 115–28.

IRELAND, Colin A., 'Boisil: an Irishman hidden in the works of Bede', *Peritia* 5 (1986), 400–3.

— 'Aldfrith of Northumbria and the Irish genealogies', *Celtica* 22 (1991), 64–78.

— 'Where was King Aldfrith of Northumbria educated? An exploration of seventh-century Insular learning', *Traditio* 70 (2015), 29–73.

— 'Some Irish characteristics of the Whitby Life of Gregory the Great', in Pádraic Moran and Immo Warntjes (eds), *Early Medieval Ireland and Europe: Chronology, Contacts, Scholarship: Festschrift for Dáibhí Ó Cróinín* (Turnhout, 2015), 139–78.

ISAAC, Graham, '*Gweith Gwen Ystrat* and the northern heroic age of the sixth century', *Cambrian Medieval Celtic Studies* 36 (1998), 61–70.

JACKSON, Kenneth Hurlstone, 'Common Gaelic: the evolution of the Gaelic languages', *Proceedings of the British Academy* 37 (1951), 71–97.

— *Language and History in Early Britain: A Chronological Survey of the Brittonic Languages*

First to Twelfth Century A.D. (Edinburgh, 1953).
— 'The sources for the Life of St. Kentigern', in N. K. Chadwick *et al.* (eds), *Studies in the Early British Church* (Cambridge, 1958), 273–357.
— 'On the northern British section in Nennius', in N. K. Chadwick (ed.), *Celt and Saxon: Studies in the Early British Border* (Cambridge, 1963), 20–62.
— *The Gododdin: The Oldest Scottish Poem* (Edinburgh, 1969).
— 'Varia 1: Bede's *Urbs Giudi*: Stirling or Cramond?', *Cambridge Medieval Celtic Studies* 2 (1981), 1–8.
JAMES, Alan G., 'A Cumbric diaspora?', in Oliver Padel and David Parsons (eds), *A Commodity of Good Names: Essays in Honour of Margaret Gelling* (Donington, 2008), 187–203.
JAMES, Heather and Peter YEOMAN, *Excavations at St Ethernan's Monastery, Isle of May, Fife* (Perth, 2008).
JAMES, Simon, 'Celts, politics and motivation in archaeology', *Antiquity* 72 (275) (1998), 200–9.
— *et al.*, 'An early medieval building tradition', *Archaeological Journal* 141 (1984), 182–215.
JAMIESON, John, *An Historical Account of the Ancient Culdees of Iona* (Glasgow, 1890).
JANKULAK, Karen, *The Medieval Cult of St Petroc* (Woodbridge, 2000).
— 'Carantoc *alias* Cairnech? British saints, Irish saints and the Irish in Wales', in *eadem* and Jonathan M. Wooding (eds), *Ireland and Wales in the Middle Ages* (Dublin, 2007), 116–48.
JARITZ, Gerhard, 'Interdisciplinarity in medieval studies', in Albrecht Classen (ed.), *Handbook of Medieval Studies: Terms, Methods, Trends* (Berlin, 2010), 711–16.
JARMAN, Catrine *et al.*, 'The Viking Great Army in England: new dates from the Repton charnel', *Antiquity* 66 (2018), 183–99.
JARRETT, Michael G., *Maryport, Cumbria: a Roman Fort and its Garrison* (Kendal, 1976).
JASKI, Bart, 'Druim Cett Revisited', *Peritia* 12 (1998), 340–50.
JENNINGS, Andrew, 'Iona and the Vikings: survival and continuity', *Northern Studies* 33 (1998), 37–54.
— and Arne KRUSE, 'From Dál Riata to Gall-Ghàidheil', *Viking and Medieval Scandinavia* 5 (2009), 123–49.
JESCH, Judith, *Women in the Viking Age* (Woodbridge, 1991).
— *Ships and Men in the Late Viking Age: The Vocabulary of Runic Inscriptions and Skaldic Verse* (Woodbridge, 2001).
— 'Speaking like a Viking: language and cultural interaction in the Irish Sea region', in Harding *et al.* (eds), *In Search of Vikings*, 51–60.
— *The Viking Diaspora* (London, 2015).
JEWELL, Helen M., *The North–South Divide: The Origins of Northern Consciousness in England* (Manchester, 1994).
JOHANSEN, Olav Sverre, 'Bossed penannular brooches: a systematization and study of their cultural affinities', *Acta Archaeologica* 44 (1973), 63–124.
JOHN, Eric, *Orbis Britanniae and other Studies* (Leicester, 1966).
— 'The social and political problems of the early English Church', in Joan Thirsk (ed.), *Land, Church and People: Essays presented to Professor H. P. R. Finberg* (Reading, 1970), 39–63.
JOHNSON, David, *Excavation of an Early Medieval Structure in Upper Pasture, Horton in Ribblesdale, North Yorkshire* (Ingleton, 2012).
— *The Crummack Dale Project: Excavation of Three Early Medieval Steadings and a Lime Kiln, Austwick, North Yorkshire* (Ingleton, 2015).
— 'Early medieval rural settlement in North Craven: a reassessment', *Contrebis* 35 (2017), 26–38.
JOHNSON, Ruth, 'Irish crucifixion plaques: Viking Age or Romanesque?', *Journal of the Royal Society of Antiquaries of Ireland* 128 (1998), 95–106.
— 'The development of Irish brooch forms and pins in the Viking Age, c. 850–1170', *Peritia* 15 (2001), 321–62.
JOHNSON-FERGUSON, Edward, *The Place-Names of Dumfriesshire* (Dumfries, 1935).

JOHNSTON, Elva, *Literacy and Identity in Early Medieval Ireland* (Woodbridge, 2013).

JOLLY, Karen Louise, *The Community of St. Cuthbert in the Late Tenth Century: The Chester-le-Street Additions to Durham Cathedral Library A.IV.19* (Columbus OH, 2012).

JONES, Barri and David MATTINGLY, *An Atlas of Roman Britain* (Oxford, 1990; repr. 2002).

JONES, G. D. B., 'Archaeology and coastal change in the North-West', in Thompson (ed.), *Archaeology and Coastal Change*, 87–102.

JONES, G. R. J., 'Some donations to Bishop Wilfrid in northern England', *Northern History* 31 (1995), 22–38.

JONES, Graham, *Saints in the Landscape* (Stroud, 2007).

JONES, Siân, *The Archaeology of Ethnicity: Constructing Identities in the Past and Present* (London, 1997).

JOPE, E., *An Archaeological Survey of County Down* (Belfast, 1966).

JORGENSEN, Tove H. *et al.* 'The origin of the isolated population of the Faroe Islands using Y chromosomal markers', *Human Genetics* 115 (2004), 19–28.

JOTISCHKY, A. and K. J. STRINGER, 'Introduction', in *eidem* (eds), *Norman Expansion: Connections, Continuities and Contrasts* (Farnham, 2013), 1–8.

JUST, John, 'The Roman roads of Lancashire Part II', *Transactions of the Historic Society of Lancashire and Cheshire* 3 (1850–1), 3–12.

KAHL, Hans-Dietrich, 'Einige Beobachtungen zum Sprachgebrauch von *natio* im mittelalterlichen Latein mit Ausblicken auf das neuhochdeutsche Fremdwort "*Nation*"', in Helmut Beumann and Werner Schröder (eds), *Aspekte der Nationenbildung im Mittelalter* (Sigmaringen, 1978), 63–108.

KAPELLE, William E., *The Norman Conquest of the North: The Region and its Transformation* (Chapel Hill NC, 1979).

KAUFFMANN, C. M., *Romanesque Manuscripts 1066–1100*, A Survey of Manuscripts Illuminated in the British Isles 3 (London, 1975).

KEEVILL, G. D. *et al.*, 'A solidus of Valentinian II from Scotch Street, Carlisle', *Britannia* 20 (1989), 254–5.

KEIGWIN, Lloyd D., 'The Little Ice Age and Medieval Warm Period in the Sargasso Sea', *Science* 274, no. 5292 (1996), 1504–8.

KELLY, Dorothy, 'The heart of the matter: models for Irish High Crosses', *Journal of the Royal Society of Antiquaries of Ireland* 121 (1991), 105–43.

— 'The relationships of the crosses of Argyll: the evidence of form', in Spearman and Higgitt (eds), *The Age of Migrating Ideas*, 219–29.

KELLY, Fergus, *Early Irish Farming: A Study based mainly on the Law-texts of the 7th and 8th Centuries AD* (Dublin, 1997).

— 'Cattle in ancient Ireland: early Irish legal aspects', in Michael O'Connell (ed.), *Cattle in Ancient and Modern Ireland: Farming Practices, Environment and Economy* (Newcastle, 2016), 44–50.

KELLY, John, *The Manx Dictionary* (Douglas, 1858).

KEMP, Eric Waldram, *Canonization and Authority in the Western Church* (Oxford, 1948).

KENDRICK, T. D., *Anglo-Saxon Art to A.D. 900* (London, 1972).

— *Late Saxon and Viking Art* (London, 1949).

KENNEY, J. F., *Sources for the Early History of Ireland: I Ecclesiastical* (New York, 1929).

KENYON, Denise, *The Origins of Lancashire* (Manchester, 1991).

KERMODE, P. M. C., *Manx Crosses* (London, 1907); repr. with an introduction by David M. Wilson and appendices (Balgavies, 1994).

— and J. R. BRUCE, *The Manx Archaeological Survey, Reports 1–6*, reissue in 2 vols (Douglas, 1968).

KERSHAW, Jane, *Viking Identities: Scandinavian Jewellery in England* (Oxford, 2013).

— and Ellen RØYRIK, 'The "People of the British Isles" project and Viking settlement in England', *Antiquity* 90, no. 354 (2016), 1670–80.

— and Ellen RØYRIK, 'Finding the English Vikings', *British Archaeology* (July/August 2017), 40–5.

KEYNES, Simon, 'Æthelred II', in C. Matthew *et al.* (eds) *Oxford Dictionary of National Biography* (2009): http://www.oxforddnb.com/
— 'The manuscripts of the *Anglo-Saxon Chronicle*', in Richard Gameson (ed.), *The Cambridge History of the Book in Britain Volume I,* c. *400–1100* (Cambridge, 2012), 537–52.
— 'Welsh kings at Anglo-Saxon royal assemblies (928–55): the Henry Loyn Memorial Lecture for 2008', *Haskins Society Journal* 26 (2014), 69–122.
— 'Wulfstan I', in Michael Lapidge *et al.* (eds), *The Wiley Blackwell Encyclopedia of Anglo-Saxon England* (Oxford, 2014), 512–13.
KIDD, Colin, *British Identities before Nationalism: Ethnicity and Nationhood in the Atlantic World 1600–1800* (Cambridge, 1999).
KILBRIDE-JONES, H. E., *Zoomorphic Penannular Brooches* (London, 1980).
KING, A. C. and A. J. POLLARD, '"Northumbria" in the later middle ages', in Colls (ed.), *Northumbria: History and Identity*, 68–87.
KING, Alan, 'Post-Roman upland architecture in the Craven Dales and the dating evidence', in Hines *et al.* (eds), *Land, Sea and Home*, 335–44.
KIRBY, D. P., 'A new survey of contacts between Celtic Scotland and pre-Viking Northumbria' (Unpublished Durham University PhD thesis, 1962).
— 'Strathclyde and Cumbria: a survey of historical development to 1092', *TCWAAS*, 2nd ser. 62 (1962), 77–94.
— 'Bede and Northumbrian chronology', *English Historical Review* 78 (1963), 514–27.
— 'The battle of Whalley', *Transactions of the Historic Society of Lancashire and Cheshire* 117 (1965), 181–4.
— 'King Ceolwulf of Northumbria and the *Historia Ecclesiastica*', *Studia Celtica* 14–15 (1979–80), 168–73.
— 'Northumbria in the ninth century', in Metcalf (ed.), *Coinage*, 11–25.
— *The Earliest English Kings* (London, 1991).
— 'Cuthbert, Boisil of Melrose and the Northumbrian priest Ecgberht: some historical and hagiographical connections', in Michael Richter and Jean-Michel Picard (eds), *Ogma: essays in Celtic studies in honour of Próinséas Ní Chatháin* (Dublin, 2002), 48–53.
KLUGE, Bernd, *SCBI 36: State Museum Berlin, Coin Cabinet, Anglo-Saxon, Anglo-Norman and Hiberno-Norse Coins* (London, 1987).
KNEEN, J. J., *The Place-Names of the Isle of Man* (Douglas, 1925).
KOCH, John T., *Cunedda, Cynan, Cadwallon, Cynddylan: Four Welsh Poems and Britain, 383–655* (Aberystwyth, 2013).
KOPÁR, Lilla, *Gods and Settlers: The Iconography of Norse Mythology in Anglo-Scandinavian Sculpture* (Turnhout, 2012).
KOSSINNA, G., *Die Herkunft der Germanen: zur Methode der Siedlungsarchäologie* (Würzburg, 1911).
Kristján Ahronson, *Into the Ocean: Vikings, Irish and Environmental Change in Iceland and the North* (Toronto, 2015).
LACEY, Brian, *Cenél Conaill and the Donegal Kingdoms AD 500–800* (Dublin, 2006).
LAING, Lloyd, 'People and pins in Dark Age Scotland', *TDGNHAS*, 3rd ser. 50 (1973), 53–71.
— 'The Mote of Mark and the origins of Celtic interlace', *Antiquity* 49 (1975), 98–108.
— *A Catalogue of Ornamental Metalwork in the British Isles c. AD 400–1200*, BAR British series 229 (Oxford, 1993).
— and David LONGLEY, *The Mote of Mark: a Dark Age Hillfort in South-West Scotland* (Oxford, 2006).
LAMBERT, Janet, *Transect through Time: The Archaeological Landscape of the Shell North-western Ethylene Pipeline* (Lancaster, 1996).
LAMBKIN, Brian, 'Blathmac and the Céli Dé: a reappraisal', *Celtica* 23 (1999), 132–54.
LANE, Alan and Ewan CAMPBELL, *Dunadd: An Early Dalriadic Capital* (Oxford, 2000).
LANG, James T., 'The Castledermot hogback', *Journal of the Royal Society of Antiquaries of Ireland* 101 (1971), 154–8.
— 'The hogback, a Viking colonial monument', *Anglo-Saxon Studies in Archaeology and*

History 3 (1984), 83–176.
— *Corpus of Anglo-Saxon Stone Sculpture Volume III: York and East Yorkshire* (Oxford, 1991).
— *Corpus of Anglo-Saxon Stone Sculpture Volume VI: Northern Yorkshire* (Oxford, 2002).
LANGDON, John, 'Inland water transport in medieval England', *Journal of Historical Geography* 19 (1993), 1–11.
LAPIDGE, Michael, 'Byrhtferth of Ramsey and the early sections of the *Historia regum* attributed to Symeon of Durham', *Anglo-Saxon England* 10 (1981), 97–122.
— 'Aediluulf and the school at York', in A. Lehner and W. Berschin (eds), *Lateinische Kultur im VIII. Jahrhundert: Traube-Gedenkschrift* (St Ottilien, 1990), 161–78.
— 'The career of Aldhelm', *Anglo-Saxon England* 36 (2007), 15–69.
LAST, C. E., 'St. Bega and her bracelet', *TCWAAS*, 2nd ser. 52 (1953), 55–66.
LAWLOR, H. C., *The Monastery of Saint Mochaoi of Nendrum* (Belfast, 1925).
LAWRENCE-MATHERS, Anne, *Manuscripts in Northumbria in the 11th and 12th Centuries* (Cambridge, 2003).
LAYCOCK, Stuart, *Britannia, the Failed State: Tribal Conflicts and the End of Roman Britain* (Stroud, 2008).
LE PATOUREL, H. E. J., 'Amounderness', in *idem et al.* (eds), *Yorkshire Boundaries* (Leeds, 1993), 113–16.
LEASK, Harold G., *Irish Churches and Monastic Buildings*, 3 vols (Dundalk, 1955–60).
LEECH, R. H. and R. NEWMAN, 'Excavations at Dacre 1982–4: an interim report', *TCWAAS*, 2nd ser. 85 (1985), 87–93.
— *The Early Christian Monastery at Dacre* (forthcoming).
LEEDS, E. Thurlow, *The Archaeology of the Anglo-Saxon Settlements* (Oxford, 1913; repr. 1970).
— 'The distribution of the Angles and Saxons archaeologically considered', *Archaeologia*, 91 (1945), 1–106.
LEERSSEN, Joep, 'Celticism', in Terence Brown (ed.), *Celticism* (Amsterdam, 1996), 1–20.
LEIGHTON, A. C., *Transport and Communication in Early Medieval Europe AD 500–1100* (Newton Abbot, 1972).
LEIMUS, Ivar and Arkadi MOLVÕGIN, *SCBI 51: Estonian Collections: Anglo-Saxon, Anglo-Norman and Later British Coins* (Oxford, 2001).
LESLIE, Stephen *et al.*, 'The fine-scale genetic structure of the British population', *Nature* 519 (2015), 309–14.
LESTER, Geoffrey A., 'The earliest English sailing directions', in Lister M. Matheson (ed.), *Popular and Practical Science of Medieval England* (East Lansing, 1994), 331–65.
LEVISON, Wilhelm, 'An eighth-century poem on St Ninian', *Antiquity* 14 (1940), 28–91.
— 'Medieval church-dedications in England: some problems', *Transactions of the Architectural and Archaeological Society of Durham and Northumberland* 10 (1946), 57–79.
— *England and the Continent in the Eighth Century* (Oxford, 1946).
LEWIS, C. P., 'Was St. Tuda buried at Whalley?', *Transactions of the Historic Society of Lancashire and Cheshire* 138 (1988), 221–4.
— 'An introduction to the Lancashire Domesday', in A. Williams and G. H. Martin (eds), *The Lancashire Domesday* (London, 1991), 1–41.
— 'Joining the dots: a methodology for identifying the English in Domesday Book', in K. Keats-Rohan (ed.), *Family Trees and the Roots of Politics: The Prosopography of Britain and France from the Tenth to the Twelfth Century* (Woodbridge, 1997), 69–87.
LEWIS, M. J. T., 'Roman navigation in northern England? A review article', *Journal of the Railway and Canal Historical Society* 23 (1984), 118–25.
LEWIS, Stephen, 'Vikings on the Ribble: their origin and *longphuirt*', *Northern History* 53 (2016), 8–25.
LHUYD, Edward, *Archaeologia Britannica* (Oxford, 1707).
LIGHTBOWN, Ted, *The Dane's Pad: a Roman Road to Nowhere?* (Blackpool, 1996).
LIND, E. H., *Norsk–Isländska Dopnamn ock Fingerade Namn från Medeltiden*, 2 vols (Uppsala, 1905–15).

LIONARD, Pádraig, 'Early Irish grave-slabs', *PRIA* 61C (1961), 95–169.

LIVENS, R. G., 'Litus Hibernicum', in D. M. Pippidi (ed.), *Actes du IXe Congrès international d'études sur les frontières romaines* (Bucharest, 1974), 333–9.

LIVINGSTON, Alastair, 'The Lanes of Galloway', *Auchencairn History Society* (Spring 2006), 4.

— 'History of Gaelic in Galloway: Part One – Expansion', *TDGNHAS* 3rd ser. 85 (2011), 85–92.

LIVINGSTON, Michael, *The Battle of Brunanburh: A Casebook* (Liverpool, 2011).

LLOYD-MORGAN, G., 'The artefacts', in S. W. Ward (ed.), *Excavations at Chester: Saxon Occupation within the Legionary Fortress, Sites Investigated 1971–1981* (Chester, 1994), 27.

LOCKWOOD, W. B., 'Some traces of Gaelic in Faroese', *Fróðskaparrit* 25 (1977), 9–25.

LONGLEY, D., 'The Mote of Mark: the archaeological context of the decorated metalwork', in Redknap *et al.* (eds), *Pattern and Purpose*, 75–89.

LORIMER, W. L., 'The persistence of Gaelic in Galloway and Carrick', *Scottish Gaelic Studies* 6 (1949), 113–36; 7 (1953), 26–46.

LOVELUCK, Christopher, *Northwest Europe in the Early Middle Ages, c.AD 600–1150: a Comparative Archaeology* (Cambridge, 2013).

— and Dries TYS, 'Coastal societies, exchange and identity along the Channel and southern North Sea shores of Europe, AD 600–1000', *Journal of Maritime Archaeology* 1 (2006), 140–69.

LOWE, Christopher, *Angels, Fools and Tyrants: Britons and Anglo-Saxons in Southern Scotland* (Edinburgh, 1999).

— *Excavations at Hoddom, Dumfriesshire: an Early Ecclesiastical Site in South-West Scotland* (Edinburgh, 2006).

— *'Clothing for the Soul Divine': Excavations at Whithorn Priory, 1957–67* (Edinburgh, 2009).

— *et al.*, 'New light on the Anglian "minster" at Hoddom', *TDGNHAS*, 3rd ser. 66 (1991), 11–35.

LOWE, E. A., *Codices Latini Antiquiores II: Great Britain and Ireland*, 2nd edn (Oxford, 1972).

LÖWE, H. (ed.), *Die Iren und Europa im früheren Mittelalter*, 2 vols (Stuttgart, 1982).

LUCY, Sam, *The Early Anglo-Saxon Cemeteries of East Yorkshire: An Analysis and Reinterpretation*, BAR British ser. 272 (Oxford, 1998).

— 'Changing burial rites in Northumbria AD 500–750', in Hawkes and Mills (eds), *Northumbria's Golden Age*, 12–43.

— 'Ethnic and cultural identities', in *eadem* and Díaz-Andreu (eds), *The Archaeology of Identity*, 86–109.

— 'Early medieval burial at Yeavering: a retrospective', in Frodsham and O'Brien (eds), *Yeavering*, 127–44.

LYON, Stewart, 'Ninth-century Northumbrian chronology', in Metcalf (ed.), *Coinage*, 27–41.

LYSONS, Daniel and Samuel LYSONS, *Magna Britannia*, 8 vols (1806–22).

MAAS, John, 'The Viking events of AD 902–19 and the Lough Ennell hoards', in Purcell *et al.* (eds), *Clerics, Kings and Vikings*, 251–62.

MACALISTER, R. A. S., *Corpus Inscriptionum Insularum Celticarum*, 2 vols (Dublin, 1945–9).

MACBAIN, Alexander, *Place-Names, Highlands and Islands of Scotland* (Stirling, 1922).

MAC CANA, Proinsias, *The Learned Tales of Medieval Ireland* (Dublin, 1980).

MCCANN, Sarah, *'Plures de Scottorum regione*: Bede, Ireland and the Irish', *Eolas* 8 (2015), 20–38.

— 'Cuthbert and Boisil: Irish influence in Northumbria', in Margaret Coombe *et al.* (eds), *Saints of North-East England: 600–1500* (Turnhout, 2017), 69–88.

MCCARTHY, Mike R., 'Thomas, Chadwick and Post-Roman Carlisle', in Pearce (ed.), *The Early Church*, 241–56.

— *A Roman, Anglian and Medieval Site at Blackfriar's Street*, CWAAS Research ser. 4

(Kendal, 1990).

— 'The origins and development of the twelfth-century cathedral at Carlisle', in T. Tatton-Brown and J. Murphy (eds), *The Archaeology of Cathedrals*, University of Oxford Committee for Archaeology Monograph 42 (Oxford, 1996), 36–8.

— *Roman Carlisle and the Lands of the Solway* (Stroud, 2002).

MCCARTHY, Mike R., 'Rheged: an early historic kingdom near the Solway', *PSAS* 132 (2002), 357–81.

— '*Rerigonium*: a Lost "City" of the Novantae', *PSAS* 134 (2004), 119–29.

— 'The kingdom of Rheged: a landscape perspective', *Northern History* 48 (2011), 9–22.

— and Caroline PATERSON, 'A Viking-Age site at Workington, Cumbria: interim statement', in Harding *et al.* (eds), *In Search of Vikings*, 127–37.

— *et al.*, *The Roman Waterlogged Remains and Later Features at Castle Street, Carlisle: Excavations 1981–2*, CWAAS Research Series 5 (1992).

— *et al.*, *Roman and Medieval Carlisle: The Southern Lanes, Excavations 1981–2* (Carlisle, 2000).

— *et al.*, 'Were there Vikings in Carlisle?', in Harding *et al.* (eds), *In Search of Vikings*, 137–48.

— *et al.*, 'A post-Roman sequence at Carlisle Cathedral', *Archaeological Journal* 171 (2014), 185–257.

MC CARTHY, D. P., *The Irish Annals: Their Genesis, Evolution and History* (Dublin, 2008).

MCCLURE, Judith, 'Bede's Old Testament kings', in Wormald *et al.* (eds), *Ideal and Reality*, 76–98.

MCCONE, Kim, 'Zur Frage der Register im Frühen Irischen', in Stephen N. Tranter and Hildegard L. C. Tristram (eds), *Early Irish Literature – Media and Communication* (Tübingen, 1989), 57–97.

MCCORMICK, Finbar, 'Cows, ringforts and the origins of Early Christian Ireland', *Emania* 134 (1993), 33–7.

— 'Iona: the archaeology of the early monastery', in Bourke (ed.), *Studies in the Cult*, 11–23.

— *et al.*, 'Excavations at Iona, 1988', *Ulster Journal of Archaeology*, 3rd ser. 56 (1993), 78–108.

MCCORMICK, Michael, *Origins of the European Economy: Communications and Commerce, A.D. 300–900* (Cambridge, 2001).

MACCOTTER, Paul, *Medieval Ireland: Territorial, Political and Economic Divisions* (Dublin, 2008).

MACDONALD, Aidan, 'Notes on monastic archaeology and the Annals of Ulster, 650–1000', in Donnchadh Ó Corráin (ed.), *Irish Antiquity: Essays and Studies presented to Professor M. J. O' Kelly* (Cork, 1981; repr. Dublin, 1994), 304–19.

MACDOUGALL, Hugh A., *Racial Myth in English History: Trojans, Teutons, Anglo-Saxons* (Hanover NH, 1982).

MCERLEAN, Thomas and Norman CROTHERS (eds), *Harnessing the Tides: The Early Medieval Tide Mills at Nendrum Monastery, Strangford Lough* (Norwich, 2007).

MACFARLANE, Robert, *The Old Ways: a Journey on Foot* (London, 2012).

MCGRAIL, Seán, *Logboats of England and Wales*, BAR British ser. 2 (London, 1978).

— *Ancient Boats in North-West Europe: The Archaeology of Water Transport to AD 1500* (London, 1987).

— and R. SWITSUR, 'Medieval logboats of the River Mersey: a classification study', in Seán McGrail (ed.), *Archaeology of Medieval Ships and Harbours in Northern Europe*, BAR International ser. 66 (Oxford, 1979), 93–115.

MACGREGOR, Martin, 'Gaelic barbarity and Scottish identity in the later middle ages', in *idem* and Broun (eds), *Mìorun Mòr nan Gall*, 7–48.

MCGUIGAN, Neil, 'Neither Scotland nor England: Middle Britain, c.850–1150' (Unpublished University of St Andrews PhD thesis, 2015).

— 'The battle of Carham: an introduction', in *idem* and Woolf (eds), *The Battle of Carham*, 1–32.

— 'Bamburgh and the northern English realm', in *idem* and Woolf (eds), *The Battle of*

Carham, 95–150.

— and Alex WOOLF (eds), *The Battle of Carham: A Thousand Years On* (Edinburgh, 2018).

MCGURK, Patrick, 'The Mappa Mundi', in *idem et al.*, *An Anglo-Saxon Eleventh-Century Illustrated Miscellany: British Library Cotton Tiberius B.V., part I* (Copenhagen, 1983), 79–87.

MACKAY, A. W. and J. H. TALLIS, 'The recent vegetational development of the Forest of Bowland, Lancashire, UK', *New Phytologist* 128 (1994), 571–84.

M'KERLIE, P. H., *History of the Lands and their Owners in Galloway* (5 vols, Edinburgh, 1870–9, repr. Wigtown, 1994).

MACKINDER, Halford J., *Britain and the British Seas* (London, 1902).

MACKINLAY, James Murray, *Ancient Church Dedications in Scotland*, 2 vols (Edinburgh, 1910–14).

MCKITTERICK, Rosamond, 'The diffusion of Insular culture in Neustria between 650 and 850: the implications of the manuscript evidence', in H. Atsma (ed.), *La Neustrie: les pays au nord de la Loire de 650 à 850* (Sigmaringen, 1989), 395–432.

— 'Conclusion', in *eadem* (ed.), *The Uses of Literacy in Early Medieval Europe* (Cambridge, 1990), 319–333.

— *History and Memory in the Carolingian World* (Cambridge, 2004).

MACLEAN, D., 'Knapdale dedications to a Leinster saint: sculpture, hagiography and oral tradition', *Scottish Studies* 27 (1983), 49–65.

— 'Maelrubai, Applecross and the late Pictish contribution west of Druimalban', in David Henry (ed.), *The Worm, the Germ and the Thorn: Pictish and Later Studies presented to Isabel Henderson* (Balgavies, 1997), 173–87.

MCLEOD, Shane, *The Beginning of Scandinavian Settlement in England: The Viking 'Great Army' and Early Settlers*, c. *865–900* (Turnhout, 2014).

— 'A traveller's end? A reconsideration of a Viking Age burial at Carronbridge, Dumfriesshire', *TDGNHAS*, 3rd ser. 88 (2014), 13–20.

MCLEOD, Wilson, *Divided Gaels: Gaelic cultural identities in Scotland and Ireland c.1200–c.1600* (Oxford, 2004).

MCMANUS, Damian, *A Guide to Ogam* (Maynooth, 1997).

MCNAMARA, M., 'Ireland and Northumbria as illustrated by a Vatican manuscript', *Thought* 54 (1979), 274–90.

MAC NEILL, Eoin, 'Ancient Irish law. The law of status or franchise', *PRIA C* 36 (1921–4), 265–316.

— 'Varia I', *Ériu* 11 (1932), 130–5.

MACQUARRIE, Alan, 'The career of Saint Kentigern of Glasgow: *Vitae, Lectiones* and glimpses of fact', *Innes Review* 37 (1986), 3–24.

— *The Saints of Scotland* (Edinburgh, 1997).

MACQUEEN, John, 'Welsh and Gaelic in Galloway', *TDGNHAS*, 3rd ser. 32 (1953–4), 77–92.

— 'Kirk- and Kil- in Galloway place-names', *Archivum Linguisticum* 8 (1956), 135–49.

— 'The Gaelic speakers of Galloway and Carrick', *Scottish Studies* 17 (1973), 17–33.

— *St Nynia* (Edinburgh, 1990; rev. edn 2005).

— *Place-Names in the Rhinns of Galloway and Luce Valley* (Stranraer, 2002).

— *Place-Names of the Wigtownshire Moors and Machars* (Stranraer, 2008).

MCROBERTS, David, 'Material destruction caused by the Scottish Reformation', in *idem* (ed.), *Essays on the Scottish Reformation 1513–1625* (Glasgow, 1962), 415–62.

MAC SHAMHRÁIN, A. S., *Church and Polity in Pre-Norman Ireland: The Case of Glendalough* (Maynooth, 1996).

MCWHANNELL, D. C., '*Gaill, Gàidheil, Gall-Ghàidheil* and the *cenéla* of Greater Galloway', *TDGHNHAS* 87 (2013), 81–115.

MADDERN, Christine, *Raising the Dead: Early Medieval Name Stones in Northumbria* (Turnhout, 2013).

MADDICOTT, John, 'Two frontier states: Northumbrian and Wessex, c.650–750', in *idem* and D. M. Palliser (eds), *The Medieval State: Essays presented to James Campbell* (London,

2000), 25–46.

MAHLER, Ditlev L., *Sæteren ved Argisbrekka. Økonomiske forandringer på Færøerne i vikingetid og tidlig middelalder* (Tórshavn, 2007).

MAINMAN, A. J. and N. S. H. ROGERS, *Craft, Industry and Everyday Life: Finds from Anglo-Scandinavian York*, The Archaeology of York: The Small Finds 17/14 (York, 2000).

MALDONADO, Adrián, 'Early medieval burial in Scotland: new questions', *Medieval Archaeology* 57 (2013), 1–34.

MANN, J. C., 'The northern frontier after A.D. 369', *Glasgow Archaeological Journal* 3 (1974), 34–42.

MARGARY, Ivan D., *Roman Roads in Britain*, 3rd edn (London, 1973).

MARKER, Margaret E., 'The Dee estuary: its progressive silting and salt marsh development', *Transactions of the Institute of British Geographers* 41 (1967), 65–71.

MÁRKUS, Gilbert, *Conceiving a Nation: Scotland to AD 900* (Edinburgh, 2017).

— 'Iona: monks, pastors and missionaries', in Broun and Clancy (eds), *Spes Scotorum*, 115–38.

MARKUS, R. A., *Bede and the Tradition of Ecclesiastical Historiography*, Jarrow Lecture (1975).

MARNER, Astrid, 'Irish saints in medieval Iceland', in Rudolf Simek (ed.), *Between the Islands – and the Continent. Papers on Hiberno-Scandinavian–Continental Relations in the Early Middle Ages* (Vienna, 2013), 141–66.

MARSTRANDER, Carl J. S., 'Det norske landnåm på man', *Norsk Tidsskrift for Sprogvidenskap* 6 (1932), 40–386.

— 'Remarks on the place-names of the Isle of Man', *Norsk Tidsskrift for Sprogvidenskap* 7 (1934), 287–344.

— 'Om sproget i de Manske runeinnskrifter', *Norsk Tidsskrift for Sprogvidenskap* 8 (1937), 243–56.

— 'Treen og Keeil', *Norsk Tidsskrift for Sprogvidenskap* 8 (1937), 287–442.

MARTIN, Toby F., *The Cruciform Brooch and Anglo-Saxon England* (Woodbridge, 2015).

MASON, David J. P., *Roman Britain and the Roman Navy* (Stroud, 2003).

MASON, Roger, 'Civil society and the Celts: Hector Boece, George Buchanan and the ancient Scottish past', in Edward J. Cowan and Richard J. Finlay (eds), *Scottish History: The Power of the Past* (Edinburgh, 2002), 95–119.

MATRAS, Anna Katrin *et al.*, 'A Viking-Age Shieling in Skarðsvík, Fugloy, Faroe Islands', *Fróðskaparrit* 51 (2004), 200–11.

MATRAS, Christian, 'Gammelfærøsk ærgi', Namn och Bygd 44 (1953), 51–67.

— 'Korkadalur', *Fróðskaparrit* 28–9 (1981), 78–80.

MATTHEWS, Stephen, *The Road to Rome: Travel and Travellers between England and Italy in the Anglo-Saxon Centuries*, BAR International ser. 1680 (Oxford, 2007).

MAWER, Allen, *The Place-Names of Northumberland and Durham* (Cambridge, 1920).

— 'The redemption of the Five Boroughs', *English Historical Review* 38 (1923), 551–7.

MAXWELL, G. S. *The Romans in Scotland* (Edinburgh, 1989).

— 'The evidence from the Roman period', in Fenton and Stell (eds), *Loads and Roads*, 22–48.

MAXWELL, Herbert, *A History of Dumfries and Galloway* (Edinburgh, 1896).

— 'Notes on a hoard of personal ornaments, implements, and Anglo-Saxon and Northumbrian coins from Talnotrie, Kirkcudbrightshire', *PSAS* 47 (1912–13), 12–16.

— *The Place-Names of Galloway: Their Origin and Meaning Considered* (Glasgow, 1930).

MAYR-HARTING, Henry, *The Coming of Christianity to Anglo-Saxon England* (London, 1972).

MECKLER, Michael, 'The Annals of Ulster and the date of the meeting at Druim Cett', *Peritia* 11 (1997), 44–52.

MEEHAN, Bernard, 'The siege of Durham, the battle of Carham and the cession of Lothian', *Scottish Historical Review* 55 (1976), 1–19.

MEEK, Donald E., *The Quest for Celtic Christianity* (Edinburgh, 2000).

MEGAW, Basil, 'Norseman and native in the Kingdom of the Isles: a reassessment of the Manx evidence', *Scottish Studies* 20 (1976), 1–44; revised version in Davey (ed.), *Man and*

Environment, I, 265–314

MEGAW, Eleanor, 'The Manx "Eary"', *Man and Environment in the Isle of Man*, ed. Peter Davey, BAR British Series 54, 2 vols (Oxford, 1978), II, 327–45.

METCALF, D. M., 'The coinage of King Aldfrith of Northumbria (685–704) and some contemporary imitations', *British Numismatic Journal* 76 (2006), 147–58.

— 'A topographical commentary on the coin finds from ninth-century Northumbria (*c.* 780 – *c.* 870)' in *idem* (ed.), *Coinage*, 361–82.

— (ed.), *Coinage in Ninth-Century Northumbria*, BAR British ser. 180 (Oxford, 1987).

MEYVAERT, Paul, 'A new perspective on the Ruthwell Cross: *ecclesia* and *vita monastica*', in B. Cassidy (ed.), *The Ruthwell Cross* (Princeton NJ, 1992), 95–166.

MIDDLETON, Robert *et al.*, *The Wetlands of North Lancashire* (Lancaster, 1995).

— *et al.*, *The Wetlands of South-West Lancashire* (Lancaster, 2014).

MIGHALL, Tim *et al.*, 'A record of atmospheric pollution and vegetation change as recorded in three peat bogs from the North Pennines Pb-Zn orefield', *Environmental Archaeology* 9 (2004), 13–38.

MIKET, R., 'Two Anglo-Saxon brooches provenanced to near Corbridge', *Archaeologia Aeliana*, 5th ser. 13 (1985), 214–16.

— and Colm O'BRIEN, 'The early medieval settlement of Thirlings, Northumberland', *Durham Archaeological Journal* 7 (1991), 57–91.

MIKOLAJCZYK, Andrzej, *Polish Museums: Anglo-Saxon and Later British Coins* (London, 1987).

MILFULL, Inge and Katrin THIER, 'Anglo-Saxon perceptions of the Celtic peoples', in Clayton *et al.* (eds), *England, Ireland and the Insular World*, 199–223.

MILLEA, Nick, *The Gough Map: The Earliest Road Map of Great Britain?* (Oxford, 2007).

MILLER, Molly, 'Stilicho's Pictish war', *Britannia* 6 (1975), 141–5.

— 'The commanders of Arthuret', *TCWAAS*, 2nd ser. 75 (1975), 96–117.

— 'The disputed historical horizon of the Pictish king-lists', *SHR* 58 (1979), 1–34.

— 'The dates of Deira', *Anglo-Saxon England* 8 (1979), 35–61.

MILNE, John, *Gaelic Place-Names of the Lothians* (London, 1912).

MOISL, Hermann, 'The Bernician royal dynasty and the Irish in the seventh century', *Peritia* 2 (1983), 103–26.

MOLYNEAUX, George, *The Formation of the English Kingdom in the Tenth Century* (Oxford, 2015).

MOMMA, Haruko, *From Philology to English Studies: Language and Culture in the Nineteenth Century* (Cambridge, 2013).

MONTGOMERY, Jane *et al.*, 'Continuity or colonization in Anglo-Saxon England? Isotope evidence for mobility, subsistence practice, and status at West Heslerton', *American Journal of Physical Anthropology*, 126 (2005), 123–34.

MOORE, Donald (ed.), *The Irish Sea Province in Archaeology and History* (Cardiff, 1970).

MORAN, Joe, *Interdisciplinarity*, 2nd edn (London, 2010).

MORELAND, John, *Archaeology and Text* (London, 2001).

— *Archaeology, Theory and the Middle Ages* (London, 2010).

MORCKEN, Roald, 'Norse nautical units and distance measurements', *Mariner's Mirror* 54 (1968), 393–401.

MORRILL, John, 'The British problem, *c.*1534–1707', in *idem* and Brendan Bradshaw (eds), *The British Problem, c.1534–1707: State Formation in the Atlantic Archipelago* (Basingstoke, 1996), 1–38.

MORTENSEN, Andras and Símun V. ARGE (eds), *Viking and Norse in the North Atlantic* (Torshavn, 2005).

MUFWENE, Salikoko S., *The Ecology of Language Evolution* (Cambridge, 2001).

MULLINS, Juliet, 'Anglo-Irish relations and the cult of St Martin', in Graham-Campbell and Ryan (eds), *Anglo-Saxon/Irish Relations*, 113–27.

MUNCEY, R. W., *A History of the Consecration of Churches and Churchyards* (Cambridge, 1939).

MUNDAL, Else, 'Færeyinga saga – a fine piece of literature in pieces', in Mortensen and Arge (eds), *Vikings and Norse*, 43–51.

MURISON, David Donald, 'Linguistic relationships in medieval Scotland', in G. W. S. Barrow (ed.), *The Scottish Tradition: Essays in Honour of Ronald Gordon Cant* (Edinburgh, 1974), 71–83.

MURRAY, Alexander Callander, 'Reinhard Wenskus on "ethnogenesis", ethnicity, and the origin of the Franks', in Gillett (ed.), *On Barbarian Identity*, 39–68.

MURRAY, Griffin, 'Irish crucifixion plaques: a reassessment', in Juliet Mullins *et al.*, *Envisioning Christ on the Cross: Ireland and the Early Medieval West* (Dublin, 2013), 286–317.

MURRAY, Kevin, 'Dialect in medieval Irish? Evidence from placenames', *Studia Celtica Fennica* 2 (2005), 97–109.

MURRIETA-FLORES, Patricia and Howard WILLIAMS, 'Placing the Pillar of Eliseg: movement, visibility and memory in the early medieval landscape', *Medieval Archaeology* 61 (2017), 69–103.

MYNORS, R. A. B., *Durham Cathedral Manuscripts to the End of the Twelfth Century* (Oxford, 1939).

NAISMITH, Rory, 'Kings, crisis and coinage reforms in the mid-eighth century', *Early Medieval Europe* 20 (2012), 291–332.

— *Medieval European Coinage VIII, Britain and Ireland* c.*400–1066* (Cambridge, 2017).

NEES, Laurence, 'The colophon drawing in the Book of Mulling: a supposed Irish monastery plan and the tradition of terminal illustration in early medieval manuscripts', *Cambridge Medieval Celtic Studies* 5 (1983), 67–91.

NEILSON, G., 'Annals of the Solway until AD 1307', *Transactions of the Glasgow Archaeological Society*, new ser. 3 (1899), 245–308.

NELSON, Janet L., 'Why re-inventing medieval history is a good idea', in Graham A. Loud and Martial Staub (eds), *The Making of Medieval History* (York, 2017), 17–36.

NETZER, Nancy, 'Willibrord's scriptorium at Echternach and its relationship to Ireland and Lindisfarne', in Bonner *et al.* (eds), *St Cuthbert*, 203–12.

— *Cultural Interplay in the Eighth Century: The Trier Gospels and the Making of a Scriptorium at Echternach* (Cambridge, 1994).

— 'The Book of Durrow', in Gameson (ed.), *The Lindisfarne Gospels*, 16–82.

NEUMAN DE VEGVAR, Carol L., *The Northumbrian Renaissance: a Study in the Transmission of Style* (Selingsgrove PA, 1987).

NEWELL, W. H., 'Decision-making in interdisciplinary studies', in G. Morcoll (ed.), *Handbook of Decision-making* (New York, 2007), 245–65.

NEWMAN, Conor, 'Fowler's Type F3 Early Medieval Penannular Brooches', *Medieval Archaeology* 33 (1989), 7–20.

— 'Further notes on Fowler's Type F3 penannular brooches', *Medieval Archaeology* 34 (1990), 147–8.

NEWTON, Michael, *Warriors of the Word: The World of the Scottish Highlanders* (Edinburgh, 2009).

NÍ CHATHÁIN, Próinséas, 'Bede's Ecclesiastical History in Irish', *Peritia* 3 (1984), 115–30.

— and Michael RICHTER (eds), *Irland und Europa: die Kirche im Frühmittelalter* (Stuttgart, 1984).

NÍ DHONNCHADHA, M., 'The Guarantor list of *Cáin Adomnáin*, 697', *Peritia* 1 (1982), 178–215.

NÍ MHAONAIGH, Máire, 'The date of *Cogad Gáedel re Gallaib*', *Peritia* 9 (1995), 354–77.

— *Brian Boru. Ireland's Greatest King?* (Stroud, 2007).

— 'Of Saxons, a Viking and Normans: Colmán, Gerald and the monastery of Mayo', in Graham-Campbell and Ryan (eds), *Anglo-Saxon/Irish Relations*, 411–26.

— 'Of Bede's "five languages and four nations": the earliest writings from Ireland, Scotland and Wales', in Clare A. Lees (ed.), *The Cambridge History of Early Medieval English Literature* (Cambridge, 2012), 99–119.

— '*Caraid tairisi* – literary links between Ireland and England in the eleventh century', in Axel Harlos and Neele Harlos (eds), *Adapting Texts and Styles in a Celtic Context:*

Interdisciplinary Perspectives on Processes of Literary Transfer in the Middle Ages (Münster, 2016), 265–88.

— 'Perception and reality: Ireland c.980–1229', in Brendan Smith (ed.), *The Cambridge History of Ireland: Volume I* (Cambridge, 2017), 131–56.

NICOLAISEN, W. F. H., '*Slew-* and *sliabh-*', *Scottish Studies* 9 (1965), 91–106.

— 'Gaelic place-names in southern Scotland', *Studia Celtica* 5 (1970), 15–35.

— *Scottish Place-Names: Their Study and Significance* (Batsford, 1976).

— 'Gaelic *sliabh* revisited', in Sharon Arbuthnot and Kaarina Hollo (eds), *Fil súil nglais: A Grey Eye Looks Back* (Brig o' Turk, 2007), 175–86.

NILES, John, *The Idea of Anglo-Saxon England 1066–1901: Remembering, Forgetting, Deciphering and Renewing the Past* (Oxford, 2015).

NORMAN, E. R. and J. K. ST JOSEPH, *The Early Development of Irish Society: The Evidence of Aerial Photography* (Cambridge, 1969).

Ó BAOILL, Colm, 'A history of Gaelic to 1800', in Moray Watson and Michelle Macleod (eds), *The Edinburgh Companion to the Gaelic Language* (Edinburgh, 2010), 1–21.

— and Nancy R. McGuire (eds), *Rannsachadh na Gàidhlig 2000* (Aberdeen, 2002).

Ó BRIAIN, M., 'Léirmheasanna/Reviews: Betha Adamnáin. The Irish Life of Adamnán', *Studia Hibernica* 27 (1993), 155–8.

O'BRIEN, Bruce, *Reversing Babel: Translation among the English during an Age of Conquests, c.800 to c.1200* (Newark DE, 2011).

O'BRIEN, Colm, 'The Great Enclosure', in Frodsham and O'Brien (eds), *Yeavering*, 145–52.

— 'The emergence of Northumbria: artefacts, archaeology, and models', in Collins and Allason-Jones (eds), *Finds from the Frontier*, 110–19.

— and Roger MIKET, 'The early medieval settlement of Thirlings, Northumberland', *Durham Archaeological Journal* 7 (1991), 57–91.

O'BRIEN, Elizabeth, 'Churches of south-east County Dublin, seventh to twelfth century', in G. Mac Niocaill and P. F. Wallace (eds), *Keimelia: Studies in Medieval Archaeology and History in Memory of Tom Delaney* (Galway, 1988), 504–24.

— 'Contacts between Ireland and Anglo-Saxon England in the seventh century', *Anglo-Saxon Studies in Archaeology and History* 6 (1993), 96–100.

— *Post-Roman Britain to Anglo-Saxon England: Burial Practices Reviewed*, BAR British ser. 289 (Oxford, 1999).

Ó BUACHALLA, Breandán, 'Common Gaelic revisited', in Ó Baoill and McGuire (eds), *Rannsachadh na Gàidhlig 2000*, 1–12.

Ó CARRAGÁIN, Éamonn, 'The Ruthwell Cross and Irish high crosses: some points of comparison and contrast', in Ryan (ed.), *Ireland and Insular Art*, 118–28.

— 'Ruthwell and Iona: the meeting of St Paul and St Anthony revisited', in M. Meek (ed.), *The Modern Traveller to our Past. Studies in Honour of Ann Hamlin* (Gretton, 2006), 138–44.

Ó CARRAGÁIN, Tomás, 'Church buildings and pastoral care in early medieval Ireland', in FitzPatrick and Gillespie (eds), *The Parish*, 91–123.

— 'Cemetery settlements and local churches in pre-Viking Ireland in light of comparisons with England and Wales', in Graham-Campbell and Ryan (eds), *Anglo-Saxon/Irish Relations*, 329–66.

— *Churches in Medieval Ireland: Architecture, Ritual and Memory* (New Haven CT, 2010).

O'CONNOR, Anne and D. V. CLARKE (eds), *From the Stone Age to the 'Forty-Five: Studies presented to R. B. K. Stevenson* (Edinburgh, 1983).

Ó CORRÁIN, Donnchadh, 'Nationality and kingship in pre-Norman Ireland', in T. W. Moody (ed.), *Nationality and the Pursuit of National Independence* (Belfast, 1978), 1–35.

— 'On the "Aithechthúatha" tracts', *Éigse* 19 (1982), 159–65.

— 'Irish origin legends and genealogy: recurrent aetiologies', in Tore Nyberg *et al.* (eds), *History and Heroic Tale: A Symposium* (Odense, 1985), 51–96.

— 'Creating the past: the early Irish genealogical tradition', *Peritia* 12 (1998), 177–208.

— 'The Vikings in Scotland and Ireland', *Peritia* 12 (1998), 296–339.

— 'Viking Ireland – afterthoughts', in Clarke *et al.* (eds), *Ireland and Scandinavia*, 421–52.

— 'The Church and secular society', in *L'Irlanda e gli irlandesi nell'Alto Medioevo* (Spoleto,

2010), 261–322.
— *Clavis Litterarum Hibernensium*, 3 vols (Turnhout, 2017).
— and Fidelma MAGUIRE, *Gaelic Personal Names*, 2nd edn (Dublin, 1990).
Ó CRÓINÍN, Dáibhí, 'Pride and prejudice', *Peritia* 1 (1982), 352–62.
— 'Early Irish annals from Easter-tables: a case restated', *Peritia* 2 (1983), 74–86.
— 'The Irish provenance of Bede's computus', *Peritia* 2 (1983), 229–47.
— 'Rath Melsigi, Willibrord and the earliest Echternach manuscripts', *Peritia* 3 (1984), 17–49.
— 'The Old Irish and Old English glosses in the Echternach manuscripts', in Michele Camillo
    Ferrari (ed.), *Die Abtei Echternach 698–1998* (Luxembourg, 1999), 85–101.
Ó CRÓINÍN, Dáibhí (ed.), *A New History of Ireland I: Prehistoric and Early Ireland* (Oxford,
    2005).
— *The Kings Depart: The Prosopography of Anglo-Saxon Royal Exile in the Seventh Century*,
    Quiggin Lecture 8 (Cambridge, 2007).
— *Early Medieval Ireland 400–1200*, 2nd edn (London, 2017).
Ó CUÍV, B., 'Personal names as an indicator of relations between native Irish and settlers
    in the Viking period', in John Bradley (ed.), *Settlement and Society in Medieval Ireland*,
    79–88.
Ó hÉAILIDHE, P., 'The Rathdown slabs', *Journal of the Royal Society of Antiquaries of
    Ireland* 87 (1957), 75–88.
Ó FLOINN, Raghnall, 'Patrons and politics: art, artefacts and methodology', in Mark Redknap
    et al. (eds), *Pattern and Purpose in Insular Art* (Oxford, 2001), 1–14.
— 'Irish metalwork: the Anglo-Saxon connection', in Graham-Campbell and Ryan (eds),
    Anglo-Saxon/Irish Relations, 231–51.
— 'Early Christianity in Ireland based on the most current archaeological research', in Orsolya
    Heinrich-Tamáska *et al.* (eds), *Christianisierung Europas: Entstehung, Entwicklung und
    Konsolidierung im archäologischen Befund* (Regensburg, 2012), 11–35.
O'HANLON, J., *Lives of the Irish Saints*, 9 vols (Dublin, 1875–1923).
OKASHA, Elisabeth, *A Handlist of Anglo-Saxon Non-Runic Inscriptions* (Cambridge, 1971).
— and Katherine FORSYTH, *Early Christian Inscriptions of Munster: a Corpus of the
    Inscribed Stones* (Cork, 2001).
O'KEEFFE, Tadhg, *Romanesque Ireland: Architecture and Ideology in the Twelfth Century*
    (Dublin, 2003).
O'KELLY, Michael J., 'Church Island near Valencia, Co. Kerry', *PRIA* 59C (1959), 57–136.
OLDFIELD, F., 'Pollen analysis and the history of land use', *Advancement of Science* 25
    (1969), 298–311.
Ó LOCHLAINN, Colm, 'Roadways in ancient Ireland', in J. Ryan (ed.), *Féilsgríbhinn Éoin
    Mhic Néill* (Dublin, 1940), 465–74.
O'LOUGHLIN, Thomas, *Gildas and the Scriptures: Observing the World through a Biblical
    Lens* (Turnhout, 2012).
OLSEN, Magnus, 'Runic inscriptions in Great Britain, Ireland and the Isle of Man', in
    Haakon Shetelig (ed.), *Viking Antiquities in Great Britain and Ireland Part VI* (Oslo, 1954),
    153–232.
Ó MAINNÍN, Mícheál, 'The mountain names of County Down', *Nomina* 17 (1994), 31–53.
— '"The same in origin and in blood": bardic windows on the relationship between Irish and
    Scottish Gaels, *c.* 1200–1650', *Cambrian Medieval Celtic Studies* 38 (1999), 1–51.
Ó MAOLALAIGH, Roibeard, 'Place-names as a resource for the historical linguist', in Simon
    Taylor (ed.), *The Uses of Place-Names* (Edinburgh, 1998), 12–53.
— 'The Scotticisation of Gaelic: a reassessment of the language and orthography of the Gaelic
    notes in the Book of Deer', in Katherine Forsyth (ed.), *Studies on the Book of Deer* (Dublin,
    2008), 179–274.
Ó MURCHADHA, Diarmuid, 'Nationality names in the Irish annals', *Nomina* 16 (1992–3),
    49–70.
Ó NÉILL, Pádraig, 'The vernacular glosses of MS. Vat. Pal. 68: evidence for cultural links
    between Ireland and Northumbria in the early eighth century', *Old English Newsletter* 14
    (1981), 47–8.

— '*Romani* influences on seventh-century Hiberno-Latin literature', in Ní Chatháin and Richter (eds), *Irland und Europa*, 280–90.

— 'The origins of the Old English alphabet', in Graham-Campbell and Ryan (eds), *Anglo-Saxon/Irish Relations*, 3–22.

O'NEILL, Pamela, 'Six degrees of whiteness: Finbarr, Finnian, Ninian, candida casa and Whithorn', *Journal of the Australian Early Medieval Association* 3 (2007), 259–67.

OPPENHEIMER, Stephen, *The Origins of the British* (London, 2006; repr. 2007).

O'RAHILLY, Thomas F., *Irish Dialects Past and Present* (Dublin, 1932; repr. 1976).

— *Early Irish History and Mythology* (Dublin, 1946).

ORAM, Richard, 'Scandinavian settlement in south-west Scotland with a special study of Bysbie', in Crawford (ed.), *Scandinavian Settlement*, 127–40.

— *The Lordship of Galloway* (Edinburgh, 2000).

— *Domination and Lordship: Scotland 1070–1230* (Edinburgh, 2011).

— 'Trackless, impenetrable and underdeveloped? Roads, colonisation and environmental transformation in the Anglo-Scottish border zone, c.1100–c.1350', in Allen and Evans, *Roadworks*, 303–25.

— 'Parishes and churches', in Stringer and Winchester (eds), *Northern England and Southern Scotland*, 197–218.

— and G. STELL (eds), *Galloway: Land and Lordship* (Edinburgh, 1991).

O'REILLY, J., 'Notes on the orientations and certain architectural details of the old churches of Dalkey Town and Dalkey Island', *PRIA* 24 C (1901–3), 195–226.

Ó RIAIN, Pádraig, 'St. Finbarr: a study in a cult', *Journal of the Cork Historical and Archaeological Society* 82 (1977), 63–82.

— 'Samson alias San(c)tán?', *Peritia* 3 (1984), 320–23.

— 'Conservation in the vocabulary of the early Irish Church', in Donnchadh Ó Corráin *et al.* (eds), *Sages, Saints and Storytellers: Celtic Studies in Honour of Professor James Carney* (Maynooth, 1989), 358–66.

— 'The Tallaght martyrologies redated', *Cambridge Medieval Celtic Studies* 20 (1990), 21–38.

— *Anglo-Saxon Ireland: The Evidence of the Martyrology of Tallaght*, H. M. Chadwick Memorial Lecture 3 (Cambridge, 1993).

— 'The saints of Cardiganshire', in J. L. Davies and D. P. Kirby (eds), *Cardiganshire County History Volume 1: From the Earliest Times to the Coming of the Normans* (Cardiff, 1994), 378–96.

— 'Finnio and Winniau: a return to the subject', in John Carey *et al.* (eds), *Ildánach Ildírech. A Festschrift for Proinsias Mac Cana* (Andover MA, 1999), 187–202.

— *Feastdays of the Saints: a History of Irish Martyrologies* (Brussels, 2006).

— *A Dictionary of Irish Saints* (Dublin, 2011).

Ó RÍORDÁIN, Seán P., 'The genesis of the Celtic Cross', in S. Pender (ed.), *Féilscríbhinn Torna* (Cork, 1947), 108–14.

ORME, Nicholas, *English Church Dedications with a Survey of Cornwall and Devon* (Exeter, 1996).

ORSCHEL, Vera, 'Mag nEó na Sacsan: an English colony in Ireland in the seventh and eighth centuries', *Peritia* 15 (2001), 81–107.

ORTON, Fred and Ian WOOD, *Fragments of History: Rethinking the Ruthwell and Bewcastle Monuments* (Manchester, 2007).

O'SULLIVAN, Aidan *et al.*, *Early Medieval Ireland AD 400–1100: The Evidence from Archaeological Excavations* (Dublin, 2014).

O'SULLIVAN, Deirdre, 'Curvilinear churchyards in Cumbria', *Bulletin of the C.B.A. Churches Committee* 13 (Dec. 1980), 3–5.

— 'Two early medieval mounts from the Crosthwaite Museum', *Medieval Archaeology* 34 (1990), 145–7.

— 'Sub-Roman and Anglo-Saxon finds from Cumbria', *TCWAAS*, 2nd ser. 93 (1993), 25–42.

— 'The plan of the Early Christian monastery on Lindisfarne: a fresh look at the evidence', in Bonner *et al.* (eds), *St. Cuthbert*, 125–42.

O'SULLIVAN, Jerry, 'Iona: archaeological investigations 1875–1996', in Broun and Clancy (eds), *Spes Scotorum*, 215–43.

— 'Excavation of an early church and a women's cemetery at St Ronan's medieval parish church, Iona', *PSAS* 124 (1994), 327–65.

O'SULLIVAN, Thomas D., *The De Excidio of Gildas, its Authenticity and Date* (Leiden, 1978).

OWEN, Olwen, 'Galloway's Viking treasure: the story of a discovery', *British Archaeology* 140 (January/February 2015), 16–23.

— and Richard WELANDER, 'A traveller's end? – an associated group of Early Historic artefacts from Carronbridge, Dumfries & Galloway', *PSAS* 125 (1995), 753–70.

OWEN-CROCKER, Gale R., *Dress in Anglo-Saxon England*, rev. edn (Manchester, 2004).

PAGAN, H. E., 'Northumbrian numismatic chronology in the ninth century', *British Numismatic Journal* 37 (1970), 1–15.

PAGE, Raymond I., 'A tale of two cities', *Peritia* 1 (1982), 335–51.

— 'Celtic and Norse on the Manx rune-stones', in Hildegard L. C. Tristram (ed.), *Medialität und mittelalterliche insulare Litteratur* (Tübingen, 1992), 131–47.

— 'The Manx rune-stones', in *idem, Runes and Runic Inscriptions: Collected Essays on Anglo-Saxon and Viking Runes*, ed. David Parsons (Woodbridge, 1995), 225–44.

PAGE, William, *The Victoria County History of York Volume III* (London, 1974).

PAINTER, Kenneth, 'Hacksilber: a means of exchange?', in *idem* and Hunter (eds), *Late Roman Silver*, 215–41.

PALLISER, D. M., 'An introduction to the Yorkshire Domesday', in A. Williams and G. H. Martin (eds), *The Yorkshire Domesday* (London, 1992), 1–38.

— 'Review article: the "minster hypothesis": a case study', *Early Medieval Europe* 5 (1996), 207–14.

— *Medieval York: 600–1500* (Oxford, 2014).

PALMER, James T., *Anglo-Saxons in a Frankish World, 690–900* (Turnhout, 2009).

PARSONS, David N., 'Clarifying Ptolemy's English place-names', in *idem* and Patrick Sims-Williams (eds), *Ptolemy: Towards a Linguistic Atlas of the Earliest Celtic Place-Names of Europe* (Aberystwyth, 2000), 169–78.

— 'Anna, Dot, Thorir ... counting Domesday personal names', *Nomina* 25 (2002), 29–52.

— 'On the origin of the "Hiberno-Norse inversion compounds"', *Journal of Scottish Name Studies* 5 (2011), 115–52.

PATERSON, Caroline, 'Insular belt-fittings from the pagan Norse graves of Scotland: a reappraisal', in Redknap *et al.* (eds), *Pattern and Purpose*, 125–32.

— *et al.*, *Shadows in the Sand: Excavation of a Viking-Age Cemetery at Cumwhitton, Cumbria* (Lancaster, 2014).

— 'The sculptural fragments', in Zant and Parsons (eds), *St Michael's Church, Workington*, 65–82.

PATERSON, James, *History of the County of Ayr* (Edinburgh, 1876).

PEARCE, Susan M., 'The dating of some Celtic dedications and hagiographical traditions in south west Britain', *The Devonshire Association* 105 (1973), 95–120.

— (ed.), *The Early Church in Western Britain and Ireland: Studies presented to C. A. Ralegh Radford*, BAR British ser. 102 (Oxford, 1982).

PEDERSEN, Unn, *Into the Melting Pot: Non-ferrous Metalworkers in Viking-period Kaupang* (Aarhus, 2016).

PEERS, C. R. and C. A. R. RADFORD, 'The Saxon monastery of Whitby', *Archaeologia* 89 (1943), 27–88.

PELTERET, David A. E., 'The roads of Anglo-Saxon England', *Wiltshire Archaeological and Natural History Magazine* 79 (1985), 155–63.

PENNEY, S. H., 'Gazetteer', *Contrebis* 5 (1977), 47–9.

— 'Gazetteer', *Contrebis* 6 (1978), 43–4.

PENNINGTON, Winifred, 'Vegetation history in the north-west of England: a regional synthesis', in D. Walker and R. G. West (eds), *Studies in the Vegetational History of the British Isles: Essays in Honour of Harry Godwin* (Cambridge, 1970), 41–79.

PEPPERDENE, Margaret, 'Bede's *Historia Ecclesiastica*: a new perspective', *Celtica* 4

(1958), 253–62.

PERRY, David R., *Castle Park, Dunbar: Two Thousand Years on a Fortified Headland* (Edinburgh, 2000).

PETTS, David, 'Cemeteries and boundaries in Western Britain', in S. Lucy and A. Reynolds (eds), *Burial in Early Medieval England and Wales* (London, 2002), 24–46.

— 'Coastal landscapes and early Christianity in Anglo-Saxon Northumbria', *Estonian Journal of Archaeology* 13 (2009), 79–95.

— 'Expanding the archaeology of Holy Island (Lindisfarne)', *Medieval Archaeology* 57 (2013), 302–7.

— and Sam TURNER, 'Early medieval church groups in Wales and western England', in Edwards (ed.), *The Archaeology*, 281–99.

— and Sam TURNER, *Early Medieval Northumbria: Kingdoms and Communities, AD 450–1100* (Turnhout, 2011).

PHILLIPS, Christine, 'Portages in early medieval Scotland: the Great Glen route and the Forth–Clyde isthmus', in Christer Westerdahl (ed.), *The Significance of Portages*, BAR International ser. 1499 (Oxford, 2006), 191–8.

PHILPOTT, Robert A., 'Recent Anglo-Saxon finds from Merseyside and Cheshire and their archaeological significance', *Medieval Archaeology* 43 (1999), 194–202.

PHYTHIAN-ADAMS, Charles, *Land of the Cumbrians: a Study in British Provincial Origins A.D. 400–1120* (Aldershot, 1996).

PICKIN, J., 'A Viking-Age silver hoard from Rey Cross', in B. Viner *et al.*, *Stainmore: The Archaeology of a North Pennine Pass* (Hartlepool, 2001), 170–1.

PICKLES, Thomas, *Power, Religious Patronage and Pastoral Care: Religious Communities, Mother Parishes and Local Churches in Ryedale, c.650–c.1250*, Kirkdale Lecture 2009 (York, 2012).

PIRIE, Elizabeth J. E., *SCBI 5: The Grosvenor Museum, Part I: the Willoughby Collection of Coins with the Chester Mint-Signature* (London, 1964).

— *SCBI 21: Coins in Yorkshire Collections Part I: Coins from Northumbrian Mints c. 895–1279* (London, 1975).

— 'Finds of "sceattas" and "stycas" of Northumbria', in M. A. S. Blackburn (ed.), *Anglo-Saxon Monetary History: Essays in Memory of Michael Dolley* (Leicester, 1986), 67–90.

— 'Earduulf: a significant addition to the coinage of Northumbria', *British Numismatic Journal* 65 (1995), 20–31.

POCOCK, J. G. A., 'British history: a plea for a new subject', *Journal of Modern History* 47 (1975), 601–22.

— 'The limits and division of British history: in search of the unknown subject', *American Historical Review* 87 (1982), 311–36.

POHL, Walter, 'Ethnic names and identities in the British Isles: a comparative perspective', in John Hines (ed.), *The Anglo-Saxons from the Migration Period to the Eighth Century: an Ethnographic Perspective* (Woodbridge, 1997), 7–40.

— 'Introduction: strategies of distinction', in *idem* and Reimitz (eds), *Strategies of Distinction*, 1–15.

— 'Telling the difference: signs of ethnic identity', in *idem* and Reimitz (eds), *Strategies of Distinction*, 17–69.

— and Helmut REIMITZ (eds), *Strategies of Distinction: The Construction of Ethnic Communities, 300–800* (Leiden, 1998).

POLLINGTON, Mitchell, 'A new survey of Blackstone Edge road: interim results', *Forum: The Journal of Council for British Archaeology Yorkshire* 1 (2012), 53–8.

POOLE, Reginald Lane, *Chronicles and Annals: A Brief Outline of their Origin* (Oxford, 1926).

POOLE, Russell, *Viking Poems on War and Peace: A Study in Skaldic Narrative* (Toronto, 1991).

POSTLES, David, *The North through its Names: A Phenomenology of Medieval and Early Medieval England* (Oxford, 2007).

POTIN, V. M., *SCBI 50: Hermitage Museum, St Petersburg, Part I: Anglo-Saxon Coins to

1016 (London, 1999).

POTTER, T. W., *Romans in North-West England: Excavations at the Roman Forts of Ravenglass, Watercrook and Bowness on Solway*, CWAAS Research ser. 1 (Kendal, 1979).

— and R. D. ANDREWS, 'Excavation and survey at St Patrick's Chapel and St Peter's Church, Heysham, Lancashire, 1977–8', *The Antiquaries Journal* 74 (1994), 29–73.

POULTER, J., 'The date of the Stanegate and a hypothesis about the manner and timing of the construction of Roman roads in Britain', *Archaeologia Aeliana*, 5th ser. 26 (1998), 49–58.

— *The Planning of Roman Roads and Walls in Northern Britain* (Stroud, 2010).

PRESTWICH, Michael, 'The royal itinerary and roads in England under Edward I', in Allen and Evans (eds), *Roadworks*, 177–97.

PREVOST, W. A. J., 'The Solway smugglers and the customs port at Dumfries', *TDGNHAS*, 3rd ser. 51 (1975), 59–67.

PRICE, Liam, *The Place-Names of Co. Wicklow*, 7 vols (Dublin, 1945–67).

PRITCHARD, Aimee, 'The origins of ecclesiastical stone architecture in Wales', in Edwards (ed.), *The Archaeology*, 245–64.

PROUDFOOT, L. (ed.), *Down: History and Society: Interdisciplinary Essays on the History of an Irish County* (Dublin, 1997).

PRYCE, Huw, 'Pastoral care in early medieval Wales', in John Blair and Richard Sharpe (eds), *Pastoral Care before the Parish* (Leicester, 1992), 41–62.

PURCELL, Emer *et al.* (eds), *Clerics, Kings and Vikings: Essays on Medieval Ireland in Honour of Donnchadh Ó Corráin* (Dublin, 2015).

PUTTER, Ad, 'Multilingualism in England and Wales, c. 1200: the testimony of Gerald of Wales', in C. Kleinhenz and K. Busby (eds), *Medieval Multilingualism: The Frankish World and its Neighbours* (Turnhout, 2011), 83–105.

QUANRUD, John, 'Taking sides: north-west England Vikings at the Battle of Tettenhall, AD 910', in Harding *et al.* (eds), *In Search of Vikings*, 71–93.

QUINE, Gillian, 'A reconsideration of the evidence of the shieling in the kingdom of Man and the Isles, with particular reference to Man' (Unpublished Durham University PhD thesis, 1990), 2 vols.

RACKHAM, Oliver, *The History of the Countryside* (London, 1986).

RADFORD, C. A. R., 'Excavations at Whithorn, 1949', *TDGNHAS*, 3rd ser. 27 (1950), 85–126.

— 'The excavations at Chapel Finnian, Mochrum', *TDGNHAS*, 3rd ser. 28 (1951), 28–40.

— 'Hoddom', *TDGNHAS*, 3rd ser. 31 (1953), 174–97.

— 'Two Scottish shrines: Jedburgh and St Andrews', *Archaeological Journal* 112 (1955), 43–60.

— 'Excavations at Whithorn: final report', *TDGNHAS*, 3rd ser. 34 (1957), 131–94.

— 'The earliest Irish churches', *Ulster Journal of Archaeology* 40 (1977), 1–11.

— 'St Patrick's Isle, Peel: the medieval ecclesiastical remains and the excavations of 1962', ed. A. Marshall Cubbon, *Proceedings of the Isle of Man Natural History and Antiquarian Society* 11 no. 3 (2001–3), 361–93.

RAFTERY, Barry, *Pagan Celtic Ireland: The Enigma of the Irish Iron Age* (London, 1997).

RAHTZ, Philip, *New Medieval Archaeology* (York, 1981).

— 'The Nuer Medieval Archaeology: theory vs history – comment on Driscoll', *Scottish Archaeological Review*, 3 (1984), 109–13.

— 'Appendix C: The building plan of the Anglo-Saxon monastery of Whitby Abbey', in D. Wilson (ed.), *The Archaeology of Anglo-Saxon England* (1976), 459–62

RAMSAY, Susan and James H. DICKSON, 'Vegetational history of central Scotland', *Botanical Journal of Scotland* 49 (1997), 141–50.

RANCE, Philip, 'Attacotti, Déisi and Magnus Maximus: the case for Irish federates in Late Roman Britain', *Britannia* 32 (2001), 243–70.

RAY, Roger, 'Bede's *Vera Lex Historiae*', *Speculum* 55 (1980), 1–21.

RCAHMS, *Seventh Report with Inventory of Monuments and Constructions in the County of Dumfriesshire* (Edinburgh, 1920).

— *An Inventory of the Ancient and Historical Monuments of Roxburghshire*, 2 vols (Edinburgh, 1956).

— *Argyll: An Inventory of Monuments, Volume IV, Iona* (Edinburgh, 1982).

REDKNAP, Mark, 'Viking-Age settlement in Wales and the evidence from Llanbedrgoch', in Hines *et al.* (eds), *Land, Sea and Home*, 156–64.

— 'Silver and commerce in Viking-Age North Wales', in Graham-Campbell and Philpott (eds), *The Huxley Viking Hoard*, 29–41.

— 'Glitter in the dragon's lair: Irish and Anglo-Saxon metalwork from pre-Viking Wales, *c.*400–850', in Graham-Campbell and Ryan (eds), *Anglo-Saxon/Irish Relations*, 281–310.

— *et al.* (eds), *Pattern and Purpose in Insular Art: Proceedings of the Fourth International Conference on Insular Art* (Oxford, 1998).

REDMOND, Angela, *Viking Burial in the North of England*, BAR British ser. 429 (Oxford, 2007).

REDMONDS, George, *Christian Names in Local and Family History* (Richmond, 2004).

— *et al.*, *Surnames, DNA and Family History* (Oxford, 2011).

REECE, R., *Excavations in Iona 1964 to 1974* (London, 1981).

— 'Sequence is all: or archaeology in an historical period', *Scottish Archaeological Review* 3 (1984), 113–16.

REES, Rice, *An Essay on the Welsh Saints* (London, 1836).

REES JONES, Sarah, *York: The Making of a City 1068 1350* (Oxford, 2013).

REEVES, William, *Ecclesiastical Antiquities of Down, Connor and Dromore* (Dublin, 1847; repr. 1992).

— *The Life of St Columba, Founder of Hy* (Dublin, 1857).

— *On the Céli-dé, Commonly Called Culdees* (Dublin, 1864).

REIMITZ, Helmut, *History, Frankish Identity and the Framing of Western Ethnicity 550–850* (Cambridge, 2015).

REKDAL, Jan Erik, 'Parallels between the Norwegian legend of St. Sunniva and Irish voyage tales', in Clarke *et al.* (eds), *Ireland and Scandinavia*, 277–87.

— 'Vikings and saints – encounters *Vestan um Haf*', *Peritia* 17–18 (2003–4), 256–75.

RENAN, Ernest, 'La poésie des races celtiques', *Revue des Deux Mondes*, 2nd ser. 5 (1854), 473–506.

RENFREW, Colin, *Before Civilization: The Radiocarbon Revolution and Prehistoric Europe* (London, 1973).

REPKO, Allen F., *Interdisciplinary Research: Process and Theory*, 2nd edn (Thousand Oaks CA, 2012).

REUTER, Timothy, *Medieval Polities and Modern Mentalities*, ed. Janet Nelson (Cambridge, 2006).

REYNOLDS, Andrew (ed.), *The Archaeology of Travel and Communication*, World Archaeology 43 (2011).

— 'The archaeology of transport and communication: an introduction', in *idem* (ed.), *The Archaeology*, 343–4.

— and Alexander LANGLANDS, 'Travel *as* communication: a consideration of overland journeys in Anglo-Saxon England', in Reynolds (ed.), *The Archaeology*, 410–27.

REYNOLDS, Susan, 'What do we mean by "Anglo-Saxon" and "Anglo-Saxons"?', *Journal of British Studies* 24 (1985), 395–414.

— *Kingdoms and Communities in Western Europe, 900–1300*, 2nd edn (Oxford, 1997).

RICHARDS, Julian D. *et al.*, 'Anglo-Saxon landscape and economy: using portable antiquities to study Anglo-Saxon and Viking-Age England', *Internet Archaeology* 25 (2009): http://intarch.ac.uk/journal/issue25/richards_toc.html

RICHARDSON, Caroline, 'A late pre-Conquest carving from Corbridge (Roman site)', *Archaeologia Aeliana*, 5th ser., 22 (1994), 79–84.

RICHMOND, I. A. and O. G. S. CRAWFORD, 'The British Section of the Ravenna Cosmography', *Archaeologia* 93 (1949), 1–50.

RICHTER, Michael, 'Bede's *Angli*: Angles or English?', *Peritia* 3 (1984), 99–114.

— *Ireland and her Neighbours in the Seventh Century* (Dublin, 1999).

— *Bobbio in the Early Middle Ages: The Abiding Legacy of Columbanus* (Dublin, 2008).

RIPPON, Stephen *et al.*, *The Fields of Britannia: Continuity and Change in the Late Roman and Early Medieval Landscape* (Oxford, 2015).

RIVET, A. L. F., 'The Brittones Anavionenses', *Brittania* 13 (1982), 321–2.

— and Colin SMITH, *The Place-Names of Roman Britain* (London, 1979).

RIX, Robert, *The Barbarian North in Medieval Imagination: Ethnicity, Legend and Literature* (London, 2015).

ROBERTS, Brian K., 'Late –bý names in the Eden Valley', *Nomina* 13 (1989–90), 25–40.

— 'Northumbrian origins and post-Roman continuity: an exploration', in Collins and Allason-Jones (eds), *Finds from the Frontier*, 120–32.

— and Stuart WRATHMELL, *An Atlas of Rural Settlement in England* (London, 2000).

ROBERTS, D. F. *et al.*, 'Genetic variation in Cumbrians', *Annals of Human Biology* 8 (1981), 135–44.

ROBERTSON, Anne S., *SCBI 2: Hunterian and Coats Collections, University of Glasgow, Part I: Anglo-Saxon Coins* (London, 1961).

ROE, Helen M., 'The *orans* in Irish Christian art', *Journal of the Royal Society of Antiquaries of Ireland* 100.2 (1970), 212–21.

ROFFE, David R., 'Domesday Book and Northern Society: a reassessment', *English Historical Review* 105 (1990), 310–36.

— 'The Yorkshire Summary: a Domesday satellite', *Northern History* 27 (1991), 242–60.

ROLLASON, David, 'A list of saints' resting-places in Anglo-Saxon England', *Anglo-Saxon England* 7 (1978), 61–93.

— 'The wanderings of St. Cuthbert', in *idem* (ed.), *Cuthbert Saint and Patron* (Durham, 1987), 46–50.

— 'Monasteries and society in early medieval Northumbria', in Benjamin Thompson (ed.), *Monasteries and Society in Medieval Britain* (Stamford, 1999), 59–74.

— *Northumbria, 500–1100: Creation and Destruction of a Kingdom* (Cambridge, 2003).

— *et al.*, *Sources for York History to AD 1100*, The Archaeology of York 1 (York, 1998).

ROPER, M., 'Wilfrid's landholdings in Northumbria', in D. P. Kirby (ed.), *Saint Wilfrid at Hexham* (Newcastle, 1974), 61–79.

ROSE, R. K., 'Cumbrian society and the Anglo-Norman Church', in S. Mews (ed.), *Religion and National Identity*, Studies in Church History 18 (1982), 119–35.

ROSENTHAL, Joel T., 'Bede's Ecclesiastical History and the material conditions of Anglo-Saxon life', *Journal of British Studies* 19 (1979), 1–17.

ROSS, Alasdair, *The Kings of Alba, c.1000–c.1130* (Edinburgh, 2011).

ROSS, Alan S. C. and E. G. STANLEY, 'Index verborum glossematicus', in Kendrick *et al.* (eds), *Codex Lindisfarnensis*, II, book 2, 45–176.

ROWE, Elizabeth Ashman, *Vikings in the West: The Legend of Ragnarr Loðbrók and his Sons* (Vienna, 2012).

RUSSELL, Paul, 'Patterns of hypocorism in early Irish hagiography' in J. Carey *et al.* (eds), *Studies in Irish Hagiography: Saints and Scholars* (Dublin, 2001), 237–49.

— '"What was best of every language": the early history of the Irish language', in Ó Cróinín (ed.), *A New History*, 405–50.

— 'The names of Celtic origin', in Rollason and Rollason (eds), *The Durham Liber Vitae*, II, 5–8, 35–43.

— 'Scribal (In)consistency in thirteenth-century South Wales: the orthography of the Black Book of Carmarthen', *Studia Celtica* 43 (2009), 135–74.

— '"Ye shall know them by their names": names and identity among the Irish and the English', in Graham-Campbell and Ryan (eds), *Anglo-Saxon/Irish Relations*, 99–111.

RUTHERFORD, A., '*Giudi* revisited', *Bulletin of the Board of Celtic Studies* 26 (1976), 440–4.

RYAN, Michael (ed.), *Ireland and Insular Art A.D. 500–1200* (Dublin, 1987).

RYNNE, Etienne, 'A bronze ring-brooch from Luce Sands, Wigtownshire', *TDGNHAS* 42 (1965), 99–113.

— 'Excavation of a church site at Clondalkin, County Dublin', *Journal of the Royal Society of Antiquaries of Ireland* 97 (1967), 29–37.

— 'The La Tène and Roman finds from Lambay, County Dublin: a re-assessment', *PRIA* 76C (1976), 231–244.

SAWYER, P. H., 'The density of the Danish settlement in England', *University of Birmingham Historical Journal* 6 (1957–8), 1–17.

— *Anglo-Saxon Charters: An Annotated List and Bibliography* (London, 1968).

— *The Age of the Vikings*, 2nd edn (London, 1971).

— *et al.*, 'The two Viking Ages of Britain: a discussion', *Mediaeval Scandinavia* 2 (1969), 163–207.

SCHARER, Anthony, 'The role of language in Bede's Ecclesiastical History', in *idem*, *Changing Perspectives on England and the Continent in the Early Middle Ages* (London, 2014), II.

SCHEIL, Andrew, *The Footsteps of Israel: Understanding Jews in Anglo-Saxon England* (Ann Arbor MI, 2004).

SCHUSTEREDER, Stefan J., *Strategies of Identity Construction: The Writings of Gildas, Aneirin and Bede* (Göttingen, 2015).

SCOTT, Allan J., *Solway Country: Land, Life and Livelihood in the Western Border* (Cambridge, 2014).

SCOTT, J. G., 'A note on Viking settlement in Galloway', *TDGNHAS*, 3rd ser. 58 (1983), 52.

SCULL, Christopher, 'Post-Roman phase I at Yeavering: a re-consideration', *Medieval Archaeology* 35 (1991), 51–63.

— and A. F. HARDING, 'Two early medieval cemeteries at Milfield, Northumberland', *Durham Archaeological Journal* 6 (1990), 1–29.

SEDGEFIELD, W. J., *The Place-Names of Cumberland and Westmorland* (Manchester, 1915).

SELKIRK, Raymond, *The Piercebridge Formula: A Dramatic New View of Roman History* (Cambridge, 1983).

SHANNON, William D., *Murus Ille Famosus (that Famous Wall): Depictions and Descriptions of Hadrian's Wall before Camden*, CWAAS Tract ser. 22 (2007).

— 'From Morikambe to Morecambe: antiquarians, *periploi* and *eischuseis*', *TCWAAS* 3rd ser. 2 (2012), 37–54.

SHARPE, Richard, '*Vita S. Brigidae*: the oldest texts', *Peritia* 1 (1982), 81–106.

— 'Were the Irish annals known to a twelfth-century Northumbrian writer?', *Peritia* 2 (1983), 137–9.

— 'Some problems concerning the organization of the Church in early medieval Ireland', *Peritia* 3 (1984), 230–70.

— *Medieval Irish Saints' Lives* (Oxford, 1991).

— 'Symeon as pamphleteer', in David Rollason (ed.), *Symeon of Durham. Historian of Durham and the North* (Stamford, 1998), 214–29.

SHEEHAN, John, 'The Huxley hoard and Hiberno-Scandinavian arm-rings', in Graham-Campbell and Philpott (eds), *The Huxley Viking Hoard*, 58–69.

— and Donnchadh Ó CORRÁIN (eds), *The Viking Age, Ireland and the West: Papers from the Proceedings of the Fifteenth Viking Congress, Cork* (Dublin, 2010).

SHENNAN, S. J., 'Archaeological "cultures": an empirical investigation', in Ian Hodder (ed.), *The Spatial Organisation of Culture* (Pittsburgh PA, 1978), 113–39.

SHEPARD, Jonathan, 'Networks', *Past and Present* 238, supplement 13, *The Global Middle Ages* (2018), 116–57.

SHERLOCK, Stephen J., *A Royal Anglo-Saxon Cemetery at Street House, Loftus, North-East Yorkshire*, Tees Archaeology Monograph 6 (Hartlepool, 2012).

SHOTTER, D. C. A., 'Numeri barcariorum: a note on RIB 601', *Britannia* 4 (1973), 206–9.

— 'Watercrook and Ravenglass: the Names and the Garrisons', in Potter (ed.), *Romans in North-West England*, 315–20.

— *Romans and Britons in North West England* (Lancaster, 1993).

— and Andrew WHITE, *Roman Fort and Town of Lancaster* (Lancaster, 1990).

SIDEBOTTOM, Philip, 'Viking Age stone monuments and social identity in Derbyshire', in Hadley and Richards (eds), *Cultures in Contact*, 213–35.

SIMPSON, Linzi, 'Forty years a-digging: a preliminary synthesis of archaeological investigations in medieval Dublin', *Medieval Dublin* I (2000), 11–68.

— 'Pre-Viking and early Viking-Age Dublin: some research questions', *Medieval Dublin* 10 (2010), 49–92.

SIMPSON, Luisella, 'The King Alfred/St Cuthbert episode in the *Historia de Sancto Cuthberto*: its significance for mid-tenth-century English history', in Bonner *et al.* (eds), *St Cuthbert*, 397–411.

SIMS-WILLIAMS, Patrick, 'The settlement of England in Bede and the *Chronicle*', *Anglo-Saxon England* 12 (1983), 1–41.

— 'Gildas and the Anglo-Saxons', *Cambridge Medieval Celtic Studies* 6 (1983), 1–30.

— 'The visionary Celt: the construction of an ethnic preoccupation', *Cambridge Medieval Celtic Studies* 11 (1986), 71–96.

— 'St Wilfrid and two charters dated to AD 676 and 680', *Journal of Ecclesiastical History* 39 (1988), 174–83.

— 'Celtomania and Celtoscepticism', *Cambrian Medieval Celtic Studies* 36 (1998), 1–35.

— 'The five languages of Wales in the pre-Norman inscriptions', *Cambrian Medieval Celtic Studies* 44 (2002), 1–36.

— *The Celtic Inscriptions of Britain: Phonology and Chronology, c. 400–1200* (Oxford, 2003).

— *Irish Influence on Medieval Welsh Literature* (Oxford, 2011).

SINDBÆK, Søren, 'The small world of the Vikings: networks in early medieval communication and exchange', *Norwegian Archaeological Review* 40 (2007), 59–74.

SISAM, Kenneth, 'Anglo-Saxon royal genealogies', *Proceedings of the British Academy* 39 (1953), 287–346.

SKENE, William Forbes, *Celtic Scotland*, 2 vols (Edinburgh, 1877).

SKRE, Dagfinn, 'From Kaupang and Avaldsnes to the Irish Sea', in Purcell *et al.* (eds), *Clerics, Kings and Vikings*, 237–46.

— (ed.), *Things from the Town: Artefacts and Inhabitants in Viking-Age Kaupang*, Kaupang Excavation Project Publication Ser. 3 (Aarhus, 2011).

SLOAN, Geoffrey R., *The Geopolitics of Anglo-Irish Relations in the Twentieth Century* (London, 1997).

SMART, Veronica J., 'Moneyers of the late Anglo-Saxon coinage 973–1016', in *Commentationes de Nummis Saeculorum IX–XI in Suecia Repertis* II (Stockholm, 1968), 193–276.

— *SCBI 28: Cumulative Index of Volumes 1–20* (London, 1981).

— 'Scandinavians, Celts and Germans in Anglo-Saxon England: the evidence of moneyers' Names', in Blackburn and Dolley (eds), *Anglo-Saxon Monetary History: Essays in Memory of Michael Dolley* (Leicester, 1986), 171–84.

— 'Moneyers of the late Anglo-Saxon coinage: the Danish dynasty 1017–42', *Anglo-Saxon England*, 16 (1987), 233–308.

— *SCBI 41: Cumulative Index of Volumes 21–40* (London, 1992).

SMITH, A. H., 'Some aspects of Irish influence on Yorkshire', *Revue Celtique* 44 (1927), 34–58.

— *The Place-Names of the North Riding of Yorkshire*, English Place-Name Society 5 (Cambridge, 1928).

— *The Place-Names of the East Riding of Yorkshire and York*, English Place-Name Society 14 (Cambridge, 1937).

— *English Place-Name Elements*, English Place-Name Society 25–6, 2 vols (Cambridge, 1956).

— *The Place-Names of the West Riding of Yorkshire*, English Place-Name Survey 30–7, 8 vols (Cambridge, 1961–3).

— *The Place-Names of Westmorland*, English Place-Name Society 42–3, 2 vols (Cambridge, 1967).

SMITH, Ian M., 'Brito-Roman and Anglo-Saxon: the unification of the Borders', in Peter Clack and Jill Ivy (eds), *The Borders* (Durham, 1983), 9–48.

SMITH, Julia M. H., *Europe after Rome: a New Cultural History 500–1100* (Oxford, 2005).

SMITH, Tom C. and Jonathan SHORTT, *The History of the Parish of Ribchester* (London, 1890).

SMYTH, A. P., 'The earliest Irish annals: their first contemporary entries, and the earliest centres of recording', *PRIA C*, 72 (1972), 1–48.

— 'The *black* foreigners of York and the *white* foreigners of Dublin', *Saga-Book* 19 (1974–7), 101–17.

— *Scandinavian Kings in the British Isles, 850–880* (Oxford, 1977).

— *Scandinavian York and Dublin: The History and Archaeology of Two Related Viking Kingdoms*, 2 vols (Dublin, 1975–9).

— *Celtic Leinster: Towards an Historical Geography of Early Irish Civilization A.D. 500–1600* (Blackrock, 1982).

— *Warlords and Holy Men: Scotland, AD 80–1000* (Edinburgh, 1989).

SOCIÉTÉ DES BOLLANDISTES, *Bibliotheca Hagiographica Latina Antiquae et Mediae Aetatis*, 2 vols (Brussels, 1898–1901).

SØRENSEN, Anne C., *Ladby, A Danish Ship-Grave from the Viking Age* (Roskilde, 2001).

SPEARMAN, Michael R. and John HIGGITT (eds), *The Age of Migrating Ideas: Early Medieval Art in Northern Britain and Ireland* (Edinburgh, 1993).

SPERBER, Ingrid, 'Lives of St. Finnian of Movilla: British Evidence', in Proudfoot (ed.), *Down: History and Society*, 85–102.

STALLEY, Roger, 'Ecclesiastical architecture before 1169', in Ó Cróinín (ed.), *A New History*, 714–43.

STANCLIFFE, Clare, 'Red, white and blue martyrdom', in Dorothy Whitelock *et al.* (eds), *Ireland in Early Medieval Europe* (Cambridge), 21–46.

— 'Cuthbert and the polarity between pastor and solitary', in Bonner *et al.* (eds), *St Cuthbert*, 21–44.

— 'The thirteen sermons attributed to Columbanus and the question of their authorship', in Michael Lapidge (ed.), *Columbanus: Studies on the Latin Writings* (Woodbridge, 1997), 93–202.

— *Bede, Wilfrid, and the Irish*, Jarrow Lecture (2003).

— *Bede and the Britons*, Whithorn Lecture 14 (Stranraer, 2007).

— 'The Irish tradition in Northumbria after the Synod of Whitby', in Gameson (ed.), *The Lindisfarne Gospels*, 19–42.

STANTON, Robert, 'Linguistic fragmentation and redemption before King Alfred', *The Yearbook of English Studies* 36 (2006), 12–26.

STEINFORTH, Dirk, *Die Wikingergräber auf der Isle of Man*, BAR British ser. 611 (Oxford, 2015).

STENTON, D. M. (ed.), *Preparatory to Anglo-Saxon England* (Oxford, 1970).

STENTON, F. M., 'The historical bearing of place-name studies: the Danish settlement of eastern England', *Transactions of the Royal Historical Society*, 4th ser. 24 (1942), 1–24.

— *Anglo-Saxon England*, 3rd edn (Oxford, 1971).

— 'Pre-conquest Westmorland', in *An Inventory of the Historical Monuments in Westmorland* (London, 1936), xlviii–lv; repr. in D. M. Stenton (ed.), *Preparatory*, 214–23.

— 'The road system of medieval England', in D. M. Stenton (ed.), *Preparatory*, 234–52.

STEVENS, Paul, 'A monastic enclosure site at Clonfad, Co. Westmeath', *Archaeology Ireland* 20.2 (Summer 2006), 8–11.

— 'Early medieval jet-like jewellery in Ireland: production, distribution and consumption', *Medieval Archaeology* 61 (2017), 239–76.

STEVENSON, Robert B. K., 'The Inchyra stone and some other unpublished Early Christian monuments', *PSAS* 92 (1958), 33–55.

— *SCBI 2: National Museum of Antiquities of Scotland, Edinburgh, Part I: Anglo-Saxon Coins* (London, 1966).

STEVENSON, W. H., 'Trinoda Necessitas', *English Historical Review* 29 (1914), 689–703.

STOCKDALE, James, *Annales Caermoelenses, or Annals of Cartmel* (Ulverston, 1872).

STOCKER, David, 'Monuments and merchants: irregularities in the distribution of stone sculpture in Lincolnshire and Yorkshire in the tenth century', in Hadley and Richards (eds),

Cultures in Contact, 179–212.

STOKES, Whitley, 'On the linguistic value of the Irish annals', *Transactions of the Philological Society* 21 (1888–90), 365–433.

STORY, Joanna, 'The Frankish annals of Lindisfarne and Kent', *Anglo-Saxon England* 34 (2006), 59–109.

— *Carolingian Connections: Anglo-Saxon England and Carolingian Francia, c.750–870* (Aldershot, 2003).

— 'After Bede: continuing the *Ecclesiastical History*', in Baxter *et al.* (eds), *Early Medieval Studies*, 165–84.

STOUT, Matthew, *The Irish Ringfort* (Dublin, 1997).

STRECKER, Karl, 'Zu den Quellen für das Leben des heiligen Ninian', *Neues Archiv* 43 (1920–1), 1–26.

STRINGER, Keith J., 'Social and political communities in European history: some reflections on recent studies', in *idem et al.* (eds), *Nations, Nationalism and Patriotism*, 9–34.

— *et al.* (eds), *Nations, Nationalism and Patriotism in the European Past* (Copenhagen, 1994).

— and Angus J. L. WINCHESTER (eds), *Northern England and Southern Scotland in the Central Middle Ages* (Woodbridge, 2017).

STRONACH, Simon, 'The Anglian monastery and medieval priory of Coldingham: *Urbs Coludi* revisited', *PSAS* 135 (2005), 395–422.

STUKELEY, William, *Abury, a Temple of the British Druids* (London, 1743).

STUMMANN HANSEN, Steffen and John SHEEHAN, 'The Leirvík Bønhústoftin and the early christianity of the Faroe Islands, and beyond', *Archaeologica Islandica* 5 (2006), 27–54.

SWEET, Rosemary, '"Truly historical ground": antiquarianism in the north', in Colls (ed.), *Northumbria: History and Identity*, 104–25.

SWIFT, Catherine, 'Irish ecclesiastical influence on ecclesiastical settlements in Scotland: a case study of the island of Islay' (Unpublished Durham University MPhil thesis, 1987).

— *Ogam Stones and the Earliest Irish Christians* (Maynooth, 1997).

— 'Early Irish priests and their areas of ministry AD 700–900', in Eugene Duffy (ed.), *Parishes in Transition* (Dublin, 2010), 20–46.

SYMONDS, Leigh *et al.*, 'Medieval migrations: isotope analysis of early medieval skeletons on the Isle of Man', *Medieval Archaeology* 58 (2014), 1–20.

SYMONDS, Matthew, 'Maryport's mystery monuments', *Current Archaeology* 289 (April 2014), 17–21.

SYMSON, A., *A Large Description of Galloway*, ed. T. Maitland (Edinburgh, 1823).

SZARMACH, Paul Edward (ed.), *Sources of Anglo-Saxon Culture* (Kalamazoo MI, 1986).

TALLGREN, A. M., 'The method of prehistoric archaeology', *Antiquity* 11 (1937), 152–61.

TALVIO, Tuukka, *SCBI 25: The National Museum, Helsinki and other Public Collections in Finland* (London, 1978).

— *SCBI 40: Royal Coin Cabinet, Stockholm, Part IV* (London, 1991).

TAYLOR, Henry, *The Ancient Crosses and Wells of Lancashire* (Manchester, 1902).

TAYLOR, H. M. and Joan TAYLOR, *Anglo-Saxon Architecture*, 3 vols (Cambridge, 1965–78).

TAYLOR, J. and L. WEBSTER, 'A Late Saxon strap-end mould from Carlisle', *Medieval Archaeology* 28 (1984), 178–81.

TAYLOR, Simon, 'Place-names and the early Church in eastern Scotland', in Barbara E. Crawford (ed.), *Scotland in Dark Age Britain* (St Andrews, 1996), 93–110.

— 'Seventh-century Iona abbots in Scottish place-names', in Broun and Clancy (eds), *Spes Scotorum*, 35–70.

— (ed.), *Kings, Clerics and Chronicles in Scotland 500–1297: Essays in Honour of Majorie Ogilvie Anderson* (Dublin, 2000).

— 'The element *sliabh* and the Rhinns of Galloway', *History Scotland* (Nov./Dec. 2002), 49–52.

— '*Sliabh* in Scottish place-names: its chronology and meaning', *Journal of Scottish Name Studies* 1 (2007), 99–136.

— 'From *Cinrigh Monai* to *Civitas Sancti Andree*: a star is born', in Michael Brown and Katie Stevenson (eds), *Medieval St Andrews: Church, Cult and City* (Woodbridge, 2017), 20–34.

TEDESCHI, Carlo, *Congeries lapidum: iscrizioni britanniche dei secoli V–VII* (Pisa, 2005).

THACKER, Alan T., 'Bede's ideal of reform', in Wormald *et al.* (eds), *Ideal and Reality*, 130–53.

— 'Bede and the Irish', in L. A. J. R. Houwen and A. A. MacDonald (eds), *Beda Venerabilis: Historian, Monk & Northumbrian* (Groningen, 1996), 31–59.

— 'Early medieval Chester', in C. P. Lewis and A. T. Thacker (eds), *The Victoria County History of Chester Volume 5* (Woodbridge, 2003), 16–33.

— 'Bede, the Britons and the Book of Samuel', in Baxter *et al.* (eds), *Early Medieval Studies*, 129–47.

— 'Bede and the ordering of understanding', in DeGregorio (ed.), *Innovation and Tradition*, 37–63.

— and Richard SHARPE (eds), *Local Saints and Local Churches* (Oxford, 2002).

THOMAS, Charles, 'Ardwall Island: the excavation of an Early Christian site of Irish type, 1964–5', *TDGNHAS*, 3rd ser. 43 (1966), 84–116.

— 'An Early Christian cemetery and chapel on Ardwall Isle, Kirkcudbright', *Medieval Archaeology* 11 (1967), 127–88.

— *The Early Christian Archaeology of North Britain* (Oxford, 1971).

— '*Rosnat, Rostat* and the early Irish Church', *Ériu* 22 (1971), 100–6.

— 'The Irish settlements in post-Roman western Britain: a survey of the evidence', *Journal of the Royal Institution of Cornwall*, new ser. 6 (1972), 251–74.

— *Christianity in Roman Britain to A.D. 500* (London, 1981).

THOMAS, Gabor, 'Strap-ends and the identification of regional patterns in the production and circulation of ornamental metalwork in late Anglo-Saxon and Viking-Age Britain', in Redknap *et al.* (eds), *Pattern and Purpose*, 38–48.

— 'Anglo-Scandinavian metalwork in the Danelaw: reconstructing social interaction and regional identities', in Hadley and Richards (eds), *Cultures in Contact*, 237–55.

THOMAS, Sarah E., *The Parish and the Chapel in Medieval Britain and Norway* (Woodbridge, 2018).

THOMASON, S. G. and T. KAUFMAN, *Language Contact, Creolization and Genetic Linguistics* (Berkeley CA, 1988).

THOMPSON, E. A., 'Gildas and the history of Britain', *Britannia* 10 (1979), 203–26.

THOMPSON, F. H. (ed.), *Archaeology and Coastal Change* (London, 1980).

THOMPSON, J. D. A., *SCBI 9: Ashmolean Museum, Oxford: Anglo-Saxon Pennies* (London, 1967).

THOMPSON, Victoria, *Dying and Death in Later Anglo-Saxon England* (Woodbridge, 2002).

THOMSON, R. L. 'Aldrediana V: Celtica', *English and Germanic Studies* 7 (1961), 20–36.

— 'The continuity of Manx', in Fell *et al.* (eds), *The Viking Age*, 169–74.

— 'The interpretation of some Manx place-names', in Peter Davey (ed.), *Man and Environment in the Isle of Man*, BAR British ser. 54, 2 vols (Oxford, 1978), I, 319–25.

— 'Language in Man: prehistory to literacy', in Duffy and Mytum (eds), *A New History of the Isle of Man: Volume 3*, 241–56.

THORNBER, William, 'Remarks on the evidences of Roman occupation in the Fylde district', *Transactions of the Historic Society of Lancashire and Cheshire* 3 (1850–1), 57–67.

THORNTON, David E., 'Hey Macc! The name *Maccus*, tenth to fifteenth centuries', *Nomina* 20 (1997), 67–94.

— 'Edgar and the eight kings, AD 973: *textus et dramatis personae*', *Early Medieval Europe* 10 (2001), 49–79.

— *Kings, Chronologies and Genealogies: Studies in the Political History of Medieval Ireland and Wales* (Oxford, 2003).

THURNEYSEN, Rudolf, *A Grammar of Old Irish*, transl. D. A. Binchy and Osborn Bergin (Dublin 1946; repr. 1998).

TINTI, Francesca (ed.), *England and Rome in the Early Middle Ages: Pilgrimage, Art, and Politics* (Turnhout, 2014).

TIPPING, Richard, 'The form and fate of Scotland's woodlands', *PSAS* 124 (1994), 1–50.

— 'Vegetational history of southern Scotland', *Botanical Journal of Scotland* 49 (1997), 151–62.

TODD, John [M.], 'St. Bega: cult, fact and legend', *TCWAAS*, 2nd ser. 80 (1980), 23–35.

— 'The pre-Conquest church in St. Bees, Cumbria: a possible minster?', *TCWAAS*, 3rd ser. 3 (2003), 97–108.

TONER, Gregory, 'Reconstructing the earliest Irish tale lists', *Éigse* 32 (2000), 88–120.

TOOLEY, M. J., 'Theories of coastal change in north-west England', in Thompson (ed.), *Archaeology and Coastal Change*, 74–86.

TOOLIS, Ronan, and Christopher BOWLES, *The Lost Dark Age Kingdom of Rheged: The Discovery of a Royal Stronghold at Trusty's Hill, Galloway* (Oxford, 2016).

TOON, Thomas E., 'Old English dialects', in Richard Hogg *et al.* (eds), *The Cambridge History of the English Language, Volume 1: The Beginnings to 1066* (Cambridge, 1992), 409–52.

TOOP, Nicola, 'Northumbria in the west: considering interaction through monumentality', in Petts and Turner (eds), *Early Medieval Northumbria*, 85–111.

TOWILL, Edwin S., 'Saint Mochaoi and Nendrum', *Ulster Journal of Archaeology* 27 (1964), 103–20.

TOWNEND, Matthew, 'Viking Age England as a bilingual society', in Hadley and Richards (eds), *Cultures in Contact*, 89–105.

— *Language and History in Viking Age England: Linguistic Relations between Speakers of Old Norse and Old English* (Turnhout, 2002).

— 'Whatever happened to York Viking poetry? Memory, tradition and the transmission of skaldic verse', *Saga-Book* 27 (2003), 48–90.

— *Scandinavian Culture in Eleventh-Century Yorkshire* (Kirkdale Lecture, 2007).

— *Viking Age Yorkshire* (Pickering, 2014).

TRENCH-JELLICOE, Ross, 'A re-definition and stylistic analysis of P. M. C. Kermode's "pre-Scandinavian" series of sculptured monuments' (Unpublished Lancaster University PhD thesis, 1985).

— 'The Skeith Stone, Upper Kilrenny, Fife, in its context', *PSAS* 128 (1998), 495–513.

— 'Manx sculptured monuments and the early Viking Age', in Peter Davey *et al.* (eds), *Mannin Revisited: Twelve Essays on Manx Culture and Environment* (Edinburgh, 2002), 10–34.

TRIGGER, Bruce G., *A History of Archaeological Thought* (Cambridge, 1989).

TRISTRAM, Hildegard L. C. (ed.), *The Celtic Englishes* (Heidelberg, 1997).

— (ed.), *The Celtic Englishes II* (Heidelberg, 2000)

— (ed.), *The Celtic Englishes III* (Heidelberg, 2003)

TUDOR, Victoria, 'St. Cuthbert and Cumbria', *TCWAAS*, 2nd ser. 84 (1984), 67–77.

TUGÈNE, Georges, *L'idée de nation chez Bède le Vénérable*, Collection des Études Augustiniennes, Série Moyen Âge et Temps Modernes 37 (Paris, 2001).

— *L'image de la nation anglaise dans l'Histoire ecclésiastique de Bède le Vénérable* (Strasbourg, 2001).

TURNER, Sam *et al.*, *Wearmouth and Jarrow: Northumbrian Monasteries in an Historic Landscape* (Hatfield, 2013).

TURPIE, Tom, *Kind Neighbours: Scottish Saints and Society in the Later Middle Ages* (Leiden, 2015).

TYLER, E. M. (ed.), *Conceptulaizing Multilingualism in England, c. 800–c. 1250* (Turnhout, 2011).

VALANTE, Mary, 'Dublin's economic relations with hinterland and periphery in the later Viking Age', *Medieval Dublin I* (2000), 69–83.

— *The Vikings in Ireland: Settlement, Trade and Urbanization* (Dublin, 2008).

VEIT, U., 'Ethnic concepts in German prehistory: a case study on the relationship between cultural identity and archaeological objectivity', in S. J. Shennan (ed.), *Archaeological Approaches to Cultural Identity* (London, 1989), 35–65.

VENDRYES, J., *Lexique étymologique de l'Irlandais Ancien: RS* (Dublin and Paris, 1974).

VEREY, Christopher D. *et al.* (eds), *The Durham Gospel: Together with Fragments of a*

Gospel Book in Uncial (London, 1980).
VON FEILITZEN, Olof, *The Pre-Conquest Personal Names of Domesday Book* (Uppsala, 1937).
WADDELOVE, A. C. and E. WADDELOVE, 'Archaeology and research into sea-level during the Roman era: towards a methodology based on the highest astronomical tide', *Britannia* 21 (1990), 253–66.
WADDEN, Patrick, 'Theories of national identity in early medieval Ireland' (Unpublished University of Oxford DPhil thesis, 2011).
— '*Trácht Romra* and the Northumbrian episode in *Betha Adamnáin*', *Ériu* 62 (2012), 101–11.
— 'Dál Riata c. 1000: genealogies and Irish Sea politics', *Scottish Historical Review* 95 (2016), 164–81.
WAINWRIGHT, F. T., 'Ingimund's invasion', *English Historical Review* 63, 145–69; repr. in *idem*, *Scandinavian England*, 131–61.
— 'Problems and policies', *Antiquity* 23 (1949), 73–82.
— *Archaeology and Place-Names and History: an Essay on Problems of Co-ordination* (London, 1962).
— *Scandinavian England* (Chichester, 1975).
WALLACE, Patrick F., 'The archaeological identity of the Hiberno-Norse town', *Journal of the Royal Society of Antiquaries of Ireland* 122 (1992), 35–66.
— *Viking Dublin: The Wood Quay Excavations* (Dublin, 2016).
WALLACE-HADRILL, J. M., *Early Germanic Kingship in England and on the Continent* (Oxford, 1971).
— *Bede's Ecclesiastical History of the English People: a Historical Commentary* (Oxford, 1988).
WALLERSTEIN, Immanuel, *The Modern World-System I: Capitalist Agriculture and the Origins of the European World-Economy in the Sixteenth Century*, 2nd edn (Berkeley CA, 2011).
WALSHAM, Alexandra, *The Reformation of the Landscape: Religion, Identity and Memory in Early Modern Britain and Ireland* (Oxford, 2011).
WALTON, Joseph, 'The medieval mines of Alston', *TCWAAS* 2nd ser. 45 (1945), 22–33.
WALTON ROGERS, Penelope, 'The copper-alloy belt set', in Crone and Hindmarch (eds), *Living and Dying*, 60–2.
WAMERS, E., 'Insular finds in Viking Age Scandinavia and the state formation of Norway', in Clarke *et al.* (eds), *Ireland and Scandinavia*, 37–72.
WARD, Robin, 'The earliest known sailing directions in English', *Deutsches Schiffahrtsarchiv* 27 (2004), 49–92.
WARHURST, Margaret, *SCBI 29: Merseyside County Museums* (Oxford, 1982).
WARNER, R. B., 'Some observations on the context and importation of exotic material in Ireland from the first century BC to the second century AD', *PRIA* 76C (1976), 267–92.
WATKIN, W., *Roman Lancashire, or a Description of Roman remains in the County Palatine of Lancaster* (Liverpool, 1883).
WATSON, William J., *The History of the Celtic Place-Names of Scotland* (Edinburgh, 1926).
WATTS, Victor, *The Cambridge Dictionary of English Place-Names* (Cambridge, 2004).
WAY, A., 'The tombs of the de Broham family', *Archaeological Journal* 4 (1847), 59–68
WEBSTER, Graham *et al.*, 'A Saxon treasure hoard found at Chester', *Antiquaries Journal* 33 (1953), 22–32.
WEGNER, Timo, 'The Dumfriesshire mounts reconsidered', *TDGNHAS*, 3rd ser. 80 (2006), 59–80.
WEINREICH, Ulrich, *Languages in Contact: Findings and Problems* (New York, 1953).
WELLS, Colin, 'Environmental changes in Roman north-west England: a synoptic overview of events north of the Ribble', *TCWAAS*, 3rd ser. 3 (2003), 67–84.
WENSKUS, Reinhard, *Stammesbildung und Verfassung: Das Werden der frühmittelalterlichen Gentes* (Cologne, 1961).
WHALEY, Diana, *A Dictionary of Lake District Place-Names* (Nottingham, 2006).
WHITAKER, Thomas Dunham, *An History of the Original Parish of Whalley, and Honor of*

Clitheroe, 4th edn, 2 vols (London, 1872–6).

WHITE, A., 'Finds from the Anglian monastery at Whitby', *Yorkshire Archaeological Journal* 56 (1984), 33–40.

WHITELOCK, Dorothy, 'The dealings of the kings of England with Northumbria in the tenth and eleventh centuries', in Peter Clemoes (ed.), *The Anglo-Saxons: Some Aspects of their History and Culture: Studies presented to Bruce Dickins* (London, 1959), 70–88.

WHITFIELD, Niamh, 'Motifs and techniques of Celtic filigree: are they original?', in Ryan (ed.), *Ireland and Insular Art*, 75–84.

— 'The filigree of the Hunterston and "Tara" brooches', in Spearman and Higgitt (eds), *The Age of Migrating Ideas*, 118–27.

WHITTAKER, C. R., *Frontiers of the Roman Empire: a Social and Economic Study* (Baltimore MD and London, 1994).

WHITTOW, Mark, 'Sources of knowledge, cultures of recording', *Past and Present* 238, supplement 13, *The Global Middle Ages* (2018), 45–87.

WHITWORTH, Victoria, 'A cross-head from St Mary Castlegate, York, and its affiliations', in Michael F. Reed (ed.), *New Voices on Early Medieval Sculpture in Britain and Ireland*, BAR British ser. 542 (Oxford, 2011), 42–7.

— 'With book and cross: a reading of the sculptural assemblage from Stonegrave, Ryedale, North Yorkshire', in Conor Newman et al. (eds), *Islands in a Global Context* (Dublin, 2017), 258–65

WHYTE, Ian D., 'Shielings and the upland pastoral economy of the Lake District in medieval and early modern times', in Baldwin and Whyte (eds), *Scandinavians in Cumbria*, 103–17.

WICKHAM, Chris, *Framing the Middle Ages: Europe and the Mediterranean 400–800* (Oxford, 2005).

— *The Inheritance of Rome: A History of Europe from 400 to 1000* (London, 2010).

WILLIAMS, B. B. and P. S. ROBINSON, 'The excavation of Bronze Age cists and a medieval booley house at Glenmakeeran, County Antrim, and a discussion of booleying in North Antrim', *Ulster Journal of Archaeology*, 3rd ser. 46 (1983), 29–40.

WILLIAMS, Gareth, *Eirik Bloodaxe* (Hafrsfjord, 2010).

— 'The Cuerdale coins', in Graham-Campbell, *The Cuerdale Hoard*, 39–71.

— 'A new coin type (and a new king?) from Viking Northumbria', *The Yorkshire Numismatist* 4 (2012), 261–75.

— 'The "Northern hoards" revisited: hoards and silver economy in the northern Danelaw in the early tenth century', in Andrew Reynolds and Leslie Webster (eds), *Early Medieval Art and Archaeology in the Northern World: Studies in Honour of James Graham-Campbell* (Leiden, 2013), 459–86.

— *The Viking Ship* (London, 2014).

— and Barry AGER, *The Vale of York Hoard* (London, 2010).

WILLIAMS, Howard, 'Citations in stone: the material world of hogbacks', *European Journal of Archaeology* 19 (2016), 497–518.

WILLIAMS, James, 'Tynron Doon, Dumfriesshire: a history of the site with notes on the finds', *TDGNHAS*, 3rd ser. 48 (1971), 106–20.

— 'An architectural fragment from Ruthwell', *TDGNHAS*, 3rd ser. 51 (1975), 29–31.

WILLIAMS, W. Wynn, 'Leaden coffin, Rhyddgaer', *Archaeologia Cambrensis*, 4th ser. 34 (1878), 136–40.

WILLIAMSON, May G., 'The non-Celtic place-names of the Scottish Border counties' (Unpublished Edinburgh University PhD thesis, 1942), available online at: http://spns.org.uk/wp-content/uploads/2017/07/MayWilliamsonComplete.pdf

WILLIAMSON, Tom, *Environment, Society and Landscape in Early Medieval England: Time and Topography* (Woodbridge, 2015).

WILLIS, Browne, *A Survey of the Cathedrals ... in Three Volumes*, 3 vols (London, 1727–30; repr. 1742).

— *Parochiale Anglicanum* (1733); repr. in vol. 3 of *A Survey of the Cathedrals* (1742).

WILMOTT, Tony, 'The Late Roman transition at Birdoswald and on Hadrian's Wall', in *idem* and Pete Wilson (eds), *The Late Roman Transition in the North*, BAR British ser. 299

(Oxford, 2000), 13–23.

WILSON, David M., *Anglo-Saxon Ornamental Metalwork* (London, 1964).

— *The Vikings in the Isle of Man* (Aarhus, 2008).

— 'Stylistic influences in early Manx sculpture', in Graham-Campbell and Ryan (eds), *Anglo-Saxon/Irish Relations*, 311–28.

— *Manx Crosses: A Handbook of Stone Sculpture 500–1040 in the Isle of Man* (Oxford, 2018).

WILSON, P. A., 'St. Ninian and Candida Casa: literary evidence from Ireland', *TDGNHAS*, 3rd ser. 41 (1964), 156–85.

— 'St. Ninian: Irish evidence further examined', *TDGNHAS*, 3rd ser. 46 (1969), 140–59.

WILSON, P. R. *et al.*, 'Early Anglian Catterick and *Catraeth*', *Medieval Archaeology* 60 (1996), 1–61.

WILSON, S., The Means of Naming: a Social and Cultural History of Personal Naming in Western Europe (London, 1998).

WINCHESTER, Angus J. L., 'The multiple estate: a framework for the evolution of settlement in Anglo-Saxon and Anglo-Scandinavian Cumbria' in Baldwin and Whyte (eds), *Scandinavians in Cumbria*, 89–101.

— *Landscape and Society in Medieval Cumbria* (Edinburgh, 1987).

— *The Harvest of the Hills: Rural Life in Northern England and the Scottish Borders, 1400–1700* (Edinburgh, 2000).

— and Alan G. CROSBY, *England's Landscape: The North West* (London, 2006).

WITHERS, Charles W. J., *Gaelic Scotland: The Transformation of a Culture Region* (London, 1988).

WOLFRAM, Herwig, *The History of the Goths*, transl. Thomas J. Dunlop (Berkeley CA, 1988).

WOOD, Ian, 'Anglo-Saxon Otley: an Archiepiscopal estate and its crosses in a Northumbrian context', *Northern History* 23 (1987), 20–38.

— *The Missionary Life: Saints and the Evangelisation of Europe 400–1050* (Harlow, 2001).

— 'Bede's Jarrow', in Clare Lees and Gillian R. Overing (eds), *A Place to Believe in: Locating Medieval Landscapes* (University Park PA, 2006), 67–84.

— 'Monasteries and the geography of power in the age of Bede', *Northern History* 45 (2008), 11–25.

— *The Modern Origins of the Early Middle Ages* (Oxford, 2013).

WOOD, Jamie, *The Politics of Identity in Visigothic Spain: Religion and Power in the Histories of Isidore of Seville* (Leiden, 2012).

WOOD, Jason, 'Roman Lancaster: the archaeology of Castle Hill', *British Archaeology* (Nov./Dec. 2017), 38–45.

WOOD, Michael, 'Searching for Brunanburh: the Yorkshire context of the "Great War" of 937', *Yorkshire Archaeological Journal* 85 (2013), 138–59.

WOOD, Susan, *The Proprietary Church in the Medieval West* (Oxford, 2006).

WOODING, Jonathan M., *Communication and Commerce along the Western Sealanes AD 400–800*, BAR International ser. 654 (1996).

— 'The figure of David', in J. Wyn Evans and Jonathan M. Wooding (eds), *St David of Wales: Church, Cult and Nation* (Woodbridge, 2007), 1–19.

WOODMAN, David, 'Charters, Northumbria, and the unification of England in the tenth and eleventh centuries', *Northern History* 52 (2015), 35–51.

WOODS, David, 'Gildas and the mystery cloud of 536–7', *Journal of Theological Studies* 61 (2010), 226–34.

WOOLF, Alex, 'Amlaíb Cuarán and the Gael', *Medieval Dublin* 3 (2002), 34–43.

— 'The Britons: from Romans to Barbarians', in Hans-Werner Goetz *et al.* (eds), *Regna and Gentes: The Relationship between Late Antique and Early Medieval Peoples and Kingdoms in the Transformation of the Roman World* (Leiden, 2003), 345–80.

— 'Caedualla *rex Brettonum* and the passing of the Old North', *Northern History* 41 (2004), 5–24.

— 'Onuist son of Uurguist: *tyrannus carnifex* or a David for the Picts?', in David Hill and

Margaret Worthington (eds), *Aethelbald and Offa: Two Eighth-Century Kings of Mercia*, BAR British ser. 383 (Oxford, 2005), 35–42.

— 'Dún Nechtain, Fortriu and the geography of the Picts', *Scottish Historical Review* 85 (2005), 182–201.

— *From Pictland to Alba, 789–1070* (Edinburgh, 2007).

WOOLF, Alex, 'Reporting Scotland in the Anglo-Saxon Chronicle', in Alice Jorgensen (ed.), *Reading the Anglo-Saxon Chronicle* (Turnhout, 2010), 221–39.

— (ed.), *Beyond the Gododdin: Dark Age Scotland in Medieval Wales* (St Andrews, 2012).

— 'A historian's view of the evidence from Auldhame', in Crone and Hindmarch, *Living and Dying at Auldhame*, 166–71.

— 'The diocese of Lindisfarne: organisation and pastoral care', in McGuigan and Woolf (eds), *The Battle of Carham*, 231–9.

WORMALD, Patrick, 'Bede, the *Bretwaldas* and the origins of the *Gens Anglorum*', in *idem et al.* (eds), *Ideal and Reality*, 99–129; repr. in his *The Times of Bede, 625–865: Studies in Early Christian Society and its Historian*, ed. Stephen Baxter (Oxford, 2006), 106–34.

— *Bede and the Conversion of England: The Charter Evidence*, Jarrow Lecture (Jarrow, 1984).

— 'Celtic and Anglo-Saxon kingship: some further thoughts', in Szarmach (ed.), *Sources*, 151–83.

— '*Engla lond*: the making of an allegiance', *Journal of Historical Sociology* 7 (1994), 1–23.

— *The Making of English Law: King Alfred to the Twelfth Century. Vol. 1, Legislation and its Limits* (Oxford, 1999).

— *et al.* (eds), *Ideal and Reality in Frankish and Anglo-Saxon Society* (Oxford, 1983).

WRIGHT, Charles D., *The Irish Tradition in Old English* (Cambridge, 1993).

WRIGHT, Joseph, *The English Dialect Dictionary*, 6 vols (London, 1898–1905).

WRIGHT, Neil, 'Gildas's geographical perspective', in Michael Lapidge and David N. Dumville (eds), *Gildas: New Approaches* (Woodbridge, 1984), 85–105.

WYATT, David, *Slaves and Warriors in Medieval Britain and Ireland 800–1200* (Leiden, 2009).

WYCHERLEY, Niamh, *The Cult of Relics in Early Medieval Ireland* (Turnhout, 2015).

YORKE, Barbara, *Kings and Kingdoms of Early Anglo-Saxon England* (London, 1990).

— *Rex Doctissimus: Bede and King Aldfrith of Northumbria*, Jarrow Lecture (2009).

— 'Adomnán at the court of King Aldfrith', in Jonathan Wooding *et al.* (eds), *Adomnán of Iona: Theologian, Lawmaker, Peacemaker* (Dublin, 2010), 36–50.

YOUNG, Robert J. C., *The Idea of English Ethnicity* (Oxford, 2008).

YOUNGS, Susan, 'A Northumbrian plaque from Asby Winderwath', in Hawkes and Mills (eds), *Northumbria's Golden Age*, 281–96.

YUVAL-DAVIS, Nira, *Gender and Nation* (London, 1997).

ZANT, John, and Christine HOWARD-DAVIS, *The Carlisle Millennium Project: Excavations in Carlisle, 1998–2001*, 2 vols (Lancaster, 2009).

— 'The stratigraphic sequence', in *idem* and Parsons (eds), *St Michael's Church, Workington*, 11–46.

— and Adam PARSONS, *St Michael's Church, Workington: Excavation of an Early Medieval Cemetery*, Lancaster Imprints 26 (Lancaster, 2019).

ZIEGLER, Michelle, 'The Ripon connection? Wilfrid, Willibrord, and the mission to Frisia', *The Heroic Age* 6 (2003), 1–19:
http://www.heroicage.org/issues/6/ziegler.html

ZVELEBIL, Marek, 'At the interface of archaeology, linguistics and genetics: Indo-European dispersals and the agricultural transition in Europe', *Journal of European Archaeology* 3.1 (1995), 33–70.

Web resources (all web addresses correct on 21 July 2019)

BAILIE, Warren R., *An Assessment of the Extent and Character of Hobbyist Metal-detecting in Scotland* (GUARD Archaeology, 2016), https://www.historicenvironment.scot/archives-and-research/publications/publication/?publicationId=3de69b89-5f55-481e-9819-a70c00 990d96

BARLOW, Natalie and Ian SHENNAN, 'An overview of Holocene coastal change in north-west England', in Ben Johnson (ed.), *North West Rapid Coastal Zone Assessment* (2009), https://historicengland.org.uk/images-books/publications/nwrcza/

BEAM, Amanda *et al.*, 'People of Medieval Scotland 1093–1314', http://www.poms.ac.uk/

'Celtic Inscribed Stones: Language, Location and Environment', http://www.ucl.ac.uk/archaeology/cisp/index.htm

BRITISH MUSEUM, *Treasure Annual Report 2005/6*, https://webarchive.nationalarchives.gov.uk/+/http:/www.culture.gov.uk/images/publications/TAR2005_2006pt1.pdf

CAMPBELL, Ewan and Cathy MACIVER, 'Excavations at Iona Abbey 2017: Data structure report', https://ionaresearchgroup.arts.gla.ac.uk/wp-content/uploads/2017/12/Iona-AbbeyDSR2017.pdf

CASSWELL, Chris, 'Lindisfarne: the Holy Island Archaeology project: assessment report and updated project design', https://digventures.com/lindisfarne/wp-content/uploads/Lindisfarne_2018_PXAUPD_V2.0.pdf

CURRIE, Allan, 'Àirighean', School of Scottish Studies SA1960.24.B6 (1960), Tobar an Dualchais/Kist o' Riches, http://www.tobarandualchais.co.uk/en/fullrecord/41169/2

'Database of dedications to saints in medieval Scotland', http://saints.shca.ed.ac.uk/

DIG VENTURES, 'Lindisfarne', https://digventures.com/lindisfarne/

DRAKEN HARALD HÅRFAGRE 'Expedition America', www.drakenhh.com

DURHAM COUNTY COUNCIL and NORTHUMBERLAND COUNTY COUNCIL, 'Keys to the Past', http://www.keystothepast.info/article/8749/KeysToThePast-Home-Page

eDIL, 'Electronic Dictionary of the Irish Language', http://www.dil.ie/#

ENGLISH HERITAGE, 'Introduction to Heritage Assets: Shielings', https://historicengland.org.uk/images-books/publications/iha-shielings/heag233-shielings/

FITZWILLIAM MUSEUM, Cambridge (Department of Coins and Medals), 'Early medieval corpus of coin finds', https://emc.fitzmuseum.cam.ac.uk/

— 'Checklist of coin hoards from the British Isles, c.450–1180', http://www.fitzmuseum.cam.ac.uk/dept/coins/projects/hoards/index.list.html

GIBBONS, P. and C. L. E. HOWARD-DAVIS, *Excavations at Walton-le-Dale, 1981–83 and 1996* (2001) http://archaeologydataservice.ac.uk/archiveDS/archiveDownload?t=arch-1352-1/dissemination/pdf/Lancashire/GL42025.pdf

GOUGH-COOPER, Henry (ed.), *Annales Cambriae* (texts A–E), http://croniclau.bangor.ac.uk

GUNN, Nik *et al.*, 'A new runic inscription', https://languagesmythsfinds.files.wordpress.com/2014/07/lmf-poster2-v7.pdf

HISTORIC ENGLAND, 'Pastscape', www.pastscape.org.uk

HISTORIC ENVIRONMENT SCOTLAND, 'The Canmore Database', https://www.historicenvironment.scot/archives-and-research/archives-and-collections/canmore-database/

IONA RESEARCH GROUP, 'Charles Thomas excavations on Iona, 1956–1963', https://ionaresearchgroup.arts.gla.ac.uk/index.php/projects/charles-thomas-excavations-1956-1963/

— 'Excavations on Iona, 2017', https://ionaresearchgroup.arts.gla.ac.uk/index.php/projects/excavations-2017/

JAMES, Alan, 'The Brittonic language in the Old North: a guide to the place-name evidence', 3 vols (Introduction, Dictionary, Index), https://spns.org.uk/resources/bliton

KIRBY, Magnus, *Lockerbie Academy: Neolithic and Early Historic Halls, a Bronze Age Cemetery, an Undated Enclosure and a Post-Medieval Corn-drying Kiln in South-West Scotland*, Scottish Archaeological Internet Report (2011), http://archaeologydataservice.ac.uk/archiveDS/archiveDownload?t=arch-310-1/dissemination/pdf/sair46.pdf

LANCASHIRE COUNTY COUNCIL, 'Lancashire, 1786',
http://www.lancashire.gov.uk/environment/oldmap/yates/

'Linguistic geographies: the Gough Map of Great Britain and its making', http://www.goughmap.org/map/

MCCORMICK, Finbar and Philip MACDONALD, *Excavations at Dunnyneil Island, Co. Down*, Data Structure report 029 (2004), https://www.qub.ac.uk/schools/CentreforArchaeologicalFieldworkCAF/PDFFileStore/Filetoupload,180988,en.pdf

MACLEOD, Kitty and Annie MACLEOD, 'Beatha air an Àirigh', School of Scottish Studies SA1958.1.3 (1958), Tobar an Dualchais/Kist o' Riches, http://www.tobarandualchais.co.uk/en/fullrecord/31686/10

MCCOMISH, J. M. and D. PETTS, *Archaeological Investigations at Fey Field, Whithorn* (2008), https://www.yorkarchaeology.co.uk/web-publications/

NATIONAL MUSEUMS SCOTLAND, 'The Galloway Hoard', https://www.nms.ac.uk/gallowayhoard

NEWMAN, Rachel *et al.*, 'The early medieval period: resource assessment' (2004), www.liverpoolmuseums.org.uk/mol/archaeology/arf/documents/EARLYMEDIEVALASSESSMENT.pdf [The North-West Regional Research Framework is currently being revised. Updates and drafts can be viewed at: https://archaeologynorth-west.wordpress.com/period-updates/]

Ó CORRÁIN, Donnchadh (revisor), 'Onomasticon Goedelicum by Edmund Hogan', https://www.dias.ie/celt/celt-publications-2/onomasticon-goedelicum/

OXFORD ARCHAEOLOGY NORTH, 'Stanwix primary school, Stanwix, Carlisle, Cumbria: Archaeological watching brief' (2010), https://library.thehumanjourney.net/1500/1/StanwixPrimarySchoolFullReport.pdf

PEREGRINI LINDISFARNE LANDSCAPE PARTNERSHIP, 'Community archaeology', http://www.peregrinilindisfarne.org.uk/community-archaeology-group/

POLLOCK, Dave, *Whithorn 6: Interim Report on the 1993 Excavations at Whithorn Priory* (Whithorn, 1995), available at: https://www.yorkarchaeology.co.uk/new-page

PORTABLE ANTIQUITIES SCHEME, 'Database', https://finds.org.uk

'Prosopography of Anglo-Saxon England', http://pase.ac.uk

QUATERMAINE, Jamie, *Aggregate Extraction and the Geoarchaeological Heritage of the Ribble Valley and Kirkham Moraine*, Oxford Archaeology North (2007), http://archaeologydataservice.ac.uk/archives/view/ribble_eh_2007/downloads.cfm?phase=phase1

RATLEDGE, David, 'Roman Roads in Lancashire', http://www.romanroads.org/gazetteer/lancspages.html

'Saints in Scottish Place-Names', http://saintsplaces.gla.ac.uk/

'*Taxatio* database', https://www.dhi.ac.uk/taxatio/

TREASURE TROVE UNIT, 'Reports and minutes', https://treasuretrovescotland.co.uk/reports-and-minutes/

VETUS LATINA INSTITUT, *Vetus Latina database*: *Bible versions of the Latin Fathers* (Turnhout, 2002–), http://brepolis.net

VIKINGESKIBSMUSEET, 'Viking ships sail again', http://www.vikingeskibsmuseet.dk/en/professions/viking-ships-on-voyages/earlier-voyages/

WESSEX ARCHAEOLOGY, 'Speke Keeill, Murray Mount Hotel, Isle of Man: archaeological evaluation and assessment of results', https://www.wessexarch.co.uk/our-work/speke-keeill-mount-murray-hotel-isle-man

YORKSHIRE MUSEUM, 'The Bedale Hoard', https://www.yorkshiremuseum.org.uk/collections/collections-highlights/the-bedale-hoard/

INDEX

In cases where the administrative entity has changed since 1974/5, both the current designation and historic county are given; for example: Manchester (Greater Manchester, Lancashire). Where provided, modern forms of Scottish Gaelic place-names derive from https://www.ainmean-aite.scot/ and modern forms of Irish place-names from https://www.logainm.ie/.

kings *see* Ælle, Edwin, Osric
Denmark 51
Dere Street 82, 88, 93, 175, 183
Derry (Doire, OIr Daire Calgaig) 97
Derwent, estuary/river (Cumbria, Cumberland) 80, 91, 112
Derwentwater (Cumbria, Cumberland) 64, 107
Diarmait, abbot of Iona (*ob. ca* 832) 111, 120
Diarmait mac Maíl na mBó, king of Leinster and over-king (*ob.* 1072) 66, 157
Dingesmere 60
dirhams 51, 84
DNA 17, 55–6, 157
Domangart Réti (Dál Riata) 40
Domesday Survey 69, 78–9, 139, 164, 172, 174,177–83, 220–1
Domnall Brecc, Dál Riatan king (*ob.* 642) 38–9
Doncaster (South Yorkshire, West Riding) 82, 87
Donnán, St (*ob.* 617) 153
Dore (South Yorkshire, Derbyshire) 82
Douglas (Lanarkshire) 136
Douglas, river (Lancashire) 85
Downham, Clare 61
Dromore (Droim Mór, OIr Druim Mór) (Co. Down) 123
Dryhthelm, visionary 106
Druim Cett, convention 35
Dubgaill/Dubgennti 52–3
Dublin (Baile Átha Cliath) 25
  excavations 53, 97, 213–15, 217
  exiled leaders 53–4, 85
  hinterland 132, 138–44, 182
  kings/leaders *see* Blákári, Echmarcach mac Ragnaill, Sigtryggr (grandson of Ívarr), Óláfr Guðrøðsson, Óláfr Sigtrygsson, Sigtryggr (son of Óláfr Cúarán)
  language 157
  mint 67
  ship-building 81
  trade 83, 87, 96
  Viking-Age polity 51–62, 65, 119, 149, 220
Duleek (Damhliag, OIr Damliac) (Co. Meath) 194
Dumbarton/*Al Clut* 'the rock of the Clyde', citadel/kingdom 46, 48, 52, 94
  kings *see* Owain
Dumfries (Dumfries & Galloway, Dumfriesshire) 80, 92
Dumville, David 49
Dunadd, citadel 48, 97, 211, 212
Dunbar (East Lothian) 40, 50, 95, 142, 211

Dunkeld (Dùn Chailleann, OIr Dún Caillden) (Perthshire) 56, 111, 152
Dúnlaith, Uí Néill princess 61, 133
Dunnichen (Angus), proposed battle site *see Nechtansmere*
Dunragit (Dumfries & Galloway, Wigtownshire) 30
Durham (Co. Durham)
  bishopric 18, 107
  manuscripts *see* manuscripts, *Liber Vitae*, Oxford University College MS 165
  raids 65
  relics 110
  sculpture 204
  texts *see Historia de Sancto Cuthberto, Historia regum, see also* Reginald of Durham, Symeon of Durham
Durisdeer (Dumfries & Galloway, Dumfriesshire) 93
Durrow (Darú, OIr Dairmag)
  Book of Durrow 100, 202, 212

Eadberht, Northumbrian king (*ob.* 768) 47–8, 71, 87
Eadred, English king (*ob.* 959) 15, 62–3
Eadwig, English king (*ob.* 955)
Eadwulf son of Ecgwulf (*ob.* 717) 45
Eadwulf Cudel of Bamburgh 69
Eadwulf of Bamburgh (*ob.* 913) 14
Ealdred son of Eadwulf of Bamburgh (*ob.* 934) 56–7
Ealdwulf, bishop of Mayo 90, 117
Eamont, river (Cumbria) 57–8
Eanflæd, Northumbrian queen 39–40
Eanfrith son of Æthelfrith, Bernician king 37–8
Eanred, Northumbrian king 82
Eardwulf, Northumbrian king 49
Eardwulf, bishop of Lindisfarne (*ob.* 900) 109, 112
Eata, abbot of Melrose, bishop of Hexham/Lindisfarne (*ob.* 686) 106–7, 109–10
Ecgberht, St (*ob.* 729) 1, 109–10
Ecgberht, bishop/archbishop of York (*ob.* 766) 47, 87, 102
Ecgberht, Wessex king (*ob.* 839) 82
Ecgfrith, king (*ob.* 685) 1, 40–2, 48, 88, 91, 107–8, 113
Ecgred, bishop of Lindisfarne (*ob.* 845) 110
Echmarcach mac Ragnaill, king in Dublin, Man and the Rhinns (*ob.* 1065) 68, 125, 144
Echternach 100
Eden
  river 30, 75, 80

STUDIES IN CELTIC HISTORY

www.ingramcontent.com/pod-product-compliance
Ingram Content Group UK Ltd.
Pitfield, Milton Keynes, MK11 3LW, UK
UKHW020324280225
455670UK00009B/130

9 781837 650279